W9-DBF-178

the psychologists

the psychologists

VOLUME TWO

edited by T. S. Krawiec

SKIDMORE COLLEGE

New York **OXFORD UNIVERSITY PRESS**

London 1974 Toronto

Library of Congress Catalogue Card Number: 78-188293
Printed in the United States of America

Preface

One way to learn about and understand psychology is to study psychologists as they reveal themselves in writing about their lives. This series came about because the psychology texts available today give the student little opportunity to explore in depth the thinking of those who work in the field.

Some of the most distinguished individuals in psychology have contributed autobiographical sketches for the series. They have written of the people and events that influenced their choice of psychology as a career and of what they have tried to accomplish in it. Each contributor is significant in at least one facet of the discipline, be it research, teaching, editing, or writing, and brings to his essay a lifetime of study in his field of special interest.

The chapters are varied, the authors having been free to choose not only their manner of presentation but also the aspects of their lives they wished to emphasize. Included in their sketches are discussions about their education, their relationships with some of the major figures in psychology, and their feelings and thoughts about their careers and accomplishments.

I am profoundly indebted to the authors of the chapters for their excellent contributions.

T.S.K.

Saratoga Springs, N.Y.
Spring 1974

Contents

the psychologists

Donald Brodine, Vermont Academy, 1973

1

Psychology: A Way of Living*

HEINZ L. ANSBACHER

It is altogether appropriate that I should begin the account of my life as a psychologist with the name of Alfred Adler. There are three reasons for this: (*a*) Adler was my first contact with psychology and encouraged me to study psychology. (*b*) Adler introduced me to my wife, Rowena Ripin Ansbacher, Ph.D. in psychology. (*c*) My work in psychology was from the beginning strongly influenced by Adler's position, which I made my own.

I was born in Frankfurt–am–Main, Germany, in1904, and came to the United States in 1924, by myself and on my own account. This was a year after my graduation from the *Gymnasium* (classical high school plus first two years of college) because I did not know what to do with myself. In New York I took a job with a stock exchange firm to whom I had a recommendation. The financial business was a family tradition. I was, however, not happy in my work, nor particularly successful.

*Since writing is not easy for me, the editor of this volume most kindly consented to interview me and to record the interview on tape. In the transcription of the tape, Professor R. John Huber, Skidmore College, gave invaluable help for which I also want to express my gratitude. As a student at the University of Vermont he took some courses with me and has become an active contributor to Adlerian psychology himself. He was very qualified to do the necessary editing. The present paper is essentially Dr. Huber's version of the transcript. I have added numerous important factual sections of which I had not thought at the time of the interview, and condensed some of the incidentals which had grown relatively large during the interview.

I shall begin my story around 1932 when my life as a psychologist began, and take up the early period at the end. The year 1932 was not only the nadir of the world-wide depression which started with the well-remembered crash of 1929, but was for me also one of personal crisis and a new beginning. The crisis came in the fall of 1932 when the girl whom I had been seeing for nearly five years broke off our relationship. We had liked each other a great deal, yet I was unable to make up my mind about marrying her. My doubts were actually justified and the break became a blessing. But at the time, it meant the collapse of my world.

ALFRED ADLER

In my despair I went to Alfred Adler for help, who during these years spent fall and winter in New York. I had attended a series of six weekly lectures given by him at Columbia University, Institute for Arts and Sciences, in the spring of 1930. This was my very first contact with psychology.

The lectures had fascinated me greatly, and I still have my notes. Adler was introduced by Professor Robert S. Woodworth, under whom I was later to do my dissertation. He presented Adler as "the 'creator' of the inferiority complex." Right from the first lecture I have in my notes: "Individual Psychology is concerned with how a person looks toward himself. How does he want to use his powers? A person is always one unit, ruled by a goal. The five year old has already formed a goal. The question is, which is a desirable goal? The goal must be a cooperative one, and the ability to cooperate is the result of proper training. The task of Individual Psychology is to see which goal a child is heading for, and how he faces the problems of life we all must solve. One child will face the problems by himself, another will look to others for help."

In the second lecture Adler discussed the three kinds of children who are in increased danger of not developing in a cooperative way—children with physical imperfections, pampered children, and neglected children. They are likely to make mistakes in their "pattern of life." It is noteworthy that he used this phrase rather than "style of life," which he had also introduced by that time. At these lectures he also preferred to talk of "cooperation," rather than social interest.

The remaining four lectures dealt with inferiority complex, superiority complex, degree of cooperation, and problems of neurosis. I was enthusiastic about Adler and the course; I had learned a great deal and told all my friends about it.

Looking at these notes today, I find they contained a good deal of what Adlerian psychology represents. It is a thoroughly humanistic psychology with a concept of man as self-determined to a larger extent than is generally recognized, forward oriented, and guided by values and goals; a methodology that is pragmatic and operational, keeping hypothetical constructs at a minimum; and the purpose to be useful for living in general and for psychotherapy in particular (1971c).* Adlerian treatment is essentially a belated teaching how to live, involving a conceptualization of the person's unworkable and useless goals and values, and enabling him to replace these by constructs and actions that are more helpful to himself and his fellow men.

I was in "treatment" with Adler approximately from October 1932 to February 1933 when I saw him about once or twice a week as I remember, and later less often. He lived then at the Hotel Gramercy Park in New York City. I remember him as very kind and friendly, comfortable and completely unpretentious, yet at the same time as very forceful. He reminded me in some ways of my long-deceased father, whom I venerated. Of course I told Adler of all my troubles, past and present.

Apparently Adler soon focused on my lack of job satisfaction, probably because this was where alternatives could be worked on. When I said I did not know what I could or wanted to do, he quickly replied, "Why not become a vocational guidance counselor?" This was the first suggestion that I become a psychologist, although Adler's lectures had already aroused my curiosity as to his relationship to the field of psychology in general.

When I expressed my thought, Adler answered, "You must get a Ph.D. Then you can develop your own ideas, and make yourself heard. Without it, nobody will listen to you." So I went to Columbia University to find out what it would take for me to obtain a Ph.D. in psychology. The requirements seemed not im-

*The references are arranged in two lists: author's publications and general references. The dates referring to the author's list are in roman type; those referring to the general list are italic.

possible to fulfill, and I registered for an evening course in introductory psychology that spring, plus one in sociology and one in English as a part of the requirements. Then Adler encouraged me to come to Vienna during the summer to take the courses with the Bühlers at the university there and attend the informal seminars which he held in his home. He made his suggestions in low key and I could easily have ignored them. But I followed them.

ROWENA RIPIN ANSBACHER

One day in the spring of 1933 Adler invited me to lunch when a young woman was also present. When it was time to part and she reminded Dr. Adler about the tea party at her house the next day, he asked whether I could not go too. I did go, and she still recalls that I was the first person to arrive.

Not only did Adler stress social interest in his theory; he lived it. Once, when two colleagues expressed their pleasure at finally having met through him, he is quoted as having said: "All my life it was my endeavor to bring people together" (Rom, *1970*). In this case it was Dr. Rowena Ripin and myself whom he brought together—at first sight a very unlikely combination.

I was immediately enormously impressed by her. Rather petite, she was charming and had all the social graces and skills and the social courage to invite to her house someone like Adler, among other distinguished guests. She had a Ph.D. in psychology, something to which I had just begun to aspire. She lived in a beautiful apartment on Central Park West in New York City with her mother and younger sister and brother. Her father had died a few years before.

It soon turned out that our cultural background and values were very similar. For one thing, although born in New York, Rowena knew German well; her mother was born in Germany and lived there until she married, and Rowena visited there often from early childhood on. We both had a strong social orientation, mine tending toward the theoretical, hers toward the practical side. Besides, we both thought that Adler had combined in his system something immensely worthwhile in many ways.

As we learned many years later we were also well matched from the viewpoint of family constellation, she being the oldest in her family, with a younger brother, and I being the younger brother of an older sister. This would be the best combination according to Toman's (*1959*) further development of Adler's views on this matter.

Two years younger than I, she had received her B.A. in 1927 at Barnard College, Columbia University, where H. L. Hollingworth was department chairman. After her graduation her family had planned to spend a year in Europe, where she would stay on to get her Ph.D. She had become interested in Adler during her studies. Hollingworth (*1930*) had called Freudian psychoanalysis "psycho-analogy." While he credited Freud with much sound observation, he found this "scattered among fantasies and allegories" (p. 323). On the other hand, he considered "certain features of Adler's account . . . entirely acceptable and useful" (p. 338).

So Rowena went to see Adler in New York to ask him where to study in Europe. He received her with the great kindliness that was his way. He suggested that she study with Karl and Charlotte Bühler at the department of psychology at the University of Vienna. He also suggested that she attend Adler's informal seminars at his home and the lectures of the Society of Individual Psychology—very much the same suggestion that he had made to me.

Rowena received her Ph.D. in 1929 under Charlotte Bühler. Her dissertation was based on a study of early responses of infants to the feeding situation. She found that bottle-fed infants responded to the person presenting the bottle earlier than to the bottle itself. The dissertation was published, in English, the following year (Ripin, *1930*). Subsequently she also contributed to Adler's journal, primarily through a general review of definitions of neurosis (Ripin, *1933*).

When we met, she was a child psychologist at the Home for Hebrew Infants in the Bronx, a position she continued on a part-time basis until we moved to Providence in 1940. She had also taught at Barnard College and at Long Island University.

We were married in June 1934. After a summer session at Columbia University we went for our honeymoon to Europe to introduce Rowena to my family there. I had uncles, brothers of my father, well established in the world of finance, in London, in Paris, and in Frankfurt, where my sister and her husband also lived.

After our return I became a full-time student, as we had

planned. I had given up the Wall Street job before our marriage; this did not mean any financial hardship because I had an "independent income," as it is nicely phrased.

We settled in an apartment right across the street from Columbia University. It had French doors with a balcony grille opening on 116th Street, and was altogether very pleasant. Rowena had a flair as a hostess and soon many of our peers and teachers came to see us there.

Nowadays wives often financially see their husbands through their studies. In our case the husband received intellectual support. My English was more imperfect than it is today, and I had no experience writing term papers, etc.

Eventually Rowena's help turned into a steady collaboration. There is hardly a piece of work I did in which she does not have a share even when her name does not appear. Our largest combined effort remains *The Individual Psychology of Alfred Adler* (1956b), where we did much translating and editing. And to this day we still work together as editors of the *Journal of Individual Psychology* and on other projects.

We are often asked how we actually go about working together. It depends on the job. When it is a matter of editing a manuscript for the *Journal* Rowena does the first digest while I go into the details. When it is a matter of translating, I may read in translation while she types. When it is a matter of my own writing, she gives it a very critical reading. And then, of course, there are mini-"conferences" all the time. In our team I am the more systematic, the pedant, while she wants to do everything quickly, and she is likely to become impatient. The cooperation is thus not without frictions. Besides, I was and am at it full time, while it was primarily she who raised our family, ran and still runs the household, and has outside interests besides.

Our first joint publication was fittingly a memorial for Adler upon his death on May 28, 1937, which we were asked to write by Helen Jennings for Moreno's *Sociometry* (1937b).

We had four children, all boys, between 1935 and 1942: Max, named after my father; Benjamin, after Rowena's father; Theodore, after one of my uncles; and Charles. In raising them we tried to follow Adler's admonition to "remove the possibility of a feeling of inferiority arising in the child" (1956b, p. 55), and to prepare them for taking their place in the world on the side of common usefulness. This precluded permissiveness. But the authority intended was one of reason and social feeling rather than of the person (Seif, *1922*). All this went along with Rowena's spunk and self-reliance which also enabled me to leave her with the four small children in Providence in 1943 to participate in the war effort against Hitler.

Today we dare say the boys have all turned out well. Max is a corporation lawyer; Benjamin, an industrial administrator and computer man, happily married to a former computer girl, and father of two sons; Theodore is a physics professor; while Charles conducts a symphony orchestra, is married to a musicologist, and has one son.

STUDYING PSYCHOLOGY

Undergraduate Study. As mentioned, my first formal course in psychology was in the spring of 1933. I was fortunate that the instructor was Otto Klineberg, a stimulating lecturer who presented fascinating material. The textbook was Woodworth, *Psychology,* 2nd edition. The studies by Klineberg (*1931*) disproving the claims of Nordic superiority over other ethnic groups in Europe were quite recent then, a blow to the racial theorists who had been prominent in the United States after World War I and were now in the ascendency in Europe through Hitler. What I learned from Klineberg then and in later contacts led to my second publication, "Recent Trends in the Nordic Doctrine." It appeared under the pseudonym of Andrew Baker (Ansbacher, 1936) for fear that otherwise relatives who had not yet left Nazi-Germany might experience increased difficulties. Waldemar Kaempffert (*1936*) reported on this paper at length in the *New York Times.* My first publication was a minor item in Adler's American journal.

The course with Klineberg was followed by the summer courses in Vienna. There were six courses, extending over four weeks, given in English, and carrying six credit points at the University of Kentucky. Two courses by Charlotte Bühler dealt with childhood and adolescence, and biographical methods, and were concerned with human lives as a whole. Her relevancy to my own development can be seen in her stress on life goals and her eventual prominence in humanistic psychology (Bühler, *1967*). A third unit consisted of demonstrations in testing children, by two assistants, Lottie Danziger and Lieselotte Frankl. The fourth course was on language and personality, by Karl Bühler, a dramatic orator.

The fifth course, by Egon Brunswik, was my first contact with experimental psychology. I remember my profound disappointment when I learned that the striking demonstrations with the color wheel actually had no further consequences of any sort, led to nothing, and proved nothing beyond themselves. Brunswik's work on object constancy was quite a different matter. In fact, I later based my dissertation on it. He was considered to be a functionalist (Chaplin and Krawiec, *1968,* p. 607) and his experimental work appeared to me from the start compatible with and meaningful to an Adlerian type of psychology, Adler being an outstanding functionalist as expressed in his phrase, "psychology of use vs. psychology of possession" (1956b, p. 205). Brunswik came to the United States in 1937.

The sixth course was given by Paul Lazarsfeld. Some years after Lazarsfeld had come to this country he became the founder and director of the Columbia University Bureau of Applied Social Research. The course I took with him dealt with market research and survey techniques and was my first preparation for my "market research" with German prisoners in England and France during World War II. At heart Lazarsfeld was also an Adlerian, his mother having been an important member of Adler's group.

The summer in Vienna was very fruitful for me for several reasons. First, I became better acquainted with Individual Psychology and Adler and his circle. I got to know his city home at the Dominikanerbastei 10 and his "country" place in Salmannsdorf, just outside the city. But I never saw one of the educational counselling centers, probably because they were not operating during the summer.

Second, the courses at the university were most valuable for my further progress, as mentioned.

Third, I got to know an important part of Rowena's world so that it was later almost as if we had studied in Vienna together. When, shortly thereafter, nearly all the faculty had come to this country by and by, we both felt as their friends. We saw Lazarsfeld especially often, and also Brunswik.

Finally, the Columbia admissions office was very generous about my studies in Vienna. On the basis of my work there plus the one course I had taken with Klineberg in the spring I was granted full standing as a graduate student beginning in September 1933. It should be added that I also had to pass an examination. For this I prepared by studying, primarily on the way home on the boat, Woodworth's introductory textbook, which I had been told would see me through. And it did. But I had no B.A. and also never obtained an M.A. degree.

Graduate Study. During 1933–1934 I was still a part-time student, taking three two-semester courses in the evening, in schools of psychology with R. S. Woodworth, comparative psychology with C. J. Warden, and statistics with Jack Dunlap. In the summer of 1934 I took experimental psychology with John Seward.

Among my further courses during the following years, now as a full-time student, were differential psychology with H. E. Garrett, learning with C. J. Warden, and the social psychology of religion with Gardner Murphy. I also took two courses in sociology, the first, the undergraduate course mentioned before, with Bernhard J. Stern, and the second with George Lundberg.

Two additional teachers were particularly significant for me: Max Wertheimer and Kurt Goldstein, both of whom had recently left Germany. My first course with Wertheimer was at the New School for Social Research which I attended with Rowena in the spring of 1934. The second course was at Columbia in the fall of the same year. Wertheimer was essentially an artist and as a young man for a while undecided whether to become a psychologist or a conductor. His idea of creativity was to follow the structure of the subject matter until one could recognize exactly where the problem lay. Often one could then see the solution directly, or else one could be playful in trying out various solutions. In any case, a solution is a restructuring, a cognitive reorganization. This has direct applications to psychotherapy—in which Wertheimer was also interested, although this is not well known. The patient can be led to a solution of his problem by an "honest" study of the structure of the confronting problem, which is, of course, also quite Adlerian. In these courses Wertheimer taught in addition to his contributions in perception essentially what became included in his posthumously published book *Productive Thinking* (*1959*).

At Columbia, Wertheimer insisted that a piano be moved into

the classroom, though he actually used it only a few times, mostly to demonstrate how differently the same notes may sound, which depends on the context they are in. At parties, we have been told, he liked to play on the piano tone sketches of persons present and let the group guess whom he was characterizing. Recently we learned that the Adlerian psychiatrist Rudolf Dreikurs also liked to do this. We became quite friendly with Wertheimer and visited him occasionally at his home in New Rochelle; I consulted him on my post-doctoral research on the perception of real movement.

The course with Goldstein provided the invaluable views of a neurologist who from his studies of brain pathology arrived at a thoroughly holistic and humanistic conception of man. The chief characteristic of the intact human organism is its ability to engage in abstract behavior and concept formation. It is the brain-injured individual who is stimulus-bound. Goldstein and Adler supplement one another. This positive relationship was pointed out years later by Alexandra Adler (*1959*), Alfred Adler's daughter. Personally I appreciated Goldstein greatly because during the war against Hitler he was one of the few who, like myself, made a sharp distinction between the Nazis and the rest of the German people.

I should also like to mention the assistants in some of the courses with whom we had subsequent contact: Norman Locke, Richard Henneman, Charles N. Winslow, and especially Frederick Thorne.

Among my peers I would like to remember here: Mary Sheehan, Ruth Conkey, Dorothy Barrett, Joseph Stone, and Aaron Nadel. Particularly significant in my life became Saul Sells, through whom I got my first start in working in psychology, and Eugene Hartley who had become editor for the publisher who contracted for our first Adler book.

Finally, there was Abe Maslow. Because of his interest at that time in dominance and submission and my Adlerian convictions, we had much in common. We also shared an admiration for Kurt Goldstein. Our friendship continued throughout the years, with him often in the role of the encourager. Around 1935 we sometimes went together to the small meetings at Adler's hotel apartment. In my first Adlerian research study I used the Maslow Security-Insecurity test (1947b). Abe was a continuous inspiration while we contemplated writing our book and while we worked on it. Later he supported our *Journal* with contributions. When Abe got his "third force" going, I became a founding sponsor, as which I am still listed by today's Association of Humanistic Psychology. I should like to note particularly that in his very last writings Abe Maslow (*1970*) expressed increasing appreciation for Adler (see also 1971c).

Despite all the stimulation, the training at Columbia had undoubtedly been limited. It was essentially confined to experimental psychology. I had not been required to take any courses in the areas of abnormal psychology, testing, child psychology, etc. Realizing this deficiency I took, after receiving a Ph.D., a course in testing at Teachers College, and a practicum at the Vocational Adjustment Bureau under Emily Burr. Ten years after my graduation, in 1947, Rowena and I took a summer workshop in the Rorschach test with Bruno Klopfer and his group, at Bard College.

EXPERIMENTAL RESEARCH: "DETHRONEMENT OF THE STIMULUS"

I was aiming for a psychology of the active individual, responding to his surroundings selectively in accordance with his beliefs, attitudes, and especially his purposes. If such a concept of man has any validity it should be possible to support some of it experimentally. This would be an area of research to meet the requirements of the dissertation.

As mentioned, I did my dissertation under Woodworth. I was attracted by his gentleness, kindness, helpfulness, and immense scholarliness and knowledge. But I was as much attracted by the similarity of his viewpoint with mine. I remember him saying on the issue of free will versus determinism that as long as one is alive, one has an alternative. Even a hold-up man is not actually forcing you to give up your money. You still have the choice to resist, and perhaps be killed, or to give him your money. This is expressed in his simple S-O-R formula, by which Woodworth broke the S-R chain. The response (R) is not the direct function of the stimulus (S), but the function of the organism (O). And furthermore individuals differ according to their situations and goals in addition to their heredity and previous environment (Woodworth, *1934,* p. 13).

The study I did under Woodworth, which was inspired by Brunswik, demonstrated that perception of number is influenced by the monetary value of the objects, value being of course an O factor, not an S factor (1937a). Subjects were asked to equate groups of 2c postage stamps and 3c stamps with regard to number of stamps. More specifically, they were briefly shown a group of thirty uncanceled 2c stamps randomly arranged and affixed on a blank 11″ by 11″ card, side by side with one card at a time of a series of similar cards with 3c stamps ranging in number from well above to well below thirty. The subjects were asked to say quickly for each presentation on which side were more stamps. In this way a point of subjective equation was established. It took a significantly smaller number of 3c stamps to appear as numerous as thirty 2c stamps. This held true, however, only in response to stamps of one's own country, i.e., Americans responding to American stamps but not to Canadian stamps, and Canadians responding to Canadian stamps but not to American stamps. The results were then due not to any physical property of the stamps but to the value or meaning they had acquired for the subject. In both countries at that time 2c was the postage for a letter within city limits and 3c for a letter throughout the country. I did the Canadian part of the study at the University of Toronto.

The study was well received. In his presidential address at the annual meeting of the American Psychological Association in 1939, Gordon W. Allport (*1940*) cited it with eight others, as reflecting growing interest in *frame of reference,* a concept expressing the importance of context. Allport recognized this as part of a new movement whose "concepts have a realistic and humanistic flavor" (p. 23). The study was subsequently cited by Bruner and Goodman (*1947*) in their well-known paper "Value and Need as Organizing Factors in Perception" and in a great many other places. Among the eight cited by Allport were studies by Cantril, McGregor, Sells, Sherif, and Stagner.

Jobs in psychology were scarce in 1937 when I got my degree. My plan was simply to keep on doing research on my own, under the assumption that sooner or later something would turn up.

My next project was an exploratory study of size constancy in a natural surrounding. Rowena and I had just acquired, in 1937, an old farm house with quite a bit of land around it in a hilly area a hundred miles north of New York City, a place which, incidentally, we still own. Some of the subjects were from the vicinity (farmers, tradespeople, road-construction workers) and some were visitors from the city. As I could get hold of them and lead them behind the barn I asked them from there to judge the size of an object in the distance—an orange-colored upright board, 8″ wide and 7′ high, that stood 1000 feet away among grass and shrubbery. Farther in the background was the woods. From informal observation of their judgments I saw that some seemed quite challenged by this task and were determined to do well while others did not seem to care how well they did. As it turned out, the former actually did worse by overestimating more than the latter. They were also primarily rural subjects, men, the less educated, and those over forty-eight years old, who as groupings—quite contrary to expectations—did worse than the urbanites, women, the more educated, and those less than forty-eight years old. Particularly the country dwellers as a group overestimated by 4.6′ whereas the urbanites overestimated by only .9′. Adequate statistical treatment required variance analysis for data from unequally represented classes. I was not capable of doing such an analysis and so I let the matter rest. But while I was in England during the war I had the opportunity of showing this problem to the statistician K. Mather. Its solution became so interesting to him that the resulting paper qualified for publication in *Psychometrika* (1945). But apparently the paper never came to the attention of any psychologist who might have been interested in the findings themselves aside from the statistics.

My last experimental effort was an investigation of what I called at first the "Harold C. Brown shrinkage phenomenon" (1938): When an illuminated arc-line one-tenth the circumference of a disk rotates continuously at less than fusion speed and is observed with eyes fixed, it appears to shrink to a fraction of its actual length, and may be seen as a mere point. It was shown to me, after my doctorate, by a fellow graduate student at Columbia, Harold C. Brown, who discovered it while working on another perceptual problem. I immediately proposed that we work on it together because he had not the time to do it alone. But he wanted me to go ahead without him.

To investigate the phenomenon I ran seven series with variations of the stimulus, leading to a tentative explanatory statement: The perceptual shrinkage is a function of the degree of overlap of retinal stimulation, under the assumption that the process of vision is not a continuous one, but one of rapid pulsations. Such a view would carry the Gestalt theory of motion perception one step further, namely, that stroboscopic motion perception is physiologically more elementary than "real" motion perception (1944a, p. 22).

The study was used by B. J. Underwood (*1949*) as one of his three "illustrative experiments using the method of average error" (pp. 34, 43–45). He reproduced a modification of Figure 1 and parts of Table 1 of the original paper. We know of several attempts to investigate the shrinkage phenomenon and our tentative interpretation further; but it is a difficult problem, even though the phenomenon itself is clear and strong. A relatively recent investigation of the phenomenon is by Gordon Stanley (*1964*) of the University of Western Australia, who assigns its paternity to me, calling it the "Ansbacher Shrinkage Effect." Stanley's purpose was to test my explanation of the phenomenon against one that is somewhat different. He found that under certain conditions my explanation still holds (p. 117).

The common aspect of these three studies on perception is that they are in a way all psychophysical studies. The emphasis, however, is not on the accuracy of perception but rather on the constant error, that is, properties of the observer, be they psychological or physiological. They were thus of the order of dethronement of the stimulus as Thurstone (*1923*) had proposed, when he wrote: "I suggest that we dethrone the stimulus. He is only nominally the ruler of psychology. The real ruler . . . is the individual and his motives, desires, wants, ambitions, cravings, aspirations" (p. 364), to which he might add, also his cognitive and physiological structures. Thurstone quoted from H. S. Jennings, "Activity does not require present external stimulation. . . . The *organism is activity*. . . . The energy . . . comes from within and is merely released by the action of the stimulus . . . what James has called 'trigger action' " (p. 367).

This then was my idea of experimental psychology within an Adlerian framework, Adler having emphasized, "We *make* our experiences" (1956b, p. 211). By this he meant there is always the individual who actively utilizes the stimulus situation, a "psychological metabolism, so to speak" (1956b, p. 178).

EMPLOYMENT IN PSYCHOLOGY, 1937–1943

My first pay in psychology came from the translation of Kurt Goldstein's book, *Der Aufbau des Organismus,* in 1937–1938. The translation came at a good time. I had been suffering more or less severely from lower back pain with sciatica, and I remember vividly lying in bed in the apartment at 116th Street, dictating to a young cousin of Rowena's who had recently arrived from Germany. Henry E. Garrett was editor of the series in which the book was to appear, and he recommended me. Although I knew the material from Goldstein's course and liked it, the translation was very difficult. The German original had been printed in Holland after Goldstein had to leave Germany and was very poorly edited. When I wanted to confer with him on various problems, he was not willing, not even once. When the translation was finally done, he was very dissatisfied. His acknowledgments in the book (*1939*) convey an idea of what happened. I made the first draft, three others helped with regard to special problems, a fifth person worked over the entire text with Goldstein, while finally Martin Scheerer passed on the entire book (p. x).

Nevertheless Goldstein and I remained good friends. When over twenty years later Eugenia Hanfmann and Norbett L. Mintz suggested that we dedicate an issue of the *Journal of Individual Psychology* which we were editing to papers in honor of Goldstein's eightieth birthday, we were glad to do so. This was the May 1959 issue, which Hanfmann and Mintz helped to edit. But we were disappointed to note then that Goldstein's following was not larger than it was.

My first formal employment was with the *Psychological Index* Project of the Works Project Administration (WPA) of the City of New York, between 1938 and 1939. The director was Professor A. T. Poffenberger and the planner and administrator on the part of the WPA was Saul B. Sells. Sells and I had become good friends at Columbia, where he had received his Ph.D. a year before I did. He offered me the job as one of the two non-relief psychologists for which the project called, and I accepted. The history, planning, and operation of the project were written up by Poffenberger (*1939*), with the two assistant project supervisors and the two non-relief psychologists as co-authors. One of the assistant supervisors was Harold C. Brown who had "given" me the "shrinkage phenomenon."

Prior to 1927 when the *Psychological Abstracts* began, the literature was recorded in the *Psychological Index,* founded in 1894. It was a yearly listing of published titles, classified by subject, with an author index. A cumulative author-title index had been maintained by Woodworth at Columbia, an updated form of which has since been published by G. K. Hall, Boston, Massachusetts, in the well-known oversized green volumes. The purpose of the WPA project was to provide a cumulative subject index. Indexing from title was not considered adequate, and it was to be done from an examination of the article or book. People trained in psychology who qualified for relief employment went to the various libraries to provide abstracts to be indexed at the office. In this process it was found that many of the titles had already been abstracted, in various journals here and abroad. In fact for over 45,000 of the total of 107,000 titles in the *Psychological Index* (that is, 42 per cent), one or more published abstracts were located. I became the editor of a compendium which lists the numbers of the entries in the *Psychological Index* for which published abstracts have been found with the references to these abstracts. This compendium was published in two volumes (1940–1941). J. R. Kantor (*1942*) in his review did "hail these volumes as important bibliographical tools."

Modest as this job was in every respect, it became a uniquely valuable preparation for the next step, becoming assistant editor of the *Psychological Abstracts.* When Walter S. Hunter, at Brown University, founder and editor of the *Abstracts,* needed a replacement for Raymond R. Willoughby, I looked like just the right man to my sponsors at Columbia, and then to Hunter.

Both Rowena and I welcomed the move away from New York to Providence. We rented an old house on Humboldt Avenue not far from the university, and with the children spent a few very good years there. Our youngest son, Charles, was born in Providence, did his undergraduate work at Brown University (and met his wife there); our third son, Theodore, at one time did some post-doctoral work at Brown.

The job consisted of going through journals and books as they arrived each day and of checking what should be abstracted. The second phase was the editing of the abstracts as they came in. The third part consisted of making tabs for the annual author and subject index. The office force consisted of myself and two part-time secretaries—Alda Hunter, Walter's wife, in the morning, and Esther Hunt, Joe McVicker Hunt's wife, in the afternoon. I thought they both were very good, but Esther was my dream of an excellent typist and she was an extremely intelligent and warm person besides. The office was just one room, adjoining Hunter's office in an old medium-size former private residence on Waterman Street on a plot where years later the Walter S. Hunter Memorial Laboratory was erected. Hunter, as editor, examined the complete manuscript of an issue only before it went to the printer, which took him but several hours at one sitting. All the rest was up to me, and generally slow as I am, it took me a great deal of time. But the job gave me much satisfaction. In fun and secretly, I considered myself the key person of all psychology.

In many ways Hunter and I were far apart; for one thing he represented objective psychology and animal research. Yet I respected him very much and learned a great deal from him. He was a most capable department chairman, had gathered a fine and very congenial faculty, and knew how to select graduate students who would amount to something later on. In addition, he was much in demand in Washington.

The first person I met upon arrival, on the stairs of the psychology building, was Joe McVicker Hunt. He gave me such a hearty welcome that I have never forgotten it. And ever since, we have always thought that each time one met Joe one felt the better for it. We became very friendly also with Harold Schlosberg and family, Clarence Graham, the Carl Pfaffmanns, and Frank Finger. Then there were Lorrin and Doris Riggs; it was Lorrin who eventually suggested to me that I apply for a teaching position at the University of Vermont, where he had taught previously. Among the younger people with whom we became friends at Brown I should like to mention Neil Bartlett, Charles Cofer, Robert Gagne, George Lehner, Fred Mote, William Verplanck, Richard Solomon, and Stanley Williams.

As the United States became increasingly involved in World War II, other opportunities presented themselves and Hunter urged me to accept one of them. My present job did not hold enough future, he declared; he felt Willoughby had overstayed his time, and he did not want this mistake to be repeated by me. So, I accepted a job with the Office of War Information in the summer of 1943. Rowena and the children stayed on in Providence until the summer of 1945, when they moved to our Elizaville house to stay the year around. Up to that time they had spent the summers in Elizaville and I visited them on weekends.

WAR AND PEACE

German Military Psychology. Actually my war effort against Hitler started several years before I joined the Office of War Information. The war in Europe began September 1, 1939, and the United States entered December 7, 1941. For me as a German and a Jew, Hitler was the enemy from his start around 1923, and the fight had become acute after he seized power in 1933. Everyone made out all the affidavits he could to help his family and friends escape from disaster.

My first effort in psychology was the paper (1936) on the Nordic doctrine mentioned earlier. Having in this context surveyed recent German psychology, I became aware of numerous publications on German military psychology and also the publication in 1938 of a Polish bibliography on military psychology. After I received my Ph.D. I applied at several places for support in one or another project on the basis of this material. But nothing came of it.

By the fall of 1940 the Emergency Committee in Psychology had been established under the National Research Council "to prepare the profession for . . . the event of a great national crisis." Walter Hunter was a member of this committee. An annotated bibliography on war psychology was to be the first step, and Carroll C. Pratt of Rutgers was made editor. Of the fifteen sections one was to be on German military psychology and Pratt asked me if I "could find time to prepare a brief statement" (Letter, November 9, 1940). I jumped at the opportunity and spent all the time I could on the project, including holidays at the New York Public Library, where most of my sources were located. When it came to the organizing and writing, Rowena worked with me for entire days. By the middle of February 1941 the assignment was done, a systematic review with 148 references, entitled "German Military Psychology" (1941a). At the same time I also wrote a brief discussion of the Polish bibliography (1941b). Both these papers were included in the larger work edited by Pratt.

The paper on German military psychology was a great success. Pratt wrote right back, "I am greatly impressed . . . and can only hope that the other sections will come up to your high standard" (Letter, February 19, 1941). On Hunter's suggestion I also sent a copy to Walter V. Bingham, Director, Personnel Research Section, Adjutant General's Office. He was "thrilled" and immediately circulated copies among the AGO, G-1 and G-2 of the General Staff, and in the office of the Secretary of War (Letter, February 21, 1941). Waldemar Kaempffert (*1941*) wrote nearly two full columns on it in the *New York Times* and Marjorie van de Water gave it further publicity through a Science Service release, March 25, 1941.

The paper was paradoxically sensational because it was so unsensational. I had no special secret sources—merely material available to everyone, which I put together systematically. The system that emerged was one of selection of key personnel on principles of clinical psychology very much in line with the theory of personality as represented by Allport, and methods in which Henry Murray and his associates had pioneered. Ideas of race with which the politicians confronted them were politely put aside by the German military psychologists.

Such considerations led to a third paper that year (1941c), comparing point by point Murray's and Simoneit's German military methods of personality study. Max Simoneit was the scientific director of German military psychology. The principal similarity between the two methods was that both exposed the subject to many varied life-like situations in which he was rated by about six observers. Murray's reaction to the manuscript was quickly positive. At a later meeting he told me that this paper had been most helpful in obtaining approval for his OSS selection procedure which has since become well known. A fourth paper with K. R. Nichols (1941d) in the *Infantry Journal* was a more popular description of German officer selection with some case material from the literature. Finally, in an unpublished fifth paper "The Theory of German Military Psychology," I noted that the Germans were functionalists and that they stressed the uniqueness of the personality and most important, the unitary character of the individual—ideas similar to those of Wertheimer, Adler, Murray, and Allport, despite the difference in political system, which I found gratifying for a science of psychology. All this was done before America's entry into the war, in December 1941. After the war, Max Simoneit asked me to write an evaluation of the work of his organization. This was published in German (1949b) and in English (1949c).

Psychological Warfare. I was hired by the Office of War Information, Overseas Branch, for their London office, in the summer of 1943. The first step was a three-week training course at the OWI Technical Center, Lloyds Neck, Huntington, Long Island. The Center was located on the Marshall Field estate in the sixty-five-room mansion where thirty trainees at a time and their instructors were housed and classes were held. The subjects that were taught included everything for a propaganda operation, from principles of leaflet writing to offset reproduction and broadcasting techniques.

After spending, subsequent to this training, some time at the OWI office in New York City, I managed to find an interesting OWI assignment in Washington with Theodore M. Newcomb, while awaiting shipment to London. The assignment was a compilation of quotations from Hitler in German and English to be used in our propaganda. By the end of September I succeeded in compiling a volume of 157 pages which was reproduced in October (1943). But later research with prisoners showed that the idea of discrediting Hitler by quoting some of his earlier statements against him—such as, "The German Luftwaffe . . . will safeguard German territory"—was not as good as it seemed. The Germans considered themselves sufficiently sophisticated to write off such statements as political rhetoric.

Before shipment I could still spend some time at home in Providence. Finally, on November 2, a small group of OWI personnel, a commercial artist, a radio technician, a secretary, and myself, embarked from Halifax on a Norwegian freighter in a huge convoy of perhaps a hundred ships. We arrived in Liverpool two weeks later, after a very good trip.

I had no specific assignment beforehand, and in London the situation was also quite fluid. I was at first to familiarize myself with the German propaganda output which reached us regularly and profusely via Portugal, an international propaganda clearinghouse so to speak at that time. It just so happened that the German newspapers then carried many quite informative articles on problems of industrial psychology. In fact there was enough for a good ten-page paper for the *Psychological Bulletin* (1944b). This paper too was reviewed by Kaempffert (*1945*), and after the war Fitts (*1946*) found its statements generally confirmed.

By the end of January 1944 I was assigned to the Psychological Warfare Division (PWD, SHAEF). I studied in a German POW camp two hours west of London the reactions of the POWs to some of our leaflets and the weekly newspaper we dropped behind the German lines.* It was one of my greatest experiences thus to talk to Germans again, after that enormous wall that was erected in my mind through eleven years of Hitler and five years of war. It was for me like going into Germany and seeing that there were still individuals there the way I had known them. I remember talking to a young German who was rescued in the Mediterranean when his submarine was forced to surrender. In civilian life he had been a violinist and very unlike the kind of person one would have expected to find on a Nazi submarine. These studies conducted at the camp yielded some interesting recommendations, such as to avoid anything that might be interpreted as propaganda (for example, a caricature of Hitler) and instead to present material factually, rationally, and in personal rather than abstract terms. The Germans liked leaflets with a lot of reading material, such as on the Atlantic Charter.

Soon we did regular opinion surveys on various issues using questionnaires that were administered to large groups at one time. I became part of a larger survey team that had come to England, consisting of Elmo C. Wilson, Jerome Bruner, Hazel Gaudet, Hans Gottlieb, and John Riley, and we had an excellent group spirit. Shortly after D-Day, the invasion of France, June 6, 1944, Jerry Bruner and Jack Riley went to France to do opinion surveys on the French population in the Normandy. It had become the custom to inscribe one's jeep with one's favorite name. They inscribed theirs $\sqrt{\frac{PQ}{N}}$, the formula for the significance of the difference between two percentages, most important in survey technique.

Soon after the fall of Paris late in August, I was sent to France.

*When at the POW camp and later in France, I wore the Army officer's uniform with special civilian insignia.

The high point was when in September we administered questionnaires to 800 newly captured German troops in an open field enclosure near Revigny not far behind the front line, 150 miles east of Paris. We did a similar large-scale survey in October. We were stationed at a hotel in Paris which still had German orders on the walls and other reminders of the previous "guests."

I eventually published some of the results of these surveys as a monograph (1948b). One of the main findings was that the followers of Hitler had an image of him quite different from the real Hitler, but in accordance with their own desires and convictions. They would flatly disbelieve his statements when these were contrary to their own convictions. My study has been included in at least two textbooks of social psychology, one by Hartley and Hartley (*1952*), the other by Krech, Crutchfield, and Ballachey (*1962*).

From my first contact with a POW camp I learned to my dismay that anti-Nazis were at a disadvantage in our camps. For our authorities it was simpler to work through the Nazi bullies who knew so well how to keep things under control. This was perhaps even worse in the United States, where between September 1943 and April 1944 six murders and two forced suicides were reported, all but one "the result of terrorism against prisoners accused of anti-Nazi activities" (Porter, *1945*). This was in part in accordance with our national policy of unconditional surrender: If we consider all Germans Nazis we can punish them all alike. At that time the draft of a *Pocket Guide to Germany,* being prepared for our troops when they were to enter Germany, was shown to me for my opinion. It said that if any German tells you he was never a Nazi, don't believe him; 95 per cent voted for Hitler. The information that this election was held under terror and that in the last free election the Nazis received only 37 per cent of the vote was omitted. The postwar U.S. Bombing Survey concluded that 8 per cent and 31 per cent had been real and lukewarm Nazis, respectively, while 61 per cent had not been Nazis at all (Peak, *1945*)—pretty much the same proportions as in the elections some ten years earlier.

I should like to mention here the Austrian socialistic journalist Julius Braunthal who was also at the PWD in London. In him I found a soul mate in deploring our unethical and short-sighted policy, and also learned a great deal from him. I reviewed one of his books (1947a) for its excellent historical examples of phenomena of social psychology.

Later in the fall I was to be transferred to a group which was to function with the Military Government that was in preparation. But since the man in charge was one of the worst non-discriminating anti-Germans and since the war was obviously won by that time, I handed in my resignation and arrived back in New York early in December 1944.

Mission to Germany. After the war in Europe had ended on May 7, 1945, V-E Day, I was asked to go on a mission to Germany for the Navy to gain first-hand information on selection methods in the German Navy and to gather pertinent material. The mission consisted of Lieutenant Commander Daniel D. Feder, officer in charge; Harold Gulliksen, Educational Testing Service; and myself. We were in Europe during August and September, with headquarters again in Paris. Travel was by jeep, no other transportation being available, and this time I was in Navy field uniform with civilian insignia.

Once in Germany we separated part of the time to cover more territory. I had a jeep and driver; the other two also had an interpreter each. I interviewed fourteen former military or otherwise applied psychologists in northern Germany. While Gulliksen covered southern Germany Feder found the big treasure, a large quantity of the files and some books and apparatus of the naval selection station in Kiel which had been evacuated to Kappeln, a small town in Schleswig-Holstein. This material was shipped to Paris where I sifted and organized it with the invaluable assistance of a former German naval psychologist. It was then sent to the Bureau of Naval Personnel in Washington.

During July 1946 I worked on this material in Washington, completing a large report by the following summer (1948a). While a great deal of concrete new material had been added, it all fitted into the outline provided by my original paper (1941a).

Of the psychologists I met on the mission I should like to mention four with whom I became good friends. Dr. Udo Undeutsch, who subsequently became professor at Mainz, arranged for my teaching there during the summer of 1950, when Albert Wellek was department chairman. Dr. Ernst Bornemann and his wife Aenne turned out to be Adlerians, students of Seif, and Aenne and I wrote a brief paper entitled "Individual Psychology in Germany" (1949a). Ernst, who later became professor at Muenster, saw to it that our first Adler book (*1972*) was finally published in German and wrote the preface for it. Without him, I don't know when this would have come about. Professor Wolfgang Metzger had been an assistant to Wertheimer before Hitler and personifies the intrinsic relationship between Gestalt Psychology and Individual Psychology. After having concentrated for years on work in the former, he became instrumental in organizing the first postwar German Adlerian society and has of late edited the new German paperback edition of Adler's important books, providing them with excellent introductions and extensive indexes. Finally, I would like to express the warmest sentiments for the late Karl Mierke, professor at Kiel. When I found him in 1945, he was teaching school in a small village, after having been director of German naval psychology. Proud of his peasant origin, he was a man of great dignity, sincerity, and social consciousness. When he later invited me to spend a year in Kiel as a Fulbright lecturer I felt he wanted to show his appreciation for the way I had met him when he was at his low point. He embodied for me the qualities of Bach's music and Dürer's art. He too appreciated Adler, and his review of our first book when it appeared in English is today quoted on the jacket of the German edition. He and his wife lived in admirable harmony and simplicity.

The mission also gave me an opportunity to visit old friends I still had in Germany. But the country was prostrate and to take pictures seemed like a desecration of the dead. What about the Nazis, the reader may ask. Well, I did not meet any at that time. (When Rowena and I were in Florida early in 1972 people told us how strong George Wallace was, and subsequently he won the primary election; but we did not meet any Wallace supporters.)

A by-product of the interviews in Germany and the material found there was a paper on personnel methods used with foreign workers in Germany during the war (1950a). It showed that even with "slave labor" the same basic psychological principles and methods are applicable as in a free society and that "industrial relations" under these conditions are not limited to simple oppression. Characteristic of the spirit of that time Ross Stagner (*1950*) saw in this paper an attempt to white-wash Nazi inhumanity, and a slur on American industrial psychologists for finding any similarity between them and those who practiced under the Nazi regime. Still Stagner and I remained on friendly terms. Work on this paper also stimulated me toward a reinterpretation of some results by the U.S. Bombing Survey on attitudes of Russian workers in war-time Germany (1950b).

TEACHING PSYCHOLOGY

From what I had seen of government agencies, I certainly wanted to go into teaching. I had taught one semester of educational psychology in the spring of 1939 at Yeshiva College, New York. The job had been passed on to me by Saul Sells who had been succeeding Henry Garrett. Before that, friends had suggested that I do something about getting rid of my German accent and I took a course for this purpose. When I was made to listen to a playback of my voice, I was so shocked that I decided I would have to succeed in spite of it, or not at all.

After returning from England I found a teaching position at Brooklyn College as a substitute in the evening session during spring and fall 1945. Because of the mission to Germany in August and September that year, I was given a leave for that time. Charles Winslow was in charge of the evening session, while Daniel Katz was department chairman. I taught general psychology, applied psychology, and personality, and I remember recommending Adler's *What Life Should Mean to You* as outside reading. My appointment was not renewed since the man for whom I was substituting returned from the Army. One of my gains from Brooklyn College was that I got to know Isidore Chein who impressed me with his general wisdom.

My family moved that summer from Providence to Elizaville to stay there until I found a position of some permanency. While at Brooklyn I stayed in a furnished room near the campus and went home on weekends. After Brooklyn, I enjoyed the winter at home in Elizaville, besides looking for a job.

The middle of February 1946 I received a wire from Donald K. Adams, Duke University, asking, "Are you available for temporary appointment March 1st to July 1st to teach three to four sections of elementary psychology?" I was, left Elizaville in snow and ice, and arrived down there in lovely spring weather. I had met Don Adams in London. I was able to give him some information he was looking for, and we got along well. Thus I had written him in December about a job. Things went very well at Duke. I even got some research done (1947b). Karl Zener, the department chairman, and Don were the first translators of Kurt Lewin, and William Stern had spent his last years at Duke. There was a congenial atmosphere. Sigmund Koch, whom I liked a great deal, was there. So were J. B. Rhine and his ESP group. In fact, my office was on the same floor as theirs, in a monumental old building with very high ceilings and enormously wide hallways. They were especially friendly and enjoyable people, and one could avoid the topic of ESP.

After Duke came an appointment at the University of Vermont where I have remained. Lorrin Riggs, who had been at Brown, had been at Vermont for a time. When Professor John T. Metcalf, the department chairman, needed someone in the spring of 1945, Riggs suggested me. But nothing came of it. In May 1946, however, Metcalf asked me if I was still interested. Burlington was for us a place of choice, alone geographically speaking. I had grown up in Frankfurt, where there was much green, and one could go hiking in the nearby mountains on Sundays. That was the way I felt it really should be, and Burlington met this criterion. Besides I liked to ski. The Metcalfs were lovely people, and once you had joined the small department you were a member of their family. When we moved, they were still on vacation and let us live in their house—small children, cat, and all—until we found something. There seemed to be just one house available in Burlington at that time which we took. With some renovations now and then, we have lived there ever since.

Professor Metcalf was a gentleman of the old New England tradition. That meant he was broadminded and liberal, except regarding Midwesterners and Catholics; in his eyes they were a certain cultural menace.

Although we were only a small department, about four or five people, and a relatively small college with an enrollment under 3000, there were at least ten sections of Introductory Psychology, which was a two-semester course. We all used the same textbook and the same questions for the objective part of the exams. This seriously interfered with my teaching what I thought was important and made me quite unhappy. But I saw no alternative but to submit. Of course there was complete freedom in the other courses.

For a number of years I taught social psychology, using Krech and Crutchfield as soon as it appeared in 1948. I profited enormously from that book. While I had a fairly good understanding of Gestalt Psychology, I had not realized before how excellently it could be applied to all problems of beliefs and attitudes. Much of it became reflected in our book on Adler. The course itself was considered difficult by the students, but always had a large enrollment nevertheless. After a number of years I traded this course for one in personality. This naturally became a course in Adlerian psychology and is my most important course.

My other important course was one of two semesters in Tests and Measurements. It was in fact an introduction to clinical psychology for seniors, with practicum. Since a practicum for undergraduates was somewhat innovative, I wrote the course up for publication (1957). Several smaller research papers resulted from this course (1952, 1956c, 1960, 1965d). Today I teach my basic undergraduate course and various clinical graduate seminars with an Adlerian orientation.

As mentioned briefly, I had two opportunities to teach in Germany, in Mainz in the summer of 1950, and in Kiel, 1954–1955. There, in addition to a course on Adler, I taught American objective methods of testing. I also learned to my amazement that German students are not so different from Americans. There always are only a few who understand and are really with you, while the rest are more interested in meeting requirements.

There was also one summer session at Brandeis University in 1960 to which Abe Maslow asked me to speak on Adlerian psychology during the second part of a course. Charlotte Bühler had taught the first part. We overlapped enough to meet with her and Karl, which was a fine reunion for us. In 1965 I taught Adlerian theory during the summer at Oregon State University in Corvallis, which had been arranged by our fellow Adlerian, the educator Maurice Bullard. Of late, I have been asked on various occasions to speak on Adler.

James P. Chaplin, a new Ph.D. under P. T. Young, came to Vermont a year after I did and we were for many years close colleagues. From 1954–1964 Jim was department chairman succeeding Metcalf. Jim resigned because of increasing pressure toward expansion into a full-fledged graduate program, which he resisted. His successor was Don Forgays, a very able and likable expansionist with an uncanny knack for securing grants—even for me, for work on untranslated writings of Adler. An experimental and a clinical Ph.D. program were developed, and the department moved into a brand-new building created inside the shell of the old medical school, John Dewey Hall, very appropriately so renamed, after the distinguished alumnus of the University of Vermont.

CONCENTRATING ON ADLERIAN PSYCHOLOGY

As I consider the course of my life, I see it in three major stages: 1904–1932, youth and floundering; 1933–1950, finding and becoming established in psychology, as well as finding my wife and getting a family started; since 1951, systematizing, disseminating, and advancing Adlerian theory.

In terms of my career the last period is unquestionably the most significant. It is treated here relatively briefly and the second period looms large but this is because I have already expressed in numerous papers what would be relevant here (see references to author's publications). On the other hand, before now the second period had almost completely sunk into oblivion. When I revived it for the present occasion I found it surprisingly interesting and thought others might also find it so.

To have dedicated myself since 1951 to one particular approach in psychology—and a less known one at that time—I must have had strong convictions about it. These are:

1. Psychology as generally taught, namely, exclusively as a natural science, implies complete determinism, a totally depleted self. This is wrong in fact, and damaging as a belief because it makes for fatalism, with feelings of helplessness and dehumanization. It is on these assumptions that Freud's (1917) credence as a "scientist" essentially rests. He prided himself in proving that man "is not even master in his own house" (p. 252), a seriously pathogenic statement. In mental disturbance man feels himself indeed a help-

less victim; but in mental health he feels in control of the situation. I was convinced that Adler's psychology was truly one of mental health, pointing to man as active and creative, "the artist of his own personality" (1956b, p. 177). And like any artist, man shapes his personality according to a guiding image, a goal of perfection. This assumption puts Adlerian psychology on a teleological rather than a causalistic basis.

2. If man is to a crucial degree self-determined, he is confronted with the necessity of making choices. Psychology as a science attempting to do justice to its subject matter must then offer some guidance for making choices. Psychology cannot be value-free. I was convinced that Adler's formulation in this respect was the simplest and most ingenious: Man, living in society and having created all the cultures and languages in communication and cooperation with his fellow men, must have an innate aptitude for social living. This being an aptitude, not a full-fledged instinct, it must be consciously developed to become operative. Once developed it becomes an interest in the interests of others, a social interest. The developed social interest becomes ultimately the most valid criterion for all our choices. It is also the criterion of mental health. (See 1968b.)

3. While the various components of Adler's theory have been expressed by philosophers before him, he developed his viewpoint as a practitioner. I was convinced that he expressed it in a way that is most teachable and widely applicable, meeting especially well the requirements of a psychology "to be given away" to the people (G. A. Miller, *1969*). Avoiding esoteric language, Adler's explicit aim was to develop a theory that "could bring greater gain to all people" (1964d, p.363n) than other theories could. At the same time its philosophy of science, founded on Kant, Marx, Nietzsche, Bergson, and Vaihinger (1965c, 1972a), is highly sophisticated. Adler's theory can be described in as few as four basic concepts: (a) the unity, creativity and goal-orientation of the individual—his style of life, as Adler introduced this term into psychology; (b) the individual's course of life as a continuous movement from a felt minus situation (inferiority), toward a felt plus situation (superiority), toward a subjective goal of success; (c) man's aptitude for harmonious living in his various social systems—social interest; (d) mental disorders as errors in method

of living which can be corrected once proper training methods have been devised, rather than disease processes.

Rowena shared these convictions. We considered our most important professional obligation to be to concentrate our efforts on the advancement of Adlerian psychology.

Books. Adler's strength as practitioner and theoretician was not matched by strength as an expository writer. His writings did not do justice to the sophistication behind his apparent simplicity. Thus it would be important to present Adler's work in a way notable to the academic world, so that the world at large would eventually recognize Adler and gain by him. This is what Rowena and I attempted with our first edited book, *The Individual Psychology of Alfred Adler* (1956b). We began to work on it in the summer of 1951, and it took nearly every minute of our available time until the summer of 1954.

Our most important conceptualization was that Individual Psychology is no more a form of psychoanalysis than functionalism is a form of structuralism or than Gestalt Psychology is a form of behaviorism. Rather the line-up is: structuralism, behaviorism, Freudian psychoanalysis *vs.* functionalism, Gestalt Psychology, Adler's psychology (pp. 3–9).

The book accomplished as much as we could have hoped. Luckily it was in proofs when Hall and Lindzey prepared their *Theories of Personality.* They heard about it, requested a set, and largely based on it their section on Adler. Many textbooks have since followed suit. In 1970 even the *Great Soviet Encyclopedia*, third edition, in a radically changed entry on Alfred Adler (*1970*), showed the influence of our book and referred to it. It has been published in paperback (1964c), in Spanish (1959c), and recently in German (1972b). It represents undoubtedly the high point of our effort and our achievement.

Allport's reaction to the book in a heretofore unpublished letter to us was:

> I keep thinking how very grateful Adler would be. He is a man whose ideas were first-rate, but whose supporting logic was second-rate, and whose exposition was third-rate. Now . . . the logical structure is made first-rate through your organization and comments; and by merciful selection and interpretative comments you even improved the exposition to a point of high readability. I have never thought it possible to enjoy reading Adler, as much as I agreed with him, but now . . . I

actually did enjoy the reading. . . . The job is simply first rate. . . . I repeat, how lucky Adler was to have your backstopping of his lifework (Letter, December 2, 1956).

Eight years later, our second edited book, Alfred Adler, *Superiority and Social Interest* (1964d), was published. While the first attempted to give an overview of all of Adler, the second presents in full Adler's important later writings which had not heretofore appeared in book form or translation. It includes Adler's essay "Religion and Individual Psychology," a biographical essay by his early co-worker, Carl Furtmüller, and a complete bibliography of over 350 titles. It has recently appeared in paperback (1972c), and a Spanish edition (1968e) has also been published. It is interesting to note that both books appeared also in separate editions in England (1958, 1965e); these, however, did not succeed and were discontinued.

We further edited somewhat and wrote new introductions for the paperback editions of Adler's *Problems of Neurosis: A Book of Case Histories* (1964b) and *The Science of Living* (1969a). Our future plans include the further editing and publishing of works by Adler.

Journal of Individual Psychology. After the first book was out Rowena and I wanted to relax for a while. Thus when in the fall of 1956 the American Society of Adlerian Psychology offered us the editorship of its journal, to succeed Rudolf Dreikurs, we declined. That same evening Fred Thorne happened to drop in for a visit. He persuaded us, with the best intentions, to change our minds—and we accepted. Jokingly, we have never forgiven him, for since then the *Journal* has not let go of us.

We considered one function of the *Journal* to integrate Adlerian psychology with the wider field by attracting non-Adlerian writers who are in essential agreement with the basic Adlerian propositions. In line with this, the following have been among our authors: Hadley Cantril, Albert Ellis, Viktor E. Frankl, George A. Kelly, Salvatore R. Maddi, A. H. Maslow, Ashley Montagu, Julian B. Rotter, Joseph F. Rychlak, Frederick C. Thorne, and Robert W. White. Through our book reviews and book notes we have consistently attempted to bring out mutual relationships for the benefit of the authors as well as our readers.

Papers. Over the years I have dealt in separate papers with numerous special topics in Adlerian psychology, often in response to specific requests for participation in a symposium or otherwise. These papers can be conveniently classified according to their topics as historical (1949a, 1959a, 1961b, 1962a, 1962b, 1968c, 1970c, 1971b), theoretical (1951, 1959b, 1964a, 1965a, 1965b, 1965c, 1966b, 1967, 1968a, 1968b, 1969b, 1972a), clinical (1961a, 1966a, 1966c, 1970a, 1971d, 1972d), and research (1947b, 1947c, 1953, 1960, 1965d). There are also four encyclopedia articles varying considerably in length and importance (1956a, 1968d, 1970b, 1971a).

Fellow Adlerians. Beginning with the time when Adler was still alive we have been on friendly terms with his children Alexandra and Kurt, both psychiatrists in New York City. They have on many occasions been most helpful with our editing and writing.

During my early days of writing on Adler the *Individual Psychology Bulletin,* which Rudolf Dreikurs started in Chicago in 1940 and which eventually became the present journal, offered me an opportunity to formulate my thoughts. Later, I contributed quite frequently to the *Individual Psychology News Letter* which Paul Rom founded in London in 1951 and still edits for the International Association of Individual Psychology.

Another platform was offered by the Alfred Adler Institute, New York City, where I was asked to speak several times. At first Danica Deutsch, who combines devotion, warmth, and energy, and later also Dr. Helene Papanek, got me involved there. Becoming acquainted with other Adlerians was greatly facilitated by the annual meetings of the American Society of Adlerian Psychology, which was founded in 1952. I had the honor of serving as its president from 1957 to 1960. At the annual meeting in New York City in 1967, Rudolf Dreikurs, upon the suggestion of Rowena, held one of his counselling sessions before an audience, in the manner Adler had introduced. We were greatly impressed by this and subsequently suggested that he be invited to Vermont the following summer to give a course of counseling demonstrations before the cameras of the Educational Television Studio of the University. The course was very successful in all respects and Dr. Dreikurs was asked to give similar courses the three following summers, until his death in May 1972. The videotapes that were made will remain valuable training aids. For us these courses were a great experience in psychotherapy, filling an important gap in our training.

SINCE 1970

In 1970 I became Professor Emeritus and find myself as the honored senior citizen in the department, with a half-time undergraduate and graduate teaching load.

The year 1970 was memorable for the Adlerian movement as the celebration of the centennial of Adler's birth, February 7, 1870. Two issues of the *Journal of Individual Psychology* were devoted to the celebration. And there was a joint meeting in New York City of the International Association of Individual Psychology and the American Society of Adlerian Psychology.

This was followed by a workshop at the University of Vermont of those engaged in training Adlerian counsellors and psychotherapists. The workshop was organized by Rowena, and has been summarized and reported by her (*1971*). In the summers of 1972 and 1973 she coordinated two further workshops in Adlerian psychology for students in general, in which I participated together with others.

In 1970–71 I was president of Division 24 (Philosophical Psychology) of the American Psychological Association. One of the president's functions was to arrange the Annual Invitational Dialogue between a distinguished philosopher and a distinguished psychologist for the meeting in Washington in 1971. Rowena suggested inviting Walter Kaufmann, the Nietzsche scholar from Princeton University, as the philosopher, and he was good enough to accept. He in turn suggested Rollo May as the discussant. Kaufmann's topic was "Decidophobia: Fear of Making Fateful Decisions," from a book that was then in preparation and has since been published (Kaufmann, *1973*). The meeting was attended by several hundred persons and Kaufmann (*1973,* pp. 261–262) expressed his gratitude to the APA for the opportunity to present his ideas to such a large and responsive audience.

Kaufmann also consented to participate in a session on "Will to Power Re-examined" at the parallel meeting of the Association of Humanistic Psychology. Kaufmann (*1972*) spoke on "Nietzsche's Concept of the Will to Power," and my topic was "Adler's

'Striving for Power,' in Relation to Nietzsche" (1972a). The third speaker was Helene Papanek, M.D. (*1972*), on "Pathology of Power Striving and Its Treatment." This session apparently led to my being invited to participate in an interdepartmental symposium on Nietzsche at Syracuse University, November 2–4, 1972. Kaufmann spoke at this occasion on "Nietzsche and Existentialism," and Rollo May the next evening on "Nietzsche's Contributions to Psychology." I followed May with a brief paper on "Nietzsche's Influence on Adler."

On March 24 and 25, 1972, the Fourth Brief Psychotherapy Conference sponsored by the department of psychiatry at the Chicago Medical School was devoted to "Adlerian Techniques of Psychotherapy." I had been fortunate in having been involved in the inception of this conference and had the privilege of being its còdirector together with H. H. Garner, M.D., chairman of the department. Rudolf Dreikurs on his seventy-fifth birthday was honoree and also main contributor. Some three hundred persons attended. The proceedings of the conference have been published in the November 1972 issue of the *Journal.*

At the end of November 1972, I was with Rowena on a two-week lecture tour in Holland and Germany, sponsored by the German Society of Individual Psychology. I spoke to Adlerian groups in Amsterdam, Aachen, Delmenhorst near Bremen, Düsseldorf, and Munich, to a psychoanalytic group in Berlin, and at the Universities of Nijmegen and Münster. It was a stimulating experience and we were impressed by the zest, caliber, and vigor of the German Society, which had only recently been revived.

As to the coming years, there are numerous projects waiting and I only hope that I shall be able to realize some of the more important ones.

EARLY YEARS

There remains to give an account of the first part of my life and to join it with the rest. Some of it may already have been mentioned incidentally.

My parents were Max and Emilie Dinkelspiel Ansbacher. They were well-to-do. We lived in Frankfurt on a very nice airy street, the Beethoven-Strasse, in a new fourteen-room apartment plus servants' quarters, with cook, housemaid, governess, etc. Relatively early I developed an opposition to certain aspects of this way of living, although I certainly appreciated the pleasantness of the entire setting. I considered earning money fine, because that was a skill, a competence, as exemplified by my father. But I did not see that the possession of money and its spending created any values, as exemplified by the women in my home and in the broader family. I felt closer to servants and others who worked for their living.

There were two children; I had a sister who was five years older than I. She made my life rather miserable in the early years, pulling my ear, refusing to go out with "such an ugly, funny-looking child," etc.

My mother must originally have been very attractive; she was cordial; she played the piano well; and she was interested in horses. But she had become quite neurotic. She was frequently "sick" in bed, or was in nearby Mannheim with her mother. The splendid apartment was hardly used properly. There was almost no entertaining, although my father would have liked this very much; we lived in the modest rear part, while the lavish front rooms remained unused. I felt sorry for my father.

My mother was very ambitious for me. It was not only important that I go to the best school but I had to be among the best in the class. Apparently I was not, and consequently I had to submit to supplementary private tutoring, which I did not like at all. Eventually I was left to my own devices, but never was among the best students, except in composition.

When I was about twelve or thirteen years old my mother had a very good gymnastic apparatus, with crossbar and all, installed in the backyard so that I would become a good athlete. This really accomplished its purpose. In 1917 the school was closed for several months on account of a fuel shortage and my good friend with whom I shared a bench in school and who was a fine athlete practiced with me. From then on I also was a good athlete and considered myself as such.

I was never afraid of getting into fights. I fought mostly for the underdogs in the class, whose side I generally took. I was also in on pranks aimed at teachers. Finally, I was one of the small anti-war group in our class, beginning in 1917. With all that, real, lasting friendships developed, and my closest friends to date are from these years in the Goethe-Gymnasium, which was the name of the school. Rowena has come to share and cultivate these friendships with me. Today even some of the next generation are good friends.

My father always had my highest respect and admiration, as he was admired by many other people. His three younger brothers and five sisters venerated him. With one of his brothers he continued the family banking and brokerage business. This had been founded in Fürth, Bavaria, in 1818, a few decades after one of our ancestors had come from Ansbach to Fürth, where he acquired the family name. After my grandfather's death in 1889 the family moved to Frankfurt. The two other brothers were also in finance, one in Paris, the other in London. Successful in his enterprises and reasonably proud of this, my father could be a fierce fighter in some litigations in which he had become involved. Yet he was a very kind and essentially very modest man who had an open mind and a good sense of humor. On Sundays, rain or shine, my father and I hiked in the nearby Taunus Mountains, always joining with friends and relatives on the way. The motto was, "There is no bad weather, there are only bad shoes." The following may illustrate what kind of father he was.

The German collapse and revolution in November 1918 provided great excitement. I used to go to the central railway station, mingle with the returning troops, and gather and collect discarded Army insignia and equipment. I also went to all kinds of political meetings and collected revolutionary newspapers. I did this quite alone. My mother must have told her physician about my doings and he asked my father what he thought of all this. My father replied, "Of course my son can do this. He must see what goes on and form his own opinion." One day I told my father of a meeting of a crackpot political group which I attended, where a collection was taken up to defray the cost. He asked, "Did you give anything?" I had not. He said, "You should have; after all, you went and got something out of it."

My father died in December 1919, when I was fifteen. Following Jewish law, for many months after his death I went to the synagogue every morning before school. Nobody told me to do so, and I had not been brought up very religiously. But I wanted to do something in the face of this event, and found in this need the support and company of an orthodox Jewish classmate. My father had taught me one or two prayers in Hebrew and I had also had some Hebrew lessons. He liked being a Jew and one reason was, as he said, that he counted for so much more belonging to a minority; I accepted this view.

My mother died in December 1920, a year after the death of my father. My sister and I continued in the apartment with the old household help. Soon my sister got married and her husband moved in. After my graduation in 1923 I had neither the courage to go into my father's business, which was now conducted by my uncle alone, nor the courage to go to the university in preparation for a profession. But I knew I wanted to get away from home. So I went to Hamburg to take a job with a stock brokerage firm to which I had been recommended. Yet I did not feel successful. I registered for university courses in sociology and economics in the evening, but I attended only a few classes. However, I became very fond of my landlord's entire family, a friendship which Rowena and I have maintained to this day.

As a "student" I had the opportunity to be hired on a boat to see the world. I became a dishwasher and pantry man on a Hamburg-America liner that went to Spain, Cuba, and Mexico. It was a great experience to see how it really is to earn a living, to be with entirely different people, and to see the world. When my uncle in London said afterwards, "Why did you not tell me? I would gladly have paid for your trip," he showed that he had completely missed the point.

After this trip I was, of course, no further along in knowing what I wanted to do than before. So I came to the United States. Again I had a recommendation to a brokerage firm. I worked for $12 a week as a "runner" until I knew the language better. Gradually I was promoted to clerk at $17 a week. I managed to live on my salary, and this gave me satisfaction. I also enjoyed the awareness that the ordinary man here had a much better chance in life than he did in Germany at that time. Eventually I earned a very good salary due to accounts that I was able to bring in through my family connections. But this did not give me a feeling of personal accomplishment. The great consolation was the girl I met one day, ice-skating in the park. But after four years of indecision on my part she ended the relationship, which resulted in the crisis with which I began my account.

CHANGE, CONSTANCY, AND FULFILLMENT

Regarding the totality of a human life there is always the problem of constancy and change in style of life. In my case, where there was a considerable change from the early to the later periods, what changed, and what remained constant?

The Adlerian approach to life is one of problem-solving, Adler having recognized three main life problems, or if you wish, existential problems. These are the problems of occupation, love and marriage, and social living in general, including friendship. I clearly had difficulty with the first two. With the help of Adler I became able to meet these problems more courageously and more responsibly than before. That was the change. It included changes in goals and in their concretization. While these changes were crucial, constancies may already have become apparent. These can be brought out further through a few additional earliest and later recollections, as the following.

In the apartment in which my family and I lived prior to the one described above, I was standing one day on the small rear balcony facing the back yard with a whip in my hand. It was a very special whip in that I had tied pieces of string together so that it would reach from the second floor, where we lived, down to the ground. In this way I hoped to control the small spitz down in the yard, perhaps whip him. Of course, this did not work. Instead, the spitz played with the end of the string as I wiggled it. I did not mind this outcome. Regarding the same spitz I am also said to have made the wise pronouncement "When the dog is behind the fence, I am not afraid."

In the closet of the children's living room in the later apartment, a corner of the lowest tier had been assigned to me, and it was crammed with my things. I remember one time sitting in front of it on the floor, pleased because I had finally succeeded in arranging everything in an orderly way.

During the later part of the war there was an ongoing salvage drive by the school children. I distinguished myself in this and still have the diploma and the medal that I earned. I also had various collections, among these the unusual one of unused ration coupons. In addition, I collected extremist newspapers, as mentioned before.

The common denominators in these stories are maintaining a certain distance; dealing with things rather than people; showing deliberation; and saving, collecting, putting pieces together, systematizing—all of which involve a certain degree of pedantry. The saving and collecting were, however, not a blind hoarding, but for some future historical use.

A certain interest in the socially useful and in efforts at social betterment can also be noted in my early attitudes, such as a dislike for the "idle rich," beginning within my own family, and identification with those earning a living and with the underdog. I had, of course, been the underdog with my sister. My interest was in earning my own living; I remember one time on a walk with my governess when I was about eleven years old that I tried to figure out how little I could live on some day.

When I was still a small boy, my father impressed upon me that if we were a royal family I would be the heir to the realm, the crown prince. But as soon as I started thinking about such matters, I was convinced that I could never in any way come even near to my father in accomplishment. With this relatively low opinion of myself I apparently created in the situation an ideal for myself of preserver of the realm. I would some day hand the trust over in good condition to the next generation, for more glorious days again. It is in line with such comforting consciousness of a continuity that I remember the title of one of my high school themes which I had selected from several options. It was, "Man as a link in the chain of his lineage."

My work in Adlerian psychology brought all these earlier tendencies into play. (a) Adlerian psychology was a very small area in psychology and was in keeping with my satisfaction with a minority position. (b) Its emphasis on social usefulness coincided with my interest in social issues and my sympathy for the underdog. (c) Its dynamics of goal striving and overcoming of inferiority feelings were quite obviously of interest to me. (d) The work on Adler's legacy was of the cast of a custodianship. I recognized in

Adler's work a great treasure ,and considered it my particular calling to present it in the best possible way to our contemporaries and so preserve it. Allport saw this when he wrote of our "backstopping" Adler's lifework. (e) Our work itself required some of the traits shown in my early recollections. Again, as Allport described it, it involved "many hours, indeed years, spent in selecting, fitting, refitting, and finding proper headings." The editing of the journal is similar in nature. The review of German military psychology was almost like a training exercise for the major work. And even before that, my first edited "book" consisted of a collection of potentially useful bits of information salvaged from the Psychological Index project.

The big change in my life, the fact that I became a psychologist, is not as relevant to my actual life style, as is where in psychology I eventually found my place. I did not continue in experimentation, although I had made a fairly good start; I did not go into attitude and opinion research, although it was fascinating to me for a while; I did not become a practicing clinician, although I was close enough to such work to do so. And I was never an administrator, nor was I ever politically effective. Where I found my place is quite in line with many early indications. And this is where the constancies in my life style are.

In a goal-oriented, holistic model of man, "The best life is that in which the goals . . . are progressively more realized" (Maddi, *1970,* p. 156), resulting in a sense of fulfillment. Maddi (*1968*) has considerably contributed to a better understanding of Adler's theory by classifying it with the "fulfillment models." Still, Adler mentioned fulfillment seldom since he looked at life not retrospectively, but prospectively. The idea was there, however, as in "a goal . . . which appears to offer fulfillment" (1956b, p. 187), and "the main line of movement [which is] in the direction of a fulfillment" (Adler, *1970,* p. 39). As I look back on my life from the viewpoint of Adlerian psychology and see the numerous goals that I was fortunate enough to be able to realize, I note a growing sense of fulfillment–side by side with still existing feelings of inadequacy and incompletion.

REFERENCES

References to Author's Publications

1936 Baker, Andrew [Pseudonym]. Recent trends in the Nordic doctrine. *Journal of Psychology,* 2, 151–159.

1937 (a) Perception of number as affected by the monetary value of the objects. *Archives of Psychology, N.Y.,* No. 214. Pp. 88.
(b) With Rowena R. Ansbacher. Alfred Adler: 1870–1937. *Sociometry,* 1, 259–261.

1938 Further investigation of the Harold C. Brown shrinkage phenomenon. *Psychological Bulletin,* 35, 701.

1940/1941 (Ed.) *Psychological Index: Abstract References of Volumes 1–35, 1894–1928.* (2 vols.) New York and Evanston, Ill.: Work Projects Administration and American Psychological Association, Northwestern University. Pp. 178, ix, and 241.

1941 (a) German military psychology. *Psychological Bulletin,* 38, 370–392.
(b) The gasiorowski bibliography of military psychology. *Psychological Bulletin,* 38, 505–508.
(c) Murray's and Simoneit's (German military) methods of personality study. *Journal of Abnormal and Social Psychology,* 36, 589–592.
(d) With K. R. Nichols. Selecting the Nazi officer. *Infantry Journal,* 49 (November), 44–48.

1943 [Anon.] *Hitler's Wartime Speeches: An Indexed Selection of German Quotations with English Translations.* Office of War Information, Overseas Intelligence, October. Pp. ii and 157.

1944 (a) Distortion in the perception of real movement. *Journal of Experimental Psychology,* 34, 1–23.
(b) German industrial psychology in the fifth year of war. *Psychological Bulletin,* 41, 605–614.

1945 With K. Mather. Group differences in size estimation. *Psychometrika,* 10, 37–56.

1947 (a) Review of J. Braunthal, in search of millennium. *Journal of Abnormal and Social Psychology,* 42, 146–148.
(b) Adler's place today in the psychology of memory. *Individual Psychology Bulletin,* 6, 32–40. Also in *Journal of Personality,* 15, 197–207.
(c) Alfred Adler's place in psychology today. *Internationale Zeitschrift für Individualpsychologie,* 16, 97–111.

1948 (a) *German naval psychology* (NavPers 18080). Washington, D.C., Princeton, N.J.: Bureau of Naval Personnel, College Entrance Examination Board. April. Pp. v and 91.
(b) Attitudes of German prisoners of war; a study of the dynamics of national-socialistic followership. *Psychological Monographs,* 62 (1). Pp. v and 42.

1949 (a) With Aenne Bornemann. Individual Psychology in Germany. *Individual Psychology Bulletin,* 7, 30–32.
(b) Bleibendes und Vergängliches aus der deutschen Wehrmachtpsychologie. *Mitteilungen des Berufsverbandes Deutscher Psychologen,* 3(11), 3–9.
(c) Lasting and passing aspects of German military psychology. *Sociometry,* 12, 301–312.

1950 (a) Testing, management and reactions of foreign workers in Germany during World War II. *American Psychologist,* 5, 38–49.
(b) The problem of interpreting attitude survey data: a case study of the attitude of Russian workers in wartime Germany. *Public Opinion Quarterly,* 14, 126–138.

1951 Causality and indeterminism according to Alfred Adler, and some current American personality theories. *Individual Psychology Bulletin,* 9, 96–107. Also in K. Adler and Danica Deutsch (eds.), *Essays in Individual Psychology.* New York: Grove Press, 1959. Pp. 27–40.

1952 The Goodenough Draw-a-Man Test and primary mental abilities. *Journal of Consulting Psychology,* 16, 172–180.

1953 "Neo-Freudian" or "neo-Adlerian"? Report on a survey conducted among members of the American Psychoanalytic Association. *American Psychologist,* 8, 165–166.

1956 (a) Adler, Alfred. *Encyclopaedia Britannica.*
(b) With Rowena R. Ansbacher (eds.). *The Individual Psychology of Alfred Adler; A systematic Presentation in Selections from His Writings.* New York: Basic Books. Pp. xxiii and 503.
(c) Social interest, an Adlerian rationale for the Rorschach human movement response. *Journal of Projective Techniques,* 20, 363–365. Also in K. Adler and Danica Deutsch (eds.), *Essays in Individual Psychology.* New York: Grove Press, 1959. Pp. 41–45.

1957 A training unit in individual testing at the undergraduate level. *American Psychologist,* 12, 151–153.

1958 With Rowena R. Ansbacher (eds.). *The Individual Psychology of Alfred Adler: A Systematic Presentation in Selections from His Writings.* London: Allen & Unwin. Pp. xxiii and 503.

1959 (a) The significance of the socio-economic status of the patients of Freud and of Adler. *American Journal of Psychotherapy,* 13, 376–382.
(b) Anomie, the sociologist's conception of lack of social interest. *Journal of Individual Psychology,* 15, 212–214.
(c) With Rowena R. Ansbacher (eds.). *La psicología individual de Alfred Adler: presentación sistemática de una selección de sus escritos.* Buenos Aires: Troquel. Pp. 570.

1960 With Robert I. Keimowitz. Personality and achievement in mathematics. *Journal of Individual Psychology,* 16, 84–87.

1961 (a) Suicide: The Adlerian point of view. In N. L. Farberow and E. S. Schneidman (eds.), *The Cry for Help.* New York: Blakiston, McGraw-Hill. Pp. 204–219.
(b) On the origin of Holism. *Journal of Individual Psychology,* 17, 142–148.

1962 (a) Rudolf Hildebrand: A forerunner of Alfred Adler. *Journal of Individual Psychology,* 18, 12–17.
(b) Was Adler a disciple of Freud? *Journal of Individual Psychology,* 18, 126–135.

1964 (a) Ego psychology and Alfred Adler. *Social Casework,* 45, 268–272.
(b) Introduction to the Torchbook edition. In A. Adler, ‡△*pγ*¯*lems of Neurosis: A Book of Case Histories.* Ed. by P. Mairet. New York: Torchbooks, Pp. ix-xxvi.
(c) With Rowena R. Ansbacher (eds.). *The Individual Psychology of Alfred Adler: A Systematic Presentation in Selections from His Writings.* New York: Harper & Row. Pp. xxiii and 503.
(d) With Rowena R. Ansbacher (eds.). Alfred Adler. *Superiority and Social Interest: A Collection of Later Writings, with a Biographical Essay by Carl Furtmüller.* Evanston, Ill.: Northwestern University Press. Pp. xxi and 432.

1965 (a) The structure of Individual Psychology. In B. B. Wolman and E. Nagel (eds.) *Scientific Psychology: Principles and Approaches.* New York: Basic Books. Pp. 340–364.
(b) With Paul Rom. An Idlerian case or a character by Sartre? *Journal of Individual Psychology,* 21, 32–40.
(c) Sensus privatus versus sensus communis. *Journal of Individual Psychology,* 21, 48–50.
(d) With Patricia A. Stone. Social interest and performance on the Goodenough Draw-a-man Test. *Journal of Individual Psychology,* 21, 178–186.
(e) With Rowena R. Ansbacher (eds.). Alfred Adler. *Superiority*

and Social Interest: A Collection of Later Writings, with a Biographical Essay by Carl Furtmüller. London: Routledge & Kegan Paul. Pp. xxi and 432.

1966 (a) With Rowena R. Ansbacher, D. Shiverick, and Kathleen Shiverick. Lee Harvey Oswald: an Adlerian interpretation. *Psychoanalytic Review,* 53, 379–390.
(b) Love and violence in the view of Adler. *Humanitas, Duquesne University,* 2, 109–127.
(c) Co-discussant with H. E. Altenberg, J. L. D. Cos, A. R. Maher, Esther Menaker, and R. V. Speck. What's in a dream? *Voices,* 2 (4), 37–42.

1967 Life style: A historical and systematic review. *Journal of Individual Psychology,* 23, 191–212.

1968 (a) Adler's theory of Individual Psychology. In L. Gorlow and W. Katkovsky (eds.), *Readings in the Psychology of Adjustment.* 2nd ed. New York: McGraw-Hill. Pp. 135–148. (b) The concept of social interest. *Journal of Individual Psychology,* 25, 131–149.

(c) Adler and the 1910 Vienna symposium on suicide: A special review. *Journal of Individual Psychology,* 25, 181–191.
(d) With Rowena R. Ansbacher. Individual Psychology. In *International Encyclopedia of the Social Sciences.* New York: Crowell, Collier, and Macmillan. Vol. 7. Pp. 213–218.
(e) With Rowena R. Ansbacher (eds.). Alfred Adler. *Superioridad e interés social: una colección de sus últimos escritos.* Trans. by María Martínez Peñaloza. Mexico: Fondo de Cultura Económica. Pp. 365.

1969 (a) Introduction. In A. Adler, *The Science of Living.* Ed. by H. L. Ansbacher. Garden City, N.Y.: Doubleday. Pp. vii–xxii.
(b) Suicide as communication: Adler's concept and current applications. *Journal of Individual Psychology,* 25, 174-180.

1970 (a) Alfred Adler, Individual Psychology, and Marilyn Monroe. *Psychology Today,* February, 3 (10) 42–44, 66.
(b) Adler, Alfred. In *Lexikon der Pädagogik.* Freiburg i.Br., Germany: Verlag Herder.
(c) Alfred Adler: A historical perspective. *American Journal of Psychiatry,* 127(6), 777–782.

1971 (a) Alfred Adler. In *Encyclopedia Judaica.* New York: Macmillan.
(b) Alfred Adler and G. Stanley Hall: Correspondence and general relationship. *Journal of the History of the Behavioral Sciences,* 7, 337–352.

(c) Alfred Adler and humanistic psychology. *Journal of Humanistic Psychology*, 11(1), 53–63.
(d) Utilization of creativity in Adlerian psychotherapy. *Journal of Individual Psychology*, 27, 160–166.

1972 (a) Adler's "striving for power," in relation to Nietzsche. *Journal of Individual Psychology*, 28, 12–24.
(b) With Rowena R. Ansbacher (eds.). *Alfred Adlers Individualpsychologie*. Munich: Reinhardt. Pp. 445.
(c) With Rowena R. Ansbacher (eds.). Alfred Adler. *Superiority and Social Interest: A Collection of Later Writings*. 3rd ed. New York: Viking Press Compass. Pp. xxi and 434.
(d) Adlerian psychology: The tradition of brief psychotherapy. *Journal of Individual Psychology*, 28, 137–151.

General References

Adler, Alexandra. The concept of compensation and overcompensation in Alfred Adler's and Kurt Goldstein's theories. *Journal of Individual Psychology*, 1959, 15, 79–82.

Adler, Alfred. Fundamentals of Individual Psychology (1930) *Journal of Individual Psychology*, 1970, 26, 35–49.

Alfred Adler in the *Great Soviet Encyclopedia*. *Journal of Individual Psychology*, 1970, 26, 183–185.

Allport, G. W. The psychologist's frame of reference. *Psychological Bulletin*, 1940, 37, 1–28.

Ansbacher, Rowena R. First workshop on training Adlerian counselors. *Individual Psychologist*, 1971, 8, 41–48.

Bornemann, E. Einführung. In *Alfred Adlers Individualpsychologie*. Ed. by H. L. and Rowena R. Ansbacher. Munich: Reinhardt, 1972. Pp. 17–39.

Bruner, J. S., and Goodman, C. C. Value and need as organizing factors in perception. *Journal of Abnormal and Social Psychology*, 1947, 42, 33–44.

Bühler, Charlotte. Human life as a whole as a central subject of humanistic psychology. In J. F. T. Bugental (ed.), *Challenges of Humanistic Psychology*. New York: McGraw-Hill, 1967. Pp. 82–91.

Chaplin, J. P., and Krawiec, T. S. *Systems and Theories of Psychology*. 2nd ed. New York: Holt, Rinehart & Winston, 1968.

Fitts, P. M. German applied psychology during World War II. *American Psychologist*, 1946, 1, 151–161.

Freud, S. *A General Introduction to Psychoanalysis* (1917). Garden City, N.Y.: Garden City Publishing Company, 1943.

Goldstein, K. *The Organism: A Holistic Approach to Biology Derived from Pathological Data in Man*. New York: American Book Company, 1939.

Hartley, E. L., and Hartley, Ruth E. *Fundamentals of Social Psychology.* New York: Knopf, 1952.

Hollingworth, H. L. *Abnormal Psychology: Its Concepts and Theories.* New York: Ronald Press, 1930.

Kaempffert, W. Germans and Nordics: Nazi ideas on race superiority analyzed. *New York Times,* May 31, 1936, XX 4.

Kaempffert, W. Selecting German officers. *New York Times,* March 30, 1941, 6D.

——. Germany gets utmost from manpower by applying psychology to boost morale. *New York Times,* January 7, 1945, 9E.

Kaufmann, W. Nietzsche's concept of the will to power. *Journal of Individual Psychology.* 1972, 28, 3–11.

——. *Without guilt and justice: from decidophobia to autonomy.* New York: P. H. Wyden, 1973.

Kantor, J. R. Review. *American Journal of Psychology,* 1942, 55, 460–461.

Klineberg, O. A study of psychological differences between "racial" and national groups in Europe. *Archives of Psychology, New York,* 1931, No. 132.

Krech, D., Crutchfield, R. S., and Ballechey, E. L. *Individual in society: a textbook of social psychology.* New York: McGraw-Hill, 1962.

Maddi, S. R. *Personality Theories: A Comparative Analysis.* Homewood, Ill.: Dorsey, 1968.

——. Alfred Adler and the fulfillment model of personality theorizing. *Journal of Individual Psychology,* 1970, 26, 153–160.

Maslow, A. H. *Motivation and personality.* 2nd ed. New York: Harper & Row, 1970.

Miller, G. A. Psychology as a means of promoting human welfare. *American Psychologist,* 1969, 24, 1063–1075.

Papanek, Helene. Pathology of power striving and its treatment. *Journal of Individual Psychology,* 1972, 28, 25–32.

Peak, Helen. Observations on the characteristics and distribution of German Nazis. *Psychological Monographs,* 1945, 59 (6).

Poffenberger, A. T., Brown, H. C., Wetmore, R. G., Ansbacher, H. L., and Miller, S. C. Indexing the Psychological Index. *Psychological Bulletin,* 1939, 36, 477–487.

Porter, R. Violence is ended in prisoner camps. *New York Times,* January 18, 1945.

Ripin, Rowena. A study of the infant's feeding reactions during the first six months of life. *Archives of Psychology, New York,* 1930, No. 116.

——. Definition der Neurose. *Internationale Zeitschrift für Individualpsychologie,* 1933, 11, 161–176.

Rom, P. Memories of an Individual Psychologist. *Freethinker, London,* February 7, 1970, 90(6), 43.

Seif, L. Autorität und Erziehung. In A. Adler, C. Furtmüller, and E. Wexberg (eds.) *Heilen und Bilden.* 2nd ed. Munich: Bergmann, 1922. Pp. 245–250.

Stagner, R. Reply to Ansbacher. *American Psychologist,* 1950, 5, 158–159.

Stanley, G. A study of some variables influencing the Ansbacher shrinkage effect. *Acta Psychologica,* 1964, 22, 109–118.

Thurstone, L. L. The stimulus-response fallacy in psychology. *Psychological Review,* 1923, 30, 354–369.

Toman, W. Family constellation as a basic personality determinant. *Journal of Individual Psychology,* 1959, 15, 199–211.

Underwood, B. J. *Experimental psychology: an introduction.* New York: Appleton-Century-Crofts, 1949.

Wertheimer, M. *Productive Thinking.* Enlarged ed. Ed. by M. Wertheimer. New York: Harper, 1959.

Woodworth, R. S. *Psychology.* 3rd ed. New York: Holt, 1934.

PURKYNĚ

2

The American Adventure*

JOSEF BROŽEK

Migration pressures, wars, and revolutions had me on the move at tender age. In 1911 my parents moved from central Bohemia to Warsaw, in the part of Poland occupied by Russia. In July 1913 my mother journeyed back to Bohemia so that I would be born "home," which I was, on 14 August 1913. We returned to Warsaw six weeks later. All was well until World War I broke out. As bearers of an Austro-Hungarian passport, we became "enemy aliens" overnight. My father was arrested and was held in a prison which, strangely enough, was one of the few buildings in Warsaw that remained standing at the end of World War II. Shortly after that, he was sent to a "concentration point" located in the Siberian Altai Mountains, south of Tomsk, on the river Ob. In time we followed, with our possessions limited to what my mother could carry in addition to me. Thus it was that Russian and not Czech or Polish became my first spoken language.

When the internees of Slavic origin were given amnesty by the Czar in 1916, my father found employment in the district of Ufa in the Central Ural Mountains, first as manager of a saw mill in Belyi Klyuch and later as a mechanical engineer in a railroad-car factory in Ust'-Katav.

*I owe debts of gratitude to many people, in many lands. None is greater than the debt to Ancel Keys as director of the Laboratory of Physiological Hygiene, University of Minnesota.

The October Revolution of 1917 eventually led to a complicated, two-year journey across Siberia (1918–1920), from the Ural Mountains in the west to the port city of Vladivostok in the east. We made longer or shorter stops along the route and an abortive expedition, on the river Yenisei, from Krasnoyarsk in mid-Siberia to Minusinsk in the south, and back again. The military situation in the area changed so quickly that we had to leave Minusinsk before my mother finished cooking the chicken she had in the pot, and we scrambled for a place on the last boat leaving the river port for the north. As "associate members" of the 5th division of the Czechoslovak legionary army we reached the Pacific late in the spring of 1920 and were repatriated by the troopship *America* via the Sea of Japan, East China Sea (with a stop at Shanghai), South China Sea (Hong Kong), Straits of Malacca (Singapore), Indian Ocean (Colombo), Red Sea, Suez Canal (Port Said), and Mediterranean Sea, arriving at last in Trieste. We reached Bohemia, by rail, in mid-summer.

Years passed, again in relative peace. Then came the partial occupation of Czechoslovakia by Hitler's armies in 1938, the incorporation of the Protectorate of Bohemia and Moravia into the Third Reich in 1939, and the outbreak of World War II in September 1939. I was scheduled to leave for the United States on 6 September even though funds to be provided by the Czechoslovak Ministry of Education and the Denis Research Fund became "unavailable." To complicate matters further, the old passport game that plagued my father a quarter of a century earlier was on again. Germans did not recognize Czech passports; Americans did not recognize German passports. Eventually I did leave Czechoslovakia, reached Italy, and left for New York from Genoa. As a temporary resident of the famous immigration station at Ellis Island, I was a "guest" of the Governor of New York on Thanksgiving Day of 1939. I would not have survived those first months without the warm hospitality that Anna and Howard Brinton, directors of Pendle Hill, a Quaker study center, extended to me at the very beginning of the American adventure.

My original plan was to return home within a year, but the war made this impossible. What started as a year's post-doctoral study in America turned into a life-long adventure. Perhaps I should use the plural—adventures, not adventure—since the thirty-odd years spent in the New World have been full of them. This is true even when I restrict myself to professional matters and disregard my personal, at times turbulent, history. The chronology of events that are typically referred to in official biographies is delightfully (and deceitfully) simple:

> A year of exploration at the University of Pennsylvania and at Pendle Hill (1939–1940).
>
> An Honorary Fellowship at the University of Minnesota (1940–1941)—the most liberal education, ever.
>
> Close to twenty years of stimulating and rewarding association with the Laboratory of Physiological Hygiene, University of Minnesota.
>
> Serving as professor and chairman of the department of psychology, Lehigh University (1959–1963), and as research professor subsequently.

The American adventure involved much more than research in "experimental, applied" psychology, focused on the impact of deficient nutrition on behavior. There were other psychological themes—including aging, illumination and vision, and an eventual shift to the history of psychology. More important, for an extended period of time I wore the hat of a physical anthropologist (or, speaking broadly, human biologist). I was active in the new, multidisciplinary field of research on the composition of the human body, with special emphasis on methods and application to human nutrition. Laboratory and field investigations in physical anthropology, in and out of the United States; shared exploration of the theoretical aspects of body composition; organization of national and international conferences; serving as book review editor of *Human Biology* and as consultant to the World Health Organization, with temporary assignments in many countries—all of this was a large and important component of my professional life. It does not belong, however, in an account of what I do as a *psychologist* and how I came to do it.

The forces at play were complex throughout, with a few ounces of "self-actualization" to each pound of "adjustment" to the biomedical, economic, and historical realities, frequently changing in unpredictable ways and beyond my control. "Purposes" were hopelessly intertwined with "accidents" and "natural causes."

EARLY STUDIES AND INTERESTS

Prior to the University. My boundless enthusiasm for a steam locomotive at one of Moscow's many railroad stations, during our trek to Siberia in the winter of 1915, earned me the approving comment of a Russian military officer: "Nastoyashchii inzhinyer"—Here is a railroad engineer for you! But this diagnosis was incorrect. My intelligence was to be verbal, not quantitative, spatial, or manipulative.

At the age of ten I had to make my first important decision regarding my course of study. Would I go to the local school for the next four years, in comfort, but reach a dead end academically at age fourteen? Or would I be willing to rise well before six o'clock, six days a week, walk some two miles to the nearest railroad station in every sort of weather, take a half-hour train ride, walk another mile to school, and return in the afternoon? In winter it would mean leaving home in darkness and, on some days, returning in darkness. In a long, serious discussion the alternatives were made clear to me by my father. I chose the discomfort and the academically oriented secondary school.

A second major decision had to be made at age fourteen. Should I pursue the study of violin in the music conservatory in distant Prague, or should I go on with my academic studies? This was a difficult choice. I loved music and loved the violin. Attending evening chamber-music concerts was the most thrilling experience of those years, despite the fact that I returned home around midnight, having made the long trek from the railroad station alone and having to rise early the next morning as if I had had a full night's sleep.

My mother, who was my first music teacher, knew all of this. She also knew how hard a musician's life was. Her counsel was: "Continue with your academic studies. Music is wonderful as an avocation but problematic as a vocation." I accepted her advice, even though at times I spent more time on music than was good for my studies. I played violin in a local chamber orchestra, a group with remarkably high standards; I played violin duets for hours with a local miller, a skillful violinist as well as a mountain-bred philosopher, filled with wonder for things of the earth and the heavens; and I greatly enjoyed trying my hand at Charles de

Bériot's violin concertos. My adolescence was steeped in music. In the seventh class of secondary school I discovered the viola and cello. I was ill a great deal that year. Having to spend much time in bed, I learned to play guitar and still today I sing Slavic folksongs to my own accompaniment.

While in secondary school, I participated as the youngest member in a summer program to train personnel for small-town public libraries. This was my first professional certificate. I put the information to use when I was in charge of the library in the department of philosophy at Charles University in Prague. This was one of the principal duties of the departmental assistant, a post which I held in 1936 and 1937. I was grateful for this appointment, which in Europe is the traditional entry to a university career. Professor J. B. Kozák, a philosopher's philosopher, was very kind and open-minded in giving the job to someone interested in psychology, and "applied" psychology at that. Years later, at Minnesota, in a setting in which administrative responsibilities were shared among the staff, I was responsible for the Laboratory's library.

The University Years. I graduated from secondary school (*Realgymnasium*) in 1932 in the city of Pilsen (Plzeň), with concentration on Latin, French, biology, and history. Intellectually, the next three years at Charles University were stormy indeed. My professional interests were shifting between areas as widely separate as theology, medicine, Slavic linguistics, and Classics. All was permeated by an absorbing interest in philosophy. This led to contact with psychology, taught at Charles University as a specialty within the department of philosophy, with an experimental and applied orientation.

A serious illness in the spring of 1935 interfered with my preparations for the state examinations in Czech literature and in Latin. These examinations were given once a year, in June. Two of these examinations had to be passed, one at the completion of the second year of study and one at the end of the fourth year, in order to qualify as a secondary school teacher. It was obvious that I would have lost one whole year because of my illness.

This interruption, with several months of enforced leisure, played a decisive role in shifting the focus to psychology as my area of primary concentration. It gave me time necessary for a critical evaluation of my plans of study. In deciding to work toward a doctor's degree, without bothering with the state examinations required for teaching in secondary schools, I was swayed, in part, by the fact that many of the courses I had taken up to that point would fit the Ph.D. program in philosophy and psychology. The decision was daring and hazardous, since at that time employment opportunities for psychologists were almost nonexistent.

With the return of good health in the fall of 1935, I embarked on the program with vigor. I supplemented the psychology offerings at Charles University by taking laboratory courses in experimental psychology and participating in the psychology seminar at the German University of Prague, under Johannes Lindworsky. I learned statistics from Josef Váňa, head of the Psychotechnological Laboratory of the city of Prague, and became familiar with instrumental test methods in the Laboratory of the Army Technological Air Institute. Part of the material utilized in my doctoral thesis, "Memory: Its Measurement and Structure," came from the Psychotechnological Institute, associated with the Masaryk Academy of Labor in Prague. I received my Ph.D. in June 1937.

In the fall of 1937 I registered in the Faculty of Natural Sciences, in Prague, planning to study physical anthropology, with philosophy of natural sciences as a minor. When I had the good fortune to receive a full-time position as applied psychologist in Zlín (today's Gotwaldov) in Moravia, these plans had to be changed. Departure for the United States in November 1939 ended altogether my formal training in physical anthropology.

Early Professional Satisfactions and Frustrations. In Prague I worked as psychometrist in a vocational guidance clinic during the spring and summer of 1937. I developed, in collaboration with Bohumil Sekla, a physician at the clinic and a budding medical geneticist, plans for interdisciplinary research on twins, including their psychological characteristics. The idea came to naught when, early in the fall of 1937, I took the position with the large and dynamic industrial complex of the Bat'a Shoe Company in Zlín.

At Zlín I was absorbed in the mechanics of a large-scale testing program, including the development of new test procedures (for example, a test of color vision), establishment of norms, and validation of the testing procedures. At the same time I established close contacts with the medical department and initiated statistical analysis of their anthropometric data, with a focus on age trends. My departure for the United States unfortunately interrupted this project.

Another project did not get off the ground at all. I had noted that an excessive number of applicants for employment who came from a nearby mountain area had a strikingly low intelligence. I wished to examine the ecology of the area systematically, with special reference to the iodine supply which appeared deficient. This clearly would have had to be a collaborative study. The problem served to stimulate my interest in the broader question of the relation between diet and performance capacity, a topic which I examined in depth at the University of Minnesota.

LEARNING AT AMERICAN UNIVERSITIES

My plan for study in America called for a semester at the University of Nebraska, under J. P. Guilford, author of *Psychometric Methods* (1936), and a semester under Morris Viteles, author of *Industrial Psychology* (1932), at the University of Pennsylvania. These were the two books I brought with me from Europe.

Lack of funds interfered with the plan. I never reached Nebraska, and spent the remainder of the fall semester and the spring semester 1939–1940 at the University of Pennsylvania, living (and learning a great deal) at Pendle Hill, in Wallingford, Pennsylvania.

The fall semester was half over before I arrived in Philadelphia. I was not in great shape either physically or psychologically, with the disastrous war developments in Europe weighing heavily upon me. I managed the spring semester substantially better, but the experience could hardly be regarded as a complete success.

By contrast, the year 1940–1941 at the University of Minnesota was most rewarding—a "total immersion" in graduate study, completely free of concern for grades and for what a dean might say to my extensive and heterogeneous menu of courses and seminars. Some of them were means for exploring new areas, such as time-and-motion studies (in the department of industrial engineering, under Everett Laitala), history of medicine (under Richard Scammon), and the relationship between psychology and cultural anthropology (under David Mandelbaum). In others I studied, in depth, topics with which I was familiar (individual differences, under D. G. Paterson; student personnel, under J. G. Darley—the best graduate seminar in which I have ever participated). I attended the general introductory course in psychology and Florence Goodenough's seminar in developmental psychology because I wished to familiarize myself with new teaching techniques and with the approaches of outstanding individual teachers.

Subsequently, while I was working in the Laboratory of Physiological Hygiene, I audited a two-semester course on physiology, given in the Medical School. Of special benefit was the laboratory part of the course. For several semesters I participated in Professor Ernst Gellhorn's seminar in neurophysiology.

Years later, I went "back to school," on a part-time basis, as a visiting fellow in Princeton University's Program in the History and Philosophy of Science (during the academic year 1966–1967). I wished to have some formal contact with the general history of science, and I did so in the fall semester. In the spring I participated in Professor Marshall Clagett's fascinating seminar in which we read fourteenth-century astrological manuscripts. The content was not of particular interest to me, but acquiring the skill of reading medieval Latin manuscripts was helpful in subsequent archival research.

WORK HABITS

My study habits became firmly established in my third year of university studies, when I was given the key to a reading and study room at Charles University. I entered the building of the faculty of philosophy at 8:00 a.m. when the gates opened; I left at 10:00 p.m. This represented a fourteen-hour workday, Monday through Friday. On Saturdays I closed my books at 7:00 p.m., and usually went to a special lecture, a concert, or the opera; I rarely worked on Sundays.

I enjoyed my student years tremendously, and regarded the daily stint as a privilege. The pattern of a fourteen-hour workday remained my "norm" for years. I cannot say that my wife and, especially, the children ever came to like it. Once, in 1959, I extended the workday to sixteen hours straight, but only for two summer months during which I attempted to complete a variety of tasks that were unfinished when I left the Laboratory in January. Within that time I prepared a long final report on work done under a governmental grant and wrote a handful of papers. Fortunately, during this time my family lived with the grandparents near Minneapolis. Two full shifts a day would have been too much for even the most understanding of wives.

An important part of my daily routine is handling the mail. I begin with the most peripheral and easily disposable parts, such as advertising material. When an advertised book is directly relevant to my interests, I order it immediately, enclosing the payment with the order whenever possible. This reduces to one-half the clerical operations involved in the acquisition of new books.

Next, I go through the journals, both special and general, such as *Science*. I scan the contents, read the relevant material, write out cards requesting reprints of papers needed for future reference, examine the book reviews, and go through the list of new publications. Of these, some may be ordered, others recommended for acquisition by the university library, and still others recorded in my file of reference works. I make the entries in the empty space on the endpapers of appropriate books or within the text as a marginal note, depending on the nature of the particular publication that is being registered.

In highly circumscribed areas of central professional interest, I have made a point of acquiring reprints or photostatic copies of all journal articles related to the topic. This has greatly facilitated an in-depth familiarity with ongoing research, the writing of papers, and the preparation of critical reviews of the literature.

It is unfortunate that my collection of books continues to be scattered. There is a library on each of the three floors of our house, in addition to bookcases in all the halls, containing collections in such areas as classic literatures; medieval Latin literature written in the Slavic countries; the writings, mostly in Latin, of John Hus (1369–1415), a Czech religious reformer, and of John Amos Comenius (1592–1670), educator and bishop of the Unity of Czech (Moravian) Brethren; and an extensive collection of Old (Church) Slavonic texts.

The library adjoining my office at the university contains reference works and psychological literature in English. Lehigh University has generously provided a large room in the Linderman

Library which houses books and journals in such areas as the science of science and history of science, and an extensive collection of Slavic, especially Russian, publications in psychology and related areas. In the absence of clerical help, the sheer mechanics of handling some 1000 acquisitions per year has consumed a distressingly large amount of time and effort.

TEACHING, IN AND OUT OF THE UNIVERSITY

I began to teach as a private tutor and have continued to teach, in one form or another, ever since. Yet I have never thought of myself as an "educator," a "professor." At the age of fourteen, I started to give lessons in school subjects, mostly Latin, to fellow students who needed help. I continued this practice through the upper grades of secondary school and the university years.

The principal mission of the Laboratory of Physiological Hygiene at the University of Minnesota was research. In addition, an undergraduate course in physiology was taught, in which I was responsible for the section on special senses and nervous function. On our own, without remuneration, Ernst Simonson and I shared for several years a course on human factors in industry, offered in the university's Institute of Technology. Dr. Simonson covered the physiological aspects and I presented the psychological aspects of the topic.

At Lehigh I served, at the outset, as Professor as well as Chairman of the department of psychology and taught whatever needed to be taught, including introductory psychology, physiological psychology, and human engineering. After 1963 I specialized in teaching the history of psychology, at both undergraduate and graduate levels.

I have never taught a course twice in the same way, although this might be viewed as a loss of time and an inefficient way to teach. Working with different textbooks and changing the format of the courses has enabled me to approach each course and each lecture with freshness and enthusiasm, which I regard as central ingredients of effective teaching. I have taught, always, as if everyone in the class were vitally interested in the subject matter. I could not do otherwise. Furthermore, I regard students as partners in learning.

Partnership in Learning and Teaching. I have always rebelled against the concept that the principal task of universities is to teach. Since my own student days I have maintained that this is an essentially distorted view: learning, not teaching, is the core of education at the university level. A university is an institution facilitating learning.

This is not a play on words. Focus on *learning* rather than on teaching unifies students and teachers into one body of learners, while focus on *teaching* tends to separate them into polarized groups and thus invites confrontation rather than a pursuit of common goals.

Emphasis on active learning helps the student feel not only that learning is a matter of self-discipline but that it has elements of genuine pleasure, of fun, of adventure. Importantly, it enables him to realize that learning is a life-long process, closely bound with the rapid and unceasing social, technological, and intellectual changes.

The image of the university as an institution dedicated to learning has far-reaching implications not only for the student but for the teacher as well. The university teacher is, in a very real sense, *ein ewiger Student*—an "eternal student." His competence as a "teacher" may well be measured partly in terms of his ability to instill an interest in life-long learning in his "classmates."

I like to teach history of psychology, since the subject is particularly suitable for an approach stressing the student's initiative and freedom of exploration and his active role in the learning-teaching process. It may be useful to consider, concretely, a specific course, History and Systems, taught to undergraduates in the fall semester of the academic year 1969–1970.

As in all the other courses, the students learned from the assigned books, from the instructor's presentations, and from classroom discussions. The distinctive flavor in this particular course came from the emphasis on the student's *learning from his peers* and on *learning by teaching,* in the form of class presentations of assigned readings, joint effort in the making up and correcting of examinations, and the presentation and discussion of term papers. Thus the course was a decidedly collaborative undertaking.

The instructor's contribution was threefold: (1) commenting on the assigned textbook materials, with stress on topics calling for clarification and on points of view that invited critique; (2) helping the students to get a "feel" for the changing temper of the times and placing the major developments in psychology in a broader scientific and cultural perspective; (3) providing additional information that reflected largely the instructor's own interests and active research involvement.

The students had full freedom in choosing the term-paper topic, provided it was presented in historical perspective. The last meeting of the class was devoted to presentation of synopses of the term papers. The level of performance, even by students who had earned low grades in the formal written examinations, was rewardingly high. This was true also of a number of the papers themselves. Reading them was for me one of the most satisfying aspects of the course, providing the opportunity to *learn from the students.* The experience reinforced my conviction that the university can be a community of scholars.

Contacts with Colleagues. Perhaps my most significant contribution to teaching has been at the "postgraduate level": working with authors of book reviews published in *Human Biology* and, during the 1960s, in *Contemporary Psychology;* as Chairman of scientific symposia and Editor of the proceedings; and as organizer and Instructor in Summer Institutes on the History of Psychology for College Teachers. I should add also teaching by correspondence, with "pupils" scattered all over the globe.

Most of my extracurricular teaching involved correspondence with reviewers of books. I have always regarded the reviewing of scientific books as a serious business in which the reviewer has a threefold responsibility: to himself and his professional growth; to the author of the book; and to the scientific public to whom the appraisal is addressed. As book review editor and editorial consultant I endeavored to instill this attitude in the reviewers with whom I worked.

OFF THE RECORD

Whereas publications are the visible fruit of one's intellectual and organizational endeavors, many professional activities are not on the "public record."

For me one of the most demanding tasks, carried out on behalf of the national and international scientific community, has been preparation of evaluative reports of applications submitted to agencies providing financial support for research. On a guest basis, I have cooperated in these matters with the National Science Foundation, National Institutes of Health, and the World Health Organization. In 1963 I was asked to serve as a member of the Nutrition Study Section of the National Institutes of Health. I was not really eager to assume this additional responsibility, since my load of reading and writing was already heavy. Yet I was fully aware of the vital importance of keeping control of the distribution of research funds in the hands of the scientific community. The remnants of my resistance were swept away by a colleague who pointed out that in years past other people had had to review and evaluate *my* grant applications, and that it was my turn.

Closely related to the evaluation of research proposals is the preparation of critical, "editorial" reviews of articles submitted by one's professional colleagues for publication in scientific journals. On numerous occasions I have provided such reviews for a variety of journals.

I welcomed the opportunity to play a more active role as Advisory Editor of *Contemporary Psychology,* a journal of book reviews, for which I have had special responsibility in the area of Slavic literatures. Since its beginning I have served on the Board of Advisory Editors of *Soviet Psychology* and its predecessor, *Soviet Psychology and Psychiatry.*

"Invisible" have been many of the activities involved in organizing symposia, conferences, and scientific programs of societies. Much of this effort was concerned with research on body composition, a new interdisciplinary view of the "inner man." Also interdisciplinary in nature were some of the conferences involving psychology, from the 1956 symposium on Nutrition and Behavior (University of Minnesota) to the 1966 conference on the Biology of Human Variation (New York Academy of Sciences). A symposium on contemporary Soviet psychology was organized in the framework of the 1963 annual meeting of the Eastern Psychological Association. I especially enjoyed organizing the Symposium on Adjustment to Aging, in the framework of the 15th International Congress on Applied Psychology (Ljubljana, Yugoslavia, summer 1964). I was pleased to be able to arrange a truly international program, with participants from France, Italy, Poland, Czechoslovakia, and the United States.

I have held few "regular" offices in scientific societies, feeling that my organizational endeavors and heavy involvement in editorial activities fulfilled my organizational professional obligations. An elected post that was particularly instructive involved a tour of duty in the 1950s as a delegate of Division 20 (Maturity and Old Age) to the Board of Representatives of the American Psychological Association.

Within psychology most of my organizational effort was concentrated on the history of psychology. I took part in the formation of Division 26 (History of Psychology) of the American Psychological Association and served as Chairman of the Division's first scientific program presented in the framework of APA's 1966 annual convention held in New York. In 1972 I had the honor of being elected the Division's President.

Over the years the extensive, world-wide professional correspondence has been a source of pleasure and, on occasion, pain. On the positive side, it has been a sure antidote to any feelings of isolation, no matter where I worked at a given time and what were the level and quality of intellectual interaction with my immediate environment. Contacts with scientists abroad continue to reinforce my faith in the scientific, intellectual unity of the world and the hope for an eventual organizational, politico-economic unity as well. On the negative side, the correspondence at times grows too heavy. Leaving my office for a week, I court the prospect of a desk that is invisible beneath its load of mail.

ON THE RECORD

The first piece of writing to appear in print, in 1935, was a review published in the *Lusatian-Serbian Bulletin (Lužickosrbský věstník,* Prague). Reports on investigations in the area of psychometrics, carried out in the years 1937–1939 in Zlín, remained in manuscript. These were the only research papers I wrote in Czech.

Books, Monographs, and Conference Proceedings. Publications in this category involve collaborative works, monographs published under my own name, and a number of volumes for which I served

TABLE 2.1.

Thematic Classification of Books, Monographs, and Conference Proceedings

Focus	*Year of Publication*
Nutrition and Behavior	1950, 1957, 1959, 1962
Nutritional Anthropometry	(1950), 1956
Body Composition	(1950), 1961, 1961b, 1963, 1963a, 1963b, 1965, 1966, 1970
Performance Capacity	1961a
Soviet Science	1964, 1970a
Human Variation	1966
History of Psychology	1968, 1968–1969, 1970b, 1972

as editor and co-author. The bibliographical details are given in the appended list of publications. Here I shall present only a thematic classification of the publications (Table 2.1), ordered chronologically. The 1950 volume *The Biology of Human Semistarvation* is relevant to three topics.

Journal Articles. In Europe I had learned to view *books* as a true measure of the significance of a scientist's contribution. In the Laboratory of Physiological Hygiene, at the University of Minnesota, I quickly realized that for an experimental research worker the writing of books is a luxury for which there is frequently neither time nor money, and that *journal articles* are the "bread and butter" form of publication. Perhaps I learned the lesson too well, welcoming the frequent "reinforcement" represented by the arrival of galley proofs and later of reprints of journal articles. This pattern persisted even when longer-term investment of time became possible.

While classification of the journal articles is not a simple matter, for general purposes the categories *Bohemica* and *Slavica,* Psychology, Physical Anthropology, *Sovietica,* and *Varia* will do. The discipline-oriented labels (Psychology, Physical Anthropology) account for the largest number of articles.

Many of the technical papers were interdisciplinary and collaborative in nature. Placing some of them in the category Psychology indicates the nature of my own contribution, not the over-all character of the studies. Most of the papers were published in such non-psychological media as the *Journal of Industrial Hygiene and Toxicology, American Journal of Physiology, Journal of Gerontology, American Journal of Clinical Nutrition,* and *Physiological Reviews.* Only a minority of the papers appeared in regular psychological journals.

Most papers placed in the category Physical Anthropology dealt not with classical anthropometry (with its emphasis on bone dimensions) but with "soft tissues" and, more broadly, with the composition of the living human body. My participation in experimental and field investigations on body dimensions and body composition ended in 1958 but the "cleaning up" operation took substantially longer than initially anticipated. Work during the 1953 sabbatical leave of absence and during four months spent in field research in 1958, both times in Yugoslavia, was devoted primarily to physical anthropology. This was reflected in the depression of "output" in psychology during the subsequent year. Similarly, intensive publishing activity in physical anthropology in 1956 was counter-balanced by a zero count in psychology.

The papers in the category *Bohemica* and *Slavica,* written during the war years, dealt with the problems of postwar reconstruction of Czechoslovakia (with special reference to university education), Czech civilization in Europe, relations to Russia, and studies of Slavic languages, literature, and culture in the framework of American universities.

Sovietica refers to papers dealing with topics which lie outside the realm of Soviet psychology or in which consideration of psychological data plays only a minor role: the effects of war-time starvation in Leningrad, political factors in Soviet science and the current five-year plan, general characteristics of Soviet science, research on arterial hypertension, nutritional research, research on aging, and trends in Soviet biomedical research.

Varia includes such heterogeneous topics as analysis of the characteristics of interdisciplinary research, measurement of elastic properties of skeletal muscles, variability of the electrocardiogram in normal young men, vasodilatation in normal individuals and in schizophrenic patients, population studies on serum cholesterol and dietary fat in Yugoslavia, multilingual reporting of scientific data, biographical entries in *The New Catholic Encyclopedia,* and the significance for university education of the "science of science."

Publications in the categories *Sovietica* and *Varia* are spread, thinly and fairly evenly, over the period under consideration.

The category Psychology, which is of central interest in this context, is anything but homogeneous over time. The appearance and disappearance of the different themes is indicated in Figure 2.1. Papers on performance capacity and fatigue, psychological methods, aging, and, especially, illumination and visual functions and visual work are concentrated in the period 1943 to 1955. Articles on nutrition and behavior cover a larger span of time but the later papers change in nature. They represent reviews of our own work and of the literature, as well as their translations into other languages, rather than experimental contributions. Soviet psychology and the history of psychology come to the fore in the 1960s, following a move from the University of Minnesota to Lehigh University.

Other papers, not included in Figure 2.1, deal with such topics as war-time psychological research in Great Britain, psychobiological rhythms, contemporary American psychology, and contemporary psychology in Czechoslovakia.

Book Reviews. Since childhood, reading has been a pleasure (more than that: a passion), ranking second only to music. In my early teens I read in Czech translation all of the available works of Jack London, Jules Verne, Karl May, and Henryk Sienkiewicz—an American, a Frenchman, a German, and a Pole. Later I enjoyed rereading Sienkiewicz in Polish. In America the balance has shifted to scientific literature, although I read lyric poetry almost every day, primarily in the Slavic languages. I enjoy Latin and, on occasion, German, Italian, Spanish, and French poetry as well. Among the American poets my favorites are Carl Sandburg, Langston Hughes, and Don Marquis, author of the hilarious *Lives and Times of Archy and Mehitabel.* Through the years I have retained an admiration for Edgar Lee Master's *Spoon River Anthology.*

I approach the reading of scientific books as a dialogue with the author. During the years spent at the University of Minnesota, where most often I was the only staff member who was professionally concerned with psychology, reviewing books was useful in

Years	43	44	45	46	47	48	49	50	51	52	53	54	55	56	57	58	59	60	61	62	63	64	65	66	67	68	69	70
Performance and fatigue	x	x					x				x																	
Methods		x x			x x x	x	x	x		x x		x																
Nutrition and behavior		x x x	x x	x x x		x x x x	x	x	x	x x	x		x x x x		x x x	x x x x x x	x	x x	x x x x x		x							x
Aging			x						x x x	x			x x											x		x		
Vision and illumination						x x x x x x		x	x	x x x													x		x			
Soviet psychology																				x x		x x x	x	x x x x		x x x	x	
History of psychology																								x		x x x	x x	x x x x x

Figure 2.1. Distribution in Time of Journal Publications Dealing with Specific Themes. Each cross corresponds to a journal article.

maintaining a "balance of conversation." Of special significance for keeping in touch with a field which eventually became the dominant focus of my research and literary activities were the reviews of books in the history of science and closely related fields. Between 1948 and 1970 about fifty books were reviewed which would fall into the category of the history of science, history of medicine (with special reference to Russia), and, in particular, history of psychology. The distribution of these reviews was fairly even, with a heavier concentration after 1963.

Labors in the Bibliographical Vineyard. Several categories of activities should be considered under this heading. In the late 1940s and the early 1950s I served as a regular abstractor for *Psychological Abstracts,* with emphasis on the coverage of industrial psychology and of foreign literature. As Book Review Editor of the journal *Human Biology,* published quarterly, I wrote several hundred book notices between 1955 and 1965. Occasionally, I have provided sets of book notices for the *Journal of the History of Behavioral Sciences.* More systematically, but in smaller numbers, I contribute book notices to *Contemporary Psychology.*

Since 1961 I have been publishing in *Contemporary Psychology,* roughly at yearly intervals, lists of recent Slavic books on psychology. These lists provide a record of publishing activity in countries, including the Soviet Union, the output of which has been increasing both in quantity and significance but is poorly known in the West due to the difficulties of communication. We cannot remain ignorant of what our colleagues in Eastern Europe are thinking and doing.

CRITERIA OF SIGNIFICANCE

Counting publications measures diligence, but says little about significance.

The concept of "significance" cannot be uniformly defined in all contexts and for all scientific disciplines. Much of the experimental work in which I was engaged could be labeled "applied psychology." It dealt with the impact of different forms of nutritional stress on behavior, effects of illumination on visual performance and visual fatigue, smoking, and the relation between personality characteristics and proneness to coronary heart disease. Significance was defined in part by the practical importance of the problems under study. Múch of the significance of the research undertaken by the Laboratory lay in translating an awareness of inherent complexity into a multidisciplinary research approach. I had the privilege and the responsibility of bringing to these studies the potential resources of psychology.

What is the measure of significance of specific publications? We may apply three criteria, from the least to the most objective and quantitative:

1. personal judgment,
2. judgment of peers, as reflected in the choice of materials selected for inclusion into various "readings," and in invitations to contribute to books, yearbooks, and symposia,
3. citation in journal articles.

Personal Judgment. If I were to choose a single work, my choice would fall on the collaborative 1950 *Biology of Human Starvation.* It dealt with a problem that has threatened man from time immemorial, emerged in force during World War II, and looks mankind grimly in the face as overpopulation marches on. The compelling reasons for undertaking the research were practical: the pressing need to know more about the effects of calorie, protein, and vitamin content of rehabilitation diets on rates of recovery. The information was required for the refeeding of pockets of populations suffering from starvation at the end of the Second World War. Of more basic, lasting significance, however, is the information obtained on the complex, profound changes in the machinery of the body and in behavior that resulted from prolonged (six months), severe restriction of food intake. The psychological aspects—sensory, motor, intellective, personality—were covered about as thoroughly as the available technology would permit.

As regards research methods, perhaps the most innovative was a work task designed for a quantitative study of visual performance and fatigue, reproducing the operation of inspecting objects transported on a conveyor belt.*

*With E. Simonson and A. Keys. "A Work Test for Quantitative Study of Visual Performance and Fatigue," *Journal of Applied Psychology,* Vol. 31, No. 5, pp. 519–532, 1947.

In the area of research on aging the most unusual in several ways (including the length of the longitudinal study—fourteen years at the time when the data were first analyzed) was the report on the personality characteristics of individuals prone to coronary heart disease.** In a group of business men and professional men, aged forty-five to fifty-five years and clinically healthy at first examination, thirty-one developed coronary heart disease. These men were at the outset significantly more "masculine" in their interests and had higher mean score on the "hypochondriasis" scale of the Minnesota Multiphasic Personality Inventory. In the Thurstone Temperament Schedule they had significantly higher scores on "Activity Drive" scale than the 138 men who remained clinically normal during the period of observation.

As it turns out, none of my three self-selected entries was noted in the *Citation Index*.

The Citation Record. Citation provides a useful yardstick of the impact of a scientist's writings on the scientific community. At present there are no workable means for tabulating citations in books. The publication of the *Citation Index* has made possible a quantitative assessment of the "echo" in the journal literature, even though the approach has its limitations, inherent as well as accidental.

Systematic, consecutive data were available only for a limited period (1964–1970). Erroneous or inappropriate citations, duplicate entries, and self-citations were removed before the data were submitted to a quantitative analysis.

The results of the analysis are indicated in Table 2.2. The total of valid entries is 511. Psychological topics account for about 16 per cent of these. The other topics are dominated by work on body composition and the closely related research on use of body measurements in characterizing man's nutritional status and its changes under a variety of conditions.

For the psychological topics (taken as 100 per cent) the subareas ranked in the order of decreasing frequency of citations are as follows: nutrition and behavior (42 per cent), aging (31 per cent), performance and fatigue (including work on vision, 13 per

**With A. Keys and H. Blackburn. "Personality Differences between Potential Coronary and Non-coronary Subjects," *Annals of the New York Academy of Sciences,* Vol. 134, Art. 2, pp. 1057–1064, 1966.

TABLE 2.2.

Entries in the Citation Index, *1964–1970, concerning psychological topics (n=77) and other topics (n=434)*

Psychological Topics		*Other Topics*	
Aging	24	Biology of Human Variation	5
Nutrition and Behavior	32	Body Composition	331
Performance and Fatigue	10	Nutritional Anthropometry	68
Soviet Psychology	7	Nutrition - Other	17
Varia	4	Soviet Science	9
		Varia	4

cent), and Soviet psychology (9 per cent). *Varia* account for 5 per cent.

It took hours of eye strain to obtain the information summarized in Table 2.2. Was the investment worth the effort? My answer is positive, while my wife is skeptical. I was aware that the new area of research on human body composition, opened up in the early 1940s, had both interesting theoretical aspects and manifold biomedical implications. Yet I was surprised by the disproportion in the citations of psychological and non-psychological publications. In terms of this criterion, I am 84 per cent "non-psychologist"! The ranking of the subareas within psychology corresponds with my "intuitive" appraisal of the relative significance of the earlier contributions.

Reprintings. In the psychological area the publications selected by editors for reprinting all dealt with research on diet and behavior, primarily with behavioral changes under conditions of prolonged, severe restriction of food intake (see Publications). This validates indirectly my judgment regarding the importance of the research in "psychodietetics" in general and the contribution to *The Biology of Human Starvation* in particular.

In the mid-1940s a paper on interdisciplinary research, written with Ancel Keys (*Science,* Vol. 100, pp. 507–512, 1944), was reprinted by a governmental agency and received wide circulation in governmental research establishments.

Psychological Contributions "Made to Order." For the most part, the publications written by invitation are included in the proceedings of symposia, conferences, and congresses. Some are chapters in books and yearbooks. The references are given in the appended list of publications. The topics are summarized in Table 2.3.

Publications Abroad. Science is a transnational enterprise. While the English language is the most widely used medium of scientific communication at present and American journals have a wide circulation, there is a point to having one's work published in journals appearing abroad, whether in English or in the language of a given country.

In the early 1950s communications on the effects of illumination on visual work and visual fatigue appeared in French and German. A paper on psychobiological rhythms came out in Russian in 1965 in *Voprosy Psikhologii* (Problems of Psychology). In a number of short reports, written in 1966 in Czech, Jiří Hoskovec and I informed our colleagues in *Československá Psychologie* about various aspects of contemporary psychology in America. This was followed in 1971 by an extensive survey, published in the same journal in English and thus more accessible to readers in the other central European and east European countries.

Most frequently translated were our accounts of experimental studies on the impact of deficient diets on human behavior, prepared in several versions. Published first in the English language in Holland, they appeared also in Spanish (in several media) and later in Russian (1960) as well as in Croatian, Czech, Polish, and Slovak (1961).

TABLE 2.3.

Topics of the Psychological Contributions "Made to Order"

Topic	*Year*
Performance and Fatigue	1943, 1944, 1948
Nutrition and Behavior	1949, 1955, 1960, 1964, 1965, 1966, and 1967
Psychological Methods	1950, 1954 (2 entries), 1961 (3 entries)
Physiological Psychology	1958
Soviet Psychology	1962, 1963, 1964a, 1966a, 1966b

CONSONANCES AND DISSONANCES

The Laboratory of Physiological Hygiene, University of Minnesota, was a multidisciplinary enterprise, with an intensive, stimulating intellectual interaction between the staff members and a high level of aspiration, individual as well as corporate. To me it was a great deal more, a dream come true: a refuge, a fortress, a living community of students of man—his structure, his metabolic machinery, his organ functions, and his behavior. The impact of this dynamic, growing, democratic organization on a receptive but not yet acculturated young European could be described only in poetic terms. There was the daily exchange of ideas, at times so intense that passersby tactfully closed the door of the little office I shared with Henry Taylor. But in addition there were the lighter moments of sharing tales of pheasant hunting with Austin Henschel, playing softball on Olaf Mickelsen's lawn, playing violin to the piano accompaniment of Ernst Simonson. In particular, I shared many intellectual interests and concerns with Ancel Keys, Director of the Laboratory but also a mentor and friend in need, and of needs there were many, especially in the 1940s. In terms of laboratory and field research and the volume of published research papers, these were my most productive years.

In principle, it was expected that the senior research workers would devote about 50 per cent of their time to team research, another 25 per cent to research on related topics (for example, the development of methods), and 25 per cent to their personal research. For a long time such a division was fully satisfactory to me. But in the late 1950s I became restive. The focus of the Laboratory's research was shifting toward the biochemistry of atherosclerosis, and I was getting older. If I were to move, this was the time.

Yes, to move! But where? I thrived in the multidisciplinary atmosphere of the Laboratory. I was a bona fide member of the American Psychological Association, American Physiological Society, and the American Association of Physical Anthropologists, but my professional identification was with "experimental human biology," a field which did not exist formally or in terms of employment opportunities within the framework of American universities.

Most of my research in the more "saleable" fields of psychology and physical anthropology was highly specialized, focused on the relationship between diet and behavior and on *in vivo* studies of human body composition, respectively. Without a degree in anthropology, however, it would have been unrealistic to think in terms of an appointment in an anthropology department.

My first choice would have been to teach and to do behavioral research in a department or school of nutrition. However, in 1958 "psychodietetics" was still viewed as an esoteric discipline. At Cornell University's Graduate School of Nutrition such a position was created twelve years later.

Fortunately, psychodietetics was not my only contact with psychology. I had worked for two years as a psychotechnologist in industry, prior to coming to the United States. In the late 1940s I was involved in research on illumination and visual performance and fatigue, and wrote a chapter entitled "Personal factors in performance and fatigue" for a widely used textbook of industrial hygiene and toxicology. Later I shared with Ernst Simonson a course on human factors in industry, offered in the department of industrial engineering, at the University of Minnesota. I participated regularly in the seminars offered by the Laboratory to students in the School of Public Health, so that I did not lack teaching experience even though my involvement in teaching had been small.

In 1958 I received an offer of a chairmanship appointment from Lehigh University, Bethlehem, Pennsylvania. I welcomed the opportunity to move "back East," with its more moderate climate, and the opportunity to become associated with a smaller University stressing academic excellence. Having worked for close to twenty years as a member of a research team, I was ready and anxious to do "my own thing," in psychology.

At Minnesota all senior staff members shared in the administration of the Laboratory by serving as principal investigators responsible for obtaining research grants and supervising research projects. This background of administrative experience was helpful when I assumed the chairmanship of the department of psychology at Lehigh University in 1959. On the other hand, identification with the friendly atmosphere of the Laboratory, united by common purposes and long-term commitments, bound by shared intellectual interests, responding with courage and enthusiasm to new challenges and opportunities, and achieving within the span of a few years national and international visibility, proved to be a "hindrance." It provided a model of social organization that was not applicable to the new situation.

It was clear to me that the psychology department at Lehigh had to change radically if it were to attain the excellence stressed by the University as a whole and achieved by many departments, particularly in the College of Engineering. The psychology department was numerically small and there was no prospect that this would change substantially. Under these circumstances, how could one combine a competent, reasonably broad coverage of psychology at the undergraduate level with a strong graduate program—the one calling for breadth, the other for depth?

I thought I had the answer: to focus on a rather well defined area which, at the same time, had many facets. Furthermore, it would have to be an area in which it was feasible to obtain grant support for research and for graduate students. Several areas were examined that would have allowed each member of the department to contribute significantly to a common goal, including aging, nutrition, and industrial and engineering psychology. Such a reorientation would have represented a radical departure from the existing pattern.

In my view, coordinated research effort was essential. However, due in part to pre-existing personality differences and strains within the department, I did not obtain a sympathetic hearing and cooperation from my colleagues. Yet without the wholehearted support of the staff the venture would have been doomed to failure. The concept of pooling intellectual resources and of pulling in the same direction was in too sharp a conflict with the traditional individualism of the academic personnel.

Seeing that a fundamental restructuring of the department's operations was not possible, I explored two other avenues. The first involved an effort to strengthen the area of industrial and engineering psychology, without making it the dominant focus of the department. This approach appeared appropriate in a university with a strong division of engineering, but it was not fruitful.

The other avenue called for building up the research in psychophysiology, in the privately endowed Bioelectrical Laboratory. I brought over a bright young man from Yugoslavia, competent in handling the hardware and in experimental design. As to research *problems,* I had enough ideas for twenty years' work on the topic of sleep alone. In preparation for research in this area I shared in the foundation of the journal *Psychophysiology* and for a time served on its editorial board. For personal reasons, the man who was to assume a pivotal position in the Bioelectrical Laboratory returned to his home country. This brought to naught endeavors in this direction.

The positive accomplishments during these different four years were personal rather than departmental, even though new men with promise, fresh research perspective and good research backgrounds had joined the department in the interim.

In 1963 I was pleased to exchange the duties of a department chairman for those of a research professor. This made possible the payment of some older intellectual debts, including a broad survey of the "biology of human variation" (1966) and, more important, an exploration of new horizons.

WHERE THE PAST MERGES WITH THE FUTURE

The current focus of my reading, writing, and even arithmetic is the history of science, with special reference to psychology. While this represents, in a real sense, a "new career," an interest in the history of psychology goes back to my student years in Prague. In 1935 I volunteered to familiarize fellow students in Professor J. B. Kozák's philosophy seminar with the content of Hans Henning's historically oriented volume on *Contemporary Psychology,* published in German in 1931. It took six weekly meetings to do so.

My interest in history was strongly reinforced by a seminar on the history of medicine, given at the University of Minnesota by Richard Scammon, in which I participated in 1940–1941.

At Minnesota my "curricular" obligations during the period 1941–1959 were to experimental research, and the interest in history was manifested, externally, in the form of book reviews. Later, several communications took the form of special (essay) reviews, with particular reference to developments in the Soviet Union. Journal and yearbook publications of the early 1960s on "current" Soviet psychology, including the literature on history, became the steppingstones to a more systematic concern with the development of psychology, in and out of Russia.

In connection with the organization of the first scientific program of Division 26 (History of Psychology), for the 1966 annual meeting of the American Psychological Association, I made a survey of current research and writing in the United States in the field of the history of psychology. The work of the Dutch physiologist F. C. Donders (1818–1889), an important contribution to the birth of experimental psychology, gave rise to several journal communications and a monograph, with Maarten S. Sibinga, entitled *Origins of Psychometry* (1970).

Recent communications have included papers dealing with writings on the history of psychology and physiology of behavior in the USSR, brief biographies of Soviet psychologists, and an account of the trends in Soviet views regarding mental tests. The results of my 1970 explorations in the history of psychology on the territory of today's Yugoslavia, with subsequent forays to the archives of Venice and Budapest, were presented at the Fourth Congress of Yugoslav Psychologists (October 1971).

History of Psychology–Organizational Activities. Several of my contributions to history of psychology have been organizational in nature. I directed two Summer Institutes on the History of Psychology for College Teachers, held in 1968 (at the University of New Hampshire, with Robert I. Watson as Associate Director) and in 1971 (Lehigh University). Each six-week Institute represented a major, time-consuming undertaking but both Institutes were for me as much a welcome learning experience as a teaching experience. The enthusiasm generated at the 1968 Institute by the activities of both the staff and the participants led to the formation of the International Society for the History of Behavioral and Social Sciences, later christened "Cheiron."

What of Tomorrow? My primary interest is shifting from a multiplicity of small jobs to a limited number of major tasks—from journal articles to monographs. The four areas I am most interested in "mining" are the history of psychology in Russia and the Soviet Union; the echoes over a period of one hundred years (1868–1968) of F. C. Donders' ideas on the timing of mental operations; the literature in Latin, from the seventeenth to the beginning of the nineteenth century, relevant to the development of scientific psychology; and the unpublished manuscripts of the physiologist J. E. Purkyně (Purkinje, 1787–1869) dealing with psychology.

SYNOPSIS

The American adventure began under the dark clouds of World War II but it led to a rewarding involvement in research, organizational endeavors, and teaching. The effects of nutrition on human behavior became the initial focus of collaborative research at the Laboratory of Physiological Hygiene, University of Minnesota. The interest in the history of psychology, manifested as early as 1935 and broadened by contacts with Richard Scammon at the University of Minnesota in 1940–1941, became an absorbing concern in the late 1960s. Early fascination with languages, both classical and modern, led eventually to concern with the birth of one branch of experimental psychology ("mental chronometry"), in the laboratory of the Dutch physiologist, F. C. Donders (ca. 1865) and to detective work on the elusive Marcus Marulus (1450–1524), apparently the author of the first treatise entitled Psychology (*Psychologia,* in Latin). While the content of the intellectual pursuits has been changing over the years, undulled curiosity remains a strong propelling force in my continuing American adventure.

SELECTIVE BIBLIOGRAPHY

Books and Monographs

With A. Keys, A. Henschel, O. Mickelsen, and H. L. Taylor. *The Biology of Human Starvation,* Vol. 1, esp. pp. 675–713, and Vol. 2, esp. pp. 767–918, The University of Minnesota Press, Minneapolis (1950).

Editor and coauthor. *Body Measurements and Human Nutrition,* Wayne University Press, Detroit, Michigan (1956); also, *Human Biology,* Vol. 28, No. 2, pp. 107–273 (1956).

Editor and coauthor. *Symposium on Nutrition and Behavior,* National Vitamin Foundation, New York, March 1957, 124 pp.; also *American Journal of Clinical Nutrition,* Vol. 5, No. 2, pp. 103–211, No. 3, pp. 332–343 (1957).

With Francisco Grande. *Neurologické Poruchy při Nedostatečné Výživě* (Neurological Disturbances Resulting from Inadequate Diet, in Czech). State Health Publishing House, Prague (1959).

Editor, with Austin Henschel, and coauthor. *Techniques for Measuring Body Composition.* National Academy of Sciences–National Research Council, Washington, D.C. (1961).

Editor, with H. Spector and M. S. Peterson, and coauthor. *Performance Capacity–A Symposium.* Quartermaster Food and Container Institute for the Armed Forces (Chicago, Ill.) (1961a).

Determinación Somatométrica de la Composición Corporal (Somatometric Determination of Body Composition). Publication No. 8, Departamento de Investigaciones Antropológicas, Instituto Nacional de Antropología e Historia, México, D. F. (1961b).

"Soviet Studies on Nutrition and Higher Nervous Activity." *Annals of the New York Academy of Sciences,* Vol. 93, Art. 15, pp. 665–714 (1962).

Editor and coauthor. "Body Composition," *Annals of the New York Academy of Sciences,* Vol. 110, Part I, pp. 1–424, Part II, pp. 425–1018 (1963).

Editor, with Austin Henschel, and coauthor. *Techniques for Measuring Body Composition.* U. S. Government Research Report, No. AD 286 506, U. S. Department of Commerce, Office of Technical Services (1963a). A reprint.

With Božo Škerlj. "Somatometric Estimation of Body Composition" (in Slovenian, with J. Brožek's "Postscript in Lieu of a Summary," in English). *Razprave* (Dissertations), Slovene Academy of Arts and Sciences, Division of Natural History, Vol. 7, pp. 317–360 (1963b).

Editor and coauthor. "Selected Aspects of Contemporary Psychology in the U.S.S.R.: A Symposium," *Medical Reports* of the Institute of Contemporary Russian Studies (Fordham University), Vol. 6, No. 1, pp. 1–21 (1964).

Editor and coauthor. *Human Body Composition: Approaches and Applications.* Vol. 7, Symposia of the Society for the Study of Human Biology, Pergamon Press, Oxford, England (1965).

Editor and coauthor. "The Biology of Human Variation," *Annals of the New York Academy of Sciences,* Vol. 134, Art. 2, 497–1066 (1966).

Quantitative Description of Body Composition–Physical Anthropology's 'Fourth' Dimension. The Bobbs-Merrill Reprint Series in the Social Sciences, No. A-275 (1966a).

Editor and coauthor. "Fifty Years of Soviet Psychology," Parts I and II, *Soviet Psychology,* Vol. 6, No. 3–4, pp. 1–125 (Spring-Summer 1968); Vol. 7, No. 1, pp. 1–72 (Fall 1968).

Editor and coauthor. "Special Issue on Georgian Psychology," *Soviet Psychology,* Vol. 7, No. 2, pp. 1–54 (Winter 1968–1969).

Editor. *Physical Growth and Body Composition: Papers from the Kyoto Symposium on Anthropological Aspects of Human Growth,* Monogr. Soc. Child Development, Ser. 140, Vol. 35, No. 7 (1970).

Editor, with E. Simonson, and translator, with Margaret Maria Brožek. *The Physiological Mechanisms of Cerebral Blood Circulation,* by A. J. Naumenko and N. N. Benua, Springfield, Ill., C. C. Thomas (1970a).

Editor, with Maarten S. Sibinga. *Origins of Psychometry: Johann Jacob de Jaager on "Reaction Time and Mental Processes"* (1865), Nieuwkoop, Holland, B. de Graaf (1970b).

Editor, with Dan I. Slobin, and coauthor. *Psychology in the USSR: An Historical Perspective,* White Plains, N.Y., International Arts and Sciences Press (1972).

Reprintings

With Nancy K. Kjenaas. "Item Analysis of the Psychoneurotic Scales on the MMPI in Experimental Semistarvation," pp. 484–491 in G. S. Welsch and W. G. Dahlstrom (eds.), *Basic Readings on the MMPI in Psychology and Medicine,* University of Minnesota Press (1956).

With B. C. Schiele. " 'Experimental Neurosis' Resulting from Semi-starvation in Man," *ibid.*, pp. 401–483.

With Harold Guetzkow and Marcella V. Baldwin. "A Quantitative Study of Perception and Association in Experimental Semi-starvation," pp. 145–162 in *Handbook of Projective Techniques,* ed. by B. I. Murstein, Basic Books: New York (1964).

"Semi-Starvation," pp. 232–239 in *Psychiatry and Public Affairs:* Reports and Symposia of the Group for the Advancement of Psychiatry, Aldine Publishing Co.: Chicago (1966).

With Harold Guetzkow. "Psychological Effects of Thiamine Restriction and Deprivation in Normal Young Men," pp. 134–145 in *The Origins of Abnormal Behavior,* ed. by W. L. Corah and E. N. Gale, Addison-Wesley: Reading, Mass. (1971).

Psychological Contributions "Made to Order"

"Psychological Factors in Relation to Performance and Fatigue," *Federation Proceedings,* Vol. 2, No. 3, pp. 134–144 (1943).

With H. L. Taylor. "Evaluation of Fitness," *Federation Proceedings,* Vol. 3, No. 3, pp. 216–222 (1944).

"Personal Factors in Competence and Fatigue." Pages 45–104 in *Personal Hygiene and Toxicology,* Vol. 1, Frank A. Patty, ed. Interscience Publishers, New York (1948).

With O. Mickelsen. "Diet," pp. 311–327 in *Human Factors in Undersea Warfare,* National Research Council, Washington, D. C. (1949).

"Eye-Movement Co-ordinations. Quantitative Analysis of Voluntary Eye Movements," pp. 199–207 in *Methods of Medical Research,* Vol. 3. The Year Book Publishers, Chicago (1950).

"Nutrition and Performance in Animals," pp. 155–157, and "Physical (read: Psychological) Performance," pp. 204–221, in *Methods for Evaluation of Nutritional Adequacy and Status–A Symposium,* ed. by H. Spector, M. S. Peterson and T. E. Friedeman, National Academy of Sciences–National Research Council, Washington, D. C. (1954).

"Psychological aspects of nutrition with special reference to experimental psychodietetics." pp. 259–276 in *Third International Congress of Nutrition,* Amsterdam, Sept. 13–17, 1954 (1955); also, *Voeding,* Vol. 16, pp. 443–460 (1955).

"Physiological Psychology," *Annual Review of Psychology,* Vol. 9, pp. 71–98 (1958).

With F. Grande. "Abnormalities of neural function in the presence of inadequate nutrition," pp. 1891–1910 in *Handbook of Physiology,* Section 1: Neuro-physiology, Vol. 3, ed. by J. Field, H. W. Magoun, and V. E. Hall. American Physiological Society, Washington, D.C. (1960).

"Current Status of Psychology in the U.S.S.R.," *Annual Review of Psychology,* Vol. 13, pp. 515–566 (1962).

"Soviet Psychology," pp. 438–455 in M. H. Marx and W. A. Hillix, *Systems and Theories in Psychology.* McGraw-Hill, New York (1963).

"Experimental Investigations on Nutrition and Human Behavior: A Postscript," pp. 1–37 in *Science in Progress,* Fourteenth Series, ed. by W. R. Brode, Yale University Press (1964); also in *American Scientist,* Vol. 51, No. 2, pp. 139–163 (1963).

"Recent Developments in Soviet Psychology," *Annual Review of Psychology,* Vol. 15, pp. 493–594 (1964a).

"Sleep Deprivation, Nutritional Deficit, and Some Soviet Work on Stress," pp. 215–242 in *Symposium on Medical Aspects of Stress in the Military Climate,* Walter Reed Army Institute of Research, Washington, D.C. (1965).

"Food as an Essential–Experimental Studies on Behavioral Fitness," pp. 29–60 in *Food and Civilization: A Symposium,* ed. by S. M. Farber, Nancy L. Wilson, and R. H. L. Wilson. C. C. Thomas, Springfield, Ill. (1966).

"Contemporary Soviet Psychology," pp. 178–198 in *Present-day Russian Psychology,* ed. by Neil O'Connor, Pergamon Press, Oxford, England (1966a).

"Nutrition and Behavior," pp. 140–147 in *Proceedings of the Symposium on Feeding the Military Man,* ed. by M. S. Peterson, U. S. Army Natick Laboratories, Natick, Mass. (1970).

History of Science (Journal publications)

Sections on "History," pp. 546–547 in "Current Status of Psychology in the U.S.S.R.," *Annual Review of Psychology,* Vol. 13 (1962); pp. 540–541 in "Recent Developments in Soviet Psychology," *ibid.,* Vol. 15 (1964); pp. 18–19, in "Current Soviet Psychology" A Systematic Review" (with J. Hoskovec), *Soviet Psychology and Psychiatry,* Vol. 4, No. 3–4 (1966).

"Russian Contributions on Brain and Behavior," *Science,* Vol. 152, pp. 930–932 (1966).

"V. Bekhterev," Vol. 2, pp. 234–235, "E. Bleuler," Vol. 2 (p. 615), and "J. Charcot," Vol. 3, p. 459 in *The New Catholic Encyclopedia* (1967).

"Fifty Years of Soviet Psychology: Guest Editor's Preface," *Soviet Psychology,* Vol. 6, No. 3–4, pp. 4–7 (1968).

With Dan I. Slobin. "Toward a History of Soviet Psychology: A Set of Bibliographies," *Soviet Psychology,* Vol. 6, No. 3–4, pp. 8–18 (1968).

"The Incomparable Georgians," *Soviet Psychology,* Vol. 7, No. 2, pp. 3–6 (1968–1969).

"Current and Anticipated Research in the History of Psychology," *Journal of the History of the Behavioral Sciences,* Vol. 4, No. 2, pp. 180–185 (1968).

"History of Psychology: Variations on a Theme," *Contemporary Psychology,* Vol. 13, No. 5, pp. 256–262 (1968).

"History of Psychology: Diversity of Approaches and Uses," *Transactions* of the New York Academy of Sciences, Ser. II, Vol. 31, No. 2, pp. 115–127 (1969).

"Soviet Contributions to History" ("History of Soviet Psychology," by A. V. Petrovskii, and "History of Psychology," by M. G. Yaroshevskii), *Contemporary Psychology,* Vol. 14, No. 8, pp. 432–434 (1969).

"Development of Biology in the USSR: An Essay Review," *Journal of the History of Biology,* Vol. 2, No. 2, pp. 438–444 (1969).

"The Science of Science," *Lehigh Alumni Bulletin,* pp. 7–10 (1969).

With Robert I. Watson and Barbara Ross. "A Summer Institute on the History of Psychology," Part 1, *Journal of the History of the Behavioral Sciences,* Vol. 5, pp. 307–319 (1969); Part 2, Vol. 6, pp. 25–35 (1970).

"Spectrum of Soviet Psychology: 1968 Model," *American Psychologist,* Vol. 24, No. 10, pp. 944–946 (1969).

"Citation 'Longevity' as Criterion of Significance: F. C. Donders and the Timing of Mental Operations," *Proceedings* of the 78th Annual Convention, American Psychological Association, pp. 787–788 (1970).

"Partnership in Learning (with Special Reference to History)," *Teaching Psychology Newsletter*, pp. 2–4 (June 1970).

"A Note on Historians' Unhistoricity in Citing References," *Journal of the History of Behavioral Sciences*, Vol. 6, No. 3, pp. 255–257 (1970).

"Wayward History: F. C. Donders (1818–1889) and the Timing of Mental Operations," *Psychological Reports*, Vol. 26, pp. 563–569 (1970).

"Contemporary Psychology in the U.S.A.: Some General Characteristics," *Československá Psychologie*, Vol. 15, pp. 496–511 (1971, in English).

"USSR: Current Activities in the History of Physiology and Psychology," *Journal of the History of Biology*, Vol. 4, No. 1, pp. 185–208 (1971).

"In memoriam: Božo Škerlj, Anthropologist (1904–1961)," *American Journal of Physical Anthropology*, Vol. 35, No. 1, pp. 1–12 (1971).

"Psicología estadounidense y psicología Soviética en 1971," *Revista Latinoamericana de Psicología*, Vol. 3, No. 1, pp. 51–72 (1971).

"Recent Russian Pavloviana," *Conditional Reflex*, Vol. 6, No. 3, pp. 157–165 (1971).

"Purkyně and Psychology in a Historical Research Perspective," pp. 105–118 in *Proceedings, J. E. Purkyně (1787–1869) Symposium*, ed. by V. Kruta, University, Brno (1971).

3

Travels in Psychological Hyperspace

RAYMOND B. CATTELL

Most psychologists have a presentiment at times that whereas the physical sciences move in a familiar three- or four-dimensional world, our own science is in some metaphorical sense in hyperspace. They may even have a foreboding that, moreover, some phase surface will ultimately appear athwart our science, separating the solid state of determinism from some ultra-deterministic, fluid domain too subtle for us yet to have apprehended. Be that as it may, the sense in which I have used "hyperspace" in the present title—though it may reach out to domains and freedoms of thought which all-too-terrestrial psychologists have neglected—is only the familiar mathematical one. It strikes the keynote of my research life in a solitary but not lonely exploration of the unknown and complex dimensions of personality.

When first asked to write this life sketch my immediate response was to declare the task impossible. My chapter for *The History of Psychology in Autobiography* (Lindzey, 1973) seemed unlikely to leave anything over as a fresh dish for the reader. But though there cannot be two different truths about a life's work, there can be distinct perspectives and areas of interest to different kinds of readers. And when I tentatively tried the formula of writing this second view for the interests of the student (as the other was written for peers and posterity) or, at least, of the student as I remembered my own early student needs, I was quite

surprised to find how many new perceptions remained to be expressed. Let the reader, therefore, recognize these two accounts as complementary, the first documented and proportioned as a historical record for official purposes; the present speaking more freely on personal aspects of those adventures in thought and emotion such as would be most relevant to the student on the threshold of a psychological career.

Apart from whatever personal unconscious kinks may help bring a man to the study of a science, there are two substantial and rational arguments for that career. One is a love of augmenting knowledge for its own sake, which some gifted mortals have been able to express in a full life. This extends from attractions of sheer knowledge into the more remote artistic fascinations of intellectual beauty. The other is a concern that a mature personality may have for the human race in terms of the benefits in health and fulfillment which science can bring to ignorant and wayward mankind. Psychology is peculiar in having a third appeal. It promises to solve the conflicts of the emotionally disturbed person himself. This is a more self-bound and limiting interest. At the time I entered psychology—soon after World War I—it was said with some truth that two psychologists out of three were "a bit strange." Certainly a penchant for fads and emotional fashions has characterized psychologists more than other scientists, at least in this generation.

To the best of my knowledge my interest in psychology was never motivated by a search for a nostrum for personal adjustment, but it was powerfully moved by the motives above and in about equal strength. I was born in England in 1905, when the flood tide of the British Empire and a ripe Victorian culture still bore on its brimming surface much of the world's political, economic, and sociointellectual life. My life at home and school had been happy, and my boyhood emotional needs had found expression in a firm home atmosphere and the relatively homogeneous and frictionless framework of the English middle class at that time. I had graduated from the university with British equivalent of *magna cum laude* (first class honors) at nineteen, my degree being in chemistry and physics. To these already matured and fascinating sciences my thoroughly stimulated intellectual interests would have held me, had it not been for the second motive—that of concern for social progress. London University stood in a city where Bernard Shaw, H. G. Wells, Bertrand Russell, Arnold Toynbee, Julian Huxley, and other equally significant writers lived and lectured. (The bones of Marx and the mummy of Bentham were within a penny bus ride.) Both by a "concerned" temperament and this major stimulation, I became intensely but, I believe, not noisily or fanatically, concerned with social problems. They were not the relatively hideous problems that youth has seen (and in part created) in the last decade—like rising crime, festering racial enclaves, and drug addiction—for apart from a certain shock at the poverty and poor morale I saw in big cities, which were in sharp contrast with my native Devonshire—my concern focused more upon positive progress at the top. That is to say, I shared a Wellsian view of mankind gaining ever greater knowledge and control of environment, and of a rising intelligence in a more gracious community life of creatively occupied citizens. I expected this to happen in the next thirty years of my life and I never dreamed that it would take so long to get the rear guard to catch up. Such steps as technically better education, birth control, city planning, and a universal adoption of racial improvement by eugenic ideals would surely eliminate very rapidly the totally unnecessary poverty, petty ignorance, and unfulfillment one saw in so many sections of society. Perhaps I have not lost my youthful impatience, for I still deplore the loss of the brave new world through progressives having to be so preoccupied with the rear guard. But I have lost some of my optimism and am prepared to recognize that in some respects and in some sections society is more backward now than then. If this sounds uncharitable I can only say that truth is a virtue as important as charity.

Although my boyhood life had been happy it had not been easy. The inherent exacting standards of parents and teachers, and the suffering and straitened circumstances of over four years of world war, meant that my generation was decidedly less casual and more intellectually tough and suspicious than most. My social idealism was not in the least sentimental, and, charity as a means hardly entered into it more than the society Lenin was at that time creating in Russia. The Bloomsbury students of my circle were occasionally "sold" on socialism or even communism, but some, and certainly I myself, despised the Marxian bible as sheer dogma and realized that new knowledge of the Great Leviathan had to be gained before rational advance could be made, though the steps mentioned above were reasonably sound. This meant that above all, society needed to advance in psychological and physiological knowledge more than in engineering, chemistry, or physics. Psychology must become a science if society aspired ever to get beyond the dreary repetition of mistakes from its existing politico-religious, rule-of-thumb methods of handling social evolution. That, and to a lesser extent, the greater scientific appeal of pioneer work in a new science rather than the physical science, eventually gained sufficient momentum to drive me into a difficult decision. From a virtually assured career as an accepted capable student in the physical sciences, I took the plunge into the uncertain future of a new, half-formed, and almost entirely socially unrecognized specialty.

The switch, and the waste of "credit" in requalifying, together with the miserably poor professional prospects in psychology, at that time, dismayed my friends, and perhaps my parents. There were then, possibly, a dozen academic positions available in psychology in the whole country, and psychology was far from being recognized as a profession. Clearly someone needed to awaken the public to the potential importance of psychology, and since no one seemed to be offering to do so I set about writing, at twenty-two, a far-ranging volume, eventually published as *Psychology and Social Progress* (1933a). But it had to be done over and above my work for the Ph.D. and required a far wider reference in history, philosophy, economics, and religion than my accustomed library resources possessed. Accordingly, I obtained entry to the British Museum Reading Room, with its boundless if slow supply. That room I cannot enter today without feeling a strange oppression for, it turned out that from overwork, snatched meals, and a cold attic, I fell ill with a stomach condition, which lasted some years.

That was in 1929–1930 and on top of my small personal problem there now fell the weight of the great economic depression. Since no job at all turned up in any such new and esoteric area as psychology, I could, if necessary, dwell on the next few Spartan years with the dreary detail of a kitchen sink novelist, but fortunately space forbids it. Suffice it to say that despite recommendations by my professors as "brilliant and with a sure future" the traumatic present continued. The perplexity of that trauma was all the greater through the contrast that it presented to the Victorian expectations of stability and sanity which I had imbibed unconsciously from several generations of middle-class English and Scottish forebears. My parents and relatives kindly refrained from saying "I told you so." They recognized that the brook I had undertaken to leap had, through no fault of mine, become a river.

To many young students today, accustomed to appropriate assistantships and well-directed traffic in the approaches to a career, it might come as a surprise to realize how far a man may pursue the paths of production he has chosen despite the lack of all such current aids, and the absence of any beaten track. Through all the experiences of the merely "fringe" jobs in psychology that I was compelled to take I was able to keep some research and writing going. But those years made me as canny and distrustful as a squirrel who has known a long winter. It bred asceticism, and impatience with irrelevance, to the point of ruthlessness. One psychological consequence, which I did not recognize at the time, was that I became more fixated on problems of practical importance than in those cushioned theoretical and purely laboratory experimental issues that my scientific interest might otherwise have dictated. Had those post-Ph.D. years from 1928 through 1932 been spent in academic security and easy opportunity I should almost certainly have chosen different themes. (This stands out if I contrast the socially serious "population intelligence" problems I then became interested in with what some of my contemporaries, and later friends—say, Mowrer and Hunt—were at that same time discussing in learning theory in the cloisters of Yale.)

I need dwell no longer on these harsher pressures and the deprivations of a suitable working environment, however, for, at the great price of giving up my country, I was rescued to a full psychological career. That came through an invitation from E. L. Thorndike, in America, who had read and been stimulated by my social research in *The Fight for Our National Intelligence* (1937a). It was like the wrench of a tooth extraction to leave the country I loved—the country in which my roots ran deep and far back. Just what I am trying to say in that sentence a reader may better appreciate by turning to a book I wrote a couple of years earlier (and which earned me a year's support for my psychological work) in 1937, called *Under Sail Through Red Devon,* and which sang the sensuous and primary love for the beauty of that countryside, and "a Shropshire Lad's" attachment to good companions, "in hearts at peace, under an English heaven." Now all this had to be left behind as I found my way with the groping of starved emotions, toward eventual satisfaction in a beauty of a more abstract and placeless kind.

This is an age when religious idioms are less well understood than formerly, but granted an intellectual transposition to a scientific age, my experience can be described as close to that which great religions have called being "reborn." American friends who know my native Devonshire and the charm of life in certain circles there have asked me point blank how I could settle down for thirty years first in arid New York and then in the stark Midwest. The answer is very simple. The good farmers and citizens of Illinois have given me the setting—the equipment and time of a research professor—in which my keenest pleasures in intellectual discovery can be exercised, and by comparison with this the physical surroundings now seem trivial.

With this sketch of the personal exodus which ended in my being research associate to Thorndike in New York (and two years later G. Stanley Hall Professor at Clark) I may perhaps be permitted to leave the personal, emotional foundations of a career and turn to some general attitudes, experiences, and insights regarding scientific work itself. It is my conviction that the two essential paradigms of scientific activity are to be found in the lives of the geographical explorer and the criminal lawyer. Actually the "court-room analysis" belongs to a later, often less important and certainly less creative analytical phase, and it has been my lot to spend much of my time, until recently, largely in the exploration phase. Here, like Columbus, one must have definite intentions of direction, but be prepared to veer off, either from a too rigid course dictated by infatuation with a theory or from the momentum of a programmatic research plan, responding alertly to new clues which nature herself may offer. Lest there be any mistake about the meaning of this flexible response to the movements of the quarry, let me be explicit that I have no use whatever for a "gypsy" scientific dilettantism, which is actually very different from exploration and often the result of a queasy intellectual stomach or a self-concerned desire to show tricks of versatility. I say this because I know that onlookers have justly wondered what I am up to in permitting such apparent digressions in my work as evidenced in wandering from personality to statistical innovation, from clinical psychology to social-cultural psychology, and so to group dynamics, to motivation, to learning theory, to the structure of abilities, to the physiological psychology of the anxiety and stress and other mood states, and finally to behavior genetics.

I can only reply that for me this apparent gypsying actually has the obvious unity of a day's fox hunt or the hunt across wide oceans for Moby Dick. Yet, since I have not paused to make this clear in a paperback overview, I can sympathize with and apologize to the student who has no time to find his way through three hundred articles. Unfortunately, only in the last few years has there been time to say, briefly, what it is all about, in one place, in a short, readable book (*The Scientific Analysis of Personality*) for students. And even for general "faculty," as distinct from specialists in the research field, it is only in the last ten years that I have made time to fill in certain obscurely sketched parts and footnote allusions, by more explicit formulae and models developed in three or four monographs, for example, "Real Base, True Zero Factor Analysis" (1972b), *Personality and Mood by Questionnaire* (1973) and "Structured Learning Theory" (1974).

However, the basic evidence for the twenty or more personality dimensions in objective tests, which constitute much of my adventure in hyperspace, was relatively early assembled in two books (1957, 1965a), as far as the experimental and statistical support for them as *patterns* (and for certain age trend and criterion relations) was concerned. Alas, I have never had time to relate them to various historical theories or to write *Personality Factors in Life and Literature,* with which it would be my pleasure to develop the meaning of these underlying structures in personality for a larger circle of readers. Other areas in which my colleagues and I have driven ahead are also only recently beginning to be linked together. For example, it is now clear that the work on objective motivation measurement and the dynamic calculus can be very potently carried over to problems of group structure and synergy in "group dynamics." And what I have recently called structured learning theory has formulae which have carried over usefully on the one hand into the psychometrics of ability structure (Cattell, 1971) and, on the other, into a new view of the nature-nurture problem in behavior genetics (in Nesselroade and Reese, 1973).

To gain sophistication on research as an art it is interesting to look back and ask what led one to decide what particular directions of reconnaissance seemed most promising at particular times. In a general way these excursions might be explained by saying that a vigilant scientist tends to play the role of a traffic helicopter over a city, spotting and releasing blockages. Often it is the appearance of some striking regularities, as in the strange repeating pattern of the U and I motivation components, or the 50 per cent larger I.Q. sigma in culture fair intelligence tests. I would say that the most important characteristic in a creative scientist—apart from realistic competence in methodological discipline—is simply an insatiable curiosity. Granted this, and an acceptance of theory as theory rather than as a rigid truth, events will show him the best way to move, as surely as the glitter of gold in a stream will attract the miner.

As for the helicopter role, some observers will recognize that I have spent appreciable time over the last forty years positively making a nuisance of myself trying to suggest traffic diversions, e.g., by getting the "experimental" psychologists to realize the inadequacy of classical, brass instrument bivariate "experimental psychology." For example, to release the traffic jam in such a domain as motivation, human or animal, I believe that multivariate and factor analytic approaches are absolutely essential. In the *Handbook of Multivariate Experimental Psychology* (1966a), I have systematized these arguments for the crucial importance of bringing multivariate methods to bear at the right place and time in relation to bivariate methods.

Since example is better than argument I have several times made forays to sow in areas in which I knew I would not have time to stay till harvest time. Such are the studies which I and my colleagues made between 1948 and 1955 in the dynamics of culture patterns. It has seemed to me that the analysis of culture patterns by Benedict, Mead, Toynbee, and many others has been either a mere "descriptive science" or, when not, has leaned on the broken reed of "subjective" explanation, by psychoanalysis or "Geisteswissenschaftlich" mysticism. The factor analysis of culture patterns which we made was most rewarding and was later taken up powerfully by Rummel (1970), Sawyer, Russett, and other political scientists and sociologists. As for the field of motivation, it is surely clear that the clinical psychologists worked for years with the concept of innate drives, but were as unable by bivariate methods to fix the numbers and natures of such structures by any objective operational procedure as a diner to eat his soup with a fork. The systematic application of multivariate methods in our laboratory, to both human and animal motivation measures, between 1950 and 1972, has left us with much clearer concepts of the actual number and nature of drives—*ergs* as I call them, to avoid the trailing traditional confusions of "instinct"—and with knowledge of how to measure their changing tension levels.

To turn to more general issues concerning the advance of science, I think it is true that most students and younger members in a research field are prone emotionally to overvalue the importance of theories *per se*. By contrast they lack due appreciation of the importance in the history of science of well-thought-out methodological inventions and advances. Theories are easier to talk about, but glibness is no substitute for decisive experiment and the guts necessary to carry it out thoroughly in the face of practical difficulties. Nevertheless, the researcher who brings innovations in methods, concepts, and terms must learn not to expect thanks from the inhabitants of the regions visited (as Kipling observed in writing of the civilized man's burden). Instead it is realistic to expect a host of intellectualized defense mechanisms, positively emotionally vicious counterattacks, and thinly disguised editorial xenophobia. The inevitability of this irrational response to anything quietly, firmly, and truly creative is written into the history of human thought. Obstructiveness has never been absent, even from the halls of science, nominally dedicated to discovery. Did not the scholars of Pisa refuse to look through Galileo's new telescope, and the medical pundits of France believe they could ignore Pasteur because he did not have a medical degree? The tragedy is not the personal disappointment of the problem solver, but the "unnecessary" lag in progress which results from students being curtained from new methods by teachers who cannot themselves master them. Of course, all new work is controversial, and this should rightly lead to its being intensively scrutinized. But the fifteen-to-twenty-year lag by the cultural anthropologists in interpreting the new cultural dimensions I have mentioned above, and of the motivation theorists (fortunately, with several striking exceptions) in failing to utilize in experiment the manifest possibilities of the dynamic calculus (despite Lindzey's good exposition as early as 1958) is surely excessive.

Despite the various diversions just described, I have never doubted that the structure and development of personality should remain for me the heartland, integrating the work of the laboratory. To explain more fully why this is so, a personal historical approach will again be of help. In the late 1920s, when I was completing my Ph.D., the domain of personality seemed to me and many other experimentalists to be loud with pretentious theories and empty of either meaningful measurement or experiment. Certainly men who wanted "safe" reputations avoided it. With my background in more established sciences, it seemed clear to me that we needed to backtrack and spend perhaps twenty years in getting sound, objective measures and a *taxonomy,* that is, a knowledge of the features and structure of personality on which to base measurement. Basically, we needed to be able to *describe and measure personality structure accurately, at a given moment in time,* if we aspired to meaningful laws about *development* and its causes. The prospects of getting either interest or support for such a low-key and laborious enterprise were depressingly small, amid the prevailing loud hysteria of melodramatic theories. I think I owe much to the personal influence of both Burt (1925) and Spearman (1927) in enabling me, despite these influences, to hold on to the longer scientific perspective. In any case, as the student of the literature will know, I then deliberately eschewed the prevailing popular, superficial (largely neo-Freudian) theories and emphasized the need for "representative" experiment from which entirely new ideas, unprejudiced by clinical fashions, might be generated. Thus began a taxonomic method and the *personality sphere* concept, and therein I recognized explicitly three possible panels of observation—L-, Q-, and T-data—and the need to coordinate them. The proper order seemed to be: first, ratings of behavior in life situations (L-data), followed by questionnaires (Q-data), and so to objective "laboratory" tests (T-data). For the meaning of structures could *first* be more readily seen in familiar L- and Q- (verbal) variables, and on that visible basis, we could hope to develop theories to guide the later construction of objective laboratory tests.

As to the means of bringing out the trait structure, I proposed what was then a novelty to 99 out of 100 psychologists, namely, that the methods of factor analysis, which had unquestionably clarified the ability field, should be turned upon personality data. When I came to work as a graduate student in Spearman's laboratory in 1926, that towering and dedicated genius had made a record contribution in psychology, from the breakthrough of his 1904 paper on the nature of intelligence ("objectively defined and measured") to the manuscript of his *Abilities of Man* (1927). The latter seemed to me to rivet down the essentials of the ability field so comprehensively that I looked for new fields to conquer, in the same spirit and with extensions of these same new methods. My first attempts to bring the latter to bear on the field of personality, then chaotic except for the semi-mystical systematizations of Freud, received a skeptical and even hostile reception. On the one hand, the clinicians chose to be slighted by my intention to begin afresh as if nothing had been proven, for example, about ego structure and the drives (though, when objective results eventually gave support and substance to those clinical adumbrations, I was more ready than most experimentalists to link with clinical terms and concepts). On the other hand, the cautious psychometrists, accustomed to the field of stable abilities, said that the structures in personality and still more in motivation would prove too shifting, subtle, and evanescent for this approach. And, finally, all those who knew nothing about factor analysis—and their numbers were considerable—sagely shook their heads and, with various rationalizations, rejected it for that very reason.

But I could logically see no other method by which the intricate unitary structures and functions in personality would be unraveled objectively, and established by replication. And the first studies that I completed (1933b), while a clinician in charge of a child guidance clinic at Leicester, England, and later at Clark and

Harvard, unquestionably revealed enough consistency and meaning to encourage an experimenter. The most stable concepts of the clinicians and analysts—ego strenth, super ego strength, as well as the cyclothyme-schizothyme polarity of temperament from Bleuler and Kretschmer's penetrating observations—emerged at once; and, in addition, there was a harvest of at least nine other novel factor patterns, each provocative of new theories.

In those days, before the electronic computer, work on large matrices was very gruelling—yet large numbers of variables and factors were indispensable to a reliable simple structure rotation in hyperspace and to significant loadings. For several dimensions must be included even though one's interests might be focused on only one dimension. (On one large study I might have given up if the boundless ingenuity of David Saunders, then a graduate student, had not made a breakthrough by finding a way to perform new operations with the IBM sorter.) Naturally, the advent of electronic computers around 1947 was at first hailed as a great blessing. Indeed, that it came just as we were needing to move into still larger matrices was an act of Providence as far as our laboratory was concerned.

Unfortunately, one is compelled in realism to add that the computer has become a dismaying source of extensive intellectual pollution in recent years. The temptation for mass-produced, push-button factor analyses, with insufficient prior sense of design and experimental planning, and poor understanding of methodology, by transient investigators who have not taken time to acquire craftsmanship in the field has produced a flood of conclusions so ill-fitting and even chaotic that the personality student unfamiliar with the technical questions involved may well be discouraged from entering the field. For example, in the domain of personality structure in questionnaires, there are at the moment at least half a dozen well-publicized solutions differing in diverse directions from the core of primary factor structures reached in the interlocking 16 PF, HSPQ, CPQ, etc., studies, and as I have shown in a recent book (1973) four-fifths of these confusing results are based on researches which omit one or more of the cardinal requirements, e.g., a test for the number of factors, a demonstration of the significance of simple structure reached, for a unique solution. Here is an instance in the course of scientific research where the power can be too high for the drivers to handle it without mishap. A machine to factor items by the hundreds and subjects in the thousands is no substitute for intelligent design and a deeper understanding of method.

Struggling for technical statistical improvements as we proceeded we entered on a long trek in the 1940–1960 period through the rating and questionnaire media of observation to the ultimate goal of objective behavior tests. This was the star to which I hitched the laboratory wagon. However, it was 1949 (the year of publication of the 16 P.F. questionnaire) before I felt sufficiently satisfied with the stability and meaning of the matching L- and Q-data source traits, to leave those areas and go ahead primarily with objective test construction.

To create entirely new objective, miniature situation tests by the hundreds—since each of perhaps twenty factors would need eight to ten good subtests to define it—was an ambitious undertaking that required the resources of a substantial laboratory. Fortunately, by 1945, Professor Woodrow and the administration at Illinois had called me to the newly created research professorship in psychology. Thus, "life began at forty" and for the first time I had adequate resources and equipment. The varied budding ideas, held frozen since their beginnings in my 1930–1940 articles until this late spring of personal opportunity, could now burst into flower. Thus, the Laboratory of Personality and Group Analysis at Illinois began that series of interlocking and increasingly converging factor analytic studies of objective personality tests which, in 1974, has come close to its goal in the work of Schuerger, Hundleby, Sweney, Burdsal, and others. Psychometrists—and many others—are apt to think of the fifty factor analyses collated from our work in the books by Hundleby, Bolz, and Pawlik as perhaps a tour de force in multivariate methods per se, or even in computer program construction. But most of this statistical methodology (or artistic finesse in multivariate methods, according to one's evaluation) could have been brought to bear by any competent statistician. The creativity on which the success of the long enterprise really hung—and sometimes waited impatiently—was the invention, in the light of insights into the theories of emerging personality factors, of the 400 new types of objective, miniature situation tests themselves.

These objective personality tests were for fifteen years available for reference only in lists of very brief descriptions in some forty articles scattered in many journals. It was the faithful labor of my colleague of several years, Frank Warburton, a heavy labor about which I sometimes have misgivings that it may have been contributory to his final illness, which brought them out of the laboratory and into one encyclopedic volume for psychologists. But even then, since only illustrative bits of each total test were given, I could not feel confident that those repeating our work could get the necessary precision of reproduction of experimental conditions. Not until Schuerger and Hundleby this year finally put complete O-A (Objective-Analytic) batteries together and persuaded IPAT to undertake the expense of publishing them were they really available for general use by psychologists. Only at that point could they and I feel that the labor of half a lifetime and many co-workers was safe and delivered. We were like bridge builders seeing the last connecting rivets driven home.

It is an interesting sidelight on the difficulties of communication in face of stereotypes that many experimentalists and theorists have seen this phase of our work as aimed at practical test construction. Instead it was, of course, a construction of firm and relevant behavioral referents by which to investigate the structure and basic functioning of personality. As that structure was revealed in such concepts as anxiety, cortertia, regression, exvia, etc., these test situations became the firm framework by which the concepts were held (more firmly than by everyday life criteria). Appearances to the contrary, psychological tests *as such* are something for which I have not had much concern; and my personal interest in what commonly goes under the name of test construction is actually very limited. The reason that I have devoted much overtime, and my wife has given many years of unpaid, onerous, and exacting editorial labor, to the publishing work of the Institute for Personality and Ability Testing (the unendowed work of which has made these reference measures available) has been that the personality concepts are scientifically trivial unless tied down operationally. The published batteries and scales, not launched as tests until many years of work established and checked the structural foundations, have provided conceptual "markers" for the discovered primary personality factors in Q-data (in the form of the ESPQ, CPQ, and 16 P.F.) and in T-data (the Child and the Adult O-A Batteries), as well as for the fluid general intelligence factor in culture fair scales, and for anxiety, arousal, and other states needing to be measured in clinical and physiological research.

The university laboratory could scarcely keep up with the basic research itself, and, except for the publications by Warburton and one or two others of actual tests, had no resources for the expensive and commercially not self-sustaining business of publishing complex test material. If the small group of researchers had not set up IPAT, as described above, much research on child development, therapy, and firm cross-cultural reference to the same basic concepts resting on standard operational measures would have been delayed many years. By the provision of scales, such as the ESPQ, CPQ, HSPQ, and 16 P.F., measuring as far as possible the same factors at different ages, an indispensable continuity of conception has been made feasible in developmental research.

I certainly would not claim that this continuity and standardization of measures has or could have been attained by so small a band of co-workers to levels satisfying to every onlooking psychometric statistician. Progress continues, but exact equivalences will never be attained for the inherent reason that factor patterns change with culture and epoch. However, the theoretical understanding of the personality source traits indexed under the numbers U.I. 16 through 36 has moved ahead, notably regarding U.I. 24 (anxiety); U.I. 23 (regression); and U.I. 16, 18, 19, 21, and 32 (extraversion) through conceptual analysis and further experiment on the dozen or so different behaviors found to have replicated loading on these "batteries."

Anyone familiar with the history of discussion in this area will know that it has been a frequent criticism, which factor analysts in all fields have to meet, that factors are mere "mathematical abstractions." Without due attention to experimental conditions, and great care in pursuing simple structure, they may well be just that! But life criterion relations, for example, the more than 100 per cent increase in predicting school achievement beyond that from intelligence tests alone, through including personality factors (Cattell and Butcher, 1968), show they are more than that. Thus, as to interest in getting beyond the "static" measurement of persons of a given moment—the taxonomic stage—into the developmental and criterion relation field, no psychologists have been more eager than our laboratory group to get to grips with such problems. Whatever appearance this group may give from a distance of lingering perfectionistically over the cross-sectional work its goal has been the study of origins and developments, as well shown in the first harvest of results from Barton, Dielman, Fozard, Rickels, Schmidt, and many others who have begun to use defined source trait measures in the last decade. But most developmental work done *without* first reaching checked structural concepts and measures turns out to achieve few significant criterion relations and conceptually to reap mainly confusion and waste. Admittedly, it has taken twenty years to reach the reasonably firmly structured personality measures requisite to start developmental work on an enlightened basis. But one cannot help commenting that if four or five hundred psychologists from perhaps a hundred departments (rather than the dozen able factor analysts, confined to three or four centers, who actually appeared on the scene), who claim to be seriously interested in personality research, had "heard the drummer," and turned up on the job, it might have been done in five years.

Such moments of stagnation in the movement of science—or at least of intense activity in some laboratories and uncertainty in others—are not really due to lack of resources, but are matters of communication alertness, open minds, and readiness for serious, consecutive planning. I believe that any realistic observer would be forced to conclude that personality research between, say, 1940 and 1960 paid dearly in wasted effort and confusion for not recognizing the importance and priority of conceptually and technically advanced measurement. But there were, fortunately, not only a few such active centers of effort as those of Guilford, Eysenck, ETS, Thurstone, and our own laboratory, but also many independent thinkers in applied psychology who could see far enough ahead to start work with structured personality measures. Someday some historically minded psychologist should investigate just how much this movement ahead of the pack, by men like Butcher, Scheier, Sweney, Tatro, Karson, Killian, Rickels, Miller, Dielman, Knapp, Barton, Delhees, Schmidt, Sells, Bjerstedt, Weckowitz, and others contributed to what has been a conceptual revaluation in personality and motivation referents. Both in factored personality and motivation it has also been evident that this change brought a higher percentage of significant predictions of diagnostic, educational, and vocational criteria where work with more arbitrary scales had been negative and discouraging.

By 1950 the small team of two to four Ph.D. full-time researchers who typically formed the Laboratory of Personality and Group Analysis at the University of Illinois had built a sufficiency of technical experience to keep the personality dimension research going steadily, thus giving us a little surplus time and energy to consider a more difficult domain. There had been assumptions since Darwin that mammalian drives are present in man; but though Freud, Murray, Drever, McDougall, and others had written on the matter, there had been little methodological advance and still less consensus. If we could measure the strengths of individuals' motives and particular interests in some objective way, and apply multivariate analysis methods to a large spectrum of measured human interests, it seemed logically certain that this approach should permit one to analyze out the number and nature of underlying human drives, if such patterns existed. Possibly we could also pick up the outline of those learned aggregates of attitudes which we called "sentiments" and which represent the impress of sociological institutions, working through "conditioning schedules."

The first factorial "photographs" of what everyone said (and we half believed) would be a "fuzzy" field were awaited in our first experiments almost with apprehension. But, lo, they proved if anything to be clearer than the factor patterns that had emerged for years from the well-known fields of ability and temperament! Sex, fear, parental protectiveness, curiosity, etc., stood out to the tune of nine "ergs" (as we called them to avoid the methodological quagmire of the terms "instinct" and "drive"). Here again, as in the general personality domain, much of the research success hinged on our ability to create a basis of new devices for objective measures of interest strength (in place of the verbal self-evaluation in such traditional measures as the Strong, the Kuder, and various existing interest-motivation scales). The story of the numerous (over 100) devices that we tried, for example, physiological response, perception, memory, attention, etc., and the mysterious refusal of this new data to fit a single "strength of motive" factor has been told elsewhere (Cattell, 1965a). Here the evidence for the concept of two fundamentally distinct components in all motivation, "integrated" and "unintegrated," was born, and out of this the theoretical framework called the "dynamic calculus," with its vectorial measurement of attitudes, of conflict, and of personality learning, grew naturally.

This instance is as good as any to illustrate the developmental difficulties which psychology as a science has suffered in this generation as a result of "the two cultures." By the two cultures (analogous within psychology to those which C. P. Snow has indicated dividing our whole higher culture), I mean scientific psychology, on the one hand, and, on the other, that literary, conversational, humanistic, pre-scientific speculation which still occupies the conversation and practice of perhaps two-thirds of psychologists. Our science has the peculiarity that *everyone* can claim to be a psychologist (and in that intuitive and conversational sense some politicians, businessmen, and teachers are actually highly capable psychologists). It seems to me probable that in fact if not in name the overgrown amoeba we call the APA will fission, not vertically into functional specific interest areas, as now, but horizontally into equally functional specific levels of technical qualification. The smaller group with rigorous scientific methods and interests is already peeling off in such societies as the Psychonomic Society, the Society of Multivariate Experimental Psychology, the Society of Experimental Psychologists, and the Psychometric Society, and these groups find it increasingly difficult to communicate with the larger remainder—a difficulty increased by the editors of the mass journals declining to expose their charges to anything they would have difficulty in reading.

Recently the search for some identity in this non-rigorous majority, which has slipped into all kinds of cults, has led to the term "humanistic." This originally was a good term from the Italian Renaissance, and inasmuch as I have always been a lover of literature and positively an addict of poetry, I might be expected to welcome this. Actually I view it as a possible disaster. Science and esthetics are for me respectively work and recreation. Beauty may enter science, as when I contemplate an intricate and perfect fit in hyperspace, but I would prefer to enjoy the magnificent language of Hamlet or Julius Caesar without psychoanalysis or factor analysis. If half of the APA wishes to follow a "humanistic psychology" they are entitled to their enjoyment, but they will not advance by those methods on Shakespeare, Goethe, Balzac—or even Plutarch or Lucretius. And one must realistically add that humanistic psychology is one thing but what it will become if fed largely by student escapees from mathematics, experiment, and logic is something else.

It is no accident that the psychologists I find most congenial, and who have contributed most to psychology, such as Hull, Thurstone, Godfrey Thomson, Tolman, and (in my immediate circle) Tucker, had been physical scientists, learning what science means, before they became psychologists. In years to come I have little doubt that the half-century from 1925 to 1975, in which my postgraduate life has been spent, will be recognized as having the same birth agonies as those in which chemistry grew out of alchemy. There is the same exasperation or indifference on the two sides now as then. The difference between the reception of, for example, my *Scientific Analysis of Personality* in departments with the scientific and the "humanistic" emphases is fantastic. And a diatribe to which I was subjected not long ago in *Contemporary Psychology* by an eloquent writer who found all this quantitative stuff beside the point could easily be matched by what the seekers of the philosopher's stone and the elixir of life had to say about Dalton, Priestly, and Lavoisier and their footling weighing, adding, and subtracting. And in the last decade and in London University where Spearman and Burt took their giant steps there have been near revolts by the more casually permissively educated undergraduates against having to face either mathematics or experiment in taking a degree in psychology. Parenthetically, there is plenty of room for intuitive psychologists skilled in emotional interaction, but their role in relation to scientific psychologists has to be that of priests to theologians, or nurses to doctors.

As I have recounted in more detail elsewhere the place where I have found this failure of conceptual training in students most frustrating of advance has been in regard to what I and my co-workers have called the dynamic calculus—the application of objective test devices and mathematical analysis to the realm of motivation. For lack of other shoulders at the wheel of the wagon we have traversed in twenty years what should have been covered in five. I am increasingly convinced that the problem is more in the teachers than the students. Statistics is taught in dry isolation from the substantive interests of students. And in several instances known to me a good personality theorist with statistical know-how has been drafted to teach straight statistics leaving a personality teacher lacking mathematical capacity to teach personality, thus impoverishing both fields. Actually the student needs no more than high school algebra and a steady logical understanding to handle the clinical and personality applications of the dynamic calculus. The problem is that his teachers are unwilling to ask of him (and possibly of themselves) that he use the simple equations of which every undergraduate in chemistry, physics, genetics, or physiology takes in his stride. If the statistics or mathematics relate to clear concepts the student is generally willing, and surely it can be said that the formulae for ergic tension, and the vector measurement of attitudes, conflict, and decision-making are close to those in use by the clinician.

My sympathy for the students' problem was first strongly provoked during the time that Allport and I shared the teaching at Harvard. Psychologists familiar with his books and mine will surely recognize that we were asking the young undergraduate to dissolve oil in water and to perfect feats of methodological reconciliation which no faculty member could perform. Incidentally the Harvard department was then more compact than the more than ten floors of William James Hall today, and I enjoyed excellent discussions over a sandwich lunch among Allport, Boring, Lashley, Murray, Mowrer, Stevens, Sheldon, Morgan, and Beebe-Center. Allport and I struggled, with the utmost goodwill, to communicate, but never successfully. One obstacle was his conviction that statistics could not deal with unique traits and it was while arguing with him over this that I clarified for myself what eventually became P-technique: the factor analysis of the single person. Among other things it also led to the addition of state (mood) factors to the behavioral specification equation and so to modulation theory.

As the reader will know, the experimental procedure in P-technique is simply the measuring of a subject on the same, say, 30 or

40 state, physiological, and motivation variables every day for a hundred or more days. When these variables are correlated over time and factored, one discovers the dimensions along which human moods fluctuate—the unitary state components. Differential R-technique—taking 100 people on the same 30 or more variables on two different days—should, by factoring differences, yield the same common state patterns, so that we have deliberately used P- and dR- (differential R) experiments as the left and right hands of psycho-physiological state investigation.

Looking back at what I set out three years later more clearly as the *Covariation Chart* (1946), and ultimately as the ten-dimensional *Data Box* (1966a), it is surprising that the conception of factor analysis as something applicable only to groups held up so long the idea of P-technique and dR-technique. I envisaged them in 1942 simply as an answer to the problem of discovering and defining states, not as a part of the splendid perspective of total analysis possibilities that appeared later in the ten-dimensional data box. But these partial glimpses and hesitating steps are absolutely typical of the story of science, where, when the light is switched on later, one is disgusted with the timidity and stupidity of the steps one made in the dark.

My wife was the literally long-suffering subject for the first P-technique experiment performed about this time; every day for nine weeks she endured the electric shocks and other indignities of the experiment. From this, a succession of interlocking state and trait experiments with combined psychological and physiological measures produced, over twenty years, a clear distinction in concepts and operational measurements, among such states as anxiety, arousal, fatigue, depression, and stress. Again, due to technical communication difficulties, medical and even psychological journals were full of studies on states during the next fifteen years that continued to rest on subjective definitions of the various states, not realizing what P- and dR-techniques could contribute to precision of findings. One result of this naïve belief that states could be defined by fiat was a harvest of contradictory physiological associations. (For example, our demonstration that cholesterol increase is associated with the state of stress, *not* the state of anxiety, has gone without either a check or a conceptual recognition in most medical literature.) A symposium to which I was recently asked to contribute (and did) at the American Psychological Association meetings in 1971, entitled "The Revolutionary Implications of the State Trait Distinction for Psychological Theory," indicates that in present climates, despite the heroic efforts of *Psychological Abstracts* to communicate, revolutions became visible only with a quarter of a century lag.

Advance in psychological laws and concepts on the one hand and in methods and statistical concepts on the other can be thought of as conceptually distinct, but only the raw student assumes that in fact they are. Pursuit of psychological findings has forced me almost constantly over forty years into methodological invention, and in most years four or five substantive articles would stand side by side with two or three essentially methodological. The tendency to separate two types of psychologists who do these things is, I believe, as misguided as with respect to those who teach these things. It is true that—not being a statistician or mathematician—I have always been mighty glad of there being specialists to call to for help. Yet fine mathematical statisticians like Hotelling, Horst, Guttman, Kaiser, and Anderson, unless pestered by people in substantive research like myself, are very prone to solve problems with their preferred, elegant mathematical assumptions, rather than those needed by the scientific model seen as necessary by the researcher. For example, most write theorems for component analysis, calling it factor analysis, or analytical programs for orthogonal rather than oblique factors, and have shown little interest in modeling higher order factors as causes, modulation theory, the riddle of motivation and dynamic structure factors in the "grid," and so on. The result is that I have shamelessly produced makeshift innovations without setting out all mathematical assumptions, and have even descended to Monte Carlo methods when no mathematician could help me in getting distributions and significance tests for what have been to me the *psychologically* important coefficients.

Nevertheless, I have enjoyed the methodological puzzles, which commonly began by appearing as thugs barring my research path and ended by being beautiful companions. There is no space here, however, to describe their abstract beauty, but only to list them. They include a solution for the number of factors (the scree test), a test of goodness of simple structure, a factor-matching evaluator (the s index), ipsative scoring in the dynamic field, real base factor analysis, the maxplane program, the taxonome program for objectively locating clinical and other types, and, especially, what ultimately became the confactor rotation method. In this "side activity" belong also the Procrustes rotation, the profile similarity coefficient, r_p, the notion of cooperative factors, true zero factor scoring, modulation theory, the isopodic and equipotent methods for comparing traits across cultures, the "heresy" (in 1935) of oblique and higher order factors, a restructuring of the earlier APA committee "reliability" and "validity" concepts (with Tsujioka, 1964), the dimensional representation measurement of focal and ambient stimulus situations, the relational simplex theory of equal interval scaling (1962, 1971), and my attempt, perhaps a little wild in parts, to reach the promised land of real base, true zero factor analysis (1972b).

Although like most mathematical propositions these developments *can* be conceived algebraically, it is perhaps of interest from the standpoint of styles of creation that in my own thinking they were not so conceived. I am, by nature, a spatial thinker (as, incidentally, were Thurstone and Thomson, but not Burt or Horst), and many times I have lain awake utilizing the quiet of the night in attempting to see the meaning of some new result (or seeming contradiction) in an extended visualized model. Once I thought I had a new perception which invalidated ten years of work and kicked the foundations from under the work of myself and many others. Fortunately, with the dawn, I found that the Devil himself could make mistakes, and with this exposure of the flaw, I got some sleep. Actually, much of the multivariate field, if approached geometrically, involves one in the tour de force of visualizing hyperspace, which is why I have titled this account of my forty years of exploration of the domain as "travels in hyperspace." It has certainly been no less exciting, though open to fewer onlookers, than that exploration, albeit undertaken in the same spirit, which the adventurers in outer space have made in this generation.

Reviewers of my three purely taxonomic books (1946, 1957, 1965a), that is, books integrating evidence on structures and types per se have—not only in my perception but in that of others—often stopped short of the vital values and technical problems. They have wanted closed, simplified solutions where I have instead sharpened up the need for sensitive concern for methodological issues. Further they have been rather unwilling to get familiar with the admittedly wide spread of new facts, concepts, and terms. The sheer volume of multivariate data handled in this area has itself been difficult for my colleagues, too. The patient and comprehensive accountancy in experimental work accompanying interlocking cross-cultural and cross-age strategies has been enormous. Nevertheless, it is pointless to ask for laws about learning more "entertaining" theoretical development regarding the inner nature of the personality factors themselves until the patterns themselves are well tied down. My reply to this impatience has essentially been that the real game of high-level, theoretical interaction simply cannot begin until the actual pieces on the chessboard have been produced, and the rules which govern their moves learned. (If one begins prematurely, the game becomes a chaotic wild goose chase.) Actually, the onlookers are free, in any case, to take the well-replicated individual trait or state patterns and make as many theories to account for the observed patterns as they wish. But, except for some good theorizing in articles on U.I. 19, U.I. 20, U.I. 24, and U.I. 28, few personality or clinical psychologists have moved from experiment to theory, and, inferentially, back to experiment.

A team of investigators such as I have worked with on these problems receives its outside evaluations from reviewers of books, journal editors, the teachers and writers of textbooks, the debates and interactions with other laboratories, and the committees who distribute grants. As innovators in literature and art also know, reviewers are erratic, and in psychology reviews by senior men, such as those which Sir Godfrey Thomson or Sir Cyril Burt used to present (often more important than the book) have become infrequent, supplanted by writings for spleen rather than instruction. Teachers and textbook writers, even when very able, are apt to lag, because the customer—the college teacher—wants what he knows. The debates and interactions with other workers in the field come nearest to the genuine indicator. Yet, if research is to continue, it is the granting committees that are immediately most important. In that fine period of national enthusiasm for research which followed World War II and was accelerated by Sputnik, the psychologists in Washington handled this new feature in our culture with remarkable maturity, penetration, and dedication. They showed imagination, and the capacity to transcend fads, and, the ability to resist purely political pressures. But seemingly this could not last. The permanent secretaries acquired skill in "research on research" but there are signs that the first enthusiasm which made outstanding people in research willing to serve on the evaluation committees has waned, and merely correct people sit where imaginative people sat before. We are in danger of Bernard Shaw's dictum transformed to the research field: "Those who can, do; those who cannot, evaluate." Perhaps I can indicate my concern over a possible trend in the quality of the life blood of science with less risk of accusation of prejudice since it has been my own good fortune to have the essential programmatic character of my work sustained from 1945 quite adequately by these committees. More help than two or three associates and a couple of research assistants and clerical help I have never wanted, because the intimately lively daily contact in research problems is lost in administrative work when the unit becomes larger. Spontaneous discussions around the blackboard in my own or an associate's office are the stuff of daily research progress.

To fit the above activities into time perspective I will relate that apart from the rhythmic "digressions" into method, the sheer mapping of personality factors proceeded steadily from 1945 to 1970.[1] In accumulating evidence on these initially as "patterns in people," we did not lose the methodological and conceptual perspective that traits are abstractions from relations between

[1] Surprisingly very few clinicians and personality theorists have yet made good use of these published empirically checked patterns as a basis for developing testable theories. They seem to have preferred to start with a long word in the dictionary and weave a theory around it, e.g., "the authoritarian personality," which has popular or personal emotional significance. However, our work toward integrating psychometric and personality theory interests has not suffered from poor communication only on the clinical-personality flank. Psychometrists continue to misunderstand the clearly explained strategy which my colleagues and I have deliberately practiced of converging on the major dimensions in the personality sphere. Starting with variables widely sampled from the personality sphere our plan has been to use *many* short (and therefore less reliable) measures, increasing the length of those which are demonstrated to be relevant to an emerging factor. It is not unusual for a psychometrist divorced from substantive research to turn up his nose at the resulting modest factor loadings. In this he has the important distinction between reliably replicating a *factor pattern,* on the one hand, and the quite different objective of producing a sufficiently valid battery *to measure it* on the other.

people and social and other environments, and are not definable and measurable just as "characteristics embedded in people."

Both for this theoretical reason, and also because of that earlier concern with social progress which helped propel me into psychology, I have constantly experienced a pressure which forced me to take intermittent "periods off" from the personality research to re-enter social psychology and work more precisely on the *environment* of personality definition. This has meant the development of models and the tackling of substantive issues in (a) small group dynamics and (b) the problems of cultural definition and dynamics. One is inevitably forced into a model which seeks to relate attributes of groups to attributes of individuals, and to the structured role relations of individuals in groups. It therefore appeared a cogent argument to me—but evidently not so cogent to many group dynamicists and cultural anthropologists, judging by their publications—that these sciences need to start by establishing a comprehensive, quantified taxonomy and measurement system for groups themselves. Of course, even before that, we need a *psychological* definition of the generic nature of these entities we call groups.

Around 1950, with the resourceful assistance of Gibb, Adelson, Stice, Meeland, and others, I factored the behavior of 100 groups of 10 men each on about 50 performances for each group. This led to actual test batteries for measuring certain uniquely determined dimensional conceptions of morale, stability, congeniality, etc. These group traits were in turn found to relate in significant and meaningful ways to the personality of group members and the roles prevailing among them. This work published as an Office of Naval Research Monograph (Cattell and Stice, 1953) has never been repeated or followed up by those interested in behavior of groups, though our work using the same model for national cultures has been taken up and pursued with imagination and rigorous methodology by political scientists like Rummel (1970). Yet the group behavior factoring in small group dynamics must someday be picked up again, for I firmly maintain (and here Miller's work, 1971, on organism-group systems fully supports my position) that the relation of individuals to groups will get nowhere until we have dependable, structurally meaningful *measures* of the characteristics of both.

Hume complained that his *Treatise on Human Understanding* "fell deadborn from the press," but with no more hollow a thud than Stice's and my own *Dimensions of Groups* (1953, 1960). By contrast as just indicated, and for reasons evidently better known to political scientists than psychologists, the formally identical approach to the dimensions of nations and national culture patterns, with Breul and Hartman (1952) "caught on." However, among psychologists pioneers like Gorsuch and Lynn have lately carried the work substantially further. Having expanded on the frontier of personality with sociology and political science I felt that a balanced concern for personality development called next for bringing understanding of genetic influences to comparability with that of our grasp of environmental influences. This move was no part of the all-too-common game of giving a sense of conceptual advance by closing one's eyes to everything but one aspect at any one time. The conceptual importance of genetics was always in our theory, but actual resources dictate research concentration first on this and then on that frontier.

In view of the substantial contribution which heredity makes to human behavior, as Darwin, Galton, and, indeed, intuitive observations of many a novelist (such as Jane Austen or Galsworthy) have witnessed, it has always been a matter of astonishment to me that Watsonian reflexology could be taken so seriously that perhaps one-half of all psychologists are content to be more ignorant than the shrewd man-in-the-street about behavior genetics. Indeed, the omission of practically any treatment of the topic from many textbooks in the 1940s was obviously more than chance and pointed to a conspiracy of silence.

Historically one may guess that the explanation lies outside science in the racist prejudices of Hitler and the ignoracist counter-prejudices of which he is the originator (as surely as a shout is the originator of an echo). Some willful or stupid misreadings of Jefferson's fine words in the Constitution setting up equality of opportunity as a condition of society—misinterpreting it to mean that men *are* born of equal intelligence, etc.—may also have contributed to the taboo. In some sections of the U.S. population, however, the taboo reaches the same threatening proportions as in Russia, where at least two great scientists, Muller and Haldane, lost their strong sympathies for Communism when genetics in Russia was formally condemned and executed as a science. The recent hooliganism of students attacking Jensen, Eysenck, and the Nobelist Shockley—not without some hounding on by biologically uneducated political scientists—illustrates Bolitho's observation that the less intelligent can be depended upon in the name of progress to embrace the exploded doctrinaire views of the last generation's avant-garde. This year, in my book *Beyondism,* I have pointed out that the great task now before progressive democracies is to utilize behavior genetics as well as learning theory in the pursuit of their ideals.

Stepping back into the purely investigatory spirit of the laboratory, as a researcher is entitled to do, I conclude that good strategy, and an economical use of research resources, call for us logically to take each newly appearing, but well-replicated source trait and ask "How much of the variance in this trait is genetic and how much environmental?" Though in determining nature-nurture ratios we cross only the first bridge along the route to an effective science of behavior genetics, the geneticist who wants, eventually, to tie behavior tendencies to genes needs to begin there. Pondering the limitations of the twin study method, I found crystallizing in my mind (actually, one day on a deserted cove near Dartmouth in Devonshire) what finally became the Multiple Abstract Variance Analysis (MAVA) method. Like some other intriguing new-borns in the world of ideas that have seemed, at first, to require only a long weekend for their development into viable adult form, this one led me on a far longer developmental journey than I expected. It included stop-offs at the friendly doors of many geneticists, and development in a series of four articles, over ten years (1953–1963), each carrying the new definition and assumptions, for example, on environment-heredity interaction, a step further. Only in the last two years have I been able, after some tussles with Jinks and Fulker in England, and refinements by Loehlin, Kempthorne, Nesselroade, Eaves, and others to bring it to a form apparently satisfactory to both psychologists and geneticists. If the application which Dr. Klein and I are now making of the ten-hour HSOA Battery to over two thousand children in six family constellations can be continued for two more years, I believe that illuminating answers, as convergent as those concerning the primary factor we call intelligence, may become available for a dozen other primary factors of personality (and these traits are at least as important, clinically and socially, as intelligence).

To leave an area fallow in one's mind and return to it after some years is often an effective research maneuver (provided distractions of teaching or excessive family cares in the interim do not result in such a general overcrowding of interests that the unconscious gains no relief and, therefore, no consolidation). One among several experiences that I have had of such action concerns my work on abilities. It transpired that after publishing on abilities from 1930 to 1940, I was so distracted by the main thrust we were making in personality that I could not return to those interests until around 1960. I believe this did the trick of enabling me to shed some older "prejudices" and to see the evidence afresh. Up to 1940 my research and thinking about intelligence moved along to what has seemed to onlookers two distinct lines, one practical, one theoretical. The first led to the construction of culture fair intelligence tests invoking the perception of complex relations on universally familiar fundaments. The second expressed itself in a theoretical conception: that Spearman's *g* was really *two* general factors, to be designated *fluid* and *crystallized* intelligence. By 1960 factor analysis techniques at the higher order had advanced sufficiently for the implications of this theory to be crucially examined. To my increasing satisfaction one sample and age group after another came out with results supporting the theory. Furthermore, the idea behind culture fair tests and the fluid intelligence concept itself then came felicitously together. The result was that I found myself in a position differing equally from Spearman, Burt, Thurstone, and Guilford—though Thurstone's work had been the clue to the step I had taken. Space precludes following the ideas which then ensued like a train of firecrackers. But the *triadic theory* of ability structure, the ADAC chart, and the bridge to structured learning theory are sufficiently set out in my recent book, *Abilities: Their Structure, Growth and Action* (1971).

As I set down these half-dozen apparently distinct directions of research endeavor above, I realize that they must appear more unrelated than they actually were. Indeed, they look like one of those gypsy-like meanderings which some scholars pursue and which I have occasionally pursued myself on the principle that the best recreation is a change of work. But in fact the excursions were mainly not of this type. To me they had a natural integration and were undertaken partly to throw light on one another, though I am told by those who glance at my articles that necessary connections are not easy to see. Thus as investigation after investigation has appeared on factor structure over twenty years across various ages, media, and cultures with an integration and a plan fully evident to my co-workers, I am told that many psychologists see only a straggling caravan of individual taxonomic studies and strange trait names.

Experimentalists of the bivariate, brass-instrument type in particular have shown no more understanding of this parade of naturalist's specimens than perhaps they would in a botanist's herbarium. Yet such patient collection and definition is essential in this area, and the game can begin only after the pieces are assembled—as Linnaeus and Darwin realized. Moreover, disappointment and poor morale have resulted for two generations before the present from psychologists finding negligible relations in developmental and clinical fields largely because of the amateurish and shoddy character of their trait measurements.

Similarly the more recent attention to the nature of dynamic traits and their measurement per se—to ergic tension levels and to sentiment structures—is reaping a long-delayed harvest. It is encouraging in this same field to see our conceptualizations and "taxonomy" throwing light on deeper issues in the work of such a penetrating systematist as Madsen at Copenhagen. Obviously in all these fields misunderstandings might be lessened if the researcher would steal time from the experimental work to write up more frequent overviews and explain what he is doing for people with little time to read. But except for a few great men like Churchill it is difficult both to make history and write it. In my own field, since my time in the laboratory is coming to an end I shall in fact probably be enabled to write that overview, yet to plan campaigns is second best to carrying them out, especially in a field where one can see that "the party has barely begun."

Finally, in this survey of areas of activity, I come to one more far out from what most psychologists deal with than the others. This last activity, recently expressed in *Beyondism* mentioned above, is rooted in my early concern with social progress and the role of psychology therein. I still find myself, forty years after my first essay, "Psychology and Social Progress," as convinced as ever that the rule-of-thumb methods by which we manage society are an unnecessarily crude comparison of what might be with the present realities of human prejudice and lack of imagination. Among other things, we are still obsessed with the right-left-wing stereotype and an arrangement of political party structure too obviously modeled on a football game. However, political action, whether arranged by scientific or by obsolete mechanisms, in the end merely trails behind whatever moral values the community has espoused or technical discoveries science has made. My book on psychology and social progress (1933) and *Psychology and the Religious Quest* (1938) set out a radical attempt at an objective approach to ethical values. Apart from intermittent action in a chapter in 1941 and a brief article in 1950, however, I was quite unable—"to the wheel of life bound dizzily"—to return to this interest until as late as 1972 in my book *A Morality from Science: Beyondism.* This questions the capacity of the method of "revealed religions," including parts of Christianity, to integrate our intellectual and emotional life. It suggests and proposes a shift of origin from intuition means whereby we may progress to a scientific derivation of ethical values by analysis of evolutionary goals. It indicates that modern Russellian "humanism" is quite as fallible and arbitrary as those ancient religious dogmas which the modernist attacks. I imagine it will be some years before the implications of this Copernican shift in the philosophy of ethics become a part of general discussion.

Neither in these domains commonly left to human emotionality nor in the area where scientific analysis is accepted as the main method have I sought controversy. The new conclusions I reached are fairly frequently described as controversial, but this is a by-product to which I pay little attention. In science preoccupation with debate is a vice to be avoided. Most often it generates more heat than light, and a descent to *ad hominen* "personalities." How then are ideas to be changed? I suggest by reading and thought. Debate rarely changes opinion and indeed, as Kuhn points out in regard to revolutions in science, though it does some good by airing new facts, wrong opinions often only disappear with the death of their holders. Both the facts and the reasoning which generates new concepts from them have generally been well stated in the literature. I frequently find myself challenged, with more belligerence than investigatory spirit, on such questions as my theories of personality structure, oblique versus orthogonal rotation in factor analysis, the abandoning of inventories for objective devices for motivation measurement, and the subordination of classical reflexological learning theory to structured learning theory. Once issues have been clearly defined in print debates merely consume time needed for creative research thought. At least half the criticisms aimed at my concepts in personality and motivation make assumptions that have already been explicitly set aside in writings a decade earlier. In fact most innovators are careful to set down their new reasons, and it is commonly the holder of the reactionary position who has never examined or set out his justifications. The criticism that "you only get out of factor analysis what you put into it" is a good specimen of this kind of criticism.

However, I hope this aversion to controversy for its own sake will not be misunderstood as lack of regard for the polity of science or the duty to interact when required. Indeed, I gather that I am considered more of a controversialist than would be expected of one holding the above philosophy. One major fracas or feud where I respond perhaps too readily to the war-trumpet concerns the whole domain of the design of experiment. There I have contended, to the annoyance of manipulative, bivariate, classical, brass-instrument experimentalists, that theirs is only half—and the less effective half—of psychological experiment. Multivariate experiment, for reasons I have set out adequately in the *Handbook of Multivariate Experimental Psychology,* has opened doors in psychology that classical approaches have beaten on in vain. It can be as manipulative as the bivariate method—a vital point which generally goes completely unrecognized by the classical "experimentalist." But even when it is not designed to include manipulation it can, by invoking sequential measurement, establish causal connection. It is not restricted to mere associative correlation, which some suppose to be its limit. Although I should have known better than to get involved in a dead issue, I arose only last week to refute yet another repetition of the stereotype that "only classical experiment can establish causality." (This was made at a meeting of leading experimenters—bivariate and multivariate—by an Oxford psychologist!)

By comparison, a minor feud has been that with factor analysts who extract only two or three factors "in order to be conservative" when decidedly more—say fifteen to twenty—are indicated by statistical tests. This underlies the present personality structure controversy between Eysenck's three and my own sixteen to twenty or more scale questionnaire. Underfactoring is anything but conservative! On this criticized trend toward dealing with twenty rather than three factors, as well as the rejection of orthogonal for oblique rotation, it is now evident that two or three investigators appearing as a small minority, can, by logic and crucial research, within a decade lead a majority.[2]

[2] It is of interest in the history of science to analyze the effect of degrees of external and internal challenge or threat on the performance of a research group. In internal administration I have always practiced "a light hand on the tiller" believing the nature of research is such that the utmost possible freedom is required. On the other hand, I value the gift of research funds so strongly that I would drop an assistant at once who indubitably lacks any sense of dedication.

The effect of outside pressures—and here I mean completely unsympathetic attacks, not the probings of independent faculty we have always been glad to have in the laboratory on their sabbaticals—has usually been to close the ranks, though I'm sure this is good. An instance of such rather useless criticism has appeared in the last decade from those availing themselves of the ease of getting questionnaire data and large computers to comment on personality structure theory. A whole scholarship of personality structure—including the personality sphere, a methodology of successive convergence, corrections from perturbation and instrument factor theory, the theory of matching across media, etc., verification by higher order relations, effects on obliqueness from selection, etc.—is lacking from these squalid, push-button computer products, and their divergence from more systematic and programmatic work is meaningless.

An equally meaningless type of criticism is that which fails to perceive the rhythm of exploration, and hypothesis formation on a broad front with rough methods, alternating with precision. In intelligently flexible research, optimally cut to the limited resources of one laboratory, there is a time for approximation and a time for great precision. It is stupid mechanically to incur the cost of working to a tolerance of .0001 of an inch, when a tenth of an inch suits the actual problem.

In later exact phases, connected with building valid batteries for each of the twenty factors we have discovered—there will be a time when larger funds and reinforcements and samples of 1000 will be necessary. Some "crystal ball gazing"—which means forming the best possible conclusion from the particulars and circumstances of many researches,

The second major feud is major indeed, since it concerns learning theory and its whole relation to personality theory. My contention, beginning as part of a general psychology text in 1940 and a general personality theory book in 1950, is that the reflexological model which, for most students, is presented as "constituting" learning theory itself, from Pavlov to Skinner, is, in fact, only half of the real domain. Had the construction of learning theory been approached by *an attempt to explain the observable and measured changes in personality structure,* the whole story would have been different. In short, if the distribution of effort had been such as to advance personality measurement between 1930 and 1940 to where it reached by 1970, with much restricted help, the story of learning theory would have been quite different. Instead of "I have a gadget called a reflex; let me show you what I can explain with it, regardless of its relevance to personality," it would have been better strategy had we begun, "I have demonstrated measured changes in a demonstrated personality structure; let me now explore the possible formulations of learning laws capable of explaining this." The learning theorists set on the reflexological highway may not have taken this new path. But it is also true that until some completion was reached in our work on meaningful, "surgical" dissection of structure, by objective means, as well as in that which led to the dynamic calculus, thus allowing measurements of human motivation strengths, the personality researcher was himself scarcely in a position to fertilize learning theory. But now that functional personality and dynamic measurement is a reality,

---

giving weight to statistically not significant loadings in some single researches, belongs to stage one. And sometimes theories of more convincing clarity than the data justified have functioned as slogans to hearten perplexed research assistants to return "once more into the breach, dear friends, once more." Thus one critic worthy of respect but capable of misunderstanding has said, "Cattell has sometimes left himself open to criticism by claiming identity of factors across behavior rating, questionnaire and objective test realms." This use of "claiming" misses the nature of a theory and the importance of a theory (resting on indications) in provoking research. My insistence from a long way back on the theory that instrument free factors will be found to span the three media of observation has led to more careful observation, as well as the concepts of instrument factors and trait view and perturbation theories. Incidentally unless these critics themselves adopt the newer, more flexible use of factor analysis they can then no more hope to see the new relations than Galileo's critics could hope to see Jupiter's moons, when they refused to put an eye to his telescope.

and structured learning theory has been sketched and given explicit operational meaning, it is time, in the board room of learning theory, for reflexology to move over and make room for radical new viewpoints around the table.

The advances to be made by structured learning theory offer two potencies unknown to present reflexology. First, in the *tri-vector* representation of the learning change itself, it offers a far richer statement of the totality of *what happens* in the learner than is available even in the Tolmanian enrichment of reflexology. Second, in the new ability to define and measure ergic tensions, state levels, magnitudes of reward, and the strength of formation of sets, it presents greater capacity—potentially—to explain and predict any given learning process. Structured learning theory bridges easily enough to reflexological concepts of reward schedules when it explains sentiment patterns as being due to repeating patterns of social reinforcement, which can be located by factor analytic study of social interactions. Indeed, in this and other respects, it is actually not at odds with reflexology, but only with those inbred characteristics therein which keep it tied to a theoretically infelicitous terminology, for example, "operant conditioning," instead of *means-end* learning, and which make reflexology unable to assimilate the manifest enlargements and new perspectives which structured learning theory offers. Part of the mutual embarrassment between personality theorists and reflexologists lies in the sense of surprise when they find themselves trying to do the same thing. As far as I was concerned pursuit of the exciting developments in objective motivation measurement and the dynamic calculus had brought me suddenly by a side door onto the stage where reflexological learning has long performed. A justifiable indignation greets a man entering from the wings with lines not fitting the play, especially by actors who have not learned the wider lesson that the drama of science requires a continually redeveloping plot.

Neither party in the interactions of scientific theories should protest too much about such upsets in communication, whether he stand on the side of conserving what is, or of breaking in with what is awkwardly new. The stories of Copernicus,

Galileo, Harvey, Rutherford, and others show that even science has not learned to examine change quite objectively and accept it gracefully. Pasteur urged the intelligent young to "live in the calm of the laboratory." But, although the student may rightly expect a life of science to proceed in a more rational atmosphere and by more enlightened canons of dispute than most, I would have to cite, without complaint, many experiences of being on the receiving end of almost vituperative comments by alleged scientific critics, resentful of radically new concepts, and using the ambush of anonymous consulting editorship to vent pure spleen. Einstein and Bohr, as their articles show, could disagree thoroughly with mutual respect and a clear understanding of the issues involved. The bulk of controversy in psychology—and in that I must naturally include the snide comments of consulting editors and equally anonymous committee members—has not reached that level. It has reached it neither in civility of discourse nor in intelligent, educated analysis of the issues. The former at least could be remedied by abolishing the traditional but quite unwarranted privilege of anonymity, which for some reason goes unquestioned. If I feel this to be important despite between 300 to 400 articles accepted for publication how much more must it be so for those who have suffered in comparative silence!

When I was a youth in my native Devonshire, it was considered a challenge to find a certain mysterious place called Cranmeri Pool, lost in the desolate mist-wreathed heart of Dartmoor. Whoever reached it deposited a card in a box on the west bank and took away the message left by the last prospector. A party of ten of us set off one day; but in the fogs and detours around morasses, the group splintered. I lost them or they lost me. Nowadays things are easier, since the road ends only five miles short of the target. With compass and occasionally glimpses of landmarks through the rolling clouds smoking from the peaks, I eventually found the pool in late afternoon, glimmering before me just when I was ready to give up. I waited for the others until as near dark as I dared, and then covered the rough miles back to civilization. This little event has turned out to be an epitome of some features of my scientific life. What I have called in the title my adventures in hyperspace, referring especially to the use of mathematical, geometric models to bring initial order into behavioral structure, have been pursued—to a degree which has always surprised me—largely alone. Except for a few original souls, like Thurstone, Guilford, Royce, Hakstian, Eysenck, and those enterprising laboratory colleagues I have listed above, the distance has somehow been too great for good communication with at least 50 per cent of leading personality and motivation theorists. Investigators in this field, vital though it is, moved like a lone caravan in the desert. That is how things were at least until the formation of the Society of Multivariate Experimental Psychology. Such research work is altogether too engrossing to complain of loneliness; but one can, at times, get indignant that so few try to train themselves to find the way to a place where every hand is needed; and the rewards for psychology are plentiful.

To raise the question of whether waste in strategic research could be avoided by some reform of the existing haphazard logistics by which research campaigns are now shaped, particularly of the means by which psychology now directs its students to the best points of attack, is again to become (as Professor Horrocks has described me) a "controversial" innovator (though, he kindly proceeds to add "of impeccable credentials"). If we are to leave the course of research activity to a host of free individuals—like the Crusade of Bernard of Clairvaux—rather than an organized army (much is to be said for both) then it behooves the researcher who has found a good pass through the mountains to turn back and let others know, then despite my calling back, I have a sense of unquestionable failure. Roland's horn has echoed emptily in the pass. Various insightful observers, for example, Berg (in Dreger, 1971), ascribe the difficulties I have had in attracting more than a small minority to these essentially rewarding hunting grounds as due to my unwillingness, politically, to attach myself to current "grass roots" cults in American psychology. Another critic, Gordon, insists I am "brilliant and contradictory," but "more respected than read." Responding directly to this painful charge that my objective, quantitative, and theory-constructing approach is poorly designed to communicate to American students, Eysenck concludes "American students of personality have embraced a curious creed made up of environmentalistic beliefs, Freudian concepts, and projective techniques . . . the [resulting] failure of clinical psychologists and personality theorists to pay sufficient attention to Cattell's contributions, is, as Dr. Johnson put it, 'ignorance, sheer ignorance.' Cattell's work cannot be understood, and should not be judged, by people who cannot tell the difference between an Eigenvalue and a non-Gramian matrix, an Oblimax and an Oblimin, or a dot product and a scalar. Technical writing requires technical competence in understanding and reviewing."

These are magnanimous words from a man with whom I have had sharply to disagree (though in a good scientific framework) on some important theoretical issues. But the agreement on the communication problem by the three psychologists just mentioned despite diverse positions and evaluations suggests that these quotations must be taken seriously as evidence that any impression I have of an excessive lag in communication, notably to undergraduate students in America (compared to say, England, Germany, Australia, or Japan) is not purely subjective. (My Penguin paperback, *The Scientific Analysis of Personality,* has run to larger publication as an undergraduate textbook in those countries than here, and "relevance" ratings in Europe give me a decidedly better position there than in my own country.) What is the rational thing to do about this? Can part of the difficulty be simply that for thirty years I have done no classroom teaching, and that our present atmosphere is such that followers depend largely on personal contacts? Are we in an age when students will watch lectures on television but not pick up books to read on their own—at least not outside the excessive but often still narrow reading required by their immediate course teachers?

Although I am asked to write here on my personal professional life I do not wish to labor this individual experience of a communication problem, and would not do so were it not that it is really a widespread problem in psychology, which psychology has to tackle itself because no other science has the disease so badly. The susceptibility lies in the fact that everyone is a psychologist, and the standards of science cannot suddenly be applied in the subject at some arbitrary point. The Ph.D. at any rate scarcely functions at that point. Mowrer has said that more Ph.D.'s in psychology were issued in the last decade than in all previous time and that according to his calculation there will soon be more psychologists than people. Certainly if the APA is considered to have its nose aimed at science we have reached a point where the tail is wagging the dog, and where the bulk of members are more interested in permissive and casual cults than in tough standards of scholarship and genuine attempts to understand the complexity of their subject. The challenging comment of McDougall, made a year or two before he died, that "psychology is too difficult for psychologists," like some other useful comments by McDougall, has never been given much popularity in America, salutary though it could be.

Yet another angle from which the slowness of utilization of multivariate experimental psychological methods might be understood is that in a rapidly developing subject (for psychology, relative to its miserable position a generation ago, has moved faster than, say, physics or medicine), perhaps teachers continue too much to teach what they were taught, instead of accepting the "threat" of formidable textbooks with new approaches, which "challenge" their own learning? I do not think the solution to this problem is for researchers in positions like mine to start an intensive personal teaching campaign in areas where rapid progress is being made. True the scholar-teacher is what the universities since medieval times have had as their ideal figure but I believe it is obsolete. And, as a psychologist who has spent less than half his professional life as a university teacher and more than half as a basic researcher, I have a duty to bring to bear a viewpoint which few will contribute. With the increasing specialization which advancing culture creates, the divided loyalty and very real mutual distraction which teaching and research create need no longer be tolerated. Research is an intensive, full-time profession. If teaching is a 45-hour week, research is a 65-hour week. And if research progress is what society needs, it should be prepared to support full-time researchers, either as research professors in universities or in special institutes, like the Max

Planck Institute in Germany or the I.R.M.A. laboratory which, at the present moment, I am trying to create in Colorado. Heaven knows, society at all levels and in all corners has benefited enough from science to be obligated to support as many pure researchers as it does, say, film stars, football players, and stock exchange "experts"!

The dangers of the teacher-scholar ideal are mainly four: (a) it wastes the man hours of a talented researcher—when this rare character turns up in a university—in routine instruction, which many equally intelligent but less creative academics could do just as well; (b) the person who teaches simplified views with dramatic emphasis to undergraduates sooner or later himself accepts these racy simplifications. By contrast the researcher must live in a world of crepuscular uncertainties, sensitively watching every shade of indication. (c) There is a failure to recognize the difference—even in the scholarly ideal—between the scholar and the researcher; that is, between the impressively stuffed mind and the agile but obsessively focused mind of the researcher. Teaching tends both to require and to generate the former, and (d) the mixed teacher and researcher stereotype creates a competitive situation which forces good teachers to become poor researchers, diluting the journals with pot-boiling articles. The universities should reward teaching as such. Meanwhile, since it takes ten to fifteen years to judge from results that a man's flair and capacity for research will justify supporting him in the life of pure research, the ideal of the teacher-researcher in the university setting has a function as a pupal stage of life in which good researchers can be evaluated and converted to the imago. After forty, academic men should primarily be either teachers, scholars, administrators, or researchers. Research institutes, independent of universities but sitting next door to them, should become the home of the mature, highly organized team researcher; and special graduate students should, by a cooperative arrangement, go there for their apprenticeship. Certain it is that my own movement at forty from half-time to full-time research did not double but quadrupled my effective research output.

My answer to what I have focused above as my "communication problem" cannot, therefore, in any consistency with the above position, be that I should teach more or set out to write "popular" books. I am obligated to write clear and well-organized books—and reviewers on the whole have granted these qualities to my thirty or so books and monographs—but after that, I must leave it to progressive teachers to be the intermediaries. Meanwhile one can accept without comment the inevitable but not the totally unnecessary part of the lag.

A minor consequence of being out on a limb in research is that bibliographies referring to supporting, prior results are confined apparently excessively to members of the laboratory team, past and present. Friends "kid" one about this, and enemies try to cut off grants on the grounds that insufficient regard is paid to other research. The fact is that one cannot mix oil and water in the realm of method. For example, the researches by Scheier and myself (1961) on anxiety would have been confused and ruined in their theoretical development by assuming that the associations found or not found with anxiety as measured by various arbitrary anxiety scales held for the unitary factor concept of anxiety with which we dealt. Some of these subjective scales, notably Eysenck's and the Manifest Anxiety Scale demonstrably, by mode of origin, contain neuroticism as well, and others wander into stress, giving a theory of association of anxiety with cholesterol which proves quite wrong when a factor anxiety scale is used. Another instance is the failure of our researches on states to interact with Nowlis's work on states also using factor analysis. But since his measures are taken on a single occasion only, they cannot be assumed to be states in the sense of our dR- and P-technique concepts derived from measures of temporal change. Until the concepts of psychology are as well tied down operationally as those of the physical sciences the work of two people who use the same word for their area of research does not mean that any useful connection in ideas or calculations can be made between them.

A more sophisticated look at research requirements will therefore show that the omission of work apparently in the same field is neither ignorant nor malign as some naive critics have stated, but an inevitable consequent of recognizing that psychology is not as conceptually advanced as a science as it pretends to be, and that results talking of the same concept often cannot yet be given a positive connection. Meanwhile our bibliographies unfortunately and regretfully have to go back, like the logistics of explorers who leave the population centers of civilization behind, to our own string of base camps. For example, in relation to the string of personality factors in objective, laboratory, and general behavioral measures, which we have pursued systematically across age groups and cultures, there exist, apart from a half-dozen studies by the London group under Eysenck, by Guilford, by Goldberg at ORI, and one or two investigators in Germany and Australia, only the sixty or so published interlocking pieces of research by psychologists in some way connected with the Illinois laboratory. In the field of objective test personality structure and of analyses of factors in objective motivation measures the degree of isolation (except for Eysenck in the former and recent work by Witkin) has been virtually complete.

Although I cannot honestly refrain from recording, and deploring as unnecessary, this isolation I recognize that it has happened many times before in science, and its deplorableness consists mainly in the fact that with so much history behind us we should be more adaptive and in the fact that a great amount of money is now being poured into science. For despite these circumstances interaction has been as interesting and brisk as we could possibly afford time for. First, there has been an exciting interaction of minds with the hundred or more psychologists with whom I have published joint studies. Second, I have had good technical discussions by correspondence with psychologists in virtually every country in the world, but particularly the British Commonwealth countries, Germany, France, Sweden, Italy, Japan, Czechoslovakia, South Africa, and India. Four of my best research associates, Pawlik, Schmidt, Schneewind, and Uberla, in terms of spiritedly "carrying the ball" to new distances in technical advance, came from the postwar revival of quantitative psychology in Germany, and seven remarkably able associates (if I may risk invidious realisms), Warburton, Butcher, Sealy, Radcliffe, Vaughan, Gibb, and Coulter from English-speaking countries.

Although from men such as these the international correspondence of science is never too much, I have to confess in realism that correspondence from all far and near has become a real burden in the last decade, interfering seriously with the time I need for thought and planning. Incidentally, I am convinced that most of the "creativity curves" which show decline after forty are due to the brutal demands of administration and correspondence that come with any access of reputation in one's field. The international quality of science is a fine and precious thing, but let us not sentimentally believe that it exists in full flower. I have been painfully aware, for example, of limitations from religion in relation to psychology in Mediterranean countries, and limitations on easy discussion of individual differences and behavior genetics in communist countries—and as a threat from below recently in America.

Another aspect of science in which fond hopes and ideals have had to accommodate, in my experience, to realities, concerns the biographical habit of representing eminent scientists as paragons of rationality. Happily their training makes them objective and imaginative beyond the average man, but a few let real emotional prejudices suffuse their work, and some—even most—can be extremely rivalrous, exhibiting "the last infirmity of noble minds." I feel I must render homage, however, to precious rivals and staunch co-workers who have always "played cricket" hard but fairly, and at the risk of omissions from space demands I want to mention Berg, Eysenck, Guilford, Horn, French, Merrifield, Stephenson, Cohen, Vernon, Harman, Royce, Fiske, Fulker, Burt, Messick, Lazarus, Thorne, Young, Hunt, Thurstone, Allport, Schuerger, Sells, Jensen, Tryon, and Thomson, with all of whom I have had technical disagreements. To be undiplomatically truthful, and show that the brotherhood of science is only an ideal which mortal men never fully reach, I could add a list of about half that length of men who have done their best to bring the insidious methods of psychological warfare into scientific debates. These methods include *ad hominem* arguments, the scrupulous exclusion of the rivals' contributions when quite relevant, and, especially, attempts on grants committees and journals to exert economic and political pressures. Incidentally a perfect example of all these diseases of science—more perfect, luckily for myself, than I have ever encountered personally—is visible currently in the treatment of men like Jensen and Herrnstein over the issue of racial differences in intelligence.

Knowing that these worms may exist in my chosen apple has not prevented my getting thorough enjoyment from the healthy intercourse of science. Conferences and conventions, however, with their often excessive sociability and politicking, should rightly be seen as the less important part of that interaction. For one must never forget that the truly original and fundamental innovations are more likely to occur in a quiet back room of a laboratory than at an exciting convention. My own conception of what the ideal balance is concerning the fruitful use of time lies farther away from the symposium and more toward the back room than most psychologists that I know would want to believe. Nevertheless, I consider personally the three years during which I did not do so much research but campaigned for my conception of a Society of Multivariate Experimental Psychology (SMEP). The ensuing formation of SMEP, limited to 60 people, with its design of expanding when necessary to further "small cells," has functioned extremely well. Furthermore it has advanced the field, and training therein, in universities, considerably.

It is no reflection on the importance and pleasure of these larger interactions, nevertheless, to add that, in the end, "there is no place like home," by which I mean the small community of three or four research associates at a time, as in my laboratory spontaneously going into a huddle whenever an intriguing possibility requires discussion.[3] The family life of discoveries and failures shared, of emergencies calling for midnight work, and of problems solved, leave few dull moments.

[3] Clearly in this space I cannot pay the tribute that substantial contribution by many individuals calls for, though I have listed them elsewhere (Cattell, 1972a) more completely. What needs to be brought out here is that in addition to what is done by organized teams serving clear-cut objectives, as in our own group, science benefits substantially from the contributions of what one might call "quaint geniuses with special hobbies." These are Kipling's "men of little showing" whose "work continueth, great beyond their knowing." I think, for example, of the substantial impetus given to the work of several laboratores, including our own by the farsighted, selfless devotion of men like Charles Wrigley and Kern Dickman to producing the programs and the technicians which gave such indispensable impetus to multivariate research.

From the standpoint of planning of research units my experience definitely favors, at the largest, one of half a dozen researchers. Such a group necessarily has its leader, and the onslaught of demands upon him for creative solutions to problems that no one before has encountered can become excessive. Routine, rule-of-thumb solutions are feasible for a single leader in a much larger group, but new structurings of ideas come into the mind only when they will. In this connection I must record that not once over the past 28 years have I been able to take the year's sabbatical leave that comes naturally to the teaching academic. New problems arise with a frequency which precludes absence, even in what may look like one of those "set piece" researches. In the context of university life, and the fact that the teaching professor is definitely apt to feel some envy of the research professor (who is "always on sabbatical"), a word of perspective might help. The teacher actually has more leisure; his emotional rewards are more immediate in the social interactions with his students; and his work does not normally present such agonizing periods where he wonders if he is really getting anywhere at all. This is another aspect of the point I have made above about the need for distinct specialists in research and in undergraduate teaching. For it becomes evident here that research, like any special mode of life, demands its own special temperament and peculiar spectrum of talents. Granted that these are given, there are few modes of life that give such lasting and uncloying satisfactions as this continual pursuit of new concepts, with their payoff in improved practice and control. The vistas I have enjoyed in what I have epitomized as my "travels through hyperspace" have been kaleidoscopic enough for anyone.

Alas, as the Roman proverb recognized long ago, "The arts are long, and life is brief." As my fellow huntsmen and our packs of research assistants gallop ever faster after the quarry, I find so much else that I thought important—all, in fact, but personal human loyalties and impersonal sense of beauty—trivial. (Gone are the traditional weekends, the sailing that was my hobby, and other diversions that I allowed to consume my time.) Yet, obviously, as the hunt goes by some dark copse, the specter of age will ultimately step out and lay an authoritative hand on the bridle of my horse. I shall scarcely blame the others in the hunt if they barely have time to wave a hand. What I have been permitted to crystallize from the unknown in my own lifetime is enough satisfaction for one man—but I cannot deny that I would dearly like to be there when the hunt reaches the ultimate mysteries at the end of the chase.

REFERENCES

Bischof, L. H. *Interpreting Personality Theories.* New York: Harper & Row, 1964.

Burt, C. L. *The Young Delinquent.* London: University of London Press, 1925.

Cattell, R. B. *Psychology and Social Progress.* London: Daniel, 1933. (a)

——. Temperament tests: II. Tests. *British Journal of Psychology,* 1933, *24,* 20–49. (b)

——. *The Fight for Our National Intelligence.* London: King, 1937. (a)

——. *Under Sail Through Red Devon.* London: Machehose, 1937. (b)

——. *Psychology and the Religious Quest.* New York: Nelson, 1938.

——. The place of religion and ethics in a civilization based on science. In R. Wulsin (ed.), *A Revolution of Our Civilization.* Albany, N.Y.: Argus, 1944.

——. *The Description and Measurement of Personality.* New York: Harcourt, Brace & World, 1946.

——. The integration of psychology with moral values. *British Journal of Psychology,* 1950, *49,* 25–34.

——. *Personality and Motivation Structure and Measurement.* New York: World Book, 1957.

——. The dynamic calculus: A system of concepts derived from objective motivation measurement. In G. Lindzey (ed.), *Assessment of Human Motives.* New York: Rinehart, 1958.

——. Group theory, personality and role: A model for experimental researches. In *Defense Psychology.* Oxford, England: Pergamon Press, 1961.

——. Research strategies in the study of personality. In S. Messick and J. Ross (eds.), *Measurement in Personality and Cognition.* New York: Wiley & Sons, 1962.

——. Formulating the environmental situation and its perception, in behavior theory. In S. B. Sells (ed.), *Stimulus Determinants of Behavior.* New York: Ronald Press, 1963.

——. *Personality and Social Psychology: Collected Papers.* San Diego, Calif.: R. R. Knapp & Co., 1964.

——. *The Scientific Analysis of Personality.* London: Penguin Books, 1965. (a)

——. Methodological and conceptual advances in evaluating hereditary and environmental influences and their interaction. In S. G. Vandenberg (ed.), *Methods and Goals in Human Behavior Genetics.* New York: Academic Press, 1965. (b)

——. *Handbook of Multivariate Experimental Psychology.* Chicago: Rand McNally, 1966 (a)

——. Anxiety and motivation: Theory and crucial experiments. In C. B. Spielberger (ed.), *Anxiety and Behavior.* New York: Academic Press, 1966. (b)

——. Taxonomic principles for locating and using types (and the derived taxonome computer program). In B. Kleinmuntz (ed.), *Formal Representation of Human Judgment.* Pittsburgh, Pa.: University Press, 1968.

——. *Abilities: Their Structure, Growth and Action.* Boston: Houghton Mifflin, 1971.

——. *A New Morality from Science: Beyondism.* New York: Pergamon Press, 1972. (a)

——. Real base, true zero factor analysis. *Multivariate Behavioral Research Monographs,* No. 1, 1972. (b)

——. *Personality and Mood by Questionnaire.* San Francisco: Jossey-Bass, 1973.

——. Structured learning theory. In R. B. Cattell and R. M. Dreger (eds.), *Handbook of Modern Personality Theory.* New York: Appleton-Century-Crofts, 1974.

——, Breul, H., and Hartman, H. P. An attempt at more refined definition of the cultural dimensions of syntality in modern nations. *American Sociological Review,* 1952, *17,* 408–421.

—— and Butcher, H. J. *The Prediction of Achievement and Creativity.* Indianapolis, Indiana: Bobbs-Merrill, 1968.

—— and Horn, J. L. An integrating study of the factor structure of adult attitude-interests. *Genetic Psychology Monographs,* 1963, *67,* 89–149.

—— and Jaspers, J. A general plasmode (No. 30–10–5–2) for factor analytic exercises and research. *Multivariate Behavioral Research Monographs,* 1967, *67,* 3, 1–212.

—— and Scheier, I. H. *The Meaning and Measurement of Neuroticism and Anxiety.* New York: Ronald Press, 1961.

—— and Stice, G. F. *The Psychodynamics of Small Groups.* Final report on Research Project NR172–369, Contract ZN80nr–79600, Human Relations Branch, Office of Naval Research, 1–207–1953.

—— and Stice, G. F. *The Dimensions of Groups and Their Relations to the Behavior of Members.* Champaign, Ill.: Institute for Personality and Ability Testing, 1960.

—— and Tsujioka, B. The importance of factor trueness and validity, versus homogeneity and orthogonality, in test scales. *Educational and Psychological Measurement,* 1964, *24,* 3–30.

—— and Warburton, F. W. *Objective Personality and Motivation Tests. A Theoretical Introduction and Practical Compendium.* Champaign, Ill.: University of Illinois Press, 1967.

Dreger, R. M. *Multivariate Personality Research. A Contribution in Honor of Raymond Cattell.* Baton Rouge, La.: Claytor Publishing Division, 1971.

Eysenck, H. J. *The Structure of Human Personality.* London: Methuen, 1953.

Hundleby, J. D., K. Pawlik, and R. B. Cattell. *Personality Factors in Objective Test Devices.* San Diego, Calif.: R. R. Knapp & Co., 1965.

Lindzey, G. *A History of Psychology in Autobiography.* New York: Appleton-Century-Crofts, 1973.

Miller, J. G. Living systems. Produced for limited circulation, February 1971, University of Louisville, Louisville, Kentucky.

Nesselroade, J. R., and H. W. Reese. *Life Span Developmental Psychology.* New York: Academic Press, 1973.

Pawlik, K. *Dimensionen des Verhaltens.* Bern, Switzerland: Huber, 1968.

Pervin, L. A. *Personality: Theory, Assessment and Reward.* New York: Wiley & Sons, 1970.

Rummel, R. J. *Applied Factor Analysis.* Evanston, Ill.: Northwestern University Press, 1970.

Spearman, C. *The Abilities of Man.* New York: Macmillan, 1927.

Thurstone, L. L. *Multiple Factor Analysis.* Chicago: University of Chicago Press, 1947.

4

A Professional Odyssey

J. McVICKER HUNT

The story of one's professional life begins with the choice of profession. While mine was one of considerable deliberation, it was forced by a seemingly irrelevant event: the expulsion of Americans and Europeans from the Military and Naval Academies of Japan in 1928.

As an undergraduate at the University of Nebraska, my interests were spread, as they have continued to be, all too widely. They ranged over athletics, campus activities, several fields of scholarship, and the selling of life insurance on the side to ease the strains of my pocketbook. For more than a decade, Nebraskans had been going to Japan for two-year stints of teaching English to the students of the Japanese Naval Academy. In the fall of 1927, John M. Allison, my predecessor as President of the Student Christian Association who became Ambassador to Japan after World War II, went for his stint. I expected to follow upon graduation in 1929. In December of 1928, I received a letter from John Allison reporting that he was selling Buicks in Shanghai. Political events in Japan had resulted in the general expulsion of Americans and Europeans from the service academies of Japan. Although John had been inclined toward pacifism as an undergraduate, he nevertheless predicted war within fifteen years. This shocked my social consciousness, but it shocked even more my personal plans; for this letter came just a few days after I had become engaged to

Esther Dahms, who has been my wife since Christmas Day of 1929. The letter meant that a two-year escape from deciding what ultimately to become and to do was gone. The first semester of my senior year was nearly ended.

Despite the time devoted to football and wrestling (with limited success) and to such campus activities as editing the University Directory, writing for the school paper, and serving as Secretary and President of the Student Christian Association and President of the League of Industrial Democracy, college courses had been exceedingly interesting to me. A focus, however, had been hard to find, and I had changed my choice of major each semester or year. As a freshman, I had started in the College of Business Administration in order to get credit for typing and shorthand, which I wanted to learn because I anticipated becoming the secretary of a politician like George Norris, the great Senator from Nebraska. This looked to my youthful eyes like a feasible route to a political career. But Professor Hartley Burr Alexander, head of the philosophy department, had admitted me as a freshman to his course labeled Humanism because I explained that I had already read my father's copy of Plato's *Republic* while convalescing from the flu. Alexander's splendid lectures and the reading were exciting. At the end of the semester I switched colleges to become a philosophy major.

Zoology had also been especially interesting. As a farm boy with a father who had taught biology in Lincoln High School for some five years, I came to it prepared with considerable knowledge of anatomy and a good deal of the technical terminology acquired from my father's conversation while we were butchering. Undergraduate laboratory assistants were common then, and Professor Wolcott invited me to become one during my sophomore year. I declined his invitation because the afternoon laboratories interfered with football practice. Nevertheless, when the philosophy courses in logic and ethics proved to be less exciting than Alexander's Humanism, I shifted my intended major to biology. Yet I continued taking and auditing courses in philosophy. William Werkmeister's lectures in the philosophy of science, which became his book entitled *A Philosophy of Science,* impressed me and introduced me to conceptual methodology. About this same time, however, someone recommended Joyce Hertzler's course in social progress. Somehow I got into it without having taken a first course in general sociology. It interested me and again I shifted my intended major. Moreover, when football season ended in my junior year, I spent my afternoons in the library reading Frazier's *The Golden Bow.*

In the 1920s, the University of Nebraska operated implicitly on what Brown's President, Henry Merrit Wriston, characterized some twenty years later as the "seat-warming theory of education." There were courses of two, three, and five hours' credit (depending on the number of one-hour class meetings a week). I registered for a good many two-hour courses, and audited more. Having started economics while a freshman in the business school, I had continued with courses in the subject. While I disliked the course in money and banking, I was delighted by Professor Virtue's course in the history of economic thought. Consequently, as a first-semester senior, I was majoring in sociology but serving as paper-grading assistant in economics. By that time I had had elementary courses in chemistry and in physics, some mathematics, and several courses each in English, history, biology, economics, and sociology. Biology, economics, and sociology were turning out to be my fields of greatest interest, but J. P. Guilford had returned to Nebraska, where he had earned his bachelor's and master's degrees, in September of 1928 to direct the laboratory of psychology in the philosophy department. This laboratory was founded by Harry Kirk Wolfe, a Nebraska graduate who had gone to the University of Berlin and then on to Leipzig for a doctorate with Wilhelm Wundt and had returned to his Alma Mater in 1889 to found what has been claimed to be the third laboratory for the "new psychology" in America. Professor Hertzler suggested that I should have a course in psychology as background for sociology. I accepted his counsel.

By custom, psychology was then a senior course given by the department of philosophy, with a laboratory. The texts had been William James' *Psychology* and James Dunlop Lickley's *Nervous System.* Guilford, with a doctorate from Cornell and a year of teaching at the University of Illinois and at the University of Kansas, substituted Pillsbury's *Psychology* for James'. The discovery that I have red-green color blindness to some degree and my learning of the existence of aptitude testing contributed strongly to my interest in this course.

When John Allison's letter came, I had the felt responsibility of being newly engaged with no clear path to the future except that stint of teaching English at the Japanese Naval Academy. His letter blocked even my path to a two-year respite from decision.

What to do? Inclinations toward academia had already cropped up in my awareness, but in what academic field? My deliberation was a worried dialogue between myself and me during Christmas vacation at home in Scottsbluff and throughout the remainder of that first semester. This worried dialogue went on as I ran, daily, to build up my wind for wrestling. It intruded into the interviews with the Mexicans of the North Platte Valley through which I was obtaining data for my senior thesis in sociology. It went on through wakeful nights.

The argument, as I still vividly recall it, went like this. Sociology was the only subject in which I could collect a major by June. Unfortunately, I had come to feel that it differed too little from the journalism that I had tried and rejected earlier. In fact, I then found myself characterizing the subject as "Jacob Riis journalism." With some six courses behind me, zoology might be feasible, but I would have to go on an extra semester to complete the required major. Anyway, zoology appeared to be too far from the human scene. Medicine did not then even occur to me. With five or six courses behind me, economics might also be feasible, especially since I had audited some other courses and might later take examinations in them. Yet this meant I would need more money and I would have to take courses in banking and accounting. What I liked in economics were the assumptions about human nature, about the springs of human action and the forces in social organization proposed by the founders: the motive of self-interest controlled automatically by the competitive operations of the market for Adam Smith, the passions which Malthus saw overpopulating the world and dooming men to starvation, the struggle for social advantage and status seen by Riccardo, and the rational development of productivity in John Stuart Mill. This concern with human nature and especially with human motivation pointed toward psychology, but psychology could hardly be considered, for I had completed but a part of one semester.

Once Christmas vacation ended, I took time away from the training for wrestling to consult with some of my teachers. I called first on Professor Whitney who had taught me both genetics and vertebrate zoology. He encouraged me and indicated that I might have a teaching assistantship in Zoology which would pay $500—$50 a month for ten months. Then, as his paper-grader, I talked with Professor Spangler, a specialist in the economics of insurance. He, too, encouraged me with the assurance that I could have an assistantship in economics that would pay $600. Professor Hertzler, my adviser and mentor in sociology, also assured me of an assistantship in sociology. It would pay $500, but he warned me all too concretely that academia was a poor man's profession.

During the week of final examinations, Professor Guilford stopped me in the hall to say that he had heard that I was thinking of graduate school: Would I like to consider psychology? When I supposed aloud that I had too little background in psychology to permit me to be considered, he responded that my major could be philosophy. Little did he then know how short of the prescribed number of courses I was. In the end, he accepted social psychology from the department of sociology, comparative anatomy from the department of zoology, and other such courses as psychology courses so that I had enough hours for a major. In retrospect, I believe my spread of courses has given me a better background than the prescribed ordering would have. Guilford's flexibility in interpreting the academic rules has been a model that I have followed. Guilford also pointed out that psychology could lead to fairly well paid careers in industry and to practice in aptitude testing or clinical work with patients in mental hospitals as well as to a career in academia. The assistantship available, however, would pay only $400. Even so, the world looked up. About aptitude testing I knew very little. Yet, perhaps because I did not then know what I wanted to do, the prospect of guiding others attracted me. Moreover, in psychology one could view as problems for investigation those assumptions made by the early economists about human nature. Finally, even though affluence was never one of my major objectives, it was good to feel that the career opportunities in psychology did not require a vow to poverty.

The spring semester of 1929 firmed my decision to become a psychologist. The general course continued to be interesting. Moreover, Esther, my fiancee, and I registered for a two-hour course in abnormal psychology that proved very interesting even though my grade was 92, while hers was 95. In June we skipped the graduation ceremonies to attend a student conference in Estes Park, Colorado. With Evelyn Hooker, who was then already a graduate student in psychology at Colorado University, I served as co-chairman of this conference. When we returned to Lincoln, I entered graduate school in psychology with a total background of three semester courses (8 credit hours in the subject). Yet, even though I continued to wander intellectually, my professional die was cast. Later, during graduate work at Cornell University, the attractions of neurology with James W. Papez stirred up an inclination to change fields again, but the Great Depression was in its depths and the added time required to achieve the doctorate curbed that inclination.

GRADUATE WORK AT NEBRASKA UNIVERSITY

At the University of Nebraska, J. P. Guilford was then the whole of psychology, at least outside the College of Education. Although his own confidence appeared not to be high in those days, he was an excellent teacher and mentor. He took obvious pleasure when any of us five graduate students got an idea or expressed a new twist on an old one.

Guilford laid out the path for me. He had me continue mathematics through integral calculus. There being no better way to learn than by teaching, I did it by finding weak students to tutor in each course. He introduced me along with the others to points of view in psychology. He pushed Rudolph Voegler and me through Garrett's book on statistics and then had us use our statistics on the data we got from our psychophysical and psychometric experiments. This course took nearly half our time. Over the next few years, it became Guilford's splendid book on psychometric methods. To earn my stipend, I assembled the apparatus and materials for and taught eight hours of the laboratory for the general course each week. Since this stipend was only $400, I continued to supplement my income with occasional sales of life insurance. One selling appointment took longer than expected. I missed a staff meeting. Guilford let me know in no uncertain terms that this should not be repeated. It was not repeated.

Three experiences, two extracurricular, at Nebraska seem, in retrospect, to have been important for my future. One came with my introduction to investigation. My study concerned William McDougall's theory that the personality trait of introversion-extraversion is a matter of the speed and ease with which nervous impulses circulate in the higher brain centers, which can be assessed in the rate of fluctuations in the perspective of such ambiguous figures as the Necker-Wheatstone cube. My first test of this theory was to get three measures of these fluctuation rates and scores on each of four tests of introversion-extraversion, seven measures each, for twenty-five subjects. It took five weeks of June and July (1930) to compute the intercorrelations among these variables on a Monroe calculator. The pencilled squares and cross-products required to check accuracy filled six of the large sheets of cross-section paper. It took another sixteen days to uncover and correct the errors (Guilford and Hunt, 1932). One pedagogical result, unanticipated by Guilford, I am confident, was skepticism of the meaning and value of correlational analysis. Even though I later taught statistics for ten years, my own investigations were based on analyses of variance with small samples. Not until I got to the University of Illinois in the early 1950s and had access to the then new Illiac did I attempt another correlational analysis.

One of the extracurricular experiences got me involved in psychoanalytic theory. I had read Freud's *General Introduction to Psychoanalysis,* with considerable irritation from the dissonance between his formulations and my beliefs, and Adler's *Individual Psychology,* with less irritation, while I was an undergraduate. Not until Willard Waller, who later became a fairly prominent sociological writer, joined the department of Sociology in the fall of 1929 did psychoanalytic ideas influence my own beliefs. The influence came through the discussions among several graduate students from various departments meeting at Waller's house in an informal seminar. I read more of the psychoanalytic literature, including, of course, Jung's writings on introversion-extraversion for my thesis. There I came upon the ideas of extreme introversion being represented in the pathology of schizophrenia and of extreme extraversion in the manic-depressive psychosis. This became the subject of my second investigation (Hunt and Guilford, 1933). Moreover, I came to believe that early experience should be directly investigated for its importance in the formation of temperament and personality, and got generally intrigued with Freud's formulations.

The second extracurricular experience got me involved in intelligence testing. Sometime during 1929–1930, the Director of the Nebraska Home for Dependent Children requested of Guilford the services of a psychometrician. Guilford encouraged me to learn to give the Stanford-Binet test (1916 version) and various performance scales. With the aid of books from the library, I learned the tests, practiced giving them to the children of friends, and got the school psychologist in Lincoln to check me out as a psychological examiner. No laws and few explicit standards prevailed in those days. During the spring of 1930, I was paid to test the children of the Nebraska Home to get the information required for recommendations on placement and adoption.

In the fall of 1930, with the M.A. completed, I became an assistant instructor: salary, $750. Not only did I teach the laboratories for the general course, but with my new experience as a psychological examiner, I had full responsibility for a course in psychological testing. My office was in the Psychological Clinic. Arthur Jenness, who joined the staff that fall with a new doctorate from Syracuse University with Floyd Allport, had the other office in the clinic. There students and even a businessman or two came for psychological counseling perhaps unwitting of what an untutored novice I was. With apparent success in helping one young woman from another department through a psychoneurotic episode with a combination of dream analysis and hypnoanalysis, I began to think of myself as something of a psychotherapist. In the period since World War II, no second-year graduate student has been allowed to take such responsibility without close supervision. I proceeded on my own, learned a lot, and I hope and believe I did no damage.

Probably no two years of my professional life have contained as many formative experiences as did those first two years of graduate work, which included teaching my first course, at the University of Nebraska. In the summer of 1931, I managed to test all of the residents at the Nebraska Home for Dependent Children and managed to use my coming departure from Lincoln for graduate work at Cornell University to close enough sales of life insurance to get me on the list of leading agents for the month of August.

This brought money enough to pay for the engagement and wedding rings that I had bought for Esther. Early in September we packed up our yellow Buick coupe and took off for Cornell, where I had been awarded the Susan Lynn Sage Scholarship in psychology. I had made applications to Cornell, Duke, and Yale. The idea of the new Institute of Human Relations at Yale had appealed strongly, but Yale had responded to my application with only a tuition scholarship. McDougall, of Duke, had come forth with the largest assistantship, but I had absorbed some of the disdain in which McDougall's theories were held. I still have a letter from Madison Bentley saying that if I was interested in McDougall's theories of introversion-extraversion I would not find Cornell congenial. These influences combined to get us off to Cornell.

GRADUATE WORK AT CORNELL

The Cornell experiences in themselves could fill a book. Although I learned much and got personal backing from Madison Bentley that was later of great importance to my career, these experiences appear in retrospect to have been only a detour in the main trajectory of my intellectual and professional odyssey.

Our arrival in the fall of 1931 followed a year when the chief, Professor Madison Bentley, had been away in Washington as executive secretary of the anthropology-psychology division of the National Research Council. Work and play had got a bit mixed during that year. Esther was a bit taken back by being asked why in the world she would bother to get married. I was teased because I was already "domesticated." In consequence of all this, the chief, M.B. as he was typically called (when out of earshot), was setting down restrictions which bothered those who had become addicted to the freedoms of the year before.

It may seem strange, but I had only one course in psychology for which I registered formally during my two years at Cornell. This was Shammai Feldman's excellent course in perception. Although I had participated actively in Guilford's seminar in Gestalt psychology, it was in Feldman's course that I came to appreciate the Gestalters' position. The investigations of size and color constancy and of seen movement intrigued me. I can still state Korte's laws. But the issues in perception seemed then too peripheral to the economist's issues which had first attracted me to psychology. While the other courses for which I registered formally were in neuroanatomy with James W. Papez, and in physiology with Professors Dye of the medical school and Howard Scott Liddell, most of my training in psychology was conducted in tutorial fashion with Madison Bentley. After one of our extended conversations, he would decide that I didn't know enough about a certain topic. He would then set me the task of doing a critical literary review of work on the topic. In recollection, my Cornell experience seems filled with writing papers for Bentley. Yet I had seminars with Harry Porter Wells and with Karl M. Dallenbach, and I had many instructive conversations with Professor John G. Jenkins, with Robbie MacLeod, and with such of my fellow graduate students as Margaret Erb, Warren Fox, Douglas Glanville, and Merrill Roff. Moreover, I learned a great deal while serving as a teaching assistant in abnormal psychology for Madison Bentley and in the general course for Karl M. Dallenbach.

James Papez was a great teacher despite his lecturing in a monotone in simple sentences of the passive voice. He described neural tracts in terms of their nuclei of origin and termination and he avoided, except in passing, the naming of tracts for the men who discovered them. He consistently related structure to function, and his book on comparative neurology was also thoroughly straightforward. Papez's concept of a "neural system," however, was not easy to come by, and most of his students were lost for months. Despite my having already studied Lickley's little book and having cut up a sheep's brain, it was Thanksgiving weekend before I "got the idea" of a system which integrated structure with function. Then, peculiarly, it was the olfactory system and Papez's version of its evolution from reptiles to the higher mammals. This was an exciting experience, and it enabled me to understand the investigative process of building models from drawings made from magnified projections through microtomic slides.

Liddell's course in general physiology and Dye's in medical physiology were informative but unexciting. What I got from Liddell in a seminar was an introduction to the works of Ivan Pavlov and to his own work on the experimental neuroses in animals. Although the influence of Bentley's psychology kept me from becoming actively involved in Liddell's work, what I learned from him became important to my later work.

Madison Bentley's was the chief influence on me while we were at Cornell. Upon the death of E. B. Titchener, Bentley had been invited to return to the post of his former teacher at Cornell from the headship of psychology at the University of Illinois. He was then in the process of revising his textbook entitled *The Field of Psychology* and was trying to classify what he called the "psychological functions." Bentley had strong opinions and he wanted followers. As his assistant in abnormal psychology, I learned the rudiments of his system fairly quickly and was rewarded by a great many signs of his support. At the end of my first semester, he said one day, "Hunt, about the end of February, you will take your preliminary examination."

It was just like that!! Instruction was individualized; there were no rules about times for qualifying examinations, etc. When I wondered aloud about how to prepare, Bentley advised me to ask myself questions, and then to answer them or find the answers. When the time came, *all too soon* (!), the first question, obviously from Bentley, asked me to discuss the relationships between clinical and experimental psychology. The second question, from Dallenbach, concerned the psychophysical methods. The other questions I have forgotten, but I typed for three days running, and learned about a week later that I had passed.

Although Bentley was chiefly concerned with the development of his own system and with revising his book, he had, while at the National Research Council, agreed to join E. V. Cowdry in editing a book to be entitled *The Problem of Mental Disorder.* Once I had passed my preliminary examination, he wondered if I would be interested in reviewing the contributions of experimental psychology to this problem. I devoted much of the spring and nearly all of the summer of 1932 to this task and managed to write a preliminary draft which Professor Bentley rewrote as one of his chapters for the book. Later, largely while I was a postdoctoral fellow of the National Research Council, I completed the review and published it under the title "Psychological Experiments with Disordered Persons" (Hunt, 1936a). I recall the great satisfaction I got from receiving a complimentary letter on the piece from Professor Clark Hull at Yale, to whom I had sent a reprint.

With the preliminary examination out of the way, Professor Bentley also began to talk about what I should do for a thesis. Recognizing that he hoped I would investigate something relevant to his system, I agreed to study the differences between what he called "perceiving" and "inspecting." I first presented my subjects with cartoons and had them search for meaning, then had them compare objects and lines presented tachistoscopically for .1 second and dictate verbal reports on their observational processes to a dictaphone. These reports Esther and I transcribed, and later, I analyzed them. On the basis of the analysis, I described "perceiving" as an uneventful process of intake leading to objects and events as products. "Inspecting," which also leads to objects and events as products, I found distinguished from "perceiving" by an active search governed by questions or anticipated ends. Such was about what was expected. To me, however, the most interesting finding concerned the sources of conflict that result in the doubtful judgments ("I don't know") so common in such psychophysical experiments. In the method of limits, for instance, the reports of my subjects would show that the trend in successive comparisons of the "comparison line" or object with the "standard," from exposure to exposure, would lead to the anticipation of a report of "equal." Yet, when the pair of lines appeared, the "comparison line" still seemed longer than the standard. In consequence, the subject was unable to choose between the two tendencies to respond, so said: "I don't know." Every subject made such reports a good many different times (Hunt, 1935).

Being intrigued with the source of the doubtful judgment reflected my persisting interest in what controls behavior. Bentley was then classifying the various determiners of behavior and incorporating them under what he called "psychological government." Among the "governors" were certain persistent tendencies, which others would call traits, self-instructions, and occasional instructions. In Bentley's system, the doubtful judgment emerged from the conflict between two different occasional instructions. I was even then inclined to view such explanations as essentially verbal, but try as I would, I could never come to grips with Bentley on such matters in discussion. He was so supportive of any of my statements that might agree with his opinions and so quiet about my own queries and doubts that we got nowhere. Moreover, I could not help but recognize that my future opportunities depended upon his support. Jobs in psychology were scarce in the spring of 1933. I heard of and was interviewed for only one, that at Bryn Mawr, which I failed to get.

As part of Professor Bentley's support, he invited me to apply for one of the postdoctoral National Research Council fellowships in psychology. I formulated a plan to examine the repeatedly reported high variability in performance of schizophrenic patients in terms of their self-instructions. The formulation was couched in the language of Bentley's system. The title of the paper which ultimately issued from this work was similarly couched: "Psychological Government and the High Variability of Schizophrenic Patients" (Hunt, 1936). At any rate, my application was approved, perhaps only because Bentley was active on the scholarship committee. Esther and I made plans for a year in New York with Dr. Carney Landis at the New York Psychiatric Institute and Hospital and Columbia University, and then for a second year with Dr. R. G. Hoskins, the endocrinologist directing the study of schizophrenia at Worcester State Hospital, and at Clark University.

NEW YORK PSYCHIATRIC INSTITUTE AND COLUMBIA

The news of winning a postdoctoral fellowship of the National Research Council relieved economic anxieties, but it was not until the first of October (1933) that we could take up residence in New York. Finishing my thesis took the summer and much of September. We settled in an apartment on 165th Street across the street from the Columbia Presbyterian Medical Center of which the New York Psychiatric Institute and Hospital are a part. Those were hard times in New York. Holy Joe McKee was the mayor of the city, and the bread lines and soup lines of the unemployed were all too evident.

At the New York Psychiatric Institute, Dr. Carney Landis, head of the Psychology Section, was my mentor and I officed with Theodore Watson Forbes who had recently earned his doctorate at Ohio State. Carney Landis introduced me to Superintendent Chaney in his office. After I described my project, Dr. Chaney remarked that it was obvious that I lacked clinical experience and understanding, but he guessed that I could go ahead.

Carney Landis had an interested, friendly shop. The prejudices acquired at Cornell and the loyalty I held for Madison Bentley hampered my freedom of learning considerably during this year in New York.

Yet, during that year at the New York Psychiatric Institute, various influences did begin to penetrate my shell of prejudice and loyalty. Ted Forbes and I bought copies of R. A. Fisher's statistics and studied them together. I saw the value of pooled variances for testing the statistical significance of differences, especially for small samples, and I used Student's t-test in my study of psychological government and the high variability of schizophrenic patients (Hunt, 1936). Forbes also taught me something about the theory and the technique of recording the galvanic skin-response, but I was too intent upon my own program to become genuinely involved with this problem in which not only Forbes but also William A. Hunt and Carney Landis were interested. Bill Hunt and Carney Landis were also starting their work on the startle pattern. I discussed often with Carney and Agnes Landis their comparative investigation of the sex histories of schizophrenic patients with those of normal subjects matched for age and social status. Zygmunt Piotrowski, Francis Strakosch, and Joseph Zubin all had studies under way in the Institute at that time which contributed to my education.

Perhaps best of all, our year in New York enabled us to become personally acquainted with a good many of the then-famous psychologists and psychiatrists. No longer were J. McKeen Cattell, Henry Garrett, Gardner Murphy, Albert Poffenberger, and Robert S. Woodworth only names on articles and books. They became professional acquaintances as did also many of the younger instructors and graduate students at Columbia. Those around the Institute, especially Carney Landis, William A. Hunt, and Joseph Zubin, became life-long friends. When I had been invited to apply for one of the fellowships of the National Research Council, I wanted to continue at Cornell and work in one of the nearby hospitals. Professor Bentley explained it was the policy of the Council to insist that postdoctoral fellows change their locales in order to broaden their horizons. My experience illustrates the wisdom of this policy.

WORCESTER STATE HOSPITAL AND CLARK UNIVERSITY

In July of 1934, as originally planned, Esther and I moved to Worcester to become associated with the neuroendocrine research on schizophrenia under the direction of Dr. R. G. Hoskins.

Worcester State Hospital was a lively place in those days. Besides the neuroendocrine research, Paul Houston and David Shakow had under way their investigations of reaction time in schizophrenics and normal subjects. The Russian girls, Tamara Dembo, Eugenia Hanfmann, and Maria Rickers-Ovsiankina, were engaged in a series of studies inspired by their background in Gestalt psychology. Andreas Angyal, a Hungarian psychologist-psychiatrist, had joined the staff and was making intriguing clinical studies of hallucinations and delusions. By watching Andreas Angyal work with patients, I learned how to take a variety of roles to foster communication, to elicit information, and to influence cooperation. Samuel J. Beck had recently returned from a year in Rorschach's clinic, and he came weekly to Worcester for a seminar in Rorschach's test about which I had first heard in an article by Loosli-Usteri which Madison Bentley had assigned to me for translation as part of my examination in French. A rotund, German neuropsychiatrist, whom I shall not name, irritated us all with his anti-Semitism and his defense of Nazi Germany. These were combined with utterly certain localizations of all kinds of symptoms in the various centers within the cerebrum. His was a simplistic neurology. Leo Alexander, a Viennese neurologist, came to Worcester at approximately the same time following more than a year in Shanghai on a neorological service for Chinese soldiers who were then fighting the Japanese. Finally, there was the psychoanalytic seminar of Earl Zinn attended by all of these people and more. Because there was some prospect of a new position for a psychologist at the Cornell Medical School, I also took courses in organic chemistry at Clark so that I might be prepared to work toward a medical degree if this opportunity should actually become available to me.

Although the year at New York Psychiatric Institute and Hospital had freed me considerably to be influenced by the lively interchanges on-going at Worcester, I still felt honor-bound to proceed with the plan I had proposed to the fellowship committee. I continued with the study "Psychological Loss in Paretics and Schizophrenics" (Hunt, 1935), and reported what I had done at the meetings of the American Psychological Association at Columbia University. I completed the review of psychological experiments of disordered persons begun at Bentley's suggestion. Then, with the counsel of R. G. Hoskins, the endocrinologist then in charge of the program of research on schizophrenia, I planned and did a study of the effects of going repeatedly on and off of thyroid medication in which the patients were tested repeatedly and asked to compete with their own records of performance as they recalled and reported them. Without thyroid medication, the patients tended to understate their records, apparently to escape the responsibility for large output, but with thyroid medication, they tended to overcome this tendency. With thyroid medication, the patients were not only likely to recall correct or exaggerated recollections of their performance, they were likely to perform better (Hunt, 1937).

The problem of obtaining cooperation from the patients who served as subjects in this study, combined with what I learned from Andreas Angyal, suggested an investigation of influencing cooperation from schizophrenics for its own sake. A start on a classification of schizophrenics in terms of the various kinds of interpersonal roles and strategies required to influence them and to obtain various degrees of cooperation provided lecture illustrations in abnormal psychology for years to come. Moreover, the strategies which I could imagine and act out would influence approximately two-thirds of the patients in my sample.

During this year at Worcester, Esther and I met not only this lively hospital group, but also the group at Clark University. Esther became a research assistant for Professor Walter S. Hunter and also helped Mrs. Hunter as editorial secretary for the *Psychological Abstracts.* I attended regularly the psychological colloquium at Clark. Moreover, we socialized perhaps even more with the group at Clark than the hospital group. This group included the Walter S. Hunters, the Edward H. Kemps, the Hudson Hoglands, the C. Lad Prossers, and often Donald B. Lindsley, who was also enjoying a second year as an N.R.C. Fellow at Massachusetts General Hospital in Boston, and his wife, Ellen. Although quite unknown to us then, these socializations were apparently important for the future. When, in 1936, Walter Hunter moved from Clark to Brown University, he invited Clarence Graham and me to join his staff. E. H. Kemp had already joined the Brown staff at the invitation of Leonard Carmichael.

During the year at Worcester, the interests in investigating the importance of conflict and of early experience which had emerged from my reading of the psychoanalytic literature returned. It occurred to me that the Cornell College of Medicine might be interested in supporting such a program of research, but the opportunity never came. In the meantime, economic worries were at least temporarily oblitered by an invitation from Carney Landis to return to the New York Psychiatric Institute to compare the sex histories of male psychotic patients with those of normal subjects matched for age, education, and socioeconomic status. This invitation depended upon the National Research Council approving his application for a grant. Approval, however, was not forthcoming.

The contrast in employment opportunities existing in the 1930s with those after World War II is instructive. Not only was there no approval of the Landis application to the N.R.C., but no other opportunities appeared. In July, we drove west toward home in Nebraska. I had earned a doctorate, had two years of postdoctoral experience in highly instructive settings, and had seven papers published or in press, yet no prospects of a position that would feed and house us seemed to exist. The only opening I had heard of was at the Medical College of the University of Chicago. A neurologist, Roy Grinker, allowed me a luncheon interview at which I had little opportunity to eat. After it, and probably fortunately for both of us applicants, he chose Ward C. Halstead. Following visits with our families, we went on to Estes Park, Colorado. There Esther's parents were having a summer home built. We suspected we might be inhabiting it through the winter of 1935–1936. I dug part of the trench for the water pipe, shingled the west side of the roof, and, together with Esther's brother, built a sandstone patio. We were not too much worried about paid employment. Esther planned to devote the winter to writing some stories, and I planned a series of articles, some of which have never got written. Little did we realize then that this cottage would one day become our own summer home where I would withdraw to write and where, thirty-six years later, this odyssey is being written.

OFFICIALLY UNEMPLOYED, BUT WORKING

It was never actually necessary to implement these plans which probably functioned chiefly to control our anxiety. About mid-

August, Esther's brother was married in Lincoln. We returned for the wedding. Immediately after came a call from J. P. Guilford who asked us to come by. After telling us that he had been invited to become visiting professor at Northwestern University for the fall semester, Guilford wondered if I was free and interested in teaching his courses at the University of Nebraska. Interested? I was delighted!!

At the University of Nebraska. My job was to teach two sections of general psychology, a course in experimental psychology, and the course in statistics and psychometric methods, using as a text the manuscript of what became the first edition of Guilford's classic textbook in *Psychometric Methods.* Teaching these courses required much preparation for I had been reading chiefly in the domains of psychopathology and endocrinology. They had the merit of getting me much better informed in the mainstream of psychology. It was also a time to renew friendships with Arthur Jenness and William Walton and to form a friendship with Donald Dysinger, who had joined the departmental staff with a new doctorate from Iowa University. The four of us were then the department of psychology at Nebraska. It was also good to see again many of my old teachers. Yet, in faculty meetings, when I wished to make a point, I had a strong feeling that having once been one of their students put me at a disadvantage. No one is a prophet in his own community—or on the faculty of his own Alma Mater.

Time did not permit writing the stories and articles which we had planned to do during a winter in Estes Park, but I used the data from Worcester State Hospital to write a paper on the effects of thyroid medication. When John McGeoch, then editor of the *Psychological Bulletin,* returned the manuscript of my "Psychological Experiments with Disordered Persons" for condensation and rather extensive revision, I managed to make them. Also, feeling a possible chance that Guilford might remain at Northwestern University, I explored the possibilities of doing one or more of the studies that I had outlined for myself at Worcester. In those days, before the impact of the studies of the Iowa Group and the writings and movies of René Spitz on the institutional rearing of infants resulted in outlawing orphanages in favor of foster placement, there were orphanages in Nebraska. Some were run by the state and some by churches. Having learned the rudiments of Rorschach's test in Sam Beck's seminar at Worcester, I thought I might use this test to uncover differences in the personalities of children who had lived from infancy under differing orphanage regimes. Such an approach could hardly test the details of Freud's theory of psychosexual development, yet it would be a start. I looked into two orphanages, one supported by the state, the other by a church. As I described my plan to the authorities at the state orphanage, I met a deluge of questions and complaints that such a study would interfere with operations which I suspected might mean interference with opportunities to profit undetected. When I explained my purpose to the head of one of the church orphanages, he told me frankly that there were not especially concerned with the personalities of the infants in their charge if they could ensure their souls for Christ. When a letter from Guilford assured me that he would return at the end of January, I ceased to explore such avenues further, but I suspect it would have been impossible to gain the access I sought to these orphanages in the next half-dozen years.

At St. Elizabeths Hospital. With no prospects for the spring of 1936, Madison Bentley came again to our aid with some funds from the Carnegie Corporation left from his grant for *The Problem of Mental Disorder.* With this support I sought and got a research associateship at St. Elizabeths Hospital in Washington, D.C.

Several experiences during those six months at St. Elizabeths Hospital were important for my later career. One involved an unusual approach to psychotherapy. Depression is a heart-rending disorder, and I included among my sample all of the manic-depressive patients then hospitalized at St. Elizabeths. One I saw first while he was still being tube-fed. As soon as he could or would talk, he confirmed the information in his case history that he was the son of a diplomat who had been first consul at Potsdam, and he had been reared in Germany. He had dropped out of college, however, had spent most of his adult life in the Army, had attained the rank of master sergeant when his depression brought him to this federal psychiatric hospital. Although his history suggested a homosexual conflict, his chief expressed complaint concerned his complete uselessness. I wondered what would happen if one got him into a social role whereby he could be obviously useful to someone of at least nominally superior status. In considering this possibility, it occurred to me that his schooling in a gymnasium in Germany might have prepared him to be useful as a tutor of German so that I might kill two birds with one stone: try my hunch about psychotherapy while at the same time improving my own mastery of German. It was painful at first, but as I acted out a strong show of gratitude for every bit of constructive help he gave me, first in reading a German translation of *Robinson Crusoe,* and then Goethe's *Faust,* he began steadily to improve. Within eight or ten weeks from the time I first saw him as a tube-fed patient, he was brought up for discharge. His sister wrote a letter of gratitude, and for several years I got occasional notes from him. After hearing me describe this experience in lecture, one of my students tried this scheme successfully with another depressed patient who had been an expert at chess. This ex-student got the patient to tutor him in the game. Recovery was unexpectedly rapid. Although one can conceive of such treatment as a special case of what we now call behavior therapy, it calls for a client-oriented conception of reinforcement, for the scheme appears to work only when the patient takes pride in the skill with which he attempts to help his "therapist-tutee."

Another experience was a serendipitous encounter with evidence of a socially induced conflict of apparent etiological importance. When one of my patients, who was recovering from a severe depression and writing poetry of considerable beauty, remarked, more or less in passing, that the boys of his neighborhood had never had a fair chance in life, I countered, tongue in cheek, with the American creed. He answered with considerable emotion that five of the fifteen boys of his neighborhood had spent most of their lives in psychiatric hospitals, and that another had died on the streets of Washington while either drunk or in a psychotic stupor. The fact that this patient was writing prompted me to ask him to write biographies of each of the fifteen boys in his neighborhood. Analysis of these biographies made it evident that all six of these boys, including the one who died, had participated both in a homosexual ring and in Pentecostal Revivals. One partial exception, however, had been unattractive to the other boys in the ring. He had resorted to prostitutes while in his early teens, and had been hospitalized with general paresis instead of depression or schizophrenia. None of those who participated in but one of these two kinds of experience had been hospitalized or had crippling personal problems. After checking certain key facts with several of the individuals named, I guessed that the information from my patient was probably valid, and I published a paper on it entitled "An Instance of the Social Origin of Conflict Resulting in Psychosis" (Hunt, 1938).

Two of the other educational experiences came from direct contact with men associated with St. Elizabeths Hospital. One was Walter Freeman, a neurologist and brain surgeon who pioneered frontal lobotomies. The other was William Alanson White, then superintendent of St. Elizabeths Hospital. I met Walter Freeman accidentally at lunch in the hospital dining room. In casual conversation, I mentioned my work with James Papez at Cornell, and he invited me to his lectures and demonstrations in clinical neurology at the George Washington University School of Medicine. I attended them regularly, and we lunched together occasionally thereafter. He was especially interested in Papez's tracing out of the extrapyramidal system, in his theory of emotion, and in the role of the frontal lobes in emotion. Some years later when Walter Freeman was planning an extensive investigation of the effects of lobotomies, he came to Brown University to invite me to make the assessments of any improvements or deficits that might result. I appreciated the compliment. But inasmuch as the offer included only temporary grant support while I had at Brown a less tenuous appointment and I had begun some of my own studies of the effect of conflict on rat behavior, I declined.

William Alanson White deserves a long essay rather than a paragraph. A young Naval psychiatrist named George Neely Raines, who was later to be chief of the Bethesda Naval Hospital, had come to St. Elizabeths for his psychiatric residency at the same time I came. Dr. White was a natural teacher. In my first interview with him, he kept me going for nearly two hours while he found out what I had read, what I wanted to do immediately, and what I saw as my future. Along the way, he shared a variety of his own significant experiences. When he learned that I had read only the books of Freud, he urged me to read the concrete case material in the *Collected Papers.* With this suggestion for reading came others and still others throughout the months to come. So far as Freud's *Collected Papers* was concerned, Raines got the same counsel that I got. We saw patients and participated in the staff conferences from about eight in the morning to some time shortly after three when we made a practice of going to the hospital library for two or three hours. Once or twice a week, Dr. White would appear in the library at about four. Either he discussed with us what we were reading, or he regaled us with his experiences and reactions to readings. Even while directing staff conferences, he continued our education. Unlike most of the clinical teachers I have observed, White never talked, either to his staff or his class, about a patient who was present. He gave his attention completely to the patient, who appeared to be made oblivious to those looking on. Probably because we were the newest and least experienced members of the staff, he often called upon one of us first for a diagnosis and a plan of treatment. This put us on the spot, but his questioning of our diagnoses and treatment plans were as humane as his interviews with the patients. White also invited us to his lectures. They were the last he gave in psychiatry for the medical students at George Washington University. Here, again, White was able so to engross patients in his demonstration-interviews that they appeared to be oblivious of the student audience. Dr. White's humanity was outstanding. Later, when I was teaching abnormal psychology for Brown students at the Butler Hospital in Providence, White's were my models of demonstration-interviews. It is highly appropriate that his name has been memorialized in the William A. White Institute of Psychiatry in Washington.

During the months I was at St. Elizabeths, I was continually on the alert for news of academic openings. From Landis, I had learned to examine the obituaries in the *New York Times* for leads. Of course I attended the meetings of the Eastern Psychological Association, but to no avail. I already knew of the two openings I heard of there.

A break came unexpectedly. At the end of these 1936 meetings of the Eastern Psychological Association in New York, Esther and I drove to New Haven to see Clark Hull at Yale. Following an interesting interview, we considered going on up to Providence to see the Kemps, our friends of Worcester days. When we called to see if such a visit would be welcomed, Eddie Kemp seemed curiously to be expecting our call. Even though I had no faith in telepathy, we were too poor to permit prolonged probing via long-distance telephone. Some hours later, we learned that the Kemps had indeed been expecting us, for Walter Hunter, who was then negotiating his move from Clark to Brown, had been trying to reach us with an invitation to come up to Providence for interviews. Even though the next day was Easter Sunday, Hunter arranged interviews with Vice Presidents Mead and Adams of Brown University and with Dr. Arthur Ruggles, Superintendent of the Butler Hospital. I was offered an instructorship with the munificent salary of $2200 a year. A possibility at the University of Maryland was pending with a rank of assistant professor and salary of $3000, but the opportunity to work with Hunter's group, to have a relatively light load of teaching, and to have access to both an animal laboratory and a psychiatric hospital made the choice easy. We were delighted to accept the instructorship with the lesser salary and were never sorry. On Monday we drove back from Providence to Washington to continue the work under way. Through fate and the kindness of two ex-teachers, we had fared well during the year without a job.

BROWN UNIVERSITY AND BUTLER HOSPITAL

Brown University was, except for below-average salaries, a most advantageous place to begin an academic career. Even as a lowly instructor, the teaching load was limited to two courses each semester and some quiz sections in the first course. One was expected to teach well, to introduce his undergraduate students to investigation, and to grow intellectually. The student evaluations of one's teaching, published annually in the *Brown Daily Herald*, counted. The library was excellent and the easiest to use that I have ever encountered. Moreover, one continued one's education almost effortlessly because the university's faculty was both excellent and small. When we arrived in the fall of 1936, it numbered only 105—not appreciably more than the staffs of the larger departments nowadays. It was not uncommon to have shop talk at lunch with colleagues from two other departments. The fates of the individuals over the years have demonstrated the high quality of that Brown faculty. The questions about work were both penetrating and from a fresh viewpoint, and they often got answered with uncommon lucidity. In such a setting, one could hardly avoid growth in both breadth and depth.

Walter S. Hunter, moreover, managed to foster in his departmental staff both enterprise and warm personal relationships. He managed this despite his overt emphasis on the impersonal and objective (Hunt, 1956). That staff, in the first years, included Clarence H. Graham, Herbert Jasper, Edward H. Kemp, and Harold Schlosberg. Later, after Jasper moved to McGill University, Donald B. Lindsley came in his place, and, still later, Carl Pfaffmann and Lorrin Riggs came during my decade of 1936–1946. As a group, we were both productive and mutually supportive. At professional meetings, we nearly always gathered to hear each other's papers. I shall never forget the supportive smiles on the faces in the first two rows when, at the meetings of the American Psychological Association in 1940 at Pennsylvania State University, I got up to present my paper, "Effects of Feeding Frustration in Infancy on Adult Eating and Hoarding in Rats" (Hunt, 1941).

The close relationship with the Butler Hospital made the situation almost ideal for my interests. With access to both an animal laboratory and a psychiatric hospital, I lacked only an orphanage, but my Nebraska experience had already discouraged such hopes, and I had already decided, at least for the time being, to focus my investigations on the role of conflict on neuroses in rats and on deficit in psychoses and brain injuries.

Walter Hunter explained that, in asmuch as we were a "service department," teaching came first. As I recall it, my courses for the first semester of 1936 were abnormal psychology, an introduction to statistics, and the lectures on the psychoses and neuroses along with two quiz sections each Friday in the first course. Because of my background in psychiatric hospitals, Dr. Arthur Ruggles invited me to bring the students in abnormal psychology once each week to Butler Hospital for demonstrations. This posed a problem. The coordinate arrangement between Brown and Pembroke had dictated the custom of meeting the men and the women in each course separately, but having two classes a week at the Butler Hospital would be too much. Hunter and Ruggles got permission for me to bring the Brown men and the Pembroke women in my course together from two to four on Tuesday in a Brown classroom and from two to four on Thursday in the conference room at the hospital. Thus, I believe I taught the first coeducational class at Brown University.

As a teacher-investigator, I have often wondered how best to foster the investigative skill of problem finding in students. Such wondering has motivated my reading autobiographical accounts of creative work such as Kekule's discovery of the benzene ring. It has also prompted me to scrutinize how I have come by the ideas I have had for investigation. Already noted is the origin of my interest in early experience from an analysis of the theory of psychosexual development in Freud's writings which led me to believe that one central issue concerns the special importance of early experience, another that behavioral disorders are a product of conflict. The existence of experimentally induced neuroses in Pavlov's dogs and Liddell's sheep suggested to me that it should be feasible to investigate the validity of the etiological importance attributed to conflict in rats. Earlier, Kurt Lewin had described three types of conflict in the behavior of children. To begin with, I investigated the behavior of rats forced into each of these types of conflict, but it soon became evident that a criterion of neurotic behavior was needed as the dependent variable. At about this point, Harold Schlosberg and I pooled our forces as collaborators. Because emotional disturbances in human beings almost always result in insomnia, we investigated the diurnal activity cycles of white rats (Hunt and Schlosberg, 1939) and then the effects of reversing the dark-light periods (Hunt and Schlosberg, 1939) in the hope of finding measurable behavioral indicators of neurosis in rats. Studies done in collaboration with our students subsequently demonstrated that conflict induced in situations outside the activity cages would decrease general activity but did not alter the diurnal cycle as the insomnia hypothesis would demand (Evans and Hunt, 1942; papers by Finger and Schlosberg). Moreover, the decrements in activity were small and barely significant statistically. I found myself wondering if the low evolutionary level of rats did not mean that the central processes of the species were inadequate to permit them to carry their conflicts around from one situation to another. Schlosberg and I hit upon the idea of pitting instinctual needs against each other continually in a situation by electrifying the water supply of the rats in the activity cages. This conflict between thirst and shock-avoidance did appreciably alter the portion of their activity occurring during the normally quiet, lighted half of the day. Moreover, this conflict produced an abundance of maladaptive behavior, which we described when the paper was finally published (Hunt and Schlosberg, 1950).

Although, in retrospect, these investigations still look interesting to me, they attracted less attention from colleagues than did two others: one concerned with the deficit associated with bilateral frontal lobectomy in a man who had earned an M.A. degree in modern languages and held executive posts (Nichols and Hunt, 1940), and the studies of the effects of infantile feeding frustration upon hoarding and the rate of eating in adult rats (Hunt, 1941; Hunt, Schlosberg, Solomon, and Stellar, 1947; Stellar, Hunt, Schlosberg, and Solomon, 1952).

The impetus for the case study came with the opportunistic presence of a case with the history of a bilateral frontal lobectomy at the Butler Hospital coupled with a bit of information. One could not know Walter Hunter without knowing also of his classical studies of delayed reaction and double alternation (Hunt, 1956). The evidence from these suggested his concept of "symbolic processes." At about this time, Carlyle Jacobsen and his collaborators at Yale had reported that capacity for delayed reaction and double alternation in primates is grossly reduced by damage to their frontal lobes. This frontal-lobectomy patient had a Binet IQ of about 120 and could define satisfactorily all but 11 words of the sample in the 1916 version of the Stanford-Binet scale. Nevertheless, when I tested him with a version of the double-alternation test with five playing cards dealt out repeatedly before him with the goal card twice on his right and then twice on his left, he failed to "get the system." Even preschool children can readily learn such double alternation, yet this frontal-lobectomy patient was still turning up "middle cards" after 63 deals and had failed through 200 deals. The test was made on the day of the great hurricane flood of 1938, but neither the patient nor I noted the howling winds during the two hours we worked. The next week he even failed a test of single alternation until, in exasperation, I complained, "Haven't you got the system yet?" He had not considered the possibility of a system. Once I had set him to look for a system, he solved single alternation and finally solved also double alternation. Even with this instruction it took a great many deals, and other procedures confirmed a deficit in planning.

At this same time, Donald Hebb was reporting little or no deficit, as measured by standardized psychometric tests, following the surgical removal of large amounts of brain tissue. We argued via correspondence. He questioned the meaning of the unstandardized tests which I had devised, and I complained that the standardized tests simply fail to bring out the deficit. Later my students got data on my tests from samples of college-trained men ranging in age from forty to eighty years. In every case this patient's performance fell well below all those aged above sixty who were without symptoms of senility. The possibility of scar tissue with disruptive firing rhythms could not be ruled out without an autopsy. Unfortunately, when Arthur Ruggles retired as the Superintendent of the Butler Hospital, no one recalled our arrangement, so this patient was transferred to a state hospital without my knowledge. He died there and was buried without an autopsy, so the question of scar tissue was never answered.

The idea for the experiments on the effects of infantile feeding frustration upon adult hoarding in rats came from reading Roger Money-Kyrle's *Superstition and Society.* There he reported a relationship between the frustrations of irregular feeding in infancy and a high valuation on hoards of food which held across several cultures. I had already seen rats hoard food pellets (Hunt and Willoughby, 1939). Even though I recognized the tenuous and analogous nature of any relationship between the hoarding of food by rats and the high valuation of food stores in human cultures, Money-Kyrle's report suggested to me the general nature of both an independent variable and a dependent variable for investigating the effects of early experience in rats. In the first experiment, there were two groups—those animals which had been submitted to feeding frustration beginning when they were twenty-one days old and their litter-mate controls. The first group, following an adult feeding frustration, hauled more than 2.5 times as many pellets as the controls from the storage cans at one end of the alleys to their home cages at the other end. Moreover, during the first day or two of the five days of adult feeding frustration, it was evident that some of the animals were eating much more rapidly than others. This gave me the idea of weighing the food dishes to ascertain the amounts eaten during the limited feeding time. As it turned out, it was the infantile frustrates who ate most rapidly. My interpretation contended that the cues of hunger elicited during the adult feeding frustration evoked in the infantile frustrates the intense hunger arousal which had been part of the intense hunger experience during the adult feeding frustration. This arousal, being absent in the control group, was presumably responsible for the difference in pellet hauling. When no such difference appeared for the group in which the infantile feeding frustration began when they were thirty-two days old, it appeared that infant rats were more sensitive to feeding frustration in infancy than they were later.

Although Walter Hunter had been highly skeptical of this idea, the results of this exploratory experiment so impressed him that he urged me to seek a grant from the Rockefeller Foundation to support a program of research on the effects of early experience. Even though the task of organizing and editing *Personality and the Behavior Disorders* was keeping me busy, I accepted his counsel, had my application approved, and in the fall of 1940 began with the collaboration of Harold Schlosberg, Richard L. Solomon, and Eliot Stellar such a program. During 1940–1941, we managed three repetitions of the main study with extensions. In general, these tended to confirm the original finding, but the differences between the infantile frustrates and the controls in pellets hoarded were substantially less than they had been in the original study. We attempted feeding frustration before weaning, but failed to develop a method that would keep the mothers lactating and the pups alive. We also investigated the effects of infantile feeding-frustration upon running in activity wheels and on measures of emotionality derived from Calvin Hall's open field. From Hull's drive theory, I had expected that the infantile frustrates would run more and would defecate and urinate more in one of the open fields devised by Calvin Hall than would their litter-mate controls, but these predictions failed completely. Inasmuch as they were tried with repetitions where the infantile feeding frustration had had less than the usual effect upon the numbers of pellets hauled and the amounts eaten, I was unwilling to give up the hypothesis. In the summer of 1941, when World War II drew Solomon and

Stellar into defense work, Carl Duncan became our assistant in the program. We managed one study in which the infantile feeding frustration failed to produce an effect upon hoarding, but produced a very large effect on the rate of eating during the first ten minutes of each feeding following the adult feeding frustration. At this point, World War II stopped the program completely. After the war, we published one paper which gave the results of the three repetitions of the original study (Hunt, Schlosberg, Solomon, and Stellar, 1947). After 1946, when I had become Director of the Institute of Welfare Research in New York, it seemed unwise to publish the results from them without the opportunity to repeat the findings of the other studies. Subsequent work by Marx (1952), however, indicates that increases in the rate of eating are a more nearly invariable consequence of infantile feeding frustration than is increased hoarding. Moreover, one of my students at the University of Illinois, Arnold Freedman, has investigated the effects of repeated periods without water in rats beyond infancy and found them resulting in increased rapidity of drinking which could be evoked by either short periods without water or injections of mild saline under the skin. These results suggest that the difference between the groups in which the feeding frustration started at twenty-one days and thirty-two days of age should be rechecked. While early experience may endure and affect adult behavior, the same kind of experience may have similar results even when it occurs later. Freedman also found that repeated periods without water did not later affect even such a closely related activity as running down an alley to get water. These findings, coupled with another that rats, once the number of pellets hauled has been approximately quadrupled by bright lights over the hoarding alleys, will continue to haul pellets at the illuminated rate in subsequent tests after the lights over the alleys have been removed, suggest an interpretation quite different from my original one. They suggest that the rate or intensity of an activity, once established, becomes an intrinsic part of that activity in the situation which elicits it. More generally, it suggests that drive and habit are less separate than Hull's theory would have them.

How one comes by professional opportunities is also of interest. Mine appear to have come from the support of those with whom events have made me acquainted. Although the studies of feeding frustration may have set a model for experimentally controlling the life history of animal subjects for investigative purposes, probably the major professional accomplishment of my decade at Brown University and Butler Hospital was the organization and the editing of *Personality and the Behavior Disorders.* Opportunities to edit major handbooks seldom go to a young man with a reputation not yet established. My opportunity occurred when Charles P. Calhoun, then Vice President of the Ronald Press Company, came in a search for someone to do a textbook in abnormal psychology. Walter Hunter named me as a likely prospect. Calhoun invited me to submit a plan. It was then early in the fall of 1939. Although my hands were already full with teaching and research, it seemed that submitting a plan could do no harm. Three years of gulping the literature in order to have a background for teaching had got me acquainted with almost every on-going investigative program in America and some of those abroad. Carl Murchison of Clark University had organized and edited successful handbooks of experimental psychology and of child psychology. It seemed to me that the time might be ripe to organize and edit a handbook in the domain of personality and personality disorders which would bring psychoanalytic thinking within the general domain of psychology and which would have as its main organizing theme that integration of psychoanalytic thought with behavioristic psychology which was developing out of Hull's psychoanalytic seminar and which would shortly be represented by *Frustration and Aggression* by Dollard, Doob, Miller, Mowrer, and Sears and by *Social Learning and Imitation* by Miller and Dollard. One October weekend with no distracting football game at Brown, I began the plan by listing domains. What resulted was a list of the eight general topics of my courses in personality and in abnormal psychology. I thought these might well become the parts or sections of such a work. They were (1) theoretical approaches to personality, (2) cross-sectional methods of assessment, (3) behavioral dynamics, (4) determinants of personality, (5) the concept of abnormality, (6) the disorders of behavior, (7) some of the investigated correlates of the behavior disorders, and (8) the prevention and therapy of the behavior disorders. Within each of these domains, I listed chapter titles, which, in total, numbered thirty-six.

For each of these titles, I listed as potential authors at least two names of individuals whom I knew to have work under way on the topic.

It seemed, in view of my youth and limited prestige, it would be important to have a contract and a plan for remuneration. On the basis of the sales of Murchison's handbooks, I reckoned that the work would sell at least 2000 copies within five years. I typed the letter describing the plan, and, on Sunday afternoon, I mailed it to Calhoun. In his answer, he noted that what I proposed was not the textbook they had been looking for, but they would be willing to give me the contract. During November and December 1939, I began writing my prospective authors for appointments. The strategy of starting with the most prestigious names first looked good and seemed to work. By April or May 1940, I had nearly all the chapters committed, taking two for myself: one on the general concept of abnormality and disorder and one on psychological deficit, for which I later got Charles Cofer as a collaborator.

The events following the disaster at Pearl Harbor forced a number of changes in the authorship of chapters and produced discouraging delays in production. Nevertheless, by about Christmas of 1942, drafts of all but two of the chapters had come, several without bibliographies. These had to be supplied. Academic psychologists and sociologists turned out to be far superior to neurologists and psychiatrists as authors and bibliophiles. By March of 1943, the manuscripts of the thirty-five chapters filled a box which had once held reams of mimeographing paper. Calhoun acknowledged receipt of what he called "your oct-opus." After a number of debates about quantity, one of which prompted me to withdraw my chapter on the meaning of abnormality, and others about whether the work should be one volume or two, the Ronald Press finally sent the manuscript to the printer. All spare time during the fall of 1943 went to proofreading. On the Saturday or Sunday following Thanksgiving, a telegram brought the news that the presses could be obtained if the index could be available within a week. Heroic efforts were in order. Esther was doing the author index. Our four-year-old daughter, Judy, was scheduled that week to have a tonsillectomy in Philadelphia, where my father's sister was an ear-nose-throat surgeon. Esther took one set of page proofs to Philadelphia. There she cared for Judy days and indexed at night. On Monday morning, I gave my nine o'clock lecture, and my good friend Harold Schlosberg agreed to take my classes for the remainder of the week. By working stretches of five hours and sleeping one hour from Monday noon until five o'clock Saturday morning, the slips of paper which comprised the index were alphabetized, shoe-boxed, taped up, and addressed for shipment to the Ronald Press Company. One afternoon in late January 1944, Esther and Judy met me with the baby buggy. In the buggy were Daddy's twins, dressed in red covers: Volume I and Volume II of *Personality and the Behavior Disorders.* A task that had endured for somewhat over four years was finally finished.

Although this is intended to be a professional odyssey, separating the various aspects of one's life completely is impossible. They run together and interact. Despite the fact that my situation at Brown was ideal from the standpoint of my investigative and teaching interests, other factors were forcing me away. Brown's salaries were relatively low, and Carol Jean had joined our family, providing me with the occasion to announce to my class in child psychology that "Henceforth my generalizations about children will be based on an *n* of two."

Two events, quite unconnected, combined to force a major change of direction and location. Within a couple of months after the two volumes appeared, Hobart Mowrer, who had recently moved from Yale to Harvard, stopped by to ask me if I would take his place in collaborating with John Dollard on assessing the results of social casework at the Institute of Welfare Research of the Community Service Society in New York. During the war, the Dollard-Mowrer project was the only one under way at the Institute.

Later in the spring, President Wriston called me to his office. As he picked up the two volumes, he said: "By the racing form, you deserve a raise. I can raise your rank, but not your salary." He went on to explain that Brown needed buildings with which to face the future, that temporarily the faculty would suffer, and that if he were in my place, he would be looking elsewhere for the future. And so in 1944, I became an Associate Professor, ironically with tenure, but the salary remained $3000 a year with a temporary supplement of $1000 because I was teaching three semesters a year. The pat on the back felt good, but it was even better that

Hobart Mowrer had called, for prices were rising. I got my courses arranged so that in May 1944, I began taking the train for New York each Thursday night and flying back on either Saturday or Sunday night. For the first few months, there were Pullmans for these trips, but during 1945–1946, the Pullmans were taken off for war service, and I learned to sleep, at least some, on two chairs.

AT THE INSTITUTE OF WELFARE RESEARCH

The Institute of Welfare Research was, when I became its director, a semi-autonomous component of the Community Service Society of New York. The Community Service Society (CSS) had come into being in 1939 from a merger of two large, old, private social agencies: the Association for Improving the Condition of the Poor (AICP), incorporated in 1848, and the Charity Organization Society (COS), incorporated in 1882. In the new name, the absence of the words *charity* and *poor* served to recognize the change of emphasis which had come with the establishment of publicly financed welfare agencies in the 1930s. The purposes of the Community Service Society were formulated under three main headings: service (Family Service Department, Department of Educational Nursing, Nutrition Service, Department of Special Services, and the Bureau of Public Affairs), professional training (New York School of Social Work), and research (the Institute of Welfare Research) (see Hunt, 1949). The roster of the Board's Committee on the Institute, chaired by Frederick A. O. Schwarz, included a number of other influential names (Dr. Frank G. Boudreau, Executive Director, the Milbank Fund; Dr. Edwin S. Burdell, President, Cooper Union; Guy Emerson, Director, Samuel H. Kress Foundation; Stanley P. Davies, Executive Director, Community Service Society; Walter S. Gifford, President, American Telephone and Telegraph Company; Keith S. McHugh, President, New York Telephone Company; and Bayard S. Pope, President, Marine Midland Bank). This committee had authorized Chairman Schwarz to direct the Institute "to determine and express how case work is carried on, at what cost, and with what success." Robert P. Lansdale, the first director of the Institute (1941–43), had invited John Dollard, then a professor at the Institute of Human Relations at Yale University, to organize and direct a program of research implied by this directive. Quite appropriately, Dollard saw "with what success" as the first question, and sought to develop a dependable and generally applicable measure of change in clients and their situations. He sought the collaboration of Hobart Mowrer, and they developed the *Distress-Relief Quotient* (DRQ), derived from reward-learning theory. This instrument, based first on the assumption that the case worker is a teacher and the client a learner, and second on the assumption that what the client learns should be associated with reduction in his distress, utilized a content-analysis of the case record.

When I entered the situation, Dollard and Mowrer had already followed Binet's use of teacher's ratings to validate tests of intelligence by correlating the differences between DRQ values for the first and last tenths of a series of thirty-nine case records with the amount of improvement in these cases as judged by caseworkers to validate the DRQ. With this validity study came objections from the caseworkers for being "researched upon." When they requested participation, Dollard and I formed what we called the "Joint Research Committee." When the correlation between changes in DRQ values and caseworker ratings of improvement proved disappointingly low, the caseworkers quite naturally saw their judgments of improvement as more valid than change in the DRQ. Inasmuch as the judgment of the worker on a case would involve the least possible expense in routine application, I decided to utilize the techniques of scaling and of anchoring scales to improve agreement among caseworkers. First, we got fifteen caseworkers to judge our thirty-nine cases and to describe the reasons for their judgments to uncover their criteria of improvement or deterioration, which they termed *movement*. We arranged the scales to focus attention on these agreed-upon criteria. In order to minimize the existence of differing standards among the workers, which had permitted some workers to see "great" improvement where others saw merely "slight" improvement, we used that case showing the largest amount of improvement and called it +4 (Hunt and Kogan, 1950), or later, +40 (Kogan, Kogan, and Hunt, 1952). We selected cases judged to show half this amount of improvement as that in this anchor to illustrate +2 or +20, and cases judged to show deterioration equivalent to half the improvement in the anchor to illustrate −2 or −20. The improvement in agreement was substantial. It occurred less in the size of the mean intercorrelation among the judgments from the various workers (from +.7 to +.82) than in the variance among the mean judgments for the sample of cases from these individuals. These mean judgments now fell within a range of .3 of a step on a 6-step scale (Hunt and Kogan, 1950) or 3 steps on a 60-step scale (Kogan, Kogan, and Hunt, 1952). In a field-test of this scale, the caseworkers' judgments of movement in their own cases agreed well with those by an independent judge (Hunt, Blenkner, and Kogan, 1950). While this work was under way, I saw social casework as a variety of psychotherapy, or helping through verbal communication. Later, at the Student Counseling Service at the University of Illinois, Rolfe LaForge, Thomas Ewing, William Gilbert, and I attempted to approximate what I had conceived as an integrated approach to the evaluation of therapeutic counseling (Hunt, 1949, 1952), and here the Movement Scale proved to be a useful tool (Hunt, LaForge, Ewing, and Gilbert, 1959). It was a source of some gratification in 1950 to have the Hunt-Kogan Movement Scale receive honorable mention for excellence in research from the American Personnel and Guidance Association, and in 1960 to have our Integrated Approach win the award for excellence from that same association.

When Mowrer came by to invite me to take his place as Dollard's collaboratory on this project, it looked like a radical change of direction for me. My Depression-based experience indicated that I would be departing from academia forever. It was a radical change, but circumstances dictated making the change despite serious qualms.

The contrast between academia and a large social agency was sharp enough to produce an emotional disturbance in any academic investigator, but I was saved from any Hebbian fear by making the change gradually. I was two years a consultant before becoming the Director. Where the academician is free to choose what he will investigate, the psychologist in such an institution must investigate the problems set in general by those who pay his salary. Such was my situation. The Committee on the Institute of Welfare Research were puzzled by the growth of public welfare which had occurred during the Depression and were equally puzzled about the role of the private social agency and the value of such services as social casework. These Committee members were highly able and influential men of affairs. They were asking representatives of the behavioral and social sciences, and of us psychologists within those sciences, for evidence that would guide them for making the choices for what they felt to be their responsibility for the program of a large private social agency with a substantial endowment. The services, which constituted the independent variable, were administered, of course, by the social caseworkers under the direction of their administrative colleagues. The social caseworkers of that day looked to psychoanalytic psychiatry for leadership, and they conceived of themselves as professionally equipped to be the arbiters of social values and how to achieve them. They welcomed research, but perhaps chiefly in the hope of obtaining evidence with which to justify their program and practices to their sources of financial support. Thus, we investigators of the Institute were caught between two proverbial fires which had to be kept low to avoid a destructive conflagration. The only useful strategy for coping with such a situation of which I knew or know now is to focus firmly on evidence from clearly formulated methodology with the implications of the outcomes for accepted goals considered so far as possible in advance. Although I accepted as sensible the focus provided by the Committee's directive when I came to the Institute, I learned a great deal both from these people and from the situation which called for a broader frame of reference than either they or I could then command. In the Movement Scale, we produced an instrument which, in combination with a classification of cases, might have been highly useful in uncovering the conditions of effective casework. Although schools of casework used this work in their courses on research, about the only use of the instrument in the fashion I envisaged for it has been that made at the Student Counseling Service at the University of Illinois.

Research in a private social agency brought home to me as nothing else ever has the open-ended nature of life and social processes. In the end, social processes are political. While evidence from the behavioral and social sciences can be powerful aids to those who participate in and lead political forces, this evidence and the methods of obtaining it need to be better understood by both the leaders and the led than it is or ever has been. The open-ended nature of life and social processes calls for a collaboration between policy leaders and social investigators. The collaboration should focus on the assessment of admittedly unwanted consequences of policy changes before these can produce such possibly irreversible damage as I fear the Depression-dictated improvisations in the domain of public welfare have done or at least helped foster.

During my first year as director of the Institute, I was fortunate enough to interest Leonard S. Kogan in the post of Assistant Director. He had special training in psychological measurement; he had headed the statistical program of the Atomic Energy Unit at Oak Ridge, Tennessee, and he was then completing his doctorate psychology at the University of Rochester. With an even temperament, a capacity to get things done, and a voice to sing, he made a wonderful collaborator. Our collaboration was enjoyable and fruitful. When I moved on, he became Director. Margaret Blenkner, who played a highly important role in the field-test of our Movement Scale (Hunt, Blenkner, and Kogan, 1950), and Phyllis Bartelme, who found and interviewed the individuals of the thirty-eight cases in our follow-up study (Kogan, Hunt, and Blenkner, 1953), joined the staff later. By the fifth year, the full-time professional staff numbered four. It was supplemented summers by such graduate students as David Freides from Yale and Nathan Kogan from Princeton. Our secretarial staff, headed by Helen Mulroney who skillfully guided our papers through the press, numbered four and was supplemented by one or two students from Antioch.

My fears of irrevocable separation from academia were quite unfounded. Within two years after I became Director of the Institute, Laurence F. Schafer of Teachers College in Columbia University invited me to give my personality course to graduate students in his program of training in clinical and counseling psychology. For two years I took the subway to Teachers College each Monday afternoon for a two-hour lecture. Early in 1950, Lyle Lanier invited me to become Adjunct Professor in the Graduate College in New York University where I gave a seminar in methodology. Accepting this latter invitation saved some long subway rides.

The decision to move back to academia came gradually through a number of considerations. With the advances in salary of professional personnel, the endowment of the Community Service Society became inadequate to support the program. I had to raise funds through foundation grants to support the work of the Institute. Moreover, just as we were ready to expand the Institute's operations outside the services of the Community Service Society, the Board of Trustees of the Society was inclining to change the status of the Institute from a semi-autonomous component for research to that of a research department within the agency. Moreover, the keenness of my long-standing interest in early experience had taken a new turn. Various professional groups were interested in telling parents how to rear their children. Such were the differences in views that one could hear on successive occasions almost diametrically opposed counsel. As Director of the Institute of Welfare Research, I had found a friendly colleague in Don Young, Executive Director of the Russell Sage Foundation. When I suggested that someone should examine the literature of the behavioral sciences for evidence relevant to the various beliefs about child rearing, he agreed with enthusiasm. On the other hand, the Committee on the Institute showed no enthusiasm for such a study. In the meantime, I had become involved in the affairs of professional associations and also in editing the *Journal of Abnormal and Social Psychology*. As a consequence, the three hours spent each day in commuting became an increasing burden, and when my good friend Lyle Lanier accepted the headship of the department of psychology at the University of Illinois and offered me a professorship with the task of coordinating training in clinical and counseling psychology, I accepted. I thought then that a regular professorship in the department of psychology at the University of Illinois would enable me ultimately to accept the invitation of the State Commissioner of Welfare to utilize part of the state hospital system as a laboratory for the evaluation of milieu therapies for mental disorders. In retrospect, this appears to have been a naïve hope of which my experience of doing evaluative research in a social agency should have disabused me. Yet, it took the change of Illinois State Administration with the Eisenhower election of 1952 finally to destroy all hope of such an opportunity for me in the state hospitals of Illinois.

In July of 1951, the Hunt family followed the century-old counsel of Horace Greely to move west, by moving to Champaign-

Urbana, home of the main campus of the University of Illinois. Then, while the family went on home to Nebraska and Estes Park, Colorado, for August of 1951, I returned for that month of August to produce the first draft of the manuscript of our *Follow-up Study of the Effects of Social Casework* (Kogan, Hunt, and Bartelme, 1953).

PARTICIPATION IN PSYCHOLOGICAL ASSOCIATIONS

Professional associations took so much of my time from 1946 to 1960 that I have sometimes adapted a term from skiing and referred to my fifteen years of intensive participation as my tour as an "association bum." Yet association affairs, seeing old friends at meetings, the joyful shouts of "Hi, Joe," yes, and the impromptu song fests have been an important source of the fun of professional life.

It all began with my paper on the program of the American Psychological Association at the meeting in Iowa City during the Christmas holidays of 1930. Again at Cornell in 1932, when the membership first passed 1000, I was assigned to the local committee to run cinema projectors. Most clearly do I recall running the cinema on the twins Johnny and Jimmy, by Myrtle McGraw.

My participation was limited to presenting and discussing papers till 1942, when I was invited to chair a session when the Eastern Psychological Association met in Providence. Then came a small part of the 1944 merger of the old American Psychological Association (APA) with American Association of Applied Psychologists (AAAP). The AAAP was composed chiefly of those professionally concerned with the various tests of individual differences, with industrial, and with clinical work who had split from the parent APA in the early 1930s to escape the dominance of those in the experimental tradition. When World War II came, the split left psychology without a unified voice for participation in the war effort. This effort brought old adversaries back together in the new APA with a divisional structure for both scientific interests and forms of professional practice. At this point, the regional associations limited their function to annual meetings for scientific communication, while the state associations concerned themselves with licensing and other professional matters.

Committees and boards serve the members of associations by

shaping and running the administrative errands. He is greatest who serves the most. My serving started with selection as Program Chairman of the Eastern Psychological Association (EPA) in 1945, then came election as Secretary in 1946–1947 when Lyle Lanier was serving as Treasurer. We "ran" the meeting at Haddon Hall in Atlantic City in the spring of 1947 when Anne Anastasi gave her presidential address on the role of education in the factor structure of tested abilities. As Secretary, I had to receive and count the nominating ballots. There I discovered that I was nominated for President along with my friends Harold Schlosberg and Lyle Lanier. When I tried to withdraw, Professor Boring wrote me one of those prized letters about how Hunt, the Secretary, had no right to use knowledge gained from his office to influence decisions by Hunt, the nominee. I ran. Much to my surprise, I was elected and was faced with the problem of a presidential address. Having then no accumulated program of research to report, I discussed a social agency as a setting for research (Hunt, 1949). My friends, I suspect, felt a bit let down.

In the spring of 1950, I received the surprise of my life. It was notification from Dael Wolfle that I had been nominated President-elect of the APA. The discrepancy between my concepts of G. Stanley Hall and William James and my self-concept was tremendous. To join the list of presidents was at that time beyond my fondest hopes. It occurred to me that others must have got an exaggerated impression of my contributions and status from those two red volumes of *Personality and the Behavior Disorders* which I had edited. I even suffered some from guilt for riding on the excellent work of the contributors to those volumes. Esther was less surprised than I and took for granted that I should accept the nomination. And I confess that once I saw the names of the other nominees, their qualifications seemed less discrepant from my own than those of Hall and James. The news of election just before the meetings at Pennsylvania State University, the last of those on college campuses, was less startling to me than that of nomination. Getting accustomed to my new self-concept was not really difficult.

A few of the things that I worked for in the American Psychological Association have been achieved. As a firm believer then in the effects of rewards on performance, it seemed highly out of order for biology, chemistry, and physics to have a variety of awards and prizes while psychology had only the Warren Medal of the Society of Experimental Psychologists. While I was a member of the Council of Representatives, I talked of this often and made motions to establish a series of prizes. These motions failed, but later the Distinguished Contribution Awards were established and I was invited to serve on the first committee on these awards. In these postwar years a few psychologists began to make fairly large amounts of money. I sought the establishment of an institutional arrangement whereby those who had achieved affluence through the profession could return some of their profits to the benefit of the profession. In consequence, I was made Chairman of the committee for the establishment of the American Psychological Foundation which was incorporated in 1953 with the seven preceding presidents of the APA as trustees. When I became the first President, we had a foundation but few funds. In order to have a program, we established the Gold Medal Award to recognize senior psychologists, usually aged over seventy, whose life-long devotion and contributions have been outstanding. We also established awards for such other contributors as science writers. As also the seventh President in 1959, it was my duty to present the Gold Medal Award to Edwin G. Boring and a science writer's award to Marjorie Van de Water of Science Service; she had collaborated with Professor Boring in writing the popular war-time book entitled *Psychology for the Fighting Man.* What a joyful duty!

THE UNIVERSITY OF ILLINOIS

According to the popular stereotype of academia, a professor is a man of leisure who has time to read and to think. Even I had absorbed some of this popular view during my absence as Director of the Institute of Welfare Research, but the experience of returning quickly dispelled it. With me to The University of Illinois I had brought the editorship of the *Journal of Abnormal and Social Psychology.* This called for reviewing about twenty manuscripts a month during 1951–1952 even though I had already sought as Associate Editor my old friend and teacher from Nebraska days, Arthur F. Jenness. My term as President of the American Psychological Association had also begun. Moreover, along with my graduate courses, I was not only to coordinate the training program in clinical and counseling psychology, but I was also asked to administer the Ford Grant to the University of Illinois for the behavioral sciences. Coordinating training in clinical and counseling psychology made me adviser to a large number of graduate students. Administering the Ford Grant called for organizing and leading an inter-disciplinary seminar composed of anthropologists, economists, interested faculty from the Law School, and interested faculty from the departments of political science, psychology, and sociology. It was a splendid way for a new member of the faculty to become acquainted with the faculty of other departments and with the graduate students of his own department, who then numbered about 250. It was all but impossible to develop a program of research, yet with collaborators including Ewing and William Gilbert of the Student Counseling Service and of Rolfe LaForge as project coordinator, the integrated program of research on therapeutic counseling, already mentioned, did get under way. The situation persisted through the year 1954–1955 which brought an end to my term as editor of the *Journal of Abnormal and Social Psychology* and an end to the Ford Grant Program.

As this state of affairs developed, I felt in need of a new course of graduate study, and my concern with early experience returned. I wrote Donald Young, then Executive Director of the Russell Sage Foundation, to remind him of our discussions of the need for an examination of the existing evidence in the literature of the behavior sciences for implications that might correct and put some empirical ballast on our swinging beliefs about child rearing and early childhood education. I asked if the Russell Sage Foundation would be interested in providing a grant that would pay my summer salary and permit me to retire to Estes Park each summer for three or four years to examine the literature and do a book on behavioral science and child rearing. The Foundation was interested, and the grant was arranged.

Before reading the literature, I believed that such a book should consist chiefly of filling in deductions already made from the drive-reduction theory of behavior formulated by the Yale group under the leadership of Clark L. Hull. This group, including especially John Dollard, Neil Miller, Hobart Mowrer, and Robert R. Sears, had become my reference group for psychological theory and faith. Nevertheless, my feelings of ignorance motivated an extended program of reading beginning in the summer of 1955. In the summer of 1956, I managed to write the first draft of a history of beliefs about child rearing extracted largely from the writings of Plato, the Hebrew fathers, the Scholastics, Rousseau, and the educational philosophers who followed him, especially Pestalozzi and Froebel. I continued with the implications from Darwin's evolution by natural selection as it came down through the genetic psychology and child study of G. Stanley Hall and through the tradition of individual differences and eugenics founded by Sir Francis Galton. I continued with John Dewey and functional psychology, with the tradition deriving from family welfare and child guidance, and ended with a description of the influence of Freud's theories of neurosis and psycho-sexual development on nursery schooling and the child guidance movement. This historical study brought out the various forms of the tension between the demands of society, which change with the social values dictated by culture and the conditions of the age, and the developmental abilities and needs of children. Thus, the rationalism of Socrates, Plato, and Aristotle made wisdom the goal of education; Christian theology set the goal as preparation for life eternal; the development of trade following the Crusades at the end of the Middle Ages led to schools to teach computation and writing for record keeping; the Reformation's emphasis on having direct access to the word of God prompted Calvin and Luther to establish schools to teach Bible reading. Lacking ability to cope with Biblical ideas, children were hardly interested. Unfortunately, St. Augustine's notion of original sin provided a ready explanation of their lack of interest and justified Calvin's approval of teachers' almost literally beating the devil out of children to force an attempt to learn. It was Rousseau who utilized the implications of John Locke's attack on innate ideas to call into question the doctrine of original sin, to assert dogmatically that "all things are good as they come out of the hands of the Creator," and, in *Emile,* to prescribe permissiveness combined with supplying "the grand motive" to keep children interested in employing "those abilities that nature has given" to acquire educational skills. Reading *Emile* inspired such educational pioneers as Pestalozzi and Froebel to arrange educational situations according to ability level to provide motivation and to introduce permissiveness by allowing children freedom of choice. Maria Montessori appears independently to have rediscovered the same principle. Permissiveness got a further boost from G. Stanley Hall's interpretation of the implications of the recapitulation doctrine, and yet another one from the support Freud's early theorizing provided when it was interpreted to mean that freedom from over-strict parental controls would prevent the development of crippling super-egos and neurotic inhibitions.

The second chapter on the theory of psychosexual development and the infant disciplines was long. It reviewed the failure of objective investigations to support expectations from the theory. The third reviewed the evidence from investigations of the effects of early experience in animal subjects and gave support to the basic, general psychoanalytic proposition that early experience endures and is important for later development. The evidence reviewed also called into question the psychoanalytic trauma theory and the behavioristic theory of acquired drives. The fourth chapter, also from the summer of 1956, examined the evidence of the significance of "mothering," defined as a one-to-one relationship, and called into question the belief in the dire effects of multiple mothering then commonly held.

What I wrote in these drafts of chapters was far different from what I had expected to write. Reading the literature turned out to be very dangerous for a number of the beliefs that I had cherished and shared with various members of the Yale group with whom I identified.

It is no easy matter, even with Festinger's (1957) dissonance theory, to look back and put a finger on just what has been effective in changing one's professional beliefs and attitudes. In all probability, reading the historical literature to which I have alluded above helped prepare the way, for in re-reading the papers which Hebb had written in the mid-1940s on emotion and on fear as well as his book *Organization of Behavior,* they seemed far more congenial than they had seemed when I was reading them while I was Director of the Institute of Welfare Research. Earlier while I was at New York Psychiatric Institute, I had read Piaget's early works on the language and thought of children, their judgment and reasoning, their conceptions of the world and of causality, and I had given them up as a blind alley. Of his books newly translated in the 1950s those on the origin of intelligence and the construction of reality had made an impression, but I continued to consider myself a Hullian behavior theorist.

In all likelihood, as the experience I shall now relate would indicate, it was probably loyalty to the colleagues with whom I had been identified in psychological theory making that inhibited a more gradual attitudinal shift as I absorbed the information already mentioned. Actually the attitudinal transition was dramatic, and it came with a relatively minor bit of information in which I happened to have a great deal of faith based on my relationship with the investigator who produced it.

Shortly after I became director of the Institute of Welfare Research in New York, a young man by the name of Seymour Levine came to my office to report the results of a study of early experience which he had made while yet an undergraduate at the University of Denver. He was about to enter graduate school at New York University. We agreed to collaborate, but other commitments crowded the agreement out of our schedules. By the time I got to Illinois, he had completed his doctorate, done a year or two as an applied experimental psychologist in Air Force research, and was taking an internship in clinical psychology. As part of his internship, he decided to force rats into encounters with noxious experience during infancy. Both he and I expected that such traumatic experience would interfere with their later adaptive or learning ability. While in Chicago I visited his project in the laboratory at the Michael Reese Hospital. Other investigators had found that handling rat pups in infancy while their eyes and ears were still closed made them as adults less "timid" and "emotional" than their litter-mate controls left continually in the nest. Levine, Chevalier, and Korchin undertook to compare in rats the effects of electrical shock associated with handling, and remaining in the nest till weaning time at twenty days of age on the amount of defecating in a strange situation and on the number of trials required to learn to avoid shock when their subjects became approximately sixty days old. Surprisingly, the group left in the nest defecated more and required substantially more trials to learn to avoid shock than did both those shocked and those handled in infancy. The number of trials for the latter two groups differed little. In later studies, Levine found that rats shocked in infancy were, as adults, more ready to drink water in a strange situation following eighteen hours without it than were either those petted or those left in the nest. These results, which were later confirmed, seemed to me to be diametrically opposite to what one would expect from either the trauma theory of psychoanalysis or the Pavlovian conditioning of behavior theory. As I was reading the prepublications of the Levine studies and considering the findings in relation to some of the other evidence I had at hand, the immensity of the implications struck me. If I was wrong in the conditioning theory of fear, which I had strongly believed and which I considered to be implicit in the trauma theory of psychoanalysis, was I wrong in many of my other beliefs? Since the welfare of children was concerned, it seemed infinitely more important to be correct than it would be were it merely a matter of academic argument. The emotional impact of this realization set me on a hike over the mountain trails. On this hike, I vowed I would indeed follow the scientist's code to hold any beliefs I might have very lightly while seeking the implications of the evidence in the literature. This was an emotional resolve probably not unlike those reported in connection with religious conversions. The way loyalty to a group may interfere with smooth information processing is illustrated in a dream that I had the following night. In this dream, I was crossing Cedar Street in front of the Yale Institute of Human Relations in New Haven, Connecticut. I was walking toward a Model T Ford which was parked on the curb opposite. It was a Ford such as I had driven from the farm on which I grew up to high school in Scottsbluff, Nebraska. As I reached the car and turned back to wave goodbye to those standing in front of the Institute, I had a strong sense of ominous anxiety. Standing there were John Dollard, Neil Miller, Hobart Mowrer, and Robert Sears, my reference group for psychological theory. As the anxiety wakened me, I recalled the resolve of the previous afternoon. Then the humor of the dream struck me. The information I had been absorbing from the evidence in the literature was clearly taking me away from those beliefs which had given me the sense of security which comes from sharing beliefs with a reference group. Such a sense of security appears to be a fundamental motive underlying membership in a church or a political party. Holding to such membership, however, can restrict the process of taking in and elaborating on information until that information accumulates to force a dramatic change.

The alterations in my theoretical beliefs during the summer of 1956 resulted in substantial changes in my graduate course in personality. Moreover, as the department at the University of Illinois had then no graduate course in developmental psychology, Lyle Lanier and I agreed that I should give one in place of my course in psychopathology. This was a boon inasmuch as it permitted work on what I then thought was to become a book on behavioral science and child rearing as part of my teaching. Never before had I been able to view what I was investigating as a major share of the domain for which I was responsible in my teaching assignments.

The plan for the proposed book on behavior science and child rearing was to continue with the role of experience in the development of competence which I then saw as a kind of amalgam of intelligence and motivation. Scrutiny of the literature on intelligence during the year brought gradually another change in belief. I had more or less accepted the view that experience can produce substantial modifications in motivation, but only slight ones in intelligence as assessed by the standard tests. As I examined the literature, however, I became convinced that these views were historical vestiges of earlier teachings and were no longer consonant with the accumulating evidence of plasticity in psychological development. It seemed to me that Francis Galton's deduction of fixed traits from the survival conception of evolution formulated by his cousin, Charles Darwin, was quite unnecessary. Yet that deduction coupled with the need to have the measurements of individuals stay put appeared to have been highly instrumental in perpetuating a belief in fixed traits and especially in fixed intelligence. Abetting this view was the belief in "predetermined development" deriving from G. Stanley Hall's faith in recapitulation. The implications of Hall's view had been buttressed by the results of Coghill's early studies of behavioral development in such lower amphibious vertebrates as the tadpoles of salamanders and frogs. Coghill saw the development in behavioral patterns as completely dependent upon neuroanatomical maturation which he thought he could detect through the microscope. Such a view of behavioral development was nicely consonant with the nativistic views of Gestalt psychology. Highly dissonant with such a view, however, were various lines of evidence. It seemed to me that findings from behavioristic method had destroyed the dichotomy between unlearned and learned behavior. Moreover, beginning with the "symbolic processes" of Hunter, and progressing through the "pure-stimulus act" of Hull, the "response-produced stimuli" of Miller and Dollard, and the "central mediating processes" of Osgood, behavioristic method had been gradually undoing the peripheralism of behavioristic theory and making a larger and larger place for the central processes deriving from experience or information processing. Such a reinterpretation seemed to me to get substantial support from the evidence for learning sets in Harlow's work, and from the effects of early perceptual experience on later problem solving to be found in the studies from the McGill laboratory deriving from Hebb's (1949) theorizing. The evidence of a hierarchy of concepts and skills in the work on adult problem solving by Robert Gagné as well as that evidence from Piaget's observations of the development in his own children seemed clearly to make this line of interpretation which I had derived from animal studies directly relevant for human intelligence. When I found a substantial number of studies yielding evidence highly dissonant with Cattell's prediction of "a galloping plunge toward intellectual bankruptcy" from the fact that a disproportionate share of each new generation derives from people in the lower socioeconomic classes with lower than average IQs, it seemed to me that the whole story hung together quite well. Yet I was still troubled by the correlational evidence for the heritability index and by the meaning of the factor analytic evidence. In the summer of 1957, I put this story together in what I expected then to be merely a chapter for the book-to-be on behavior science and child rearing, but the piece went to well over two hundred triple-spaced pages.

The next chapter in the plan was to concern motivation. During the academic year 1957–1958, I devoted all of my spare time to reading in this domain. I re-read the papers of Neil Miller, with which I was already familiar, read the complete file of papers in the Nebraska Symposia on Motivation, read Kelley's book on personal constructs and saw the parallel between his view of motivation and that of Carl Rogers, got excited about Old's discovery of a physiological mechanism of reward through direct stimulation of the brain, re-read Hebb's studies of fear, studied the long series of papers by Berlyne and by Montgomery along with those of Harlow and his collaborators, re-read the work on the achievement motive by McClelland and his collaborators, and re-read Helson on the adaptation level. I also searched historically for the roots of both drive theory and the physiological theory of arousal. In physiological terms, drive theory seemed to go back through the work of Walter B. Cannon to that of Claude Bernard, but conceptually it went back through Freud to Schopenhauer and the romantic revolution against rationalism in the late eighteenth and early nineteenth centuries. I accumulated a lot of notes and a fair store of information which ultimately got published as "Toward a History of Intrinsic Motivation" (Hunt, 1971).

Perhaps I should have read less, for the conceptual substance would not jell. Whereas I had gone to Estes Park the year before with a fairly clear imaginary outline of what I could say about intelligence, I had no such outline for the topic of motivation. I forced one, wrote about a hundred pages on the basis of it, then the organization fell apart. I forced another and wrote some more, then another and wrote some more. The result, not all in 1958, was 400 or 500 pages, but leading off in various directions.

The year 1958–1959 brought me a sabbatical semester, which I entered in an unhappy frame of mind. I was distressed by failing to get together the manuscript of the book on behavioral science and child rearing that I had promised Don Young and the Russell Sage Foundation. Even though the topic of motivation had frustrated me, I could not give up trying somehow to make it jell. Except for two or three weeks devoted to writing a presentation for the dedication of the Hunter Laboratory at Brown University, which brought honorary doctorates of science to those of us who had been there in the 1930s, I persisted. With the impetus coming from invitations to present a paper at the Eleventh Annual Institute in Psychiatry and Neurology of the Veterans Administration at Little Rock, Arkansas, and colloquia for the department of psychology at Vanderbilt and the department of psychiatry at the Colorado Medical School, I put together a paper which I entitled "Experience and the Development of Motivation, Some Reinterpretations" (Hunt, 1960). In this paper I began to separate the topic into what I call the motivation questions, to explain the limitations of drive theory and the notions of conditioned fear and anxiety, and to offer a supplementary notion of motivation in terms of the incongruity-dissonance principle. I had found this principle illustrated in diverse ways in the writings of Festinger, Hebb, Helson, Kelley, Piaget, and Rogers. The closing sentence was: "Perhaps the task of developing proper motivation is best seen, at least in nutshell form, as limiting the manipulation of extrinsic factors to that minimum of keeping homeostatic need and exteroceptive drive low, in favor of facilitating basic information-processing to maximize accurate anticipation of reality" (Hunt, 1960, p. 504). In retrospect, the picture presented was amorphous, but I still like that last sentence.

Having failed to get out the major work during my semester of sabbatical in 1958, I sought a Fellowship for Senior Scientists from the Commonwealth Fund in New York with a plan to write a book on the development of *intelligence and motivation.* When it became clear at the end of 1959 that I would have too much manuscript for one book and that what I had to say about motivation had still failed to jell, I decided to limit the work to intelligence. I revised and elaborated the chapter I had written on the role of experience in the development of intelligence during the summer of 1957. The result was *Intelligence and Experience,* which appeared in 1961. I sent it to the Ronald Press with a good deal of foreboding about the reaction of colleagues, but negative reactions failed to appear. Moreover, people who should know have told me that this book had some influence with the Kennedy-Johnson administrations in the early 1960s. Along with Michael Harrington's *The Other America,* and Kenneth B. Clark's *Dark Ghetto,* these people have said that it was a factor in the decision to launch Project Head Start. At heart much of the optimism of the late nineteenth century about the perfectibility of man and human society remains with me, so such reports were gratifying. Although the unrealistic goals for Head Start created dangers of an oversell that could lead to an overkill, which in 1967 I described in an invited address before Psi Chi (Hunt, 1969, Chapter 5), I believe the ferment created by Project Head Start has been basically positive, and I hope it will continue to be so in the future.

The publication of *Intelligence and Experience* had other consequences for my life. It got me tagged as an environmentalist. It has also got me so involved in early childhood education that it has been impossible to complete the books I began.

The tag of environmentalist I resent. If tags are necessary, I prefer that of *interactionist.* To be sure I have emphasized the importance of the circumstances encountered early in life for both the rate and the ultimate level of behavioral development. To be sure I have emphasized the evidence of a broad norm-of-reaction in the achievement of competence. I have pointed out the evidence indicating that both plasticity and the norm of reaction for competence increase up the evolutionary scale with what Donald Hebb has termed the A/S ratio which I prefer to call the intrinsic/extrinsic ratio (see Hunt, 1963a). Yet, never have I denied the importance of heredity. Rather, I have contended that the higher the quality of the genotype in whatever it is that influences intelligence, the larger will be the norm of reaction (Hunt, 1961, pp. 323–336; 1969, Chapter 5). Thus, if one of a pair of identical twin mongoloids and one of a pair of typical identical twin infants were reared in an orphanage with a child-caretaker ratio of the order of 10 to 1 while the other identical twin in each case was reared in the fashion that Myrtle McGraw reared her trained twin, Johnny, the difference in mental age between the identical twins in each pair would be much less for the mongoloid than for the typical children. From this standpoint, in other words, the genotype determines the cumulative degree of effect which the successive environmental encounters in life can have on measured intelligence and upon competence. It seems to me that the relationship between heredity and environment in development and the concept of interactionism are probably the most poorly understood of any in the lexicon of psychology.

Here I am supposed to be focused on my professional odyssey. This debate is a side issue. Yet its coming in illustrates how hard it is to avoid the debates which take up time and energy once what one has said chances to be controversial.

In 1960, the Carnegie Corporation approved an application for a grant to pay my summer salary to get on with what I hoped would be a book entitled *Motivation and Experience.* I did get on with the formulation of eight separate motivational questions, saw what I thought for a time was a clear picture of what I called

"Motivation Inherent in Information Processing and Action" (Hunt, 1963a), and intrinsic motivation with a central role in psychological development (Hunt, 1965). Later results from the dissertations of my own students showed that I could not consider "incongruity," my central concept, to be generic. In all I got together nearly a thousand pages of first-draft manuscript, but they failed to hang together as a proper theory. Even so, various portions which appeared to be relatively clear have been separately published (see Hunt, 1963b, 1966, 1971a, 1971b) upon invitations to give papers or write chapters on motivation.

In the meantime, those tentative new beliefs achieved while examining the literature have suggested investigations. After 1960, I began wanting more time for these and my theoretical synthesis than the two or so months of each summer. I am indebted to Wayne Holtzman for suggesting that I see Bert Boothe, Chief of the Fellowship Section of the National Institute of Mental Health, about applying for one of the Research Career Awards. When Dr. Boothe encouraged me, I applied and my application was approved. I hope my productivity justifies the judgment of the Fellowship Committee. It has motivated me, and it perhaps has even exaggerated the most troublesome quirk in my character, which is to find it too easy to formulate hypotheses and plans without foreseeing all the time and effort required to see them through. Without the interest and collaborative help of ex-students, my productivity would have been far less. Two of these collaborations deserve special mention.

Dissatisfaction with the longitudinal prediction implied in the IQ together with the idea inspired by Piaget's observations that it should be feasible to construct ordinal scales of psychological development prompted me to talk a good deal about this possibility of ordinal scales while I was working on *Intelligence and Experience.* Ina C. Uzgiris, then one of my graduate students completing her doctorate, got interested. We applied for and got a grant from the National Institute of Mental Health for the purpose. Five years of work, in which she especially worked ingeniously through successive approximations of ordinality, resulted in a set of six ordinal scales and six sound-cinemas, one illustrating each scale (Uzgiris and Hunt, 1968). Although these scales have been or are being used in approximately a score of investigations, they still exist only as mimeographed prepublications. At this writing, however, the manuscript of the monograph describing them and the investigations leading to them is about to go to press (Uzgiris and Hunt, 1974).

The other line of empirical investigation concerns the consistency of trait-indicators across situations. Its inception goes back to 1940 at a meeting of some personologists who then gathered fairly regularly in New England. R. B. Cattell reported with disappointment the low agreement among raters of the personality traits of their acquaintances. Remembering how camp counselors would disagree about the characteristics of campers from seeing them in different kinds of situations, I contended that such low agreement would be expected. Cattell disagreed. Driving back to Providence after the debate, I found myself formulating a lecture which I gave next morning and for some fourteen years thereafter to classes in my personality course. It did not occur to me to do more than present the argument until Alvin J. Rosenstein, who had heard that lecture once before and once after two years in the Army devoted to social research, noted upon the second hearing that the idea had the basis for an inventory. In planning his doctoral thesis on the effects of anxiety on performance, he was searching for instruments with which to assess anxiety. Within about two hours after he came to my house with his idea, we constructed what became the first version of the S-R (Situation-Reaction) Inventory of Anxiousness. Rosenstein gave this instrument to some sixty-seven undergraduates serving as his subjects. Although he scored it and used the scores, it was not till about a year later that Norman S. Endler, who had completed his dissertation early, undertook the almost endless calculations of the statistical analyses required. After obtaining data from a second sample of subjects and analyzing them, the result became first a monograph (Endler, Hunt, and Rosenstein, 1962) and then a program of research showing that the largest contributors to the variance in indicators of anxiousness are the interactions: situations with persons, persons with responses, and situations with responses (Endler and Hunt, 1966), and the triple interactions (Endler and Hunt, 1968a). By giving several versions of the S-R Inventory of Anxiety to samples of individuals varying in age and social status, we demonstrated that our estimates of the sizes of the contributions from the various sources of variance could be generalized (Endler and Hunt, 1969). Generalizability across traits, for example, from anxiety to hostility, is limited (Endler and Hunt, 1968b). Moreover, focusing on indicators of a trait-like anxiety in the specific criterion situations increases the validity correlation of inventory scores with behavioral criteria from those typically of the order of .2 for omnibus inventories to coefficients of the order of .6 or .7 for those with situations specified (D'Zurilla, 1964; Paul, 1966). In other words, people can report with considerable accuracy on the way they respond in specific situations.

The original monograph reported that situations contribute about eleven times as much of the variance as do persons. This was based on the ratio of mean squares to which Endler had objected as a false way to partition variance. When an outstanding statistical authority approved such a ratio, however, I overruled him at the time of our publication. After publication, he persisted. He had a hard time convincing me that he had been correct, but he did, and we finally corrected the matter (Endler and Hunt, 1966). It pays to listen to students and ex-students; all too often their judgment or knowledge surpasses that of their teachers.

My personal program of theoretical synthesis and investigation was interrupted by an involvement with early childhood education growing out of my writing on intelligence. In the early fall of 1962, Martin Deutsch, who was then Director of the Institute for Developmental Studies then at New York Medical College, was organizing an Arden House conference on preschool enrichment for socially disadvantaged children. Having read *Intelligence and Experience,* he invited me to give the first presentation which became the paper entitled "The Psychological Basis for Using Pre-School Enrichment as an Antidote for Cultural Deprivation" (Hunt, 1964b). This quickly written paper has appeared in more than a dozen anthologies and appears to have been instrumental in bringing more invitations to talk on the topic than I could possibly accept.

The big interruption, however, began in 1966. The preceding year I had decided that the topic of motivation and experience was like a proverbial pot that will not boil while being watched. I had decided to give up for a time, and to turn to a book on early experience which would bring my work in that domain up to date.

In Estes Park during the summer of 1965, I put together drafts of five chapters, about half of the intended content, had a seminar on the topic in the fall, then devoted myself to a collaboration with Ina Uzgiris on our sound-cinemas in the spring of 1966. In the summer of 1966, I went to Tehran to get under way the investigation of how effective auditory and visual enrichments contingent upon self-initiated efforts would be in preventing the retardation and apathy that Wayne Dennis had in 1957 found there in orphanage-reared infants. After returning via the International Congress at Moscow, I fully expected to return to the book on early experience. About the first of October, however, Joseph Califano, Chief of Lyndon B. Johnson's staff of advisers at the White House, asked me to chair a Task Force to recommend what the role of the federal government should be in early child development. I hesitated until John Gardner, an old friend from days at both Brown and New York who was then Secretary of the Department of Health, Education, and Welfare, told me that it was important and that I should do this job. The roster of this Task Force included an anthropologist, pediatricians, psychiatrists, social workers, and six psychologists (Jerome S. Bruner, Urie Bronfenbrenner, Susan Gray, Nicholas Hobbs, Lois B. Murphy, and myself).

Following the first meeting, I went home in a quandary about how to get people with such disparate assumptions and languages to come up with a coherent document. At a second meeting, we formulated a series of questions and hit upon the device of having each member of the group write out answers to these questions. A scrutiny of the answers brought out a surprising degree of agreement despite the differences. In the course of some six one-day-long or two-day-long meetings, we came up with a series of documents from which, during the first three weeks of December—with the help of members of the Civil-Service staff from the Bureau of the Budget and the Children's Bureau—I got together a draft of our report entitled "A Bill of Rights for Children." The Summary portion was then submitted to President Johnson's staff in the White House, and the whole document was circulated to the members of the Task Force for emendations over the Christmas holidays. In January of 1967, I lived for several days on the telephone, long distance, discussing emendations and shaping them for incorporation within the document. Once they were incorporated, Mrs. Bonnie B. Stone, my secretary, got her Washington baptism at the Bureau of the Budget seeing these emendations through the process of incorporation into the document for the White House.

Throughout this process, those on this Task Force were requested to keep the contents of our discussions completely confidential. A great deal of satisfaction came with reading President Johnson's message to Congress for February 8, 1967. It contained two of our most important recommendations: (1) an extension of the Project Head Start upward in the age range as the Follow-Through Program and (2) an extension of the project downward in the age range through the establishment of a limited number of Parent and Child Centers. These two recommendations were accepted, but their success is still uncertain and the effort to learn from evaluative studies has been woefully inadequate. We also recommended the establishment of the Office for Children to be administered by someone reporting directly to the Secretary of Health, Education, and Welfare. This recommendation has been implemented by President Nixon, but perhaps without his knowledge that it was earlier recommended to President Johnson.

For reasons unexplained, our document *A Bill of Rights for Children* remained confidential until it, along with the reports of other task forces on aspects of education were released during a symposium on education in January of 1972 at the Johnson Library on the campus of the University of Texas in Austin.

Another part of the interruption of my personal program came almost simultaneously. Within a day or two after my return from Tehran and Moscow, I got a call from the Office of Education asking me to become a member of an *ad hoc* committee with the task of choosing the centers to be incorporated into a new National Laboratory for Early Childhood Education. Since the appeal came from Marian Sherman whom I had already known as a Brown classmate and good friend of my daughter, Judith, I accepted, albeit somewhat reluctantly. At the meeting, I wondered aloud whether it would be possible to create a collaborative amalgamation of established centers in universities with on-going programs under the direction of established investigators. When it was made clear that this was the plan, I went along, but with strong doubts. Yet, when, during the work of my Task Force, I was invited to become the Chairman of the National Advisory Board, my involvement with the welfare of children had grown to such proportions that I accepted.

When the Office of Education decided to locate the Coordination Center at the University of Illinois, I questioned whether my serving as Director of the Advisory Board might not imply a conflict of interest. When I was reassured by both representatives of the Office and representatives of the University, I went along. With the work of the Task Force completed, the failure to find a Director for the Coordination Center resulted in a request for me to change roles and become that Director. At the time, it seemed that the purpose of this National Laboratory was so close to that of my Research Career Award, that it might be feasible to combine them. When Bert Boothe in the Fellowship Branch gave me permission to try the office for a year or two, I accepted.

I should have known better. I should have recognized the wisdom of my original questioning of whether it would be possible to establish a collaborative relationship among established centers in universities with on-going programs. Yet, the idea of a program of national scope focused on early childhood education was exciting, and for some months following March 1967, I had myself convinced that one might gradually achieve coordination among such a group of already established individual programs with a focus on the central issues which would broaden greatly the sampling possibilities and the generalizability of results obtained from the single centers. But this effort involved far more than merely writing a report as a basis for recommendations which the President could use in a message to the Congress. It got down to the nitty-gritty of agreement about how to formulate hypotheses, about how to evaluate programs, about which hypotheses to investigate, and about which innovations to launch. The investigators in each established center already had under way what they wanted to do. Even so, it seemed that theoretical leadership and persuasion might gradually produce a common focus. But there was another strong element in the situation consisting of an advisory board. The National Advisory Board was created to prevent the leaders of the established centers from becoming a pool of mutual support. Men and women of experience and wisdom accepted membership on this Advisory Board, and they came to the meetings. Late in that year, however, it became clear that the directorship of the Coordination Center of this National Laboratory would absorb all of my time with problems of organization and persuasion, and leave none for either theoretical synthesis or empirical investigation. During the spring of 1968, I helped find a new director, and took a place on the Advisory Board where what I observed indicated that my original qualms were well founded. I returned to my program of theoretical synthesis and empirical investigation concerned with the role of early experience in the development of intelligence and motivation, but this program now also includes early childhood education.

This intellectual and professional odyssey is incomplete. Although the calendar puts me among the senior citizens, I still feel like a young man who might possibly do something important some day. I have under way two programs of empirical investigation. One is concerned with the effectiveness of auditory and visual enrichments tied to the self-initiated actions of infants in preventing the retardation associated with orphanage rearing. This project is under way at the Orphanage of the Farah Pahlavi Foundation in Tehran where my collaborator is Professor Khossrow Mohandessi, who was once a student in my graduate courses at the University of Illinois. As part of this same project, a collaboration with John Paraskevopoulos in Athens has shown that the child-caretaker ratio in orphanage rearing has substantial effect on the ages at which children achieve the successive levels of object permanence and vocal imitation defined by the scales that Uzgiris and I have developed (Paraskevopoulos and Hunt, 1971). For instance, the average ages at which children achieve that level of object construction at which they can follow an object through one hidden displacement varies from 33 months in an orphanage where there are approximately 10 children for each caretaker to just under 22 months for children in an orphanage where there are only about 3 children for each caretaker. Ordinal scales provide landmarks and levels of psychological development which permit one to use age as the dependent variable and differing conditions of rearing as the independent variable. In a Parent and Child Center, David Schickedanz and I have found that eight successive babies from families of poverty, all of whom have had the advantage of a special enrichment program, have achieved this landmark of following an object through one hidden displacement before they are a year old.

In another program under way at the University of Illinois, Girvin E. Kirk and I have developed several criterion-referenced tests of semantic mastery (color, position, shape, and number) which we believe to be taken for granted in children coming to school. We have found that four year olds in a Head Start program can process both color and position information perceptually as well as children who have a middle-class background and are in nursery school. Yet these Head Start children show far less semantic mastery as either speakers or listeners than do the nursery schoolers, and they commonly fail to incorporate color and placement information in requests (e.g., give me the blue block) to another child, whereas the nursery schoolers manage such communications almost perfectly. Head Start children, however, vary widely. We hope to determine how the within-family communication patterns for those with high and low communication ability differ. We also hope to identify a series of the landmarks in the development of ability to communicate which may enable us to develop an ordinal scale of communicative ability which can help to guide the teaching of such ability.

The student disturbances of 1968–1969 convinced me that no one should hold a professorship in a university without trying to communicate with undergraduates. I have returned to giving a course in developmental psychology for undergraduates. I am also continuing to work on my book on early experience. Once it is finished, I still hope to find a conceptual structure for human motivation that will enable me to do the book which I had in view a decade ago.

This odyssey, I repeat, is incomplete. I like what I am trying to do. While I was about Columbia University as a National Research Council Fellow, I came to know Robert S. Woodworth. He worked throughout his eighth and ninth decades. He completed his last book somewhat after he became ninety. I would that Fate had something similar in store for me.

REFERENCES

1931 With J. P. Guilford. Some further experimental tests of McDougall's theory of introversion-extroversion. *Journal of Abnormal and Social Psychology, 26,* 324–332.

1933 With J. P. Guilford. Fluctuation of an ambiguous figure in dementia praecox and in manic depressive patients. *Journal of Abnormal and Social Psychology, 27,* 443–452.

1935 (a) A functional study of observation. *American Journal of Psychology, 47,* 1–39.
(b) Psychological loss in paretics and schizophrenics. *American Journal of Psychology, 47,* 458–463.

1936 (a) Psychological experiments with disordered persons. *Psychological Bulletin, 33,* 1–58.
(b) Psychological government and the high variability of schizophrenic patients. *American Journal of Psychology, 48,* 64–81.
(c) A preliminary study of some psychological effects of thyroid medication in schizophrenic patients. *Journal of Psychology, 2,* 367–376.

1938 An instance of the social origin of conflict resulting in psychoses. *American Journal of Orthopsychiatry, 8,* 158–164.

1939 (a) With H. Schlosberg. General activity in the male white rat. *Journal of Comparative Psychology, 28,* 23–38.
(b) With H. Schlosberg. The influence of illumination upon general activity in normal, blinded and castrated male white rats. *Journal of Comparative Psychology, 28,* 285–298.
(c) With R. R. Willoughby. The effect of frustration on hoarding in rats. *Psychosomatic Medicine, 1,* 309–310.

1940 With I. C. Nichols. A case of partial bilateral frontal lobectomy: A psychopathological study. *American Journal of Psychiatry, 96,* 1063–1083.

1941 (a) The effects of infant feeding-frustration upon adult hoarding in the albino rat. *Journal of Abnormal and Social Psychology, 36,* 338–360.
(b) With R. O. Fleischer. A communicable method of recording areas in the Rorschach Test. *American Journal of Psychology, 54,* 580–581.
(c) With J. T. Evans. The "emotionality" of rats. *American Journal of Psychology, 55,* 528–545.
(d) With R. L. Solomon. The stability and some correlates of group-status in a summer-camp of young boys. *American Journal of Psychology, 55,* 33–45.

1943 How men meet defeat. In E. G. Boring and Marjorie Van de Water (eds.), *Psychology for the Fighting Man.* New York: Penguin (Special 212), pp. 312–321.

1944 (a) (Ed.) *Personality and the Behavior Disorders.* (2 vols.) New York: Ronald.
(b) With C. N. Cofer. Psychological deficit. In J. McV. Hunt (ed.),

Personality and the Behavior Disorders. New York: Ronald, Vol. II, pp. 971–1032.

1945 With W. S. Hunter and H. Schlosberg. Raymond Royce Willoughby: 1896–1944. *Psychological Review, 52,* 113–115.

1946 (a) Experimental psychoanalysis. In P. L. Harriman (ed.), *Encyclopedia of Psychology.* New York: Philosophical Library, pp. 140–156.
(b) With H. Schlosberg, R. L. Solomon, and E. Stellar. The effects of infantile feeding-frustration on adult hoarding in white rats. *Psychological Cinema Register,* Supplement to No. 5, Film PCR-86.

1947 (a) Measuring the effects of social case work. *Transactions of the New York Academy of Sciences,* Series II, *9*(3), 78–88.
(b) With H. Schlosberg, R. L. Solomon, and E. Stellar. Studies of the effects of infantile experience on adult behavior in rats. I. Effects of infantile feeding frustration on adult hoarding. *Journal of Comparative and Physiological Psychology, 40,* 291–304.

1948 (a) A discussion of "Failures in social casework," by Lucile Austin. In P. H. Hoch (ed.), *Failures in Psychiatric Treatment.* New York: Grune & Stratton, pp. 216–223.
(b) Measuring movement in casework. *Journal of Social Casework, 29,* 343–351.
(c) Personality. *Collier's Encyclopedia.* New York: P. F. Collier, Vol. 15, pp. 575–579.
(d) Technical methods of research. In *Research in Social Work: A Report of the Workshop on Research in Social Work* (June 16–20, 1947). Cleveland, Ohio: Western Reserve University, School of Applied Sciences, pp. 9–14.

1949 (a) Measuring social work results: Researchers at CSS seek answers to service questions of long standing. *Better Times: New York City's Welfare News Weekly, 30*(36), 1–2, 8.
(b) The problem of measuring the results of psychotherapy. *Psychological Service Center Journal, 1,* 122–135.
(c) A social agency as a setting for research—The Institute of Welfare Research. *Journal of Consulting Psychology, 13,* 69–81.

1950 (a) Editorial. *Journal of Abnormal and Social Psychology, 45,* 3–6. (On journal policy.)
(b) A memorandum to all psychologists in New York State. *Bulletin of the New York State Psychological Association, 3* (2), 1.
(c) *New York State Psychological Association: Its Functions and Purposes.* New York: Bulletin of the New York State Psychological Association.
(d) Year-end report of NYSPA president to all psychologists in New York State. *Bulletin of the New York State Psychological Association, 3* (3), 1, 3.

(e) With L. S. Kogan. *Measuring Results in Social Casework: A Manual on Judging Movement.* New York: Family Service Association of America.

(f) With Margaret Blenkner and L. S. Kogan. *Testing Results in Social Casework: A Field-test of the Movement Scale.* New York: Family Service Association of America.

(g) With L. S. Kogan. Problems of multi-judge reliability. *Journal of Clinical Psychology, 6,* 16–19.

(h) With L. S. Kogan. The need for psychological theory in evaluating the results of psychotherapy. *Psychological Service Center Journal, 2,* 77–82.

(i) With Margaret Blenkner and L. S. Kogan. A field-test of the Movement Scale. *Social Casework, 31,* 267–277.

(j) With H. Schlosberg. Behavior of rats in continuous conflict. *Journal of Comparative and Physiological Psychology, 43,* 351–357.

1951 (a) With Margaret Blenkner and L. S. Kogan. A study of interrelated factors in the initial interview with new clients. *Social Casework, 32.*

(b) With Wilma Winnick. The effect of an extra stimulus upon strength of response during acquisition and extinction. *Journal of Experimental Psychology, 41,* 205–215.

(c) The nature of the traces of early experience. In J. P. Scott (ed.), *Minutes of the Conference on the Effects of Early Experience on Mental Health* (September 6–9, 1951). Bar Harbor, Me.: Roscoe B. Jackson Memorial Laboratory, p. 13.

1952 (a) Toward an integrated program of research on psychotherapy. *Journal of Consulting Psychology, 16,* 237–246.

(b) Psychological services in the tactics of psychological science. *American Psychologist, 7,* 608–622.

(c) With E. Stellar, H. Schlosberg, and R. L. Solomon. The effect of illumination on hoarding behavior. *Journal of Comparative and Physiological Psychology, 45,* 504–507.

(d) With N. Kogan and L. S. Kogan. Expansion and extension of use of the Movement Scale. *Social Casework, 33,* 10–12.

1953 (a) The American Psychological Foundation. *American Psychologist, 8,* 740–741.

(b) With L. S. Kogan and Phyllis F. Bartelme. *A Follow-up Study of the Results of Social Casework.* New York: Family Service Association of America.

1955 Professional liability insurance for psychologists. *American Psychologist, 10,* 243–244.

1956 (a) Comments on Scientifically predicting and understanding human behavior, by Ernest Dichter, in R. H. Cole (ed.), *Consumer Behavior and Motivation.* Urbana: *University of Illinois Bulletin, 53* (45), pp. 38–41.

(b) Walter Samuel Hunter: 1889–1954. *Psychological Review, 63,* 213–217.

1957 (a) Foreword to *The Three Faces of Eve,* by C. H. Thigpen and H. M. Cleckley. New York: McGraw-Hill.

(b) What is a community mental health program like? In *Proceedings of the Mental Health Workshop for Psychologists and Social Workers* (May 14–15, 1957). Phoenix: Arizona State Department of Health, pp. 1–23.

(c) With R. C. Beck, T. N. Ewing, and L. J. Cronbach. *Interpersonal Perception and Interpersonal Relationships in Therapeutic Counseling.* First Annual Report, Contract Nonr–1834 (11), Group Psychology Branch, Office of Naval Research. Urbana: University of Illinois Department of Psychology and Student Counseling Service.

1958 With Marie-Louise Wakeman Cole and Eva E. S. Reis. Situational cues distinguishing anger, fear, and sorrow. *American Journal of Psychology, 71,* 136–151.

1959 (a) Comments. In E. A. Rubinstein and M. B. Parloff (eds.), *Research in Psychotherapy.* Washington, D.C.: American Psychological Association, pp. iii, 58, 119, 123, 221, 273–275.

(b) Comments (entitled Wertheim: What about fathers?) on a joint-interview technique with mother and child, by Eleanor S. Wertheim, *Children, 6,* 78.

(c) Christmas with mother. Comments. In S. W. Standal and R. J. Corsini (eds.), *Critical Incidents in Psychotherapy.* New York: Prentice-Hall, pp. 202–205, 110–111, 138–139, 223–225, 280–283, 337–338.

(d) Gold Medal and Distinguished Scientific Writing Awards: American Psychological Foundation, *American Psychologist, 14,* 794–796.

(e) On the judgment of social workers as a source of information in social work research. In Ann W. Shyne (ed.), *Use of Judgments as Data in Social Work Research.* New York: National Association of Social Workers, pp. 38–53.

(f) With T. N. Ewing, R. LaForge, and W. M. Gilbert. An integrated approach to research on therapeutic counseling with samples of results. *Journal of Counseling Psychology, 6* (1), 46–54.

1960 Experience and the development of motivation: some reinterpretations. *Child Development, 31,* 489–504.

1961 (a) Suggestions for intervention and prevention with their rationale. Comments. In R. H. Ojemann (ed.), *Recent Research Looking Toward Preventive Intervention: Proceedings of the Third Institute on Preventive Psychiatry* (April 20–21, 1961). Iowa City: State University of Iowa, pp. 67–72, 85–86.

(b) *Intelligence and Experience.* New York: Ronald Press.

(c) With H. C. Quay. Early vibratory experience and the question of innate reinforcement value of vibration and other stimuli: a limitation on the discrepancy (burnt soup) principle in motivation. *Psychological Review, 68,* 149–156.

1962 (a) Comments on evoking change in psychotherapy. In H. H. Strupp and L. Luborsky (eds.), *Research in Psychotherapy, II.* Washington, D.C.: American Psychological Association, pp. 293–295.
(b) With N. S. Endler and A. J. Rosenstein. An S-R inventory of anxiousness. *Psychological Monographs, 76,* No. 17 (Whole No. 536), 1–33.

1963 (a) Motivation (and institutional management). In *Proceedings of the Second Conference on Institutional Management* (Urbana, April 25–27, 1963). Columbus: Ohio State University (for American Home Economics Association and American Dietetic Association), pp. 25–47.
(b) Motivation inherent in information processing and action. In O. J. Harvey (ed.), *Motivation and Social Interaction: The Cognitive Determinants.* New York: Ronald Press, pp. 35–94.
(c) Piaget's observations as a source of hypotheses concerning motivation. *Merrill-Palmer Quarterly of Behavior and Development, 9,* 263–275.
(d) With H. C. Haywood. Effects of epinephrine upon novelty preference and arousal. *Journal of Abnormal and Social Psychology, 67,* 206–213.

1964 (a) Przykłady modyfikacji teorii osobowośći przez wyniki baden. *Psychologia Wychowawcza* (Warsaw, Poland), 7 (21), 254–265. Translation of a paper entitled "Five instances where investigative observations are modifying personality theory," read at XVII International Congress of Psychology, Washington, D.C., August 25, 1963.
(b) Concerning the impact of group psychotherapy on psychology. *International Journal of Group Psychotherapy, 14,* 3–31.
(c) The implications of changing ideas on how children develop intellectually. *Children, 11,* 83–91.
(d) "Revisiting Montessori," Introduction to *The Montessori Method,* by Maria Montessori (1912 transl. by Anne E. George). New York: Schocken, pp. xi–xxxix.
(e) The psychological basis for using pre-school enrichment as an antidote for cultural deprivation. *Merrill-Palmer Quarterly of Behavior and Development, 10,* 209–248.
(f) With A. A. Salama. "Fixation" in the rat as a function of infantile shocking, handling, and gentling. *Journal of Genetic Psychology, 105,* 131–162.

1965 (a) Comments (entitled Hess-Shipman: room for all) on early blocks to children's learning, by R. H. Hess and Virginia Shipman (*Children, 12,* 189–194). *Children, 12,* 248.

(b) Intrinsic motivation and its role in psychological development. In D. Levine (ed.), *Nebraska Symposium on Motivation, 13,* 189–282. Lincoln: University of Nebraska Press.

(c) Traditional personality theory in the light of recent evidence. *American Scientist, 53,* 80–96.

(d) *What You Should Know about Educational Testing.* New York: Public Affairs Committee (Pamphlet No. 375).

1966 (a) The epigenesis of intrinsic motivation and early cognitive learning. In R. N. Haber (ed.), *Research in Motivation.* New York: Holt, Rinehart and Winston.

(b) Toward a theory of guided learning in development. In R. H. Ojemann and Karen Pritchett (eds.), *Giving Emphasis to Guided Learning.* Cleveland: Educational Rcsearch Council, pp. 98–160.

(c) With N. S. Endler. Sources of behavioral variance as measured by the S-R Inventory of Anxiousness. *Psychological Bulletin, 65* (6), 336–345.

(d) With Ina C. Uzgiris. An instrument for assessing infant psychological development. Mimeographed paper, Psychological Development Laboratory, University of Illinois, Urbana. (Prepublication.)

1967 (a) On fostering the development of intellectual competence. In R. C. Orem (ed.), *Montessori for the Disadvantaged.* New York: G. P. Putnam's Sons, pp. 54–64.

(b) With Ina C. Uzgiris. The development of visual pursuit and the permanence of objects (sound-cinema title: *Object Permanence*). Urbana: Motion Picture Production Center, University of Illinois.

(c) With Ina C. Uzgiris. The development of means for achieving desired environmental events (sound-cinema title: *Development of Means*). Urbana: Motion Picture Production Center, University of Illinois.

(d) With Ina C. Uzgiris. The development of gestural and vocal imitation (sound-cinema title: *Imitation,* Part 1, *Gestural;* Part 2, *Vocal*). Urbana: Motion Picture Production Center, University of Illinois.

(e) With Ina C. Uzgiris. The development of operational causality (sound-cinema title: *Operational Causality*). Urbana: Motion Picture Production Center, University of Illinois.

(f) With Ina C. Uzgiris. The development of object relations in space (sound-cinema title: *Object Relations in Space*). Urbana: Motion Picture Production Center, University of Illinois.

(g) With Ina C. Uzgiris. The development of schemas for relating to objects (sound-cinema title: *Development of Schemas*). Urbana: Motion Picture Production Center, University of Illinois.

1968 (a) Evolution of current concepts of intelligence and intellectual development. *American Montessori Society Bulletin, 6* (4).

(b) Toward the prevention of incompetence. In J. W. Carter, Jr. (ed.), *Research Contributions from Psychology to Community Mental Health.* New York: Behavioral Publications, pp. 19–45.
(c) Foreword to N. S. Endler, L. R. Boulter, and H. Osser (eds.), *Contemporary Issues in Developmental Psychology.* New York: Holt, Rinehart and Winston.
(d) With N. S. Endler. S-R Inventories of hostility and comparisons of the proportions of variance from persons, responses, and situations for hostility and anxiousness. *Journal of Personality and Social Psychology, 9* (4), 309–315.
(e) With N. S. Endler. Triple-interaction variance in the S-R Inventory of Anxiousness. *Perceptual and Motor Skills, 27,* 1098.
(f) Rip Van Winkle returns: Then and now. *The Clinical Psychologist, 22* (1), 7–11.
(g) With David Greenberg and Ina C. Uzgiris. Hastening the development of the blink-response with looking. *Journal of Genetic Psychology, 113,* 167–176.
(h) Conceptions of learning with implications for styles of teaching. In P. Olson (ed.), *Proceedings of the Conference of the Tri-University Project* (Denver, Colorado, September 19, 1967). Lincoln: University of Nebraska Press.
(i) With Ina C. Uzgiris. Ordinal scales of infant psychological development: Information concerning six demonstration films. Mimeographed paper, Psychological Development Laboratory, University of Illinois. (Prepublication.)

1969 (a) With N. S. Endler. Generalizability of contributions from sources of variance in the S-R Inventories of Anxiousness. *Journal of Personality, 37* (1), 1–24.
(b) The impact and limitations of the giant of developmental psychology. In D. Elkind and J. H. Flavell (eds.), *Studies in Cognitive Development: Essays in Honor of Jean Piaget.* New York: Oxford University Press, 3–66.
(c) Has compensatory education failed? Has it been attempted? *Harvard Educational Review, 39* (2), 278–300.
(d) Black genes—white environment. *TransAction, 6* (7), 12–22.
(e) Parent and Child Centers: One alternative model. *The Clinical Psychologist, 22* (2), 71–77.
(f) Potpourri and the Hall-Nebraska "model." *The Clinical Psychologist, 22* (3), 127–136.
(g) Graduate training: Some dissents and suggestions. *The Clinical Psychologist, 22* (4), 182–188.
(h) Kenneth S. Carlston. *Law Forum* (1), p. xiii.
(i) *The Challenge of Incompetence and Poverty: Papers on the Role of Early Education.* Urbana: University of Illinois Press.

1970 (a) Poverty versus equality of opportunity. In V. L. Allen, *Psychological Factors in Poverty.* Chicago: Markham, pp. 47–63.
(b) Attentional preference and experience: I. Introduction. *Journal of Genetic Psychology, 117,* 99–107.
(c) With Ina C. Uzgiris. Attentional preference and experience: II. An exploratory longitudinal study of the effect of visual familiarity and responsiveness. *Journal of Genetic Psychology, 117,* 109–121.
(d) With D. Greenberg and Ina C. Uzgiris. Attentional preference and experience: III. Visual familiarity and looking time. *Journal of Genetic Psychology, 117,* 123–135.

1971 (a) Parent and Child Centers: Their basis in the behavior and educational sciences. *American Journal of Orthopsychiatry, 41* (1), 13–38.
(b) Using intrinsic motivation to teach young children. *Educational Technology, 11* (2), 78–80.
(c) Intrinsic motivation: Information and circumstance. In H. M. Schroder and P. Suedfeld (eds.), *Personality Theory and Information Processing.* New York: Ronald Press, Chapter 4.
(d) Intrinsic motivation and psychological development. In H. M. Schroder and P. Suedfeld (eds.), *Personality Theory and Information Processing.* New York: Ronald Press, Chapter 5.
(e) Foreword. Edith H. Grotberg (ed.), *Day Care: Resources for Decisions.* Washington, D.C.: Research and Evaluation, Office of Planning, Office of Economic Opportunity (Pamphlet 6106–1), pp. vi–viii.
(f) Early childhood learning. In L. C. Deighton (ed.), *The Encyclopedia of Education,* Vol. 3. New York: Macmillan Co. and The Free Press, pp. 173–186.
(g) With G. E. Kirk. Social aspects of intelligence: Evidence and issues. In R. Cancro (ed.), *Intelligence: Genetic and Environmental Influences.* New York: Grune & Stratton, pp. 262–306.
(h) With T. D. Wachs and Ina C. Uzgiris. Cognitive development in infants of different age levels and from different environmental backgrounds: An exploratory investigation. *Merrill-Palmer Quarterly of Behavior and Development, 17* (4), 283–317.
(i) With J. Paraskevopoulos. Object construction and imitation under differing conditions of rearing. *Journal of Genetic Psychology, 119,* 301–321.

1972 (a) (Ed.) *Human Intelligence.* New Brunswick, N.J.: Transaction Books. (Distributed by E. P. Dutton & Co., New York.)
(b) Toward a history of intrinsic motivation. In H. I. Day, D. E. Berlyne, and D. E. Hunt (eds.), *Intrinsic Motivation: A New Direction in Education.* Ontario: Holt, Rinehart and Winston of Canada, Ltd.
(c) The shape of the needed investigation into the development of human competence. In R. C. Doll and Maxine Hawkins (eds.), *Educating the Disadvantaged.* New York: AMS Press, pp. 20–28.

(d) Psychological assessment in education and social class. In *The Legal and Educational Consequences of the Intelligence Testing Movement: Handicapped and Minority Group Children.* Columbia, Mo.: The University of Missouri, Proceedings of the Missouri Conference, pp. 7–33.

5

What Is the Question? What Is the Evidence?

ARTHUR R. JENSEN

WHAT KIND OF PSYCHOLOGIST AM I?

By a number of formal criteria I am properly classified as an educational psychologist, and I am more an educational psychologist now than I was five, ten, or fifteen years ago. But there are many kinds of educational psychologists doing all kinds of things, and so the label is not very descriptive of actual interests and work. To get a more precise idea of what I have been doing, I have tabulated those items in my bibliography that can be classified at all roughly into several broad categories, much as they would be classified in the *Psychological Abstracts,* with the following result.

General Topic	Per Cent
Human Learning and Memory	33
Intelligence and Other Abilities	24
Personality and Clinical	20
Educational Research	13
Human Behavioral Genetics	10

Surely the percentages will markedly change in the coming years. But I doubt that any new categories will be added. I think of a career as lasting at least forty years, and by this reckoning I am less than halfway along. Since I could not have predicted the

Sam Falk

course of my interests and activities thus far, I would not attempt to do so for more than the immediate future. One does not have complete freedom of choice in these matters anyway. The further one digs into a research problem, the more is the unexpected work that it generates and the more impossible it becomes to extricate one's interest and commitment. This is the position I find myself in with respect to my own present work. While I continue to enjoy viewing, as from the outside, many interesting and important developments in the behavioral sciences, I find it increasingly difficult to become very deeply involved with subjects other than the problems that continually grow out of my own research. Thus, except for pleasure reading (mostly biography and books about music and musicians), I read in psychology and related fields mostly what I think I must read, and I learn mainly what I must learn, in order to get on with the job at hand. Earlier in my career, I was influenced more by what others may have thought most interesting or important, or by what at any moment may have seemed more attractive. But now I find a certain inexplicable satisfaction in being more and more engrossed in the problems that arise out of my own research, and I doubt that I would be as happy without this rather introverted condition in my work. This may be desirable for a research worker. That it makes one an all around better professor, I am not sure, except for those few good graduate students who can profit from working with an engrossed and experienced researcher in the actual day-by-day problems of investigation.

APPRENTICESHIP

For me, at least, it is hard to recall anything that I learned in my courses as a graduate student at Columbia that later proved as valuable as what I acquired in this apprenticeship fashion, as a research assistant to the late Professor Percival M. Symonds. True, there is practically nothing in common between my current interests and orientation and Symonds's interests at that time. But it is really not the substantive aspect of the subject that is the most important thing one gets from a good professor. (One can get that by reading.) It is more a matter of acquiring certain general intellectual attitudes and work habits, of getting the benefit of many little practical "pointers," "know-how," and insights into psychological phenomena, and of being actively involved in the excitement of doing research alongside a mentor for whom this was apparently the main pleasure in life. These are the things I now most value from my association with Symonds. In retrospect, it seems to me Symonds was really more a learned scholar than an original investigative scientist. But the fact that his interests, his own research, and his whole approach to psychology at that time, so strongly influenced by psychoanalytic theory, were all nearly diametrically opposite to the paths I have come to prefer, now seems of little consequence. The lasting influences that have really mattered I could have gotten only from a dedicated scholar, and for that I have always felt indebted to Symonds. He is among the most admirable persons I have known. I have observed that outstanding persons, regardless of the differences in their particular specializations, generally have more in common with one another than with more mediocre persons who claim the same specialty.

Probably the most valuable piece of advice Symonds ever gave me was when I got my Ph.D. "If you want to become a researcher," he said, "don't be attracted by the best paying job you're offered at the outset. Don't get tied down to routine clinical work or heavy teaching assignments. Work a year or so with someone you're sure knows a lot more than you about doing research. Find the psychologist whose research is the most interesting to you and get a job in his lab." Symonds mentioned postdoctoral fellowships and suggested a couple of prominent psychologists I might consider; he offered to write to them on my behalf. But I was undecided about them; I knew their work; they were too much in the same vein as Symonds; and my own ideas about psychology, I felt, were already beginning to depart from Symonds's orientation. Besides, I still had a year's clinical internship ahead of me in which I could discover how best to proceed after that.

I never had the intention of becoming a psychological clinician as a career. I had wanted to become a professor and a researcher in some applied field of psychology—*applied* because of some general philosophical notions and ideals I had held since adolescence concerning how one should use his life in ways relevant to serving his fellow man. (For reasons that are only open to speculation, since my boyhood I had an overwhelming fascination with Mahatma Gandhi, whose writings influenced me considerably in my formative years, even to the point of becoming a vegetarian for a time!) The clinical field seemed the most obvious and likely for socially valuable research contributions, and I couldn't see being a researcher without first gaining some of the practical experience of a clinician. My graduate training and the work with Symonds had well prepared me for it, and it proved to be a valuable experience. There could have been no adequate substitute for seeing for myself the highly varied raw materials for psychological research that I was exposed to in the well-rounded internship provided by the Psychiatric Institute in Baltimore. But while it was all very interesting and instructive for me, I felt most dissatisfied with what clinical psychologists were actually doing. The usual diagnostic procedures and techniques, as well as the psychological theories which were the basis for the "dynamic" interpretations in our clinical reports, seemed to me much too pat, speculative, and inadequate for understanding the psychological problems of the patients we were trying to help (3, 4, 5, 23). I learned how to obtain, assemble, organize, and interpret clinical diagnostic information from psychiatric patients, and to write it up as a coherent psychological report. But gradually, and especially as I became more skilled in it, it all came more and more to seem to me to be a kind of literary, rather than scientific, activity. I came to believe less and less in the objective validity of what we as clinicians were thinking and saying in our case conferences and writing in our psychological reports. In this frame of mind, I was naturally open to the circumstances that determined my next move.

Symonds's advice about working with an outstanding researcher was still uppermost in my mind. Nearly every evening throughout my internship was given to reading in psychology, even more intensive and extensive reading than I had done as a graduate student, since now I was mainly groping for the kind of psychological research I could fully believe was worth investing myself in as a life's work. Personality theory and clinical assessment were still fascinating to me and, in terms of my humanistic values, seemed more important than other areas of psychology. But I was already quite disenchanted with the psychoanalytic approach that so dominated American clinical psychology, including my own training, at that time. In all my reading that year, I finally found a book that made a much greater impression on me than all the rest: *The Scientific Study of Personality* by H. J. Eysenck. Interestingly enough, it was given to me by Symonds on one of my visits to New York. He'd received a review copy of Eysenck's book and asked me to read it to see what I thought of Eysenck's criticisms of some of his (Symonds's) work on personality diagnosis with projective techniques, work of the kind I had been assisting Symonds in (8). Eysenck's book determined all the rest of my reading that year. Besides reading many of Eysenck's journal articles, I studied his *Dimensions of Personality* and *The Structures of Human Personality,* which virtually compelled me to study also L. L. Thurstone's *Multiple Factor Analysis* and Charles Spearman's *Abilities of Man.* In my study of these works, I felt considerable excitement as well as the satisfaction of finding so much clear expression of my own vague intuitions of what was needed in this area of psychology, which, broadly conceived, is the scientific study of individual differences. This, I felt sure, was the kind of psychology for me. The quantitative and experimental approach to personality research espoused by Eysenck had much greater appeal to me, and seemed a much sounder basis for investigating and understanding human behavior than the more literary and speculative psychoanalytic variety of theory and research, based mostly on interviews and projective techniques, with which, up to that time, I had been predominantly involved.

I finally wrote to Professor Eysenck and asked if I could spend a year in his lab. He sent an encouraging reply, so I applied for and received a postdoctoral fellowship from the U. S. Public Health Service, which made it financially possible. At the end of the year I was off to Eysenck's research department in the University of London's Institute of Psychiatry located at London's old and famous Maudsley Hospital.

LAUNCHED IN LONDON

My two years at the Maudsley were the most important to me. Nearly all my work since then has directly or indirectly grown out of the kinds of problems I became involved with during this period in Eysenck's department. From then till now I can perceive an essentially unbroken continuity in the things I have been doing as a researcher. The external details of many of the studies may seem quite varied, and there have been many byways, detours, and sidetracks, but the direction and central theme have remained the same. Basically, I am most concerned with how and why persons differ behaviorally from one another, as they so obviously do. So essentially I have always been a differential psychologist. The fact that I am now concerned with the implications of differential psychology for education is more or less fortuitous and incidental. I became really interested in educational problems because of my interest in differential psychology, rather than the other way around. This was a lucky accident for me. I have found that too many students who begin with an interest in educational problems per se never learn enough psychology or sufficiently acquire the basic tools of scientific investigation to do good research on the most fundamental problems of education, which involve the psychology of human learning, developmental psychology, individual differences in mental abilities and their measurement, the socialization of behavior, and the social psychology of the classroom, to name a few of the more general topics (18).

Eysenck ran a lively shop. Almost everyone in his department—the professional staff, postdoctoral fellows, and graduate students—was working on some facet of Eysenck's theory of extraversion-introversion. From Eysenck and all the others, I quickly learned what was going on and began to think about how I could become actively involved in their program of research. Because Eysenck was an incredibly productive researcher and writer, I was warned long before arriving in London, by persons who only surmised what it was like in Eysenck's department, that he would probably be very inaccessible to students and postdoctoral fellows. As it turned out, nothing could have been further from the truth. He was easily the most accessible professor I have ever known, either before or since then. He was always there and one only had to knock on his door. It seemed he was glad to discuss any problem at any time. He was always "all business" and when the "business" part of any discussion was over, that was that. He never engaged in social pleasantries or idle chitchat. Nearly every dealing with him was in some way intellectually rewarding. In his discussions he brought to bear an exceptionally quick, incisive intelligence, a greater verbal and ideational fluency than I'd seen in anyone else, and a vast erudition, seemingly always at his fingertips. He was clearly a great professor and I felt lucky to be at the Maudsley. His staff, too, was a stimulating group of workers. We all talked shop and little else every day at morning coffee, at lunch, and at afternoon tea. Rarely have I encountered a group of researchers more involved and excited in what they were doing. Eysenck's own powerful commitment to his research, I felt, had a lot to do with it.

By applying factor analysis to a large variety of measurements of personality characteristics as these are reflected in self-report questionnaires, projective tests, ratings by observers, objective behavior tests, and physiological indices, Eysenck found that two main factors, or "dimensions of personality," accounted for most of the personality differences among individuals in the general population. He called these factors *N* for neuroticism and *E-I* for extraversion-introversion. These two basic dimensions are uncorrelated with one another; that is, you cannot tell a person's position on one dimension from knowing his position on the other. Eysenck devised highly reliable questionnaire measures of *N* and *E-I*. During the years I was at the Maudsley, the major research emphasis focused on the extraversion-introversion factor. The psychological reality or construct validity of this important dimension of human differences had been established by means of factor analysis, an important quantitative method in differential psychology invented by Charles Spearman and developed further mainly by Sir Cyril Burt and Sir Godfrey Thomson in England and L. L. Thurstone in America. The next step in Eysenck's program was to apply the methods of experimental and physiological psychology and quantitative genetics to the problem of discovering the causal basis of human differences in the extraversion-introversion dimension. By comparing monozygotic (MZ or identical) twins with dizygotic (DZ or fraternal) twins—a common method in human genetical studies—Eysenck found that extraversion-introversion (or *E-I* for short) had high *heritability*. That is to say, individual differences in this trait are largely attributable to genetic, inborn factors, with environmental factors accounting for only a minor part of the differences. In other words, the chief determinants of where persons stood on the *E-I* dimension were their own internal processes, physiological and biochemical, which are conditioned by the genes one inherits from his parents. (The same also proved true of basic neuroticism, that is, proneness to anxiety.) If *E-I* has a biological basis, what is its nature? This was the problem Eysenck had set about to solve.

Like the great American psychologist and learning theorist Clark L. Hull, Eysenck at that time extolled the so-called hypothetico-deductive method of scientific research. This means, in brief, that one proposes an explanatory postulate or set of postulates—call it theory—and then deduces from these basic postulates certain hypotheses concerning the empirical consequences that must arise under carefully specified conditions if the postulates are true and if the deductive logic is correct. Validation of the theory or the postulates, then, consists of subjecting the derived hypotheses or predictions to empirical, usually experimental, test. If the resultant data do not accord with the theoretical prediction, and no fault can be found with the experiment or with the deductive logic, then the postulate must be seriously questioned and must either be discarded or, if possible, revised so as to accord with the facts. Then new deductions are made and are empirically tested for agreement with fact, and thus the process repeats itself, again and again. This is the way of establishing scientific truth. We cannot really *prove* any theory in science; we can only *disprove* theories. Whichever theory has not been disproved, despite considerable rigorous attempts to do so, is regarded for the time being as true. It remains true so long as it continues to accord with new facts that come under its purview. Also, it may be displaced by a new and better theory, one which accords with all the facts handled by the old theory as well as with a broader range of facts that could not all be comprehended by the old theory. Putting forth such a new theory is regarded as a major step forward in the progress of science.

For reasons I cannot go into here, Eysenck's initial postulate about extraversion-introversion was that individual differences in this personality dimension are mainly due to individual differences in the build-up and dissipation of cortical inhibition. Higher degrees of extraversion were postulated as being associated with greater build-up and slower dissipation of inhibition in the central nervous system. Cortical inhibition is a hypothetical construct in the Pavlovian theory of conditioning, used to explain a variety of phenomena in classical conditioning, particularly extinction, spontaneous recovery, inhibition of delay, trace conditioning, discrimination, and conditioned inhibition. The counterpart to Pavlovian inhibition in C. L. Hull's theory of learning is the somewhat narrower concept of reactive inhibition (symbolized as I_R), which is involved in extinction in both classical and instrumental conditioning and is more or less synonymous with the concept of "work inhibition" which figures so prominently in all accounts of motor-skill learning and in the phenomenon in motor learning known as "reminiscence"—that is, the sudden improvement in motor performance following a brief rest period after the initial period of practice. Reactive inhibition is itself a hypothetical construct—a most useful one—and much more was known about it than about the causes of extraversion-introversion. Since an aim of science is to explain the unknown in terms of the known, and more complex phenomena in terms of simpler, established laws and principles, Eysenck was following a standard scientific procedure in attempting to explain *E-I* in terms of cortical inhibition, about which a good deal was already known concerning its behavioral manifestations. The main thrust of the research going on in Eysenck's laboratory at that time consisted of obtaining groups of individuals who were high or low in behavioral extraversion and comparing them on a wide variety of performances in which cortical inhibition plays a part. (Usually just the correlation between the personality scores and experimentally produced behavior of subjects in the laboratory was determined.) And, in line with the theory, introverts and extraverts were found to differ in many of those behaviors which are explainable, at least in part, in terms of cortical or reactive inhibition, such as rates of conditioning and extinction, and reminiscence in motor (rotory pursuit) learning. Also the effects of stimulant and depressant drugs on cortical inhibition were being studied in rats and in humans.

How did I fit into all this? I was slow at finding my way into it. But I think it is rather worth describing, because as I look back, I see that it is all fairly characteristic of the way I have proceeded with nearly every problem since then. First of all, I felt a need not to leave too many loose ends and unfinished business from my previous work with Symonds and the little research I had begun during my clinical internship. So first I finished up this work—

mostly on projective techniques—and wrote it up for publication (1, 2, 4). At the same time I was learning more about the work in Eysenck's lab. I was vague about the concept of inhibition as it figured in this work and found many others were not much clearer in their thinking about this central construct. So I donned the scholar's hat and did an intensive review of the literature on inhibition, from Sherrington and Pavlov up to Hull and more recent research. With all this material more or less thoroughly organized and digested, I decided that Hull's formulation of reactive inhibition, I_R, was most clearly relevant to Eysenck's theory of extraversion-introversion and also the most clearly formulated in operational terms of any of the inhibition concepts in psychology at that time (6). I_R figured in many types of conditioning, extinction, and learning, as indicated by its prominent role in Hullian learning theory. And the attempts to measure individual differences in I_R were based on human subjects' performance in conditioning and motor learning situations, all of which involved also other important processes such as (in Hullian terminology) habit strength ($_SH_R$), drive (D) and conditioned inhibition ($_SI_R$). There were also conceivably individual differences in all these other processes involved in learning, and the investigator had to read through, so to speak, all the "noise" created by IDs and $_SH_R$, D, and $_SI_R$, in order to discern individual differences in I_R, the reactive inhibition which was what we wanted to relate to individual differences in extraversion as measured independently by a questionnaire (the Maudsley Personality Inventory). (A more recent revised and improved version is known as the Eysenck Personality Inventory.) I was unhappy with the ambiguities created by measuring I_R in situations that also involved learning and the various other sources of IDs associated with it. What was needed was a measure of I_R which eliminated or at least minimized individual differences in all other factors. I set about to invent such a measure. Hull formulated I_R as being a function of three variables: rate of response (R), number of responses (N), and the amount of work (W) involved in each response. Work had the same meaning as in physics, that is, force $\times$ distance. The simplest setup I could think of that would embody these features and permit the measurement of individual differences in I_R and little else consisted of three Morse telegraph keys mounted on a circular board with the pushbuttons equidistant (forming the points of an equilateral triangle). The three keys were set so as to move through equal distances (say, 0.5 cm) when depressed to make contact and turn on a small light bulb. But the springs on two of the keys were set tight, so as to require 7 ounces of pressure to depress them, while the third key was set to require only 1.5 ounces of pressure to turn on the light. Thus there was a work differential between the two "heavy" keys and the one "light" key in the ratio of 1 to 4.6. Response rate was controlled by a metronome. Subjects were required to tap the three keys in random order strictly in time with the metronome for a period of exactly four minutes. Two additional four-minute work periods were given, separated by rest periods. The subjects were told that this was a personality test of rigidity-flexibility: a "good" score requires that the subjects come as close as possible to tapping each of the three keys an equal number of times during the four-minute period and at the same time tap them in as random an order as possible, avoiding as much as possible any repetition of the same order of tapping the buttons.

Obviously there is little or nothing for the subject to learn in this simple situation. His over-all response rate is controlled by the metronome. The only thing free to vary is the number of taps made on each of the keys. According to the Hullian formulation, the most I_R should build up in responding to the keys requiring the most work (that is, the two heavy keys) and the least I_R should build up in response to the key requiring the least work (the one light key). Since there should be less inhibition of the response of tapping the light key, it should be tapped more often during each four-minute work period, and throughout the work period the subject's responses should unconsciously gravitate more and more to the light key. Electrical counters were connected to each of the keys. Persons who build up more I_R in responding should show a greater discrepancy between the number of taps on the light key (L), and the average number of taps on the two heavy keys (H). So the measure of I_R was $L - (H_1 + H_2)/2$. It was shown that under various experimental manipulations, such as different tapping rates, this measure of I_R behaved in accord with predictions from the Hullian formulation (27). Also, the measurements had high reliability, comparing favorably with the reliability

of individual tests of intelligence. Correlations of the I_R with extraversion, though not large, were also in the predicted direction. So my results did not contradict Eysenck's theory of *E-I*. Most of us were seeking experimental evidence that would clearly not accord with the theoretical predictions. Repeated attempts to *disprove* a hypothesis is, in the final analysis, the only method available to science for reducing uncertainty.

Thus there was some excitement in the lab at the time that one of Eysenck's experiments yielded negative results—a virtually complete lack of any difference between extraverts and introverts in a task supposedly involving I_R and consequently on which extraverts and introverts should show a difference. The task was serial rote learning—the learning of a 12-item list of nonsense syllables presented by a memory drum. Each 3-letter nonsense syllable appears for 2 seconds, and the subject has to anticipate aloud which syllable will appear next in the series. The same order is constantly repeated until the subject reaches criterion; that is, he can anticipate every item in the list without a single omission or error. An interesting and highly lawful phenomenon in serial learning is the so-called serial position effect or SPE, which is the fact that the middle items in the serial list are apparently harder to learn than the items at the beginning or at the end of the list. If for a group of subjects one plots the frequency of errors made throughout the course of learning on each item in the list as a function of its position, a serial position curve like that shown in Figure 5.1 is the typical result. The hump in the curve is called "bowing" because of its resemblance to an archer's bow. The asymmetry of the bow (with the peak of errors just past the middle position and more errors in the last half than in the first half of the series) is called "skewness." Without going into the rather complicated details of Hullian learning theory (which I am afraid is now dead but which in the early 1950s was still very much alive) let it suffice to say that Hull explained the bowing effect in terms of inhibition. For reasons it would take much too long to explicate, Hull's theory held that throughout the course of learning a serial list, more inhibition accrued to the items near the middle of the list, causing them to take longer to be consistently anticipated correctly and thereby producing the familiar bowed serial position curve of errors, as shown in Figure 5.1. If Hull's

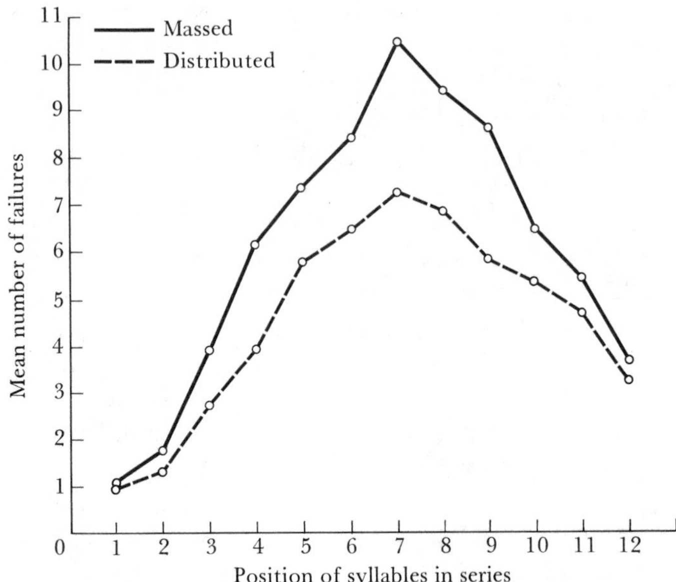

Figure 5.1. Typical serial position curves showing mean number of errors made at each position in a 12-item list of nonsense syllables learned to a criterion of mastery (i.e., one errorless trial) under conditions of massed and distributed practice. The two "curves" become almost identical when plotted as the percentage of total errors at each position.
(From C. I. Hovland, *Journal of Experimental Psychology,* 1938, *23,* p. 178.)

theory of the serial position effect was correct, as we assumed it was at the time, then according to Eysenck's theory of *E-I,* extraverts, since they build up inhibition more rapidly and dissipate it more slowly than introverts, should produce a more severely bow-shaped serial position curve than introverts. The prediction was clear cut. And so were the results when the experiment was analyzed. There was not an iota of difference between the serial position curves of even the most extreme introverts and extreme extraverts.

The question raised by this result had one of three possible answers: either (a) Eysenck's theory of extraversion-introversion was wrong, (b) Hull's theory of the serial position effect was wrong, or (c) *both* Eysenck and Hull were wrong.

INDIVIDUAL DIFFERENCES IN LEARNING

Then and there I decided that, as for myself, the problem of individual differences in basic learning processes (which at the time I thought of almost exclusively in terms of Pavlovian and Hullian constructs) was more "fundamental" or "basic" than the problems of personality. And I saw the career before me as being devoted to the study of individual differences in basic learning processes. I figured these more "basic" problems would have to be solved before one could make much progress in the study of the more complex behaviors that constitute personality. The idea of what is more "basic" is actually a rather mystical concept which at the time influenced my thinking considerably but in which now I put practically no stock at all. I now take the much simpler view that science is just rational, empirical problem solving. I give little thought to whether the problems to be solved are "basic" or "practical," "theoretical" or "applied." In recent years I have found satisfaction in working more on problems that seem to me to have some practical or social consequence. They can be just as interesting, just as amenable to scientific investigation, and if the results are of consequence outside the field of theoretical psychology, such as in affecting educational practices and policies in ways that others might benefit, so much the better.

So I set about to study IDs in learning, and the serial position effect seemed as good a place to begin as any. I began this work in Eysenck's lab and took it with me when I went to Berkeley, which generously provided everything I needed in the way of lab space and equipment to pursue this line of investigation (for example, 17). I devoted the next several years mainly to individual differences in serial learning and particularly to the serial position effect, work that involved many experiments, some of which have been reported in psychological journals in a dozen or more articles on serial learning (9, 10, 12, 13, 14, 15, 16, 19, 20, 21, 24, 25).

In many ways, to me, this work on serial learning has been the most fascinating I have ever engaged in. Although it is hard to think of any conceivably practical importance of most of the research problems arising from serial rote learning, they have their own fascination, much like the game of chess. Strangely enough, serial learning is the only line of research about which I have had dreams. I often go to sleep at night thinking about some research problem, but for some strange reason the only problems that ever persist into my dreams, and even turn into quite pleasantly exciting and entertaining adventures, are those involving serial learning and particularly the serial-position effect!

But I am forced to make a long story short. It turned out that Hull's theory of the serial position effect was quite wrong. Inhibition, I concluded, has nothing to do with the serial position curve. And while there are marked individual differences in the over-all rate of learning a serial list, I could never find any reliable individual differences in the degree of bowing of serial position curves once they were equated for over-all speed of learning. The bowing of the curve, when plotted in terms of *percentage* of total errors at each position, was always the same, within the limits of reliability, for every subject and for all kinds of lists, under both massed and distributed practice, and under various pacing rates. The relative (that is, percentage) serial position curve appeared to be invariant (10). With one exception: there are reliable individual differences in the *skewness* of the curve, that is, the degree to which errors pile up more toward the end of the list. Fast learners produced slightly more skewed curves than slow learners, especially on lists of less than 12 items. For longer lists there were virtually no differences of any kind in the shape of the relative serial position curve. I discovered that the basis of individual differences in the skewness of the curve was individual differences in memory span, that is, the number of items the subject can repeat correctly after a single presentation (19). I found a substantial correlation between individual differences in memory span and speed of serial learning. So here was a definite link between serial learning phenomena and what seemed to me to be the more basic processes of memory span and short-term memory in general. Again, my reductionist proclivity showed itself in my growing belief that the route to understanding individual differences in learning was via research on individual differences in short-term memory. Memory span, being a part of some standard intelligence tests, such as the Stanford-Binet and the Wechsler scales, thus also seemed an important link between the learning domain and that of psychometric testing. Here, I thought, was the link that could

bridge the disturbing gulf between the experimental psychology of learning and the differential psychology of mental abilities as represented by intelligence and aptitude testing.

While beginning a long-term program of research on individual differences in short-term memory, I continued in my efforts to understand the cause of the serial-position curve. It was a more dependable, more lawful, more robust, and more invariant phenomenon than just about any I knew of in the whole experimental psychology of human learning. If Hull's explanation of the phenomenon was wrong (since some of the most important predictions from his theory were not borne out experimentally), what *was* the true explanation? I found that the items in a serial list got learned in a highly regular order and that a person would take the same amount of time (or number of learning trials) to learn each item, once the previous items in this regular order of learning had already been learned. The order of learning, after the first two or three items in the list (the number depending on the subject's memory span), alternated systematically between items from the beginning and end of the series, thus

Serial Position: 1 2 3 4 5 6 7 8 9

Order of Learning: 1 2 4 6 8 9 7 5 3

This all appeared to be very simple and lawful. The question of the serial position effect was reduced to the more fundamental question of why subjects learned a series of items in this particular order (9). I found that when children learned to spell words, they even learned the letters in this order, and that spelling errors, when plotted as a function of their position in the word, formed a perfect serial position curve (11).

Notice that since item 1 in the series is seen first it is most likely to be learned first, and from that point on the items nearest to it get learned next, as if they "stick on" to what has already been learned. This is more apparent when viewed as follows.

Serial Position: 6 7 8 9 *1* 2 3 4 5

Order of Learning: 9 7 5 3 1 2 4 6 8

What is the "adhesive" property that causes as-yet-unlearned items to "stick" to the nearest already-learned item? I postulated a more basic process than the serial position effect which I called the *adjacency* effect (26). This hypothesis states simply that an unlearned (that is, not previously recalled) item in a list has a higher probability of being learned when it is presented adjacently in temporal sequence to an already-learned (that is, recalled on a previous trial) item. Thus, a given unlearned item (U') would be hardest to learn if it were adjacent on both sides to other unlearned items: U, U', U, for example. It would be easier to learn if it were adjacent to one already-learned item, (L); for example, U, U', L, or L, U', U. And it should be easiest to learn if it were adjacent to two learned items, one before it and one after it in temporal sequence; for example, L, U', L.

I tested this adjacency hypothesis in a task that did not involve serial learning. Lists of 40 words were presented one at a time at a 2 seconds rate for each of 6 trials, each time in a completely random order, and on each trial 20 words were eliminated and 20 new ones were added. After each trial subjects had to write down as many of the 40 words they had seen in any order that they came to mind. Analyses of the free recall data showed that the adjacency effect, precisely as described above, was manifested to a high level of statistical significance (26). This meant that the serial position effect could possibly be explained as a product of a simpler, more basic and more general psychological phenomenon—the adjacency effect, which operates also in free recall learning. But then how can we explain the adjacency effect? Is it a result of an even more basic process? Yes, of course. It takes a certain investment of time to learn each item. (The amount of time required per item differs from one person to another and from one type of item to another.) This time is required for the action of whatever mental or neural processes are involved in fixing the item in the short-term and long-term memory stores so that it can be recalled on a later occasion—call the process what you will: rehearsal, encoding, neural consolidation, etc. The process is not instantaneous (no natural process is), but requires some finite period of time. Now then, if a new (unlearned) item temporally precedes an old (already-learned) item, the processing of the new

IQ tests called for information and skills that the testee was expected to have had the opportunity to acquire before taking the test. In short, most IQ tests assessed what the subject had learned outside the testing situation. If it could be assumed that all subjects had had roughly equal opportunities for learning prior to being tested, their scores could well be an accurate reflection of their learning ability. But in cases where this assumption could not be made, as in the case of children with a quite different cultural background, it struck me that perhaps the best way to assess learning ability (which at that time I more or less equated with intelligence) was not to test what the child had learned at some time prior to the test situation but to measure his rate of learning something new, right in the testing situation itself. This could be called a "direct learning test."

I devised several such tests, using the simplest possible materials (1961). One test consisted of the free recall of familiar objects. These were common things for which all school-age children already have some name; I did not care whether the name was given in English or Spanish, or even if it was the usual name given to the object (book, pencil, bag, car, doll, water glass, shoe, for example), so long as the child had some consistent label for the object. In various versions of the test anywhere from 12 to 20 objects were shown one at a time to the child, who was asked to name them. The objects were then hidden from the child's view and he was asked to name as many of them as he could recall. This procedure was repeated until all the objects in the set could be recalled. Other tests consisted of the serial learning and the paired-associates learning of familiar objects, and trial-and-error selective learning with auditory and/or visual reinforcements for "correct" responses. (I later found that digit span and other tests of short-term memory served the same purpose with a higher degree of reliability.)

What I found in my first studies was that EMR children who were "culturally disadvantaged," meaning they were of low socio-economic status (SES), performed much better on the direct learning tests relative to middle-SES EMR children of the same low IQ. On the other hand, somewhat to my surprise, low SES children of *average* IQ performed no better on my learning tests than middle SES children of average IQ. In subsequent studies I found this to hold true not only for low-SES Mexican-American children, but for low SES Negro and white children as well (22, 33, 34). In other words, my direct learning tests reflected the behavioral differences between low-SES and middle-SES EMR children which were not at all reflected in scores on the usual IQ tests. In fact, on the learning tests many of the EMR children performed as well as children of average IQ and some even performed as well as children at the so-called "gifted" level of IQ (that is, IQs above 130 or 140).

All this was quite startling to me and my graduate student assistants. What did it mean? At first I thought perhaps I had found the first culture-fair test that actually worked, for we found in testing representative samples of disadvantaged children, who generally score 10 to 20 points lower than middle-class white children on standard IQ tests, that there was practically no difference between the score distributions of low SES and middle SES children, or between racial minority and majority children, on the direct learning tests. Thus, in attempting to understand these findings, my first thought was that the usual intelligence tests were more culturally biased against low SES individuals and that therefore, for any given IQ, the low SES person was really more intelligent than the high SES person. This difference would be revealed in the presumably less culture-biased direct-learning tests. The fact that the IQ predicts scholastic performance equally well for low SES as for middle SES children is usually explained by saying that schooling itself is culturally biased, as are the IQ tests, in favor of the middle-class child. At the time, I viewed my research with the direct-learning tests as an attempt to formalize these notions in the psychological laboratory and thereby to demonstrate, by more precise and rigorous methods than had yet been applied, that the much higher incidence of retardation among children of low SES, and particularly among minority children, was the fault of the IQ tests and also, possibly, of the schools. However, my own research findings in this vein have since led me to reject this view.

THEORY OF LEVEL I AND LEVEL II ABILITIES

It has become quite apparent that the essential ability measured in common by all intelligence tests, that is, the factor originally called *g* (for "general") by Spearman is a quite different ability from the learning and memory abilities I was measuring by means of my direct-learning tests. For convenience I labeled the two kinds of abilities *Level I* (that is, rote learning and memory) and *Level II* (the *g* of intelligence tests, conceptual or abstract reasoning and problem solving). What all Level I tests have in common is that they call for little or no transformation of the stimulus "input" in order for the subject to arrive at the response "output." Stimulus and response are highly similar. What the tasks require essentially is accurate registration of sensory experiences, immediately giving already well learned names or labels to these, and at some later point in time repeating these labels in response to partial stimulus cues. It is a kind of recording and playback on cue, as contrasted with more *g*-loaded tasks, which involve considerable transformation and mental manipulation of the input in order to produce the answer. It is the difference between being able to repeat a string of 9 digits after hearing it once and answering the question: "If three men can mow a field in four days, how many men will be needed to mow it in half a day?" Both items may be equally *difficult* in terms of the percentage of the population who are able to perform successfully. But the tasks involve quite different kinds of mental processes, which I now believe represent a very fundamental division of mental abilities with different genetic and physiological bases. I am now entertaining the hypothesis that the locus of Level I abilities is in the electrochemical processes involved in short-term memory and the neural consolidation of memory traces. Level II abilities, on the other hand, are hypothesized to depend upon the structural aspects of the brain—the number of neural elements and the complexity and organization of their potential interconnections.

The idea that Level II tests are merely more culture-loaded than Level I tests as an explanation of why low SES children do better on Level I than on Level II has not stood up. For example, I have found no tests, either verbal or nonverbal, with any appreciable complexity or a substantial *g* loading on which properly diagnosed retarded children score in the average range or on which representative samples of low SES children score as high, on the average, as middle-class children. Surprisingly enough, low SES Negro children actually score slightly higher on the verbal and the more obviously culture-loaded tests than on nonverbal tests of the type that attempt to minimize cultural content. Also, the experimental manipulation of task variables in laboratory experiments so as to either maximize or minimize the importance of Level II processes in performing the task leads me to the conclusion that the Level I-Level II distinction is not a matter of the culture-loading of the tests that measures each type of ability but of different kinds of mental processes required in the two classes of tests. The essential distinction between Level I and Level II is in the complexity of the mental transformations or operations required for successful performance on the task (37, 38). Moreover, twin and sibling correlations and the estimates they yield of the heritability (that is, the proportion of the total variance in test scores attributable to genetic factors) of the best Level I and Level II tests give no indication of significantly lower heritability of Level II than of Level I tests. If Level II tests reflect environmental and cultural influences to a greater extent than Level I tests, one should expect lower heritability values for Level II tests. But this is not the case, and, if anything, the opposite seems to be true.

In order to study the relationship between Level I and Level II abilities, my research assistants have administered a number of representative tests of each type to large samples of the school-age population now totalling some 15,000 children in all, including the full range of socioeconomic levels that exist in California as well as representative samples of the three largest minority populations in the state—Negroes, Mexicans, and Orientals. These large-scale data obtained from the general population put my earlier findings with the mentally retarded into a proper perspective and show that they are not isolated phenomena peculiar to retardates but are a consequence of certain population characteristics.

The regression of Level I test scores on IQ (or Level II) scores in all samples appears to be linear throughout the IQ range from about 50 to 150. The slope of the regression line (and consequently the coefficient of correlation) between Level I and Level II abilities differs from one subpopulation group to another. The correlation is lower in low SES groups and higher in high SES groups. It is lower also in Negro than in white samples. In various studies the correlation (which is the *slope* of the regression line when both variates are expressed as standard scores) between Levels I and II have ranged from .10 to .40 in low SES groups,

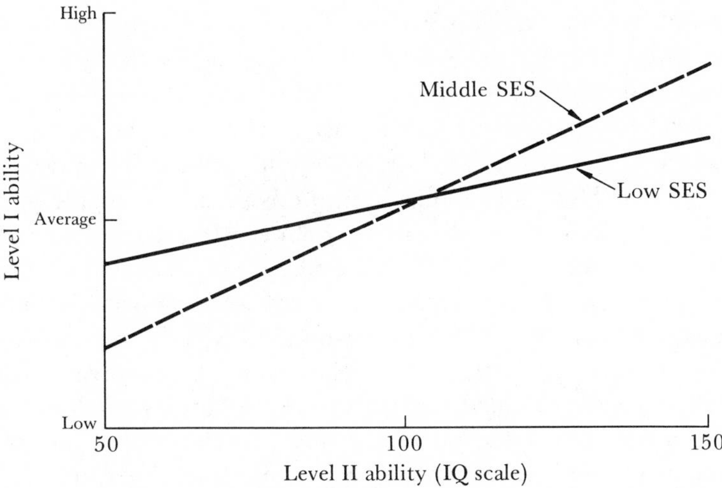

Figure 5.2. Typical regression lines of Level I upon Level II ability in middle and low socioeconomic groups.

comprised largely of Negro children, and from .50 to .70 in middle SES groups comprised largely of white children. Because the regression of Level I on Level II has a steeper slope (that is, higher correlation) in higher than in lower SES groups, the regression lines of lower and upper SES groups must inevitably cross. Consequently, in the region of low IQ that characterizes mental retardation, the lower SES group obtains higher average scores on Level I tests, as I found in my first studies. These relationships are shown in Figure 5.2. Thus the phenomenon of higher Level I ability among lower than among upper SES retardates, on the average, is seen to be a consequence of the lower correlation between Levels I and II in the low SES group as compared with the higher SES group. But what I did not expect to find prior to testing children in adequately large numbers throughout the entire range of IQ is the *reverse* phenomenon at the higher end of the IQ scale, that is, the finding that low SES children (most of whom are Negro in these studies) with high IQs perform significantly less well than their middle SES counterparts in IQ. From a scientific and theoretical standpoint, this finding is a simpler, more regular picture than we would see if the regression were not linear and the consequent reverse symmetry at the low and high ends of the IQ scale did not obtain. This finding, furthermore, helps to clarify a point about which there was a major question in the earlier stages of my research. This was the question of whether low SES retardates performed better on Level I tests, relative to those of middle SES, simply because Level I tests were less culturally biased than the IQ tests. This culture-bias hypothesis seems untenable in view of the fact that in the range of IQ above 100, low SES children perform relatively *less* well on Level I tests. Also, when I have given various Level II tests which differ obviously in culture loading, such as the highly culture-bound Peabody Picture Vocabulary Test and the more culture-fair Raven's Progressive Matrices, and then have examined the regression of the less culture-loaded on the more culture-loaded test, I find no crossover of the regression lines of the low and middle SES groups; the lines, in fact, are quite parallel. In brief, comparison of lower and upper SES groups on Level I vs. Level II tests gives a quite different picture from that of comparing the two groups on culture-loaded vs. culture-fair tests.

Another question of both theoretical and practical importance is whether the correlation between Level I and Level II abilities represents a *functional* dependence of Level II upon Level I. For example, is above-average Level I ability a necessary but not sufficient condition for above-average Level II ability in the sense, say, that knowledge of subtraction is a necessary but not sufficient condition for solving problems in long division? Obviously some degree of learning and memory (that is, Level I ability) is essential for intellectual development. But above some low threshold of Level I ability, is there any functional dependence of individual differences in Level II upon individual differences in Level I? We know, of course, that there is some correlation, often quite substantial, between Levels I and II. But correlation does not necessarily imply functional dependence of one set of processes upon another, in this case Level II upon Level I. This question has puzzled me for some time. It probably cannot be answered definitively on the basis of the evidence now available. A number of lines of evidence, however, suggest a hypothesis that seems most likely to be true.

First, the wide range of correlations between Levels I and II, going from .20 to .80 (after corrections for attenuation and restriction of range) in various subpopulations, seems inconsistent with a high degree of functional dependence between the two types of ability. If the correlation were completely a result of functional dependence, it is difficult to see why the dependency should be so much higher in one population group than in another. Second, a high degree of functional dependence would imply an increasing correlation between Levels I and II with increasing age from early childhood to early maturity, since this is the period of marked development of Level II abilities. But we have found no evidence of greater correlation between Levels I and II with increasing age, and, if anything, slightly the opposite is the case. Subjects with high IQs but low Level I ability are somewhat less common among younger children between the ages four and seven than among children beyond ten years of age. It is as if Level I ability acts as scaffolding for the development of Level II abilities and then falls away in importance as the Level II abilities are consolidated. The child who is below average in Level I and above average in Level II will appear to be a slow developer in Level II in early childhood; he is in a sense a slow learner who, because of good Level II ability, is able thoroughly to understand and consolidate everything he learns and incorporate it into the cognitive structures we call intelligence. Later in development these Level II cognitive structures become relatively more important in educational attainments, and the child who is relatively low in Level I but high in Level II becomes much less handicapped in school than the child who shows the opposite pattern of abilities. The low I-high II child is one who learns with difficulty in school when the learning is more or less rote and affords little opportunity to grasp concepts and relationships; he is slow in acquiring skills that require sheer repetition; but once it has been acquired, he can fully bring it to bear in logical reasoning and problem solving. He *understands* what he learns, though he may have learned it slowly. Such children, who often seem to get off to a slow start in the early grades in school, appear to become brighter and intellectually more capable as they progress in school and as the academic subject matter makes increasing demands on conceptual and abstract thinking and involves relatively less sheer acquisition of simple skills and factual information. The high I-low II child, on the other hand, presents a very different picture. In early childhood he may appear quite bright and quick in picking up all kinds of simple skills and verbal knowledge; he may appear linguistically precocious; he may do quite well in scholastic subjects and skills that depend upon learning by repetition such as penmanship, spelling, mechanical arithmetic, memorizing the words of songs, etc., but he experiences increasing difficulty and frustration—sometimes to the point of hating school—as the conceptual and abstract demands of the subject matter increase from earlier to later grades. It becomes increasingly difficult to understand what is learned, and, when ultimately in some academic subjects learning and understanding become one and the same, the pupil with a marked deficiency in Level II is almost totally handicapped. While one can find some small percentage of pupils of below-average Level I ability who are doing very well, say, in algebra or science, there are virtually no below-average Level II pupils who are succeeding in these subjects.

If there is at most only a slight degree of functional dependence of Level II upon Level I, as suggested by the fact that some few older children with very high Level II ability are found to be well below average in Level I, what is the basis for the correlation between Levels I and II and for the fact that it differs so markedly in different populations? The most plausible explanation is in terms of genetic assortment. If Levels I and II are controlled by two different polygenic systems, these can become assorted together to any degree in a given population through selective and assortative mating. I have rejected the idea that only Level I ability is genetically determined and that Level II abilities are learned, acquired, or developed out of Level I abilities entirely as a result of environmental influences. If this were the case, the heritability of intelligence (Level II) should not be as high as we know it to be—about .70 to .80 in present-day populations. Also, according to this notion, Level I should have much higher heritability than Level II. But the correlations obtained on siblings and twins give no indication that Level I abilities are significantly more heritable than Level II abilities, and, if anything, Level I ability appears slightly less heritable than Level II. It seems much more likely that both Level I and Level II are controlled by distinct polygenic systems and are correlated to varying degrees in different population groups because these groups have differed in the kinds of demands that would cause the genetic factor underlying Levels I and II to become assorted together. We know there is a high degree of assortative mating (that is, correlation between mates) for intelligence in European and North American Caucasian populations. In fact, in Western society there is probably a higher degree of assortative mating for intelligence than for any other trait.

This should not be too surprising since educational attainments, occupational level, and socioeconomic status, which are the basis for assortative mating, are highly correlated with intelligence. If Level I ability also has some correlation with occupational and socioeconomic status independently of intelligence (Level II), we should expect the genetic factors involved in Levels I and II to become associated through assortative mating. This is consistent with the observation that omnibus-type intelligence tests which involve an admixture of both Level I and Level II (for example, the Stanford-Binet and Wechsler tests) show a higher correlation with practical criteria such as educational achievement and occupational status than do factorially more pure tests of Level II, such as the Raven Matrices. Populations that have not long been stratified educationally and occupationally would have had less assortative mating for these abilities, and consequently would show a lower correlation between them, as we find, for example, in the American Negro population as contrasted with the white. Also, Level II ability, being more highly related to the academic and intellectual demands of schooling and higher occupational status is more subject to assortative mating and consequently to genetic stratification in terms of socioeconomic status. Good Level I ability, on the other hand, is more or less equally advantageous in all cultures and walks of life and would therefore become less differentiated than Level II among various population groups.

I have argued that this formulation, if it proves essentially correct, could have important educational implications, especially for the education of many of the children now popularly called culturally disadvantaged, most of whom have normal Level I ability but a majority of whom are quite far below the general population average in Level II ability. Such children might benefit educationally from curricula and instructional methods which make the acquisition of basic scholastic skills less dependent upon

Level II abilities and more fully engage Level I abilities as a means of improving their educational attainments (43, 46).

GENETIC FACTORS IN ABILITY DIFFERENCES

Not all the factors that cause persons to differ in their abilities can be found in their *external* environments, that is to say, in their life experiences and opportunities for learning. Some part of the psychological and behavioral differences among individuals, just as is true of differences in their physical appearance, is the result of differences in individuals' *internal* environment, particularly the structural, physiological, and biochemical aspects of the brain. And just as the development of all the physical structures and functions of the organism are conditioned by inherited genetic factors, so too are those features which are the most closely linked with behavior, namely, the central nervous system. Therefore, we cannot achieve scientifically a complete account of the causes of individual differences in mental abilities (or in any other traits) without attempting to discover the degree to which psychological differences are attributable to genetic factors as well as to influences in the external environment.

While conducting my experiments on the learning characteristics of school children from various social classes and ethnic groups, I became deeply immersed in the then rapidly growing literature on the psychology of the culturally disadvantaged—a term used for the children of the poor, particularly racial minorities such as Negroes, Mexican-Americans, Puerto Ricans, and American Indians, as well as poor whites. Much of this literature was then still in the form of unpublished research reports on projects supported by the federal funds that had been poured into attempts to understand and ameliorate the educational plight of the nation's poor. So much material was accumulating so rapidly (I already had two filing cases full) that I felt a need to scan all these reports, winnow them to find the most substantial and methodologically sound studies, classify them, and digest and organize the results into a reasonably coherent body of knowledge which could be summarized in a book, along with the results of my own research in this area. My decision to begin this project coincided ideally with my being invited to spend a year as a

Fellow at the Center for Advanced Study in the Behavioral Sciences at Stanford. This freed me for one year from teaching and the other routine academic chores of a professor, so that I could devote my full time to working on my projected book on the psychology of the culturally disadvantaged. At the same time, I was co-editing a multi-authored book on the same general theme (48).

What struck me as most peculiar as I worked through the vast bulk of literature on the disadvantaged was the almost complete lack of any mention of the possible role of genetic factors in individual differences in intelligence and scholastic performance. In the few instances where genetics was mentioned, it was usually to dismiss the issue as outmoded, irrelevant, or unimportant, or to denigrate the genetic study of human differences and to proclaim the all-importance of the social and cultural environment as the only source of individual and group differences in the mental abilities relevant to scholastic performance. So strongly expressed was this bias in some cases, and so inadequately buttressed by evidence, that I began to surmise that the topic of genetics was ignored more because of the author's social philosophy than because the importance of genetic factors in human differences had been scientifically disproved. It seemed obvious to me that a book dealing with the culturally disadvantaged, which after all is merely a specialized topic in the field of differential psychology, would have to include a chapter that actually attempts to come to grips scientifically with the genetic issue.

I was largely but not utterly ignorant of the research on the genetics of mental abilities. I would have been even more ignorant had I not gone to England as a postdoctoral fellow, for American psychology textbooks and the courses during the years of my education were, almost without exception, totally lacking any adequate account of findings in this field of research. But fortunately, while in London I had had the privilege of attending the Walter Van Dyke Bingham Memorial Lecture, sponsored by the American Psychological Association, and delivered that year (May 21, 1957) by Professor Sir Cyril Burt and entitled "The Inheritance of Mental Ability." I did not go to the lecture out of interest in the topic, but simply because Sir Cyril Burt, who was then in his late seventies and an emeritus professor in the University of

London, was England's greatest and most famous psychologist, and I merely wanted to see him in person. His lecture was impressive indeed; it was probably the best lecture I have ever heard. (It was later published in the *American Psychologist,* 1958, 13, 1–15.) But at the time, the message of Burt's lecture met no immediate need in my thinking or research and was merely stored away in my memory for future reference.

So in preparation for the chapter of my book that was to deal with the genetics of intelligence, I began by reading Burt's Bingham Lecture, which led me to all his other articles in this area, and soon I found myself reviewing the total world literature on the genetics of abilities. One could not go far into this topic without getting into that branch of genetics called population genetics or quantitative genetics, and so I began to study this subject in its own right. Quantitative genetics was not entirely foreign territory to me, since it is based largely on statistical concepts, mainly the analysis of variance, of which I already had a good grasp.

I then began to write articles about genetic research on intelligence and its relevance to current problems in education (30, 32, 39, 44, 45). Meanwhile, my chapter on the genetics of intelligence had grown to almost the length of a book, but it was neither a suitable book, nor a chapter, nor an article. I realized it would have to be completely reworked.

As a result of my first few articles on the genetic issue, I was asked by the editors of the *Harvard Educational Review* to contribute an article summarizing my position on this topic and its relevance to the current educational scene. The article, they said, would be followed by commentaries on it by four or five psychologists and a geneticist, all presumably selected to represent differing viewpoints, some of them highly critical of my own. I agreed and began with the intention of writing a rather succinct article, but my manuscript seemed to grow and grow to something like 500 handwritten pages, which boiled down to 200 typed pages, and 123 pages of print in the *Harvard Educational Review (HER)* (35, 36). This article, "How Much Can We Boost IQ and Scholastic Achievement?" was followed in the next issue of the *HER* by seven lengthy commentaries, and, as if that were not enough criticism, the next issue continued a dozen or more commentaries on my article, which also sparked off innumerable accounts in the popular press as well as heated discussions in a host of professional journals—even the *Bulletin of the Atomic Scientists* (42). If my article had been faulty, one competent critic should have been sufficient to put it down. The fact that dozens of criticisms of the article have steadily appeared for more than five years after its publication is a social-psychological phenomenon perhaps worthy of study in its own right. Space does not permit recounting some of the astonishing details of the aftermath of this article's publication; I have done that elsewhere (see 45). Attempts were made, and are still being made, by various groups and individuals (professionals and students alike) to have me censured by the American Psychological Association, or put out all together, and to have me censured by my University or fired from my professorship. Disturbances created by outsiders invading my classes and research institutes where I have been a guest lecturer have called for intervention by the police. At one period during the controversy the university authorities assigned two plainclothes police officers to accompany me to and from my classes and to the parking lot when I left for home. The voluminous and often bizarre mail I received, the alienation of some of my former friends and colleagues, and the intrigue and underhandedness involved in some of the attempts to discredit me and my research, are all phenomena which I have taken pains carefully to record as grist for further study in their own right at some time in the future when they can all more easily be viewed in some proper impersonal and historical perspective. My equanimity throughout all this, which others have sometimes mistakenly attributed to courage or sheer foolhardiness, is really, I believe, more a result of the fact that I have for a long time viewed even my own most personal experiences as not essentially different from any other natural phenomena that can be subjected to observation and analysis, much as one would attempt to study any other subject matter. It is possible for a part of one's self always to view as a third party one's own involvements, problems, and emotions.

What had set off all the furor, of course, was the 10-page section (pages 78–88) of my 123-page article (35) in which I touched upon the subject of race differences in intelligence. To juxtapose the words "race," "intelligence," and "genetics" was virtually taboo in academic circles, and that is mainly why what I wrote seemed so shocking to many persons. Actually, the articles as a whole dealt with the much broader topics of the apparent failure of large-scale compensatory education programs, the evidence for a large genetic component in individual differences in intelligence, and my own two-level theory of mental abilities. The issue of the causes of racial differences in intelligence was incidental to these other more general topics, but altogether avoiding any mention of racial differences in this context, it seemed to me, would have been most contrived and dishonest. *HER* asked for my views on this and the other topics, and I expressed them. What I said that caused such a stir was summarized in essence in one paragraph:

> The fact that a reasonable hypothesis has not been rigorously proved does not mean that it should be summarily dismissed. It only means that we need more appropriate research for putting it to the test. I believe such definitive research is possible but has not yet been done. So all we are left with are various lines of evidence, no one of which is definitive alone, but which, viewed all together, make it a not unreasonable hypothesis that genetic factors are strongly implicated in the average Negro-white intelligence difference. The preponderance of the evidence is, in my opinion, less consistent with a strictly environmental hypothesis than with a genetic hypothesis, which, of course, does not exclude the influence of environment or its interaction with genetic factors (p. 82).

I have no regrets about this statement; in fact, quite the contrary: I think it was necessary.

In a free society, one which permits freedom of speech and of the press, both to express and to criticize diverse views, the social responsibility of the scientist, it seems to me, is perfectly clear. It is simply to do his research as competently and carefully as he can, and to report his methods, results, and conclusions as fully and accurately as possible.

The scientist, when speaking as a scientist about his research, should not make it subordinate to his nonscientifically arrived-at personal, social, religious, or political ideologies. We have seen clear examples of what happens when science is corrupted by servitude to political dogma—in the bizarre racist theories of the Nazis and in the disastrous Lysenkoism of the Soviet Union under Stalin.

Unfortunately, we have been witnessing similarly ideologically motivated dogmatism concerning the cause of obvious differences in average educational and occupational performance among various subpopulations, socially identified as racial groups. In the United States this means mainly the Negro population as compared with the majority white population. These groups differ, on the average, by about one standard deviation in measures of intelligence and scholastic performance.

Serious consideration of the question whether the observed racial differences in mental abilities and scholastic performance involve genetic as well as environmental factors has been taboo in academic, scientific, and intellectual circles in recent years. Nevertheless, it remains a persistent question. It is scientifically and socially irresponsible not to try and establish the truth of the matter. I maintain only that the causes of differences in IQ and scholastic performance among different racial groups is still an open question. The nation's scientific community cannot in good conscience ignore it or slight it with superficial slogans and arbitrary or dogmatic, sometimes political, positions.

There is perhaps an understandable reluctance to come to grips scientifically with the problem of race differences in intelligence—to come to grips with it, that is to say, in the same way that scientists would approach the investigation of any other phenomenon. This reluctance is manifested in a variety of "symptoms" found in most writings and discussions of the psychology of race differences, particularly differences in mental ability. These symptoms include a tendency to remain on the remotest fringes of the subject; to sidestep central questions; to blur the issues and tolerate a degree of vagueness in definitions, concepts, and inferences that would be unseemly in any other realm of scientific discourse. Many writers express an unwarranted degree of skepticism about reasonably well-established quantitative methods and measurements. They deny or belittle already generally accepted facts—accepted, that is, when brought to bear on inferences outside the realm of race differences—and they demand practically impossible criteria of certainty before even seriously proposing or investigating genetic hypotheses, as contrasted with extremely uncritical attitudes toward purely environmental hypotheses. There is often a failure to distinguish clearly between scientifically answerable aspects of the question and the moral, political, and social policy issues; a tendency to beat dead horses and to set up straw men on what is represented, or more often misrepresented, as the genetic side of the argument. We see appeals to the notion that the topic is either too unimportant to be worthy of scientific curiosity or too complex, or too difficult, or that it will be forever impossible for any kind of research to be feasible, or that answers to key questions are fundamentally "unknowable" in any scientifically acceptable sense. Finally, we often see the complete denial of intelligence and race as realities, or as quantifiable attributes, or as variables capable of being related to one another—in short, there is an ostrich-like dismissal of the subject altogether.

Our disturbed conscience over the historical mistreatment of Negroes in America may hinder our ability to ask the right questions and to seek the answers through research. Scientists must take the lead in facing up to this question, and not repeatedly sweep it under the rug. I see a danger to our nation, and to Negroes especially, in saying what we might prefer to believe instead of trying to find out what is actually true.

I believe these obstructive tendencies will be increasingly overcome the more widely and openly the subject is researched and discussed among scientists and scholars. As some of the taboos against open discussion of the topic fall away, the issues will become clarified on a rational basis. We will come to know better just what we do and do not yet know about the subject, and we will be in a better position to deal with it objectively and constructively.

We must distinguish clearly between research on racial differences and *racism*. Racism usually implies hate or aversion and is aimed at the denial of equal rights and opportunities to persons on the basis of their racial origin. Racism should be attacked in the spheres in which it operates, by enacting and enforcing laws and arrangements that help to ensure equality of civil and political rights and to guard against discrimination in educational and occupational opportunities on the basis of racial membership.

To fear research on genetic racial differences, or the possible existence of a biological basis for differences in abilities, is, in a sense, to grant the racist's assumption—that if it should be established beyond reasonable doubt that there are biological or genetically conditioned differences in mental abilities among individuals or groups, then we are justified in oppressing or exploiting those who are most limited in genetic endowment. This is, of course, a complete non sequitur. Equality of human rights does not depend upon the proposition that there are no genetically conditioned individual differences or group differences. Equality of rights is a moral axiom: it does not follow from any set of scientific data.

I have always advocated dealing with persons as individuals, each in terms of his own merits and characteristics, and I am opposed to according treatment to persons on the basis of their race, color, national origin, or social class background. But I am also opposed to ignoring or refusing to investigate the causes of the well-established differences among racial groups in the distribution of educationally relevant traits, particularly IQ.

I believe that the causes of observed differences in IQ and scholastic performance among different ethnic groups is an important question and a researchable one (40, 46, 47). I believe that official statements, such as "It is a demonstrable fact that the talent pool in any one ethnic group is substantially the same as in any other ethnic group" (U.S. Office of Education, 1966), and "Intelligence potential is distributed among Negro infants in the same proportion and pattern as among Icelanders or Chinese, or any other group" (U.S. Department of Labor, 1965), are without scientific merit. They are dogmatic pronouncements lacking any factual basis and must be regarded only as hypotheses.

The fact that different racial groups in the United States have widely separated geographic origins and have had quite different histories which have subjected them to different selective social and economic pressures makes it highly likely that their gene pools differ for some genetically conditioned behavioral characteristics, including intelligence or abstract reasoning ability. Nearly every anatomical, physiological, and biochemical system investigated shows racial differences. Why should the brain be an exception? The reasonableness of the hypothesis that there are racial differences in genetically conditioned behavioral characteristics, including mental abilities, has been expressed in writings and public statements by such eminent geneticists as Kenneth Mather, Cyril D. Darlington, Ronald A. Fisher, and Francis Crick, to name a few. Of course, this question cannot be settled by agreement of opinion, but only by a consensus of fact and converging lines of evidence.

In my *HER* article, I indicated several lines of evidence which support my assertion that a genetic hypothesis is worth considering, and I spell these out in detail in my book, *Educability and Group Differences* (47). The fact that we still have only inconclusive conclusions with respect to this hypothesis does not mean that the opposite of the hypothesis is true. Yet some social scientists, perhaps more for ideological than for scientific reasons, would prefer to believe that the question has already been answered—that all intelligence differences are due entirely to social injustices, poverty, and racism, and that there is no question of any genetic difference.

I challenge this view. It is based on wishful thinking. The 100 per cent environmental theories have not been put to any proper test. For these environmental theories to stand up, genetic theories must be ruled out by scientific evidence. This has not yet been done. Scientific investigation proceeds most effectively by means of what Platt has called "strong inference," pitting alternative hypotheses that lead to different predictions against one another and then putting the predictions to an empirical test.

Is the question I have raised only of academic interest? I think not. As I said in my *HER* article, probably even more important than the issue of racial differences per se is the probability of dysgenic trends in our urban slums, as suggested by census data showing markedly higher birth rates among the poorest segments of the Negro population than among successful, middle-class Negroes. This social class differential in birthrate appears to be much greater in the Negro than in the white population. That is, the educationally and occupationally least able among Negroes have a higher reproductive rate than their white counterparts, and the most able segment of the Negro population has a lower reproductive rate than its white counterpart.

If social class intelligence differences within the Negro population have a genetic component, as in the white population, the condition I have described could create and widen the genetic intelligence differences between Negroes and whites. The social and educational implications of this trend, if it exists and persists, are enormous. The problem obviously deserves thorough investigation by social scientists and geneticists. Or consider one of our most grievous human problems—mental retardation. This handicap occurs at a rate five or six times higher among Negro children than in the rest of our population, and this rate may be increasing. Trends show that in the next decade more than half a million retarded children, with IQs below 70, will grow up in our urban slums. The amount of frustration and suffering implied by this prospect is a misfortune that no humane person can view with complacency.

Is it entirely caused by racism and poverty? I now doubt it. Real solutions to these problems will depend upon accurate, objective diagnosis of their causes. The consequences of failure to tackle such problems with our best scientific resources may well be viewed by future generations as this society's greatest injustice to Negro Americans.

Some research questions are undeniably disturbing and painful to any thoughtful person, and we would prefer that they not have to be raised. Yet when we come face to face with the really hard problems, we cannot gain by shying away. The researcher who ventures into the territory of differential psychology which deals with group differences, with the aim to sharpen the questions, to evaluate the old evidence and to produce new evidence, thereby hopefully to increase our understanding of the nature of population differences in psychological characteristics, treads a most difficult, not to say treacherous, path. Probably the most fearsome aspect is the struggle with one's own feelings and conscience. The enemy is indulgence of one's sentimentality. True sensitivity, on the other hand, is principled and clear-sighted, not blind and self-indulgent. Fortunately, quite aside from whatever practical or social implications one's research might have, such work has an engrossing fascination of its own, much like the game of chess and working a puzzle. It is mainly this intrinsic aspect of research activity that keeps up one's enthusiasm day to day. Each step generates the next, so that as a researcher one is never at a loss for something interesting that next needs to be done. Each step essentially comes down to trying always to be as clear in one's mind as possible about two things: What is the question? What is the evidence?

SELECTED BIBLIOGRAPHY

1. Jensen, A. R. Aggression in fantasy and overt behavior. *Psychological Monographs,* 1957, *71,* No. 445, Whole No. 16.
2. ——. Authoritarian attitudes and personality maladjustment. *Journal of Abnormal and Social Psychology,* 1957, *54,* 303–311.
3. ——. Personality. *Annual Review of Psychology,* 1958, *9,* 295–322.
4. ——. The reliability of projective techniques: Review of the literature. *Acta Psychologica,* 1959, *16,* 3–31.
5. ——. Review of the Thematic Apperception Test. In O. K. Buros (ed.) *Fifth Mental Measurements Yearbook.* Highland Park, N.J.: Gryphon Press, 1959. Pp. 310–313.
6. ——. On the reformulation of inhibition in Hull's system. *Psychological Bulletin,* 1961, *58,* 274–298.
7. ——. Learning abilities in Mexican-American and Anglo-American children. *California Journal of Educational Research,* 1961, *12,* 147–159.
8. Symonds, P. M., and Jensen, A. R. *From Adolescent to Adult.* New York: Columbia University Press, 1961. Pp. viii and 413.
9. Jensen, A. R. An empirical theory of the serial-position effect. *Journal of Psychology,* 1962, *53,* 127–142.
10. ——. Is the serial position curve invariant? *British Journal of Psychology,* 1962, *53,* 159–166.
11. ——. Spelling errors and the serial position effect. *Journal of Educational Psychology,* 1962, *53,* 105–109.
12. ——. The von Restorff isolation effect with minimal response learning. *Journal of Experimental Psychology,* 1962, *64,* 123–125.
13. ——. Temporal and spatial effects of serial position. *American Journal of Psychology,* 1962, *75,* 390–400.
14. ——. Extraversion, neuroticism and serial learning. *Acta Psychologica,* 1962, *20,* 69–77.
15. ——. Transfer between paired-associate and serial learning. *Journal of Verbal Learning and Verbal Behavior,* 1962, *1,* 269–280.
16. —— and Blank, S. S. Association with ordinal position in serial rote-learning. *Canadian Journal of Psychology,* 1962, *16,* 60–63.
17. ——, Collings, C. C., and Vreeland, R. W. A multiple S-R apparatus for human learning. *American Journal of Psychology,* 1962, *75,* 470–476.
18. ——. The improvement of educational research. *Teachers College Record,* 1962, *64,* 20–27.
19. —— and Roden, A. Memory span and the skewness of the serial-position curve. *British Journal of Psychology,* 1963, *54,* 337–349.
20. ——. Serial rote-learning: Incremental or all-or-none? *Quarterly Journal of Experimental Psychology,* 1963, *15,* 27–35.
21. —— and Rohwer, W. D., Jr. Verbal mediation in paired-associate and serial learning. *Journal of Verbal Learning and Verbal Behavior,* 1963, *1,* 346–352.

22. ——. Learning ability in retarded, average, and gifted children. *Merrill-Palmer Quarterly Journal of Behavior and Development,* 1963, *9,* 123–140.
23. ——. Review of the Rorschach test. In O. K. Buros (ed.) *Sixth Mental Measurements Yearbook.* Highland Park, N.J.: Gryphon Press, 1965. Pp. 501–511.
24. —— and Rohwer, W. D., Jr. Syntactical mediation of serial and paired-associate learning as a function of age. *Child Development,* 1965, *36,* 601–608.
25. —— and Rohwer, W. D., Jr. What is learned in serial learning? *Journal of Verbal Learning and Verbal Behavior,* 1965, *4,* 62–72.
26. ——. An adjacency effect in free recall. *Quarterly Journal of Experimental Psychology,* 1965, *17,* 315–322.
27. ——. The measurement of reactive inhibition in humans. *Journal of General Psychology,* 1966, *75,* 85–93.
28. ——. Individual differences in concept learning. In H. Klausmeier and C. Harris (eds.), *Analyses of Concept Learning.* New York: Merrill, 1966. Pp. 139–154.
29. ——. Varieties of individual differences in learning. In R. M. Gagne (ed.), *Learning and Individual Differences.* Columbus, Ohio: Merrill, 1967. Pp. 117–135. (a)
30. ——. Estimation of the limits of heritability of traits by comparison of monozygotic and dizygotic twins. *Proceedings of the National Academy of Sciences,* 1967, *58,* 149–156.
31. ——. Social class, race, and genetics: Implications for education. *American Educational Research Journal,* 1968, *5,* 1–42. (a)
32. ——. The culturally disadvantaged and the heredity-environment uncertainty. In J. Hellmuth (ed.), *The Culturally Disadvantaged Child.* Vol. 2. Seattle, Wash.: Special Child Publications, 1968. Pp. 29–76.
33. ——. Patterns of mental ability and socio-economic status. *Proceedings of the National Academy of Sciences,* 1968, *60,* 1330–1337. (c)
34. ——. Intelligence, learning ability, and socio-economic status. *Journal of Special Education,* 1969, *3,* 23–35. (b)
35. ——. How much can we boost I.Q. and scholastic achievement? *Harvard Educational Review,* 1969, *39,* 1–123.
36. ——. Reducing the heredity-environment uncertainty. *Harvard Educational Review,* 1969, *39,* 449–483.
37. ——. A theory of primary and secondary familial mental retardation. In N. R. Ellis (ed.), *International Review of Research in Mental Retardation.* Vol. 4. New York: Academic Press, 1970, Pp. 33–105.
38. ——. Hierarchical theories of mental ability. In B. Dockrell (ed.), *On Intelligence.* Toronto: Ontario Institute for Studies in Education, 1970. Pp. 119–190.
39. ——. IQ's of identical twins reared apart. *Behavior Genetics,* 1970, *1,* 133–148.

40. ——. Can we and should we study race differences? In J. Hellmuth (ed.), *Disadvantaged Child,* Vol. 3, *Compensatory Education: A National Debate.* New York: Brunner/Mazel, 1970, pp. 124–157.
41. ——. Individual differences in visual and auditory memory. *Journal of Educational Psychology,* 1971, *62,* 123–131.
42. ——. Race and the genetics of intelligence: A reply to Lewontin. *Bulletin of the Atomic Scientists,* 1970, *26,* 17–23.
43. ——. Do Schools Cheat Minority Children? *Educational Research,* 1971, *14,* 3–28.
44. ——. Controversies in intelligence: Heredity and environment. In D. W. Allen and E. Seifman (eds.), *The Teacher's Handbook.* Glenview, Ill.: Scott, Foresman & Co., 1971. Pp. 642–654.
45. ——. *Genetics and Education.* New York: Harper & Row, 1973.
46. ——. *Educational Differences.* London: Methuen, 1973.
47. ——. *Educability and Group Differences.* New York: Harper & Row, 1973.
48. Deutsch, M., Katz, I., and Jensen, A. R. (eds.). *Social Class, Race, and Psychological Development.* New York: Holt, Rinehart, and Winston, 1968.

6

The Making of a Neobehaviorist

HOWARD H. KENDLER

My decision to major in psychology in 1938 led inevitably to a professional career. Surprisingly the choice itself was easy, more difficult than choosing which novel to read or which movie to attend, but not much more.

Why was such a significant decision made with relative ease? This question has more than academic interest to one who has watched his two sons suffer through a career choice during their college days. Two major reasons facilitated my choice. The Great Depression, while encouraging concern with getting a job, offered limited opportunities to an eighteen-year-old boy whose middle-class family was suffering economic hardships. Psychology seemed to offer reasonable possibilities for a self-supporting graduate education and an economically secure career.

The other reason, less obvious to me at that time, was forces that directed me toward an intellectual life. Although neither of my parents, American-born children of Jewish immigrants, went to college, they both rewarded ("reinforced" is the proper technical term) intellectual efforts. My mother—who was more influential because she raised me (marital difficulties resulted in frequent separations and finally a divorce)—encouraged me, in the traditions of Jewish mothers, at least fictional ones, to excel. Her praising my report cards and exhibiting my precocious arithmetical abilities, although embarrassing to a shy youngster, were

nevertheless reinforcing. The praise helped maintain my high scholastic performance. My father also encouraged me to use my wits, but more indirectly. He was master of the fast quip and sarcastic wisecrack, and in order to cope with him, I was forced to compete with him. Thus I learned to use and appreciate humor. I suspect humor helped sharpen my intellectual skills, trained me to be sensitive to the subtleties of language, and to perceive problems in unconventional ways.

Although neither of my parents had scholarly interests, they instilled in me a reverence for books. A book was to be read and treasured. What was the origin of their respect for books? The answer to this question became apparent to me when I read M. Zborowski and E. Herzog's *Life Is with People,* an anthropological study of life style of Jews in small towns in eastern Europe. My grandparents had emigrated from one of those towns. Cultural traditions were such that harming a book was a crime. Education for boys began when they were as young as three, and in order to make their initial contacts with books pleasant, honey and money were used as reinforcements. Through my parents, not by design but simply by family tradition, I was conditioned to have positive reactions to books characteristic of the Jewish boy in eastern Europe.

FORMATIVE YEARS

My parents' influence in directing me toward an intellectual life was less than that of my brother Joel, fifteen months my senior, whom I admired and loved deeply. Joel was a vociferous reader and an exceptionally talented poet and artist. After my parents were divorced, my mother, Joel, and I went to live with my mother's parents and her three brothers, all of whom in varying degrees assumed some of the roles of a father. Horace, nine years my senior, an excellent athlete and a considerate person, provided warmth, understanding, and encouragement in football, tennis, baseball, and other sports I played with intensity and enjoyment. Jack, three years older than Horace, the intellectual of the family, was the apple of my grandmother's eye because of his outstanding scholastic performance in both high school and college. Jack majored in Greek and Latin and seemed to be knowledgeable about everything from ancient history to modern economics, but was primarily interested in literature and art.

Within our family circle there was a natural affinity among Jack, my brother, and me, but for the most part the major interactions occurred within the realm of literature and art, areas that interested me but for which my talents, of a modest degree, failed to match theirs. My aptitudes were in science and mathematics but these subjects tended to be ignored at home, except for those books that stoked my imagination. Paul De Kruif's *Microbe Hunters* and Sinclair Lewis's *Arrowsmith* generated visions of discovering fundamental truths and applying them for the benefit of mankind. But during my early high school days science played more of a role in fantasy than in real life. My only direct contact with science was in high school where I received good training in physics, chemistry, and mathematics but these experiences failed to generate any self-directed science-oriented activities at home. In retrospect, I'm sure that with encouragement and guidance I would have developed active interests. But probably of greater significance in blunting my scientific interest were forces that attenuated any effort on my part to strike out on my own. One was economic, the other psychological, and in both my brother Joel played a central role.

We were in the midst of the Great Depression and all the adults of the household were making valiant efforts, not always successful, to make ends meet. Our economic difficulties also began a life-long interest in politics, generating a conviction that a society must be better engineered than the United States was at that time, or is today, so it may provide everybody with dignified opportunities for economic security. My brother, Joel, had developed a rheumatic heart condition when he was five, and he could not physically exert himself. Because my mother was employed and my grandmother was elderly, many household chores became my responsibility, particularly shopping for a family of eight, which in the days before the supermarket took time and effort, especially since we did not have an automobile.

I could not avoid thinking about the future and wondering how Joel, who had a physical disability and whose artistic talents, although considerable, were of little value in an economically depressed society, would be able to support himself. A possible solution was suggested indirectly through my interest in Vincent van Gogh, the postimpressionist Dutch painter. I resonated strongly to the beauty and intensity of van Gogh's paintings and began to read avidly about him. Because his brother Theo, financially successful in commercial art circles, supported Vincent at numerous times during his career, the idea began to take hold that my responsibility should be to support Joel's artistic career. I attempted to obtain a part-time job in Wall Street as a first step to becoming a financier. Not only was this attempt unsuccessful; so was my effort to become a delivery boy at the corner drug store.

In spite of these problems, I was essentially happy except for the threat of an impending disaster. Joel's heart was seriously defective. Although I was not told directly, I knew his survival was obviously in doubt. I could not tolerate the thought that he might die. But he did, when he was seventeen and I was sixteen. Despair overwhelmed me. During my next three years, my senior year in high school and my first two years in college, I lived in a trance; I was confused, dispirited, and depressed, and I responded to fantasies while ignoring reality.

In some manner unclear to me now, I graduated high school, and for nothing better to do I began Brooklyn College, just before turning seventeen. I thought of majoring in psychology without any clear conception of what it was. A passing remark by my uncle Jack about a friend who had become a psychologist, and was happy with his choice, encouraged me to choose psychology as my tentative major when enrolling in college. My commitment to this choice could not have been very strong both because my selection of courses was uninfluenced by it, and my involvement with my studies was slight. Although freshmen were required to attend classes, I cut classes frequently, and consequently became well acquainted with an assistant dean who in a compassionate fashion encouraged me to become both more responsible and academically motivated. His arguments were sound and compelling, but they had little effect on my preference to see a movie instead of attending a class, particularly if the class was in Spanish or German. Because five years of languages were needed for entrance into Brooklyn College and I had had only three, I was required to take five years of languages in college, two of which were to compensate for my high school deficiency. I despised languages, no doubt a combined effect of my lack of talent in learning them and my embarrassment in speaking them. Perhaps if I knew at that time how useful it would have been to know French and German, I would have expended more effort, but my behavior then was dominated more by the past than by the future. As a result my first two years in college were both uninteresting and unrewarding. Economics and constitutional law appeared interesting but not sufficiently so to awaken me from my doldrums. Biology was a disappointment; instead of the excitement of discovery I was offered tedious laboratory work and painful rote memorization of long lists of terms. This might have been tolerable if the professor justified such efforts in the larger context of the nature of science. But such support never came.

INTRODUCTION TO PSYCHOLOGY

In the last semester of my sophomore year I entered an introductory psychology course, free of any commitments to other fields but still withdrawn and depressed. My introduction to psychology did not turn me on, but more importantly neither did it turn me off, and consequently the haphazard decision to major in psychology remained in force, if only as a result of inertia. Perhaps the most positive aspect of my introductory psychology course was the textbook we used. It was John F. Dashiell's *Fundamentals of Objective Psychology*. Psychological principles expressed with clarity were buttressed by empirical evidence. Appearing less vague and more objective than either economics or law, and even more importantly, being able to evaluate competing principles by experimentation, made psychology the most attractive alternative.

The summer that intervened between my sophomore and junior years was spent in working in a canteen associated with a summer camp. My job was a combined counter man and short-order cook and although the wage was small ($150 for the summer), the total experience was pleasurable and beneficial. I was away from home for the first time and I achieved an independence that I had badly needed. My grandmother had recently died and the atmosphere of the household, still not fully recovered from the death of my brother, weighed heavily with depression and apathy. The beauty of the Berkshire Hills in western Massachusetts and new-found friends, one in particular who was a brilliant philosophy student, helped me to forget the loss of my brother for longer stretches of time than I had previously been able to.

Two events in my junior year reinforced my decision to major in psychology. The first was academic, the second was romantic, and both meshed in directing me to psychology.

A requirement for a major in psychology was Experimental Psychology, and I registered for the course in the first semester of my junior year. It proved to be a dreary experience. The textbook was Kurt Koffka's *Principles of Gestalt Psychology,* an unusual selection for an undergraduate text because the obscurity of its prose was matched only by the complexity of its ideas. Much of Gestalt theory is embedded in the metaphysical traditions of German philosophy, but at that time I was unaware of this. As a result I was disturbed by my difficulty in understanding the text. Perhaps I was not qualified to pursue a career in psychology? But that doubt was rejected by the knowledge that my professor had difficulty in comprehending the text, too.

The major significance of my first course in experimental psychology was that it led to my second one, Experimental Psychology of Thinking taught by Solomon E. Asch. It was Professor Asch who gave me the necessary encouragement and direction to produce a firm commitment to experimental psychology.

Asch looked and behaved as a professor should. He was thoughtful, soft spoken, shy, and absent minded. When asked a difficult question he would sometimes ponder and delay his answer for as long as five minutes, removing his glasses, placing the end of one earpiece in his mouth, closing his eyes, tilting his head back. Suddenly his sensitive face would light up, and a slow, decisive, and appropriate answer would come forth. His performance was impressive and the students, especially those who were considering graduate school, were both proud and pleased to be students of Professor Asch.

Asch had received his Ph.D. from Columbia University where functionalism, the school of American psychology that emphasized the adaptive functions of mind and behavior, dominated. But he soon came under the influence of Max Wertheimer, the founder of Gestalt psychology, who, because of the Nazi persecution, fled from Germany to the United States where he became associated with the New School for Social Research, a graduate school organized in New York City for distinguished European scholars.

Gestalt psychology emphasized the organization, the quality of wholeness, that inheres in both behavior and experience. The analysis of perception, the major source of Gestalt psychology's theoretical assumptions, led to the adoption of the principle that *the whole was different from the sum of its parts.* In Figure 6.1, for example, there are twelve separate dots but you don't perceive them that way. Instead you perceive them in an organized manner, as the corners of three squares. The discovery of the principles that governed such organization was the task the Gestalt psychologists set for themselves.

At the time I was in Dr. Asch's class, he was working closely with Wertheimer who was completing his book *Productive Thinking* and as a consequence this topic served as the central theme of the course.

One of the major theses of the Gestalt viewpoint was that mechanical habits of thought can prevent problem solving. To illustrate this point Dr. Asch offered the following demonstration:

Consider the following series of problems, each of which you must solve by obtaining a prescribed volume of water. For example, if you have a 29-pint jar, a 3-pint jar, and an unlimited supply of water, how do you measure out exactly 20 pints of water? You do this by filling the 29-pint container and then pouring 9 pints from it by filling the 3-pint jar three times: 29–3–3–3 = 20. Now *you* solve the *first* of the following six problems:

	Capacities of Jars (in pints)			Pints To Obtain
1.	21	127	3	100
2.	14	163	25	99
3.	18	43	10	5
4.	10	41	8	15
5.	18	41	8	7
6.	23	49	3	20

You probably had no difficulty in solving the first problem. By initially filling the 127-pint container and then from it filling the 21-pint jar once and the 3-pint jar twice you would have 100 pints

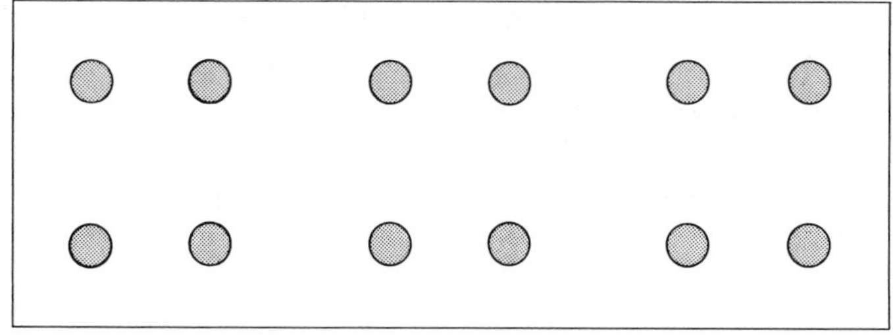

Figure 6.1. Do you perceive 12 isolated dots or 3 squares of 4 dots each?

remaining in the 127-pint container: 127–21–3–3 = 100. Now do the remaining problems.

If you are a typical subject you will solve the sixth problem by filling the 49-pint jar and from it fill the 23-pint container once and the 3-pint container twice: 49–23–3–3 = 20. But note that the problem can be solved more simply! The 23-pint can be filled and then three pints can be poured into the 3-pint container, leaving 20 pints: 23–3 = 20.

To Wertheimer and Asch, and other Gestalt psychologists, this demonstration illustrated the blinding effects of sheer habit. By solving a series of similar problems in the same fashion (first fill the middle jar, and pour from it an amount that would fill the first jar once, and the third jar twice) one learns a mechanical mode of thinking that prevents sensible problem-solving. In essence, repetitive drill produces stupid behavior.

I entertained reservations about the relevance of this *einstellung* (German for *mental set*) demonstration for condemning drill as an educational technique. After all, efficiency is frequently better served by responding to similar problems in a pat way. It would be burdensome to be required to think through each time one is confronted with a problem of why, for example, 8 times 7 is 56. Responding automatically and mechanically can be efficient. Offering an over-all judgment about drill appears inappropriate. The fundamental problem is not whether drill is good or bad but instead to understand its consequences and then decide under what conditions its applications are beneficial. The einstellung demonstration essentially shows that a set method of problem-solving persists when consistently rewarded.

I was, however, more interested in the experimental problem than in its implications for educational practice. In seeking to design an "original" experiment, a task Asch set for us, I was influenced by some of Kurt Lewin's notions which suggested to me an experiment that investigated the influence of time of delay between the last training problem, number 5, and the critical problem number 6. My theory assumed that the tendency to respond in a set manner increased over time and this led to the counter-intuitive prediction that as the aforementioned time delay increased so would the percentage of set responses.

Dr. Asch encouraged me to research the problem and this led to my most significant educational experience in college. Designing the experimental procedure and collecting and analyzing the data proved to be both challenging and stimulating. In retrospect this was not surprising because experimenting for me had the quality of playing chess, solving problems, and formulating unconventional proofs in Euclidean geometry, intellectual activities that were fun.

I was not terribly disappointed or surprised when the data failed to support my hypothesis. The results indicated that as the time interval increased between the fifth and sixth problems the percentage of set responses decreased. But in spite of these negative findings, positive information was obtained. The proportion of set responses, even after a week's interval, was rather high. In short, the einstellung effect persisted over lengthy time periods.

While doing my einstellung project, I was becoming romantically involved with an attractive, articulate, bright young lady named Tracy Seedman, whom I had previously met in the picturesque setting of a logic class. She too was a psychology major and was also in Dr. Asch's class. More than anybody else she was responsible for my emergence from the depressing shroud that had encompassed me since the death of my brother. We had similar backgrounds, similar interests, similar attitudes, but sufficient differences to generate mutual attraction.

In our senior year we did an honors study together, an extension of the einstellung problem to the behavior of rats. The experiment proved to have many benefits aside from romantic ones. It reinforced my attraction to original research and encouraged me to go to graduate school. Since Tracy was also interested

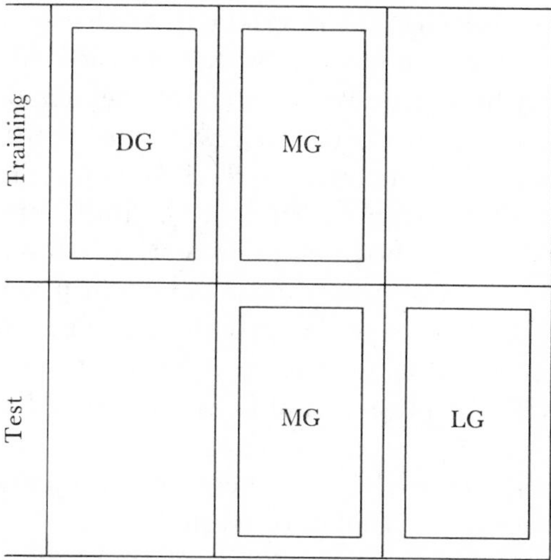

Figure 6.2. Stimuli that are used to test transposition. First, subjects are trained to choose a medium gray in preference to a darker gray. After learning this discrimination, they are confronted with a new pair of stimuli, the same medium gray and light gray. Transposition occurs when a subject chooses the light gray.

in pursuing a career in psychology, we naturally discussed graduate school possibilities. The alternatives were few and it seemed obvious from the beginning that the University of Iowa would be the best choice. Many of our professors, including Dr. Asch, recommended the University of Iowa because of the presence there of Kurt Lewin. Another attractive feature was that tuition for graduate students was fifty dollars a semester, a small amount even in those days. Finally, the graduate program in psychology emphasized learning, an area of psychology that appeared attractive to me and was consistent with the kind of experimental work that I enjoyed. One of the members of the staff was the behaviorist Kenneth W. Spence, a thirty-three-year-old associate professor. Dr. Asch, who had very little sympathy for behaviorism (more about behaviorism later) and paid little attention to it, had discussed Spence's theory of transposition critically but in great detail, thus assigning it considerable significance.

The phenomenon of transposition is illustrated by the experiment in which chickens are trained to peck at the brighter of two gray cards, a medium gray in preference to a dark gray, in order to get food. After learning this discrimination they are confronted with the same medium gray they had learned to choose and another still brighter gray. Which one did they choose—the same medium gray, the choice of which was reinforced, or the new brighter stimulus? The majority of chickens chose the new brighter stimulus, the lightest gray. That is, the birds *transposed* their choice response to the brighter of two stimuli from the original training pair to the test pair. Köhler, a Gestalt psychologist who originally reported the experiment with chickens, interpreted the results to suggest that animals learn to respond to a relationship, not to a specific positive stimulus as suggested by theories of conditioning.

Spence cleverly showed how a theory based upon conditioning principles involving principles of stimulus generalization could account for the phenomenon of transposition. In addition Spence's formulation went a step further than Köhler's conception. Köhler's relational interpretation failed to explain why in some test trials subjects chose the absolute rather than the relational stimulus. In addition Köhler's relational formulation fails to account for how the amount of transposition is influenced by the particular pair of test stimuli that are used. In Figure 6.2 the pair of test stimuli are only one of many. A still brighter pair could be selected. If it were, would the proportion of relational responses be the same? Experimental evidence suggests that the amount of transposition decreases as the difference between the test pair of stimuli and the original training pair increases, a finding that one would expect from Spence's conditioning interpretation of transposition. The subtleties of this theoretical dispute cannot be examined here; further experimental analysis indicates that the problem of transposition is much more complex than was suggested by either formulation. But the significant factor, in terms of my own development, was that Spence's formulation was clearer than that of Köhler's, both in conception and deductive implications and, as such, was closer to what I intuitively thought a theory should be. In retrospect it seemed inevitable that if I were to go to the University of Iowa even with the idea of studying with Kurt Lewin, I would end up working with Kenneth Spence. And that is exactly what happened.

GRADUATE SCHOOL

When planning their postgraduate education in psychology, college seniors would be well advised to pay more attention to the professor with whom they plan to work than to the school they wish to attend. The prospective graduate psychology student should read the publications of those professors in his major area of interest and then choose to study with the one with whom he has the greatest affinity. This recommendation stems from my own experience. Although I received excellent graduate training at the University of Iowa during the 1940–1943 period, my most significant and important experience was the apprenticeship I served with Kenneth W. Spence.

My initial association with Kenneth Spence resulted more from accident than design. Some of the first-year graduate courses in psychology were closed and Tracy and I wandered around in despair because of our difficulty in planning a satisfactory program. Kenneth Spence observed our dejection and inquired if he could be of help. When informed of our difficulty he encouraged us to register for his advanced seminar in *Conditioning and Learning*. Although our preparation for the course was inadequate, previous experience had impressed him with the quality of Brooklyn College graduates. In addition, he frankly admitted to a mission to save the minds of students who had yet to perceive the virtues of a neobehavioristic approach to the science of psychology.

Although Kenneth Spence and I emerged from different backgrounds (a native-born American citizen, he grew up in Montreal, the son of a successful electrical engineer) and disagreed markedly about politics (he was appreciably to the right of Franklin D. Roosevelt whereas I was slightly to the left of Norman Thomas, the socialist candidate for President), we nevertheless shared common qualities that drew us close together. We both prided ourselves for being able to think clearly and it rapidly became obvious to me that Spence was a master of lucid thought when it came to psychological experimentation, theorizing, and methodology. We both shared a fascination in designing and conducting experiments that tested theoretical notions. As boys we both had enjoyed competitive sports and research seemed to possess for us similar excitement and fun. In spite of our aversion to pedantic and abstruse intellectual discussions, we were both predisposed to the philosophy of science, and under Spence's tutelage this interest developed into a lifelong concern but only with those issues that were relevant to the task of the psychologist as an experimenter and theorist.

All in all I resonated to Spence's approach to psychology with its strong and intimate relationship between theory and research and its heavy emphasis on objectivity. In addition Spence proved to be a source of inspiration. In college my work habits were atrocious but in order to meet Spence's demands for scholarship, I rapidly became a hard-working (seventy to eighty hours a week) student. In attempting to explain Spence's impact I wrote the following paragraph when confronted with the sad task of preparing his necrology after his death at the age of fifty-nine:

> By example and dedication, and by a quaint and charming mixture of childish enthusiasm and stern paternal demands, he was able to transmit to students the excitement of theoretical psychology and the essential role that experimentation played. All of his doctoral students carry with them some of Spence's ideas and commitments and a desire to achieve a level of quality in their own work that would be acceptable to their Professor (Kendler, 1967, p. 341).

The one difficulty I experienced doing research with Spence, was his dominant personality. When I told him that I was interested in doing a master's thesis he suggested several interesting possibilities from a file of experimental designs that he wanted executed. His forceful manner of persuasion made it difficult for me to ignore his recommendations. But I had a strong need to express my independence and as a result a compromise was reached. I did three small experiments, one that he desired, a related one which I designed, and finally a third one the design of which was a result of our joint efforts. All three studies, done with white rats in a T-maze, were concerned in general with how learning is influenced by motivation and reward variables and specifically with some theoretical differences between Edward C. Tolman's cognitive theory and the Hull-Spence stimulus-response formulation. Clark Hull, who was at Yale when Spence did his graduate work there, was the founder of the neobehavioristic approach in psychology.

My three studies (1946, 1947, 1948) along with some that had already been completed at Iowa and several that were executed in the ensuing years became known as the Iowa latent learning studies, and became the center of an intense theoretical controversy in the 1940s and 1950s that expressed itself in well over a hundred published papers. I, myself, in my postdoctoral days, contributed related studies to those of my master's thesis (Kendler and Kanner, 1950; Kendler and Levine, 1953; H. H. Kendler and Mencher, 1948) as well as some theoretical notes (Kendler, 1952a, 1952b; Spence and Kendler, 1948). Later on it became apparent that the theoretical issues were not as clear and precise as originally thought. The result of the latest learning controversy was that psychologists became aware that their leading learning theories had failed to achieve a level of maturity that many had hoped for. Although this encouraged some to eschew theory it simultaneously encouraged others to improve the precision of their own formulation.

Spence recognized my need for independence and even encouraged it by giving me free rein to carry out whatever research interested me. As a result my Ph.D. thesis was done in the relatively unexplored area of drive interaction. Hull had proposed a hypothesis on how the presence of a hunger and thirst drive would affect the performance of a rat in an instrumental (bar-pressing) situation. The results of my study proved to be inconsistent with Hull's theory. Although one might believe that my disproof of Hull's predictions would lead to a disenchantment with his formulations, it had the opposite effect. I became more interested in his formulations because they *could* be proven wrong. I realized that worse than being wrong was being vague. Many vaguely stated formulations survive in psychology not because they are correct but instead because they are so ambiguous that they remain forever beyond attempts to test them empirically. In science, being proven wrong can help lead to finding something right. In actual fact, scientific theories sooner or later get disproven and are replaced by better theories. Although great works of art may live forever, those of science do not.

Of course, other events transpired during my days as a graduate student, besides doing research and completing theses. Tracy and I got married at the beginning of the second year of graduate study. In spite of difficulties for women that were greater in those days than they are now, she completed her doctoral research with Kenneth Spence.

Although Spence was the dominant intellectual influence during my graduate training, his was not the only one. Other professors provided the necessary training in varied areas of experimental psychology, psychological tests, and clinical psychology, the latter study fulfilling my requirements for a minor field of study (experimental psychology was my major). Being interested in learning theory I was naturally interested in therapy and had some experience treating a five-year-old boy whose parents were incapable of controlling him. Of particular importance was my association with Gustav Bergmann, a Viennese philosopher of science who emigrated to the United States in order to escape Nazism and later became collaborator with Kenneth Spence on some important articles on methodological issues in psychology. Bergmann whetted my interests in methodological and historical issues in psychology and in addition became a close friend to Tracy and myself. His interest in us, and the guidance and encouragement he offered, proved to be most helpful.

One of the most pleasant and rewarding experiences during my three years as a graduate student was the social interaction with other students, some of which developed into lifelong friendships. The University of Iowa, because of its well-known faculty and the significant role it has played in the history of psychology, had attracted many exceptionally talented students, as their later careers demonstrate. As a result an atmosphere of intellectual excitement pervaded the psychology building, and numerous discussions, including intense arguments about theories and experiments, made important contributions to my education. And the informal gatherings and parties were usually fun, and sometimes hilarious.

All in all, graduate education was a turning point in my life. I made the transition from adolescence to adulthood, while acquiring both professional skills and an involvement that led to a life's work. But graduate training was not simply a period of transition. In its own right it proved to be a significant, exciting experience—some of the best years of my life.

PROFESSIONAL CAREER

I was particularly fortunate to be able to complete my graduate training in the summer of 1943. Some of my fellow graduate students had their studies interrupted by military service during World War II. Because of defective vision I was not acceptable to the draft nor to an Air Force program that was recruiting graduate psychology students.

After receiving my Ph.D., I stayed on at Iowa as an Instructor, teaching half-time in a program designed to train soldiers for a variety of jobs requiring psychological skills and doing research for an Air Force project the purpose of which was to improve the selection, training, and performance of Air Force personnel such as pilots, navigators, and bombardiers. Although I desired an academic position, I had reservations about my teaching ability. When I did start teaching, my fears were confirmed. I prepared my lectures for my course in Tests and Measurement, which was not my field of specialization, with such thoroughness that my notes contained every word of my lecture. My careful preparation, however, did not allay my anxieties. The night before lecturing I would awaken several hours after midnight, stomach tense, and overwhelmed with worry. Needless to say, my reactions were not conducive to clear and exciting lectures. But the students, most of whom were older than I, were compassionate and understanding, perhaps because they knew I was trying.

Before the end of 1943 I was approached by the Psychological Corporation to accept a job as a research psychologist in Chicago on a government contract, one of the purposes of which was to develop improved methods of teaching radio code. Since my field of specialization was the psychology of learning, I accepted the position but a turn of events prevented me from completing an experimental project to test the effectiveness of a training program which I helped design. During the early portion of 1944, the United States had difficulty meeting its military manpower needs. My draft status, at that time, was not based upon my severe nearsightedness but instead on the military significance of the research in which I was engaged. In order to cope with the manpower shortage, a governmental decision was made to eliminate any professional deferments for men under twenty-six. In addition the visual requirements were relaxed. Being twenty-five, I became eligible again for military service. I attempted to get a commission in the Navy in the hope of continuing my research on our new method of teaching code, the initial evaluation of which proved positive. But I failed the physical examination because of defective vision. Only if I were qualified to be a chaplain, I was informed, could a medical waiver be given. As a result I was drafted into the Army and held at the induction center until an appropriate assignment for a Ph.D. in psychology turned up. This waiting period lasted thirty days, marred only by my doing a six-day stint on KP as punishment for making a wisecrack that my corporal failed to appreciate. Finally the special assignment came. I was to be trained as a heavy machine gunner in the infantry. I never understood the rationale for assigning a nearsighted Ph.D. in psychology to be trained as a machine gunner, but perhaps the difficulty is mine since my knowledge of military strategy is limited.

During the fourth month of my training as a machine gunner, my background as a psychologist was rediscovered and I was assigned to a psychiatric unit in an infantry training camp. My job was to interview and give psychological tests to soldiers who were having difficulties coping with infantry training and then to make recommendations as to whether their training should continue or whether they should be reassigned, or discharged. During this time the Army recognized its need for clinical psychologists and started recruiting among enlisted men by offering commissions to qualified candidates. I applied and soon received a commission. After some special training, I was assigned as the clinical psychologist at Walter Reed General Hospital in Washington, D.C., where I stayed until my discharge from the Army in September 1946.

I was lucky to be able to function as a clinical psychologist in the Army, especially when considered against the alternative of being a machine gunner. I was also fortunate in being assigned to Walter Reed General Hospital, a distinguished institution. During war time it was staffed by outstanding physicians, many of whom were professors in various medical schools throughout the country.

My reaction to practicing clinical psychology was ambivalent. Although I found the task interesting, challenging, and rewarding, especially when conducting psychotherapy with individuals and with groups, it proved not to be as intellectually satisfying as experimental psychology. Whereas experimental research afforded me an opportunity to develop hypotheses and then obtain evidence that threw light on their validity, the practice of clinical psychology frequently left me in the dark about the effectiveness of my efforts. Although a majority of my patients seemed to improve during treatment (see Kendler, 1947) I realized that a detached evaluation of my efforts would have to be inconclusive. Spontaneous improvements among psychiatric patients sometimes occur; even patients suffering from severe psychotic reactions suddenly get better without any psychotherapeutic intervention. Perhaps some or all of my patients would have improved without my help. In addition, improvements in the conditions of psychiatric patients are frequently transitory. Perhaps my patients would later suffer a relapse or even deteriorate below their condition on admission. I remember the case of one soldier, a talented pianist in civilian life, who seemed to be improving with treatment. One day he ran down the corridor of the ward and leaped head first into the wall. He fractured his skull and fortunately he recovered, but I did not because I could not escape from the thought that something I did or did not do during therapy was responsible for his action.

Some therapists take full credit for any improvement their patients exhibit. When a patient fails to improve, or his condition declines, the explanation is offered that the therapy failed to reach the patient or he was not motivated to be helped. My position is that if a therapist wants to take credit for his successes he must also assume responsibility for his failures.

Even though attractive opportunities were available for me to pursue a career as a clinical psychologist, I had no difficulty opting for experimental psychology. This decision was not made because of any conviction that basic research in the psychology of learning was in any sense superior to the practice of clinical psychology. My choice was simply made in terms of my own needs. I enjoyed experimental psychology more than clinical psychology.

I became an assistant professor at the University of Colorado after leaving the Army in 1946 and had the good fortune of becoming associated with Professor Karl Muenzinger, who was the chairman. In spite of having an age difference of almost thirty years as well as conflicting theoretical attitudes, we became close friends. In addition to being interested in the psychology of learning he was also actively concerned with the difficult problem of developing an integrated picture of all of psychology, from sensory processes to social behavior. He attempted such an integration in his introductory textbook and encouraged me to write an introductory textbook, believing it to be the best way of learning about all of psychology. About a decade later (Kendler, 1963, 1968, 1973; Kendler and Kendler, 1971) I took his advice. Although I do not deny the tremendous educational benefits that accrue from such an effort, I wonder whether there may be easier ways available to achieve the same goals.

At Colorado teaching was not the chore it had been at the University of Iowa. At Walter Reed General Hospital I was required to lecture on various aspects of clinical psychology, sometimes at a moment's notice. The combination of a more relaxed Army atmosphere and increased maturity reduced my anxieties and improved my teaching. And as is usual in such cases, my improved performance made me more relaxed, which in turn improved my performance further.

In spite of my close relationship to Muenzinger, I left the University of Colorado after only two years. My salary was low, my teaching load high, and the laboratory facilities mediocre. In addition the University of Colorado had a policy of not matching offers from other universities. I had better offers, an infant son, and ambition. I accepted a position as an associate professor at New York University in 1948 and during my fifteen years there I was blessed with many excellent graduate and undergraduate students, and with some talented colleagues with whom I became close friends. During the time I taught experimental psychology, 1948 to 1951, at University College, a small college in NYU's large complex of different schools, about 25 per cent of the students went on to graduate school and obtained their Ph.D. degrees.

In the 1960–1961 academic year I accepted a visiting professorship at the University of California, Berkeley, and the year there made me realize how much effort I was spending commuting to New York from my suburban home in Long Island, how much time was being consumed by my chairmanship duties at University

College, and how much I detested winter. I returned to NYU the following year but resigned the chairmanship and, when an offer came from the University of California, Santa Barbara, beginning in the fall of 1963, I accepted it.

A summary of my own professional career would be incomplete without describing that of my wife, Tracy, whose research and theoretical efforts became intertwined with that of my own. The decisions that were made, which seemed natural enough to me at that time but would qualify me today as a male chauvinist pig, were dictated primarily by my own career needs. When I left the University of Iowa to do research in radio code learning in Chicago, Tracy stayed on in Iowa City to complete her thesis work and then joined me after a few months and got a position as a clinical psychologist in a large state psychiatric institution. When I was drafted into the Army she followed me east and took a position with the College Entrance Examination Board in Princeton, New Jersey. She left that position and joined me in Texas when I became a clinical psychologist. When I received my commission I was transferred to a hospital in a nearby infantry training base, where Tracy volunteered her services. In Washington, D.C., when I was stationed at Walter Reed General Hospital, she worked as a statistician in the headquarters of the psychology program of the Army Air Force. At the University of Colorado she was employed as a part-time member of the department teaching a variety of courses at a pay scale appreciably below that of the regular members. In New York City, when adequate domestic help became available, Tracy returned to professional work as a research psychologist for the Committee on Community Interrelationships of the American Jewish Congress, the mission of which was to gain insights into the causes of social conflict with the hope that such knowledge could be used to reduce it. However, our domestic help proved to be less than adequate in caring for our son, Joel, and Tracy returned to the task of being a housewife and mother, keeping up as best she could with her professional interests, sometimes by doing part-time work on a project designed to improve educational films. Six years later, when our second son, Kenneth, who was named after Spence, was four years old, Tracy accepted a part-time teaching position at Barnard College of Columbia University which in 1955 developed into a full-time job, at an assistant professor level (I had been a full professor since 1951). In 1959 she became an associate professor.

Because of my intense desire to move to California, Tracy was willing to settle for a non-tenured position as a research psychologist at the University of California, Santa Barbara, with the proviso that she be permitted to obtain government research funds to support her effort. In spite of this arrangement, in which the university had everything to gain and nothing to lose, the nepotism rule—the rule that prevents relatives from being employed in the same department—had to be waived annually. Because of the uncertainty that the waiver would always be forthcoming we decided that other academic possibilities, where both of us would have secure positions, should be explored. Finally the Chancellor of UCSB acknowledged the fact that any productive research scientist requires tenure and set into motion a series of events (after a decision on the part of the members of the psychology department to support Tracy's appointment) that led to a waiver of the nepotism rule and Tracy's appointment as Professor of psychology.

These details are not simply cited for the purpose of historical accuracy. They illustrate the difficulties confronting a woman who wishes to pursue a professional career without denying herself marriage and a family. Both Tracy and I had similar graduate training and common interests but it proved much easier for me to pursue mine. There is no doubt that in our present society the obstacles confronting a person who desires a professional career and a family are greater for a woman than a man. In some cases, especially in war time, there are unavoidable conflicts between careers and marriage. But is it not possible for a society that values equal rights and opportunities for all to eliminate social obstacles, such as the nepotism rule, which makes it difficult, if not impossible, for married women to pursue a professional career?

Endorsing equal opportunities for men and women does not imply, at least for me, that either sex is entitled to a certain percentage, reflecting their proportion of the total population, of professorships in universities or positions in professional organizations. Positions should be filled in all areas in society, universities as well as track teams, in terms of abilities, regardless of race, creed, and sex. The important point is that everybody should have equal opportunities to develop their potentialities and exploit their skills.

NEOBEHAVIORISM

Over the years my greatest effort has been expended in research. But research, in my estimation, cannot be separated from theory, and theory, in turn, cannot be insulated from broad philosophical issues about the nature of psychology. This mandate is particularly true when one teaches introductory psychology, although I must confess with a great deal of regret that many students resist this notion. Why can't psychology be taught, the complaint goes, like other sciences, without getting enmeshed in all these complex philosophical issues? One reason is that many, if not most, introductory students have erroneous preconceptions about psychology. Only by being exposed to relevant philosophical issues can they understand psychology.

In my estimation several different interpretations, some conflicting, are possible about the nature of psychology. The reader will not be surprised to discover that my view of psychology is within the tradition of behaviorism but he probably will be surprised to learn what behaviorism really is. In anticipation of our discussion about different viewpoints of the nature of psychology, two points will now be stressed. First, different approaches in psychology (for example, behaviorism, structuralism, humanistic psychology) cannot be evaluated as right or wrong as a factual statement can, such as the earth is flat or sound travels faster in water than in air. The point at issue in choosing among different approaches in psychology is not a matter of truth but of preference (Kendler, 1970). Different conceptions of psychology lead to different kinds of knowledge and a choice among these conceptions should be made in full light of the kind of knowledge they produce. Second, behaviorism is not a monolithic conception characterized by a unity of beliefs about all aspects of psychology. For your purposes, the essence of behaviorism can be conceived as a methodology, a technique of investigation, that values objective data, that is, data that are publicly observable.

One variety of behaviorism is neobehaviorism (Kendler and Spence, 1971), a general methodological approach that was initiated by Hull and developed by Kenneth Spence. Although my present position is certainly an outgrowth of Spence's conceptions, it represents an extension, influenced, no doubt, by my shift of research interest from animal learning to human cognitive development, and my concern, as an author of an introductory psychology text, with facts and theories that range over the entire spectrum of psychology.

Perhaps the simplest method of understanding the major characteristics of neobehaviorism is to examine its development within a historical context. Behaviorism rose in opposition to structuralism, the German school of psychology founded by Wilhelm Wundt (1832–1920), that conceived the task of psychology to be the analysis of conscious experience into its basic elements. As the task of the chemist was to analyze a chemical compound into its basic physical elements the task of the psychologist was to analyze conscious experience into its basic psychical elements. For example, when perceiving chartreuse we can break down the experience into its component color sensations, which for me would be blue and green. Or when we taste a coffee ice-cream soda we can analyze the taste into its basic elementary flavors. Or when feeling love or hate or joy we can, in principle, reduce the complex emotion into its fundamental feelings. Or when we try to solve a mathematical problem we can analyze our thoughts into mental images.

Structuralism possesses two significant characteristics. One is that the subject matter of psychology is mind, or what some might prefer to call conscious experience, inner experience, or mental processes. The second is that conscious experience can be analyzed into basic psychical elements. It should be obvious that the second feature does not logically flow from the first. It would be quite possible to study mind, as many other approaches to psychology suggest, without attempting to analyze it into basic experiential elements.

Behaviorism developed as a protest against structuralism. John B. Watson (1878–1958), the self-styled "behaviorist," denied that psychology has a unique subject matter, mental processes observable only by the experiencing individual. Instead, like other sciences, physical and biological, psychology deals with objective data, events accessible to all. Watson concluded that the proper study of psychology was behavior, not conscious experience. To demonstrate that psychology need not study the mind, Watson showed how psychological research could be conducted with organisms, infants and lower animals, that were incapable of reporting inner experiences.

For some of Watson's critics, behaviorism represented an unfortunate development in the history of psychology. By previously separating itself from religion psychology had lost its soul, and under his leadership psychology was losing its mind. Such a statement is true when soul is equated with a set of religiously inspired ethical principles by which individuals and societies can guide and judge behavior, and mind is considered equivalent to conscious experience. According to neobehaviorism psychology neither has the responsibility to reveal a true set of human values nor to reflect faithfully conscious experience. To clarify this position neobehaviorism will now be contrasted with some varieties of humanistic psychology.

Whereas behavioristic psychology views behavior, whether of animals or men, from the outside, just as a natural scientist observes phenomena, the humanistic psychologist desires to understand behavior from the inside, in terms of inner experience. How a person feels inside, not how he behaves outside, becomes the focal point of psychology.

This difference in orientation leads to divergent criteria for understanding psychological events. Understanding for the neobehaviorist is equated with deducing an event from a set of theoretical principles. A classic example of deductive explanation is the theory of gravitation, the attraction that masses of matter have for each other. From this theory one can deduce such phenomena that apples fall downward from trees, that stones thrown up ultimately descend, that the time taken for any particular pendulum to swing back and forth is constant regardless of the size of the arc, and the movement of planetary bodies. Such a theory serves two functions: first, it integrates a set of separate phenomena into a coherent body of knowledge and, second, it predicts new events. For example, in the nineteenth century the planet Uranus was noted to follow a peculiar and variable path around the sun. From the theory of gravitation the mathematical prediction (deduction) was made, and later confirmed in the discovery of Neptune in 1843, that some unknown planetary body was exerting gravitational pull on Uranus.

Psychology, too, has its theories, although of a more restrictive range of implications than physical theories. Nevertheless numerous phenomena in learning, perception, and other areas can be deductively explained from a set of theoretical assumptions. But deductive explanation of publicly observable behavioral events is not sufficiently satisfying for a humanistic psychologist who aspires to share the experience of another, to know the entire spectrum of his own inner experience as well as those states of consciousness of which humans are capable. What he desires is not deductive explanation of behavior, but what may be called an intuitive understanding of the human mind. For me, intuitive understanding occurs when I read a perceptive novelist, like Dostoyevsky, Camus, or Bellows. I can empathize with their characters, to "share" their inner experience. In clinical situations, as well as in everyday life, empathic reactions are common. Ignoring for the time being whether such empathic reactions truly represent another person's inner experience, the important point to remember is that such reactions possess no clear deductive consequences as does a logically constructed theory and therefore do not qualify as scientific explanations in spite of the intuitive understanding generated.

A neobehaviorist neither denies the existence of conscious experience nor the ability to investigate it. Experimental psychologists have gained some information about states of consciousness: depth of sleep, dreams, hypnotic trances, altered states of consciousness induced by meditation or drugs, and so forth. Such research efforts are entirely consistent with neobehaviorism since they relate publicly observable events; for example, self-reports with changes in the electrical activity of the brain, both of which are recordable for future examination. In interpreting such data one cannot, however, simply assume that verbal reports mirror conscious experience with perfect fidelity. We must accept the principle that our own personal conscious experiences, as well as those of others, are guarded by an impenetrable fortress whose privacy cannot be invaded. Each of us is prevented from knowing directly whether we share a particular experience with others or whether our experience is unique.

Perhaps in the future, if the scientific fiction of today achieves reality, we will be able to compare *directly* the inner experiences of different individuals. For the time being, however, our knowledge of another person's conscious experience must of necessity be inferred, and one can choose to evaluate the adequacy of such inferences in one of two ways. One possibility, consistent with neobehaviorism, is to formulate a theory capable of generating deductions about verbal reports, physiological measures, and other publicly observed evidence that are used to infer states of consciousness. Such a theory can be evaluated as any other formulation is, by discovering whether the theoretical deductions agree with the empirical data. Another approach is to accept a radical subjectivism; one's own intuition can serve as the litmus test for knowing another person's conscious experience. No outside criteria need be met, one's own personal conviction is sufficient. As previously indicated one cannot evaluate which of the two criteria is the correct one. They each represent different conceptions of "truth": either a preference for deductive explanations or intuitive understanding.

In comprehending my preference for deductive explanation, which is consistent with the tenets of neobehaviorism, one must appreciate that this choice does not reflect a simple desire to emulate physics but instead represents an admiration for the conclusiveness of a deductive explanation. A deductive explanation does not rely on the intuitive conviction of a single individual but instead upon socially accepted rules of logic and proof.

My reading of humanistic psychology and some related enterprises such as encounter groups, sensitivity training, co-counseling, and other social efforts designed to increase conscious awareness is that they are not interested in formalizing psychological knowledge by constructing theories capable of deductively explaining psychological events. Instead the major concern is to understand intuitively the inner experience of oneself and others and to develop techniques by which conscious experience can be changed, altered, expanded, and so forth. And the ultimate criterion of success in such an enterprise is intuitive conviction. Truth, like beauty, resides in the mind of the beholder.

Another core problem, different from the nature of explanation, that distinguishes humanistic psychology from neobehaviorism, is that of the role of values in science—what are the criteria for good and bad, virtue and vice? According to neobehaviorism science is ethically neutral. What this means is that scientific facts and theories do not lead *logically* to the adoption of one set of values over another. Should violence be banned from news reports on television? Violence is contagious. Hearing and seeing television broadcasts about assassinations and airplane hijackings encourages imitation. If violent stories were banned from television news reports, one cause of criminal acts would be eliminated. But, which is more important, reducing crime or maintaining freedom of communication? Individuals would opt for different alternatives depending on their relative concern for crime reduction and for freedom. In order to resolve the issue society must possess a decision-making mechanism to choose between policies that reflect different values. Democracy, in principle, although its methods are not always perfect, makes such choices by the will of the majority, in terms of votes of the citizens or their elected representatives. Dictatorship provides an alternate method, social policy decisions are made by a person whose competence is perceived, usually by the dictator, as superior to that of the majority.

Humanistic psychology denies that science in general and psychology in particular is value free. Man, according to humanistic psychology, possesses innate potentialities for goodness. By understanding these potentialities one can discover the set of human values that society should adopt and by so doing provide life with meaning.

The significant question, which this position fails to answer to my satisfaction, is by what means are these universal human values revealed? Like the concept of intuitive understanding, the acceptance of these values rests upon a radical subjectivism in which the intuition of an individual serves as the final arbiter. Such an orientation suffers from three related drawbacks. First the intuitions of different individuals can be opposed and no method is available to resolve differences. To highlight this point, let us deal with an oversimplified example. One psychologist concludes that humans realize their potentialities when they free themselves from competitive drives while another insists that the nature of man is to be highly competitive. What objective means are available to determine who is correct? Second, these psychological insights as to the true image of man frequently represent social advocacy in the guise of scientific evidence. That man is basically competitive has been frequently maintained by those who espouse an unregulated capitalistic system while those who insist that man is innately cooperative favor a socialistic society. Since a wide range of human competitive and cooperative behavior is possible, a conclusion that either is in some sense innate, is both naïve and misleading. Such a judgment rests upon the faulty interpretation that complex social behavior is rigidly determined by genetic factors completely insulated from the influence of environmental shaping. Finally, the insistence that subjective experience of one individual can reveal the fundamental value system that should govern all reminds me of the devastation that such views have wrought in the history of mankind.

Another alternative, consistent with neobehaviorism, is to recognize that science is ethically neutral and that a multiplicity of value systems is possible. Within such a framework the problem of morality becomes redirected from the sterile issue of the search for true basic human values to the more productive task of discovering from where values emerge and how they influence behavior.

In line with this last point it should be recognized that to assume that science is value free does not imply that psychology must ignore problems of ethics. The neobehavioristic position is that psychology can study morality without moralizing about it. What are needed are genuine scientific theories of morality that throw light upon the acquisition of ethical principles and their influence on behavior. Such theories necessarily based on empirical evidence can provide important information about the consequences of certain value systems on the behavior of individuals and their implications for society. Such scientific efforts can be accomplished without advocating one value system in preference to another. This does not mean that I as a person must abstain from moral judgments or political advocacy. It only means that when so doing I divest myself of whatever authority and prestige resides in my position as a psychologist.

As a result of my background and experiences, some as a psychologist, I do favor a democratically organized society in which a multiplicity of values can operate simultaneously with a minimum of friction. Psychology and other behavioral sciences can provide information as to how such a goal can be achieved. But science can never in my estimation demonstrate logically the intrinsic superiority of one basic set of values over another.

RESEARCH AND THEORY

I was initially interested in human problem-solving behavior. However, when I began to work with Spence the learning behavior of white rats attracted my attention. Practical considerations were involved in this switch. If I were to profit fully from my association with Spence I should do research in problems that were of interest to him. But it also seemed sensible to attempt first to understand the relatively simple learning behavior of animals before proceeding to attack the more complex cognitive behavior of humans. The history of biology demonstrates the advantages of doing research with simpler organisms before attempting to cope with more complex ones.

This line of reasoning still has some validity although I have become wary of prescriptions about what constitutes the most fruitful research strategy. Science itself is a large experiment, and sometimes a counter-intuitive approach proves productive. Perhaps returning to problems of problem-solving would be fruitful. This line of reasoning, or rationalization, was followed in 1950 when I was encouraged to apply for a government research grant, which I did, to investigate some basic laws of human cognitive behavior.

Initially, I tried several research techniques but none paid off in generating a significant research problem. In 1954 (Kendler and Vineberg), however, I did a simple concept identification study in which college students were required to classify different geometrical patterns. The results suggested that two different processes were used; the subjects either responded directly to the stimulus pattern itself or transformed the patterns into some abstract representation. To clarify this distinction let us examine the experimental paradigm I used in the next study (Kendler and D'Amato, 1955) which sought to test some implications of the distinction between the two modes of classificatory behavior.

Figure 6.3 illustrates the experimental operations that distinguish a reversal from an extradimensional shift in a problem in

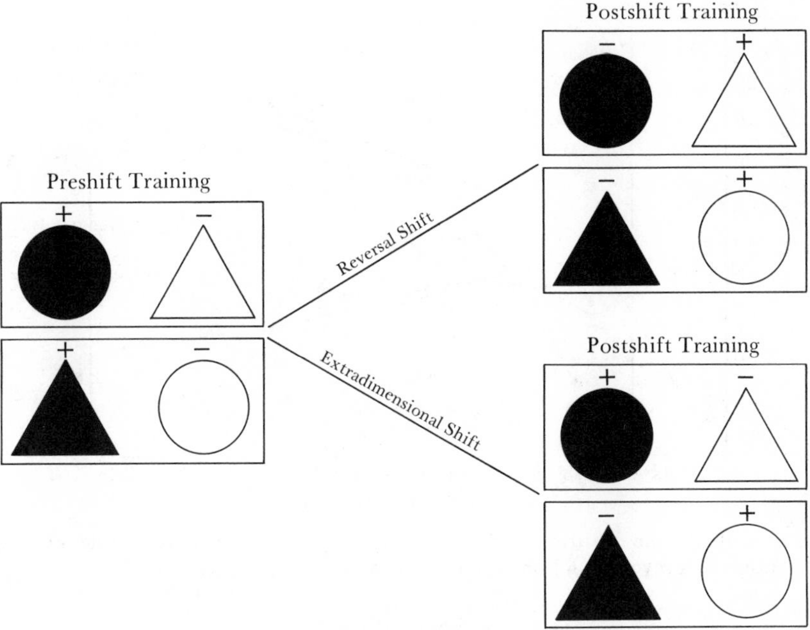

Figure 6.3. A comparison between reversal and extradimensional shifts. Reinforcement is indicated by +, nonreinforcement by −.

which subjects must solve two successive discrimination tasks. In the first task the subject is confronted with a choice between two stimulus compounds that vary on two dimensions, *brightness* and *shape*. In the initial discrimination the choice of *black* is the correct stimulus while the choice of *white* is incorrect; the *shape*, either *circle* or *triangle*, is irrelevant. After the first discrimination is learned a shift in reinforcement contingencies occurs with the same set of stimuli. In a *reversal shift* the response contingencies are reversed; the previously incorrect stimulus *white* is now correct while the previously correct stimulus *black* is now incorrect. In an *extradimensional shift* the reinforcement contingencies are shifted to the previously irrelevant shape dimension.

Which kind of shift do you believe would be easier to execute? An unqualified answer must of necessity be incorrect because the relative difficulty of the shifts depends on the subjects. College students find a reversal shift much easier than an extradimensional shift. The reason is that the students conceptualize the problem in

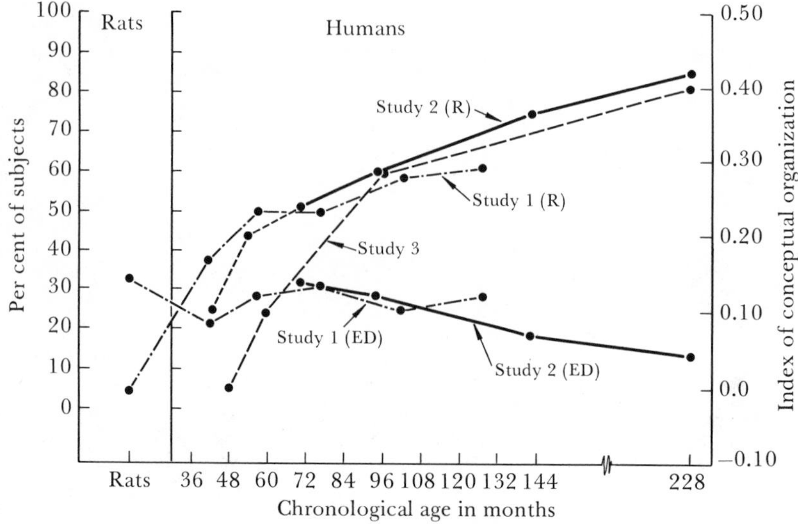

Figure 6.4. The results of three studies that compared the tendencies to respond in a reversal (R) or extradimensional (ED) manner.

terms of *brightness;* they choose *black* stimuli and avoid *white* stimuli. In a reversal shift if they can transfer their conceptualization from the initial discrimination, they have to learn only to change the choice responses to the individual stimuli. In contrast, an extradimensional shift requires abandoning the previous mode of conceptualizing the problem and acquiring a new one—for example, switching from representing the problem in terms of *brightness* to conceptualizing it in terms of *shape.*

According to Spence's influential theories of animal discrimination learning, which was primarily concerned with the behavior of rats, an extradimensional shift should be easier than a reversal shift. This would follow because rats do not respond to the concepts of *brightness* and *shape* but instead respond directly and nonselectively to each particular stimulus. For example, in Figure 6.4 when the subject chooses the *black circle* in the first discrimination problem his habit to choose each of these cues, *black* and *circle,* increases. When a rat makes an error and chooses a *white circle* in preference to a *black triangle* the tendencies to choose *white* and *circle* decrease. As a result *black* would be consistently reinforced; at the end of preshift training the tendency to approach it would be stronger than the tendency to approach any of the other three stimuli. *White*, in contrast, would never be reinforced; it would possess the weakest tendency to evoke an approach response. In between these two extremes would be the irrelevant stimuli, *circle* and *triangle*, a choice of which would be reinforced approximately 50 per cent.

The logic of this simplified analysis is that at the end of preshift training the difference between the tendencies to approach *black* and *white* is much greater than the difference in the tendencies to approach *black* and *triangle* (or *circle*). As a result, executing an extradimensional shift from *black* to *triangle* (or *circle*) would be easier than a reversal shift from *black* to *white*. Roger Kelleher, a Ph.D. student of mine, tested this theoretical analysis and found that the behavior of rats was consistent with it.

As already indicated, explaining the behavior of organisms in reversal and extradimensional shifts requires postulating two different models of behavior. The model appropriate for the behavior of rats is a single-unit model in which the stimuli directly control behavior. The model appropriate for college students is a mediational model in which the subject conceptualizes the incoming stimulation and then responds to the transformed information.

What happens to organisms that "fall between" the rats and college students, such as children of different ages? This is the question that was responsible, in part, for Tracy's and my beginning a professional collaboration (Kendler and Kendler, 1962) that is still in effect. Tracy was assigned the responsibility of teaching Child Psychology at Barnard College and as a result became interested in developmental psychology, a problem that tended, at that time, to be ignored by American experimental psychologists. Being aware of my discrimination-shift research, she began discussing the problem with me and we decided to combine our talents. As an aside I might mention that a good test of the durability of a marriage between two strong-minded individuals is a close working relationship. To the inevitable conventional disagreements about child-rearing, mothers-in-law, and politics are added disputes about research design, statistical analysis, and theoretical interpretations.

Our most significant developmental research is represented in Figure 6.4. Studies 1 (Kendler, Kendler, and Learnard, 1962) and 2 (Kendler and Kendler, 1970) measured the tendencies of individual subjects to respond in a reversal or extradimensional manner in a discrimination-learning task involving geometric patterns that differed simultaneously on two dimensions. As can be noted for the rat, located on the left side of the figure, a preference was exhibited for an extradimensional shift indicated by ED, but the developmental relationship for children from three to ten years of age was one of an increasing tendency to prefer a reversal, indicated by R, to an ED shift. Study 2 used a wider age range as well as a greater variety of stimuli and as can be seen a similar relationship prevailed: an increasing tendency to prefer an R to an ED shift. Study 3 (Kendler, Kendler, and Marken, 1969) sought to demonstrate that the results of the initial two studies could not simply be attributed to an increased tendency for subjects to look at, that is to attend to or focus on, the relevant dimension that is being reinforced. Thus pictures of conceptual instances (*apple, banana; shirt, pants,* for example) were substituted for two-dimensional geometrical patterns and because the pictures of each set (for example, *fruit, clothing*) do not share simple physical properties such as *shape* or *brightness* the subject was not able to sort the stimuli correctly by attending to any specifically located segment of the stimuli. Because the results of Study 3 were consistent with the previous two in showing that reversal shifts tend to become easier with increasing age the conclusion is that the age-related changes in all three studies reflect changes in ability to conceptualize discrete stimulus events. A simple summary statement of all three studies is that a single-unit model accounts for infrahuman behavior while the younger a child is the more likely he is to behave according to this model in which behavior is under direct control of the external stimulus. The older he is the more likely his performance will be consonant with the mediational mechanism involving conceptual transformations.

One of the fundamental problems in any sort of scientific research program is to develop an experimental technique that reflects clearly the operation of some important process. The discrimination-shift technique that has been described, and variations of it, in my estimation, are powerful research tools to help understand the development and nature of conceptual behavior.

Our research program, at this writing, has blossomed into three distinct problem areas: (1) the mathematical formulation of the single-unit theory in which behavior is directly governed by incoming stimulation, (2) the discovery of principles that govern the transition from external stimulus control to mediational control, and (3) the analysis of the mediational processes that underlie conceptual behavior.

1. If one equates scientific explanation with the rules of deductive logic one must strive to formulate a mathematical theory. Although neobehaviorists, and other experimental psychologists, are in general agreement with this aim, differences of opinion prevail about when such mathematical attempts should be initiated. Since a solid core of empirical relationships is presently available, it seemed productive to extend and refine some of Spence's early mathematical theorizing to problems of discrimination-shift behavior. This has been done by Tracy Kendler who has shown that a single-unit formulation can be used to explain the behavior of rats in a discrimination-shift study in which the components of each stimulus compound (for example, *black* and *circle*) vary in their power to control behavior. According to our coordinated single-unit and mediational theory the learning behavior of a child in his early years of life is not unrelated to that of the rat; both are governed by the single-unit principles.

2. The transition from single-unit to mediational functioning does not occur suddenly. A period of transition occurs during which time the child, although capable of mediational functioning, fails to operate in that manner. Such a failure is referred to as a "mediational deficiency." For example, a child capable of using the word *fruit* appropriately may be unable to do so when responding to separate pictures of *apples, pears,* and *oranges.* This deficiency in producing an available representational response is known as a "production deficiency." Another kind of mediational deficiency is a "control deficiency," which can be illustrated by a child describing the correct response, such as "black is right," but continuing to choose white stimuli. Control deficiency, in essence, refers to failure of a potential mediator, once produced, to control behavior.

These two kinds of mediational deficiency, production and control, have been shown to be correlated with developmental changes. Tracy Kendler has recently shown that from kindergartners to college students, there is more production deficiency than control deficiency. Moreover, control deficiency declines rapidly after the kindergarten level and becomes practically negligible by the fourth grade. In contrast production deficiency stays about the same level from kindergarten to fourth grade and then begins to decline but not as completely as control deficiency.

Another approach to the transition between stimulus control to mediational control is to develop techniques that would hasten the transition. Obvious educational benefits could accrue from techniques that would encourage representational behavior. Some training techniques have proved effective in helping the child to conceptualize (Kendler, 1971).

3. Philosophers have discussed the nature of concepts for centuries with no final solution. This is not unexpected because the problem is psychological, not philosophical. Experimentation, not armchair speculation, is required. As already indicated the changes observed in human discrimination-shift behavior have been attributed to developmental changes in conceptualizing ability. In understanding these differences, a distinction must be made between categorizing behavior and conceptual processes. For example, a rat can categorize triangles of various shapes by making a common response to them that differs from his response to non-triangular forms. A college student can behave in the same way. But the similarity between their behavior does not necessarily imply a common underlying process. The rat's behavior is based upon a single-unit mechanism in which the choice of a triangle is controlled by some stimulus feature such as the apexes of the various triangles. In contrast college students when confronted with such a discrimination transform the variety of triangles by representing them symbolically as "three-sided figures" or in some equivalent abstract fashion.

The assumption being currently tested is that categorizing behavior of young children is initially governed by single-unit mechanisms in which behavior is controlled by specific stimulus characteristics such as the apexes of triangles. This can result in an overgeneralized concept which occurs for example when an infant calls different men "Da-Da." When mediational control first takes hold narrow concepts are formed such as when a particular cat is called "kitty" as if that were its proper name. With development the child becomes capable of more abstract representations and becomes capable of broader concepts that represent a wider variety of stimuli such as *dogs, cats,* and *birds.* According to such an analysis the conceptual development of a child cannot be described by a single unitary set of principles but instead must be understood in terms of different behavioral processes operating in a developmental sequence.

A FINAL COMMENT

Now that this essay about my life and thoughts has been concluded the question of whether psychology has provided a satisfying career can be entertained. The answer is definitely affirmative. Psychology is an intellectually challenging discipline. It is not dull! Numerous fascinating problems are available to anyone who wishes to dedicate his talents, time, and effort. Psychology will, however, test the patience and perseverance of any scientist. The rewards of deep insights, of giant steps forward, that have studded the history of physics and biology, have for the most part been absent from the annals of psychology.

Psychology, if we date its origin from its first laboratory established by Wundt in Leipzig in 1879, is approaching its first centennial. Being younger than physics and biology, psychology's relatively crude state of knowledge can be attributed to its immaturity. But even this apparently reasonable excuse loses some of its impact when it is realized that genetics, with its highly sophisticated body of knowledge, is as youthful a discipline as is psychology.

Perhaps the fundamental reason for psychology's backwardness—and this comment is applicable to all behavioral sciences—is the intrinsic complexity of human behavior. The precision of the science of physics, or even that of biology, may prove to be an unobtainable goal for psychology. But since the future of any science cannot be predicted with certainty, these remarks may reflect the pessimistic reactions of one who began his career in a period of easy optimism when rapid theoretical progress was expected. Whatever the reasons for the failure of psychology to achieve the goals that many psychologists, including myself, set for it in the 1940s, only one alternative for future efforts seems reasonable. Only by frankly recognizing psychology's theoretical immaturity and by adopting firm commitments to the ideals of rigorous logic and rules of evidence will real progress be possible. Although such an orientation does not guarantee giant steps forward, it nevertheless increases the probability of their occurrence.

REFERENCES

1946 The influence of simultaneous hunger and thirst drives upon the learning of two opposed spatial responses of the white rat. *Journal of Experimental Psychology, 36,* 212–220.

1947 S. F., A case of homosexual panic. *Journal of Abnormal Social Psychology, 42,* 112–119.

An investigation of latent learning in a T-maze. *Journal of Comparative and Physiological Psychology, 40,* 265–269.

1948 A comparison of learning under motivated and satiated conditions in the white rat. *Journal of Experimental Psychology, 37,* 545–549.

With K. W. Spence. The speculations of Leeper in regard to the Iowa studies. *Journal of Experimental Psychology, 38,* 106–108.

With H. C. Mencher. The ability of rats to learn the location of food when motivated by thirst—an experimental reply to Leeper. *Journal of Experimental Psychology, 38,* 82–88.

1950 With J. Kanner. A further test of the ability of rats to learn the location of food when motivated by thirst. *Journal of Experimental Psychology, 40,* 762–765.

1952a Some comments on Thistlewaite's perception of latent learning. *Psychological Bulletin, 49,* 47–51.

1952b "What is learned?"—a theoretical blind alley. *Psychological Review, 59,* 269–277.

1953 With Levine, S. A more sensitive test of irrelevant incentive learning under conditions of satiation. *Journal of Comparative and Physiological Psychology, 46,* 271–273.

1954 With R. Vineberg. The acquisition of compound concepts as a function of previous training. *Journal of Experimental Psychology, 48,* 252–258.

1955 With M. F. D'Amato. A comparison of reversal shifts and nonreversal shifts in human concept formation behavior. *Journal of Experimental Psychology, 49,* 165–174.

1962 With T. S. Kendler. Vertical and horizontal processes in problem solving. *Psychological Review, 69,* 1–16.

With T. S. Kendler and B. Learnard. Mediated responses to size and brightness as a function of age. *American Journal of Psychology, 75,* 571–586.

1963 *Basic Psychology.* New York: Appleton-Century-Crofts. Pp. 750.

1967 Kenneth W. Spence, 1907–1967. *Psychological Review, 74,* 335–341.

1968 *Basic Psychology,* 2nd ed. New York: Appleton-Century-Crofts. Pp. 755.

1969 With T. S. Kendler and R. S. Marken. Developmental analysis of reversal and half-reversal shifts. *Developmental Psychology, 1,* 318–326.

1970 The unity of psychology. *The Canadian Psychologist, 11,* 30–47.
With T. S. Kendler. An ontogeny of optional shift behavior. *Child Development, 41,* 1–27.
With T. S. Kendler. *Basic Psychology: Brief Edition.* New York: Appleton-Century-Crofts. Pp 495.

1971 With J. T. Spence. Tenets of neobehaviorism. In H. H. Kendler and J. T. Spence (eds.), *Essays in Neobehaviorism: A Memorial Volume to Kenneth W. Spence.* New York: Appleton-Century-Crofts.
Environmental and cognitive control of behavior. *American Psychologist, 26,* 962–973.

1974 *Basic Psychology,* 3rd ed. Menlo Park, California: W. A. Benjamin.

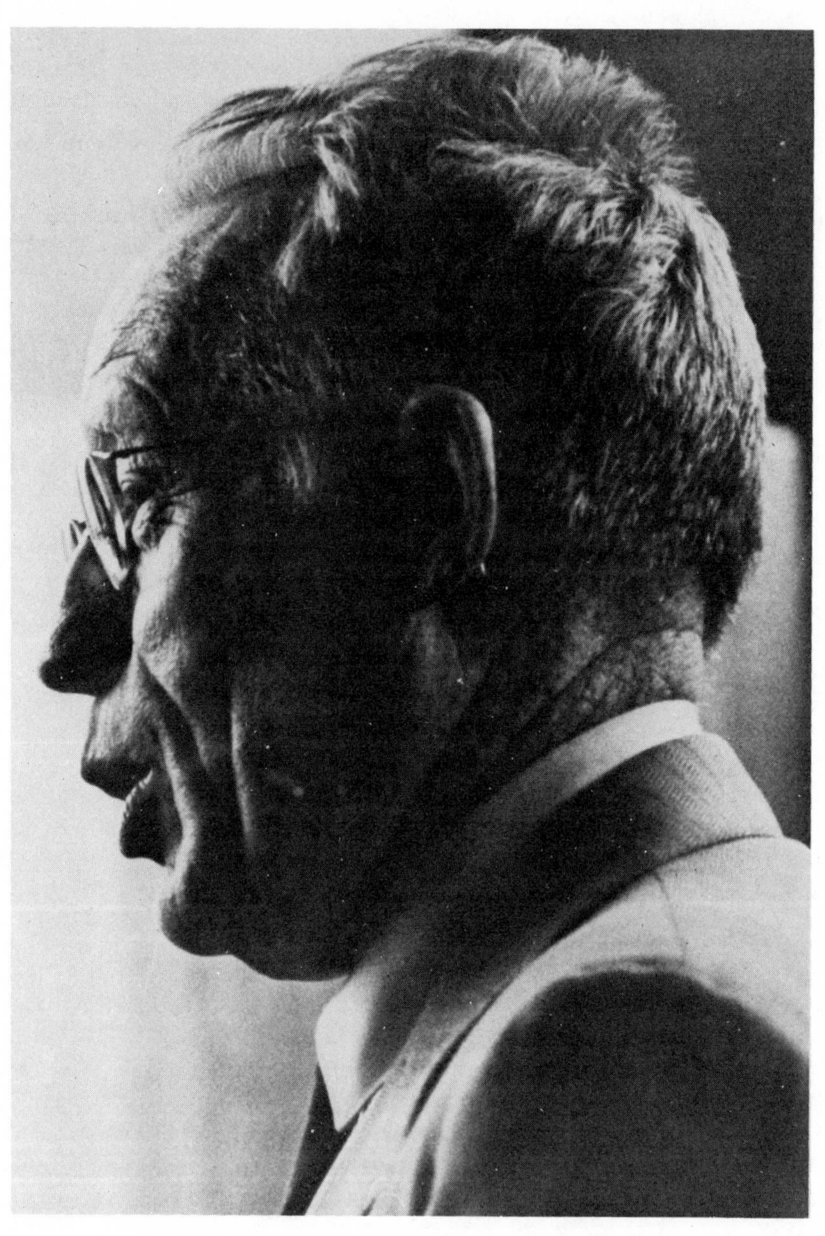

7

Gulp! So It's a Theoretical Psychologist I Am, Eh!

ROBERT WARD LEEPER

In the field of personality psychology, it is well known that people often have difficulty in re-shaping their self-images to match the realities of their lives. I had an experience of this sort a few years ago. It was in the summer of 1965. I was participating in a conference on human fear (financed by a generous grant from the National Institute of *Dental* Research!). When it became my turn to speak, I started by confessing that I had experienced a real emotional jolt when I had first seen how I was listed on the program. When I had read down through the list of main speakers, it had seemed to me as though Richard Evans, who had organized the symposium, had taken unusual pains to indicate that the participants were really dedicated research scientists and, even more specifically, *experimentalists.* Thus, what I had read (adding the italics as I went along) was "Hans Selye, *experimental*-biological medicine; Richard Solomon, general-*experimental* psychology; John Spiegel, clinical-*experimental* psychiatry." Irving Janis was labeled by only "social psychology," but I realized he was so widely known for his splendid empirical research on personality and attitude change that he needed no label as an empiricist. But, when my eye came to my own name, what I read was "Robert Leeper, *theoretical* psychologist"! I forget whether I reported that I had said "ouch" when I had read this. But I know the ouch had been felt, even if not said.

Really, I explained to the conference, this designation should have produced no surprise in myself. Thus, for at least a dozen years, in the annual *Directory of the American Psychological Association,* I had been listing my chief interests as "learning theory, personality theory." Furthermore, I knew full well that, after a small handful of experimental papers which I published in the first six years after I completed my graduate work in 1930, none of my further publications or papers at meetings had been on anything except questions of a theoretical sort.

Still further, to clinch the matter, a memory had flashed into my mind which seemed to indicate that, even as a young child, I was already fated to go into theoretical work of some sort or other. This memory—and quite a vivid one—concerned an incident that occurred when I was about five or six years old. According to the memory, we kids had left the dining table and were playing hide-and-seek, using the adjacent kitchen for base, and the dining room and subsequent rooms for hiding. My mother and father, grandmother, and two aunts were still sitting at the table. To provide my hiding place, I asked my father if I might climb up and sit astride his shoulders while he remained sitting at the table in the middle of the room. "People never look in the most obvious places," I explained. He cooperated without protest. But, to my great chagrin, when the child who was "it" emerged from the kitchen to start his search, he immediately spotted me and dashed back to base to count me out.

It might seem odd that I mentioned that incident to the conference and that I repeat it now. After all, kids do all sorts of crazy things. My answer is that I believe that Alfred Adler (1933) contributed a really valuable idea when he proposed that, when an incident stays vividly in a person's memory from his early childhood, this signifies that the memory must have been serving as a vivid and efficient symbol of the approach to life of that person. Adler did not assert, it is worth noting, that any early incident which is thus remembered was necessarily the primary or by any means the only source of the outlook which it expressed. Nor did he say that such memories necessarily reflect what actually happened. Nor that the action portrayed in the memory is the sort of thing that the individual is likely to repeat later. For, as Adler said, a crucial feature in such memories is what the person remembers as the *outcome* of his action and also what he remembers as what he *felt* about that outcome.

At any rate, my own impression is that this memory actually does express two things about myself. First, that I have a tendency to use rather general or highly abstract propositions and an interest in using them. But, second, that I had concluded from that incident (and possibly from a good many others) that a person must be awfully careful about believing any sweeping generalization, even when most people endorse it and even though he, himself, might easily find a multitude of instances that would support the generalization. And, in fact, when I look back over the work that I have done as a theoretical psychologist it is obvious that a great part of that work has been a matter of taking broad generalizations that different psychologists, or groups of psychologists, have strongly advocated and then showing that much of the empirical knowledge relevant to these generalizations simply does not support them, but calls for some more defensible interpretations instead. So, I told the conference, even though I felt I had to accept the description of myself as a theoretical psychologist, I hoped I could claim that I had been an empirically oriented theoretical psychologist.

Even with some such qualification, it is probably obvious that I still feel somewhat defensive about this description. This may well call for some explanation, because a good many readers might ask, What's wrong with being a theoretical psychologist? There are theoretical physicists who don't mind parading the label—why should it be different in psychology?

I believe the answer is that there are some good reasons and some poor reasons why the attitude toward theoretical work is different in physics and in psychology. In physics, with highly technical and difficult empirical material to work from, strongly quantitative in character and yet also calling for unusually imaginative solutions, it has been quite clear that theoretical work could well be a respected specialty. In psychology, on the other hand, it has not been so apparent that much could be done by working just on the theoretical side. In addition, psychology has had the experience only recently of separating itself from philosophy, and the general feeling of psychologists is that psychology has made progress only as it has been willing to replace abstract hypothesizing with the hard, grubby work of empirical research. And, indeed, a fair portion of psychologists believe that any theoretical developments that may be needed in psychology will naturally come as incidental by-products of such empirical research.

As a matter of fact, I share the common skepticism about theoretical psychology to this extent: my strong conviction is that those psychologists who have made the most significant contributions to psychological theory have been those psychologists—such as Wolfgang Köhler, Kurt Lewin, E. C. Tolman, K. S. Lashley, Jean Piaget, Irvin Rock, Jerome Bruner, and Roger Brown—who have moved naturally back and forth between theorizing and exploring things empirically. I would like to have been one of such persons. But, even aside from the fact that I have not been particularly resourceful in translating abstract ideas into researchable problems, my heart has not so strongly been in that other sort of work. So, the question still remains, why have I been willing to operate in a way which, even in my own conception of an optimal pattern of work, I regard as a definitely one-sided way to try to develop the theoretical side of psychology?

Part of the answer to this question lies in the fact that I have become convinced that, because of the jaundiced view which psychologists commonly have held regarding theoretical efforts in psychology, the growth of psychology has been seriously one-sided. In many respects, psychology has achieved a considerable maturity in its factual material and fact-gathering techniques. But, psychologists have failed to make corresponding progress in utilizing those empirical observations to develop the conceptual side of psychology. As Conant (1947) and many others have said, what distinguishes a science from a technology is the much greater interest of a science in developing highly abstract, generalized principles—principles that will facilitate just as precise predictions as less abstract statements would, but principles that cover surprisingly broad ranges of concrete phenomena. Such principles, of course, need to be of different scope in different matters and need to be part of a whole hierarchical conceptual system. Thus, research on motor-skill learning may establish some principles that apply only to that one form of learning. And, if there are such relatively restricted principles, motor-skill learning must be understood both by reference to them and by reference to more abstract principles that apply, say, to all kinds of learning. Even the principles of such sub-areas, however, definitely need to be abstract. Thus, there presumably are laws of motor-skill learning that will apply not only to pole vaulting but also to violin playing, brick laying, and surgical work.

Our reason for interest in highly abstract principles is, as Conant said, not merely a matter of economy of statement. Even more important is the heuristic or discovery-favoring properties of such highly abstract principles. Different concrete materials have quite different potentialities for revealing what also is present in larger territories where the crucial processes and crucial variables are much harder to identify. The psychologist who chooses to work only in some miniature area and who gives little thought to discoveries and concepts outside his professional specialty simply is not using an optimal procedure even for making progress within his own specialty. The best clues sometimes come from the oddest places. Georg von Békésy's Nobel Prize-winning research on hearing, for example, was made possible by a principle that he got from visual research, and that visual research in turn had developed because of some baffling contradictions in some astronomical observations.

My own feeling is that psychology has a great deal more empirical knowledge than it uses—especially if psychologists are willing to include observations that they can make, or have made, in real-life situations, rather than require that their knowledge of psychological phenomena must be restricted to what has appeared in print. But, as I see things, there simply hasn't been enough recognition by psychologists of how much hard work needs to be done to work out the implications or significance of our empirical knowledge. There hasn't been enough recognition of how much gold "is in them thar hills."

As an example that illustrates the difficulties of utilizing the empirical knowledge in psychology, a specific problem that often comes to my mind is a problem studied first by Frederic Bartlett (1958) and more recently and intensively by Newell and Simon (1972). Among all the "cryptarithmetic" problems that I know of, this one is a special gem for illustrating the point that merely possession of requisite factual knowledge is not sufficient to produce fruitful use of that knowledge. The problem usually is presented as the task of decoding the statement that GERALD + DONALD = ROBERT, but it is better to change the names a bit to avoid confusion between zero and the letter "O." Thus, a subject can be given the material in this form:

$$\begin{array}{r} \text{GERALD} \\ +\ \underline{\text{DUWALD}} \\ \text{RUPERT} \end{array}$$

The subject is told that he can translate this into a correct specimen of ordinary arithmetic, starting only with the knowledge that T stands for zero, and that each other letter stands for a different digit from 1 through 9.

A person is likely to feel that the problem must be virtually insoluble. A problem with 9 "unknowns"! He may even go through a bit of calculation and come up with the correct statement that if he systematically but mechanically explores all the possible pairings of letters with numbers, he might have to go through 362,880 combinations before finding the solution.

But, the beauty of this particular cryptarithmetic problem is that it can be solved without taking a single false step—without *any* trial and *error.* Anyone who knows how to add numbers has the "empirical knowledge" required for an efficient and errorless solution. Thus, to illustrate: since adding D + D calls for replacing T with a zero, and since D itself cannot equal zero since T has monopolized that digit, D must equal 5. Also, since 5 + 5 = 10, a 1 must be carried to the next column, and R, as the total of L + L + 1, must be some odd number. And, since G + D (plus perhaps a carried-over 1) = R, R must be either 7 or 9.

And, thus one can proceed—without having to assert anything or try out anything, even, that he will have to retract—all the way to the solution. However, if the reader has not met this problem before, he ought to wrestle with it now. Actually, the hardest part has been reserved for you, and it is more instructive to learn, through your own experience, that possessing the requisite background knowledge regarding some problem is not sufficient to preclude the need for a lot of hard, baffling work to grasp some relationships which eventually will seem so obvious that you will wonder why it took you so long. (I myself, I must admit, had to take hours on this problem.)

The theoretical problems of psychology are usually a good deal more complex than this example, and the relevant data are often much more confusing, partly because the data in some cases come from faulty observations or from special experimental factors that tend not to be taken into consideration. But, sometimes the needed theoretical development is a basically simple thing, somewhat like the case in the fable about the emperor's new clothes, where all that was needed was a child's naïve reaction, "Yes, but he ain't got nothing on!"

It seems to me that my role has been much like that child's when I have written some of my papers regarding the theory of emotions. This topic gets into more technical points, too, but the basic concept that I have proposed is really a part of everyday knowledge. Let me explain a bit.

In the 1930s and 1940s, psychologists almost invariably described "emotions" and "motives" in strongly contrasting terms—as was done by P. T. Young in three important books (1936, 1941, 1961). Motives were described as *constructive* factors in the life of the organism—as processes that *arouse, sustain, and direct activity,* as when hunger makes an animal or person go searching for food. Emotions, on the other hand, were described as hampering processes. They were described as processes that *disrupt* or *disorganize* the adaptive activity of the individual, as when stage-fright produces difficulties for a student-musician in his recital, or loneliness and discouragement tend to interfere with a person's work. This disruptive influence was described as most evident in very strong emotions, but as characteristic of milder emotions or feelings, as well. According to this interpretation, therefore, the task in emotional development is primarily a task of learning how to minimize the role of emotion in the person's life.

This was no new concept of the 1930s. The famous French psychiatrist, Pierre Janet, had been asserting the same idea back in the 1890s. And, still earlier, such ideas were really a product of our modern technological society, long before Pierre Janet. Technological and scientific work tends to put emphasis on intellectual factors and tends to call for suppression of emotional processes. Not that they *should* call for this, because studies of scientists show that the driving forces back of their persistent, strenuous work are rarely hunger or any other motives such as the chapters on motivation usually discuss, but are more on the side of their emotional life—their interests, enthusiasms, their craving for recognition, and so on.

At any rate, in my own thinking, the concept that I naturally held was that emotions are motives. And, not merely that, but also that they are especially important motives in the higher animals and in man—particularly if we recognize that the main influences of any motive (as with thirst) are usually exerted by milder stages of that motive, rather than by what exists in extreme situations. I realized well enough that emotional processes tend to interfere with various other goal-directed processes; but I regarded this as nothing unusual about emotions. All of the ordinarily recognized motives interfere, too, with what is irrelevant to activities that those motives call for. A bad toothache, for instance, drives a person to a dentist, but it of course would interfere with his enjoying a concert or his solving difficult intellectual problems.

I am not sure, now, when I formulated such notions, but I know that it must have been in 1932 or earlier, because it was in that year, in my second paper at any major psychological association meeting, that I presented a paper entitled "The Evidence for a Theory of Neurological Maintenance of States of Emotional Motivation." In other words, without any hemming or hawing, I was assuming that emotions are, "of course," motives. The same approach was used in 1937 and 1941 when I published some preliminary versions of a book on personality.

Quite possibly I might have let the matter rest with such incidental comments if it had not been for a discussion I had with a close friend of mine at a meeting of the American Psychological Association in 1946 or 1947. Talking with this man, whose general-psychology text has been one of the most used texts over a long span of years, I said, "Listen—why in the world, in your discussion of emotions, do you interpret emotions as processes that disrupt or disorganize? Of course emotions do that in some respects, just as motives like hunger or thirst or sex drive would tend to disrupt some things as incidental consequences of organizing the individual for something else. But isn't it true that affection, or esthetic enjoyment, or pride in one's work, or fear, or sense of guilt, or hate, or any other emotion is basically an organizing and directing influence?"

We talked about various angles of the matter. Then finally my friend said, "Well, you may be right, and I'm inclined to believe you are. But what you are saying isn't what *most* psychologists believe. And, what would be the use of writing a textbook if no one would use it!"

Somewhat the same response came when I discussed the matter with another outstanding author. So, I decided, if psychologists write such things because that is what their public demands, then I had better try to change the thinking of their public. So, in all of my free time for the next year or so, I tried to summarize the current view of emotions, tried to analyze the basis for that view, and tried to suggest that a motivational theory of emotion would fit our empirical knowledge a lot better. The resulting article (1948) has been reprinted in about a half-dozen books of readings, including two recent ones edited by Magda Arnold (1968) and by Karl Pribram (1969). It has had, I believe, a fair degree of influence.

That article led me into puzzling further about a more difficult question about emotions which I had never been able to work out in my 1932 paper. I had never submitted that paper for publication because I had never been able to come to a conception that seemed satisfactory to me as to what emotions can be said to be (other than that they are processes that are often set off by rather weak stimulations and that tend to "arouse, sustain, and direct" the activities of the individual). Finally, along in the late 1950s, the conclusion that I came to was that we have generally made a serious mistake in thinking about emotions (or any other sorts of motives, for that matter) as "lower-order processes" (visceral processes, subcortical processes, or whatever). I came to realize, more and more clearly, that emotions are not just some vague affect or feeling, or some general state of arousal, devoid of intellectual or factual content. Instead, when a person avoids something because of "fear," the "fear" which has this effect is a specific fear—a pressure-producing representation of the effects that are likely to be experienced in the given situation if such and such things are done. In other words, an emotion is basically like a taste perception or an olfactory perception—a process that simultaneously is both perceptual in an "information-processing" sense and also motivational in some slight or perhaps even intense degree.

Any such view, I have said, does not call for any neglect of whatever subcortical centers may help to contribute to the emotion as a perceptual or representational process. After all, we now know that all perceptual and intellectual processes depend, analogously, on processes in the brain-stem reticular system. In short, we have no reason for saying that emotions, in the intact organism, are any less truly complex cortical processes than for saying that thoughts and perceptions are cortical processes.

My own best statement of this interpretation has been given in a long paper in the Nebraska Symposium on Motivation in 1965, and in a much compressed version in the book edited by Magda Arnold which appeared in 1970. Before that, the idea had been stated briefly in the book on personality by Peter Madison and myself in 1959. Actually, as I discovered a few years after that, George Klein had published a beautiful paper (1958) telling how, in some long experimental studies of the influence of thirst, Klein and his co-workers had been driven to the same basic conception with reference to thirst. Klein's paper has had, I believe, rather few citations, but it seems to me an extraordinarily capable and significant contribution. It will take time for such notions to soak in; but, personnally, I think they give a better synthesis of what psychology knows.

Such, in brief, is one main line in which I have tried to make some progress in psychological theory. There is no space for comparable descriptions of work in other areas. Even more time has been invested, however, in my efforts to make progress in the basic psychology of learning. My early experimental papers were all in that area. Two of these studies (1932, 1935b) sought to develop some Gestalt concepts about relations between perception and learning. The third study (1935a), using a maze planned on the basis of Tolman's theory of learning, sought to determine whether rats could learn to use one route when hungry and a different route when thirsty. Several weeks after I started this experiment, a paper by Clark Hull (1933) was published from which I learned that he had been conducting an experiment on the same problem, but using a maze arrangement consistent with his S-R-reinforcement theory of learning. I believe that most psychologists would have said our two maze-designs were not only superficially similar, but also fundamentally similar. However, my rats learned in eight days what Hull's rats required seven months of almost daily training to learn. This extreme difference prompted a series of experiments by other psychologists. Controversies still exist as to why the difference occurs, but the empirical findings have been confirmed in case after case.

After the experimental studies described above, any further work on learning got side-tracked for almost a decade. Part of the reason was that I had shifted to a small college in Iowa (Cornell College) where my main teaching responsibilities were in the personality field. In addition, another new factor suddenly opened up. In the fall of 1936, my wife remarked to me: "You know, when you were finishing your graduate work at Clark, you used to talk about wanting to go to the University of Berlin to study with Kurt Lewin on problems of motivation. You realize, don't you, that Lewin is now teaching at the University of Iowa, about twenty miles away, and that he might be giving a seminar you could attend?"

Her logic was unimpeachable, as it sometimes is. So, I drove over to Iowa City and found that there was indeed such a seminar, every Thursday evening, in which Lewin was discussing a monograph which he was just completing on "psychological forces" (1938). The seminar proved to be an exceedingly interesting affair, as Lewin's teaching apparently always was. Furthermore, those attending were very interesting persons, including the philosopher Herbert Feigl and several psychologists who were to become good friends of ours, particularly Roger Barker, Tamara Dembo, and Daniel Adler.

At the conclusion of the year, I asked Lewin whether he would like to have me go over his manuscript to catch any problems of idiomatic expression, since this was the first publication he had ever written in English. He welcomed this and also my offer to read the galley proof. Engaged in this, I realized that most psychologists, not having had the supplementary discussions from that seminar, would experience considerable difficulties with some of the technical points. So I decided to write an article to clarify such matters. My first draft proved too long. I reworked it to shorten it. In the effort, it about doubled in length. The same on further efforts. The difficulty was that the more I worked on Lewin's interpretations, the more I became aware of places where

I thought some revisions were in order. Before I got done, the thing had grown into a monograph of 225 pages—*Lewin's Topological and Vector Psychology: A Digest and a Critique* (1943). From the reviews it received and from comments in subsequent books, I believe this has been regarded as a more scholarly and useful publication than anything else I have produced. All of which goes to show that there are advantages in having a discerning and understanding wife.

After this Lewinian interlude, what brought my work back to the psychology of learning was the publication in 1943 of Clark Hull's *Principles of Behavior.* I knew this book was a "must" for anyone like myself with a major interest in the psychology of learning. For, at that time (much as remained the case for another dozen years or more), the spectacularly influential theory of learning was that of Hull. So, I went over the book very carefully, checked various references, and then decided that I might as well write a book review and submit it to one of the journals. When I sent it in, following a number of very laudatory reviews, the editor replied that it was obviously too long for a book review (it ran fifty pages in print), but that he considered it important and would give it immediate publication as the lead article.

Some psychologists have taken me to task for being so severe in my criticisms of the book. But, on the other hand, nothing else that I have written has brought as many letters of hearty appreciation, including letters from nine psychologists who either previously or subsequently have been presidents of the American Psychological Association.

The trouble with Hull's book, I said, was that although it was pretentious and very impressive on first examination, it was not a piece of careful and responsible theoretical work. Its chief terms were not defined and used consistently. It was not dependable in its reporting of experimental studies. In connection with each of its sixteen main principles or "postulates," it cited only very limited material and had refused to mention well-known studies that weighed heavily against Hull's conclusions. As I said at the conclusion of my review, "there is hardly a principle in the whole collection that can stand up under careful criticism" (1944, p. 49). "Why," I asked, "would it not be possible, instead, to combine Hull's respect for theoretical formulations with much more of wholesome respect for homely factual material? A theoretical system is exciting when it is an interpretation of the best of scientific observations; when it is a substitute for that, it is wearisome" (p. 50).

This evaluation contrasted quite sharply with Sigmund Koch's review. Koch wrote that Hull's book "represents the most potent blow thus far struck against . . . the complementary disease cluster of literary, programmatic, verbal or speculative theorizing independently of—sometimes in spite of—empirical evidence. . . . *Principles of Behavior* is one of the most important books published in psychology during the twentieth century" (1944, p. 269).

Within the next ten years, however, Koch (1954) reversed his opinion and published a devastating criticism of Hull's theory. And, generally, there has been such a change of opinion among former Hullians that they have tended rather generally to deplore interest in highly abstract principles of learning and have called for "miniature models" instead. It has been as though their feeling is, "We got our fingers burned once on that sort of thing, and we don't want to do it again."

When Hull's two later books on learning were published in 1951 and 1952, I reviewed them at the request of the *American Journal of Psychology* (1952, 1954)—in some detail, but not on the scale of the first.

In the last two decades, my work on theoretical problems in learning has funneled through three important multi-author books—first in the *Handbook of Experimental Psychology,* edited by S. S. Stevens in 1951, then in 1963 in Volume 5 of the six-volume set on *Psychology: A Study of a Science,* edited by Koch, and most recently in the book *Learning: Theories,* edited by Melvin Marx in 1970. In these treatments, my emphasis has been on problems of developing an adequate perceptual or cognitive theory of learning. The chapter in Stevens suggested that research on concept-formation ought to have a major place in the psychology of learning, rather than being almost neglected, as was still the case at that time. This may sound wild, but I was suggesting that concept-formation probably would prove a better paradigm for the psychology of learning than any other form of learning.

The chapter in Koch's volume was a much broader discussion. I believe it took about all of my spare time for three years to write that 123-page chapter, but I think it was well worth it. The four chapters in Marx's book took about the same amount of time, even though they had the Koch chapter to build on. The attempt in the Marx chapters was to identify the major concepts and particularly crucial research from the group of persons who generally would be known as "cognitive learning psychologists" (men such as Köhler, Duncker, Tolman, Krech, Lashley, Woodworth, Bartlett, and Norman Maier from the experimental field, and personality psychologists such as Adler, Horney, Rogers, George Kelly, and Maslow) and then try to work out a systematic, integrated conceptual system from these contributions.

My other main theoretical work has been in the psychology of personality, which had originally aroused my curiosity about psychology and which has remained a main teaching area and main interest of mine ever since. I have published some scattered papers on personality (1951, 1953, 1963a) and two very early drafts (1937, 1941), primarily for my own classes, of a projected book on personality. However, my main effort in this field has been a joint publication with Peter Madison, a very close friend of mine whose great ability is illustrated by two later books of his own (1961, 1969). What we sought was particularly to see what fresh concepts about personality could come from unifying a basically Gestalt type of interpretation of psychological functioning with material from therapeutic observations and observations of personality in real life.

Most of my time, therefore, since my graduate-school years, has been invested in theoretical work, and most of this work has been along lines which have been rather strongly at odds with main tendencies in American psychology. I don't see this as anything to regret or feel apologetic about; but I think it does call for a bit of explanation. I had chosen Clark University for my graduate work because some writing by Walter S. Hunter strongly appealed to me. I continued to have a very high regard for him as my major professor. Nevertheless, I never became convinced by his behavioristic outlook on psychology nor by his basic formulations regarding the psychology of learning, as a good portion of the other graduate students did. So, what needs explaining is not merely the fact that I went so one-sidedly into theoretical psychology, rather than also having some primary interest in doing empirical research. What needs to be explained is also why I became the kind of theoretical theorist that I did.

Part of the answer fairly certainly is to be found in the very stimulating contrasts of viewpoint that I met in graduate school and soon afterward. Thus, in the psychology department at Clark University, there was the extreme contrast between Walter S. Hunter, the leading behaviorist of that period, and John Paul Nafe, the last of the structuralist or introspective psychologists trained by E. B. Titchener at Cornell University. Still another outlook was represented by Raymond Willoughby, who was at Clark as Assistant Editor of the *Psychological Abstracts.* One rarely finds a person of high statistical skill who also has a primary interest in the ideas of Freud and Jung, but this was the case with the non-credit seminars that Willoughby offered, and which were greatly appreciated by us graduate students. This contact with clinical thinking was further developed by the fact that I worked one summer as an attendant at the Worcester State Hospital, in the same town, and subsequently took advantage of seminars there.

Late in my graduate work and soon afterward, two books helped tremendously to broaden my horizons. The first was Wolfgang Köhler's *Gestalt Psychology* (1929), which I believe even now remains the best basic introduction to Gestalt thought. The other was Edward C. Tolman's *Purposive Behavior in Animals and Men* (1932). Both Köhler and Tolman, through their writings and through some few personal contacts that I had with them later, had more impact on me than any professor that I ever had. It was like an experience of "Where have these people been all of my life?"

So, there was a lot of encouragement for my theoretical interests. However, this still does not seem like a sufficient explanation. For, after all, the other doctoral students whom I knew at Clark, such as Clarence Graham, Norman Munn, Wayne Dennis, Frank Geldard, Dorothea Johannsen, and Mason Crook, all became primarily experimentally oriented research psychologists, and generally followed either the field of sensory psychology that Nafe had represented or the behavioristic interests of Hunter. So, the question still remains as to what took me off to a different pattern of work.

To answer this question, I believe I need to go back to my

experiences before I even dreamed of becoming a psychologist. Near the start of this chapter, I mentioned my memory of a childhood incident in a hide-and-seek game. I said I felt that this memory expressed not only a lively interest in abstract propositions, but also a strong conviction, learned from incidents like that, that a person must always be ready to re-examine what is asserted by other persons, and that improvements in such cases can often be found. Partly this attitude seems to have come from my own experiences; but it certainly also came partly from the example of my father. Let me speak about his influence first.

To provide the setting for this, I need to mention that I grew up in the small steel-mill town of Braddock, Pennsylvania—a town of about 20,000 people, about ten miles east of Pittsburgh. My grandfather on my mother's side was a worker in charge of a Bessemer converter in the steel mill; my other grandfather had been, by all accounts, a rather unsuccessful grocery-store owner. My father had to leave school at fourteen or so because of an invalid condition of his father; when he married at the age of twenty-seven he was reading light-meters for the electric company. Later he was a bank teller, then a worker in the paymaster's office in the steel works, and finally paymaster until he retired.

When I was about eleven years old, we moved several miles out of town to a semi-rural location, but my father continued his work in the steel mill, and we still depended on Braddock for high-school education and church activities. I would not describe our church as a fundamentalist one—all such things are relative—but at least as communicating the orthodox Christian theology of typical Protestant churches of the early 1900s.

My mother had had two years of education beyond high school, in one of the "normal schools" or teacher-training schools scattered throughout Pennsylvania. My father, naturally, had had relatively little schooling, his family situation having been what it was. He later had some very valuable intellectual stimulation from an exceptionally thoughtful minister that the church had for a while. This preacher would give a typical sermon each Sunday morning but, in the evening service, would summarize and comment on some book he had been reading. As an indication of the outlook my father previously had held, I ought to mention a discussion which my mother once described to me that she and my father had had during their engagement. He told her he did not believe her father could go to heaven when he died because he was not a member of a church. My mother was conventional in her own religious views, at that time, but she had felt keenly hurt by her fiancé's statement and felt he must be wrong. Her father was a good man, she said. And, with his seven-day-a-week, twelve-hour-a-day job at the steel works, she felt it was understandable that he was not a church member.

From that as a base-line, however, Dad did a lot of changing. Before I was in high school, he had purchased and read Darwin's *On the Origin of Species*. It seemed reasonable and the ideas well supported, so he changed his thinking accordingly, even though he was probably the only member of the church who accepted such views. Also, he took advantage of some special opportunities to learn about astronomy. The astronomer at the Pittsburgh Observatory, John Brashear, was a man who had started as a lens-grinder and then worked his way up. He took keen interest in sharing his field with the general public, and Dad seized the opportunity to attend his public lectures and visit the observatory to see the instruments and look through the telescope. One of my vivid childhood memories is of Dad's telling two of us older children about the concept of the galaxy that astronomers were developing.

Dad never spoke to us about most of his reading, but, from the splendid small library that he developed and used, and at least from a fair number of discussions, I know that his reading and thinking explored one area after another that had been completely unknown to him before, but which he greatly enjoyed, such as the plays of Shakespeare, the essays of Carlyle, Ruskin, and Emerson, and various books of biblical criticism. And, under such influences, his thinking changed more and more. I remember something my mother told me late in her life, when she was about eighty. "Your Dad and I," she said, "have come to feel that some of the beliefs of the Methodist Church aren't necessarily true. Like the part of the Apostles' Creed that speaks of Jesus as 'born of the Virgin Mary.' When the Creed is being recited each Sunday morning and it comes to that part, Dad and I just keep quiet." I think it is fairly certain that my father led in this change, but it is interesting, too, that she was able to go along with him on it.

In political matters, Dad had always been rather conventional.

When my younger brother and I were in college, we tried one time to convert him to a socialist outlook, but Dad would have none of it. Such notions, he said, simply didn't recognize economic realities. But, along in his fifties or later he heard Norman Thomas speak in one of his many campaigns as the socialist candidate for President. He heard Thomas argue that no country could ever use the concepts of Christianity if it preached brotherhood on Sunday and then went out on the other six days to engage in a dog-eat-dog, devil-take-the-hindmost economic system. There would be a lot of problems, Thomas said, to work out a socialist type of economic organization, but modern man had handled many other complex problems and he could handle those problems, too, if he really wanted to. So, as with his earlier shift to Darwinian views, Dad shifted over to a socialist view of modern society.

So, even though my father was a rather taciturn person, the model he provided for my own thought patterns was one of assuming that a person has to be skeptical, critical, and independent. I think the same thing showed up in some simpler ways, too. When different sorts of work needed to be done around the house to stretch the family finances, he proceeded, in turn, to teach himself what was needed in carpentry, cabinet making, brick laying, concrete work, wall papering, plumbing, electric wiring, and finally making repairs on the motor of the car we eventually got. It was as though he said, "If there's something to be done, and if you have enough time to work on it, you ought to be able to do most anything—not like an expert, of course, and without his speed, but still in a good, substantial way." In my own adult years I haven't covered as wide a range of things as he did; but a good deal of his attitude rubbed off on me and is an attitude that I value. One of the most memorable disappointments I can remember from my childhood occurred when we children and my mother returned from a vacation at a small resort. We found the kitchen had pieces of wood spread all over it, along with a terrific profusion of wood shavings and tools. My father had wanted to make a porch swing for my two maiden aunts, and he had taken advantage of our absence to have space for his "workshop." I was probably no more than four or five at the time, but I remember feeling that it would have been much more fun to have stayed home and to have been involved in all that.

It is obvious, I suppose, that I felt a great deal of respect and affection for my father, and that much of my basic outlook came from him. My own experience, however, also operated to build up my attitude that I would have to do a good deal of questioning and revising. Thus, possibly in my early high-school years, what my father had told me about astronomy led to thoughts like these: If the universe is as vast as astronomy is showing, and if there are millions and millions of suns like our own, then presumably there must be many other planets, and presumably there must also be people on many of these other worlds, because it hardly would seem likely that there would be people merely on one planet and not on a great many others. But, if this is so, what does this signify for various beliefs that seem central to the usual presentation of the Christian religion? For example, what does it signify for the belief that Jesus was "the Son of God, sent to earth to live and bring the truth about God to the world, and then to die as a sacrifice for the sins of the people on this earth"? If there are other people on other worlds, can we imagine that our earth was singled out just for such special consideration? Or, are we to believe that Jesus was sent to one earth after another to play out this same role? This hardly seemed possible to me.

What with the background of concepts that I had been given, I could hardly have avoided raising such questions in my mind. Yet, I also had real fears that perhaps I was doing something that was terribly wrong and that would be very displeasing to God. Yet, I could not keep from coming to the conclusion that, when Jesus taught his followers to pray, "Our Father . . . ," what he meant was that all men, including himself, were sons of God and were to live as brothers. While in college, I happened to read John Woolman's *Journal.* I still have profound respect for that early Quaker. It led me on to an interest in other Quaker writings, as by Rufus Jones. The practices and outlook of the Quakers (including the view that doctrinal matters are something for each person to decide for himself) appealed to me far more than the view in which I had been brought up. I have never joined the Quakers, but have attended a good many of their services in a country district near Philadelphia, in Detroit, in Swarthmore, and in London. In most of those services, no one ever said anything; but to me they were really vital experiences.

Not all of the challenges to my established ideas had to do with theological matters. When I was in high school, there was a major strike in the steel industry. My father, as an office worker, was not involved in it. But I remember that a classmate friend of mine asked me whether I thought that his father, a worker out in the mill, ought to join the strike. My answer was, "From what I understand, the strike is led by Communists, so I would think he shouldn't."

That was in 1919. Two years later, a commission set up by the Interchurch World Movement published a very careful two-volume report on the steel strike. These are, to my knowledge, two of the most notable books that have been published about such a conflict. They explained what issues had been at stake, what beyond-the-law means had been employed to combat the strike, and (what impressed me most) how fantastically distorted and one-sided the supposedly factual presentations about the strike had been in in the newspapers in all of the steel-mill towns. My father purchased the two volumes, and they were a liberal education for me.

So also was a fact which became known to me because my aunt was Assistant Librarian in the Carnegie Library of Braddock. The Superintendent of the local Carnegie Steel Works, as an important member of the Board of Trustees of the library, had insisted that the library must not merely discontinue its subscriptions to the *New Republic,* the *Nation,* and the *Survey Graphic* (all "liberal" magazines) but also burn the bound volumes from past years. She told how heartsick the library staff was about this; but they saw no means of resisting, and the burning was done.

This change of conceptions about industrial questions did not come to me merely from secondhand observations, however. During two different summers while I was in college, I worked in laboring jobs in the steel mill in Homestead, another nearby steel-mill town, and I came to know directly some of the conditions that had brought about that strike. For example, one of the jobs to which I was assigned required a replacement because the man who had been doing that work had been killed on the job the previous day. He had been helping to draw off the excess molten slag and steel that accumulated each day in the ovens where the steel slabs were heated to yellow heat for rolling into steel plates.

Because of the lack of certain simple safety devices, he had backed into one of the buggies of molten material that he already had pulled aside, sat down in it, and was of course so terribly burned that he soon died. For some time after I was put on the job, some hinged lids were attached to the front edge of the buggies so that, after each buggy was filled, the lid could be closed over the glowing material, not only safeguarding against any such fatal burns, but also making it easier to work because of being shielded from the half-blinding glow, particularly in the night-time shifts. The heat tended to corrode these covers, however, and it was not long until the equipment was as before.

About a third of the buggies available for use ought to have been on the scrap heap. Some of them actually had holes in the bottom of them as large as about three inches across and pieces of broken slag from earlier runs had to be put over those holes so that the new material would cool around these pieces and prevent leakage. Also, about ten feet from where we would have the stuff pour out into our squat little carts from a few of the ovens, there were leaky connections on some of the hydraulic systems used for lifting the fire-brick-lined doors to the ovens. I was cautioned that I would have to be very careful not to have any of the molten stuff slosh out on such damp spots on the floor—that the resulting steam would splatter the stuff in all directions as though from an explosion. The most dramatic incident occurred one night when we were filling a buggy that had a crack in the front of it. The molten stuff started to flow through the crack and gradually burned the buggy in two. The glowing contents spilled over the steel plates of the floor and it was impossible to take care of the additional flow that occurred before the ovens could be cooled so as to retain part of what had been ready to flow out. This of course meant that, on the succeeding night, the stuff would come out with more of a rush. The men knew this, and when we had to work on that oven the next night, an audience of forty or fifty men were standing around in the shadows to see what would happen. Things went without mishap, but I could not have handled my part of the job if I had not had a month or so of practice behind me.

Another summer, one of the men said he ought to show me where a few men were working, down under the steel-plated floor where we worked. He took me down to a network of tunnels under the "soaking pits"—ovens of a different sort where the huge ingots of steel were reheated to yellow heat for rolling into the slabs for the later ovens. With pick and shovel and wheelbarrow, four men were working down there (paid 3¢ an hour extra to compensate for the working conditions). They had only a few hours of work each shift, and they were provided with all of the ice-water they could drink, but when my guide put one of the big burlap hoods over me and led me by hand into one of the tunnels where the men had to work, it felt as though I were walking into and breathing a wall of flame. A conveyor system could have handled the work, but perhaps at more cost.

One further happening provided the final touch for these observations. In this same period, since my father happened to own five shares of stock in the steel company, he was a participant in a stock dividend—a device which companies long have used when their profits have climbed so high that the companies deem it wise to hide the extent of such gains. It was not because of lack of funds, in other words, that some jobs still were dangerous or physiologically harmful.

Since at that time I was so strongly interested in economic and industrial problems, it may seem odd that I got into psychology. And, as a matter of fact, in my last three years of college, I was planning to go to theological seminary after my college work and become a minister. What particularly interested me about such work was that I felt it would give me some means to help solve social and industrial problems. However, on leaving college, I felt it would be rushing things to go directly into a theological seminary. I knew that I had been an excessively bookish sort of child—probably partly because I was younger than most of my classmates and because, even in comparison with other boys of my own age, I was of rather slight build. Also, even though I had had some direct contact with social and industrial conditions, I realized I knew far too little about such matters. So, I formed the plan of spending the next two years working in different industries, in different parts of the country, to remedy such deficits. This involved some risk that it would not be a very feasible program financially, since I knew there would probably be some sizable interludes before I would be able to get each successive job. But, I was a vegetarian on principle in those days, primarily because of what I knew about working situations in the stockyards. I felt quite satisfied with food which I could eat without cooking, and I thrived on this. So financially the scheme worked out, and I did not need to ask my parents to subsidize a program which I felt they might not regard as a very wise venture.

This plan was pursued for fifteen months. I worked in a shipyard in Philadelphia, on a farm in a Quaker region near Philadelphia, then in an automobile factory in Detroit, a shoe factory in Chicago, and as a worker in a small riveting gang in a structural steel plant near Pittsburgh.

It was about halfway through that program that my interest in psychology was first aroused. In Chicago, six weeks passed before I landed my next job, and I soon learned that there was no point in going to employment offices after the early morning, because the few jobs that were open were always filled early in the day. So, I had plenty of time to go to the libraries at the University of Chicago and Northwestern University to browse around. At the Northwestern Library, I happened to see a book that had been put on special display. It was Carleton Parker's *The Casual Laborer, and Other Essays* (1920), published to report Parker's study of I.W.W. labor troubles in California. In this book, Parker (an economist and one-time head of the School of Business Administration at the University of Washington) was telling how, in his studies of labor unrest and labor conflicts, he came to the conviction that a deeper analysis of the motives and thinking both of labor and of management groups was required to understand what was happening. So, Parker had turned to the social psychologists and personality psychologists of that day to try to get such a deeper understanding.

I had taken an introductory course in psychology in college. As a matter of fact, as a sophomore, I signed up for a major in it, because the psychology professor had advised me that, as a prospective minister, I obviously would want to know a lot about human nature, and psychology would be the field where I could get that knowledge. However, the course went into long discussions on the different theories of mind-body relations, it called for our learning the anatomy (but not the functions) of all the main trunk-lines in the spinal cord, and in general was mostly along the lines of the old sensory psychology of Wundt and Titchener. The degree of my interest in this course may be indicated by the fact that this was the only college course in which I frequently had hallucinations of hearing the big bell in Bentley Hall toll to give notice that the class period was over and students should shift to their next classes. In no other course did I have this problem, but in introductory psychology, as taught by Professor Henke (who also taught philosophy and education), I had the experience, time after time, of looking around and seeing, to my surprise, that I was the only student who was stirring to leave the room. So, I took no further courses in psychology in college, but changed my major to Greek, and later thought better of that and ended with a major in history and political science—partly because I had been on the intercollegiate debate team for four years and was allowed one credit for each main debate issue on which I had been involved, most of which could be rationalized as "really in the political science field." I should say, incidentally, that I think the intensive and keenly critical workouts and preparations that were required in this debate work were the best part of my intellectual training in college. The one topic that stands out in my memory, by the way, was the question as to whether there ought to be some limitations on the power of the U.S. Supreme Court to declare legislation unconstitutional. This required our going to the local courthouse and reading a lot of the decisions and arguments by the members of the Supreme Court. My expectation had been that this would be utterly preposterous effort on our part, but it was eye-opening to see that the Supreme Court Justices were quite human too, and that in these matters they weren't really dealing with technical legal points, but questions that we could consider with real warrant.

To return to Carleton Parker, though—the psychology he was talking about was of a sort that I had never met in college but that had a powerful appeal to me, much greater than the typical discussion of industrial problems in terms merely of wages, hours, and working conditions. Parker's material led me to read some other books in psychology, and especially Floyd Allport's *Social Psychology*, then recently published. These books did not arouse in me any ideas about a new type of career, but they did inspire a change of plan for the rest of that two-year period. They helped me to realize that I knew very little about the South and about problems of race relations. True, in labor gangs in the steel mill, I had sometimes been the only non-black. But, still, such work had not taught me much. So, I decided to look for a one-year teaching job in a southern Negro college, and then go on to a seminary. I was hired by Paine College, in Augusta, Georgia, where there were about a hundred students in the college division.

This was one of the most strenuous and interesting years I have ever had. It involved teaching eight different courses, five each semester—including some courses I had never had in college. I taught American history, European history, history of religions, introductory political science, introductory economics, social pathology, family welfare, and (last to be added to my responsibilities) the course in introductory psychology, in which I used Allport's *Social Psychology* as my text. The hardest courses for me to teach were those in history, where I had the greatest background, and the most natural and interesting course was the one in psychology.

During that year, I came to realize that my theological views, my interests, and other factors had changed so much that I no longer could think in terms of a minister's work. I decided I should try to get some graduate training in psychology. Choosing a school was like groping in the dark. If departments had existed then with programs in clinical psychology, I would probably have chosen one of those. I visited Johns Hopkins with the idea that I might combine work in psychiatric social work with work in the psychology department, but neither department warmed up to the idea. The University of Pittsburgh ruled me out because I had had no more than one semester of psychology, and I ruled them out because the department looked weak. Chance came to my rescue again. Returning for a visit to my alma mater, Allegheny College, probably to attend the commencement of my brother, I happened to see, in the library, the book *Psychologies of 1925,* published at Clark University from a series of lectures there. I was particularly impressed by the lecture of Walter S. Hunter (1926), a presentation in what seemed to me beautifully clear thinking. So, I applied to Clark, was granted a tuition scholarship, started there in the fall of 1927, and had Hunter as my major professor at both the master's and the doctoral levels. It turned out that I disagreed with him on a good many matters, but I never had to worry when I did so. I deeply respected him both as a person and as a careful, capable psychologist. The other graduate students of the department were a fine bunch, too. The three years at Clark were one of the happiest and most helpful periods of my life.

So, that is how I came to be a psychologist and why I became a theoretical psychologist. However, this still leaves some major questions. Thus, one might wonder why, even though I had such a hearty admiration for Professor Hunter, I did not become favorably impressed with his behavioristic theory, either as regards his definition of the subject matter of psychology or as regards his interpretations of learning. Other students were thus impressed, such as Norman Munn, Clarence Graham, Wayne Dennis, and Louis Gellerman. The problem is, why did I become so much more receptive to the purposive behaviorism of Tolman, the Gestalt psychology of Köhler and Lewin, and the ideas on personality of workers like Karen Horney, Carl Rogers, and A. H. Maslow?

To answer these questions I believe we need to consider, once more, some of my background experiences. And, to begin with, let me cite another early memory—one which Adler would have particularly stressed, since it is the earliest memory that I can recall. When I was about three, our family went for a very special vacation to Chautauqua Lake, in western New York. One day, my father took me and my sister, who is two years older than I am, to play on the edge of the lake. We had either carried our lunch in a cardboard shoe box or found such a box on the beach. My father proceeded to show how it could be made into a small sailboat by finding some small sticks for a mast, etc., using sand for ballast, and using a handkerchief for a sail. The breeze was blowing out from the shore, and when we launched the little boat it sailed straight out, dancing over the successive small waves, with the sun shining on it, until it finally sailed out of sight. I remember this as one of the most beautiful and delightful scenes I have ever experienced. When we returned to our cottage later, my sister and I were still bubbling with excitement. However, when we told my mother about it, her response was to scold my father, saying that, since we were having a vacation that stretched the family finances so seriously, the family simply couldn't afford to waste a handkerchief like that.

Long afterwards—in fact, when my father was in his eighties—I mentioned the incident and asked him whether he remembered it. He described it as I have outlined above, except for the final detail. Over a period of more than fifty years during which time I believe I had never spoken to him about it, he had remembered the incident in the same terms I did. It had apparently been a notable experience for him, too. But when I asked him, "Do you remember that when we returned to the cabin, Mother scolded you for wasting a handkerchief?", he laughed and replied, "No—I suppose she might have said something like that, but I wouldn't have paid any attention to it." (Such a reaction on his part, I might add, would have come from no spendthrift tendencies; he too was very careful about his expenditures, and had to be.)

In this memory, it seems to me there are two themes that have been really basic in most of my life. The first and very notable aspect, it seems to me, is the memory of the world as a beautiful and wonderful place—and, not just in its own characteristics, as something that one might passively observe, but as having some potentialities of beauty and delight that could come through working, even just with very simple, humble materials, to help produce some beauty that otherwise would not have been manifested. That is, it was not simply a view that the world is good in itself, nor that what we ourselves had done was so gratifying, but that we were working together with the lake and wind, and so on, to have made such a thing occur. Furthermore, this experience which was so memorable was a *social* experience, and not just something done by myself alone. It is partly when you are participating with others that things that are treasurable can happen.

The other theme which the memory embodied, it seems to me, was the notion that one can also expect that some of the things that are most significant and beautiful and well intentioned, as far as oneself is concerned, can bring disapproval and adverse reactions of a serious sort from other persons. In fact, since my father did not question what my mother said, the impression that the whole incident perhaps left in me was that those who disapprove are likely to be more powerful or important than those who help in the creation of beauty, and hence that a person has to be careful about revealing to other persons some of the experiences and thoughts that have meant most to him.

There have been many experiences, subsequently, which have strengthened both of these themes. Thus, there are hundreds of experiences which I can recall that similarly reflected the beauty and the wonder of the world. Some of the earliest are from summer vacations which my younger brother and I used to have in the foothills of the Allegheny Mountains on the farms of some relatives of my mother. There are memories of building dams in the small brook of one farm, and of the crayfish and water-skaters who shared that stream with us. There are memories of the sounds of music, as it were, from the larger creek on the other farm. At night, away from city lights and smoke, the skies were thick with stars in a way that I had never seen before and had not seen elsewhere until, a few years ago, I went out one autumn from Eugene to the high mountain pass where the Bohemian gold mines used to operate and, before going back into the old bunkhouse for a night's sleep, stretched out on the ground for a while so that I could really enjoy the sky. (Most persons in this "civilized" world, it saddens me to realize, have never really seen the stars.) On those farms, as my brother and I grew older, there was a lot of hard work helping harvest the hay and grain. The farms were old-fashioned ones, with a lot of hand work to be done, and we two boys were particularly appreciated during the harvesting and threshing seasons. However, to my brother Donald and myself, these were wonderful times. At home, too, after we moved from town when I was about eleven, we had a scraggly sort of woods nearby. We roamed the woods for dead trees we could saw up and haul home for beautiful wood fires in the winter, and also simply for trees to climb and "caves" to discover. On my own, I searched for different sorts of plants that I could transplant into a small wild-flower garden I had.

From later years, there are a number of particular paintings from various art museums that I saw with deep gratitude. The same with regard to the privilege of participating in several choirs and chorus groups, even though my singing is decidedly weak. Various friendships have been truly precious to me. Or, woods flaming with color in the fall, especially in New England. Snow-covered hills in Iowa with their wonderful colors at sunset. Even the winter rains in Oregon are something to delight in, and the sound of wind through the big fir trees on our lot. Voices of children at play. . . . The list is endless. In short, one of the most fundamental beliefs or attitudes of my life is what is so well symbolized for me by the first part of that little incident at Chautauqua Lake. It did not surprise me at all, therefore, when I recently found myself unhesitatingly buying the hard-cover version of Rachel Carson's posthumously published book, *The Sense of Wonder,* when I found it recently in the bookstore, read some parts of it, and looked through the beautiful photographs her friends had provided of her treasured bit of the Maine coast. This was a book, I knew, that I would want to share with a good many persons.

As regards the other theme in the Chautauqua Lake incident, various later experiences have nourished it, too. It would be wrong to describe my mother's relations with us children as having been solely on the side of reproofs and restrictions. In some ways she was the more emotionally open and responsive of my parents. My father had grown up as an only child of a mother not much given to displays of affection. There are many things I remember which expressed my mother's genuinely positive interest in her children and her enjoyment in opening up activities for us. Even when some of our projects brought a lot of inconvenience to her, but were good, innocent, healthy fun, she was extremely patient. But, many things in her background had left her with persistent fears of doing wrong and of being scolded or rejected. Such fear concerned not merely herself, but also those of her family for whom she felt particularly responsible. I might well skip smaller examples and mention an instance from later times. When I was about thirty-five, I was on a visit to see my folks. My mother was expressing her disappointment, especially since I had once intended to be a minister, that I was no longer a church-goer. Both for the sake of my children, she said, and for the sake of my students, she felt that I ought to participate in some church group or other. She described it as a bitter disappointment to my father and herself to have had things turn out as they had. "I wish," she then said, "that I had buried you as a child." "That's an awfully strong statement," I replied. Her answer was, "Yes, but I mean it." About twenty years later, I learned that similar comments had been made to two of my four siblings (whether possibly to the other two, I don't know, but probably not). However, I also should mention that, late in her life, she had spoken to me in different terms, saying "I hope your children will be as great a comfort to you as you have been to Dad and myself." So, there was ambivalence on her part. Nevertheless, the picture of my family background would not be honestly given if there were no mention of this sort of sharp, quick criticism that occurred so often, even over little things. One of my brothers has told me that his two children finally served notice that they were going to no more Thanksgiving Day dinners at Grandma's. "*You* can go," they said, "but there's no fun for us in going and getting scolded and lectured on all sorts of things." And, in fact, it seemed that such tendencies became accentuated as she grew older, just as it is true that sometimes people grow more consistent as the years pass.

I believe it is fairly safe to say that the experiences I had with reference to my mother tended particularly to make me more guarded and cautious in my personal relationships, and more guarded and cautious in my work, than would have been desirable. I can easily spot instances of this. Yet, on the other hand, such tendencies did not prevent me from developing a considerable number of fine friendships in college, graduate school, and subsequently. Probably part of the reason for this has been the experiences with my father and also the fine comradeship of my wife Dorothy, who had been a fellow graduate student in my last year at Clark. I owe a great deal to the rich experience of life with our four children. But part of it, too, has been simply good fortune in being thrown with a remarkable number of persons who are as fine as one could imagine.

It may well be true, too, that my mother helped me indirectly on a point which, I believe, has been very helpful both in my psychological thinking and in my relations with other persons. What I refer to is my belief that, both in psychology and in ordinary life, there is a great need to recognize and emphasize more subtle factors and more subtle relationships than generally are emphasized. I do not mean that there are no important tangible factors, but that the tangible factors are never the whole story in psychological matters. If there were some tragic aspects to my mother's life, as there apparently were, and in many other lives, I think part of the reason for that is well symbolized by that Chautauqua Lake incident. She was greatly concerned to care for her family's needs, but sometimes she was unable to see how much more was going on than just the loss, say, of a handkerchief.

So, when it is asked why I took an interest in theoretical questions, and why I tended to come to the sorts of conclusions that I did with reference to learning, motivation, perception, and personality, I think the answer cannot be given merely or even basically in terms of the technical training and experience I had, but must go back also to what I had experienced from life and from the world. My account has been very incomplete, of course. But I have tried to make it representative.

In the last few pages that remain, I possibly ought to deal very briefly with a few other matters. One such topic might be the question of what is required for work in theoretical psychology, as I see the matter from my own experience with it. I would emphasize five things. It seems to me the first requirement is the development of as broad and intensive a background as possible. In this connection, I feel that Walter Hunter was wise in urging me not to launch out too quickly into theoretical problems and to get some experience in empirical research first. A theoretical psychologist is going to be talking about the research results and research methods of other psychologists. To some extent, he ought to know about empirical research at first hand. For breadth of experience, I think there are some advantages or at least compensations for those who teach in smaller universities and colleges where their teaching has to spread over more fields. In large departments, the pressures are strong for narrow specialization. There are some values in that, of course, but I believe work on basic principles tends to suffer when a person stays too much just in some miniature area.

Second, I believe a theoretical psychologist needs to have the practice of trying to restate things in the simplest and clearest terms that he can. Fancy terms and fancy language, it seems to me, often make things difficult for the theorist himself, and not merely for the reader. Egon Brunswik, Clark Hull, and even Kurt Lewin, on some matters, seem to me to illustrate this difficulty.

Third, I believe that the theoretical psychologist needs to be ready to recognize and utilize good ideas no matter where they come from. E. R. Guthrie, for example, has seemed to me in some respects one of the most undisciplined or irresponsible learning psychologists, and yet it was from his writing that I got one of the notions which is most essential in my own thinking about the psychology of learning.

Fourth, as I have already tried to illustrate above, it seems to me the theoretical psychologist must be willing and interested in turning things over and over in his mind, not just a few times, as the ordinary psychologist will take the time to do, but, say, ten or a dozen times. His role, as I see it, is to try to select questions that really deserve extremely careful and protracted thought, and then to give those questions some long, hard work that most psychologists cannot afford the time to give.

Fifth, a theoretical psychologist has to remember that thinking is partly a social process. Even in his teaching of introductory courses, it is not merely that a teacher provides intellectual stimulus for his students; the debt is reciprocal. And, a theoretical psychologist depends a great deal on his professional colleagues. In my own work, I have been particularly indebted to Rolland Waters at the University of Arkansas in 1930-1933, to David Krech in our year with Lashley in 1933-1934 and subsequently, and to the truly friendly, intellectually stimulating group of psychologists at the University of Oregon, where I have taught for the last thirty-five years. I ought to make special mention of the suggestions and constructive criticisms from Leona Tyler, Dick Littman, Jacob Beck, and my son-in-law, Fred Attneave. I have already spoken of the extraordinary value of my work with Peter Madison. There is a great deal that other psychologists can do to help you know about significant work and to point out deficiencies which otherwise might take much time to correct in your own work, or that you might never escape from.

The editor of this volume has suggested that the contributors make some mention of the recognition their work has had. In my own case, I feel there have been no indications that my work has been world-shaking, and I don't think there should have been any such praise or honor. But, for what I have done, I think the recognition has been very generous. Thus, the National Research Council Fellowship in 1933-1934, the Guggenheim Memorial Fellowship in 1948-1949, and the Fulbright lectureship at the University of Aberdeen in Scotland in 1955-1956 were important both as honors and as providing the means for some very valuable experience. I have been elected to some different offices, such as President of the Western Psychological Association in 1952 and as President of the Division of General Psychology (Division I) of the American Psychological Association in 1959 and 1972. The recognitions that I count most important, however, have been the opportunities to participate in various important collaborative volumes such as S. S. Stevens's *Handbook of Experimental Psychology* in 1951, volume 5 of the Koch set, *Psychology: A Study of a Science* in 1963, Melvin Marx's *Theories in Contemporary Psychology* in 1963, the *Nebraska Symposium on Motivation* in 1965, the volume on Egon Brunswik's work edited by Kenneth Hammond in 1966, Melvin Marx's *Learning: Theories* in 1970, and the volume edited by George G. Haydu on *Patterns of Integration from Biochemical to Behavioral Processes* in 1972.

I have enjoyed the privilege of giving special lectures, and engaging in discussions on them, at other universities. I tend to think of myself as somewhat shy and retiring, but when I count up the number of such occasions and see that there were about twenty-seven of them in the United States and Canada, about a dozen in England and Scotland, and a couple in Norway, I am not so sure that this self-image, too, does not need some remolding.

The last question might be whether I feel that the time for theoretical psychologists (even one-sided ones like myself) has passed, or whether there is still much to be done. My own view on this is particularly related to the recent book by D. H. and D. L. Meadows, Jørgen Randers, and W. W. Behrens—*The Limits to Growth* (1972). I feel that this volume, more powerfully than any other book on ecology, has given extremely good grounds for saying that our modern world is going to have to transform many of its basic patterns of outlook and modes of life within the next half-century or else have our civilization collapse. I used to believe that the threat of nuclear war was the most serious danger, but I think these authors have built a strong case for saying that the far more serious danger is coming from what we accept, ordinarily, as simply the normal growth activities of a highly technological society. We are going to have to change our functioning in very fundamental ways, and there will not be too much time in which that can be done. Populations that are dying of hunger and cold are not going to be fussy about protecting beautiful forests—or any forests or any wild life—nor will it seem important to conserve irreplaceable natural resources for later generations. I have no illusions that psychology can make more than some minor contributions to whatever will be needed, because it will have to be a matter of practical action, and not merely of scientific understanding. But psychology needs to play as much of a role as possible. And, consequently, I feel that by far the hardest and most important work in theoretical psychology is required from now on. What we have done, so far, simply does not cut deeply enough.

REFERENCES

Adler, Alfred. *Social Interest.* London: Faber & Faber, 1933.

Arnold, Magda B. (ed.), *The Nature of Emotion: Selected Readings.* Baltimore, Md.: Penguin Books, 1968.

Bartlett, Frederic. *Thinking.* New York: Basic Books, 1958.

Békésy, Georg von. *Sensory Inhibition.* Princeton, N.J.: Princeton University Press, 1967.

Carson, Rachel. *The Sense of Wonder.* New York: Harper & Row, 1956.

Conant, James B. *On Understanding Science: an Historical Approach.* New Haven, Conn.: Yale University Press, 1947.

Hull, Clark L. Differential habituation to internal stimuli in the white rat. *Journal of Comparative Psychology,* 1933, *16,* 255-272.

—— *Principles of Behavior.* New York: Appleton-Century-Crofts, 1943.

Hunter, Walter S. Psychology and anthroponomy, pp. 83-107, in Carl Murchison (ed.), *Psychologies of 1925.* Worcester, Mass.: Clark University Press, 1926.

Interchurch World Movement of America. *Report on the Steel Strike of 1919.* New York: Harcourt, Brace & Howe, 1920.

Interchurch World Movement of America. *Public Opinion and the Steel Strike.* New York: Harcourt, Brace & Howe, 1921.

Klein, George A. Chapter 4, Cognitive control and motivation, pp. 87-118, in Gardner Lindzey (ed.), *Assessment of Human Motives.* New York: Rinehart, 1958.

Koch, Sigmund. Special review: Hull's *Principles of Behavior. Psychological Bulletin,* 1944, *41,* 269-286.

—— Section 1: Clark L. Hull, pp. 1–176 in William K. Estes et al., *Modern Learning Theory.* New York: Appleton-Century-Crofts, 1954.

Köhler, Wolfgang. *Gestalt Psychology.* New York: Horace Liveright, 1929.

Leeper, Robert W. The evidence for a theory of neurological maintenance of states of emotional motivation. *Psychological Bulletin,* 1932, *29,* 571 (abstract).

—— and Dorothy O. Leeper. An experimental study of equivalent stimulation in human learning. *Journal of General Psychology,* 1932, *6,* 344–376.

Leeper, Robert W. The role of motivation in learning: A study of the phenomenon of differential motivational control of the utilization of habits. *Journal of Genetic Psychology*, 1935a, *46*, 3–40.

—— A study of a neglected portion of the field of learning—the development of sensory organization. *Journal of Genetic Psychology*, 1935b, *46*, 41–75.

—— *Psychology of Personality and Social Adjustment: A Handbook for Students.* Mt. Vernon, Iowa: privately printed, 1937.

—— *Psychology of Personality.* Ann Arbor, Mich.: Edwards Brothers, 1941.

—— *Lewin's Topological and Vector Psychology: A Digest and a Critique.* Eugene, Ore.: University of Oregon Press, 1943.

—— Dr. Hull's *Principles of Behavior.Journal of Genetic Psychology*, 1944, *65*, 3–52.

—— A motivational theory of emotion to replace "emotion as disorganized response." *Psychological Review*, 1948, *55*, 5–21.

—— Theories of personality, pp. 21–56, in Wayne Dennis et al., *Current Trends in Psychological Theory.* Pittsburgh, Pa.: University of Pittsburgh Press, 1951a.

—— Chapter 19. Cognitive processes, pp. 730–757, in S. S. Stevens (ed.), *Handbook of Experimental Psychology.* New York: Wiley, 1951b.

—— Clark Hull's *Essentials of Behavior. American Journal of Psychology*, 1952, *65*, 478–491.

—— What contributions might cognitive learning theory make to our understanding of personality? *Journal of Personality*, 1953, *22*, 32–40.

—— Clark Hull's *A Behavior System. American Journal of Psychology*, 1954, *67*, 375–379.

—— and Madison, Peter. *Toward Understanding Human Personalities.* New York: Appleton-Century-Crofts, 1959.

Leeper, R. W. Theoretical methodology in the psychology of personality, pp. 389–413, in Melvin Marx (ed.), *Theories in Contemporary Psychology.* New York: Macmillan, 1963a.

—— Learning and the fields of perception, motivation, and personality, pp. 365–487, in Sigmund Koch (ed.), *Psychology: A Study of a Science*, Vol. 5. New York: McGraw-Hill, 1963b.

—— Some needed developments in the motivational theory of emotions, pp. 25–122, in David Levine (ed.), *Nebraska Symposium on Motivation, 1965.* Lincoln, Nebr.: University of Nebraska Press, 1965.

—— Chapter 14. A critical consideration of Egon Brunswik's Probabilistic Functionalism, pp. 405–454, in Kenneth Hammond (ed.), *The Psychology of Egon Brunswik.* New York: Holt, Rinehart, and Winston, 1966.

—— Chapter 11. The motivational and perceptual properties of emotions as indicating their fundamental character and role, pp. 151–168, in Magda Arnold (ed.), *Feelings and Emotions: The Loyola Symposium.* New York: Academic Press, 1970a.

—— Part V, Cognitive learning theory, pp. 237–331, in Melvin H. Marx (ed.), *Learning: Theories.* New York: Macmillan, 1970b.

—— The structure and functional unity of psychological processes, pp. 200–216, in George G. Haydu (ed.), Patterns of integration from biochemical to behavioral processes. *Annals of the New York Academy of Sciences,* 1972, *193.*

Lewin, Kurt. *The Conceptual Representation and the Measurement of Psychological Forces.* Durham, N. C.: Duke University Press, 1938.

Madison, Peter. *Freud's Concept of Repression and Defense.* Minneapolis: University of Minnesota Press, 1961.

—— *Personality Development in College.* Reading, Mass.: Addison-Wesley, 1969.

Meadows, D. H., et al. *The Limits to Growth.* New York: Universe Books, 1972.

Newell, A., and Simon, Herbert A. *Human Problem Solving.* New York: Prentice-Hall, 1972.

Parker, Carleton H. *The Casual Laborer, and Other Essays.* New York: Harcourt, Brace and Howe, 1920.

Pribram, Karl H. (ed.). *Brain and Behavior IV: Adaptation.* Baltimore, Md.: Penguin Books, 1969.

Tolman, Edward C. *Purposive Behavior in Animals and Men.* New York: Century, 1932.

Young, Paul T. *Motivation of Behavior.* New York: Wiley, 1936.

—— *Emotion in Man and Animal.* New York: Wiley, 1943.

—— *Motivation and Emotion.* New York: Wiley, 1961.

8

There Is More Beyond

GARDNER MURPHY

For the mariners of the ancient world there was a "known world" and an "unknown world." For some of them, especially those of Viking blood, the barriers into the unknown were broken. But for our own Western tradition, it was the "admiral of the ocean sea" who in 1492 could deny the legitimacy of the phrase *ne plus ultra* as applied to the pillars of Hercules. It was not just the reefs of the Azores and not just the west coast of Africa, but the vast new world of power and wealth that was broken open in 1492, and the word *ne* was no longer appropriate. The only rightful phrase to describe the new world was *plus ultra*, or "there is more beyond." Trying to keep one foot solidly on the scientific and historical ground while the other treads forward precariously on uncertain footing, my image of myself as an exploring psychologist is exactly defined by *plus ultra;* or still more romantically, one might say with Heinz Werner that for me the scientific psychologist is like a turtle, with four feet solidly on the ground but always ready to stick his neck out.

What has this got to do with the vividness, warmth, snapping electrical vitality of the childhood memories that come back to me with a bang whenever I ask them to? What is the meaning of the brilliant golden sunshine that plays through the leaves, and lights from the mosses in a fairyland forest which I encountered in Massachusetts and Tennessee and Alabama, and long afterward, in

India and in Mars Hill in Athens? It comes back too, as I think of the oboes and horns to which I listened as I perched at the horseshoe tip of the family circle in Carnegie Hall. Is there any connection between my sentimental delights in discovery—in the world of science, travel, music, painting, conversation—and my love of sheer theory-building; sheer conceptualization?

I think these tastes are interrelated; but my love of psychology is first a love of experience as it comes through senses, affects, complex association patterns, and memory or creative fantasy. I believe every experience has a good warm personal quality, whatever other qualities it may also possess, and that science and the arts are not so different, or indeed psychology not so different either from the art that one encounters in Shakespeare and Rembrandt or the art one discovers in Darwin's and Einstein's perceptions of reality. The thing about all these experiences that has such a crashing impact for me is the primary vitality of raw experience. I discovered in kindergarten how lovable a bright blue water-color painting can be. I discovered in college what Schubert's Unfinished Symphony can be, and I discovered while teaching at Columbia, how exciting the probing of human sense perception, image, and thought can be—for example, as my wife Lois and I read together Rorschach's masterful book *Psychodiagnostics.* My love of psychology is predictable from my love of human experience for its own sake. This I think is what most people mean by being sentimental. I am not in the least injured if these thoughts are regarded as sentimental, and I may claim the company of Lawrence Sterne, William James, and Harry Murray in selecting the term.

How I got this way has been briefly told in two narratives (1957; 1967), and I will go on my way as if the story were wholly new. The genes that went into my composition belonged to that very confusing conglomerate of northern European stocks and families which came by way of Ireland, England, and Scotland, and—far enough back—many other European stocks. These were assembled and then, biologically and culturally, individualized in various American communities stretching from Texas and Ohio to Massachusetts, Connecticut, and New York. In eastern Massachusetts, we loved the exciting floral image to which Van Wyck Brooks refers under the term "the flowering of New England"—

the Emerson statue by Daniel Chester French greeted us as we made our way into the Concord Public Library. Sally Bartlett, the librarian, was one of the gay souls whom I took canoeing on the Concord River. In that world William James was a well-known and respected figure, and I heard a fair amount of philosophy and psychology discussed in the grandparental home in which much of my bringing up went on. The issue between Lamarck and Darwin, and John Fiske's conception of lengthening human infancy offered psychological tidbits avidly picked up by any of the grandchildren who proved to be nearby.

There was psychical research too, notably in the person of Mrs. L. E. Piper, the medium for whom William James had deepest respect, about whose extraordinary phenomena he wrote at considerable length. And in a world in which I was steeped in literary and historical studies, with an emphasis upon Greek and Latin both at the New Haven High School and at the Hotchkiss School in Lakeville, Connecticut, I acquired a slight knowledge of psychical research, solidified, organized, and well built up within me by reading William Barrett's book *Psychical Research* in my grandfather's library when I was sixteen. I connected these phenomena with religion, as phenomena having to do with a personal soul which survived after death, and could in some cases make its continued existence known. I was a devout young Episcopalian, confirmed at thirteen, and sophisticated enough to have read very attentively an introduction to comparative religion under the title *Faiths of the World*. I took this Anglican Christianity quite evangelically and continued to do so during the years at Hotchkiss, and at Yale, which I entered in 1912.

Freshman year at Yale gave me the extraordinarily intense experience of really *great* teaching as exemplified in Chauncey Tinker, who made English literature simply glow, and this was continued in a new dimension in sophomore year by John Chester ("Jack") Adams, who not only inspired, but loved me, and gave me a resonance for all English literature, which from my point of view marks him as a very great benefactor of all my life. At Hotchkiss, Ralph Theller had taught me the rudiments of English expression, and my father had an exquisite sense of literary form, as shown in his various books dealing with the Anglican Church, with "The Problems of the Present South," and also "A Beginner's

Star Book." There was no generation gap since my parents respected and trusted my interests in reading books in various disciplines.

In my sophomore year I took elementary psychology, and a mixture of solid facts and high, wide, and handsome speculations suited me to a tee. With Thorndike's theory of bonds and William James's theory of habits leading me on into more complex conceptualizations in the Titchener-dominated experimental psychology which was the core of my "psychology major," I was being drawn into psychology in part because I loved all that stuff about the mind, and was good at it as far as academic standards go (I did a little experimental paper on word association which was not good enough to be published, but *was* published in the *American Journal of Psychology*). At the same time, I was sure I wanted to go into psychical research, and as it became clear to me that I needed a Ph.D. in psychology to achieve that goal, I became henceforth a double personality, one personality adapting to the environment known as scientific or laboratory psychology, the other personality being concerned with a vast array of interesting phenomena which looked like telepathy, clairvoyance, precognition, and all the rest of what William James was talking about under the head of psychical research, all of which was of course rejected and gently—or not so gently—smiled at by the members of the official establishment.

As to ways of using my psychology as a prime support in life, there was no question that I was going to be a teacher. This was very real to me because Jack Adams, coach of the Yale debating team, believed in me and helped greatly in the development of my skill in organizing and presenting ideas. There was no problem about shifting from written to oral material or vice versa. My Hotchkiss and Yale education, my home background, my debating experiences made it easy and delightful to address audiences.

A delight in teaching and a love of the teacher's craft first came to me through high school debating: "We of the affirmative intend to establish . . ." etc. It called for careful preparation in terms of large blocks of ideas in an intelligible order; it called for documentation (at first, of course, always through the *World Almanac*). No such refinements as the difference between "primary sources" and "secondary sources" having penetrated that far from the library, one learned to earmark the transitions from one point to another and to "recapitulate" at the end, showing the abysmal traps into which one's opponents had fallen or must fall, and winding up with a clinching (and clenching) peroration.

At Yale too I became a member of the debating team. Jack Adams, the coach, taught us always to see things from all points of view. The debates themselves were one-evening teaching sessions. We taught and were taught by the necessities of the intrinsic logic of the problem on the one hand and the audience capacities and predilections on the other. I found later that all of this had given me a most generous and satisfying launching pad for a college teaching career.

Although I never overcame stage fright (I've had a dash of this in all teaching situations all my life) I could usually keep the prepared address at one point in my perspective, and my audience at another point, and carry out the necessary dance step to move rather rhythmically from one to another with the aid of notes, blackboard, and continuous scanning of faces and postures in the room to see what kind of contact I was making. I have always been amused by the people who have said that I speak without notes. The very idea terrifies me. The notes may be hidden—on an envelope, for example—but they are the anchorage point. Teaching is delicately reminiscent of the debating world in which it is essential to be ready for what the other fellow has to *say,* but also ready, as Jack Adams pointed out, to understand and feel one's way into an opposing point of view in order to deal with it honestly. The important thing is to learn how to organize an hour's worth or a year's worth of material by getting all of it spread out like a map. I learned in various English classes how to define a main idea in such a way that the sub-ideas fall into intelligible relation to one another and into the main idea, and when the material was sufficiently detailed, having even sub-subheads together with recapitulations and over-all interpretations which were offered then (as now) as guides to the essayist or the teacher. Perhaps this is enough to explain why the presentation of the material to graduate seminars in the beginning of my formal teaching at Columbia went easily and pleasantly.

When Robert S. Woodworth asked me in 1919, on my arrival from the Armed Expeditionary Forces, to make a "seminar" presentation of my fragmentary little study of free association, there was "no problem" about laying out a forty-five-minute presentation with the use of the blackboard and the major headings which I wanted to make clear. Woodworth looked at me in a dreamy, "can't-believe-it" way when I came out at the end of my talk at exactly the forty-five-minute point. He could not have known that as a debater I had been trained to use my time; neither less than nor more than all of it. Actually, it was because I could do the things that Ralph Theller and Jack Adams had taught me to do, more than for any skill as a psychologist, that Woodworth and Poffenberger and the other friends of the department entrusted me with beginning psychology classes.

Most important, Ralph Theller, Jack Adams, and others had given me a sense of the delight in playing with ideas, trying to communicate them in vivid ways, and in reaching students or other audiences dynamically. That is, "getting to them" so that they became aroused or involved in the intellectual problem. Another way to involve students is by phrasing abstract principles in terms of metaphors, similes, or other images that are part of the student's own mental furniture; and a third is to use paradoxical questions. Chauncey Tinker, one of the most brilliant teachers at Yale, gave me a sense of how it is possible to stretch the scope of the student's mind and contribute to greater integration at the same time.

The belief in a kind of organized clarity went very deep. The main thing that kept it from being dull was the occurrence of anecdotes or whimsies from point to point which I would immediately shovel into the stream of verbiage as it flowed forth, getting as a rule good "reinforcement" through the chuckles of those who did not regard it as too corny. Whether corny or not, I knew that something of this sort was necessary in the predominantly logical intellectualist undertaking that we were involved in.

Although I was delighted by the specific facts I learned in the three laboratory courses in psychology which I took, it never occurred to me to define for myself a specialization which would lead to more and more mastery of technical detail. I don't think the word "generalist" ever reached my ears, but that was what I wanted to be. My college minor in anthropology, and the courses I took in zoology, mathematics, language, and literature, etc., were all precious to me. My hobbies were diverse. Response to music and to painting both meant more and more to me the more deeply I got into them during the college years. As I made up my mind to be a psychologist, I would not have known what was meant if somebody asked, "what kind of a psychologist?" or "what types of psychology interest you?"

The thing that I missed was a good course in philosophy, and I made that up by spending the summer of 1916 at the Widener Library at Harvard, where I had a delightful time going through the history of philosophy by myself. I vaguely realized though that all of psychology, plus all of parapsychology, plus a good deal of philosophy and various crazes, hobbies, and excitements, in music and the arts, were going to mean overextended lines or thinness, or actual superficiality; or all that goes into the Yankee realism of the phrase "Jack of all trades, master of none." There may be a way to be a generalist without being a jack of all trades, but I have not discovered it.

Upon graduation from Yale, I went to Harvard for graduate work and got a good mix of philosophy, psychology, and parapsychology, with such delicious extras as Parker's course the Structure and Function of Central Nervous Organs and George F. Moore's delightful course History of Religions. I learned much in a self-study in Yerkes's course on Ontogenetic Psychology in which he urged us to bring in absolutely everything that we could find out about our past, and I took him literally. In a more personal way, the encounter with the literature from psychical research which I made during my period of association with Leonard Troland forced upon me the necessity of deciding what all this material really meant in terms of my philosophical outlook on life; and I decided that although rich and good, the material was not strong enough to indicate a mind-body dualism of the sort which I personally craved. I had to give up my dualism, which meant giving up my religious faith, and I did this with one clean, if bloody, stroke. I did however determine that psychical research was very important and that I was going to stay with it.

The United States entered World War I in April 1917 and I joined the Yale Mobile Hospital Unit. We were stationed in a sector which was quiet most of the time, and I did not learn anything much from the two years except to talk passable French and to see through French middle-class eyes. I came back in July 1919 and went to see R. S. Woodworth about matriculating as a Ph.D. candidate. I was generously accepted and settled down (with about $1000 in my pocket, saved in the Army) to take the requisite courses. The courses were decidedly good, but even better was the extraordinary course by Harry Emerson Fosdick at Union Theological Seminary entitled The Use of the Bible, and two courses at the new school, one by Harry Barnes, entitled Modern Industrialism, and the other by James Harvey Robinson called the History of the Human Mind. I don't know whether experiences of this sort are to be had nowadays. I don't say they are not; I'm just wondering. But when students come and tell me of the work they have had, they tell me about their *psychology* courses—all sorts. But I don't hear much about courses marked by extraordinarily rich content or extraordinarily brilliant teaching skills, or courses which give sheer broadening of outlook. When there is so much complaint that undergraduate students do not get a chance to hear a great teacher (who is supposedly occupied with his magnum opus) I don't know what it's all about. A large part of my general education came from a small number of classroom hours spread over a small span of years, often dominated by an absolutely tremendous teaching personality. The teachers were great because they were intensely and passionately in love with their subjects, had held them up to the light on a thousand and one occasions, were utterly familiar with the different ways of seeing them, fascinated by the capacity to share this multiple vision for generation after generation of inquiring minds. They were specialists, but that was not the point. Suppose my reader happens to know that Chauncey Tinker was the world's authority on the Age of Johnson; but what has that got to do with his teaching of Shakespeare or Ruskin in a way that made them come to life? Precious little. Most great teaching is epic poetry punctuated by fiery or by lyrical moments. Can you teach science this way? Yes. I say yes because it was my good fortune to take Anthropology A-1 given by A. G. Keller and Zoology A-1 given by L. L. Woodruff, who, incidentally, did the protozoan experiments that Freud emphasizes in *Beyond the Pleasure Principle.*

My colleagues at City College from the years 1940 to 1952, notably Eugene L. Hartley and John Peatman, in kindly emphasizing some of the teaching arts that meant much to me, were aware that everything I had ever learned at Hotchkiss or at Yale or at Harvard or at Columbia, or for that matter hiking in the Pyrenees, or reading Popeye aloud to my son, somehow worked its way into my lectures. I think I began this habit as I listened to my Grandpa King in Concord, Massachusetts, around 1902, because it was a Yankee habit which he had cultivated to a fantastic degree; and since I was always "reinforced" for far-fetched literary allusions I assumed that any old kind of far-fetched allusions, whether literary or not, would bring commensurate reinforcements, and they always did. I found, too, at the Menninger School of Psychiatry in recent years that while this was very puzzling to the young doctors it was not subject to a heavy taboo, and if I could get a few smiles from the gallery it counterbalanced the slightly disturbed faces in the front rows. To some it meant that "Doctor Murphy had tremendous erudition"; for others, more perceptive, it meant just a skein of free association, or what William James called "impartial redintegration."

I learned whatever I was capable of learning about the teacher's craft during those first years at Columbia in the early and middle 1920s, teaching partly in the "extension" or "general studies" and partly in Columbia College. Soon I added Abnormal Psychology to my offerings and a little later the History of Modern Psychology. As I was spreading out to prepare for these classes, I also learned something about anthropology from Ruth Benedict, Margaret Mead, and Otto Klineberg.

In the course on the History of Modern Psychology, which I first offered in 1923, my students included some inspiring colleagues, only a year or two my junior. Warren McCulloch was one; Frank Lorimer, another; Ruth Munroe, a third. They knew enough philosophy and history of Western thought to keep me humping. And Ruth was beginning a career in clinical psychology so richly expressed later in her Rorschach work and in her Schools of Psychoanalytic Thought. Ruth and I took walks along the Hudson and on one occasion she asked me over to supper to meet her roommate.

Her roommate turned out to be Lois Barclay, a Vassar graduate with a background in economics, comparative religion, and clinical psychology, and last but not least, some reading knowledge in psychical research. There were electrifying conversations which went on to include the courses which she and I were taking and continued to take in Union Theological Seminary. She began to teach me some of the levels and forms of humanistic psychology in which I was weak, and she had a kind of objectivity, a kind of intellectual honesty, which for me had been an unrealizable ideal. During the college year 1925–1926 she was teaching in Baltimore and I went frequently to see her. We were married the following year. It would be completely impossible to say anything meaningful about my subsequent path in psychology without indicating that this has been a dance of constant new steps being taught me by one who is herself deeply committed to the teaching world.

The first research which the family conducted—about 90 per cent hers, 10 per cent mine—was a study of sympathy in small children carried out at the Speyer Nursery School, associated with Teachers College, Columbia University. We had both read much current research about aggression, fights, miseries of small children. Her way was to pick cooperation and sympathy as the center for her ingenious development of new methods of observing and recording children's behavior—largely as functions of interpersonal situations. The nature of children's groups and of teachers—the situational definition—brought out different aspects of the latent individuality of each child. Lois got so deep into child psychology that she switched her Sarah Lawrence College teaching assignment from comparative religion to child psychology. She worked with me 1929–1931 on *Experimental Social Psychology,* the second edition of which appeared in 1937 and on which T. M. Newcomb collaborated.

This professional world was a very closely personal world for us. I have already mentioned several, but I'll round out the list of those who gave shape to our lives in the early married years, over and above members of Lois's family and mine: Ruth Benedict, Harold and Mary Jones, Otto and Selma Klineberg, Rensis Likert, Margaret Mead, and at a slightly later date Lawrence K. Frank and Robert and Helen Lynd.

Our son, Alpen Gardner Murphy, was born in June 1930. His intense response to, then preoccupation with, music was evident even in his early months, both radio and good recordings being available even in the New York apartment of the day. We shared the fantasy world with him very early. He taught me a good deal of psychology, particularly the things one would think the psychologist would have learned before he had children of his own (usually he doesn't). To our family a daughter, Midge, was added in 1932. She, being warm and earthy and for awhile somewhat tomboyish, helped to correct our over-literary background.

Lois and I decided in 1934 that the Amsterdam Avenue and 118th Street world was too dirty, too noisy, and too crowded for us, and we moved our home to Westchester, where we remained till 1952. Not only Midge and Al, but also their parents became better people in the process. In Westchester we lived in three different places but all three were close to Sarah Lawrence College in Bronxville, where Lois began to teach in 1928. The Sarah Lawrence world was extremely creative; a world of individualized work, each student conferring with each of her teachers every week, and having a don for individual conference in addition. There were no grades; there were simply standards of understanding and excellence, which student and staff member and don worked for together. I have never seen such educational morale in my life; nor could it exist without the individualized work—and the very high care and selection of teachers as well as students—which pervaded the whole experiment. The second major piece of work done by Lois had to do with the educational process at Sarah Lawrence and was carried on parallel to her third study, a study of personality in young children which made use of her Miniature Life Toy approach inspired by contact with Erik Erikson and by Harry Murray's work; experimental procedures developed by Eugene Lerner and L. Joseph Stone; and observations by the other gifted members of the Sarah Lawrence Nursery School group. The fourth major study by her will be noted later.

I learned also from my graduate students, especially Rensis Likert, Muzafer Sherif, Eugene Hartley, Ruth Levy, L. Joseph Stone, and my colleagues, Otto Klineberg, Goodwin Watson, and Ted Newcomb.

My teaching load at Columbia was light, and after a year or two of experience teaching each course, I had plenty of time for research, reading, and writing. They were combined with the responsibility for masters' essays and doctoral dissertations which I continued to carry all through the 1930s, and during that time, I set up and carried the main responsibility for the elementary psychology class of Columbia College. This was two hours a week of lecture to large groups which were then split up into individual discussion groups, with twenty in a class. I thought at the time that it was very superior lecturing and rather good discussion work. At age seventy-seven I think somewhat less approvingly of the lecture procedure. I played much too safe and sane, stayed with standard and acceptable topics, whether they were fairly important or not, and I did very little to encourage individual thinking or question-formulating, except as part of the discussion group work. I did not learn from my mistakes at the time. I began to learn about a quarter of a century later as I saw creative things that can be done even with lectures to large classes. I think my work for graduate students was pitched high, used all the best that I had to offer, and was very good, better than the undergraduate work.

I state these opinions now for two reasons: (1) I think it is important for a good teacher to keep on re-evaluating his work, decade by decade. I think that my experience of gradual detachment may perhaps have some value for others who will come along the same path; (2) I think that the full modern student "movement" in all its phases and forms represents a demand for more active learning and a larger share in the organization and planning of the whole educational enterprise, to be borne by students whenever they are willing to take on some of the responsibility. I think I did not do anywhere near as much as some others were doing in that era. I think my classroom style, my way of presenting material, was decidedly good. What I lacked was in a dimension which could properly be called the philosophy of education, of which I had insufficient knowledge and for which I had insufficient respect at the time.

What was the general character of the approach to psychology that I offered at Columbia in those years 1930–1949? It was broadly outreaching, a collector's interest in everything. It was middle of the road, as Woodworth would say, in method as in content. It was comprehensive; it was eclectic. I used constantly and gratefully the ideas of Columbia colleagues like Klineberg, Margaret Mead, and the Lynds; I rejoiced in all the contacts I had with Kurt Lewin, Harry Murray, and Erik Erikson. I took on easily, and rather well, responsibility for the undergraduate program as a whole and for the social psychology that was offered for the doctorate after Lois and I had presented *Experimental Social Psychology* in 1931. The social psychology course that I taught began with a rather narrow emphasis upon experimental work but broadened rapidly, and when the Lynds's *Middletown* appeared, I used it in the spring semester as basic reading, making the course essentially a study of American urban life as seen through the Lynds's eyes, but with a rich utilization of all available psychological materials. It was an eclectic approach but a proud one, and a sophisticated one, and I have no regrets about it because my eclecticism goes even further. When I hear psychologists lambasting each other as to whether man is a machine or a purposive being, I suspect that they have not closely read their Epicurus or their LaMettrie or their Bergson or their James, and that they have really not tried very hard to see the *all* that is in itself just as perceptible as are the components, or the aspects which are more easily isolated for certain scientific purposes. Gordon W. Allport, working with William Stern at Hamburg and then in the Harvard Psychological Laboratory with Philip Vernon, presented a reality which is for me as beautiful and systematic and adequate as is the beautiful, systematic, biological model of Sherrington—the models being abstractions and conceptual tools constituting a fraternity of eager voices all of which have something to say.

These attempts of psychologists to jump immediately to final interpretations, sweeping their adversaries off the board, seem to me to be scientifically immature and, in practice, a likely roadblock to research progress. The battle lines change a little but the war had already started when Galvani's studies of the electrical phenomena of the frog's *sciatic* nerve meant exactly opposite things to two schools of thought: to one school they showed tremendous differences between the living and the non-living; to the other group, they supplied a physical bridge from a laboratory phenomenon to all of life. This is no place for the recapitulation of so vast a scientific battle; it is just my own little report on a major modern instance of the fact that there always really is "more beyond." In fact, as Spinoza (1677) pointed out, there are not just two but perhaps an infinity of ways of looking at reality. "Double aspect" theories of reality have been part of what I learned from Troland at Harvard, and it has been enriched by subsequent reading, discussing, thinking, especially teaching.

I sometimes encounter a bewildered look on the faces of my colleagues if I sit down at an APA Program dealing with behavior genetics or psychophysiological feedback, as if people of my cast of thought could not possibly be interested in "mechanistic science," and those of a "humanistic" persuasion find themselves much puzzled that I cannot see the need for a "third force" or "fourth force" psychology. What I have no stomach for is exclusiveness of any sort, or that kind of final evaluation according to which we simply do not have to listen to new findings, new concepts, new integrations.

During those same years (mid-1930s) I was giving about one quarter of my time to psychical research, having become a trustee of the American Society for Psychical Research, and working with three younger persons, Ernest Taves, Laura Dale, and Joseph L. Woodruff, in small experimental projects which we published mostly in the *Journal of the American Society for Psychical Research.* We gradually strengthened the scientific standards and gradually succeeded in drawing more and more attention to the experimental work, notably the work of J. B. Rhine et al., at Duke University—work that was casting new guidelines for the gradual creation of a new science. In 1938, for example, I took part in the Symposium on Extrasensory Perception organized by J. L. Kennedy at the American Psychological Association, and in 1942, I taught a summer session course at Harvard on psychical research at the invitation of E. G. Boring, in part as a way of honoring the centennial of William James.

The period at Columbia offered many opportunities for a rapid growth in many fields, but it became more and more crowded with duties which could not be refused. We all served on all sorts of Ph.D. committees in many departments. For example one spring I was on the dissertation committee of twenty-two different candidates, including not only psychology but education and the social sciences, and one could not even pretend that one could read the dissertations on which the candidates were supposed to be examined. That was one of a number of reasons why I began actively to look around for other possibilities.

A peculiarly favorable invitation was offered me by City College in 1940; J. G. Peatman had thought of me as a suitable person to lead the psychology department at City College and the rest of the staff had supported him. It involved a very considerable lightening of my teaching load, and the time to continue work in psychical research was a benefit. I had also long been planning a systematic book on personality, and I now made a start on it. It was the City College opportunity that made it a reality. I worked several hours a week from 1940 to 1947 in preparation of that book which finally appeared after the war: *Personality: A Biosocial Approach to Origins and Structure.* During the war years I had also been working on a book entitled *Human Nature and Enduring Peace* which I edited for the Society for the Psychological Study of Social Issues.

I found at City College a superb opportunity for guiding the research of able and eager honors students, with five of whom—Robert Levine, Joseph Levine, Leo Postman, Harold Proshansky, and Roy Schafer—I published studies of the influence of drive or affect upon perceptual and cognitive functions, one of the interests which has arisen in my eclectic concern with the development of personality theory. These studies were very close to my heart.

When, in 1945, the students began returning from the armed forces, it was hard to continue these honors studies except on a low-priority basis; students wanted clinical training, not laboratory research. The teaching continued to be very satisfying, but the research opportunity after 1947 began to fizzle out, and I was very glad to accept a position with a somewhat larger free space for research at The Menninger Foundation in Topeka, Kansas, in 1952. Here my former student George S. Klein and other colleagues, such as Sibylle Escalona, Philip S. Holzman, and Martin Mayman, conspired to build up the type of position for me, with title of Director of Research, that I could seize upon with avidity. Fortunately, there was a research position for Lois which she could define in practically any way that she wanted. Sibylle Escalona had bequeathed her rich data on 128 infants who could very well be studied further at the preschool stage, with unusual research facilities. It was from this that her study of ways in which young children cope with their problems was launched—*The Widening World of Childhood* (1962)—and led to a series of intensive studies from 1953 to 1969. Just as was the case in the study of sympathy, the emphasis was on the constructive aspects of individual adaptation in American life. Her emphasis was not on pathology but on the ways in which children overcome, master, or work creatively through the personal, family, and community experiences which from another point of view are often studied in terms of psychopathology. One of my great gratifications about the Topeka work was the intimate relation between these studies of Lois's and the personality studies which some other members of our department were carrying on.

My own research at Topeka lay largely in the influence of motivation or the affective life upon the perceptual-cognitive life. Much of what we feel we established in this field was published in 1960 by Charles Solley and me (1960c), and a considerable number of other collaborators, and brought out new aspects of this concern in that it viewed the problem of the relation of motive to the perceptual-cognitive life as the core of a personality theory.

Now as to some very broad perspectives which might be called personal philosophy. This may appear to involve a paradox in the relation of two deeply ingrained principles: (1) the principle of *order,* in which each phase of reality takes its meaning from its context, particularly its context in the next higher phase of reality above it in an architectural system; an essentially Gestalt notion of "membership character," in which each large detail has its structural relation to the whole just as each small detail has its structural relation to the large detail; (2) the conception of *openness,* eclecticism, receptivity to each new fact or each new opinion which comes in an open-ended spirit to attach itself and find its own membership character in the system as best it can. I am inclined to think that the first principle is one of broad perspective serving as a map along the way of research, whereas the second is a tool, an instrument by which the open-ended investigator tries always to relate the new to the existing structure. This is very much like J. F. Herbart's conception of the process of apperceiving, and of the apperception mass which determines what each new component can be as it offers itself for membership in the system. To speak in more modern terms, it could be related to Piaget's accommodation and assimilation or to Dewey's and Bentley's transactionalism. At any rate I do not see the paradox or conflict, and I espouse both aspects of this general philosophy of method.

But my philosophy involves more than that. It involves the personal belief that the universe is, as William James said, both a universe and a pluriverse, that it has its own orderly oneness and its own relatively autonomous or free-determining components, insofar as new elements encountered by a moving system must accommodate themselves to what is possible within the system. It is in this sense that I am wholeheartedly eclectic in psychology, not just in relation to perception or motivation or psychoanalysis or what-have-you, but basically in terms of maintaining a very large vulnerable or open sector for the admission of fresh content and fresh method; in particular, really radical new ideas like Pavlov's classical conditioning, or Freud's psychoanalysis, or Weiner's cybernetics. They are all welcome; they can be taught to speak each other's languages so that they can communicate within one house, and taught like good children where they can make their contribution to the total without disrupting the next one.

It is in the same spirit too that I welcome parapsychology and, for that matter, various types of altered states of consciousness and mystical types of cognition and re-definition of personal identity; they all deal with some aspect of personality. The long-range danger for psychology is that it will get stuck in blind alleys of denial. Positive mistakes are relatively easily corrected, but the blind spots lead to mistakes in which it becomes taboo to look in unfamiliar directions; and this is almost never corrected except by thunderbolts from outside. Psychology was stuck with associationist doctrine and could not deal with unconscious dynamics; it was stuck with sensationalism and could not deal with Gestalt; it was stuck with mechanical association and could not deal with creativity; it was stuck with the medieval principle "There is nothing in the mind which was not first in the senses" and it missed the opportunity to look closely at the world of extrasensory perception. Above all, it was stuck with a competitive individualistic definition of personality and it could not see the nature of human collaboration, group integration, dynamic social and intellectual history, and, most important, the occasional transcendence of individuality both in the human group and in some sort of cosmic awareness. The eclectic may be accused of being a worshipper of odds and ends; in my judgment, it is only with this kind of eclecticism that the awesome unity of the system of the real is capable of being apprehended at all.

Most of the scholastic warring that goes on in psychology seems to me to be based on the narrow addiction to certain data, certain methods, certain assumptions, and a consequent blindness to other modes of observing. "Is man," for example, "a knower and seeker, or is he a machine?" Patently, in the light of his history, his genetic makeup, his social learning process, his struggle to apprehend the real, he is *both* a seeker and a machine. He derives attributes from his evolutionary, physical, and biochemical origins, from his social membership, etc., in defiance of all attempts to pin him down.

Finally, a few more words about teaching. I think the satisfactions are many. It is exciting to organize an area or field of knowledge or thought. It is satisfying to see a structure emerging whether it be a lecture or course or projected article or book. Errors to be corrected and afterthoughts to be included are always a thorn in the flesh, but one gradually outlives the annoyance and finds an articulated unity which is gratifying in itself and of course manyfold more gratifying when one's listeners and readers respond to it as it is intended. I would say that the gratification in teaching a really systematic course like the history of psychology or a comparison of systems of psychology can be gratifying for many different kinds of people. As for myself, I think this is satisfaction number one.

I think satisfaction number two is social-conversational. The pleasure in communicating with students is related to my pleasure in all levels of communication—with two year olds, with dogs, with truckers (for example, the day Lois and I hitchhiked in the White Mountains before we had a car of our own), with taxi drivers, with friends, with traveling companions.

Related to the delight in communicating is the parent-like satisfaction in sharing the best one has, so as to give the young a good foundation and send them on their way. And as part of this to foster potentialities, whatever they are, so as to release the maximal creativity in each one.

The joy in reciprocal communication just passes over into joy number three, which is sheer "narcissism," the "falling in love with one's own words," which of course calls for friendly honesty on the part of my wife and students and a little holding of the mirror to allow the more ridiculous aspects of the process to be corrected. I believe in what Van der Waals calls "healthy narcissism," and I think it's as healthy in teaching as it is in other activities. It is when it causes sheer blindness that it may need successive jolts from the reader or the audience. But I would add sadly that for the most part we don't learn without "knowledge of results."

But of course there were more specialized satisfactions from the teacher's craft. The history of psychology gives one a chance to do legitimate hero-worshipping all the way. I simply could not teach history of psychology without passionately extolling the tremendous genius of Pythagoras; I could not make the transition from medieval to modern without allowing myself several jumps over the table in honor of Hobbes, Hartley, and Herbart; of course I simply could not live or breathe if the world denied me the companionship of William James. Anyone teaching science needs at times to look at the individual contribution. I cannot think of evolution without thinking of Charles Darwin and the *Beagle,* and what he saw on the islands of the Pacific. I cannot think of quantum principles in psychology without thinking of Planck and Köhler in a context in which there is a wide theater of observations dominated by such personalities as Helmholtz, Madame Curie, and Einstein. This personalistic way of looking at science had grown slowly in my thinking for decades; it is Abe Maslow in *The Psychology of Science* who has articulated the reality.

The teaching of social psychology offered me something very broad—I realized very late in life how inadequate I was to the demand—for it offered a chance to look at society through a psychologist's eyes. For the most part my job at Columbia, where I taught social psychology, was to inculcate respect for solid research method, and this was one of the various things which delayed my gradual recognition that here and there in psychology a social philosopher is needed. Despite the inspiration of James Harvey Robinson's "The History of the Human Mind" I did not venture into so broad a system. I did however get a great deal of satisfaction in applying rather systematically both Robinson and the Lynds, and my own integration of the work of Ruth Benedict,

Margaret Mead, and Abram Kardiner. One who tries to teach social psychology in more or less anthropological terms will need a kind of anthropological field work which I never had and a much richer understanding of economics, political science, and intellectual history than I achieved.

Finally, the teaching craft includes of course the individual conference in a small classroom or an office or a library or a laboratory room or a field situation, and here I enjoyed myself very thoroughly in the years of teaching. This individualized way of working with psychology means an enormous opportunity for the teacher to learn, to share, to enjoy mutual challenge and response, and to consolidate the work of many individuals as they and he develop almost an orchestra-to-conductor kind of relationship. Teacher and students have a chance to know each other and—without forming an exclusive school—the teacher can help to orchestrate their thinking. This is the kind of satisfaction that R. S. Woodworth allowed me at Columbia, and that the honors system at City College made so rich for me. The seminar method as developed at Columbia, at City College, and at The Menninger Foundation proved to me in fact that each member of the group could rightfully take his turn at being Socrates; and that teaching could be a supremely satisfying form of learning from a rocking-chair perspective in which there is still an attempt to understand the flow of psychology and the meaning of the teaching relationships. I would say that I have been delighted and fulfilled in three ways. First, I have tried vigorously to maintain the perspective that "there is more beyond," helping to extend the conception of openness to all areas of method and content concerned in any way with psychological realities, especially social psychology, personality, and parapsychology, trying in and out of season to show that this open, or catholic, approach can offer more and more riches than any hyperspecialization can offer. Second, I think that the situational, or as we would say today, the ecological approaches to psychology may have been enriched a bit by the early forms of my psychological field theory which I developed in the 1930s and 1940s. And third, I think I may have contributed a little bit of something to a profound skepticism as to the adequacy of the psychological establishment as it has taken shape in the last few decades. I don't think of this in a negative way. I think establishments are attempts at order and coherence. I would rather say that the establishment is a peculiarly serious source of rigidity when it hits a new and unformed science like psychology and that prevention of premature ossification is a primary service for many of a maverick cast of thought.

This is no place for "systematic psychology" but I do want to underline that during the 1930s, while I was still at Columbia, I developed a conception of the interdependence or reciprocity of organism and environment for which I thought the term "field theory" appropriate. I attempted in great detail while writing the personality book to show that there are no psychological events expressive of the organism as demarcated and separated from the environment; neither are there any events going on in the immediate environment, as contrasted with the organism. It is the reciprocity of the two that makes the psychologist's world of observations. He literally does not see the organism and he does not see the situation as a psychologist unless he sees the reciprocity and it is the reciprocity which is the psychology. Later on, feeling an affinity with Kurt Lewin, I used various forms of expression which implied that I accepted my own formulation as roughly an equivalent to Lewin's conception of the "life space." Actually, I was and remain profoundly grateful for Lewin's life-space conception, but psychological life space as a function of a living organism is not the same thing as the reciprocity which I have just tried to describe. I have been rather wistful that my biosocial theory has so often been confused with his form of field theory. I think history will show that there is room not only for these two but for several other varieties of theory in which organisms are defined in intimate association with the moment-by-moment interchanges which make up their life. Organisms do not respond to situations. Certain aspects of the organism are observed in certain relations with certain aspects of the environment. Failures of prediction and understanding of behavior appear every day because it is assumed that the organism which is observed to make a certain response on a certain day in a certain setting will make a response identical with this when it later confronts a situation of a different cast and texture.

Actually, I never pushed this far enough. The ecologies burgeoning today will undoubtedly give biosocial theory a clarity and practicality for which there is a great need. Indeed, the study of the environment today, which has burst upon us so largely through Rachel Carson's studies of pollution (*Silent Spring*) will begin to make their deeper impact upon psychology, along with the recognition of the individual human being as continuously responding not to a stimulus, and certainly not to a situation, but to a delicately modulated changing texture of pressures from without, interacting with a similar continuous texture of modulations from within. It will be fun to watch and to see how far this prediction can be fulfilled in the years remaining to me.

REFERENCES

Selected Publications by the Author

1929 *Historical Introduction to Modern Psychology*. New York: Harcourt, Brace, & World.

1929 (Ed.). *An Outline of Abnormal Psychology*. New York: Random House.

1931 *Experimental Social Psychology*. New York: Harper & Row.

1932 With F. Jensen. *Approaches to Personality*. New York: Coward-McCann.

1935 *A Briefer General Psychology*. New York: Harper & Row.

1937 With L. B. Murphy and T. M. Newcomb. *Experimental Social Psychology* (rev. ed.). New York: Harper & Row (original edition, 1931).

1938 With R. Likert. *Public Opinion and the Individual*. New York: Harper & Row.

1942 a With H. Proshansky. The effects of reward and punishment on perception. *Journal of Psychology, 13*, 295–305.

b With R. Levine and I. Chein. The relation of the intensity of a need to the amount of perceptual distortion: A preliminary report. *Journal of Psychology, 13*, 282–293.

1943 a With R. Schafer. The role of autism in figure-ground relationships. *Journal of Experimental Psychology, 32*, 335–343.

b With L. Postman. The factor of attitude in associative memory. *Journal of Experimental Psychology, 33*, 228–238.

1945 (Ed.). *Human Nature and Enduring Peace*. Boston: Houghton Mifflin.

1947 *Personality: A Biosocial Approach to Origins and Structure*. New York: Harper & Row.

1949 *Historical Introduction to Modern Psychology*, rev. ed. New York: Harcourt, Brace & World (original edition, 1929).

1951 a With J. E. Hochberg. Perceptual development: Some tentative hypotheses. *Psychological Review, 58*, 332–347.

b *An Introduction to Psychology*. New York: Harper & Row.

1953 *In the Minds of Men: A UNESCO Study of Social Tensions in India.* New York: Basic Books.

1954 With A. J. Bachrach, eds. *An Outline of Abnormal Psychology* (rev. ed.). New York: Random House (original edition, 1929).

1956 Affect and perceptual learning. *Psychological Review, 63,* 1–15.

1957 Notes for a parapsychological autobiography. *Journal of Parapsychology, 21,* 165–178.

1958 *Human Potentialities.* New York: Basic Books.

1960 a Organism and quantity: A study of organic structure as a quantitative problem. In B. Kaplan and S. Wapner (eds.), *Perspectives in Psychological Theory: Essays in Honor of Heinz Werner.* New York: International Universities Press, pp. 179–208.

b With R. Ballou, eds. *William James on Psychical Research.* New York: Viking.

c With C. M. Solley. *Development of the Perceptual World.* New York: Basic Books.

1961 a With the collaboration of Laura A. Dale. *Challenge of Psychical Research: A Primer of Parapsychology.* New York: Harper & Row.

b *Freeing Intelligence Through Teaching: A Dialectic of the Rational and the Personal.* New York: Harper & Row.

1963 Robert Sessions Woodworth, 1869–1962. *American Psychologist, 18,* 131–133.

1964 Lawfulness versus caprice: Is there a "Law of Psychic Phenomena"? *Journal of American Social Psychological Research, 58,* 238–249.

1967 In *History of Psychology in Autobiography,* edited by E. G. Boring and G. Lindzey. New York: Appleton-Century-Crofts.

1972 With Joseph K. Kovach. *Historical Introduction to Modern Psychology.* New York: Harcourt, Brace, Jovanovich.

9

Exploration in Semantic Space: A Personal Diary*

CHARLES E. OSGOOD

My Grandfather Osgood—a graduate of Harvard University in the 1880s and a successful dentist in Boston—always felt frustrated because he had not become a college professor. As early as I can remember, he played all kinds of word games with me, teasing out subtle distinctions in meaning, giving me short lists of rare words to memorize, and rewarding me with penny candies when I used them spontaneously and correctly. I was thus one of the first M & M children, although the reinforcers were actually jelly beans. Miss Grace Osgood—or Auntie Grae as I called her then and still do—was at that time a student at Wellesley College and soon to become a history teacher at Thayer School in Braintree; she was a participant-observer in these word games, giving me a helping hand from time to time behind the scenes, and on my tenth birthday (I believe it was) gave me Roget's *Thesaurus*—probably to even the odds a bit with Grampa O! I remember spending hours and hours exploring the *Thesaurus*—not then as a tool but as an object of aesthetic pleasure.

I also recall my visual representation of the *Thesaurus*—a vivid image of words as clusters of starlike points in an immense space. I have always been a visualizer, which may explain why I did well in

*Portions of this chapter appeared in the author's Kurt Lewin Award address (American Psychological Association Convention, 1971), published in *The Journal of Social Issues,* 1971.

geometry but miserably in algebra. It was soon after this that I began what I thought was to be a career as a writer. Since I was already devouring all of the fantasy, horror, and science fiction I could lay my hands on—an appetite acquired from my father and appeased during long morning hours in the attic while everyone else was asleep—naturally my earliest efforts dealt with oozy monsters rising from the crypts of ancient castles, armies of giant ants sweeping the earth, and such-like. At Brookline High I became editor of both the weekly newspaper and the monthly magazine, and soon became skilled at working reporter-style with a few fingers of each hand on a second-hand Royal #10 that my Grandfather Egerton had given me (the same machine that wrote *Method and Theory in Experimental Psychology,* by the way). And I turned to more psycho-dynamic stories about my family and my own budding romances. I collected my full share of rejection slips from editors of short-story magazines, a few of which I prize because they were intimate and encouraging.

Why I subtitle this paper "A Personal Diary" must now be obvious. But why do I title it "exploration" in semantic space? It is not just because I was for many years Director of an institute of communications research organized within a college of journalism—and "exploration in semantic space" *does* have a certain swing in an age of human exploration of outer space; it is rather because, for me, it *has* been an exploration—in time, in methods, and in geographical space, as well as in the inner, subjective space of meaning.

ORIGINS

The notion of a concept-studded semantic space—potentially quantifiable—lay dormant until I had been at Dartmouth College for a couple of years. I had gone there with the vague idea that I would get experience on the college newspaper while studying English literature and creative writing. And then I would support myself by newspaper work while writing The Great American Novel. But during my sophomore year—after trailing Youth in a massive racoon coat as a date-less reporter of the Winter Carnival for the *Daily Dartmouth*—I happened to take Introductory Psychology and then an advanced course with the late Professor

Theodore Karwoski, affectionately known on campus as "The Count." I found what I had been, unknowingly, looking for all the time—the right combination of demand for rigor and room for creativity—and I forgot about writing The Great American Novel.

Ted Karwoski was a most remarkable person—quietly insightful, capable of thinking simultaneously on several levels and moving fluently among them, warmly supportive of students from whom he felt a returning spark, and thoroughly disorderly. My own father had died when I was thirteen, and in any case he had been a remote every-other-weekend-and-holidays figure since a divorce when I was only six. Although I did not realize it at the time, Professor Karwoski became for me the intellectual goad that my Grandfather Osgood had been and the intimate confidant that my father had never been. If one could dedicate this report on my own explorations in semantic space to someone, it would certainly be to Ted Karwoski. At the point when I moved into his life, he was doing casual experiments on color-music synesthesia and, more important, was thinking deeply about their implications for human cognition. He had the notion of "parallel polarity" among dimensions of human experience—the Yin and Yang of things—and conceived of synesthesia, not as a quirk of sensory neurology but as a universal semantic process of translation across equivalent portions of dimensions thus made parallel. This, of course, is a complex and continuous case of what is called "metaphor" in language.

It would be hard to imagine an intellectual environment better suited to a young man with visions of semantic space in his head. Karwoski's associate in research was a younger man from Harvard, Henry Odbert, who had done his thesis research on the semantics of personality traits under Gordon Allport. Later Ross Stagner brought to Dartmouth his skills in attitude measurement and his intense concern with issues of peace and war—with World War II just over the horizon. Out of my apprenticeship with these men—and apprenticeship much more intimate and exciting than most graduate students in these crowded days are likely to enjoy—came studies of parallelism of visual and auditory dimensions, as observed both in complex synesthetes and in the use of descriptive adjectives in ordinary language. Being a minor in anthropology as an undergraduate at Dartmouth, I tried to determine the generality of such dimensional parallelisms across cultures, using first-hand ethnographic reports. With Ross Stagner, I studied the changing meanings of critical concepts as the United States moved closer to, and then, with Pearl Harbor, fully into World War II. The latter studies, along with research on occupational prestige with Professor Chauncey Allen, represented our first use of 7-step scales defined by adjectival opposites—which was later to be embodied in the Semantic Differential Technique—but the multidimensional concept was lacking, nearly all scales being Evaluative (attitudinal) in nature.

After an extra year at Dartmouth beyond my bachelor's degree—during which I served as everything from research associate to mimeograph operator, and also got used to being married—I went to Yale for graduate work. Like nearly everyone else at Yale at the time, I got swept up into the monumental edifice of learning theory that Clark Hull was building. I had the heady feeling that there, with appropriate elaborations, lay the key to even the most complex of human behaviors, including language. Visions of semantic space receded, but the problem of dealing with meaning in learning-theory terms came to the fore. My doctoral thesis, among other things, was a test of a theory of meaning based upon sets of reciprocally antagonistic reaction systems—an extension and elaboration of Hull's notion of anticipatory goal reactions serving as mediators of overt behavior. I owe a debt of gratitude to Donald G. Marquis for keeping my interest in language alive, as well as to Charles Morris, who came to Yale as a Visiting Professor in time to help me defend my thesis. I am also grateful to the Powers That Be for seeing to it that I never became one of Hull's research assistants—else I almost certainly would have become, not a rat pusher, but a clinician.

My Yale years were also the war years. By 1944 many of the faculty were on leave in Washington, and as a third-year graduate student I suddenly found myself teaching all of Introductory Psychology—two lecture sections (one for regular Yalies, another for Navy V-12 students) and eight smaller discussion sections on Thursdays and Fridays. Never having taught before, I was always just one little hop and skip ahead of the students, and since I was younger than many of the V-12s, I generated the little mustache that you can still see today, if you look close enough. I was also just one little hop and skip ahead of my draftboard—one child and then two when one wouldn't do, then teaching Navy V-12, and at last when nothing would do, I had my degree and was whisked off to the Smokey Hill Air Force base in Salina, Kansas, as a civilian doing research on training B-29 gunners. Herein lies a story of frustrated experimental genius that I won't bore you with.

I wish more present-day students could have the experience I did—not necessarily of draft dodging, but of *independent* teaching while still in graduate school. I think that teaching is at its best when the ideas are being freshly molded by the instructor as well as the instructed, and there is no better way to discover what you really *don't* understand than to try to teach it to someone else. The same thing applied to writing textbooks—which is (or should be) a kind of teaching, too—as I discovered during three busy years at the University of Connecticut after the war, more or less simultaneously writing my *Method and Theory in Experimental Psychology* for the Oxford University Press (1953) and teaching graduate experimental psychology.

Then, in the spring of 1949, came one of those academic bonanzas that all young scholars hope for—a chance for an associate professorship with tenure *and* a half-time research appointment for research of one's own devising to boot. (I must remind you that those were the days when we had bona fide Ph.D.'s as instructors.) From faraway Illinois—which is much farther from Boston than Worcester, as you all know—came a "feeler" about just such a position along with an invitation to pay them a visit. So onto the overnight sleeper and off to the cornfields, where I discovered that Ross Stagner, with whom I had worked at Dartmouth, and Hobart Mowrer, whom I had known at Yale, along with Wilbur Schramm, Director of a new institute of communications research, were looking for a young man to develop research and teaching on the psychology of language—in short, *a psycholinguist* (although it would be several years before that title came into vogue).

Needless to say, the people at Illinois were interested to know just what I might do by way of research in their new institute—should I in fact be offered the position. So, back in Storrs, Connecticut, I began, for the first time, to try to put together, and down on paper, first a *behavioral theory of meaning* (based on

Hullian learning theory, but with a general representational twist), second a *measurement model* (based on the earlier attitude scaling studies with Stagner but tuned to the what were then new developments in multivariate statistics, in which I had discovered Illinois to be a hotbed of activity, what with Lee Cronbach, Ray Cattell, and others on the scene), and third *an image of a semantic space* (based on my childhood explorations of Roget's *Thesaurus* and drawn wherever one stores such things).

My original "vision" of a concept-studded space was refined to specify an *origin* or neutral point of the space, defined as "meaninglessness" (analogous to the neutral gray of the color space), and to conceive of meaningful concepts as the end-points of *vectors* extending into this space, with lengths of the vectors indicating degrees of "meaningfulness" (like saturation in the color space) and their directions indicating the "quality of meaning" (analogous to both the brightness and hue dimensions of the color space). Thus two concepts might be similar in quality of meaning (same direction in the space) yet be quite different in intensity of meaning (distance from the origin), like HATRED and ANNOYANCE; or two concepts might be equally intense in meaning, yet be very different in quality of meaning, like GOD and DEVIL. And one could nicely specify adjectival opposites, like *hot* vs. *cold* or *hard* vs. *soft,* as points equidistant and in opposite directions from the origin of the space, connecting them with an imaginary line through the origin—thus analogous to complementary colors which, when mixed in roughly equal amounts, cancel each other out to neutral gray (or meaninglessness).

This spatial model lent itself directly to factor analysis as a mathematical means of bringing order out of the apparent chaos of lines (defined by adjectives or qualifiers) and points (defined by concepts or substantives). In semantic differential (SD) measurement operations a sample of concepts (for example, TORNADO, SYMPATHY, MOTHER-IN-LAW, JUDGE) is rated against a sample of scales (for example, *fair-unfair, hot-cold, tough-tender, quick-slow*) by a sample of native speakers of a given language—in our early work, American English speakers, of course. This generates a cube of data—concepts X scales X subjects—and each cell in the cube contains the judgment of a particular subject about a particular concept on a particular scale, for example:

TORNADO

fair ____:____:____:____:____:____:X unfair

Thus each cell is a kind of implicit sentence produced by a particular speaker—here, John Jones "saying" that *a tornado is very unfair.* (I use this example of a "sentence" which would not ordinarily be said in English deliberately; we shall return to the methodological and theoretical implications.) This cube of data is correlated (each scale against every other scale, across both concepts and subjects) and factor analyzed, to determine the smallest number of underlying factors, or semantic features, which will account for the largest amount of the variance in judgments.

My behavior theory attributes the meaning (M) of all signs, both linguistic and non-linguistic or perceptual, to *representational mediation processes* or r_M's. These mediating processes are developed via the association of signs (words, perceptual images) with significates (referents or things signified, objects and events with which humans interact); some distinctive representation of the total behavior made to the Things comes to occur to the Signs of these things, and thereby the signs come to "mean" these things and not other things. Although such r_M (note that the subscript is a capital *M*) *as wholes* bear a unique one-to-one relation with the total behavior made to the things signified (R_T), they are analyzable into sets of *component mediators* or r_m (note the lower case *m*), these components representing those aspects of behavior to things which have made a difference in adjustment to those things, and hence have been differentially reinforced. These meaningful mediation processes are (a) hypothetical constructs in total behavior theory, (b) have response-like functions in decoding (language understanding) and stimulus-like functions in encoding (language creating), and (c) render functionally equivalent both classes of signs and classes of behaviors—the "emic" principle of behavior theory.

By the time LAD (popular acronym for Language Acquisition Device) is launching himself into linguistic sign learning, perceptual signs of most of the entities in his familiar environment (utensils, food objects, pets, toys, faces that smile, and faces that frown) have been meaningfully differentiated in terms of distinctive mediators. Not only can such pre-linguistic processes serve as "pre-fabricated" mediators in the subsequent learning of linguistic signs, but, even more important, many of the distinctive features of meaning have already been established.

During the past decade there has been considerable debate—notable perhaps more for its heat than for its light—over the adequacy of *any* behavioristic theory, based on associative principles, for language and meaning. Beginning in 1959 with the brilliant critique of B. F. Skinner's *Verbal Behavior* by generative grammarian Noam Chomsky—to which Skinner never replied—and continuing with attempts by philosopher-psychologist Jerry Fodor to show that representational mediation theory can be reduced to single-stage associationistic theories (Fodor, 1965, 1966)—to which I have replied (Osgood, 1966, 1969)—this debate still goes on, the most recent contribution being a formidable, formal analysis by a young Finnish philosopher of science named Raimo Tuomela. I am happy to be able to say that Tuomela (1971) concludes that Fodor did fail to make his case! Further details of this debate would be out of place here.

I have been accused—by some of my close associates as well as by some of my dissociates—of being schizophrenic as far as my SD measurement model and my representational mediation theory of meaning are concerned. There is, they claim, no obvious relation between loadings on factors and little r_m's. This is, of course, disturbing to one who considers himself reasonably neat and internally consistent. My answer is that the relation is not obvious simply because these critics have a feeble grasp of multivariate statistics, learning theory, or both. But this assertion—obviously—requires some elaboration.

Let us look first at the relation between spatial and measurement models. In the spatial model the meaning of a concept (its *M*) is represented by a point in *n*-dimensional space. And, of course, since the psychological opposites which define each bipolar scale are also concepts (albeit adjectives rather than nouns), they too are represented as points in the common semantic space, connected by an imaginary line running through the origin, and they therefore have their *M*'s, too. Now, when a subject is asked to create a "sentence" of the specified type (*N is Quantifier Qualifier*), using a given noun concept and adjectival scale-pair, what he does, in effect, is to drop the shortest line from the concept point

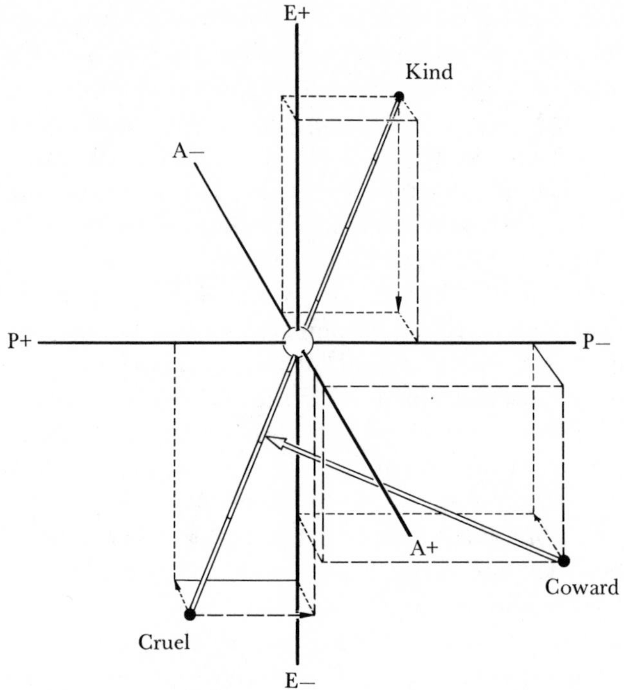

Kind-cruel: E+ 0.70 P– 0.35 A– 0.15 loadings
Coward: E– 0.50 P– 0.70 A+ 0.20 score

Figure 9.1.

to the adjective-pair line (which is necessarily at right angles to that line and therefore the projection of the point onto the line), thereby generating the most nearly congruent judgment. If MOUNTAIN projects close to the *large* end of a *large-small* line, then *MOUNTAIN (is) very large* (checkmark on +3 of the scale) is the most congruent "sentence" for this item. If SYMPATHY projects just a little toward the *hot* side of a *hot-cold* line, then *SYMPATHY (is) slightly hot* is the most congruent "sentence."

As shown in Figure 9.1, application of the factor-analytic measurement model provides a framework of underlying dimensions *which is common to both concept-meanings and scale-meanings* and in terms of which both can be described in relation to each other. These underlying dimensions thus have the functional properties of *semantic features.* Anticipating our results for those who are unfamiliar with this research, SD technique typically yields three dominant affective factors (or features): Evaluation (Good-Bad), Potency (Strong-Weak), and Activity (Active-Passive). We refer to scales as having *loadings* on these underlying factors; the scale *kind-cruel,* for example, has loadings of +.70 on E, -.35 on P (that is, *cruel* is more Potent than *kind*), and -.15 on A. From these loadings we can assign *kind* and *cruel* their reciprocal locations in the space. We can characterize *kind* as being Very Good, Quite Weak, and Slightly Passive affectively, and *cruel* as being Very Bad, Quite Strong, and Slightly Active. We refer to concepts as having *scores* on the same underlying factors; if the concept COWARD, for example, had scores of -.50 on E, -.70 on P and +.20 on A, its affectivity paraphrase would be a COWARD is Quite Bad, Very Weak, and Slightly Active. Making the projection from the COWARD point to the *kind-cruel* line in the three-factor space, we predict that COWARD will be rated as "slightly cruel" on the *kind-cruel* scale. Predictions of all concept-scale mean judgments can be made in this fashion—which is not at all remarkable, of course, since the factor loadings and scores were derived directly from these original judgments.

How does representational mediation theory relate to this spatial measurement model? First, you will recall that the mediation process associated with a sign and symbolized by r_M is *not* the representation of a simple response in a single reaction system but rather is the representation of a set of simultaneous responses in a number of different reaction systems. In other words, r_M is *componential* in nature. Second, the components (r_m's) which do become part of the total mediation process, or meaning, of a sign represent those aspects of the total behavior to things which have made a difference in adjustment toward these things and hence have been differentially reinforced. It follows that the most common and therefore shared components of the meanings of different signs will be derived from those reaction systems which are behaviorally significant, which *make a difference in meaning.* The affective reactions underlying E, P, and A have just such properties. Third, it will be recalled that, although representational mediators are presumed to be entirely central (cortical) events, in theory they retain the functional properties of "responses" as subsequent events and of "stimuli" as antecedent events.

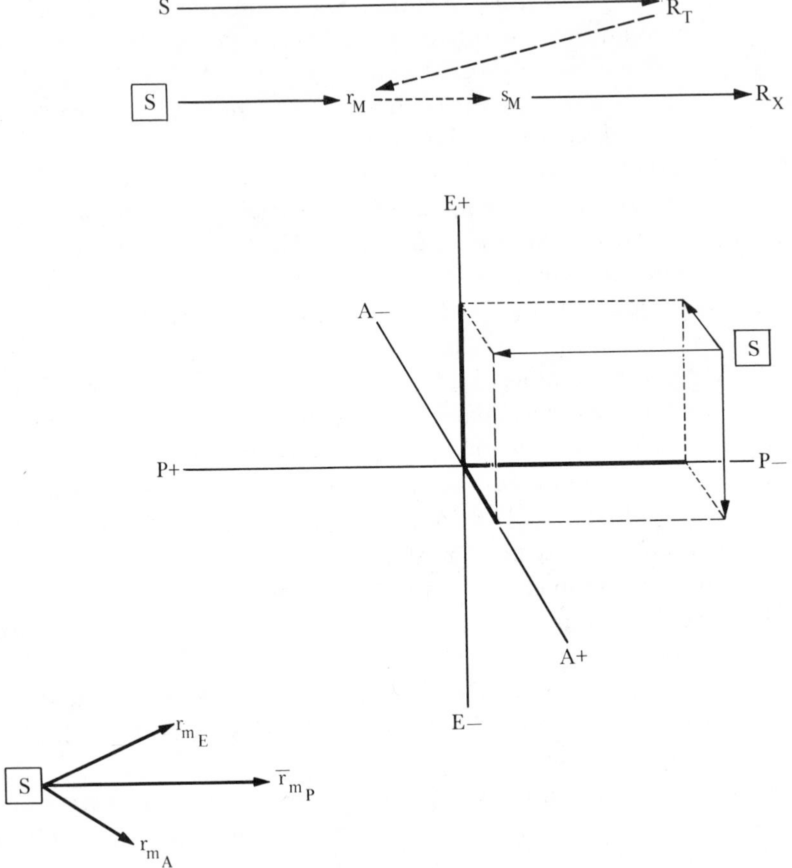

Figure 9.2.

Several theoretically relevant properties of mediation processes flow from this: (a) Since the overt reaction systems which central mediators represent are organized on a reciprocally antagonistic basis, as Sherrington and many others have shown—for example, the muscles which contract in making a fist are inhibited in making an open hand, and vice versa—it follows that *the* r_m *components derived from such systems will also function in reciprocally antagonistic fashion.* (b) Since overt reaction systems vary in the intensity with which they respond to various stimuli (here, intensity of motor contraction, etc.), *so should their central repre-*

sentations vary in intensity (here, presumably rate of neutral activation). And (c), since the same reaction system cannot assume reciprocally antagonistic "postures" at the same time, but rather must display compromise between excitatory and inhibitory tendencies, it follows that *simultaneous tendencies toward antagonistic* r_m's (for example, toward +E and −E) *must cancel each other toward neutrality or meaninglessness.* This last property of representational mediation processes is the entree of behavior theory into cognitive dynamics generally (for example, the "balance" theories of Heider, 1958, Festinger, 1957, and Osgood and Tannenbaum, 1955) and into semantic anomaly specifically.

Now, with the help of Figure 9.2 we can demonstrate the isomorphism of behavioral and measurement models. I chose this old figure from *The Measurement of Meaning* deliberately to show that way back in 1957 the componential notion of meaning was part of our thinking. I have simply changed the subscripts in the upper diagram to capital *M*'s and it comes up to date. *I identify the underlying semantic factors or features derived in the measurement model with the affective components* (r_m's) *of representational mediation processes.* That such features are characteristically bipolar in nature is consistent with the reciprocally antagonistic nature of the reaction systems from which such mediator components arise. That semantic factors should be ordered in productivity (frequency and diversity of usage as aspects of meaning) is consistent with the behavioristic notion of differential reinforcement of those mediating behaviors which make a difference in adjustment. Thus in the affective meaning system Evaluation (the Good vs. Bad of things) has more weight than Activity, just as Sex (the Masculine vs. Feminine of things) has more weight than Maritality in the semantics of kinship. *I identify the points in the measurement space which represent the meanings of concepts* (whether they be nominals like COWARD or adjectivals like *kind* and *cruel*) *with the total and unique mediation processes* (r_M's) *presumed in theory to be elicited by signs.* Such total representational processes, however, are analyzable into simultaneous bundles of mediator components which vary in polarity and intensity (the directions and lengths of vectors in Figure 9.2). But these components are *not* unique to particular signs; rather they are shared in different combinations by many signs.

I am not making the claim, of course, that representational mediation theory is the *only* theory appropriate to the SD spatial and measurement models; I am merely claiming that it is entirely consistent with these models. I must also point out that my semantic theory is not really inconsistent with many views held by linguists and philosophers, including as it does componential and polarity principles. It differs from most others, however, in its specification of continuous features as the general case (with discrete + or - codings being a result of non-discriminate, high-frequency usage) and in its derivation in the history of the organism of semantic features from actual behavior toward things signified. I would argue that derivation of semantic features from behaviors which have differential adaptive significance has the advantage of sharply constraining the proliferation of such features while enhancing the prospect of discovering ones that are universal in human languages.

ETHNOCENTRICS

Well, somehow I got the job at Illinois in 1949 and have been there ever since. The rationale I then gave for my coming research was not exactly as I have given it here—much troubled methodological and theoretical water has flowed under the bridge in twenty-two years—but the essentials were all there and have not changed. Aided mightily by George Suci, the first research assistant I ever had, and abetted by interested students and colleagues like Percy Tannenbaum, Al Heyer, and Larry O'Kelly, I started exploring semantic space in earnest. We began, of course, by demonstrating in a 1952 *Psychological Bulletin* article the abject wrong-headedness and futility of all previous psychological attempts to measure that elusive thing called "meaning"—including association, generalization, and salivation techniques—and set forth both a mediation theory and the fragile beginnings of the SD technique.

Our first major experimental effort involved 50 bipolar adjectival scales, selected on the basis of frequency of usage, and 20 concepts, selected casually for their diversity; the subjects were, as you might guess, college sophomores taking Introductory Psychology. The correlational and factorial analysis of this 50-variable problem was done—*not* on the exciting new ILLIAC I computer, to which I had been introduced on my earlier visit, since no programs were then available for mundane problems of our sort—*but* on a desk calculator by George Suci. I remember old George well, day after day, swearing over that little machine and gradually filling in the cells of monstrous tables; this one analysis took him about 4 months, but it could be done in much less than 4 minutes today. Because of this labor, George worked out a rather beautiful short-cut method for factoring—not quite as elegant mathematically as the procedures Thurstone was developing, yet serviceable—but before he could publish on it the computers had caught up with him.

Our second analysis involved the same 50 scales, but no concepts. We used a forced-choice procedure, with each scale paired with every other scale and the subjects (again college sophomores) instructed to circle that member of the second pair which seemed closest in meaning to the initial, capitalized member of the first pair, for example, HARD-soft: fair-unfair. For our third analysis (still with college sophomores) we selected some 76 scales from Roget's *Thesaurus*—yes, we were now programmed for ILLIAC I—and had another 20 carefully diversified concepts, like MOTHER, STATUE, and KNIFE, rated against them.

To cut a long story very short, all three analyses yielded nearly identical factorial results—three massive factors clearly identifiable as Evaluation, Potency, and Activity (and in that order) along with tails of minor factors which varied and were hard to interpret. You may reasonably ask, "what do you mean by saying the first three factors were 'clearly identifiable as E, P, and A'?" All I can do is ask you to note the highest loading scales in all cases—which (just giving the positive terms) were *good, nice, beautiful, honest, sweet,* etc., for E, *strong, large, thick, hard, heavy,* etc., for P, and *active, fast, sharp, excitable, hot,* etc., for A—and leave it to your own intuitions as native speakers as to what the underlying features are.

The results of these factor analytic studies of meaning were written up, and a paper was submitted to the Editor of *The Journal of Experimental Psychology*. It was returned with rather unusual promptness, even for those days. The underlying reasons for rejection were two: first, "meaning" was hardly a suitable subject for report in THIS JOURNAL; second, experiments are supposed to be tests of hypotheses, and factor analysis can hardly be viewed as a hypothesis-testing procedure. It was in reply to this rejection that I first gave a defense of "meaning" as a legitimate topic in experimental psychology—which happily needs no repetition now—and of factor analysis as a hypothesis-testing procedure. The latter goes like this: although the results of any single factor analytic study in a given domain may indeed be attributed to the happenstance of a particular sampling from that domain, the factor structure initially obtained may be considered a hypothesis to be tested in subsequent analyses—*as long as the subsequent sampling from the same domain is completely independent of the results obtained in prior analyses.* Although I have had arguments with some of my own colleagues over this operating principle, we have stuck to it in all of our SD research. In any case, I am happy to say that the paper was finally accepted by *The Journal of Experimental Psychology.*

While all this was going on, our little group was busily pushing the SD measurement technique into various nooks and crannies of psychology—into studies of attitude formation and change (Joan Dodge and Percy Tannenbaum), of source credibility (Jean Kerrick), of the authoritarian personality, semantically speaking, and into the prediction of voting behavior (George Suci), into psychotherapy, with a study of dream symbolism (Scott Moss), another on the semantics of identification (Lionel Lazowick), another on the factor structures of schizophrenics as compared with normals (Joan Bopp), and yet another (with Zella Luria) on *The Three Faces of Eve,* that well-known case of triple personality, and even into the semantics of advertising (William Mindak), visual art (William Tucker), and sonar signals (Larry Solomon). Such "applications" of SD technique paralleled more basic research on the methodology itself, and each contributed to the other. The "little group" was expanding, too, attracting graduate students in psychology, anthropology, communications, speech, and elsewhere.

In these days, when so much of research is "administered"—relatively senior people, like myself, having practically nothing to do with it between original designing and final writing-up—it is a real pleasure to look back on those early days when we literally lived and breathed our research from morning to night. I used to be my own first guinea pig in every experiment, to try to get a seat-of-the-pants feel for what might go on in the real subjects' heads. In the midst of doing an experiment, several other experiments were always aborning—over coffee, over sandwiches and beer, and even over cocktails and dinner, much to the amusement but never irritation of our spouses. I am minded of an enlarged photograph on the wall of my office which caught Percy Tannenbaum and myself, glasses in hand, in animated mid-flight on something or other; a caption had been appended reading, "BUT THERE *MUST* BE A MEDIATION PROCESS!" And I remember one full weekend spent with Al Heyer constructing a three-dimensional distance model of colored rubber balls and wooden dowels to represent the semantic similarities among 40 facial expressions of emotions. With practically no sleep we reached that point in exhaustion where every comment, every move, every facial expression of our own would reduce us to helpless laughter. I still have that old distance model in my office, but ANGER and CYNICAL BITTERNESS have fallen off and SURPRISE has somehow gotten attached to ADORATION—by a bemused janitor, no doubt.

In the comparatively brief period from 1950 through 1955, some 70 studies—some separately published, many not—were completed, and in the summer of 1955 the Osgood family departed for its first sabbatical, in Tucson, Arizona. Packed in the trunk of the second-hand Buick Roadmaster (freshly painted in Dartmouth Green) was just about everything about meaning and the measurement thereof that I could put my hands on, including all the reports of our own studies in various stages of polish. My main job during that sabbatical year was to put into one document all the diverse things we had been doing with University of Illinois Research Board, and, later, Social Science Research Council monies. As each section was drafted I sent it to George Suci and Percy Tannenbaum—by then my closest colleagues in this exploration—for commentary as well as for additional analyses and even new experiments that had been suggested in the course of scholarly composition. They showed copies of some early chapters to the Editor of the University of Illinois Press, and he suggested making a book out of it. So *The Measurement of Meaning* was published in 1957. (Because it had originally been planned as merely a research report, the first, hardcover edition had no index. I firmly recommend the later paperback edition, which *does* have an index, to any who would like to explore these early studies further.)

To the enduring amazement of Osgood, Suci, and Tannenbaum, this little book has proved to be one of the best sellers on the lists of the University of Illinois Press. It also got some solid reviewing—some of the major ones being by Roger Brown ("Is a Boulder Sweet or Sour?") and by Harold Gulliksen ("How To Make Meaning More Meaningful") for *Contemporary Psychology*, by the late Uriel Weinreich ("Travels Through Semantic Space") for *Word*, and by Jack Carroll (simply titled "The Measurement of Meaning") for *Language* (all are included in Snider and Osgood, 1969). These reviews were uniformly thoughtful and critical, but they were also generally supportive. In preparing this chapter I re-read them to see how well we'd met the legitimate criticisms in the decade of work since they were written.

Psycholinguist Brown took us to task for inadequately defining the meaning of "meaning" we were trying to measure and for "not even observing the distinctions of which (philosophers) feel most confident" (*we have not found most philosophical distinctions particularly useful in our work*); but, anticipating our cross-cultural work, he observed that "just over the horizon lurks the (contra-Whorfian) generalization [*that*] the various languages of the world operate with the same basic semantic dimensions." Psychometrician Gulliksen concentrated, appropriately enough, on scaling problems, suggesting that our 7-step scales were too coarse and that 20- or even 30-step ones would be better (*but very cumbersome for ordinary subjects*), that the SD technique is highly susceptible to concept-scale interaction (*which we remain acutely aware of but have not been able to resolve in any entirely satisfactory way*) and that non-significant differences found with small numbers of subjects (for example, in factor structures) are not reliable indicators of similarities across groups (*our cross-cultural studies now seem to answer this criticism*); but he concluded that "the studies form an impressive demonstration."

Linguist Uriel Weinreich really lambasted us for claiming to offer too much to the linguist-lexicographer but in fact offering very little (*our claim was really minimal, but the failure to deliver was maximal, for reasons we now know*) and for claiming to be measuring connotative meaning when in fact we were measuring affect and not meaning at all (*although I have dropped the term "connotative" and now use "affective," I would still insist that we are measuring a sub-set of features of meaning*); yet Weinreich concluded that the lexicographer should be grateful for the new entree to systematic description of the "affective space" of a language and the notion of dimensional structure. Finally, psycholinguist Carroll criticized us for a too grandiose title, *THE Measurement of Meaning,* when very few aspects were actually measured (*but one can't put a book into a title*) and for using too few concepts in our factorial studies to permit definition of more than four or five factors (*this has been corrected in our later cross-cultural studies, as will be seen*); however, Carroll did conclude that our SD research " . . . provided a kind of componential analysis" of meaning and that he was inclined to characterize the book by asserting: "it is *good*, it is *active,* it is *potent.*"

The notion of a quantifiable semantic space apparently caught the imagination of others—perhaps because it offered at least the possibility of measuring some important aspects of a very important variable in human affairs, *meaning*—and the past decade has witnessed a minor explosion of studies about or applying the SD technique. The bibliography appended to *Semantic Differential Technique: A Sourcebook,* edited by James G. Snider and myself and published in late 1969, lists a relevant literature of nearly 1500 items, and it is steadily growing. I must confess that sometimes I feel like the Geppetto of a wayward Pinocchio who has wandered off into the Big City—and Lord knows what mischief he's getting into. In recent years Pinocchio has been trotting around the world, introducing himself to people speaking different languages and enjoying different cultures; but in these travels, at least, Geppetto has been able to keep a hand on the puppet's strings.

ANTHROPOCENTRICS

In the near-decade of work from 1950 to 1957, the generality of the Evaluation-Potency-Activity (E-P-A) structure of what I now call "affective meaning" had been amply demonstrated for the American English language-culture community. Since this generality has been shown to hold across various methods of obtaining judgments and factoring, across various types of subjects (males vs. females, age and I.Q. levels, Republicans vs. Democrats, and even schizophrenics vs. normals), across various independent procedures for sampling bipolar adjectival scales, and across various samples of concepts (whether they be ordinary nouns in English, pictorial signs, or even whole paragraphs, for example, describing Charles Morris's "Ways To Live" (Osgood, Ware, and Morris, 1961), we seemed to have the answer to one of the major questions with which we had begun our exploration: *given diversified samples of concepts, scales, and native informants, the E-P-A structure of the semantic space obtained in replications of the SD technique is non-arbitrary.* Just as there is non-arbitrariness of the geophysical space, determined by gravity, the rotation of our planet, and the location of the magnetic pole, so there seemed to be non-arbitrariness in the affective meaning space.

There was one serious limitation upon this conclusion, however; nearly all of our research up to this point had been highly *ethnocentric*—focused on humans sharing a common (American) culture and speaking a common (English) language—and the few exceptions (for example, Kumata and Schramm, 1956, and Suci, 1960) had been subject to the bias of translation. It was at least *conceivable* that the dominance of Goodness-Badness, Strength-Weakness, and Activity-Passivity in our data was attributable to something peculiar, either about American culture or about the English language—or both. In 1958-1959—while I was a Fellow at the Center for Advanced Study in the Behavioral Sciences at Palo Alto and had a chance to sit back and look at the larger pattern of things—it became clear that the next step in our exploration of semantic space should be a shift from ethnocentrics to what might be called *anthropocentrics,* with a focus upon mankind in general and a hope of discovering something universal about human semantic systems.

There are many hypotheses about human nature that demand cross-cultural and cross-linguistic designs, if we are to successfully disentangle what is common to the human species from what is peculiar to specific segments of it. Comparisons across cultures are particularly difficult, however, when what anthropologists term *non-material* traits are under study. It is one thing to compare skull shapes, scraping tools, potsherds, and other artifacts; it is quite another to compare values, feelings, stereotypes, and, most generally, meanings—what I have come to call "subjective culture." Whereas elements of objective culture may leave their physical traces on and in the earth, elements of subjective culture certainly cannot. But more important, subjective culture is most naturally and directly assessed through the medium of language, and therefore what is called "the language barrier" must somehow be pierced.

So, in 1960, with initial support on a small scale from the Human Ecology Fund, Geppetto and his Pinocchio set out across the world looking—not for fame and fortune—but for friends in foreign lands who might catch some of their excitement and join in the exploration of semantic space. Put a bit more mundanely, my purposes were twofold: first, on the theoretical side, to test the generality—or lack thereof—of the E-P-A structure of affective meaning across a matrix of human communities differing in both language and culture; second, on a more practical bent—*if* the generality of the E-P-A system could be demonstrated as common dimensions of variation in meaning—to devise comparable semantic differential tools in various languages for measuring similarities and differences in subjective cultures.

On the Strategy of Cross-cultural Research. There is much that I could say about the "strategy" of cross-cultural research, but space limits me to only a few matters which, in retrospect, seem most critical (compare, however, Osgood, 1967). There is also much that I think I have built into myself by experience—and understand intuitively as a kind of "grammar" of cross-cultural behavior—which would be difficult, if not impossible, to communicate. And there are oh-so-many anecdotes, accumulated over the years in many places, that would give a better "feel" for what really goes on in this sort of research, but again, I must ration myself very strictly. Some are reflections of language barriers:

> *I have arrived late in a hotel in Padova, Italy, where for the next five days I am to work intensively on Atlas translations with our colleague, Professor Giovanni Flores d'Arcais. Early a.m. I pick up the phone.*
> "This is Mr. Osgood in room 412; could I have my breakfast, please?" (*All very slowly, in crisp Bostonian English.*)
> (*There is a long pause, and then, "Un momento, un momento!" Strange telephone noises, and then another Italian voice with questioning intonation.*)

"This is Mr. Osgood in . . ."
("Un momento, un momento!" More strange noises, and then a female voice which says "Buon giorno!")
"This is *Professor* Osgood in room 412 and I would like . . ."
(*"Disa elana gibsa, disa elana gibsa." "Look, habla español? Yo quierro mi caffe y mi . . ."*)
"Charlie . . . This is Eleanor Gibson, next door, 414!"
"What! What are *you* doing here?"

It turned out that I had awakened the Gibsons, Jimmie and Eleanor, from far-off Cornell, who were in Padova on a lecture tour; apparently the hotel personnel had assumed that I was trying to contact my fellow countrymen. However, I must say that I feel simultaneously grateful and a bit guilty that English—for reasons entirely extrinsic to its properties as a language—has become a kind of *lingua franca* in most urban places around the world; I'd hate to have been a monolingual Uzbek-speaking psychologist from Tashkent trying to initiate this same twenty-five-community project! There are other anecdotes which reflect cultural incongruities:

It is my first full day in Tokyo, at the beginning of our first colleague-seeking trip in 1960. A delegation of Japanese psychologists is visiting with me at the International House, and I am invited to join them for lunch in a restaurant that specializes in *sushi*—varieties of raw seafood on rolls of rice which, sight unseen (*following one of the canons of cross-cultural research*), I assure them I will enjoy. We start out, and I discover to my egalitarian horror that, being a Distinguished *and* Visiting Professor, I am leading a hierarchical train of Nipponese through the madly busy streets of Tokyo without having the foggiest idea of where I am going! At each choice point a senior professor taps me lightly on the shoulder and, with a polite smile, points the direction of the next segment of our journey. We did reach the restaurant and I did enjoy my *sushi*—as long as I inhibited visual inspection.

Here are a few retrospective comments on strategy. First, *who are the planners?* Viewed idealistically, cross-cultural research should be planned as cooperatively as it is executed, but realistically joint planning among social scientists who often differ markedly in theoretical biases and methodological traditions, and who may even be near strangers to each other, usually ends in a shambles. Far better, I think, is the careful "exportation" of research designs which have been adequately tested within the culture and language of their origin. I realize that this may sound very parochial, and indeed may be a rationalization of what we did in our own research—which was "exported" only after some ten years of indigenous work.

But, even given a solid background of indigenous work, the *values of piloting* must be stressed. Procedures (for example, in group dynamics) and even instructions (for example, in ordinary word-association tests), which seem entirely acceptable and self-evident in the American English context, may produce quite unanticipated results elsewhere. In our own case, we had to re-do our sampling of adjectival qualifiers (a kind of association test) in both Tokyo and Hong Kong—and for opposite reasons: it appears that the translation of "give the first adjective that occurs to you" was understood by the Japanese teenagers to mean "give what most people would say" (yielding extraordinarily high homogeneity) and by the Chinese teenagers to mean "give what is most uniquely my own idea" (yielding extraordinarily high heterogeneity).

And there is the *socio-political context* within which cross-cultural research necessarily transpires. Behavioral scientists face a dilemma here: they recognize the need for accurate information about other peoples—their motivations, their hopes, their fears, their conceptions about the world—but they also must recognize the political sensitivity and the possible misuse of such information.

In general, I have tried to work on a "professor-to-professor" basis and avoid entanglements with governments, our own as well as foreign—leaving matters of obtaining informed consent, from government, school, and parental authorities, to our foreign colleagues; we have encouraged the people collaborating with us to exercise their own judgment and eliminate any materials which might be sensitive or embarrassing within their own cultures (there has been a minimum of this, by the way); and all of the data and analyses involved in this project are the common property of all participants, including the right—indeed, encouragement—to publish themselves in their own journals on the basis of the shared materials.

And this leads me to another general comment on strategy—the absolutely critical business of *finding the right senior colleagues* with whom to work in each place. Given the long distances, the necessarily infrequent and much-too-short visits in both directions, and the inevitable problems of communication—face-to-face as well as through the mail—there is a very high premium on mutual trust and on a sense of reciprocal obligation if a cross-cultural project of any magnitude is to succeed. I consider myself exceptionally fortunate—I could almost say blessed—that over the past decade we have drawn together some sixty colleague-friends in some twenty countries around the world, and there have been very few dropouts. Most of these people have been able to get to know each other as well as our Center staff at two meetings-of-the-whole, held in Dubrovnik in 1963 and in Teheran in 1967—and now, it is well worth noting, there is considerable research interaction among them, quite apart from our project on affective meaning systems per se. I wish I could mention all of them by name—since they are co-investigators in the full sense of the term—but obviously space does not permit.

I have talked about my foreign or external colleagues in this work, but the internal staff at the Center for Comparative Psycholinguistics is equally important. I refer to Bill May—programmer, data processer, business manager, tutor and confidant of our research assistants, and now Co-director—fondly and accurately as "my right hand." Murray Miron and Sharon Wolfe were major contributors during the formative years of the project, and Leon Jakobovits, as Co-director, kept things moving in the later years. During his year as staff anthropologist, Jan Brukman served as intellectual goad, for which many thanks. More than twenty graduate students have also helped shape this research, while earning their bread and their degrees; at least half of them have been from foreign countries, usually serving first as field workers on the project in their own native communities.

Last but not least, I should mention William Kay Archer—ethnolinguist, ethnomusicologist, conversationalist, cartoonist, and bibliophile—who has been associated with the cross-cultural project from its inception and has accompanied me on many of my research trips. In fact I engaged Bill Archer both because of his earlier research experiences in Afghanistan, India, and elsewhere, and because of his apparent sensitivity in cross-cultural contexts. Prior to 1960, *my* only foreign excursions had been occasional trips to Canadian national parks and regular trips to neighboring Nogales, Mexico, while on sabbatical in Tucson. I thought that Archer could serve as a sort of "cultural antenna" for me, signaling nuances I might not catch and priming me for cross-cultural contacts—but herein lies a story:

> On our first trip, after visits in Tokyo, Taiwan, Hong Kong, Bangkok, and Calcutta, we are in Mysore—staying in the guest house of the Maharaja of that state because Archer happened to have organized a concert for him in New York the previous year. Toward the end of our stay, during which we successfully get the first phases of our research under way, we have our audience with the Maharaja, at which time Bill is to present him with several recent hi-fi classical recordings and I am to give him an over-all picture of our research. After waiting in rather impressive surroundings for a while, we are ushered up a wide but dark staircase, and on one of the turns I see a shadowy figure; per Archer's instructions, I quickly press my palms together under my chin in the Indian form of greeting; Archer taps me on the shoulders and whispers, "That's a statue of his father." At the door to His Highness's private suite upstairs, Bill starts to take his shoes off while I stare in sheer horror. (You see, he had failed to instruct me about *this* and, after some two months of travel, I had a hole in my sock that exposed my right big toe completely.) But the door opens, there stands His Highness, and off come my shoes. I hobble in, trying to keep my left foot in front of my right, and sit down, trying to keep my left foot on top of my right. Every so often, in the excitement of the discussion, I see the Maharaja's eyes drift downward and I quickly re-cap my big toe. Somehow, my most miserable half-hour was finally over.

However, this was one of Bill Archer's rare failures as an antenna, and I still think the principle—of making initial contacts in the company of a colleague with some sophistication in the cultures concerned—is a valid one; if he happens to have a good sense of humor, and you can laugh both at and with each other, then this minimizes the likelihood of experiencing culture-shock as well.

Hypothesis-testing and Tool-making. We wished to test the hypothesis that the major dimensions of affective meaning are independent of variations in both language and culture. Ideally, the whole world should be our oyster, but the funds available in 1960 were very limited and our estimates of expense for travel, for field work, for data processing, for salaries, and for all those other mundane matters strongly suggested an initial sample of only six language-culture communities. We settled upon six locations which we felt would maximize linguistic and cultural differences and yet provide literate speakers of "national" languages, that is, "high cultures": Finnish in Finland (Finno-Ugric language family), Arabic in Lebanon (Semitic), Farsi in Iran (Indo-European, but remote from English), Kannada in Mysore, India (Dravidian), Chinese in Hong Kong (Sino-Tibetan), and Japanese in Japan (its own language family)—with American English in central Illinois as a kind of "control," since it was necessarily the source language for translation.

If you could imagine a map of the world, with all of the twenty-five locations in which we are now working indicated by pins with city names on them, three things would immediately become apparent to you: (1) we have something of an over-representation in Europe, ten of our twenty-five if you include two Scandinavian groups and three Mediterranean ones (this is the result of the availability of interested and trained people, in large part); (2) the Southern Hemisphere is very poorly represented, with no site as yet in South America and only the Nigerian samples (Hausa and Yoruba in Ibadan, and this work was disrupted by the Biafran conflict) in Africa; (3) the two largest countries in the world, the Soviet Union and the People's Republic of China, are not included (in the former case we have made unsuccessful overtures and in the latter it seemed completely infeasible until very recently). Otherwise, the sample seems reasonably representative and extensive.*

Rather than trying to obtain representative samples in each place—which would certainly be non-equivalent in grossly different cultures—we have used homogeneous samples of teenage male students in average high schools. Rather than literally translating materials and instructions—which would impose a foreign "Western" mold and press out valueless data—we have "adapted" our tasks to each language and culture, trying to guarantee that they would be functionally equivalent and yet maximize the opportunity for cultural uniqueness to appear. At the very beginning of the sequence of tool making tasks we did employ a standardized, carefully translation-equivalent, and culture-common set of 100

*We gratefully acknowledge support from the National Institute of Mental Health (#07705) and the National Science Foundation (GS360) for support of this research from 1963 through the present.

concepts (nouns in English). These were used—in a word-association task modified to elicit qualifiers (adjectives in English)—to obtain one qualifier for each of the 100 nouns from each of 100 boys, thus a "basketful" of 10,000 modes of differentiating concepts from each of 25 language-culture communities.

I would like to say one more thing about the role of translation in our research. This initial point—translation of the 100 substantives to be used in qualifier elicitation—is the *only* point in the entire research at which translation bias could in any way *affect the data,* the actual results. Everything else is done entirely in the native language, blindly, by computers—although non-Roman scripts must be transliterated, of course, according to a set of rules (our computers read only Roman!). In other words, beyond this point the data are untouched by (American) human minds! This applies only to the quantitative facts, of course; we do obtain translation at each stage to keep an eye on what's happening, and when at last we come to *interpretation* of the data, translation problems—both linguistic and cultural—return with a vengeance.

The 10,000 qualifier tokens collected in each location were analyzed "blindly" by our computer, using a program designed *to select and order the most productive types of qualifiers* (that is, the most frequently and diversely used across the 100 nouns) and then *to prune from the ordered list redundant modes of qualifying* (that is, lower-ordered items which correlated significantly in usage with higher-ordered items across the 100 nouns). In the absence of Thorndike-Lorge lists and thesauri, this procedure seemed reasonable, combining properties of both and being standardized for all languages. These productivity-ranked and pruned lists were returned to the field where—with no difficulties—opposites were obtained for the qualifiers from which the usual seven-step scales could be made.

Using the same 100 translation-equivalent nouns, another sample of teenage boys in each community judged them as concepts against 50 scales, following the usual SD instructions (as adapted, of course). These data were tabulated and shipped to our Center in Illinois, where our computer performed two types of factor analyses: (1) *Indigenous.* Each of the 20 or so data cubes was analyzed independently, just as had been done with our AE (American English) data in the early studies, and the factor structures were compared. The first factor in magnitude was always Evaluation and the second two were usually Potency and Activity, in that order (in four of the 20 communities a unique factor displaced P or A in order). But our interpretations here were necessarily dependent upon the semantic similarities of qualifiers *as translated into English.* (2) *Pan-cultural.* To eliminate dependence of interpretation upon translation entirely, a monstrous factor analysis was engineered, with each scale from every community correlated directly with all other scales from all communities *across the 100 translation-equivalent concepts.* If a JP (Japanese) scale—say, *iwa-matsu* (which is actually the last name of one of our research assistants in Tokyo!)—correlates very highly with AE *good-bad* across the 100 concepts, then we can say that *iwa-matsu* is used *functionally* by the Japanese in differentiating among the 100 culture-common concepts in the same way the Americans use *good-bad*—and this is entirely independent of any translation of *iwa-matsu.*

The proof of this particular pudding, however, lies in the *results* of the factoring. If nothing easily interpretable in the way of factors comes out, then we can make no strong claim for universality of our affective meaning structure, despite the results of indigenous analyses—because of their dependence on translation into English. If, on the other hand, E, P, and A come out loud and clear, then we have a strong case for universality, indeed, since identification of the factors is entirely independent of translations from particular languages and all errors of measurement (differences in the actual meanings of translation-equivalent concepts) are working against us. But, of course, we must still rely upon translation for communication to an American English audience, and also leave it to that audience to judge the strength of the case.

The following three tables give, for 20 language-culture communities,* their four highest loading scales (identified only by their positive terms, to save space) on each of the first three factors of a pan-cultural factor analysis.

*Communities are represented by two-letter symbols, usually with the location indicated by the first letter and the language by the second (thus AE for American English, AF for Afghan Farsi, BF for Belgian Flemish, and so forth); where locus and language coincide, and there is no ambiguity, the two letters simply stand for the language (thus FR for French, GK for Greek, IT for Italian, JP for Japanese, and so forth).

TABLE 9.1.

Pan-cultural Principal Component Factor Analysis
Factor 1: Evaluation

AE	AD	BF	CB	DH
94 Nice	88 Good	91 Good	93 Beautiful	83 Glad
92 Good	85 Well	89 Magnificent	93 Lovely	83 Good
90 Sweet	84 Safe	88 Agreeable	91 Kind	81 Ambrosial
89 Helpful	82 Lovely	88 Beautiful	91 Finest	80 Superior
FF	**FR**	**GK**	**HC**	**IF**
88 Nice	90 Pleasant	93 Superb	92 Lovable	92 Good
87 Pleasant	89 Good	91 Good	92 Good (not bad)	89 Worthwhile
86 Good	88 Nice	88 Friendly	91 Good (not poor)	88 Best
81 Light	86 Magnificent	85 Useful	90 Respectable	88 Auspicious
IT	**JP**	**LA**	**MK**	**MS**
93 Valuable	93 Good	90 Sound	78 Merciful	93 Admirable
92 Beautiful	92 Pleasant	90 Good	76 Good	93 Agreeable
92 Desirable	91 Comfortable	90 Beautiful	75 Delicate	92 Good
92 Good	91 Happy	89 Enlivening	74 Calm	92 Friendly
ND	**SW**	**TH**	**TK**	**YS**
91 Pleasant	86 Good	88 Useful	91 Beautiful	93 Pleasant
91 Happy	84 Nice	87 Comfortable	90 Good	92 Good
90 Good	82 Right	87 Right	90 Tasteful (art)	91 Lovable
87 Nice	82 Kind	87 Loving	90 Pleasant	89 Beautiful

Table 9.1 shows the first factor, and it is clearly identifiable as Evaluation. The numbers shown are the factor-loadings of the scales, where the maximum (omitting the decimal point) would be 100. Note that with a single exception—MK, Mysore Kannada—the four scales for each community all have loadings on the 1st pan-cultural factor in the 80s and 90s. This, as anyone familiar with the results of ordinary factor analyses will acknowledge, is most remarkable. And, as casual inspection will show, all scales are clearly evaluative in nature.

Table 9.2 gives analogous data for the second pan-cultural factor. The loadings here are lower, ranging in the 40s through 60s—indicating that this factor is less concentrated in the space—

TABLE 9.2.

Pan-cultural Principal Component Factor Analysis
Factor 2: Potency

AE	AD	BF	CB	DH
68 Big	55 Great	57 Strong	62 Huge	47 Strong-of -its-kind
68 Powerful	45 Military	57 Big	60 Powerful	47 Brave
57 Strong	40 Absolute	54 Heavy	55 Big	46 Heavy
57 Deep	37 High, loud	50 Deep	54 Strong	44 Difficult
FF	**FR**	**GK**	**HC**	**IF**
60 Large	68 Large	60 Big	76 Tall, big	62 Heavy
59 Sturdy	59 Strong	59 Strong	75 Big	50 Severe
51 Heavy	57 Huge	46 Brave	72 Strong	47 Thick
40 Rough	52 Heavy	39 Difficult	68 Significant	42 Stout
IT	**JP**	**LA**	**MK**	**MS**
68 Big	66 Heavy	51 Large	44 Wonderful	60 Giant
55 Strong	63 Big	42 Strong	41 Huge	58 Big
54 Wide	59 Difficult	41 Long	41 Big	55 Major
49 High, tall	56 Brave	38 Heavy	34 Great	54 Strong
ND	**SW**	**TH**	**TK**	**YS**
57 Big	50 Difficult	50 Heavy	67 Big	72 Big
55 Heavy	50 High	49 Deep	58 Heavy	67 Bulky
54 Strong	46 Strong	43 Old	53 Large	67 Strong
48 Special	45 Long	42 Big	51 High	55 High, tall

but they are very respectable nevertheless. The semantic flavor is quite consistent, the terms as translated representing variations on the themes of physical magnitude and strength (*great, big, strong, deep, heavy,* and the like); qualifiers like *brave, important, high, difficult,* and *severe* also appear. I think you will accept my identification of this second pan-cultural factor as Potency. Factor III in magnitude, shown in Table 9.3, has more varied loadings across these 20 communities. Quite high loadings, in the 60s and even 70s, appear for Belgian Flemish (BF), Finnish (FF), Hong Kong Chinese (HC), Dutch (ND), and Swedish (SW); relatively low loadings, all in the 30s, appear for Lebanese Arabic (LA) and

TABLE 9.3.

Pan-cultural Principal Component Factor Analysis
Factor 3: Activity

AE	AD	BF	CB	DH
61 Fast	51 Fast, rapid	69 Quick	47 Alive	47 Gay
55 Alive	41 Sharp	65 Active	43 Fast	36 Thin (slim)
44 Young	40 Tender, soft	42 Bloody	43 Active	34 Soft
42 Noisy	36 Narrow	40 Impetuous	38 Light	30 Loquacious
FF	**FR**	**GK**	**HC**	**IF**
67 Fast	61 Lively	55 Quick	68 Agile	53 Active
66 Flexible	57 Fast	52 Young	54 Fast	52 Exciting
64 Agile	56 Living	39 Active	49 Alive	41 Fast, sharp
52 Lively	42 Young	39 Thin	46 Red	31 Warm
IT	**JP**	**LA**	**MK**	**MS**
66 Fast	48 Noisy	35 Fast	35 Loose	56 Active
47 Mortal	45 Active	31 Infirm	34 Unstable	46 Young
47 Young	44 Soft	30 Thin	33 Fast	44 Fast
40 Sensitive	42 Fast	29 Alive	27 Few	37 Soft
ND	**SW**	**TH**	**TK**	**YS**
72 Active	66 Bloody	56 Agile	50 Fast	63 Lively
71 Fast	63 Swift	44 Fast	47 Living	54 Fast
51 Fascinating	62 Lively	39 Thin	43 Soft (flexible)	45 Young
48 Warm	54 Sensitive	28 Naughty	42 Young	41 Soft

Mysore Kannada (MK). As to semantic flavor, the most frequent and generally highest-loading scales, as translated, are *fast* or *quick, active, alive* or *lively,* and *young,* and these seem to justify labeling this pan-cultural factor as Activity. Whether the highest-loading scales for DH (Delhi Hindi—*exuberant, thin, soft, talkative*) and MK (Mysore—*loose, unstable, fast, few*) warrant this label is certainly questionable, but I must remind you that we are dealing with single-term translations.

On the Powers and Limitations of Semantic Differential Technique. The SD was my very first vehicle for exploring semantic space. It has proved to be a hardy, space-worthy ship, and I am still traveling in her, but she does have her limitations. Let me now say something about her virtues and her vices—which I can do without embarrassment, since she responds only to feeling, not reason! The strength of the SD technique lies, first, in its natural adaptability to the very powerful procedures of *multivariate statistics,* in which factor analysis is a means of discovering semantic features and distance analysis is a rigorous means of specifying semantic similarities and differences among concepts. It lies, second, in the fact that it is a *componential model* and has all of the efficiency of such models—describing the meanings of a large number of concepts in terms of a relatively small number of distinguishing features—but, unlike most componential systems, its features are continuous rather than discrete in coding and paradigmatic rather than hierarchical in organization (that is, there is no *logical* priority of certain features over others). Its power lies, third, in the fact that it provides a *systematic sampling* of the distribution of usage of terms rather than the haphazard "compelling examples" characteristic of most linguistic and philosophical semantics.

We have seen that when the SD technique is applied cross-linguistically and cross-culturally it yields strong evidence for the universality of Evaluation, Potency, and Activity as affective features of meaning. And—reflecting back on my discussion of the pitfalls in cross-cultural research—let me emphasize that, although the procedures at all critical points were standardized, the subjects in each language-culture community were free to create *any* kind of semantic space their minds might hold. Even though they had to produce qualifiers to substantives as stimuli, *what* qualifiers they produced and with *what* frequencies and diversities was entirely in their minds; even though they had to create all possible "sentences" involving 100 concepts and 50 scale-pair adjectives, *what* "sentences" they created, for example, *TRUST is quite strong* rather than *TRUST is slightly weak,* were entirely in their minds. Therefore, the overwhelming dominance of Evaluation, Potency, and Activity as semantic features of language stands as a universal fact about Humanness.

But *why E, P, and A?* It has nothing to do with connotations of the term "connotation" (which I used to call what the SD measures), but rather, I think, with the importance of emotion or *feeling* in human affairs. I believe it was M. Brewster Smith who first pointed out to me the essential identity of our E-P-A factors to *the dimensions of feeling,* as described in introspective studies of feeling by Wundt in the last century and in studies of communication via facial expressions by Schlosberg and many others, including myself (Osgood, 1966), in the present century. Consistent with my behavioristic theory of meaning, it is these pervasive affective features which dominate much of our behavior, including language behavior; we really are—Chomsky and the mentalists to the contrary—still animals at base. I simply refer you to the latest news for confirmation. What is important to us now, as it was way back in the age of Neanderthal Man, about the *sign* of a thing is: First, does it refer to something *good* or *bad* for me (is it an antelope or a saber-toothed tiger)? Second, does it refer to something which is strong or weak with respect to me (is it a saber-toothed tiger or a mosquito)? And third, for behavioral purposes, does it refer to something which is *active* or *passive* (is it a saber-toothed tiger or merely a pool of quicksand, which I can simply walk around)? These "gut" reactions to things and their signs, by every criterion used by linguists, lexicographers, and philosophers, have the properties of semantic features, and to deny their importance is to fly in the face of everyday common sense as well as much scientific data.

But this leads us to another question: *why does the SD technique,* as ordinarily applied, *yield these massive affective features* (which lexicographers usually take for granted) rather than equally ubiquitous, denotative features, like Concrete-Abstract, Animate-Inanimate, and Human-Nonhuman (which lexicographers regularly exorcise)? The answer, in a nutshell, is that the SD technique literally *forces* the metaphorical usage of adjectival scale terms, *and shared affective features appear to be the primary basis for metaphorical extension.* If I were to predict what little essence of my life's work might go down in history—assuming there *is* a history for our species—I would say it would be the demonstration of this simple fact, that the shared affective meaning of concepts is the common coin of metaphor.

But, let's get back to reality. Since, in SD technique, *every* concept must be rated against *every* scale, this means that TORNADO must be judged *fair* or *unfair,* MOTHER must be judged *hot* or *cold,* and SPONGE must be judged *honest* or *dishonest.*

While the philosophers among you writhe, let me add the fuminous fact that, among the 100 concepts used in our cross-cultural studies, only a few will be denotatively relevant for making "sentences" with, for example, *hot-cold* and *hard-soft;* yet our subjects must somehow deal with *hot defeat* vs. *cold defeat* and *hard power* vs. *soft power.* The fact that they *do* deal with such items—and deal with them in a very consistent way—is the fact to conjure with.

The "why" of E-P-A is simultaneously the reason that the SD technique is insufficient as a vehicle for discovering the features of semantic space. This pressure toward metaphorical usage of scale terms means that most scales used with most concepts must rotate in the semantic space toward the affective feature on which they have their dominant loading—*sweet-sour* toward E, *hard-soft* toward P, *hot-cold* toward A. Since, in factor analysis, the major dimensions are mathematically inserted through the largest clusters of variables, this means that the shared affective features, E, P, and A, will be amplified and the many subtler denotative features of meaning will be damped. This is why the SD does not provide a sufficient characterization of meaning. For example, both the pair NURSE and SINCERITY and the pair HERO and SUCCESS have near identical E-P-A factor-scores, that is, near-identical affective meanings; yet, I can say *she is a cute nurse* but I cannot say *she's a cute sincerity,* and I can say *our hero plead with them* but not *our success pled with them.* But let me hasten to point out that *any* sub-set of semantic features must be equally insufficient; if I use only the familiar hierarchical features Concrete-Abstract, Animate-Inanimate, and Human-Nonhuman, then all of the semantic ways in which humans differentiate humans—male vs. female kin-cepts, skilled vs. unskilled occupation-cepts, and old vs. young organism-cepts—will disappear, and WIFE will have the same meaning as HUSBAND, LAWYER will have the same meaning as BEGGAR, and BOY will have the same meaning as MAN.

However, it is because of these insufficiencies of the SD technique that, in recent years, I have invested in a new semantic-space vehicle, called the Semantic Interaction Technique. So far it has been applied only to limited semantic domains, the meanings of interpersonal verbs (with Kenneth Forster, cf. Osgood, 1970), and the meanings of emotion nouns (with Marilyn Wilkins, not as yet published). Briefly, this procedure utilizes the rules of usage of words in *systematically varied syntactic combinations* (phrases, sentences) as a means of inferring the minimum set of features necessary to account for exactly those rules of usage. This involves new speaker-elicitation procedures, new computer programming, and much philosophizing—which I will not bore you with. But, for example, from arrays of many linguistic facts, like *sudden surprise* being judged "apposite" or fitting by native English speakers, *sudden melancholy* being judged strange or "anomalous," and *sudden excitement* being judged at least "acceptable" by the same speakers, we are able to infer a feature that might be labeled intuitively Terminal-Interminal. And we find that this same feature operates within interpersonal verbs as well, as witness *meet suddenly* vs. *console suddenly,* and also nouns, as witness *sudden movement* vs. *sudden infinity.* This vehicle has much greater range for semantic space exploration—and philosopher-linguists certainly will prefer it—but for getting down into the guts of human behavior, the old SD still has its values. So now back to our exploration of semantic space, via the SD.

PROBING SUBJECTIVE CULTURE

For making cross-cultural comparisons—or cross-element comparisons within any domain of human concern, for that matter—the essential requirement is that there be relevant dimensions of variation (for example, height, length, volume for physical objects) which are *shared* by all elements in the domain; it is only in terms of such shared dimensions that the elements can be compared. Since what I have called "subjective culture" is mediated by and is describable primarily through language, this means that common dimensions of variation among languages must be established if one is to compare cultural elements within the societal domain. Successful demonstration of the universality of Evaluation, Potency, and Activity as common dimensions along which all humans differentiate concept-meanings provides at least a minimal basis for rigorous cross-cultural comparison. The practical side of the "tool-making" phase of our research was therefore the development of short, efficient, and demonstrably comparable SD instruments for this purpose.

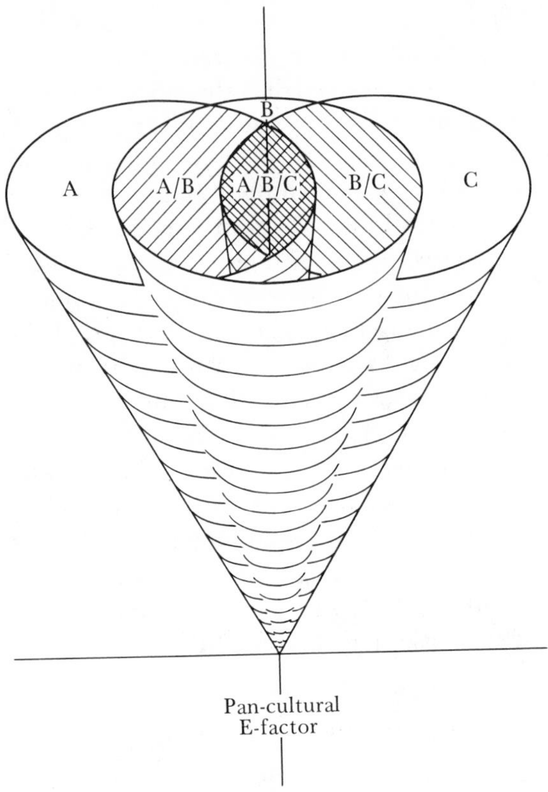

Figure 9.3.

Figure 9.3 illustrates the underlying logic of selecting E, P, and A scales for these instruments, but for only three language-culture communities. As this figure shows, the cones in the semantic space representing the evaluative factors for cultures A, B, and C have a region of mutual overlap; it is through this region, of course, that the pan-cultural E-factor runs. By selecting those evaluative scales for all language-culture communities which fall within this region of overlap—and thus have the highest loadings on the pan-cultural factor—we guarantee maximum equivalence across cultures in the measurement of this dimension of affective meaning. The same logic holds for the Potency and Activity factors, but, as you have seen, they are not as tightly interlocked as is the Evaluative factor. What we did, then, was to select from the pan-cultural factor analysis for each community the four highest loading E-scales, P-scales, and A-scales—the ones you saw in the previous tables—as an instrument for measuring the affective meanings of concepts. We also added a *familiar-unfamiliar* scale. These 13-scale instruments—pan-cultural SD's, as we call them—are thus reasonably "common yardsticks" for measuring at least the affective aspects of subjective culture.

An Atlas of Affective Meanings. The main use of the pan-cultural SD's on the part of our Center has been the development of what we rather grandiosely call *An Atlas of Affective Meanings.* I say "grandiose" because it includes only 620 concepts, as sampled, of course, in only our present set of 23 language-culture communities. Nevertheless this proved to be a very complex and time-consuming endeavor which has taken up most of our energies over the past five years or so. I wish I could claim that we had some rationale for the selection of the Atlas concepts, but we didn't then—and still do not—know of any rationale for sampling the conceptual domains of human cultures. We wanted concepts which would be intrinsically interesting and potentially differentiating among cultures; we wanted concepts which might tap possible human universals in symbolism; but we also wanted to sample those everyday aspects of human life—kinship, food, animals, technologies—which ethnographies usually explore. So we consulted the Human Relations Area Files, solicited suggestions from all of our colleagues, and held numerous "brain-storming" sessions ourselves. The resulting hodge-podge of items of subjective culture runs from A to Z, however, as an atlas should—from ACCEPTING THINGS AS THEY ARE, ACCIDENT, and ADOLESCENCE through MARRIAGE, MASCULINITY, and MASTER to YESTERDAY, YOUTH, and ZERO.

The Atlas testings, carried on over a period of several years, involved some 500 subjects in each community, with at least 40 subjects rating sets of 50 concepts against the short-form, 13-scale pan-cultural SD's developed in the "tool-making" stage. These subjects were again teenage boys, for the reasons already given; in interpreting our Atlas data, therefore, it must be kept in mind that we do not have representative samples of the 23 cultures by any means.

At this point I'd like to take a little side-trip—to a place that might be called "if I'd only known then what I know now . . ." This whole cross-cultural project has been a very novel experience for me and my colleagues, and I guess for social science generally. Practically every step in the process had to be devised pretty much *de novo,* and many could have been done much better with the benefit of hindsight. I offer you a couple of glaring examples.

You will recall that we included a *familiar-unfamiliar* scale along with the E-P-A scales for Atlas testing. This seemed simple and innocuous enough. BUT it turns out that all across our little world the meaning as translated keeps shifting in usually unknown degrees between "familiar-as-a-term" and "familiar-as-a-referent"—and in Yucatan it ended up as "familial-nonfamilial"! *If* I'd known then what I know now, we would have used *two* familiarity scales, one for " . . . as a term" and the other for " . . . as a referent"; thus DEATH might be rated highly familiar *as a term* but as quite unfamiliar *as a referent* by most teenagers.

My other example is much more glaring and caused us a great deal of extra time and labor. Although we were very careful in checking the translation fidelities of the original 100 concepts used in the tool-making phases, we did not exercise the same care on the translations of the 520 additional Atlas concepts. Most of the concepts were single words like SPHERE, DOWN, PROGRESS, BELIEF, and EVOLUTION and our colleagues were facile bilinguals—so what's the problem? BUT, *after* the first and largest part of the Atlas testing had been completed in most places, it was gradually borne in upon us by case after case that there were many translation failures—and hence grossly misleading data—in the Atlases. For example, my colleague at Illinois Harry Triandis (a native speaker of Greek), pointed out with great good humor that the translation of DOWN (which we had intended as "the nether direction") would come back into English as "the soft, under-feathers of a duck used for stuffing pillows, etc.," and that the translation of SPHERE into Greek was correct, but it was a homonym also meaning "bullet." You can imagine the lusty guffaws that would arise in academia if we attempted an interpretation of the low E, high P, and extraordinarily high A of SPHERE for the Greeks in terms of their culture and history!

I will only briefly outline what we did about this: (1) For all Atlas concepts, we listed the most viable senses given in a large and recent American English dictionary. (2) We had fluent bilinguals—usually our colleagues who had done the original Atlas translations—check the list, circle the dominant sense of their translation (if it was listed), put an X next to other listed senses which applied, and add on blank lines additional senses of their translation terms. (3) After inspecting these results, and now fully realizing the enormity of the problem, we spent many, many long afternoons at the Center creating a new "dictionary"—unlike any dictionary presently available—in which the dominant AE sense (or senses) of each Atlas term was listed first, followed by those senses judged to be close to the dominant, followed by those judged to be large or remote (and indicated by an L symbol), followed by those judged to be homonyms, like "horizontal level of a building" for the word STORY (indicated by an H symbol), and followed finally by additional senses of the translation term in other languages. And (4), I went on a five-month trip around the world, spending from four days to a week in each of our locations, carefully checking the adequacy of translations against this new dictionary. (Incidentally, I have great trouble convincing my Illinois associates and friends that such a world trip is not necessarily all fun and games; flipping from place to place with about two hours of flight time in between, in and out of suitcases, and working hard—except when your foreign friends plan lectures and social activities for you, since, for each of them, the rest of your trip is just a dull, gray nothing—is not exactly a pleasure trip.) (5) The upshot of all this, of course, was the scheduling of retesting sessions for all translation failures or large differences in sense. *If* I'd known then what I know now, of course, we would have prepared our special AE Atlas "dictionary" in advance and, using it, our colleagues could have done a much more precise job of finding words in their own languages which share the same dominants as the AE terms and even share some or most of their polysemous patterns.

Analyzing the Atlas Data. Imagine some 620 probes inserted into the bared "brains" of each of our 23 cultures—which I think you'll agree is a vivid image, even if perhaps a bit disturbing one. Given the (now) pretty tight translation-equivalence of our 620 concepts, these probes should have roughly corresponding loci in the various "brains." However, our probes are designed to give only three types of signals—Evaluation "whistles," Potency "rumbles," and Activity "tweetles"—but each type of signal is quantitatively variable in direction and intensity.

We shall be looking for *patterning* in the signals arising from various sets of probes: If all or nearly all of the "brains" give forth the same types of signals for a given set of corresponding probes (for example, +E, -P, and -A for Domesticated as compared with Wild Animals), then we shall infer potential *Universals* in subjective culture. If certain definable sub-groups of our cultures give forth signals that are distinctively different from those coming from most others (for example, THURSDAY and FRIDAY being more +E and +P than SATURDAY and SUNDAY for LA (Lebanon), IF (Iran), and AD (Afghanistan), all Moslem communities), we shall infer *Sub-universals* and look for the reasons—which, in this example, are quite obvious (Thursday and Friday being culturally equivalent to our Saturday and Sunday, respectively). If a particular language-culture community yields clearly deviant signals for a certain set of probes (for example, YC (Mayan Indian subjects in Yucatan) giving forth unusually intense +P and +A signs for all In-law concepts, WIFE, MOTHER-IN-LAW, and FATHER-IN-LAW), then we shall infer *Uniquenesses* in subjective culture and again look for the reasons—in this case, many of our YC subjects were actually married, and a successful marriage is the "make or break" point in this near-subsistence-level culture.

The Atlas project has generated a tremendous amount of information. With some 40 subjects in each of some 25 cultures judging each of some 600 concepts against 13 SD scales, we have about 7,800,000 "bits" of raw data. Even when these raw data are statistically compressed into summary measures—the three factor composite scores (means of 40 subjects X 4 scales on each) and the mean score on the familiarity scale—we still have some 60,000 items of information to deal with. And when this basic information is then amplified by the 10 or so derived measures included in the Atlases, the total information units to be dealt with come to about 600,000. Obviously, this mass of numbers has to be organized into chunks and formats that can be encompassed by human minds.

One way of *chunking* the data was to assign the 620 Atlas

TABLE 9.4.

47 Categories of Atlas Concepts by XII Super-categories

I–TIME
- A. Age continuum
- B. Months, seasons
- C. Time units
- D. Future-present-past

II–EGO IDENTIFICATIONS
- A. Kinship
- B. Races, religions, continents directions, -isms
- C. Male-female
- D. In-group, alters, outgroup
- E. Intimacy-remoteness

III–ABSTRACT SYMBOLISMS
- A. Emotions
- B. Numbers
- C. Colors
- D. Geometricals
- E. Days

IV–CONCRETE SYMBOLISMS
- A. Natural and potentially aesthetic
- B. See-hear-touch-smell-taste- (ables)
- C. Means-expressives-ends

V–ENVIRONMENTALS
- A. Food objects
- B. Animals
- C. Habitations

VI–CARNALITIES
- A. Body parts
- B. Body characteristics, processes
- C. Sex and sensuality
- D. Health, sickness

VII–HUMAN ACTIVITY
- A. Occupations
- B. Commercial, economic
- C. Work-play
- D. Success-failure

VIII–INTERPERSONAL RELATIONS
- A. Private-public
- B. Social status
- C. Moral-immoral
- D. Inter-group relations
- E. Affiliative-achievement

IX–SOCIETY
- A. Institutions
- B. Modern-trans-traditional (technology)
- C. Modern-trans-traditional (values)

X–COMMUNICATIONS
- A. Literacy
- B. Language and Literature
- C. Communications

XI–PHILOSOPHY
- A. Philosophicals
- B. Supernaturals
- C. Idealism-realism
- D. Concrete-abstract
- E. Cognitive-gut

XII–THINGS AND STUFFS
- A. Static, dynamic (nature)
- B. Static, dynamic (artifacts)
- C. Stuffs

concepts, with some overlapping, to approximately 50 categories of manageable size for analysis—these being organized under 12 "super-categories," as shown in Table 9.4. Thus Super-category I, TIME, includes the Age Continuum (from BIRTH to DEATH with stops in between at concepts like BABY, YOUTH, BRIDE-GROOM, MATURITY, PARENTHOOD, MIDDLE AGE, and OLD AGE), Months and Seasons, Time Units (from MOMENT to ETERNITY and including HOUR, DAY, MONTH, YEAR, and CENTURY as well as the concept TIME itself), and the trichotomous category Future-Present-Past (contrasting sets of concepts like THE FUTURE-THE PRESENT-THE PAST, TOMORROW-TODAY-YESTERDAY, and PROGRESS-WORK-TRADITION). Table 9.4 gives an idea of the wide variety of concept-categories covered in the Atlas; some are rather obvious, like Kincepts, Emotions, Food Objects, Animals, and Occupations, but others are less so, like Intimacy-Remoteness (from Ego), Means-Expressive-Ends, Affiliative-Achievement, Supernaturals, and Stuffs. I publicly apologize for the super-category entitled CARNALITIES, but I couldn't think of any better term to cover Body Parts, Body Characteristics and Processes, Sex and Sensuality, and Health-Sickness! These ways of categorizing the totality of human culture are obviously both limited and, to some extent, arbitrary. However, I would like to emphasize that the underlying Atlas data are stored in such a way on magnetic tapes that anyone can go into it via teletype and pull out a complete analysis of any category he desires—in about 3 minutes or less if the computer happens to be idling.

To organize the data of each category into *formats* interpretable by the human mind, we prepared: (1) *transfers of the basic measures* from the individual culture Atlases into 23 sequential strips, from AE (American English) through JP (Japanese), under each concept in each category; (2) *correlations across cultures* of these basic measures; (3) *intra-cultural ranks of the concepts* in each category on each of the primary measures; (4) *componential analyses* of these ranks in terms of underlying semantic features; and (5) *samplings from pan-cultural distance matrices,* designed to isolate the inter-concept relations for each community and the inter-culture relations for each concept.

To illustrate these data formats, I will use our Color Category—

Table 9.5.

Basic Measures for Color Category

	E	P	A	E-Z	P-Z	A-Z	F-Z	D-O	P-I	P-Z	CI	CI-Z
COLOR												
AE	1.5	0.9	−0.2	0.6	−0.1	−0.5	1.1	1.7	1.4	1.0	0.4	−0.6
FR	1.3	−0.1	1.0	0.8	−0.8	0.9	0.7	1.7	1.2	0.9	0.3	−0.9
BF	1.3	0.3	−0.1	0.7	−0.2	−0.5	1.0	1.4	1.2	0.7	0.5	−0.7
ND	1.0	−0.1	0.5	0.5	−0.7	0.2	0.5	1.2	1.2	0.6	0.6	−0.5
GG	2.0	0.2	−0.3	1.0	−0.5	−0.5	0.3	2.1	1.6	1.1	0.6	0.1
etc.												
MN	1.4	0.2	0.3	0.6	−0.5	0.1	0.8	1.5	1.3	0.8	0.5	−0.5
S	0.4	0.4	0.4	0.3	0.4	0.7	0.9	0.4	0.3	0.2	0.2	0.6
BLACK												
AE	−0.5	0.4	−0.1	−1.3	−0.7	−0.2	−0.5	0.6	1.5	0.5	1.1	2.7
FR	−1.1	1.3	−1.1	−1.6	1.5	−2.2	−0.8	2.0	2.3	1.2	1.1	1.5
BF	−0.1	1.1	−0.7	−0.6	1.4	−1.4	−2.0	1.3	1.6	0.7	0.9	1.7
ND	−0.7	1.3	−0.6	−1.2	1.2	−1.3	0.4	1.6	1.8	0.9	0.9	0.8
GG	−0.9	0.5	−1.3	−1.4	−0.1	−1.5	0.6	1.7	1.4	0.9	0.5	−0.5
etc												
MN	−0.4	0.7	−0.5	−1.1	0.2	−1.2	−0.2	1.2	1.5	0.7	0.8	0.8
S	0.7	0.6	0.6	0.6	1.0	1.0	0.8	0.7	0.4	0.4	0.3	1.2

it involves only eight concepts, COLOR, BLACK, GRAY, RED, YELLOW, BLUE, GREEN, and WHITE, and thus lends itself to economic tabular representation; yet it also yields some interesting data. You will note in Table 9.5 that (based on the means of 20 cultures) COLOR is both more E and more A than BLACK, but BLACK is more P and has more CI (intra-cultural disagreement). There is a significant correlation across cultures on the Evaluation of color terms, but YC (Yucatan Mayans) is an isolate, with quite different evaluations of colors. You will see from the ranks in Table 9.6 that COLOR and BLUE are universally *good* concepts, but GRAY and BLACK are *bad* concepts, across "our world." But you will also note that it is BLACK and RED that are *strong* and YELLOW and WHITE that are *weak*. For our two Scandinavian

TABLE 9.6.

Ranks for Colors

EVALUATION

	AE	FR	BF	ND	GG	SW	FF	YC	MS	IT	YS	GK	LA	TK	IF	DH	MK	TH	HC	JP	MEAN	
COLOR	1	1	1	1	1	3	1	⑧	1	1	2	2	4	1	1	4	1	2	1	5	2.1	U+
BLACK	8	8	8	8	8	8	8	④	8	8	8	7	8	8	6	8	8	8	8	7	7.6	U–
GREY	7	7	7	7	7	7	7	7	7	7	7	8	5	7	7	③	7	6	7	8	6.8	U–
RED	2	5	2	6	2	5	4	5	6	6	5	5	7	5	5	5	4	7	5	4	4.8	
YELLOW	6	6	6	4	6	1	2	6	4	5	6	6	6	6	⑧	①	3	①	6	6	4.8	
BLUE	3	2	3	2	3	2	5	1	2	4	1	4	1	4	2	2	⑥	4	3	2	2.8	U+
GREEN	5	3	4	3	5	4	6	2	3	2	3	1	2	3	4	7	5	5	4	3	3.7	
WHITE	4	4	5	5	4	6	3	3	5	3	4	3	3	2	3	6	2	3	2	1	3.5	

POTENCY

	AE	FR	BF	ND	GG	SW	FF	YC	MS	IT	YS	GK	LA	TK	IF	DH	MK	TH	HC	JP	MEAN	
COLOR	2	6	5	4	4	4	6	6	5	5	①	4	6	5	3	4	6	5	2	3	4.3	
BLACK	5	1	2	1	3	3	1	1	2	4	5	2	5	1	1	⑧	1	1	6	1	2.7	U+
GREY	8	3	7	5	5	7	②	8	7	8	8	6	7	3	7	5	7	3	8	4	5.9	
RED	1	2	1	2	1	2	⑤	2	1	2	2	1	4	2	2	2	4	2	1	2	2.0	U+
YELLOW	6	8	6	8	7	5	8	7	8	7	7	5	8	6	8	7	8	7	7	7	7.0	U–
BLUE	3	4	3	3	2	1	4	5	3	1	3	⑦	3	8	4	1	5	6	4	5	3.8	
GREEN	4	7	4	6	6	6	3	4	4	3	4	3	①	4	5	3	3	4	5	6	4.3	
WHITE	7	5	8	7	8	8	7	3	6	6	6	8	②	7	6	6	②	8	3	8	6.0	U–

Note: The symbol U signifies apparent Universals; U, Sub-universals; and Q, Uniquenesses.

TABLE 9.7.

Componential Analysis for Colors (III-C)

Components: (1) Brightness (bright^{+}/dark^{-})
(2) Hue (red^{+}/blue^{-})
(3) Saturation (rich^{+}/pale^{-})
(4) Color/non-color (+/−)

Codings:	Br	Hue	Sat	Color
Color	00	00	00	+
Black	−	00	00	−
Gray	0	00	00	−
Red	00	+	+	+
Yellow	00	+	−	+
Blue	00	−	+	+
Green	00	−	−	+
White	+	00	00	−

Tests:
(1) *Brightness:* White^{+}/Black^{-}; White^{+}/Gray^{-}; Gray^{+}/Black^{-}
(2) *Hue:* Red^{+}/Blue^{-}; Yellow^{+}/Green^{-}
(3) *Saturation:* Red^{+}/Yellow^{-}; Blue^{+}/Green^{-}
(4) *Color:* Color^{+}/Gray^{-}; Color^{+}/White over Black

(most Northern) communities, SW and FF, warm YELLOW has high E as a sub-universal.

Table 9.7 gives the componential analysis for Colors—the features or components being Brightness, Hue, Saturation, and Color (vs. Non-color). You will observe that the tests—for example, RED vs. BLUE on Hue—are based upon attempts to find *minimal contrasts,* that is, concepts which differ only on the semantic feature in question. Table 9.8 presents the results of this componential analysis for the Color Category: Note that the top row, comparing WHITE-BLACK as one test on the Brightness feature, shows that all 20 cultures (in the sample shown) rate WHITE more E than BLACK, and the entire set of three tests show Brightness to be more E than Darkness—perhaps because we are, after all, primates that depend upon vision for survival. The universal affective correlate of Saturation (richness of color) is Potency and the

TABLE 9.8.

Componential Analysis Results for Colors

EVALUATION:	AE	FR	BF	ND	GG	SW	FF	YC	MS	IT	YS	GK	LA	TK	IF	DH	MK	TH	HC	JP	RATIO
(1) Brightness																					
W/Blk	+	+	+	+	+	+	+	+	+	+	+	+	+	+	+	+	+	+	+	+	20/20 U+
U+ W/Gy	+	+	+	+	+	+	+	+	+	+	+	+	+	+	+	Θ	+	+	+	+	19/20 U+
GY/Blk	+	+	+	+	+	+	+	−	+	+	+	−	+	+	−	+	+	+	+	−	16/20
(2) Hue																					
Rd/Bl	+	−	+	−	+	−	+	−	−	−	−	−	−	−	−	−	+	−	−	−	5/20
Yl/Grn	−	−	−	−	−	(+)	(+)	U −	−	−	−	−	−	−	−	(+)	(+)	(+) U	−	−	5/20
(3) Saturation																					
Rd/Yl	+	+	+	−	+	−	−	+	−	−	+	+	−	+	+	−	−	−	+	+	11/20
Bl/Grn	+	+	+	+	+	+	+	+	+	−	+	−	+	−	+	+	−	+	+	+	16/20
(4) Color																					
U + Color/Grey	+	+	+	+	+	+	+	(−)	+	+	+	+	+	+	+	Θ?	+	+	+	+	18/20 U+
Color/Bl-W	+	+	+	+	+	+	+	(−)	+	+	+	+	0	+	+	+	+	+	+	0	17/18(20) U+

POTENCY:

	1	2	3	4	5	6	7	8	9	10	11	12	13	14	15	16	17	18	19	20	
(1) Brightness																					
W/Blk	−	−	−	−	−	−	−	−	−	−	−	−	−	⊕?	−	⊕?	−	−	⊕?	−	3/20 U−
U− W/Gy	+	−	−	−	−	−	−	+	+	+	+	−	+	−	+	−	+	−	+	−	9/20
Gy/Blk	−	−	−	−	−	−	−	−	−	−	−	−	−	−	−	⊕?	−	−	−	−	1/20 U−
(2) Hue																					
Rd/Bl	+	+	+	+	+	(−	−)	U +	+	−	+	+	−	+	+	−	+	+	+	+	15/20
Yl/Grn	−	−	−	−	−	⊕	−	−	−	−	−	−	−	−	−	−	−	−	−	−	1/20 U−
(3) Saturation																					
U+ Rd/Yl	+	+	+	+	+	+	+	+	+	+	+	+	+	+	+	+	+	+	+	+	20/20 U+
? Bl/Grn	+	+	+	+	+	+	−	−	+	+	+	−	−	−	+	+	−	−	+	+	13/20
(4) Color																					
Color/Grey	+	−	+	+	+	+	−	+	+	+	+	+	+	−	+	+	+	−	+	+	16/20
Color/Bl-W	+	−	0	0	0	0	0	−	0	0	+	0	−	0	0	+	−	0	+	0	4/8 (20)

Note: The symbol U signifies Universals; U, Sub-universals; and Q, Uniquenesses.

near-universal correlate of Hue is Activity (the red end of the spectrum being more active than the blue).

From the distance matrices, computed pan-culturally like the pan-cultural factor analyses described earlier, we extract both intra-cultural concept relations (for example, BLUE is closest to generic COLOR in feeling-tone for 12/23 cultures, but for Finns it is RED and for Swedes it is YELLOW) and the inter-cultural relations for the same concepts (Americans should get along fine with Iranians in communicating their feeling about colors, but miserably with the Swedes; the Mayans in Yucatan have a cultural "thing" about BLACK, arising from their mythology, and the Swedes have a "thing" about YELLOW, deviant from all others—but why?).

Interpreting the Atlas Data. Ideally, any global study of human cultures should entail both representativeness in terms of including diverse societies and representativeness in terms of aspects of culture within each society. That is, ideally we would like to maximize both breadth and depth. But, in practice, this ideal can hardly even be approached; funds and time, to say nothing of investigator energies, just simply do not permit simultaneous study, in depth, of 20 or 30 different language-culture communities. The anthropological approach is typically "vertical," emphasizing depth at the necessary expense of breadth: at any one time, the ethnographic field-worker investigates intensively one very limited community of humans, striving to come out with an integrated picture that illuminates the interrelations among the various layers of its culture—a kind of cultural cameo. The psychological approach is more likely to be "horizontal," emphasizing breadth at the necessary expense of depth: using measuring instruments assumed to be comparable cross-culturally and cross-linguistically, the investigator obtains a thin slice of information about one layer of culture across as large a number of different societies as he can manage—at least, this has been true in our case.

But, being well aware of the ideal, both vertical and horizontal "slicers" then try to relate their findings to other parts of the human pie: Cultural anthropologists try to integrate the vertical studies of many investigations into a general cross-cultural picture (for example, the integrative interpretations of kinship systems by Murdock, 1949, or the Human Relations Area Files more generally)—and they run into trouble owing, mainly, to incomparability of methods. And we are now trying to relate our reasonably rigorous and quantitative data on the attribution of affect to other layers of the cultures of our 23 communities—and we are running in troubles due, mainly, to the intricacies of culture and the questionable validities of the intuitions of native informants, even very highly motivated ones like our colleagues.

Over the past two years I have organized and participated in eight intensive two-week meetings of sub-sets of our colleagues and their associates on interpretation of our Atlas data. The first was a pilot-run of procedures for such meetings held in Oaxtepec, Mexico, for our MS and YC colleagues, who happened to be closest to our home base. Then, in the spring and summer of 1970, there were three such meetings with our Western European (French, Belgian, Dutch, and German), Scandinavian (Swedes and Finns), and—after much translation checking in other locations—our East Asian (Thai, Hong Kong Chinese, and Japanese) groups. And in the summer of 1971, meetings were held with our Mediterranean (Italian, Yugoslav, Greek, and Turkish), West Asian (Turkish, Lebanese, Iranian, and Afghan), and Indian (Hindi, Bengali, and Kannada) groups. You will note that the Turkish delegation split itself—appropriately enough, since they span the Bosphorus and thus two continents—between the Mediterranean and West Asian meetings. Another meeting with our Mexican and Yucatan colleagues was held in the winter of 1971. The main reason for these particular sub-sets is intensely practical—the costs of bringing some 12 to 15 people together for one meeting require that they be as close geographically as possible—but it is also fairly reasonable in terms of over-all cultural similarities, as inspection of the group compositions will indicate.

The amount of preparation for these meetings (and dependence upon the mail to get things there) is almost incredible—and I must thank all of our Center staff for always getting everything there at the appointed place when I arrived myself! The meetings themselves are at once exhilarating, exhausting, and "mind boggling"—as when Swedish colleagues struggle with "why is Swedish Ego (I, MYSELF) so close to HERO?" and Yucatans struggle with "why is FOG so *good* and *active?*" The Center staff at these meetings (myself and usually either Bill May, Gordana Opacić, or Bill

Archer and his wife) spend the in-between times trying to keep ahead of the group of informants, by isolating what appear to be the most interesting items in the data. There is a marked "group" effect that has appeared regularly: motivation is high during the first, orientation days, takes a gradual dip as more and more "don't knows" are encountered, and then—always behind schedule by the middle of the period—begins to pick up as participants "learn the ropes," begin to perceive patterns in their own sets of cultural deviations, and become intensely aware of how much there is still to cover. The "delegation" from each community usually included our senior colleague, a cultural anthropologist and/or linguist, and a young person who was a teenager at the time of Atlas testing.

The staff provides each participant with (a) a mimeographed booklet giving the componential codings and tests for each of some 50 categories of concepts, (b) a mimeographed booklet of apparent universals (all measures marked with Red U's on the computer outputs for each category), (c) lists of apparent sub-universals, involving their communities and others either in the group or neighboring, (d) lists of uniquenesses involving their own communities, and (e) the complete Atlases (both English-to-X and X-to-English forms) for their own communities. At the meetings, following an orientation to the work—which includes a summary of the total project procedures and a detailed examination of the Color Category computer output, as used here for illustration—we take up each category as given in Table 9.4, starting with a review of apparent universals (to give a frame of reference for interpretation), moving on to detailed and animated discussion of the sub-universals involving the participants' cultures, and then (usually after all categories in a given Super-category, for example, TIME, have been covered) we break up into small intra-cultural groups for consideration of the uniquenesses of each language-culture community, discussed privately in their own language—giving particular attention to their exceptions from near-universals, to their "sore-thumbs" (marked deviations from all other communities), and their remaining translation problems—and at this point, inevitably and poignantly, fine differences in the meanings of terms in different languages come back to haunt us. We instruct the participants to "scale" their interpretive comments with exclamation points (!! = sharp and agreed-upon intuition), no mark (agreed-upon probable interpretation), question-marks (?? = a possible, but "far-out," explanation), and DK's (just "don't know").

The *Universals* in our data (with less than 6 of 23 communities being exceptions) are our hardest data—most independent of informant interpretations. They include many instances of simple face validity (for example, ANIMAL being more A than TREE, the +Moral concepts being more E than the -Moral concepts, the Supra-ordinate concepts, like LEADER and HERO, being more P than the Sub-ordinate concepts, like FOLLOWER and BEGGAR), but these evidences of face validity lend credence to the many less obvious universals—that PRIDE has high CI (cultural ambivalence) everywhere except AE, YS, and TH, that the Future-oriented emotions like COURAGE, HOPE, and DETERMINATION are both more E and more P than their matched Past-oriented emotions, GUILT, PRIDE, and SHAME, and so forth. Many of our *Sub-universals* would be obvious (but not trivial) to students of comparative cultures (for example, the fact that the SUMMER season and its months, JUNE, JULY, and AUGUST, are highly evaluated in the West but lowly evaluated in India and Thailand), but others are by no means obvious (for example, that School-related concepts, like TEACHER, EDUCATION, EXAMINATION, are low E throughout the West (up to and including Yugoslavia) but very high E all through Asia (from Turkey to Hong Kong, but *not* Japan) and that in the Indian Sub-continent Future-oriented concepts have low E and very low P and A, particularly PROGRESS). All of our *Uniquenesses* cry for interpretation—like the affective *closeness* of EGO and FRIEND (vs. RELATIVES) for AE and HC and the affective *distance* of EGO from FAMILY, FRIEND, RELATIVES, and MOST PEOPLE for Yugoslav teenagers as compared with closeness to STRANGER—but often we get DK's on such matters from our colleagues. In general, it is when *patterns* of uniquenesses appear—like the Food preferences of Indians—that the data leap into intuitive clarity.

IN MID-FLIGHT

And this is exactly where we are at the moment of my writing this paper—right in the middle of our attempt to integrate all of our hard data and all of our colleague interpretations of it into a

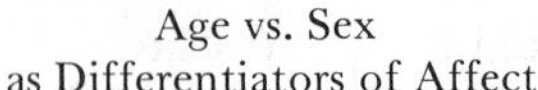

Age vs. Sex
as Differentiators of Affect

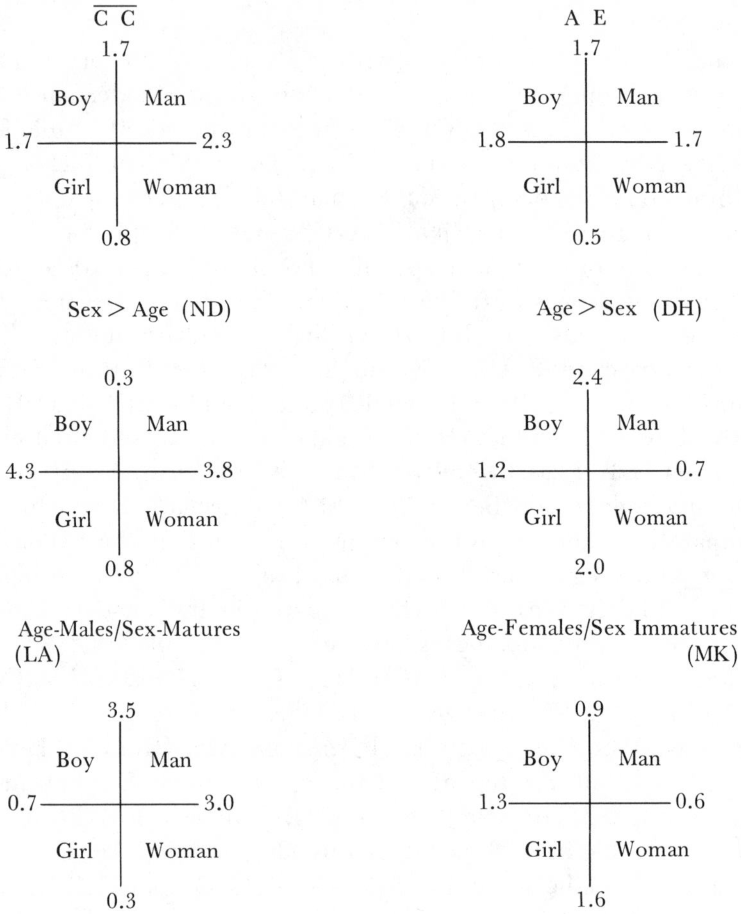

$\overline{\text{C C}}$

1.7

Boy Man

1.7 — 2.3

Girl Woman

0.8

Sex > Age (ND)

A E

1.7

Boy Man

1.8 — 1.7

Girl Woman

0.5

Age > Sex (DH)

0.3

Boy Man

4.3 — 3.8

Girl Woman

0.8

Age-Males/Sex-Matures
(LA)

2.4

Boy Man

1.2 — 0.7

Girl Woman

2.0

Age-Females/Sex Immatures
(MK)

3.5

Boy Man

0.7 — 3.0

Girl Woman

0.3

0.9

Boy Man

1.3 — 0.6

Girl Woman

1.6

Figure 9.4.

coherent picture of the whole. I won't regale you with detailed descriptions of the (literally!) feet of marked computer outputs and 23-community commentaries we must somehow put into meaningful discourse. I feel like that man with "a bear by the tail"—so big and juicy, but, Oh!, so clamorous and perplexing. I confess that I feel overwhelmed by the magnitude of this task, and I wish that there were dozens of Edward Sapirs and Julian Stewards to help me—you see, I do *not* think that our "horizontal" approach to subjective culture has supplanted the "vertical" approach. Yet, ours *is* an approach that should mesh with the richness of cameo studies of human cultures.

I won't regale you with our Atlas data either, since we are in the midst of trying to interpret it. Yet, a few tiny samples of it may serve to bemuse—or amuse: Figure 9.4 presents data on the relative distances in affective feeling-tone for BOY-MAN-GIRL-WOMAN concepts in cultures displaying very different Sex vs. Age determinants. For all cultures (average, top-left), the Sex of Matures (MAN-WOMAN) and the Age of Males (BOY-MAN) are more significant determiners of differential affect than, respectively, the Sex of Immatures (BOY-GIRL) and the Age of Females (GIRL-WOMAN)—for our teenage male sample, of course. Americans (AE), along with nine other human communities, come close to this cross-cultural tendency. The Netherland Dutch (ND) typify the Sex, but not Age, groups—including most West Europeans (FR, BF, ND, GG, SW, and FF) and also Mexicans, Italians, Greeks, and Iranians. Age is a more important differentiator of feeling than Sex for both the Delhi Hindi (DH, in the table) and the Yucatan Mayans (but not others). The Age of Males and the Sex of Matures as affective differentiators is shown in exaggerated form in LA (Lebanese Arabic). The only culture (in our sample) for which the Age of Females and the Sex of Immatures are apparently the most important determiners of differentiation in feeling is MK (Kannada-speaking teenagers in Mysore, India).

From this same Male-Female Identification Category we also draw a very unexpected finding about the affective meanings of teenagers around this world: when the closeness in affect of the concept WIDOWER to *Male* concepts (MALE, MASCULINITY, MAN, BOY, FATHER) is compared with its closeness to the matched *Female* concepts (FEMALE, FEMININITY, WOMAN, GIRL, MOTHER), it turns out that for 14 of our 23 cultures WIDOWER is closer to Female concepts than their masculine counterparts (the most marked exceptions are Finland, Mexico, Turkey, Thailand, and Japan). There seems to be an affective emasculation of WIDOWER in the minds of teenagers around the world, but this does *not* happen for WIDOW (she is consistently closer to Female concepts)!

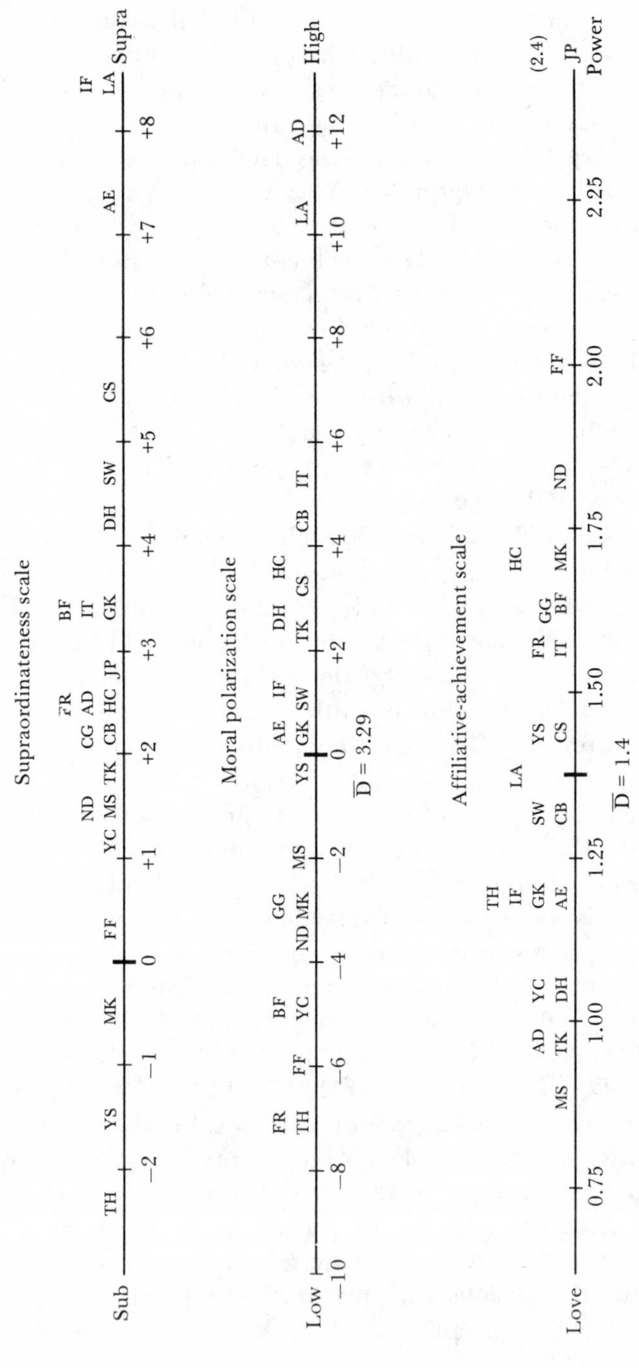

Supraordinateness scale

Sub — TH — −2 — YS — −1 — MK — 0 — FF — +1 — YC ND MS TK — +2 — CB CG FR HC AD JP — +3 — GK IT BF — +4 — DH SW — +5 — CS — +6 — +7 — AE — +8 — LA IF — Supra

Moral polarization scale

Low — −10 — −8 — TH FR — −6 — FF — YC BF — −4 — ND MK GG — −2 — MS — YS — 0 — GK AE SW IF — +2 — TK DH CS HC — +4 — CB IT — +6 — +8 — +10 — LA — +12 — AD — High

$\overline{D}$ = 3.29

Affiliative-achievement scale

Love — 0.75 — MS — TK AD — 1.00 — DH YC — AE GK IF TH — 1.25 — CB SW — LA — CS YS — 1.50 — IT FR — BF GG — HC — MK — 1.75 — ND — FF — 2.00 — 2.25 — JP (2.4) Power

$\overline{D}$ = 1.4

Figure 9.5.

And, finally, Figure 9.5 shows the distribution of our 23 cultures on three "scales" drawn from the Social Status, Morality, and Affiliative-Achievement Categories. The "Supraordinateness Scale" presents the mean distances between the concept-pairs LEADER-FOLLOWER, POLICEMAN-BEGGAR, AUTHORITY-ILLITERATE, RICH PEOPLE-POOR PEOPLE, and MASTER-SERVANT; you will note that teenagers in most cultures "identify" more with Supraordinates than with Subordinates, this being most marked for Iranians, Lebanese, and Americans—with only Thais, Yugoslavs, and Mysoreans going more with Subordinates. The "Moral Polarization Scale" presents the mean distances between the contrastive concept-pairs CHARACTER-SIN, CHARITY-GREED, DEVOTION-ADULTERY, DISCIPLINE-CHEATING, DUTY-LYING, FORGIVENESS-GUILT, HONOR-GRAFT, JUSTICE-CRIME, KINDNESS-MURDER, and MISSIONARY-PROSTITUTE; you will note that the French, Thais, and Finns make relatively low differentiations, as compared with the Lebanese and Afghans who make extremely large "morality" differentiations. The "Affiliative-Achievement (or Love-Power) Scale" shows the average affective distances between RESPECT-POWER, FRIEND-LEADER, COOPERATION-COMPETITION, DEVOTION-ENVY, SYMPATHY-GREED, ACCEPTING THINGS-TAKING THE INITIATIVE, FAMILY-SUCCESS, GROUP-CHAMPION, and FRIENDSHIP-WORK; you will note that Mexicans, Turks, Afghans, Mayans (YC), and Delhi Hindis are high on the Love end of the spectrum, while Finns, Dutch, Chinese (HC), and Mysoreans are high on the Power end of the spectrum.

Well, I have tried to give you some idea of the whys and wherefores of my own explorations in semantic space. As you can see, we are still in mid-flight—and, Powers That Be willing, we will stay in flight for at least a little while. Most of this space remains unexplored, and I am sure that vehicles radically different than the SD will need to be devised. Even so, the cross-cultural application of the SD has revealed a big and complex, but very intriguing, picture of human subjective culture. Meaningful patterns will emerge, I am sure. This cross-cultural research has been very expensive—as such things go in the social sciences—but it has been spread over nearly fifteen years in time and some 150 people in space around the planet. However, when I am told by the press that the development of just one major-league baseball player costs an average of half a million dollars, I conclude that our attempts to probe into the ways many diverse cultures attribute affect to a wide range of significant "things on their minds" is worth at least one pitcher and a couple of left fielders. Be back in a decade or so.

REFERENCES

Chomsky, N. Verbal behavior (a review). *Language*, 1959, *35*, 26–58.

Festinger, L. *A Theory of Cognitive Dissonance.* Evanston, Ill.: Rowe, Peterson, 1957.

Fodor, J. A. Could meaning be an r_m? *Journal of Verbal Learning and Verbal Behavior*, 1965, *4*, 73-81.

Fodor, J. A. More about mediators: A reply to Berlyne and Osgood. *Journal of Verbal Learning and Verbal Behavior*, 1966, *5*, 412-415.

Heider, F. *The Psychology of Interpersonal Relations.* New York: Wiley & Sons, 1958.

Kumata, H., and Schramm, W. A pilot study of cross-cultural methodology. *Public Opinion Quarterly*, 1956, *20*, 229-238.

Osgood, C. E. The nature and measurement of meaning. *Psychological Bulletin*, 1952, *49*, 197–237.

Osgood, C. E. *Method and Theory in Experimental Psychology.* New York: Oxford University Press, 1953.

Osgood, C. E. Meaning cannot be an r_m? *Journal of Verbal Learning and Verbal Behavior*, 1966, *5*, 402–407.

Osgood, C. E. Dimensionality of the semantic space for communication via facial expressions. *Scandinavian Journal of Psychology*, 1966, *7*, 1–30.

Osgood, C. E. On the strategy of cross-national research into subjective culture. *Social Sciences Information*, 1967, *6*, 5–37.

Osgood, C. E. Is neo-behaviorism in a blind alley? Unpublished mimeo. 1969.

Osgood, C. E. Interpersonal verbs and interpersonal behavior. In J. L. Cowan (ed.), *Studies in Language and Thought.* Tucson, Arizona: University of Arizona Press, 1970.

Osgood, C. E., G. J. Suci, and P. H. Tannenbaum. *The Measurement of Meaning.* Urbana, Illinois: University of Illinois Press, 1957.

Osgood, C. E., and P. H. Tannenbaum. The principle of congruity and the prediction of attitude change. *Psychological Review*, 1955. *62*, 62–73.

Osgood, C. E., E. E. Ware, and C. Morris. Analysis of the connotative meanings of a variety of human values as expressed by American college students. *Journal of Abnormal and Social Psychology*, 1961, *62*, 62–73.

Snider, J. G., and C. E. Osgood (eds.), *Semantic Differential Technique: A Sourcebook.* Chicago, Ill.: Aldine Publishing Company, 1969.

Suci, G. J. A comparison of semantic structures in American Southwest culture groups. *Journal of Abnormal and Social Psychology*, 1960, *61*, 25–30.

Tuomela, R. Theoretical concepts in neo-behavioristic theories. Unpublished manuscript, University of Helsinki, 1971.

10

de Gustibus (Mark II)*

CARL PFAFFMANN

I was born in Brooklyn on May 27, 1913, the first born of my parents, Charles Pfaffmann and Anna Haker Pfaffmann. My four grandparents had emigrated from Germany and raised their own families in New York City. My paternal grandfather, Adam Pfaffmann, had been a wheelwright but died when my father was quite young, leaving my grandmother widowed with two small daughters besides my father. For them life was financially difficult, and my father went barefoot in the summer to save shoe money. He started working at a very early age, having left school after only a few elementary grades. My mother's family was slightly better off and she completed grade school but not high school. By the time I came along, however, my father had achieved moderate success in business and was able to purchase a two-family dwelling in Queens, Long Island.

Arbeit und Ordnung were strong Germanic values in our house-

*I gratefully acknowledge the support for the program of research described herein by contracts and grants over the years from the Office of Naval Research, National Science Foundation, National Institutes of Health, General Foods Corporation, Nutrition Foundation, Army Quartermaster Corps, Guggenheim Foundation. An important part of this support has been for graduate students and postdoctoral fellowships and trainees. Without this support, research and its intimately related educational functions would not have been possible.

But most of all I have enjoyed and profited personally from the close association with my many students and postdoctoral collaborators. We have remained good friends as each has gone on to his or her own academic and scientific career.

hold. One was expected to advance himself by hard work and effort, and education was essential to this process. So it was natural as I progressed through the schools of the New York City system that I take the college preparatory course. I was the first member of the family anywhere to attend college. My choice of Brown University was influenced by a neighbor's son who was a junior at Brown when I graduated from high school. In those innocent years I made only one application, that is, to Brown, and was accepted in 1929 as one of the youngest members of the class of 1933, having graduated from high school two years ahead of time.

I had no clear career plans, and looked forward only to the adventure of college. I think my father hoped that I might study economics and business administration, and possibly join him in business after graduation. But in his helping me financially I was not made to commit myself to that course. Although the 1929 era was one of serious financial depression, my father's income was sufficient to provide significant help toward my undergraduate education. With the aid of scholarships, summer dance-band jobs (I played the sax and clarinet), busing in the college cafeteria, and so on, I was able to contribute the rest of my educational expenses.

My first semester at college yielded a mixture of A's and B's without special effort on my part. I found the lectures and the laboratory work to be very rewarding, and I had the thrill of discovering a new world, that of the intellectual realm, with its associated cultural as well as social aspects. My own children later on missed this experience. They grew up close to university circles, attending school with other professors' children and with middle- and professional-class children. For them college life was to some extent an anticlimax, a continuation of what they had known in prep school and high school. Such a difference in early background, it seems to me, may be one important contributant to some of the disenchantment and questioning search by the younger generation today. Most of their parents have had a college education and they take for granted this aspect of life. My own children, I should add, however, did enjoy and graduate from college; one went on for a master's degree, another for the D.M.D.

In any case, by my sophomore year I had decided on the

academic life, yet was uncertain as to field. The real turning point came when I took introductory psychology with Leonard Carmichael, then the youngest full professor on the Brown faculty. He had come from Princeton to build a modern department of psychology. Professor Edmund Burke Delabarre, his predecessor, taught in the more philosophical Jamesian tradition. Carmichael later went on from Brown to become Dean of Faculty at the University of Rochester, then President of Tufts University, then Secretary of the Smithsonian Institution, and then the active Vice President for research and exploration of the National Geographic Society. In my own academic and professional history he was clearly the most important and influential figure.

Psychology at Brown in those days was housed in two wooden buildings that were formerly residences; the dining and living room areas had been converted to classrooms and the basement, kitchen, and attic to laboratory space. Before Carmichael was married he actually rented one of the rooms on the second floor of 89 Waterman Street as a bedroom, which made it easy for him to work late hours, and he often did. I think he still does so, for he continues his prodigious output of editorial and scholarly work and research while being an administrator and public figure. At any rate, he soon discovered me and I discovered him and I began a major in psychology. Like many another undergraduate, I said I was interested in abnormal psychology. Actually Carmichael, as a physiological sensory psychologist (the Brown laboratory was designated the Laboratory of Sensory Physiology and Psychology), did not discourage me outright but he did note that someone with such an interest would do well to obtain an M.D. The psychologists of reputation then in the field were often regarded as second-class citizens in the medical setting in which they worked. Although this situation may have changed with the modern growth of clinical and research psychology, I still wonder whether a combined Ph.D.-M.D. of psychology and medicine does not make the soundest combination for work in abnormal psychology, or even psychology generally. Psychology has come of age since I began graduate work witnessed by the increasing effectiveness of psychological methods, and the increasing collaboration of biomedical researchers and practitioners with psychologists with the Ph.D. However, the great traditions and legal position of medicine, and the responsibility of the M.D. for patient care and research seem to me to recommend both degrees. The M.D.-Ph.D. combination is widely current in other basic biomedical disciplines: biochemistry, pathology, physiology, and I see no reason why psychology and behavioral science generally should not be included. The combined degree requires so little additional time out of the long span of one's lifetime that it clearly seems worth doing. In fact, at this time we are hoping that the recently established Ph.D.-M.D. joint program at Rockefeller University and Cornell Medical College in New York will provide new opportunities for such a combination.

Once launched as an undergraduate major I began to spend more and more time around the lab, with fellow undergraduates, graduate students, and faculty, and began a series of research projects in courses, in honors work, and for fun. Among my fellow students was the planner and editor of this series, Phil Krawiec, who went on to his Ph.D. at New York University after a master's at Brown. Among the faculty was Harold Schlosberg with whom I did an undergraduate course project, an experimental study of the ease of conditioning the knee jerk in psychotic patients (4). Later I served as a member of the faculty at Brown under his chairmanship and benefited from his wise counsel and friendship (54). At about this time Herbert Jasper also joined the faculty with a joint position as chief psychologist at Bradley Hospital near Providence. When Jasper arrived he immediately began to set up an electrophysiological laboratory for experimental and clinical electrophysiology. Berger's work in Germany on recording electrical "brain waves" (EEG) in man had just become known. Jasper and Carmichael reported some of the first EEG recordings on humans in the United States on me as one of their prize subjects with a good alpha rhythm. Jasper ultimately went on to the Montreal Neurological Institute, where with Dr. Wilder Penfield he developed his world famous laboratory for clinical EEG and neurophysiology.

As an undergraduate I did another project on the effect of rotating the maze on rats' learning performance. I remember building the Hampton Court maze of plywood floor and alley walls, the whole thing covered with a frame and screen of hardware cloth. I immediately made two discoveries; one was that I could not see the animal through the galvanized hardward cloth;

but a little flat black paint reduced the glare of the screening and made the rat visible. Second, I had left one-inch space between the top of the alleys and the hardware cloth cover. The rats soon began to "short cut" over the top of the alley walls rather than traverse long way round on the floor. This was easily rectified by re-mounting the framed cover so that the hardware cloth wire made close contact with the tops of the alleys. At that time it did not occur to me to raise the more interesting question of why the rat wanted to take the shorter route.

In deciding on an honors thesis, Carmichael reviewed the possibilities and made one statement which sent me on research that became the major interest of most of my scientific career. He pointed out that very little was known about olfaction and taste so that there was lots of room and little competition. Good research would be highly visible! This turned out to be a correct prediction. Although my honors project was a psychophysical study of taste I began to think of other more physiological approaches. Herb Jasper allowed me to use his electrophysiological equipment to record from the frog's dorsal cutaneous nerve upon chemical stimulation (3). I remember my first thrill on hearing the discharge of impulses in the audio monitor. I have never extinguished that "gut feeling" when I hear the crackle of single unit discharges.

My interest in sensory mechanisms, especially chemical senses, was set by my graduate years, 1933-1939. Problems were cast in the context of the "basis of sensation" and the specificity of afferent sensory processes. Electrophysiological recording employing the electronic amplifier and oscillograph was the latest thing in the 1930s. At long last the sense organs, the nerves, and the brain could be probed directly to provide direct information in place of indirect inferences from psychophysical, phenomenological, or behavioral observation (1,2).

Physiologists and psychologists entered the rapidly expanding field of electrophysiology and electrodes were put on every accessible sense organ, nerve, or brain center. It was apparent, however, that I needed more basic training in physiology. The opportunity to study physiology at Oxford with a Rhodes scholarship was a Godsend. I would not have applied for the Rhodes except for Carmichael's urging. I had not been particularly active in athletics, only middlingly so in freshman swimming and intramurals, but had been involved in campus affairs, especially in the orchestra and the band. My academic record was good: Phi Beta Kappa, Sigma Xi, magna cum laude, etc. Carmichael saw the opportunity for study in the Final Honors School of Physiology at Oxford where neurophysiology was still pre-eminent even though Sir Charles Sherrington had recently retired. J. C. Eccles was a young man then, a fellow of Magdalen College, with an active research program in synaptic transmission in the autonomic ganglia. He had not yet moved to the study of units in the spinal cord or the CNS, work for which he later shared the Nobel Prize. My course of study included physiology, biochemistry as well as neurophysiology. During the two years at Oxford I became an undergraduate again and research was temporarily put aside. In some respects this was irksome, but Oxford was intellectually stimulating and pleasant. Among the many undergraduates I came to know was Hortense Louise Brooks at St. Hilda's College; she later became my wife. My social and cultural world was greatly expanded not only by Oxford and England, but by the Continent with its great wealth of museums, art galleries, cathedrals, etc., all just a channel crossing away in that pre-jet age.

After two years I returned to research as a graduate student at Cambridge under Professor E. D. Adrian, later Lord Adrian, one of the founders of modern electrophysiology. Before being accepted as a student, I first had to propose a program of research to a sponsor, in this case Adrian. He accepted my plan to study the electrophysiology of taste in which Yngve Zotterman and Donald Barron had made some beginnings. Zotterman shifted to pain, touch, and temperature sensitivity and returned to taste only later. Barron shifted to other subjects. My Oxford degree excused me of one year's residence requirement so that I was able to complete the research and the dissertation in two years. There was no course work for the Ph.D., only research, and no general examination, save the defense of the thesis. Prior study in the undergraduate honors program provided the equivalent of Ph.D. course work and preliminary examinations.

The classical conceptions of taste derived from such studies in man as punctate tongue stimulation of single papillae and of selective drug action. Gymnemic acid, for example, blocked sweet and bitter but left salt and sour sensations undiminished. The four primary tastes were thought to be salty, sour, bitter, and sweet, and it was from these that all other taste sensations were compounded. My thesis problem was to search for individual chorda tympani nerve fibers in the electrophysiological responses of the primary taste receptors in the cat's tongue.

Let me first describe the apparatus we used. Bryan Matthews, now Sir Bryan and Professor of Physiology at Cambridge, had invented the moving iron-tongue Matthews oscillograph while still an undergraduate. Light from a high intensity source was reflected from the mirror of the oscillograph to a moving film camera. The slow emulsions of the recording film at that time required an arc light which could produce the high intensity required. This was long before cathode ray oscillographs with high actinic phosphors and pre-packaged amplifiers. The arc I used ran by wind-up clock work; it smoked and sputtered and sometimes went out at crucial moments. I also recall having built my own two-stage preamplifier, bread-board style, which I used for all my thesis work. It was mounted in a celotex-muffled, aluminum-screened wooden box resting upon an inflated inner tube to protect it from vibrations. This assembly was conveniently placed on the floor beneath my recording table so that with a well-directed kick I could stop microphonic oscillations to which it was prone. A proper power amplifier was made by the Cambridge Instrument Company powered with a bank of wet high-tension "accumulators," that is, batteries.

The lingual nerve contains fibers for taste, temperature, and general mucosal sensitivity. When I first placed this nerve on the electrode, I could find no recordable response to taste. It turned out that the great number of nontaste fibers in the lingual nerve "shunt out" the electrical activity in the smaller taste fibers. However, since the chorda tympani nerve leaves the lingual nerve to form a separate branch composed of mostly taste fibers and salivary efferents, it is relatively easy to record from the chorda tympani itself. But several months passed before my first successful recording from single fibers dissected with the aid of a binocular microscope, fine tweezers, and sharpened needles. The uniform height of spike trains on the oscillograph indicated when the chemical stimulus had activated but one nerve fiber. This then was photographed and the frequency of firing counted under different stimulus conditions. Since taste fibers are smaller in diameter, they are more fragile and difficult to dissect, which partly explains why, until recent years, few had studied this sensory system.

The main thesis result was that although there were chemical differences among fibers, the patterns of sensitivity were clearly unexpected. I found three fiber types, one sensitive to acid alone, one to acid plus sodium chloride, and one to acid plus quinine. None responded to sugar. Lord Adrian became more interested in my problem by these unexpected findings. I also remember very well his view of a thesis supervisor's role. When I had completed the first draft, I brought it to him for approval. "Oh," said he, "I'd better not read it until after you submit it and have been examined. I might make some suggestions now and it wouldn't be your own work." I sometimes wonder, do we now spoon-feed our students too much?

My thesis results set the stage for a long line of investigations by my students, postdoctorals, and myself. Insight into the spectrum of taste sensitivity has become clearer only in recent years. The chemical selectivity of the taste endings was amply demonstrated by these different so-called types of fibers, only one of which was selective to one specific stimulus, acid, and with which the other sensitivities were combined. Yet this posed a conceptual problem! How could the brain know which chemical had activated any particular single fiber at the periphery if it was possible to stimulate that fiber with more than one chemical? It seemed to me that the same stimuli would also activate other receptors with different relative responses. Thus, in a pair of acid-quinine fibers, acid might cause a higher impulse frequency than quinine in one fiber (A), while quinine might activate the higher frequency in the other fiber (B). Therefore, the ratios of activity in two or more simultaneously active fibers could provide the needed information. Acid would be signalled by $A > B$, quinine by $B > A$. This was the first enunciation of what has come to be known as the "across-fiber pattern theory" for the perception of taste quality (9, 32).

We immediately wondered about the general applicability of this principle to other senses. In much later work, single olfactory units and other senses were found to display very similar ratio relationships. I was in the fortunate position, thus, of having a thesis that opened up many more questions than it solved. Much of my later scientific research grew out of solving these and related questions.

In addition to this theme there is a kind of raw empiricism about my research. For example, on one afternoon when the taste nerve itself had become unresponsive, I played around with other nerves from the oral cavity. I had dissected branches of the trigeminal nerve along the floor of the orbit and placed one large trunk on the electrodes. I vividly remember my surprise and excitement when I tapped the upper canine tooth with a glass rod. There was such a tremendous response that the oscillograph almost "bounced off the bench." The tap had stimulated a massive synchronized volley in many of hundreds of large fibers from receptors in the periodontal membrane. This was one of the first recordings from a dental nerve. I followed this up on a number of preparations, comparing the impulses from the periodontal receptors with those from the pulp, the latter giving a disappointingly small response, because of their small diameter. I also studied the effect of vibratory stimulation. The thesis based on these researches on taste and teeth was submitted in the spring of 1939 with the oral examination in June (6, 7, 9).

Upon returning to the United States, I accepted a postdoctoral fellowship at the Johnson Foundation for Medical Physics, originally founded by and then headed by Dr. Detlev W. Bronk. Included among the scientific workers were H. Keffer Hartline, Frank Brink, Martin Larrabee, and others of note with whom I did some work in biophysics (8, 10).

I had met Dr. Bronk earlier on one of his visits to the Cambridge laboratory. His and Adrian's early classical single unit recordings (1929) showed that individual motoneurons discharge repetitively and rhythmically in evoking muscle contractions. Increased contraction was associated with an increase in motoneuron frequency. Although I remained at the Johnson Foundation for only one year this was the beginning of a long friendship that was strengthened especially during the 1950s when Bronk was President of the National Academy of Science National Research Council, and when I served as Chairman of the NRC Division of Behavioral Sciences. Later I was to serve under him again at the Rockefeller University from 1965 to 1970, for the last five years of his presidency there. I went as a Vice President to help recruit a group of behavioral scientists and to develop a program of research and graduate education in that field. Bronk is thus another of the key figures in my scientific and professional life.

After that year at the Johnson Foundation, Professor Walter S. Hunter, the distinguished psychologist and early behaviorist, offered me a position at Brown University as an instructor. This appointment lasted only about a year and a half until the United States became involved in World War II.

The year 1939 marked the advance of the Nazis upon Poland and the low countries. After my orals at Cambridge I had returned home on the last normal trip of the great French liner *Normandy*. The political and military problems of that period were very much on the horizon. I wanted "to do something" and soon sought out Dr. Ross MacFarland at the Harvard Fatigue Laboratory. He was a physiological psychologist who had pioneered psychological research on high altitudes and in aircraft including piloting and training. I joined him and a group of civilian scientists at Pensacola Naval Air Station, where a battery of physiological, psychomotor, and psychological tests were to be administered to naval air cadets at the beginning of flight training. Most of us eventually joined the Naval Reserve and were in uniform by the middle of the following year as converts to applied science in aviation psychology (12) and/or physiology for the duration.

At the war's end, I, like the majority of academics, returned to the campus. I re-examined my thesis to see whether it still held promise for further exploration. Not only was there the specific question of sensory coding in taste, but also the classical conceptions of highly specific afferent nerve fibers in other senses which were under attack. Weddel (117) doubted the fixed specificity of cutaneous nerves and end organs. Wever and Bray (118) suggested that the temporal patterning of impulses of the auditory nerve might be the basis for pitch discrimination. The return to a modified specificity formulation in hearing was to take place later based upon single unit recording with microelectrodes by David, Galambos, and others and the physical measurement of von Békésy (84, 91).

I was to remain at Brown for over twenty years, beginning with Walter Hunter's firm yet wise and understanding chairmanship. He

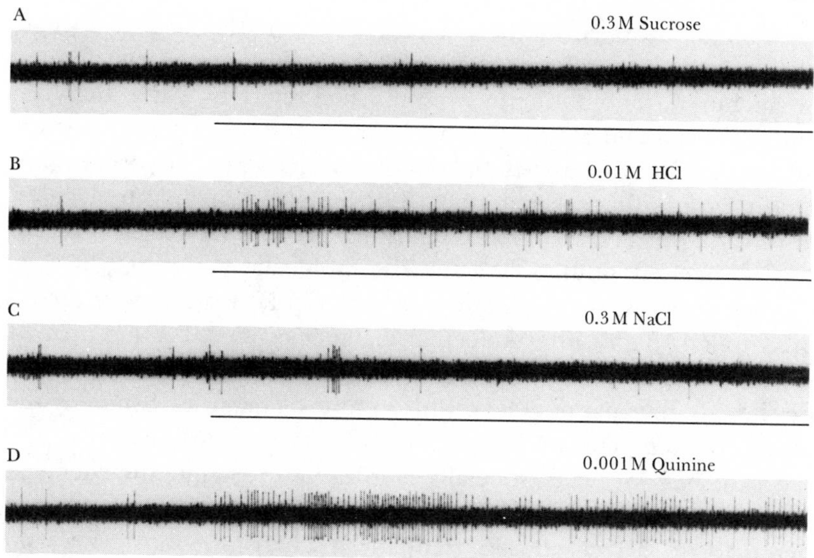

Figure 10.1. The electrophysiological response of one glossopharyngeal fiber to four stimuli. Four seconds of record is shown. The line beneath each record indicates application of the stimulus.

had spent the war years as Head of the Applied Psychology Panel under the National Defense Research Council where he administered an extensive program of behavioral and human factors research. As chairman of the department at Brown he supported and encouraged his junior staff, and I'm forever grateful for his support and sponsorship as a young academic reconverting to peacetime with my own program of academic research. He was another key figure in my professional development.

Progress on taste proved to be slow for a variety of reasons. For one thing a true sampling of individual taste receptors required long preparations with a wide array of stimuli of different intensities. It has taken many years, even down to the present time, for the ideal experiment to be realized. It was of great satisfaction to me, however, that as other investigators began to work on taste—Lloyd Beidler in the United States (82), Zotterman in Sweden (90), and M. Sato in Japan (110)—verification mounted on the fact of multiple sensitivity of single taste afferent nerve fibers in many species (18, 24). Figure 10.1 is a record from a recent study showing an acid-quinine fiber.

A major obstacle in the chemical senses is the lack of a single physical or chemical dimension to which the sensory metric may be anchored. One of the best established relations is that between hydrogen ion and sourness. The effectiveness of different acids is influenced by the associated anions which affect hydrogen ion binding on biological materials (83). Salts and organic molecules, however, give more complex relations. Recently sweetness receptor has been attributed to a specific molecular acceptor AB-A; A, the acceptor; B, the associated protein (114). Bitterness is attributed to a different intermolecular distance of an AB-A acceptor. It seems clear that the same single physicochemical parameter cannot be the effective parameter for different taste qualities. Studying the effect of temperature change of the taste solution or of the receptor has not been especially helpful in untangling the chemical character of taste stimulation. Although tongue and solution temperature do affect chorda tympani discharge (Abbott, 79, and Sato et al.), the changes may be attributed to modifications of the nerve, blood supply, or other factors. There is no simple Q_{10} relation* as in most chemical processes.

It is in this context that the electrophysiological study of the multiple sensitivity of single receptors is important. Erickson gave quantitative form (93, 94) to my earlier qualitative formulation (32) of across-fiber patterns. His across-fiber correlation analysis showed in population of units, how activation of any one receptor-fiber unit by one chemical correlates with the activation by other chemicals. In the rat, for example, sensitivities to sodium and to lithium salts are highly correlated; if sodium chloride stimulates a single fiber, lithium also stimulates. On the other hand, potassium chloride sensitivity is highly correlated with ammonium but not with sodium-lithium reactivity. There appear to be at least two classes of monovalent cation receptor: the sodium-lithium cluster, the ammonium-potassium cluster. A divalent ion, such as calcium, partially overlaps both. Such correlations also permit a type of factor analysis from which to derive a metric.

*Q_{10} is a common temperature coefficient and refers to change of rate of a chemical reaction with an increase of 10° Celsius. Most common chemical reactions have a Q_{10} on the order of 3. In most taste experiments the relation between taste and temperature is not monotonic except in a limited range.

Erickson (93) and his own students further showed that stimuli that are highly correlated physiologically are judged as similar by animals in behavior tests; they are difficult to discriminate from each other. Those that are uncorrelated (that is, stimulate quite different families of fibers) are more readily discriminated. Morrison (106) has also shown that Erickson's physiological model predicts the outcome of behavioral tests of generalization in more sophisticated preference tests. These results seem to me to justify the basic assumption of the across-fiber pattern theory, namely, that all the information of the entire afferent input is utilized for discrimination. The brain does not throw away information contained in the multiple sensitivity.

More recent experiments show that the specific receptors sensitive to only one of the four basic tastes make up about 25 per cent of the population of taste receptors, but the remainder show multiple sensitivity. Frank and Pfaffmann (64, 68) showed that in the rat the relative occurrence of units with one, two, three, or all four sensitivities, could be predicted from a simple probability formulation, assuming that sensitivity to each of the four basic tastes is independent of each other and showed random combination. Very recently microelectrode studies (98, 113) of impaled individual taste receptor cells have confirmed that individual taste cells themselves respond to one or more of the basic tastes. The relative occurrence of these sensitivities in the peripheral receptors fits the probab lity model. Thus the afferent nerve of the rat appears to reflect the multiple sensitivity within individual receptor cells of the taste bud.

Most recently Frank has made an extensive quantitative analysis of a large number of single taste fibers in the hamster. She ordered the stimuli sweet, salt, sour, and bitter (Sucrose, NaCl, HCl, and Quinine) and plotted frequency of firing for each fiber for all stimuli. Each fiber was assigned to one of these four basic categories by its best frequency. Seventy-six out of seventy-nine fibers peaked, that is, showed a highest frequency to one stimulus. The second highest responses always occurred to a stimulus or stimuli directly to the side of the best frequency when plotted in the above order. Figure 10.2 shows the response profiles of fibers so classified and indicates that there are three peaks of responses to sugar, to salt, and to acid. Little peaking of quinine appears in the

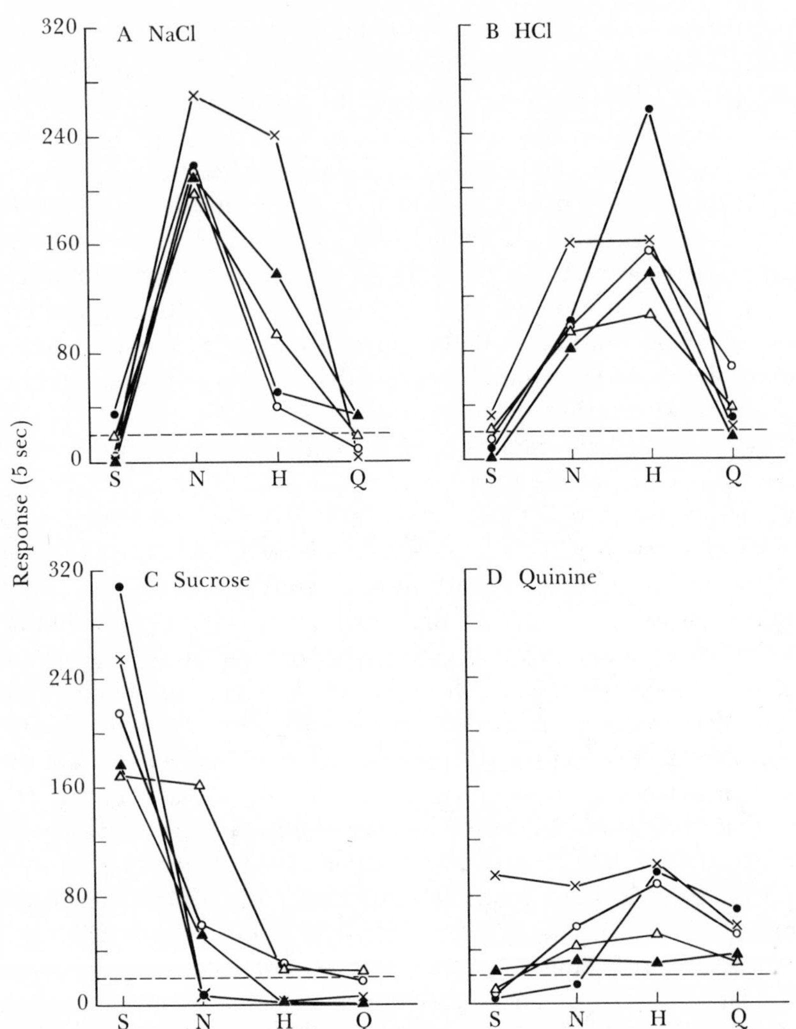

Figure 10.2. Response profiles across the basic tastes: 0.1 *M* sucrose (S), .03 *M* NaCl (N), .003 *M* HCl (H), and .001 *M* quinine hydrochloride (Q), of 20 hamster chorda tympani fibers.

hamster chorda tympani probably because of a paucity of quinine receptors.

Thus a labeled line "peaking" with side bands of sensitivity emerges from the across-fiber analysis. Specificity is not rigid or "all or none." This is a more sophisticated version of the coding mechanism which encompasses both specificity and across-fiber components not unlike that found in other sensory systems.

But what is the effect of the many anatomical branches of the taste nerve terminals as they approach and entwine among taste cells? In the rat (71, 116), taste fibers do in fact branch to innervate a receptor field composed of 4.5 (range 1 to 9) taste buds per fiber. Such branching does not account for the multiple sensitivity. Indeed, present evidence suggests that each fiber, whether of single or multiple sensitivity, tends to innervate cells of the taste bud with a similar sensitivity profile. Other cells of the taste bud with different sensitivity profiles, may be innervated by other fibers (109). It appears that the specificity resides in sites within the receptor cell but that the information clumped together as it funnels by way of the cells and their associated nerve fibers to the CNS. Further verification of this scheme was provided in experiments carried out by Dr. Bartoshuk (80) at my request on the gymnemic acid blockade of sugar sensitivity in the hamster, a species with good sugar sensitivity. Individual fibers examined before and after treatment with gymnemic acid show that it is only the sensitivity for the sugar that is blocked. Thus on a single fiber responding to salt and to sugar only the presumed terminal sugar site is affected, the fiber itself is not blocked and the salt sensitivity remains (65).

A new observation (72, 78a) showing that cross-adaptation yields the same relations as does the across-fiber-correlation does much to support such theorizing on multiple sensitivity. In the rat, sodium chloride flowed over the tongue produces an initial transient response followed by a steady state response (50, 56). Prior adaptation to NaCl itself eliminates or reduces the initial response only; the steady state is unaffected. Prior adaptation by another stimulus may have no effect, some effect, or completely eliminate the transient response, as in the case of sodium upon lithium salts. When the amount of such cross-adaptation is tabulated against the across-fiber correlation coefficients, there is nearly a perfect match, r = .92. Cross-adaptation is another measure then of across-fiber overlap or communality of stimulation.

McBurney and Bartoshuk's work (51) and that of their students on sensory adaptation have vastly advanced our knowledge of taste function. In McBurney's first study (48) he continuously rinsed the tongue with water or with various concentrations of salt. This gave evidence of an impressive degree of total adaptation in taste. Ambient salivary sodium, the normal background adaptation, elevated the threshold by 100 or more times above the level of water adaptation. Threshold elevation was proportional to concentration of the adaptant and was complete such that no sensation of saltiness remained. Earlier work by Dallenbach, v. Békésy, and others had shown some of these features.

Use of the magnitude estimate method of Stevens has been most important in clarifying taste adaptation. After adaptation, weaker subadapting concentration of NaCl elicited a contrasting sour-bitter taste quality which in very dilute salt solutions down to and including water seemed subjectively as strong as or stronger than the saltiness elicited by the adapter just prior to adaptation. Adaptation o other taste stimuli gave water a variety of other strong "after-tastes"—sweet, salty, or sour, or bitter—in a manner reminiscent of contrasting after images of color. The taste of water, therefore, reflects not only weak contaminants but the state of adaptation of the taste receptors before water is applied. These relations among taste are quite systematic and suggest a kind of "opponent process" mechanism for taste that is still being actively investigated in current experiments.

In terms of human sensitivity, of course, these issues question the classical conception of taste. Do the taste buds of man respond to one of the basic tastes, or to two or three or four in combination? v. Békésy (85) reported that most single taste buds possessed only one sensitivity which remained unchanged over time and that multiple sensitivity was rare. This is in contradiction to the earlier classic reports that all four qualities in any combination as well as singly were elicited by punctate stimulation of individual papillae in man. Recent attempts to replicate v. Békésy's results have confirmed the fact of stable multiple sensitivity of human fungiform papillae (McCutcheon (103), Harper et al. (96)).

Another important line of investigation that we have pursued concerns the taste pathways of the central nervous system. Although prior studies of CNS anatomy and function of taste had been made, the information was relatively sketchy and, in a number of instances, debatable. In the late 1940s and 1950s the evoked potential method came into widespread use as an aid to locating central pathways. It was obvious that the taste system needed study in this way, and a program of mapping taste from the periphery via the brainstem and thalamus to cortex was in order. One of my first students to use the evoked potential method was Robert M. Benjamin (25), who electrically stimulated the chorda tympani to outline a taste-receiving area on the orbital cortex of the rat. This then was ablated and the animal tested for changes in detection and preferences in behavioral tests. His studies ultimately identified the cortical and thalamic taste area. The defects in taste produced by thalamic lesions were more severe and longer lasting than those from cortical ablations. (See Burton and Benjamin (87) for up-to-date review.)

Frommer and Oakley (39, 43) added further details of the thalamic function. Studies of the solitary nucleus filled in the way station between the periphery and the thalamus in work by Halpern, Makous, Nord, and Erickson (47). In all of these experiments, the rationale was more or less the same, that is, to search by combined anatomical and physiological means for the cell body clusters and synaptic junctions of the receiving stations from the periphery to cortex. However, one point remained unclear until very recently, that is, the exact delineation of the pathway between a solitary nucleus and the thalamus. No clear thalamic degeneration had been reported from solitary nucleus lesions. Norgren and Leonard (108), in my laboratory at The Rockefeller University, discovered an ipsilateral synaptic relay in the pons between the solitary nucleus and thalamus. Above this locus there is partial decussation and thus a bilateral projection to the thalamus. Drs. R. Bernard and Nord, also in my laboratory, also found taste responses in the pons of the cat.

Such a pontine nucleus has added importance not merely because a new synaptic relay has been identified, but because this nucleus may give rise to parallel pathways to other parts of the brain, such as hypothalamus and/or limbic system. Indeed, degeneration has recently been traced from pontine lesions to the far lateral hypothalamus. Taste in the hypothalamus and limbic system presumably related to motivated behavior: to preferences and aversions and appetitive behavior generally. Here we see another success for the electrophysiological method combined, in this instance, with histology.

It should be clear that the most powerful attack on problems of neural organization comes from a combination of approaches. One is neuroanatomical, the oldest and most classical approach with the attendant use of lesion, degeneration, and histological procedures. Really careful analytical degeneration studies from small lesions are often possible only with the addition of electrophysiological localization to confirm that the electrode is in the right area. It is also possible to characterize functional differences in different parts of the nucleus or target area by the electrophysiological response. Having validated the position of electrode in a taste area, one can then make small lesions and study them with one of the Nauta methods to follow degenerating nerve fibers to their termination. To complete the understanding of these central nervous systems requires the third method, the behavioral one. This may take the form of simple preference tests or more elaborate behavioral techniques entailing operant or classical conditioning. The changes in the behavior give a clue both as to the discriminatory functions and the motivational properties of parts of the nervous system. Indeed it can be said that without behavioral study, hand in hand with physiological and anatomical methods, one gets only a partial insight; telling where! and to some degree how! but not for what!

Ever since the beginnings of my research on taste, I have followed the strategy of correlating physiology with behavior (28, 42). The widely employed summator method, introduced by Beidler, gives a good over-all measure of the frequency of firing in all the fibers. Figure 10.3 illustrates one such correlation between magnitude of the chorda tympani afferent nerve discharge and preference behavior. Different species show quite significant differences in taste sensitivity, and the across-species correlation with the standard two-bottle preference method is quite good (89). The correspondence between the electrophysiological input and behavior is not simple, however. In Figure 10.3, although the concentration values over which the physiology and behavior occur are in agreement, two of the neural discharge functions are associated with aversion responses and two with an initial preference followed by an apparent aversion at higher concentration. The fact that there are two different behaviors, approach on the one hand, aversion on the other, indicates that the total nerve response must

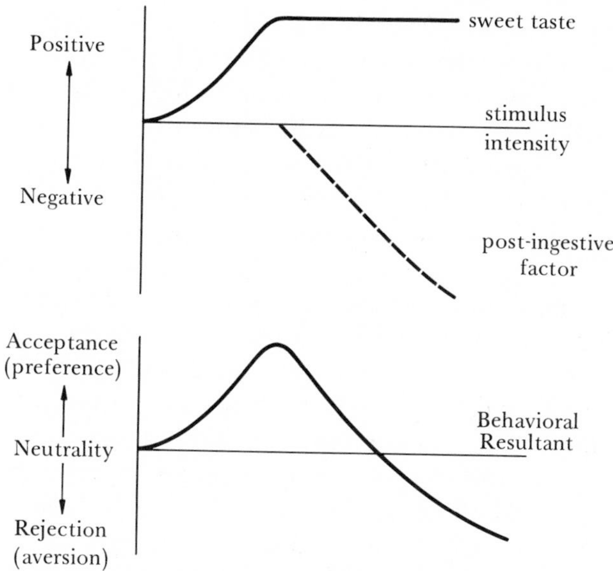

Figure 10.3. Hypothetical reconstruction of mechanisms underlying biphasic preference-aversion behavior. Reprinted by permission from *Reinforcement and Behavior,* Academic Press.

carry different qualitative information. The single fiber analysis previously discussed accounts for the difference in reaction to inputs with the same apparent electrophysiological magnitude.

In experiments employing lingual denervation there was a disappointingly small albeit perceptible effect upon both preferences and the aversion (17), presumably because of our inability to exclude all the taste sensory nerves and/or post ingestional information from the stomach. Bypassing taste with a chronic gastric intubation completely eliminates all preferences and aversions (86). The salt preference was later shown by Mook and others (104) to be very influenced by osmolarity of the stomach contents. With gastric intubation of high salt concentrations, the volume of fluid ingested by mouth increased even when either salt solutions or water was taken by mouth. From the large volume intake seen in the intact animals, salt preference appears to reflect a positive feedback between the stomach and mouth factors. For sweetening agents, on the other hand, the mouth factor appears to have a more direct influence pre-eminent over gastric factors so that intake correlates directly with the relative effectiveness of different sugars on the sensory nerve input. Indeed the ingestion pattern when taste is activated but only water enters the stomach in the behaving animal with an "electronic esophagus" directly mimics nerve input discharge for sucrose and glucose (31). Where behavior and taste afferent input diverge this divergence can be explained usually by the interaction of other factors we are now coming to recognize. The biphasic response curve for such attractive stimuli as sugar or salt leads to the theoretical formulations in Figure 10.3. "Sweet stimuli" (sugars) are positively attractive in their own right. The new-born organism finds the sweet taste attractive and its behavior may be reinforced or rewarded by its presentation (5). We found aversive stimuli to retain their aversiveness in spite of efforts to modify the response to this taste quality in early life (30). Indeed until recently, the hedonic value or attractiveness of taste stimuli seemed rather resistant to attempts to modify them by learning. Now the conditioned aversion technique has proved successful with the more drastic consequences of associating taste with nearly lethal poisoning or radiation trauma. Indeed a flip-flop of the hedonic value of stimuli has been achieved under experimental control so that pleasurable stimuli become aversive (95).

In addition to physiological factors which may dissociate the afferent input from behavior are other purely behavioral processes. For example, McCutcheon (102) preadapted rats to various solutions before they were confronted with these same solutions as preference stimuli. Account of both sensory adaptation and incentive contrast was necessary in order to explain the observed behavior. The responses to "sweeteners" (sugar) in the squirrel monkey are compelling both in the sensory nerve and at the behavioral level (57). One paradox here has attracted our attention. The different sugars show a clear quantitative seriation: fructose most effective, sucrose next, and glucose least in the chorda tympani nerve response. Other sugars were studied, but I shall restrict my discussion to these three. In preference or in reinforcing a bar-pressing response for a drop of solution, however, sucrose is most effective, fructose next, and glucose least. Our interpretation of this discrepancy is that the animal can distinguish not simply amount of afferent input (sweetness) but the quality of afferent input (kind of sweetener) by virtue of the relative across-fiber response pattern. Not all single fibers respond in precisely the same way to these different sugars, and it is on this basis that the animal may distinguish the kind as well as amount of sugar (59, 69, 71).

Most of our earlier work on humans had been concerned with the more traditional sensory psychophysical question of intensity scaling of sweetness (100) or how electrical stimulation of the tongue elicited taste sensation (111). Richard Warren and I (33) studied the effect of gymnemic acid (G. A.) as a specific blocker of sweet sensation for saccharin and sugar in man. The elevation of threshold is quantitatively related to the degree by which sweetness is weakened in suprathreshold solutions. One recent study with my old friend Professor Zoran Bujas of the University of Zagreb, utilized combined stimulation by electrical currents and application of gymnemic acid to the tongue. This agent blocked sweetness of saccharin solutions while the sweetness elicited by electrical stimulation still remained. The G.A. apparently blockades some intervening sensory step or process (76).

The study of hedonic effects in humans has been a much under-explored subject but one that holds great promise for better understanding the additional dimensions of human experience and determinants of behavior. In the experimental psychology laboratory, I have noted that it is much easier for naïve human observers to report on the pleasantness or unpleasantness of tastes or odors than to adopt a more analytical attitude to report on sensory quality per se. Hedonic value was often the first thing reported, the sensory quality often secondary.

Engen, McBurney, and I had studied the relation of hedonic judgment to sweet and salty stimuli in confirmation of the earlier classical work of Engel (92) (see Figure 10.4). We were able to divide our subjects into two groups, those who found increasing concentration of sugar increasingly pleasant and those who found them increasingly unpleasant. We reported on this only briefly in a symposium paper (41). The role of hedonic factors in behavior has been stressed from time to time by what were essentially lone voices calling them to our attention. Beebe-Center (81) and P. T. Young (119) were such champions. In what I consider one of my more important papers, "The Pleasures of Sensation" (38), I

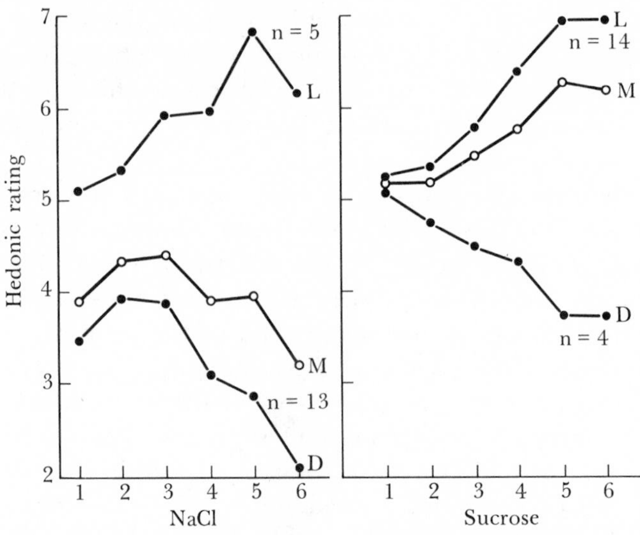

Figure 10.4. Average hedonic ratings of increasing concentrations of NaCl and sucrose on a nine point hedonic scale. M, average ratings for all 18 Ss; L, average curve for Ss liking the solution; D, average curve for Ss disliking the solution. (41)

joined the fray. Most recently a very important advance has been made by Cabanac (88), who has shown that the hedonic value of gustatory stimuli can be modified by the postingestive effects of glucose in the stomach. Hedonic ratings of sugar solutions upon repeated tasting without swallowing are more or less stable. Where sugars are ingested or stomach loaded, there was a significant shift in the hedonic rating toward the unpleasant side. Furthermore hedonic shifts were not unique to taste alone but occurred for olfactory experience and for thermal sensation, the latter in relation to internal body temperature. Pathologically obese individuals may show significant differences from normals in their hedonic ratings of taste.

At a much earlier period we had studied behavioral preferences of animals for taste solutions together with the effect of salt need upon these preferences. Indeed my first Ph.D., John K. Bare, and I studied the problem of whether or not sensory receptor processes in adrenalectomy were themselves associated with the greatly increased preference for salt solutions. We found no change in receptor sensitivity (13) and subsequently Nachman and I confirmed this in more detail (49). Hagstrom and I (26) were able to show that acutely lowered blood sugar had little effect on taste responses to sugar in the chorda tympani whereas gymnemic acid applied to the tongue surface did reduce chorda tympani activity to sugar. Thus I believe that so-called "sensory enhancement" observed in modified need or motivational states reflects a change in hedonic value, not a change in sensitivity per se. There still remains the possibility of changes in the efferent control of taste receptors which has been documented, but its possible role in motivated behavior needs further study.

Further insights into the role of taste in behavior have come from the studies of feeding in animals with lateral or ventromedial hypothalamic lesions. Both cases seem to show an enhancement of reactivity to taste stimuli, sometimes called "finickiness." In the lateral animal, taste appears to become especially important for eating and is possibly the main instigator. The ventromedially lesioned rat becomes hyperphagic and obese. But when it must bar press in order to deliver food directly into the stomach, it refuses to press the bar frequently enough to obtain sufficient food. A weak saccharin solution delivered into the animal's food cup at the same time that the liquid diet is delivered intragastrically transforms an apathetic starving animal into a vigorous hyperphagic. Teitelbaum (115) calls taste a "psychic energizer" that increases the urge to eat. When motivation for food is impaired, the pleasure provided by the taste of food is necessary for regulation. Here also there is no evidence for a change in sensory function (105). There is no lowering of threshold in preference tests, whereas the animal is hyper-reactive to suprathreshold stimuli. This can best be described as a multipler effect which enhances the stimuli once past the threshold. It would be possible to schematize these relations as in Figure 10.5.

There is thus a vast domain relating sensory processes to motivated behavior, hedonic effects, and activation of the hypothalamic and limbic system. This in a way has brought "the senses" back into psychology. During the last decade, the study of sensory mechanisms in psychology per se seemed in danger of neglect and disregard (41, 42, 52, 53).

The sense of olfaction plays an unusually important role ana-

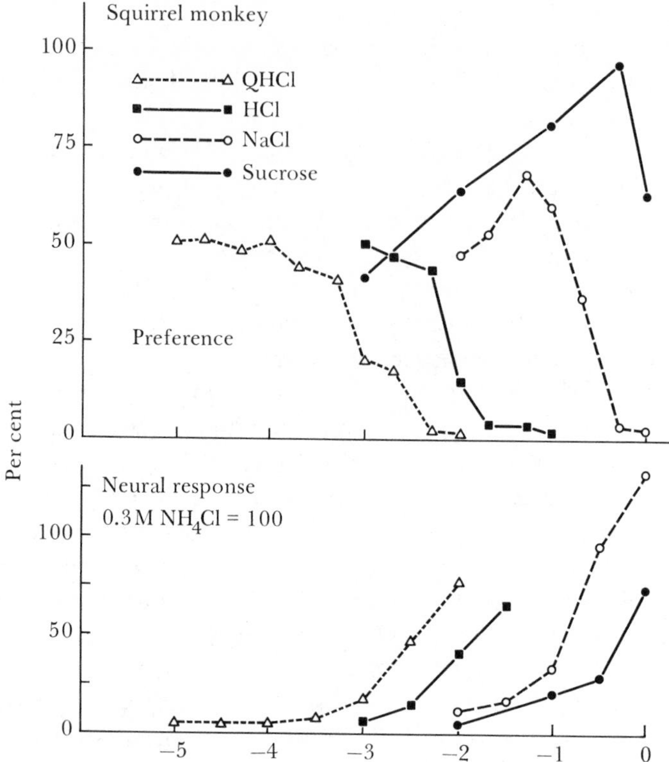

Figure 10.5. Comparison of neural responses of squirrel monkey chorda tympani nerve and 2-bottle preference behavior.

tomically and evolutionarily in relation to the hypothalamic and limbic structures. Far better known is the structural relationship of olfaction to the hypothalamus than the exact specification of its role in motivation. Certain behavior patterns as mating are of course highly controlled by olfaction in many different animal species. Earlier work seemed to emphasize the multiple sensory determinants of mating such that no one sense organ seemed predominant. This had the effect of underplaying the contribution that olfactory stimuli were later found to have on sex behavior. Heimer and Larsson's (97) quantitative analysis showed that the latency and frequencies of mounting on the part of the male were seriously affected by rendering the animal anosmic. Olfactory bulbectomy renders the male hamster essentially impotent (107).

This must be interpreted with some caution because the olfactory bulb has a large afferent, efferent, and interneuronal interconnection with the basal brain structures over and above its sensory input. Nevertheless the role of olfaction in mating behavior is becoming more and more clear (77).

Over the years several of my students and colleagues and I have examined the behavioral and physiological aspects of olfaction. Engen and I (35, 37) examined the judgment of odor quality and odor quantity in the human observer using information concepts. The practiced subject can transmit two bits of information about odor intensity, but four bits for odor quality. The greater capacity for odor quality was expected but we were surprised it was not greater in view of the range and variety of odor qualities reported by man anecdotally. Mozell (22) and Mathews (101) analyzed the patterns of stimulation in the olfactory bulb and mitral cells. Goff, Bare, and I (29) developed an olfactometer for behavioral measurements of olfactory thresholds using operant conditioning methods. With Carr and Solberg (45), we used this device to determine whether the olfactory sensitivity of the male rat to the odor of an estrus female was modified by removal of testosterone by castration. No loss was observed when the odor was used as a conditioned stimulus in spite of the fact that the normal male's attraction to the female is essentially eliminated after castration. More recently Don Pfaff and I (63, 67) turned to such issues using physiological recordings in olfactory bulb and preoptic area of the diencephalon. We found that direct infusion of the sex hormone, testosterone, could affect neurons of the olfactory system, but we do not know yet whether this is a specific or nonspecific effect. More interesting was the discovery that preoptic neurons appear to differentiate better between biological odors, that is, estrus versus nonestrus urine, than between arbitrarily chosen nonbiological chemicals. This selective responsivity (which Pfaff refers to as sharpening) is not affected by castration or by glandular state of the organism. We interpret this to mean that the hormone's effect on behavior occurs closer to the motor outflow than to the sensory input. Much more work on this vein is, of course, needed. In particular we should re-examine the significance of the olfacto-hypothalamic pathway in the lateral hypothalamus that Scott and I (61) found in electrophysiological confirmation of prior anatomical evidence. Added to this is the increasing evidence of the role of odor pheromones in many species produced by special glands which are important to sexual mating activity (112) as an aspect of their signalling and communicative role in social behavior.

I must say that I am somewhat amused by the editor's wording of one of his questions: "What significant question or questions do you raise before you hurl yourself into the details of an experimental investigation?" I find it hard to imagine "hurling myself" at this day and age. I tend to approach matters in a somewhat more measured way. I now also depend to a greater degree than formerly upon the collaborative work with younger colleagues who have less interference from administrative and other demands and distractions (44, 55, 58, 60).

This change was enhanced perhaps by my move from Brown University to The Rockefeller University where I assumed additional duties as a Vice President. On the other hand, the unique character of Rockefeller as a purely graduate university with a relatively small number of graduate students makes research a way of life. As the former Rockefeller Institute for Medical Research, the tradition for research, magnificent support facilities, relatively small size, as is a minimum of administrative detail make it ideal for research.

The editor's query of what questions are raised before we undertake an experiment can be best illustrated by a recent case history. One of my most recent students, indeed my first Rockefeller Ph.D., Robert Johnston, now Assistant Professor at Cornell University, expressed an interest in olfactory communication in mammals. As a possible thesis problem, he elected to study "scent marking," by which many organisms deposit the product of their odor producing glands.

There is a wide literature on the anatomical side, with somewhat less analytical behavior study. As a starter, Johnston reviewed this literature with several requirements in mind; an animal should be of convenient size and adaptable to the laboratory; it should have an identifiable gland and specific marking behavior. One species, the golden hamster, seemed ideal, but we didn't choose this just because it was present in the animal colony. It was a specific selection. The first task was to determine the situations which elicited scent marking. Having outlined the general problem, having selected the animal, he set about testing animals. A clean cage and its own home cage stimulated little scent marking, but one containing the scent of another prior inhabitant male was very effective. The scent of a female (female absent at test) elicited a cyclic pattern of flank marking by the male, which was least on the estrus day, most on anestrus days. Johnston then made an extensive and elegant study of the hormonal and social factors that influenced scent marking of both males and females. Of course he uncovered a number of phenomena that were not anticipated. An important principle in research is a certain open-mindedness to be "prepared for the unusual and unexpected."

In concentrating upon research and research issues I have followed the editor's guide lines. However, no account of an academic and research career would be complete without at least mentioning the teaching of psychology—especially physiological psychology, with which I have been actively and pleasurably engaged for over thirty years. I've enjoyed teaching at all levels, undergraduate introductory and advanced courses and graduate seminars. Even though at Brown University elementary psychology courses tended to be large lecture sections, they rarely exceeded 100 students in size. All faculty members took a hand at introductory courses as part of a tradition where everybody taught both undergraduate and graduate students. Like many another faculty member I became disenchanted with the usual textbook approach to the beginning course. A new, campus-wide approach to instruction was carried out at Brown in 1954 under the rubric "the identification and criticism of ideas." Small sections of no greater than twenty freshmen, sophomores, and some upperclassmen met for discussion of assigned readings. Although textbooks were to be discarded, some crept back into use. Harold Schlosberg and I developed a course around the theme "Psychology as the Science of Behavior," beginning naturally enough with Pavlov's original lectures on conditioned reflexes. Then followed Skinner's *Science and Human Behavior,* supplemented by Keller and Schoenfeld's text plus additional classics from the history of psychology. Harold Schlosberg carried the first semester, I took the second. We began with Freud's *Introduction to Psychoanalysis,* then some Adler and Jung, followed by the neo-Freudians. The shock effect was something to behold as we struggled with psychoanalysis after the initial behavioral orientation. I accused the class of having suffered a behavioristic "brainwash." I had to read long and hard in a literature with which I had little prior acquaintance. The denouement came in the middle to latter part of the semester with Miller and Dollard's approach to learning theory and psychoanalysis and Hilgard's and other writing on psychoanalysis as science. In presenting these attempted integrations, I strove not for their acceptance as a final answer but as examples of efforts to bridge and to understand an important domain of science as applied to man. This course proved to be intellectually exciting for me, and I think for the students. Because of the great student demand, extra sections were required, more faculty members hired for that purpose, more formal organization, until, of course, success spelled the doom of the whole enterprise. Still it was a great intellectual adventure and contained the guise of the only way I would want to approach introductory psychology again (27). Over the years I had also developed several laboratory teaching aids (11, 34), which was a fun outlet for my gadgeteering tendencies. It was in advanced courses in physiological psychology where I could relate my own research studies more directly to course content and teaching. Teaching was an integral part of my scientific "life of the mind."

I also have not said much about our occasional forays into research with a more applied orientation (16, 19, 20, 21, 23). Taste and olfaction have many applications in food research and in flavor acceptance and in dental and oral physiology. I was amused to see how often food technologists, employing psychophysical and psychometric methods, often of their own design, have rediscovered basic laws of psychophysics. The time error was ever a classic for rediscovery.

I think it should be clear that my approach to scientific research tends to be empirical fact finding set in a loosely theoretical framework. Predictions of outcome and system building with tightly knit formulations is not my style. Over-all there have been four main themes in my work: (1) the basis of sensation and the afferent code for taste and odor; (2) the physiology and anatomy of the central nervous system pathways and nuclei for taste and olfaction; (3) the behavioral mechanisms and correlates of taste and olfaction; and (4) the study of taste and olfaction as model systems for the study of motivated behavior, its sensory determinants, and the "pleasures of sensation."

I have come to the belief, strengthened in recent years by my experience in physiological psychology, that system building, except in a limited way, is somewhat premature and perhaps downright foolhardy. The empirical base from which psychology takes off even after all these years of investigation is still not broad enough or scientifically well established. I think that, for example, many of the questions asked of a typical "learning" point of view just do not make much sense in a total biological framework. The organism is not just a physiological behavioral machine, it is an adapting organism with a long history of evolution. Recent experiments on "bait shyness," for example, show that the so-called general laws of learning, especially their temporal characteristics, do not extrapolate to all situations (95).

This brings me to my concluding thoughts, namely, the mammoth conceptual task ahead for behavior theory. In this I do not imply simply psychological theory alone but behavior theory broadly conceived as related to many different approaches addressed to the study of behavior. I know best the biological side of the study of behavior in the laboratory. The field study, ethological approach has come to reveal many new insights and given "meaning" to behavior patterns and their environmental and ecological determinants. The emphasis upon adaptiveness of behavior, its evolutionary roots and genetic determinants raise issues that for many years were excluded almost by fiat from the psychologist's concern. Lorenz (99) has objected that the study of the species-specific behaviors that make a dog a dog, a cat a cat, a rat a rat were submerged in the search for the commonalities of learning and conditioning. The search for commonalities of behavior, of learning and adaptation, is the path of science along which psychologists have pushed with diligence and vigor but often almost too exclusively. In doing so, psychologists have felt more at home with the analytical approach of such disciplines as anatomy, neurophysiology, and neuroendocrinology. The maze, conditioning stand or Skinner box, fits the laboratory style of this scientific paradigm. The genetic-environmental clash often seen in ethologist-learning psychologist confrontation is not so apparent between physiologists and psychologists because both share a common concern for the machinery of the organism. Cats, dogs, rats, and other domesticated species are well adapted to the laboratory by generations of selective breeding. Such animals as monkeys and other primates are often preadapted to the laboratory before work begins.

Combining just the three approaches, physiological, ethological, and psychological, into building a unified behavior theory is yet to be achieved, even though attempts to integrate these points of view are being made (70). When one adds the facts of human psychology, perception and cognition, and the ontogenetic, clinical, personality, social and cultural domains, the intellectual task of constructing a unified comprehensive theory seems staggering. Biological science in general, it seems to me, has achieved such a unity by way of the concept of evolution. The broad domain includes molecular biology, genetics, physiology, neurobiology. The treatment of behavioral biology is wanting in some aspects. In behavior theory it is at the individual organismic level especially on adaptive functioning by way of new learning that a major problem arises. Man shares much of the machinery of vertebrates, often the same sense organs (but not always), a similar ground plan of nervous system and hormones, and many similar functions physiologically and behaviorally. Determining the proper balance of interactions of genome with experience, that is, solving the old heredity-environment problem, still eludes us. Until this can be better understood, if not settled, the groundwork for a unified theory of all behavior, animal and human, will continue to be tenuous. The organism as a whole, the brain as a computer, feedback system analysis, computer simulation, all promise to give better tools and methods of study, but as models of behaving organisms these still fail to give the key to the unity we as scientists ultimately hope for.

REFERENCES

The author's bibliography contains over a hundred items. This reference list gives only the major scientific articles on the various research items reviewed in the text. In addition, a series of handbook review chapters and symposium volumes, the most relevant to the subject of this review are cited: 14, 15, 36, 40, 49a, 53, 62, 73, 74, 75, 78.

1. Pfaffmann, C. An experimental comparison of the method of single stimuli and the method of constant stimuli in gustation. *American Journal of Psychology, 48,* 1935, 470–476.
2. Pfaffmann, C. Apparatus and technique for gustatory experimentation. *Journal of Genetic Psychology, 12,* 1935, 446–447.
3. Pfaffmann, C., and Jasper, H. H. Sensory discharges in cutaneous nerve fibers following chemical stimulation. *Psychological Bulletin, 32,* 1935, 565–566.
4. Pfaffmann, C., and Schlosberg, H. The conditioned knee jerk in psychotic and normal individuals. *Journal of Psychology, 1,* 1936, 201–206.
5. Pfaffmann, C. Differential responses of the new-born cat to gustatory stimuli. *Journal of Genetic Psychology, 49,* 1936, 61–67.
6. Pfaffmann, C. Afferent impulses from the teeth due to pressure and noxious stimulation. *Journal of Physiology, 97,* 1939, 207–219.
7. Pfaffmann, C. Afferent impulses from the teeth resulting from a vibratory stimulus. *Journal of Physiology, 97,* 1939, 220–232.
8. Pfaffmann, C. Potentials in the isolated medullated axon. *Journal of Cellular and Comparative Physiology, 16,* 1940, 1–4.
9. Pfaffmann, C. Gustatory afferent impulses. *Journal of Cellular and Comparative Physiology, 17,* 1941, 243–258.
10. Pfaffmann, C., and Aird, R. B. Pressure stimulation of peripheral nerves. *Proceedings of the Society for Experimental Biology and Medicine, 66,* 1947, 130–132.
11. Pfaffmann, C. A multiple cubicle-bench for the student laboratory. *American Psychologist, 2,* 1947, 559–560.
12. Pfaffmann, C. Aircraft landings without binocular cues: A study based upon observations made in flight. *American Journal of Psychology, 61,* 1948, 323–334.
13. Pfaffmann, C., and Bare, J. K. Gustatory nerve discharges in normal and adrenalectomized rats. *Journal of Comparative Physiological Psychology, 43,* 1950, 320–324.
14. Pfaffmann, C. Taste: A monitor of diet? *Research Reviews,* Aug. 1951, 16–21.
15. Pfaffmann, C. Taste and smell. In S. S. Stevens (ed.), *Handbook of Experimental Psychology.* New York: Wiley, 1951, 1143–1171, Chap. 29.
16. Manly, R. S., Pfaffmann, C., Lathrop, D. D., and Keyser, Joan. Oral sensory thresholds of persons with natural and artificial dentitions. *Journal of Dental Research, 31,* 1952, 305–312.
17. Pfaffmann, C. Taste preference and aversion following lingual denervation. *Journal of Comparative Physiological Psychology, 45,* 1952, 393–400.
18. Pfaffmann, C. Species difference in taste sensitivity. *Science, 117,* 1953, 470.

19. Giddon, D. B., Dreisbach, M. E., Pfaffmann, C., and Manly, R. S. Relative abilities of natural and artificial dentition patients for judging the sweetness of solid foods. *Journal of Prosthetic Dentistry, 4,* 1954, 263–268.
20. Schlosberg, H., Pfaffmann, C., Cornsweet, Janet, and Pierrel, R. Selection and training of panels. In *Food Acceptance Testing Methodology.* Washington, D. C.: National Research Council, Advisory Board on Quartermaster Research, 1954, 45–54.
21. Pfaffmann, C. Variables affecting difference tests. In *Food Acceptance Testing Methodology.* Washington, D. C.: National Research Council Advisory Board on Quartermaster Research, 1954, 4–17.
22. Mozell, M. M., and Pfaffmann, C. The afferent neural processes in odor perception. *Annals of the New York Academy of Science, 58,* 1954, 96–108.
23. Pfaffmann, C., Young, P. T., Dethier, V. G., Richter, C. P., and Stellar E. The preparation of solutions for research in chemoreception and food acceptance. *Journal of Comparative Physiological Psychology, 47,* 1954, 93–96.
24. Pfaffmann, C. Gustatory nerve impulses in rat, cat and rabbit. *Journal of Neurophysiology, 18,* 1955, 429–440.
25. Benjamin, R. M., and Pfaffmann, C. Cortical localization of taste in albino rat. *Journal of Neurophysiology, 18,* 1955, 56–64.
26. Pfaffmann, C., and Hagstrom, E. C. Factors influencing taste sensitivity to sugar. *American Journal of Physiology, 183,* 1955, 651 (Abstract).
27. Pfaffmann, C., and Schlosberg, H. The identification and criticism of ideas: A new approach to the introductory course in psychology. *American Psychologist, 11,* 1956, 78–83.
28. Pfaffmann, C. Taste mechanisms in preference behavior. *American Journal of Clinical Nutrition, 5,* 1957, 142–147.
29. Pfaffmann, C., Goff, W. R., and Bare, J. K. An olfactometer for the rat. *Science, 128,* 1958, 1007–1008.
30. Warren, R. P., and Pfaffmann, C. Early experience and taste aversion. *Journal of Comparative Physiological Psychology, 52,* 1958, 263–266.
31. Hagstrom, E. C., and Pfaffmann, C. The relative taste effectiveness of different sugars for the rat. *Journal of Comparative Physiological Psychology, 52,* 1959, 259–262.
32. Pfaffmann, C. The afferent code for sensory quality. *American Psychologist, 14,* 1959, 226–232.
33. Warren, R. M., and Pfaffmann, C. Suppression of sweet sensitivity by potassium gymnemate. *Journal of Applied Psychology, 14,* 1959, 40–42.
34. Church, R. M. and Pfaffmann, C. A respondent-conditioning apparatus for the student laboratory. *American Journal of Psychology, 72,* 1959, 267–270.
35. Engen, T., and Pfaffmann, C. Absolute judgments of odor intensity. *Journal of Experimental Psychology, 58,* 1959, 23–26.

36. Pfaffmann, C. The sense of taste. In *Handbook of Physiology*, Vol. 1, Sec. 1, *Neurophysiology*. Baltimore, Md.: Williams & Wilkins, 1959, 507–533, Chap. 20.
37. Engen, T., and Pfaffmann, C. Absolute judgments of odor quality. *Journal of Experimental Psychology, 59,* 1960, 214–219.
38. Pfaffmann, C. The pleasures of sensation. *Psychological Review, 67,* 1960, 253–268.
39. Pfaffmann, C., Erickson, R. P., Frommer, G. P., and Halpern, B. P. Gustatory discharges in the rat medulla and thalamus. In W. A. Rosenblith (ed.), *Sensory Communication*. New York: Wiley, 1961, 455–473.
40. Pfaffmann, C. Smell and Taste. In *Encyclopaedia Britannica,* Vol. 20. Chicago: Encyclopaedia Britannica Press, 1961, 819–823.
41. Pfaffmann, C. The sensory and motivating properties of the sense of taste. In M. R. Jones (ed.), *Nebraska Symposium on Motivation,* 1961. Lincoln: University of Nebraska Press, 1961, 71–108.
42. Pfaffmann, C. Sensory processes and their relation to behavior. In S. Koch (ed.), *Psychology: A Study of a Science*. Vol. 4: *Biologically Oriented Fields: Their Place in Psychology and in Biological Sciences.* New York: McGraw-Hill, 1962, 380–416.
43. Oakley, B., and Pfaffmann, C. Electrophysiologically monitored lesions in the gustatory thalamic relay of the albino rat. *Journal of Comparative Physiological Psychology, 55,* 1962, 155–160.
44. Miller, N., Pfaffmann, C., and Schlosberg, H. Aspects of psychology and psychophysiology in the U.S.S.R. In R. Bauer (ed.), *Some Views on Soviet Psychology*. Washington, D. C.: American Psychological Association, 1962, 189–252, Chap. 7.
45. Carr, W. J., Solberg, B., and Pfaffmann, C. The olfactory threshold for estrous female urine in normal and castrated male rats. *Journal of Comparative Physiological Psychology, 55,* 1962, 415–417.
46. Pfaffmann, C. Taste stimulation and preference behavior. In Y. Zotterman (ed.), *Olfaction and Taste*. Oxford: Pergamon Press, 1963, 257–273.
47. Makous, W., Nord, S., Oakley, B., and Pfaffmann, C. The gustatory relay in the medulla. In Y. Zotterman (ed.), *Olfaction and Taste.* Oxford: Pergamon Press, 1963, 381–393.
48. McBurney, D. H., and Pfaffmann, C. Gustatory adaptation to saliva and sodium chloride. *Journal of Experimental Psychology, 65,* 1963, 523–529.
49. Nachman, M., and Pfaffmann, C. Gustatory nerve discharge in normal and sodium-deficient rats. *Journal of Comparative Physiological Psychology, 56,* 1963, 1007–1011.
49a. Pfaffmann, C. Discussion: On the code for gustatory sensory quality. In R. W. Gerard (ed.), *Information Processing in the Nervous System.* Amsterdam: *Excerpta Medica International Congress Series No. 49,* 1964, 273–279.

50. Pfaffmann, C., and Powers, J. B. Partial adaptation of taste. *Psychonomic Science, 1,* 1964, 41–42.
51. Bartoshuk, L. M., McBurney, D. H., and Pfaffmann, C. Taste of sodium chloride solutions after adaptation to sodium chloride: Implications for the "water taste." *Science, 143,* 1964, 967–968.
52. Pfaffmann, C. Taste, Its sensory and motivating properties. *American Scientist, 52,* 1964, 187–206.
53. Pfaffmann, C. De Gustibus. *American Psychologist, 20,* 1965, 21–33.
54. Pfaffmann, C. Harold Schlosberg (1904–1964). *American Journal of Psychology, 78,* 1965, 148–152.
55. Pfaffmann, C. Behavioral Sciences, *Basic Research and National Goals, A Report to the Committee on Science and Astronautics.* U. S. House of Representatives, by the National Academy of Sciences, 1965.
56. Pfaffmann, C. L'Adaptation Gustative, *Extrait des Actualités Neurophysiologiques,* Sixth Series, 1965.
57. Fisher, G. L., Pfaffmann, C., and Brown E. Dulcin and saccharin taste in squirrel monkeys, rats, and men. *Science, 150,* 1965, 506–507.
58. Pfaffmann, Carl. The modern study of behavior. In *The Future of Biology.* A symposium sponsored by The Rockefeller University and State University of New York, November 1965, 42–48.
59. Pfaffmann, C., Fisher, G., and Frank, Marion. The sensory and behavioral factors in taste preference. In *Olfaction and Taste,* Vol. II, T. Hayaski (ed.). Oxford: Pergamon Press, 1967, 361–381.
60. Pfaffmann, Carl. Statement before the Subcommittee on Government Research, Committee on Government Operations, United States Senate. *American Psychologist, 22,* 1967, 205–210.
61. Scott, John, and Pfaffmann, C. Olfactory input to the hypothalamus: Electrophysiological evidence. *Science, 158,* 1967, 1592–1594.
62. Pfaffmann, Carl (ed.). *Olfaction and Taste,* Vol. III. New York: Rockefeller University Press, 1969.
63. Pfaff, Donald W., and Pfaffmann, C. Behavioral and electrophysiological responses of male rats to female rat urine odors. In *Olfaction and Taste,* Vol. III, C. Pfaffmann (ed.). New York: Rockefeller University Press, 1969, 258–267.
64. Frank, Marion, and Pfaffmann, C. The distribution of taste sensitivities among single taste fibers. In *Olfaction and Taste,* Vol. III, C. Pfaffmann (ed.). New York: Rockefeller University Press, 1969, 488–491.
65. Pfaffmann, C. Summary of taste roundtable. In *Olfaction and Taste,* Vol. III, C. Pfaffmann (ed.). New York: Rockefeller University Press, 1969, 527–532.
66. Pfaffmann, C. Summary of olfaction roundtable. In *Olfaction and Taste,* Vol. III, C. Pfaffmann (ed.). New York: Rockefeller University Press, 1969, 226–231.
67. Pfaff, Donald W., and Pfaffmann, C. Olfactory and hormonal influences on the basal forebrain of the male rat. *Brain Research, 15,* 1969, 137–156.

68. Frank, M., and Pfaffmann, C. Taste nerve fibers: A random distribution of sensitivities to four tastes. *Science, 164,* 1969, 1183–1185.

69. Pfaffmann, C. Taste preference and reinforcement. In *Reinforcement and Behavior,* J. Tapp (ed.). New York: Academic Press, 1969, 215–240.

70. Pfaffmann, C. The behavioral science model. *American Psychologist, 25,* #5, May 1970, 437–441.

71. Pfaffmann, C. Physiological and behavioural processes of the sense of taste. In *Ciba Foundation Symposium on Taste and Smell in Vetebrates,* G. E. Wolstenholme and Julie Knight (eds.). London: J. & A. Churchill, 1970, 31–50.

72. Smith, David V., Frank, Marion, and Pfaffmann, Carl. Cross adaptation between salts in the chorda tympani nerve of the rat. *Psychonomic Science, 21,* No. 5, 1970, 281 (Abstract).

73. Pfaffmann, Carl. Taste (human). In *McGraw-Hill Encyclopedia of Science and Technology,* 3rd ed., 1971, 422–424.

74. Pfaffmann, Carl. Smell. In *McGraw-Hill Encyclopedia of Science and Technology,* 3rd ed., 1971, 435–437.

75. Pfaffmann, Carl. Sense, chemical. In *McGraw-Hill Encyclopedia of Science and Technology,* 3rd ed., 1971, 227.

76. Bujas, Zoran, and Pfaffmann, C. Potassium gymnemate and the sweet and bitter taste provoked electrically. *Perception & Psychophysics, 10(1),* 1971, 28–29.

77. Pfaffmann, C. Sensory reception of olfactory cues. *Biology of Reproduction, 4,* 1971, 327–343.

78. Pfaffmann, C., Bartoshuk, L., and McBurney, D. Taste psychophysics. In *Handbook of Sensory Physiology,* Vol. IV: *Chemical Senses,* Part 2, Lloyd M. Beidler (ed.), Berlin, Heidelberg, New York: Springer-Verlag, 1971, 75–101.

78a. Frank, M., Smith, D., and Pfaffmann C. Cross adaptation between salts in the rat's chroda tympani response. (Paper presented at International Symposium on Oral Physiology, Stockholm, August 1971.)

Other References Cited

79. Abbott, P. The effect of temperature on taste in the white rat. Unpublished Ph.D. thesis, Brown University, 1953.

80. Bartoshuk, L. Unpublished. (Cited in Pfaffmann, C., No. 65.)

81. Beebe-Center, J. G. Feeling and emotion. In *Theoretical Foundations of Psychology,* H. Helson (ed.). New York: Van Nostrand, 1951, 254–317.

82. Beidler, L. M., Fishman, I. Y., and Hardiman, C. W. Species differences in taste responses. *American Journal of Physiology, 181,* 1955, 235–239.

83. Beidler, L. M. Taste receptor stimulation with salts and acids. In *Handbook of Sensory Physiology,* Vol. IV, *Chemical Senses 2, Taste,* L.

M. Beidler (ed.). Berlin, Heidelberg, New York: Springer-Verlag, 1971, Chap. 11.

84. v. Békésy, G. *Experiments in Hearing.* (Translated and edited by E. F. Wever.) New York: McGraw-Hill, Inc., 1960.

85. v. Békésy, G. Taste theories and the chemical stimulation of single papilla. *Journal of Applied Physiology, 19,* 1966, 1–9.

86. Borer, K. Disappearance of preferences and aversions for sapid solutions in rat ingesting untasted fluids. *Journal of Comparative Physiological Psychology, 65,* 1968, 213–221.

87. Burton, H., and Benjamin, R. M. Central projections of the gustatory system. In *Handbook of Sensory Physiology,* Vol. IV, *Chemical Senses 2, Taste,* L. M. Beidler (ed.). Berlin, Heidelberg, New York: Springer-Verlag, 1971, Chap. 8.

88. Cabanac, M. Physiological role of pleasure. *Science, 173,* 1971, 1103–1107.

89. Carpenter, J. A. Species differences in taste preferences. *Journal of Comparative Physiological Psychology, 49,* 1956, 139–144.

90. Cohen, M. J., Hagiwara, S., and Zotterman, Y. The response spectrums of taste fibers in the cat: A single fiber analysis. *Acta Physiologica Scandinavica, 33,* 1955, 316–332.

91. Davis, H. Excitation of auditory receptors. In *Handbook of Physiology,* Vol. I, Sect. 1. American Physiological Society, 1959, Chap. 23.

92. Engel, R. Experimentelle Untersuchungen über die Abhängigkeit der Lust und Unlust von der Reizstärke beim Geschmackssinn. *Archiv Für die gesamte Psychologie, 64,* 1928, 1–36.

93. Erickson, R. P. Sensory neural patterns and gustation. In *Olfaction and Taste,* Vol. I, Y. Zotterman (ed.). Oxford: Pergamon Press, 1963.

94. Erickson, R. P., Doetsch, G. S., and Marshall, D. A. The gustatory neural response function. *Journal of General Physiology, 49,* 1965, 247–263.

95. Garcia, J., and Koelling, R. A. Learning with prolonged delay of reinforcement. *Psychonomic Science, 5,* 1966, 121–122.

96. Harper, H. W., Jay, J. R., Erickson, R. P. Chemically evoked sensations from single human taste papilla. *Physiological Behavior, I,* 1966, 319–325.

97. Heimer, L., and Larsson, K. Mating behavior of male rats after olfactory bulb lesions. *Physiological Behavior, 2,* 1967, 207–209.

98. Kimura, K., and Beidler, L. M. Microelectrode study of taste receptors of rat and hamster. *Journal of Cellular and Comparative Physiology, 58,* 1961, 131–139.

99. Lorenz, Konrad. Is descriptive natural science dispensible? Invited lecture. International Congress of Physiology, Munich, 1971.

100. MacLeod, S. A construction and attempted validation of sensory sweetness scale. *Journal of Experimental Psychology, 44,* 1952, 316–323.

101. Mathews, D. F. Response of patterns of single units in the olfactory bulb of the unanesthetized, curarized rat to air and odor. Unpublished Ph.D. dissertation, Brown University, 1966.

102. McCutcheon, N. Sensory adaptation and incentive contrast as factors affecting NaCl preference. *Physiology & Behavior, Vol. 6*, 1971, 675–680.

103. McCutcheon, N. B., and Saunders, J. Human taste papilla stimulation: Stability of quality judgments over time. *Science, 175*, 1972, 214–216.

104. Mook, D. G. Oral and postingestional determinants of the intake of various solutions in rats with esophageal fistulas. *Journal of Comparative Physiological Psychology, 56*, 1963, 645–659.

105. Mook, D. G., and Blass, E. M. Quinine aversion thresholds and finickiness in hyperphagic rats. *Journal of Comparative Physiological Psychology, 65*, 1968, 202–207.

106. Morrison, G. R. Taste psychophysics in animals. In *Olfaction and Taste*, Vol. III, C. Pfaffmann (ed.). New York: Rockefeller University Press, 1969.

107. Murphy, M. R., and Schneider, C. E. Olfactory bulb removal eliminates mating behavior in the male golden hamster. *Science, 167*, 1970, 302–304.

108. Norgren, R., and Leonard, C. M. Taste pathways in rat brainstem. *Science, 173*, 1971, 1136–1139.

109. Oakley, B. Altered taste responses from cross-regenerated taste nerves in rat. In *Olfaction and Taste*, Vol. II, T. Hayaski (ed.). Oxford: Pergamon Press, 1967.

110. Ogawa, H., Sato, M., and Yamashita, S. Multiple sensitivity of chorda tympani fibers of the rat and hamster to gustatory and thermal stimuli. *Journal of Physiology* (London), *199*, 1968, 223–240.

111. Pierrel, R. Taste effects resulting from intermittent electrical stimulation of the tongue. *Journal of Experimental Psychology, 49*, 1955, 374–380.

112. Ralls, K. Mammalian scent marking. *Science, 171*, 1971, 443–449.

113. Sato, M., and Ozeki, M. Transduction of stimuli into electrical events at the gustatory cell membrane in the rat fungiform papillae. In *Olfaction and Taste*, Vol. IV, D. Schneider (ed.), Stuttgart, Wissenschaftliche Verlagsgesellschaft MBH, 1972, pp. 252–258.

114. Shallenberger, R. S., and Acree, T. E. Chemical structure of compounds and sweet and bitter taste. In *Handbook of Sensory Physiology*, Vol. IV: *Chemical Senses 2, Taste*, L. M. Beidler (ed.)., Berlin, Heidelberg, New York: Springer-Verlag, 1971, Chap. 12.

115. Teitelbaum, P. Appetite. *Proceedings of the American Philosophical Society, 108*, 1964, 413–418.

116. Wang, M., and Frank, M. Unpublished. (Cited in Pfaffmann, No. 71.)

117. Weddell, G. Somesthesis and the chemical senses. *Annual Review of Psychology, 6*, 1955, 119–136.

118. Wever, E. G., and Bray, C. W. Action currents in the auditory nerve in response to acoustical stimulation. *Proceedings of the National Academy of Sciences, 16*, 1930, 344–350.

119. Young, P. T. The role of affective processes in learning and motivation. *Psychological Review, 66*, 1959, 104–125.

11

Industrial Psychology: Reminiscences of an Academic Moonlighter

MORRIS S. VITELES

In March 1920, arriving with the suddenness of a flash of lightning in a quickening spring storm, came a letter from The Milwaukee Electric Railway and Light Co. asking me to spend the summer investigating the possibility of developing a test for the selection of streetcar motormen. Donning the uniform and taking on the duties of an apprentice motorman, in July 1920, to learn the job and analyze its "man requirements," constituted my entry into industrial psychology. Hardly known in 1920 even to most psychologists, industrial psychology is today a flourishing source of principles and methods for dealing with problems of *productivity*, individual *adjustment to work,* and *harmonious labor-management relations* in modern industry.

FACTORS IN THE MAKING OF A CAREER

Looking back, I recognize a series of forces which chiefly account for my start in a budding field of research and practice in psychology and for my subsequent achievements. These include "accidental occurrences"—coincidental matchings of opportunities with capacity, interest, skills, aspirations, and other characteristics.

Family Background and Early Schooling. I was born on March 21, 1898, in Zvanetz, a small Russian village bordering on Roumania. My family and I emigrated to Leeds, England, in the fall of

1898. We later proceeded to the United States, arriving in January 1904, shortly before I reached the age of six. My schooling started in a kindergarten, in Leeds, when I was approximately five, and was continued in a public school in Philadelphia, shortly after my arrival in this country. I was able to complete the eight-year elementary school program within six years (in 1910), thereby setting the stage for graduation from college at age twenty (in 1918), for acquiring a Ph.D. degree at the age of twenty-three (in 1921), and for an early start in a professional career.

As is often true in the case of even economically lower-middle-class Jewish families, my family emphasized learning and intellectual accomplishments as a way of life. Great respect for scholarship, aspirations toward an intellectual career, and the drive to achieve were stimulated and supported by parents ready to sacrifice their personal welfare in order to help their children find satisfaction for such needs. Furthermore, the interests of my father and the general atmosphere of the family structure were such as to promote the desire to read widely and to know music and art—to develop broad cultural and aesthetic perspectives.

With this background, it was a matter of course for me to choose the "classical" program upon entering the Central High School of Philadelphia, in the fall of 1914. Strong preparation for even the best universities was provided by a curriculum which included extensive content in English language and literature, history, mathematics, art, the basic sciences, four years of Latin, three years of Greek, two years of French, and elective courses, capped by the award of a B.A. degree. I feel sure that my devotion to the humanities and also my views on "humanistic teaching," expressed later in this chapter, have their roots in this high school program. These, however, were also well nourished by a highly eclectic selection of courses at the college level.

The Choice of a Career in Psychology. At the time of graduation from high school, I was planning to become a teacher of history at the secondary school level. Within less than a year, this career choice was supplanted by the decision to go into psychology. The change was the result of a course in mental testing (following an introductory course in psychology) taken at the Philadelphia School of Pedagogy, which I attended for a year (1914-1915) while waiting for the materialization of a scholarship for undergraduate studies at the University of Pennsylvania. The impetus toward psychology came from the interest in individual differences, in objective measurement, and in utilizing knowledge of human behavior to promote the adjustment of the individual and of his society aroused by a teacher (Melville) who, although not himself an outstanding psychologist, managed to influence his student to an extent not achieved by many more scholarly teachers.

Factors in Career Choice. In retrospect, it appears to me that my original commitment to teaching history was well founded. My major academic interests were in the humanities, especially in history and the social sciences. Biography and autobiography, historical novels, books dealing with social issues and social change, and also those describing the projected utopias of the day appeared frequently among the many books which I read. Furthermore, teaching, in which I became involved even in my high school days as an instructor in religious schools, was a fittingly honorable occupation from the viewpoint of family expectations, especially in the absence of any desire to become either a physician or a lawyer.

The shift to psychology was not so radical a move as might appear at first glance. Teaching remained a central goal since, at the time, psychology hardly existed as a profession completely divorced from teaching. Furthermore, even in these early years the focus of my interest in history was on people and their behavior rather than on dates and events. Within this context, the change to psychology may simply represent the realization, arising from Melville's course, that this was a discipline which could better than history satisfy an already existing and deep-seated interest in the variety and sources of human behavior.

I would be happy to be able to report with conviction that the need to contribute to the social good was also a well-defined goal, but to say this could be no more than a possibly self-serving conjecture. Here, as in other respects, a post facto assessment of motives in the choice of a career can well be of dubious validity. In fact, I suspect that, as J. B. Haldane says of himself, "my subjective account of my own motivation is largely mythical on almost all occasions" and that like Haldane, "I don't know why I do things" (Crichton, 1972). However, I am at least certain that anticipation of large financial rewards was not a factor in the original and final occupational choices, since low pay for teachers in both secondary and higher education was an established and well-known fact.

The Beginnings of a Career as a Psychologist. My undergraduate program at the University of Pennsylvania (1915–1918) included a heavy load of courses in psychology although officially my major subject was history. Involved here was preparation for self-support as a high school teacher while pursuing graduate studies in psychology.

This purpose was served, since I actually was certified for teaching both history and social science, but the need for teaching in a high school never arose. Enrolment, in the fall of 1918, in the Student Army Training Corps (SATC)* at the University of Pennsylvania provided an opportunity to undertake graduate work in psychology with full support. Moreover, in December 1918, a few days after discharge from military service, I was offered and I accepted a position as an Assistant in the Department of Psychology which provided full tuition costs as well as a salary of $600 per year. The following day I turned down without a moment's hesitation an invitation to become an Instructor in the Department of History at twice the salary!

The Influence of the Program in Psychology at Pennsylvania. By the end of my first year of graduate studies, which led to an M.A. degree (1919), I was well on my way to a career in applied psychology in an educational program which was extremely well suited to progress in this direction. The program was characterized by a strong emphasis on the experimental foundation of psychology. This, I am sure, helped lead to my repeated emphasis on the need for a solid experimental substructure to support the practice of psychology (1923b, 1932a, 1941a, 1953, 1959b, 1964, 1969, 1972). However, the major impact on my development came from aspects of the program which bore more directly on the interests which led me into psychology.

The study of individual differences and their measurement was strongly featured in the instructional and research programs. It seems likely that J. McKeen Cattell, the first Professor of Experi-

*Organized by the U.S. Army to make available a pool of officer training candidates during World War I.

mental Psychology at the University of Pennsylvania (1889) and the first to hold this title anywhere, contributed to this pattern. Undoubtedly, he brought with him what his teacher at Leipzig, Wilhelm Wundt, had described as his radical and "wholly American ideas" on the need for studying individual differences, and for applying knowledge about human variability and measures of human potential in the "world of human action."

It is also clear that the chief architect of the program in psychology at Pennsylvania was Lightner Witmer another of the "radicals" from Wundt's laboratory who, in 1892, succeeded Cattell as Director of the Psychological Laboratory. Witmer, like Cattell, was a strong exponent of an applied psychology. He saw "no valid distinction between a pure science and an applied science. . . . what fosters one," he noted "fosters the other." "In the final analysis," he added, "the progress of psychology, as of every other science, will be determined by the amount of its contribution to the advancement of the human race" (Witmer, 1907).

Along with such views was a novel conceptual and methodological approach to the study of human behavior, formulated by Witmer, to which he gave the name "clinical psychology." This took the form of the study of the total individual from the viewpoint of his adaptation and maladjustment to diverse life situations (Witmer, 1925), representing a reaction against the "atomistic" viewpoint of the prevalent psychological system—a general outlook which appeared only later in experimental psychology in the form of the *gestalt* orientation (1930b). A Psychological Clinic—the first in the world—established by Witmer in 1896, as a part of the Department of Psychology, provided an agency both for research utilizing clinical concepts and methods and for helping individual clients achieve optimal adjustment.

Witmer stands first among those whose influence I detect in what I became as a psychologist. His influence is to be seen directly in my long-continuing involvement in measurement and in my activities and publications, especially in the earlier years of my career, in the area of clinical psychology. He also had a strong impact in molding my general outlook with respect to psychology as science and profession, as detailed elsewhere in this chapter. It seems highly probable that Witmer would also have written, as I did, that "*the practitioner in industry must first be a psychologist before he can be an industrial psychologist,*" if he had become the author of *Industrial Psychology* (1932a).

Although Witmer fostered the emphasis upon experimental psychology and laboratory work at Pennsylvania, he took no part in instruction or in guiding individual research in the traditional areas of experimental psychology. This was the responsibility of Edwin B. Twitmyer, who for many years alternated with Witmer as Chairman of the department and who, in 1937, succeeded Witmer as Director of the Psychological Laboratory and Clinic. Twitmyer's influence looms large in what I have done well in the way of laboratory research and, on a larger scale, in the rigorous standards which I have employed as a reviewer and author in the evaluation of both laboratory and field studies. What I learned from Twitmyer found expression also in my activities, during and after World War II, as an administrator concerned with the quality of design, conduct, evaluation, and publication of research in many areas of experimental and applied psychology.

Twitmyer's contribution as a teacher in the field of experimental psychology may seem unbelievable to those who might be tempted to seek his name in the literature. Twitmyer gave up research and publication after conducting an experiment in which, for the first time in this country, and before Pavlov's work was known here, he observed the phenomenon later labeled "conditioning," in the form of a patellar tendon response to the sound of a bell in the absence of direct stimulation (Twitmyer, 1902, 1905). Withdrawal from research represented the reaction of a young and highly sensitive man to the apathy with which the report on the experiment, given at a meeting of the American Psychological Association in 1904, was received, and the readiness with which the pundits of the day, steeped in their narrow paradigms of research, rejected his observation as representing, at most, an "experimental error." However, Twitmyer made his mark as a teacher and was also responsible for significant contributions to speech therapy in his role as a clinical psychologist.

THE REORDERING OF CAREER GOALS

Acknowledgment of Twitmyer's influence does not mean that courses and research in experimental psychology represented a substantial portion of my graduate studies. My concentration was in applied psychology, in a study program designed as preparation for a career of teaching, research, and practice as a clinical psychologist concerned chiefly, as was Witmer, with the adjustment of children in school and in the home. Fittingly, soon after appointment to the department, I also started teaching and doing research in the area of individual differences (1919), and assumed professional responsibilities as an assistant in the Psychological Clinic.

This flow of events took an unexpected turn during my first year of graduate studies when, as a result of a request for assistance, Witmer suggested that I visit the Philadelphia office of the U.S. Bureau of Vocational Rehabilitation and look into the possibility that a psychologist could be helpful in improving the quality of counseling provided by the agency to disabled veterans of World War I. The interview with the director, Arthur J. Rowland, took an unpromising turn when he politely but firmly expressed his skepticism as to whether a psychologist had anything worthwhile to offer in the counseling or in any other "practical" situation. Nevertheless, probably reflecting his attitudes as a former teacher and Dean of Engineering of what is now known as Drexel University, Dr. Rowland suggested that I come in and spend time "looking over the counseler's shoulder" in order to learn what was being done and what a psychologist might be able to do in the situation.

This I agreed to do. My role soon changed from on-looker to participant when I resolved a severe crisis precipitated by the fact that a veteran had been sent to a distant point for training as a bookkeeper, in spite of his inability to read, to write, and to perform simple arithmetical operations. My achievement in producing brief reading and arithmetic tests, to be used for screening purposes, not only brought conviction that a psychologist could be of service, but also an opportunity to engage in counseling and, later, a paid job as a counselor for the summer of 1919. My work during the summer led to the further offer of a permanent appointment for what, in 1919, was a most attractive salary of $1800 a year. This I turned down to return to the university as an assistant, although a promotion to the rank of Instructor came within weeks.

A Shift to Vocational Counseling. This almost fortuitous association with the rehabilitation agency had an important long-range effect in directing my attention toward vocational guidance and in leading me into what, at the time, was still a barely emerging area of teaching, research, and professional practice in psychology. In fact, it was my work in this field, rather than that in industrial psychology, which brought me my earliest credit for a *first*—that of having established, in 1921, the first psychological clinic devoted to vocational guidance (1922c; 1925b; Brewer, 1942; Borow, 1964; Reisman, 1966). Organized within the complex of the larger program of clinical psychology fostered by Witmer, the Vocational Guidance Clinic, along with a clinic devoted to speech therapy organized earlier by Twitmyer, represent developments of historic interest in relation to the current diversification of specializations in the field of clinical psychology.

My orientation in vocational guidance was distinctly that of a clinical psychologist. It is almost exclusively in this field, and hardly ever in industrial psychology, that the titles of my publications include such phrases as "clinical approach" or "clinical viewpoint" (1925b, 1928b, 1931). Nevertheless, here as also in the case of personnel selection and classification, I functioned as a vigorous and even abrasive advocate of the need for validating guidance instruments and for the evaluation of outcomes from guidance programs. In fact, I was responsible for one of the earliest or even possibly the first follow-up study of the application of clinical methods in vocational guidance, although the criteria for measuring the vocational progress of those who "accepted" in comparison with those who did "not accept" the advice given were far from sophisticated, although quite characteristic for the era (1929a).

The criterion problem was, and continues to be, the central problem in efforts to evaluate guidance programs (1961). Consideration of the goals of vocational counseling led me to what I called a "dynamic criterion" for assessing the outcomes of vocational counseling (1936a, 1941c). This represents an internalized index of vocational success which focuses attention upon self-realization in terms of achievement and satisfaction in relation to the potential, resources, values, aspirations, and expectations of the individual, instead of upon external standards imposed by industry and other societal microcosms. However, by the time psychological tests, statistical methods, the computer, opportunities for career studies, and other facilities necessary for examining the viability of such a criterion became available, I had become inactive in the general field of guidance.

Close involvement with the guidance movement ended in the late 1930s, although I continued as Director of the Vocational Guidance Clinic at Pennsylvania until the late 1950s, and published in the area as late as 1961, to pay tribute to my friend Donald G. Paterson, well known for his years of productive efforts in both vocational counseling and industrial psychology. Involvement in the general field was largely in the form of associations with the National Occupational Conference, the Occupational Analysis Section of the U.S. Employment Service, and with other groups concerned with fostering research and providing a solid foundation for psychological practices in vocational guidance. One deeply satisfying outcome of such activity was a book, *Vocational Guidance Throughout the World,* written in collaboration with Franklin J. Keller (1938c), widely viewed as the first significant comparative evaluation of progress in the field covering psychological as well as traditional procedures used in guidance programs in the United States and elsewhere.

AN APPRENTICESHIP IN INDUSTRIAL PSYCHOLOGY

My early interest in vocational guidance was deep-seated but, even in the early 1920s it became secondary to the exciting appeal of industrial psychology, the field with which I am most closely identified in my mind and in those of others. Interestingly enough, it was the almost fortuitous meeting with the highly skeptical Dr. Rowland, which led me into vocational guidance, that also brought me into industrial psychology. Late in 1919, he had left the rehabilitation agency to become Director of Education for The Milwaukee Electric Railway and Light Co., and it was he who wrote the letter inviting me to spend the summer of 1920 looking into the possibility of developing a test for the selection of streetcar motormen.

By this time, nearing the end of two years of graduate studies, I had acquired some understanding of test construction, standardization, and validation. I was familiar with a few books bearing upon the preparation and use of vocational tests including, particularly, the early and significant volume *Vocational Psychology: Its Problems and Methods* by Harry L. Hollingworth (1916) and *Employment Psychology* by Henry C. Link (1919) which was the earliest comprehensive treatment of this topic published in the United States. I also already had under way a study involving an analysis of job requirements and the development of selection tests in the Naval Aircraft Factory at the U.S. Navy Shipyard in Philadelphia.

Otherwise, I had only sparse knowledge of the field of industrial psychology. Certainly, I knew of the field and was also familiar with the standard text of the time, *Psychology and Industrial Psychology,* by Hugo Münsterberg, published in this country in 1913. However, I had not yet considered his program in detail and, even like the more mature and sophisticated psychologists of the day, I was essentially unaware of the broad scope of industrial psychology. It is because of this ignorance that I describe my association with The Milwaukee Electric Railway and Light Co. as an *apprenticeship* in industrial psychology. My *education* as an industrial psychologist began only when, after approximately two years of part-time work with the company, I decided to reject full-time employment and to focus my attention on an academic career combined with research and practice in industry.

An Historical Interlude. This would appear to be an appropriate time for dealing with the question of what I learned and what I accomplished during the apprenticeship. However, there seems to be merit in departing from a chronological sequence of events specific to my career, as I shall do quite frequently from now on, in order to further understanding of what industrial psychology was like when I started, and of the ways in which I may have influenced the development of the field.

The beginnings of the application of psychology in industry are to be found in scattered experiments on employee selection, learning of industrial tasks, employee fatigue, and so forth, conducted in Europe and the United States during approximately the first decade of the present century. Later events were foreshadowed also in a volume, published in the United States in 1911, which presented, for the first time, an analysis of workers' motives and of the potential value of non-financial incentives in industry prepared by one trained in the theories and procedures of psychology (Scott, 1911). Nevertheless the problems and program of industrial psychology were first systematically formulated by Hugo Münsterberg, another of the "dissenters" from Wundt's laboratory who, in the last years of his life, left Germany to serve as Director of the Psychological Laboratory at Harvard University.

In the volume referred to above, first published in Germany in 1912, Münsterberg outlined definite proposals for the use of tests in the selection of workers and for the application of findings and research on learning in training industrial personnel. Included also was discussion of the potential value of psychology in dealing with the effects of conditions and methods of work on fatigue and monotony; the influence of financial incentives and of the social atmosphere upon "working power," and the general problem of adjustment of technical to psychological conditions. "Scientific vocational guidance" and advertising and sales were also perceived as being within the purview of the field. Although, as can be seen, the scope of the program had breadth, Münsterberg placed major emphasis on measuring human adaptability to industrial tasks, and it was generally only within this area that he provided findings from industrial studies, including his own investigation on the selection of motormen, telephone operators, and ship personnel to support the practicability and advantages of applying psychology in industry.

As appears clearly in the history of applied psychology, the early decades of the twentieth century were marked, in the United States, by a strong interest in individual differences and their measurement. It is therefore not surprising to find that research in the application of psychology in industry during this period was predominantly in the field of vocational selection. Furthermore, methods which could increase the probability of hiring qualified workers attracted the attention of businessmen as a promising means of reducing unit labor costs in industry. Interest was intensified as businessmen became familiar with the principles of scientific management, as first formulated in this country by Frederick W. Taylor (1911), and with what Taylor had accomplished in the way of increasing production in the steel industry by using only highly qualified men.

The impulse toward this new application of psychology gained strength from the development and fruitful large-scale application of tests in the selection and classification of military personnel in the United States (Bingham, 1919; Yoakum and Yerkes, 1920) and in other countries involved in World War I. The development of group intelligence tests, following the achievement of U.S. army psychologists in producing such tests for literates (*Alpha*) and illiterates (*Beta*), was succeeded by a rush to use intelligence tests—frequently inappropriately and without validation for the specific industrial situation in question—as a panacea for achieving economic goals in industry (1921, 1922a).

Learning and Achievement During an Apprenticeship. In terms of such developments, the invitation to undertake a project directed toward the selection of streetcar motormen qualified to avoid accidents was in the spirit of the times. To some extent, in comparison with what was already going on in industry, it was ahead of the times, since validation was viewed as an essential feature of the project. This intent became more apparent when I was shown the major device recommended by Münsterberg for selecting motormen, and was told that it had not been found useful for this purpose. I could not, however, learn what was done in the way of evaluation, or who did it.

My analysis of the man requirements of the job, made while learning to operate a streetcar, pointed to the need of an entirely different kind of instrument than that developed by Münsterberg. Preliminary work during the summer of 1920 was followed by the construction, standardization, and validation of a test (1925a), later cross-validated by Shellow (1925), which held up well for many years, especially in comparison with other devices in the area.

Although I succeeded in completing the mission which took me to Milwaukee, I do not consider this as a major accomplishment in vocational selection as compared particularly with later achievements in the way of safeguarding human lives, lowering costs of property damages, and reducing customers' discomforts and public risks during blackouts by the construction and validation of a test battery for the selection of electric substation operators (1929b, 1949a, b; Wainwright, 1961). Developed in 1928 for the Philadelphia Electric Company, with which I was associated for thirty-seven years (1927-1964), the test battery has yielded useful outcomes not only in this company, but also elsewhere. I am inclined to evaluate as even more significant, in another context of vocational classification, a program in the same company which discards psychological tests and makes use only of objectively scored measures of (1) trade knowledge and (2) skill in the completion of representative work samples for the promotion of workers from level to level and to the rank of foreman.

Analyzing and Describing the Man-Requirements of the Job. The belittlement, by comparison, of the test for streetcar motormen does not mean that I consider this to represent an achievement of no consequence. It is, however, an achievement of far less consequence than, for example, a new approach to the analysis and description of requirements imposed by the job upon a worker, also developed during my "apprenticeship" with The Milwaukee Electric Railway and Light Company.

It was well recognized at the time that success in matching men and occupations requires, as a start, an understanding of what each job demands in the way of intellectual capacity, special abilities, and other traits as well as in the way of education, physical attributes, prior experience, and so on (Hollingworth, 1916; Link, 1919; Viteles 1934d). However, the analysis and description of mental requirements were characterized by vague terminology and failed to assess and state, in standard terms, the relative importance of specific traits or the amount of each required for success on the job. I had become aware of this problem in my work in vocational counseling (1924a). This awareness was reinforced as I reviewed job descriptions in preparation for a project involving the development of tests for the selection of clerical employees for the Auditing Division of the company, undertaken, in part, for use in meeting the thesis requirements of the Ph.D. degree.

Consideration of the problem led to the development of what I called the "job psychographic method" for analyzing and stating abilities required for success on a job. The method involves a list of thirty-two terms descriptive of mental capacities, such as coordination, observation, space perception, and the like, each defined, with illustrations, so as to convey the same meaning to independent investigators. Included also is standard 5-point scale, ranging from 1—negligible to 5—of utmost importance, for designating the importance of each ability for job performance. Ratings are graphically recorded on a form that yields a job psychograph, which shows at a glance the relative importance of the listed abilities for success on the job. Clearly apparent in the profile pattern are those keystone abilities (rated 5) which must be particularly considered both in subjective evaluations of an applicant and in planning a program for the construction and validation of tests for employee selection and placement (1922b).

The job psychographic method is listed as another *first* in the history of vocational guidance (Brewer, 1942; Borow, 1964). However, it has had an even greater impact on selection and placement of personnel, since it became the model for the Occupational Characteristic Check List,* developed by the U.S. Employment Service, that has been widely used in the placement and test construction program of the U.S. Employment Service.

The U.S. Employment Service adaptation is in some ways an improvement on the job psychographic method, in that it simplifies terminology and, more important, substitutes an estimate of the *amount* of each trait required by a job for an importance rating. However, an even more useful approach is to be found in work carried on under my direction during World War II. Here ratings on importance and on amount, in terms of minimum scores on tests of vision, intelligence, and of other applicable measures, were combined for use in the differential assignment of naval personnel to gun crews, in the classification of men for assignment to billets aboard ships, and in other connections. An interesting recent application of the basic model, directed toward promoting individual job satisfaction, is to be found in the Occupational Reinforcement Patterns developed at the University of Minnesota for use in rehabilitation programs (Dawis et al., 1968; Rosen et al., 1972).

Job Families and Differential Aptitude Testing. The study which produced the job psychograph also led to another significant development in demonstrating the possibility of grouping into one "family" jobs which are alike from the viewpoint of specific abilities and specific skills required for performance. Analysis of the requirements of nineteen jobs classified under the single title of "clerk" showed, for example, that for seven of them there

*Described by one of those responsible for the instrument as "an adaptation of the Viteles Job Psychographic Method" (Shartle, 1946).

was a similar pattern of requirements in spite of differences in specific duties among the jobs constituting the "family." A quite different pattern of requirements was shown to be common to six other specific jobs, constituting another "family." A later phase of study showed that different combinations of smaller numbers of tests from a total battery of ten tests could be used for the prediction of success for all clerical jobs classified as belonging in the same "family."

Here again, as in the case of the job psychographic self, the concept of "job families" was far from fully developed in comparison, for example, with the later use of such groupings in the U.S. Employment Service job analysis program. Furthermore, the use of a standard battery of tests yielding differential predictions for a variety of jobs was primitive in comparison with the proposal for the development of a comprehensive and sophisticated program of differential aptitude testing formulated by Clark Hull, in the 1920s, for utilization in vocational guidance (Hull, 1928), but applicable also in employee selections and classifications. Nevertheless, having decided to be in this presentation what Gian Carlo Menotti (1971) has described as "candidly immodest," I am moved to describe the grouping of jobs on the basis of specific abilities and skills, combined with differential prediction from a standard test battery, as another "first"—perhaps all the more unusual because it came out of a Ph.D. thesis. Nevertheless, I am also at this point inclined to share strongly with Somerset Maugham the wish that "I had not started to write this chapter in the first person singular." Certainly, as Maugham notes, "it is charming to write about yourself when you see on the reader's eyelash the glittering tear and on his lips the tender smile"; but as he goes on to say, "it is not nice when you have to exhibit yourself as a plain damned fool" (Maugham, 1930). This, I indeed accomplished, in the study under discussion, by using the value of coefficient correlations between individual test scores and the criterion measure to weight individual tests, as though r = .60 had twice the predictive value of r = .30, and so forth.

The Role of General Intelligence Tests in Vocational Selection. Underlying the concepts of the job psychograph and job families, was dissatisfaction with the role assigned to the general intelligence test in appraising vocational competence. As noted earlier, the situation in the 1920s was one of rapidly increasing use and commercialization of such instruments for the selection of qualified workers for all jobs. This came about largely because of an analysis of Army general intelligence test scores in relation to civilian occupations held by Army personnel prior to induction which led to the conclusion that individuals within a given range of scores, representing the middle 50 per cent of the group, were equally suited for all of the jobs held by men within that range (Yoakum and Yerkes, 1920).

I took issue with this position in my first article bearing directly on industrial psychology, published in the *Journal of Applied Psychology* (1921). Here, I questioned, for example, whether all men who average C on Army general intelligence tests (with scores ranging from approximately C– to C+) are equally qualified for such diverse jobs as bricklayer, baker, cook, general machinist, and shop carpenter. I noted that the analysis of the jobs of streetcar motormen and streetcar conductors, which make approximately equal demands on general intelligence, showed marked differences between the two with respect to requirements imposed by the jobs in the way of distribution of attention, depth perception, reaction speed, coordination, alertness, and planfulness.

This does not mean that I discarded intelligence test scores. In fact, I noted the potential of *empirically validated* minimum intelligence test scores for selection purposes. I drew attention, as demonstrated in a later study of department store cashiers, to the possible value of maximum limits, as a device for curtailing boredom, turnover, and the like (1924b). Nevertheless, my plea was for the measurement of specific abilities and skills along with general intelligence in vocational selection and placement. The impact seems to have been noted since, as recently as 1960, attention has been called to the fact that "Morris Viteles forcefully argued, that 'the tests which are being used successfully in industry are those which measure specific abilities of individuals for particular jobs, and not tests for general intelligence' " (Baritz, 1965; see also Barrett, 1972).

Generalizations of the type referred to above were supplemented by a study which showed far from high correlations among three widely used tests of general intelligence and, also, no significant correlation of any of these with grades obtained by university students (1922a). I raised questions as to the generality of "general intelligence" as measured by the tests. Once more I stressed the importance of measuring specific abilities, directing attention toward the need for *ability-group-patterns* described, in this instance, as constellations of specific abilities necessary for success in one of a number of specialized professional and technical occupations, such as business, engineering, and medicine.

To anyone who has been trained in psychology within the past thirty-five years or so, such statements must have an appalling triteness. In the 1920s, however, research of this kind was just getting under way and, in fact, the study appears among those cited by Charles Spearman as presenting "damaging criticism" of assumptions pertaining to the dimensions of human ability and of work in intelligence testing (Spearman, 1927).

A Study of Negro Intelligence. As this is written, I recall also that it was an analysis of army general intelligence tests which helped promulgate the view that the intelligence of Negroes is inferior to that of Whites. Findings from this analysis contributed heavily to the assertion that the difference between Negroes and Whites discovered by practically all investigators describes a true intellectual difference between a superior and inferior race that cannot be explained in terms of dissimilarities in educational and social opportunities (Brigham, 1923). This conclusion I described as wholly untenable, following a comprehensive and critical examination of studies of the intelligence of American Negroes that were available in the mid-1920s (1928c). What I thought of the rush to find the Blacks guilty of genetic inferiority found expression in the citation, at the close of my article, of the charming observation by W. S. Gilbert that

> . . . . headstrong youths
> Of decent education,
> Determine all important truths,
> With strange precipitation.
>
> The over-ready victims they
> Of logical illusions
> And in a self-assertive way
> They jump at strange conclusions.
>
> "The Periwinkle Girl," W. S. Gilbert

Other Aspects of the Apprenticeship: Employee Training. The period of work with The Milwaukee Electric Railway and Light Co. brought, among other gains, strong awareness of the possibility of applying more or less well-established principles of learning and the research methods of psychology for improving training programs in industry. My experience in learning to operate a streetcar showed, for example, that practically each of the motormen who trained me had his special "tricks"—individual ways of handling the controller and the air-brake handle. Instead of receiving from day to day uniform training in a definite series of responses involving the same muscular combinations, there were variations in the pattern of movement from day to day. For handling the air brake, for example, one motorman recommended "long bites" of air; another recommended "short bites." One man employed one pattern of arm movements for closing the door and starting the car simultaneously; another used a second method, involving an almost antagonistic series of muscular responses.

Obvious to even an embryonic industrial psychologist were the interference effects arising in such a training situation and the needs for (1) arriving at the generally best suited methods of work and (2) reorganizing the program so as to ensure instruction only in such methods of work. Apparent also was the possibility of redistributing practice periods and of considering other steps consistent with findings from laboratory studies of learning and from research in industry to provide optimal conditions for learning desired responses in the shortest time, and at the lowest cost. Recommendations that I made to the company, following further study of the situation, led to a complete overhaul of the training program. This experience was also the beginning of many years of work directed to the improvement of industrial and also military training programs.

The End of an Apprenticeship. Such then were the major outcomes of an apprenticeship covering about two years of part-time work. During this time I continued as an Instructor at the University of Pennsylvania and I spent the summer months and university holidays in Milwaukee. In the intervening periods, work on the program was continued by a full-time assistant under direction by mail from Philadelphia.

The apprenticeship provided almost unadulterated pleasure. Under the circumstances, I showed little hesitation, following the award of a Ph.D. degree in 1921, in accepting an offer for full-time employment with the company, to start at the close of the 1921-1922 academic year. But, I soon began to question the wisdom of this decision and, in the spring of 1922, withdrew from this commitment.

This decision had actually started to take form in late December 1921, following a gentle but firmly worded reprimand by Dr. Rowland brought about by my occasional lateness in reporting for work in the morning. He acknowledged the fact that I was not shirking work, since he and others knew that I regularly remained at work after "quitting time," frequently until and beyond midnight. However, it was felt that my lateness set a bad example for other employees and could not be tolerated for this reason.

I am not inclined to derogate this position. Neither do I think that later withdrawal from the commitment represents a juvenile response to a scolding. The incident simply contributed to the surfacing of a deep-seated rejection of submission to a lifetime of rigid conformity by one who had already learned to enjoy the freedom in the patterning of activities and the distribution of time available in an academic career. Although, not so clear at the time, the decision reflected also a strong interest in learning and in scholarship. At least, such was the view held by both my father and by a number of my teachers and associates who, at the time I announced my intention to leave the university, predicted that I would return to an academic life.

My years at the university, which at retirement in 1968 amounted to fifty, and also my *education* as an industrial psychologist, started to take form on the day of the reprimand in December 1921. Later on that day I found in one of the psychological journals a notice concerning post-doctoral fellowships for study in France offered by the American Field Service. That evening I stayed in my office well beyond the midnight hour doing what was required to apply for a fellowship for study at the University of Paris and Collège de France.

The impulse to do so was, in a sense, a sudden one. Underlying it, however, was awareness, acquired in part during the apprenticeship, that there were gaps in my knowledge, particularly in the areas of motivation and psychopathology, which needed to be filled. I knew also that much was going on in the field of industrial psychology in Europe, and I saw the year abroad as an opportunity to become familiar with these developments. Considerable competence in reading, understanding, and some skill in speaking French, combined with marked interest in French literature and the civilization of France, added to the attractiveness of the American Field Service Fellowship. The notification, in April 1922, that the fellowship had been granted, started me on the way to a learning experience that contributed much to my roles as a teacher and as a psychologist.

A YEAR OF STUDY IN EUROPE, 1922-1923

The highlight of the year in Paris was attendance at lectures on "the evolution of memory and the notion of time" given by Pierre Janet. His always lucid and scintillating lectures, embodying materials from experimental psychology and psychopathology, brought new understanding, both of normal processes and of theory and practice in dealing with mental aberrations. The fashioning and delivery of his lectures raised the level of my aspiration with respect to achievement as a teacher, although I was sufficiently realistic to question the possibility of matching his skill in the lecture hall.

Regular attendance at courses was limited to those with Janet and to a series of lecturers and clinical demonstrations by Georges Dumas. Within the framework of freedom available to students (1923a), I attended many other courses irregularly, not alone in psychology but also in other areas, especially history, sociology, and philosophy. Unfortunately, I found little of interest in the area of motivation, but the breadth of exposure to psychology and other disciplines more than compensated for this lack.

As anticipated, the stay in Paris provided opportunities for furthering my education as an industrial psychologist. These came largely through J. M. Lahy who, as early as 1905, had conducted an investigation of psychophysiological factors in learning and performance as a typist. He had also become interested in the selection of streetcar motormen and, at the time of my stay in Paris, he was involved in the validation of tests in this area. He was engaged, also, in planning research in fatigue and in other areas. I was not attracted to his work, because it was done within a framework of psychotechnology as described later in this chapter, rather than within that of psychology as science. Nevertheless, my visits to his laboratories marked the beginnings of a friendship, strengthened by our common interest in the International Association of Psychotechnology (now the International Association of Applied Psychology), which lasted until his death in the 1940s.

Exploring Industrial Psychology in England, France, and Germany (1922-1923). From the viewpoint of my development as an industrial psychologist, the greatest returns from spending a year in Europe came from extended visits to universities and other centers of work in industrial psychology in England, France, and Germany. I found that, as in the United States, psychologists were conducting studies in the areas of job analysis, selection, and training. However, especially in Germany and England, they were extensively involved in research on work methods; on problems of fatigue and boredom as related to both individual differences and conditions of work; on accident prevention; and to some extent on industrial organization. In general, especially in England, I found a concern with the total interaction between man and machine of the sort that became evident in the United States only in later years.

These and other observations enlarged my understanding of the scope of industrial psychology. More important, I think, was what the visits brought in the way of deeper insights into problems affecting the development of industrial psychology. One of these involved the very identity of industrial psychology. In Germany, for example, largely under the influence of W. Moede and G. Piorkowski, the application of psychology in industry was largely in the context of psychotechnology, described as an offshoot of psychology having somewhat the same relation to the science as engineering bears to physics (Bingham, 1923).

In contrast were the efforts of a number of German psychologists, such as F. Giese and O. Lippmann, to relate the practice of psychology in industry to basic laboratory research in experimental psychology and to pertinent theory. This was the position taken by the noted French psychologist Henri Piéron. It was also that of Charles S. Myers who, in 1921, had left his post as Director of the Psychological Laboratory in Cambridge to become the principal officer of the National Institute of Industrial Psychology in London, which he had helped to organize. Most particularly, Myers saw industrial psychology not only as a recipient of benefits from the pure sciences of psychology and physiology but as bringing important returns to these sciences in the way of revealing wide gaps in knowledge and suggesting important problems for laboratory research. Exposure to such views, especially as expressed by Myers, strengthened my aversion to a psychotechnical orientation in industrial psychology. It fortified my conviction that solid experimental and theoretical foundations were prerequisites for the sound application of psychology in industry.

Another major outcome from a visit to England was reinforcement of my views, derived from my background in clinical psychology, on the necessity of strongly emphasizing individual adjustment, as a major objective in the application of psychology in industry—a position taken more frequently and expressed more emphatically by British psychologists than by those in the United States (Myers, 1920, 1926, 1929). Thus, in studies on fatigue, conducted under the auspices of the Industrial Fatigue Research Board of Great Britain, the concept of efficiency was viewed not as related solely to productivity, but as output achieved under conditions which fully safeguard the "fitness" of the worker. Such views, as well as a somewhat similar approach by a number of psychologists in this country (Thorndike, 1917; Poffenberger, 1927), undoubtedly influenced the position which I have taken that, from the viewpoint of industrial psychology, efficiency in industry is a state in which maximum output of the highest quality in the shortest possible time is achieved with the least expenditure of energy and with maximum well-being of the worker (1923b, 1932a, 1934a, 1953).

Major Outcomes of the Fellowship Year. Both my knowledge of psychology and my intellectual horizons were expanded by the post-doctoral year at the University of Paris and Collège de France. However, the major impact on my career came from visits to institutions and from associations with those engaged in research and practice in industrial psychology. These not only provided knowledge about what was going on, but led me into the European literature, thus opening the road to productivity and recognition as a scholar and not solely as a practitioner in the field of industrial psychology. This effect first became evident, I think, through the publication, in 1923, of a comprehensive, comparative evaluation of industrial psychology in England, France, and Germany, against the background of work in the United States (1923b). The full effect became evident only approximately ten years later, and after many, many hours of digesting a voluminous literature, in the publication, in 1932, of my first book, *Industrial Psychology.*

ACHIEVING MATURITY AS AN INDUSTRIAL PSYCHOLOGIST: THREE FACETS OF A CAREER

My return to the university in the summer of 1923 marked the beginning of a period, covering about a dozen years, in which I achieved maturity as an industrial psychologist. The return also set the pattern of a career which included teaching, research and publication, and professional practice in industry. In passing, it seems well to recall that this was the prevalent pattern of the time in the United States. The combination of an academic with a business career is still to be found, but industrial psychology today is predominantly a profession involving psychologists—sometimes only in name—employed in industry, or representing consulting firms, or engaged in private business as consultants. The problems in industrial psychology discussed in later pages stem largely from this patterning of professional activities.

The Psychologist as "Moonlighter." The pattern in which my life's work has been carried out is now often described as "moonlighting." However, I engaged in multiple job holding, with the full knowledge of the university and at a reduced salary, under arrangements which provided free days for research and practice in industry, although I consistently carried a full teaching load and otherwise fully met my other academic responsibilities.

I have often been asked how I managed the heavy work load, increased during World War II by extensive involvement in military research and consultation. I recognize certain assets which helped me to do this, and to achieve recognition simultaneously both as an innovator in industry and as a scholar in university circles. I am, for example, able to turn from one activity to another with negligible loss of efficiency. I have considerable resourcefulness in recognizing problems and rearranging cognitive elements to produce, frequently, a novel solution. Most important, from the viewpoint of the size of the work load I carried, was a large reserve of energy. Indeed, I sense great insightfulness and a certain prophetic quality on the part of the student editor who chose the phrase *Di omnia laboribus vendunt* for entry under my name in our high school class yearbook.

In this connection, I find of particular interest results from recent research which show that factory workers with more than one job are more energetic than those with only one job. "The moonlighter," it is noted, "is a very energetic person with a great capacity for activity" (Mott et al., 1965). This, it is added, accounts not only for multiple job holding, but for the fact that moonlighters get more education, maintain higher levels of activities in voluntary associations, and so forth, than do non-moonlighters (Mann, 1965). Moonlighters, it was also found, tend to engage in less sedentary activities than do non-moonlighters during their leisure time. In this, too, I meet the criterion of the stereotype, since my leisure activities, apart from the reading in which I engage in heavily, have included active sports such as swimming, sailing, horseback riding, and tennis, activities which, with the exception of tennis, I continue to this day.

A Career as a Teacher. It is not the prime purpose of this chapter to discuss my career as a teacher. Nevertheless, my work as a university teacher took precedence over other activities—except during World War II, and even then I took many long and strenuous trips to get back to the university to meet a class. My influence on both the undergraduate and graduate programs in psychology at Pennsylvania was extensive. My area of specialization was an important factor in the initiation of a rigorous introductory course in psychology and of a number of advanced courses in the curriculum of the Wharton School of Finance and Commerce. Industrial psychology became and remained a significant area of graduate studies in the Department of Psychology for almost half a century. My influence was felt in other areas of applied psychology—even in the improvement of teaching in the field of statistics, an area responsible, as noted earlier, for one of my outstanding displays of ignorance.

I have always enjoyed teaching and worked at doing it well. I had the reputation of being a stimulating and effective teacher of undergraduate students, although both they and graduate students thought me a "tough teacher" with respect to demands made in the classroom and to outside assignments. I think that my reputation as a stimulating teacher was based, to some extent, upon an approach in the classroom which I have described as the humanistic teaching of psychology (1970).

The Humanistic Teaching of Psychology. A common and justifiable criticism of higher education is that increases in knowledge are not accompanied by a commensurable increase in wisdom. A "better understanding of man and his experiences," the "capacity for entering sympathetically into the experiences of all men," and the assessment and "ordering of values" are among the attributes of wisdom. Above all, it is the "awareness of the limits of established knowledge" that distinguishes the truly "wise and humane" man from the "merely knowledgeable man" (Thirring, 1956; Aubrey, 1959).

It has long been assumed that the achievement of wisdom could be promoted only through exposure to the "humanities." Progress toward wisdom is not, however, solely a function of subject matter but relates perhaps even more to the spirit and aims of teaching. Particularly important here is what the teacher does in the way of utilizing the fruitful insights of the novelist, the playwright, the poet, the historian, and other humanists to provide the connective tissue between the *knowledge* characterizing his discipline and a *wise appraisal* of what has been learned.

Of the various scientific disciplines represented in a university curriculum, psychology is especially adapted to promoting the development of wisdom through the medium of humanistic teaching. The science is devoted to the objective examination of the perceptions, thoughts, emotions, and behavior of man. However, although facts are present in abundance, they are generally only the outcomes of observations made in a restricted field, frequently within a narrow theoretical context, often separated from realities of life by the use of animals for subjects and by the barriers of other constraints in laboratory experiments.

Under these conditions, there is particular need and scope for consideration, as part of the teaching process, of what the humanistic disciplines contribute to the description and understanding of human attitudes and behavior. Within this context, I know, for example, of no better way of introducing the nurture-nature controversy, in the consideration of individual differences, than by reference to Aldous Huxley's *Brave New World,* or by quoting, from W. S. Gilbert, the soliloquy:

> For nature always does contrive
> That every boy and every gal
> That's born into this world alive
> Is either a little liberal
> Or else a little conservative.
> "Iolanthe"

Similarly, William Stryon's *The Confessions of Nat Turner;* Gerda Lerner's *Black Women in White America;* Margaret Mead and James Baldwin's *A Rap on Race* provide a medium, generally better than research reports, for enhancing the student's comprehension of the realistic human issues embodied in the concept "race differences."

In quite another context, it has been suggested that "possibly we are saved from the solemnities of Freud by the sanity of Rabelais" (Anon., 1956). It is also possible that a humanistic teacher can protect the student from the inanities of behaviorism. For example, it is interesting to find, as shown in laboratory research, that there is a direct relation between the amount of restraint imposed upon rats engaged in jumping and upon chimpanzees engaged in drawing water from a spigot, on the one hand, and level of subsequent performance, on the other (Finch, 1942). By stretching the imagination, it is even possible to perceive this finding as being analogous to Balzac's observation that the duration of the passion of two persons susceptible to love is in proportion to the original resistance on the part of the woman, or to the obstacles which society puts in the way of their desires (Cohen, 1956). But, it is clear that reference to this analogy by the teacher needs to be accompanied by a reminder that the student must go to the *Song of Songs,* the *Decameron,* the letters and poems of Aretino, and to the poetry of the ages, and not to the psychologists—most particularly not to the behaviorist—to seek understanding of the sensations, perceptions, thoughts, feelings, and dynamics of passion.

A humanistic orientation in teaching does not mean that the

"intuitions" of the humanist must always be accepted as well founded, or as more meaningful than the outcomes of psychological research. Even in such cases, consideration of the views of the novelist, the historian, the philosopher, and other humanists can contribute to a more balanced evaluation of psychological phenomena. Thus, discussions of boredom and alienation as related to specialized and mechanized work (1934a, 1939a, 1951b) can be enriched by consideration of what Georges Friedmann (1955) has called the "fine sentiments; intuitions, personal affirmations" of the humanists *along with* findings from studies of factory workers, which show that although simplicity, repetitiveness, and pacing play a part, it is not an outstanding part in depriving production workers of a sense of "personal significance, accomplishment, and self-fulfillment in work. . ." (Kornhauser, 1965).

Whatever may be the merit of humanistic teaching, I feel sure that it was largely my achievement as a teacher that brought a promotion to the rank of Assistant Professor in 1925. The pleasure of this was mixed with sadness, since the department Chairman, under instructions from higher administration, found it necessary to inform me that I should not anticipate promotion beyond this level because there was already one Jew (Samuel W. Fernberger) in the department and two more in other departments of the university. However, the fact that such barriers can be overcome appears in my promotion to Associate Professor in 1935, and to Professor in 1940. An additional appointment as Professor of Psychology in the School of Medicine, in 1955, and the award by the University of an honorary degree (LL.D.), in 1973, testify to the ineptness of the early decision and warning concerning my future at the university.

More important is the absence, today, of such intolerance at higher administrative levels and in nearly all departments of the University of Pennsylvania, and the evidence of similar changes affecting minority groups in universities throughout the country. Perhaps this may even provide comfort for the WASPs, described with increasing frequency as the new minority group in the United States (Canaday, 1972; Schrag, 1972).

The Backgrounds of an Opus Magnum. As noted earlier, upon returning from France in 1923, I started a program of intensive reading of the American and foreign literature in industrial psychology. This was enlarged and further intensified when, in 1925, I was asked to prepare a review of the field for publication in the *Psychological Bulletin*. Reviews published in 1928 and 1930 following the first in the series (1926, 1928a, 1930a), covering close to 1100 titles, had widespread effects in bringing recognition by psychologists of the broad scope of industrial psychology and of the highly important developments in the way of research and practice in European countries. Reprinting of the review in the *Reprint and Circular Series* of the *Personnel Research Federation* helped, in addition, to bring the scope and accomplishments of psychology to the attention of industrial relations personnel and executives in business and industry.

Reproduction of the review series reflected the important work carried on for many years by Walter V. Bingham, another pioneer in industrial psychology, in stimulating interest in this field through the *Personnel Research Federation* and in other ways. In addition, he did much in the way of encouraging and helping younger men in the area, including myself, by providing opportunities for participation in meetings of the organization and by bringing them and their work to the attention of others in his journal and elsewhere.

During 1931, at the request of W. W. Norton, then President of the publishing firm which he founded, I agreed to prepare a book on industrial psychology. I suspect that he was prompted to ask me to do so, in part, by his knowledge of the review series. It may well be, however, that Bingham was one of those whom he consulted before approaching me with his request to write the book.

Because of the extensive reading I had done in preparing the review articles, I was able to "give birth" to the book in nine months, in spite of much concomitant labor in my university and business jobs. *Industrial Psychology* was ready as promised for publication in 1932, to be followed shortly thereafter by a condensed, semi-popular version entitled *The Science of Work* (1934a).

The "Bible" of Industrial Psychology. It seems unnecessary and also quite impossible to deal with the content, the orientation, and the evaluation of a closely printed text of approximately 650 pages. Views concerning psychology as science and profession which had taken form during the years—as voiced to some extent in earlier pages of this chapter—found expression in the book. These became apparent to reviewers who called attention to them, as well as to other aspects of the text. Thus, according to Bruce V. Moore (1933), long associated with industrial psychology at Pennsylvania State College (now University),

> The author has been consistent with his previously stated thesis that the industrial psychologist should be more than a technician with a kit of tools and statistical tricks. The book is a scholarly treatment by a psychologist of the fundamental assumptions and principles as well as techniques involved in promoting industrial efficiency through happier individual adjustment. . . .
>
> The unusually extensive but well organized data and findings concentrated into one volume include not only results from research in industry but also pertinent results from investigations in other fields of psychology. . . .
>
> As the author states . . . the new techniques, new equipment, and new viewpoints of industrial psychology have thrown light on general principles of interest to the psychologist regardless of his field (Moore, 1933).

Reference to such features of the book were found in other of the many and quite consistently favorable reviews. Present also were comments on other aspects of the book which I considered and still consider to be important, *viz* an historical perspective, enriched by materials taken from the humanistic disciplines; the treatment of social and economic forces as well as changes within psychology itself which helped set the stage for the application of psychology in industry; consideration of such conceptualizations and of more systematic theoretical formulations as were to be found in reports on investigations covering research in industrial psychology; and so on.

Not all reviewers were satisfied with all aspects of the book. Nevertheless, most of the reviewers seemed to be in agreement with statements by Moore—reported here with "candid immodesty"—that "the book is written by a master of the field who can comprehend a mass of isolated findings, see the form of the whole, and present them as an integrated body. . . . Although rapid progress is being made in the field of industrial psychology," the reviewer added, "the soundness of this author's work will make it a standard text for some time" (Moore, 1933).

This, indeed, proved to be a sound prediction, since here and there I still hear the book described as the "bible" of industrial psychology, and it is still used widely as a text in Asian countries. I suspect, however, that like the Bible, it is to be found more frequently on the book shelves than on the reading tables of industrial psychologists in this country. In this context, I find particular pleasure in a letter received about three years ago (1970) from an author of one of the better books in the field and the recipient of an American Psychological Association award for his contributions to industrial psychology—who writes:

> On a shelf by my desk I keep a series of books to which I often refer. . . . Just minutes ago, I needed to refresh my thinking on a point and reached for the appropriate book—Morris Viteles' *Industrial Psychology*. . . . Of all books on my shelf, that has been used far, far more than most. . . . [It] has always been a source of inspiration as well as a source of knowledge. That is where I go first. Someone was just inquiring of me about the use of application blanks, and that was why I reached for your text. Perhaps needless to say, I got my answer in it.
>
> Seeing the physical state of my copy of your book made me nostalgic. For when I first went into industrial psychology, I studied this particular copy of your "*Industrial Psychology*," and it is in sufficiently usable shape to last me the three more years until my retirement. So one copy of your text has served one industrial psychologist throughout his career, and served him well.
>
> Thanks again for writing it. (E. E. Ghiselli)

Further Comments on Industrial Psychology. As noted earlier, not all comments on the book were favorable. For example, questions were raised as to the need for two quite lengthy and detailed chapters on the nature, distribution, and origin of individual differences. I also had my doubts, especially with respect to the chapter on origins, as evidenced by a suggestion to lay readers made early in the chapter that they could by-pass much of this chapter without great loss. However, I had strong conviction that students and also their teachers needed to be well informed about issues and research bearing on the nurture-nature controversy, especially in approaching problems in the areas of vocational selection and industrial training.

Among comments made by critics were those of my friend Arthur Kornhauser, well known for his work in industrial psychology, who deplored, most particularly, what he described as a failure to deal adequately with the findings and implications of social psychology for work in industry. I rejected the criticism at the time and still do. Any treatment more extensive than that embodied, for example, in chapters on motivation and management, would have involved going beyond research findings pertinent to industry, available from social psychology, which started to come to fruition as an experimental discipline only in the 1940s. When the time was ripe, social psychology found its place in still another book, *Motivation and Morale in Industry* (1953), that represents another milestone in my development as an industrial psychologist.

Achievement of Maturity as a Scholar. Publication during the dozen years or so (1922-1934) on which the last twenty pages or so have been chiefly focused was not limited to the literature reviews and *Industrial Psychology.* As noted in passing, in 1934 there appeared a non-technical condensation of the latter, *The Science of Work.* Starting with an historical chapter entitled "Work Through the Ages" the volume proceeded to cover essentially the same ground as the larger book but, as noted by a reviewer, "in a style which can readily be understood by business executives." There is, of course, the possibility, stated in a Peanuts cartoon in today's newspaper (June 3, 1972) that "No book on psychology can be any good if one can understand it." Nevertheless, the book also showed up as a second text in introductory courses to illustrate developments in applied psychology. Undergraduates as well as businessmen were attracted by the style and also, I think, by a few charming sketches drawn for the book by my assistant Kinsley R. Smith who subsequently represented industrial psychology for many years as member of the faculty of Pennsylvania State University.

Included among publications of the period are reports on research conducted in industry and elsewhere (1924b, 1925a, 1929b; Viteles and Gardner, 1928d; Viteles and Smith, 1932b; Viteles, Fernberger, and Carlson, 1934c), as well as more general papers. Nevertheless, my outstanding intellectual accomplishment of the period is represented by the book *Industrial Psychology.* It is this, which I have described as my *opus magnum,* that testifies to the achievement of maturity as a scholar. It was this, I think, more than anything else, which led my colleagues in psychology to select my name, in the early 1940s, for "starring" in the *American Men of Science,* a sign at the time of scholarly achievement in a field.

RESEARCH AND PRACTICE IN INDUSTRY

The period under discussion was also one in which I established associations with two industrial organizations which became the major media for research and practice as an industrial psychologist for over forty years. It is impossible to discuss here in any detail my work with these and other organizations. A few illustrations may serve, however, both to indicate the directions taken by my professional activities and the varieties of problems which challenge the interest and skill of the psychologist in industry.

Yellow Cab Company of Philadelphia. In 1924 I established a consulting relationship with the Yellow Cab Company of Philadelphia which continued until 1965, except for a nine-year period (1927-1936), during which I continued to work as a consultant to the former President (E. S. Higgins) in New York. I returned to the Yellow Cab Company of Philadelphia, in 1936, when Higgins was called upon to reorganize the moribund company and again became its chief officer. My work during my earlier years with this company had been largely in the areas of selection and training, directed toward lowering the accident rate and improving sales productivity. Of interest, in the latter connection, was the quite successful use of application blank items in hiring men capable of building up good records in selling cab rides (1932a), representing one of the earliest programs to use autobiographical data for the prediction of job performance. In later years, I became involved also with labor relations and conducted a number of studies which, for example, established an objective base for the evaluation of the productivity of taxicab drivers, for use both in labor negotiations and in the arbitration of grievances.

It was in the Yellow Cab Company that I found suitable conditions for a study of men and women taxicab drivers operating under comparable conditions. Findings from an initial study, showing that women were responsible for three times as many accidents per 100,000 miles as men (1928d), were confirmed in a repeat study conducted almost twenty years later. By contrast, the revolutionary practice of hiring Blacks as cab drivers, initiated in the 1940s, was strengthened by findings, in repeated comparisons, that there was no significant difference between Blacks and Whites in accident rate.

Philadelphia Electric Company. In the fall of 1927, a few days after temporarily severing my relations with the Yellow Cab Company, I was asked by the Philadelphia Electric Company to look into the possibility of developing tests for the selection of electric substation operators. As noted previously, the project turned out well. During the year allotted for the construction and validation of the test battery, my relations with the company and its people had developed to an extent that led to close to forty years of productive and rewarding service.

Much of my work continued to be in the areas of employee selection and advancement. As noted earlier, this included what I consider to be a quite unique and highly significant program of objective qualifying examinations which made job knowledge and skill the basis of promotion and provided, also, realistic criteria of job performance for the evaluation of selection tests. Nevertheless, I became particularly interested in opportunities which arose for the development, administration, and evaluation of training programs covering a large variety of jobs at all levels of the organization.

Such opportunities grew, in large part, out of an initial demonstration that it was possible to shorten the training program and produce better qualified overhead linemen by interpolating periods of intensive, carefully supervised instruction in knowledge and skills at a central location with periods of practice on the job (1933a). Although the training of new employees produced significant outcomes, I found greater satisfaction in the development, starting in the 1930s, and in the utilization of "refresher" or retraining programs to "update" the knowledge and skills of experienced employees. I saw the latter as a way of both guarding against obsolescence on the employee's present job and of maintaining a "learning set" which could facilitate transfer to other jobs made necessary by technological change (1936b, 1939a, 1941b). Observations made during the Great Depression of the 1930s aroused further awareness of retraining as an aid in the readjustment of unemployed (1933b, 1934b, 1935, 1936b) and contributed to what is a continuing interest in the problem of anticipating the effects of technological change, appearing now in the form of accelerated automation (1939a, 1962b).

New vistas were still opening when, in 1964, I sought retirement from the Philadelphia Electric Company because of an urgent request at the university that I accept an appointment as Dean of the Graduate School of Education (1963-1967) so that I might help bring about an intellectual reform and enrichment of the goals and curriculum of the school.

Other Professional Activities: The Bell Telephone Company of Philadelphia. I have carefully refrained from casual short-term consultation, but I have had a few associations, lasting in each case for a few years, which provided worthwhile opportunities for both research and practice. In addition, in 1951, I agreed to spend ten days during the year "looking into" what appeared to be a high frequency of severe boredom (1951a) among clerks in the Accounting Department of The Bell Telephone Company of Pennsylvania.

Examination of this situation suggested that some of the usual approaches, such as job enlargement, could be helpful in dealing with the problem. It also became clear that much more was needed, especially in the way of reducing the size of the work group and in dealing with barriers to effective relations between work groups and their supervisors. As I worked with the problem, I became involved in other matters and was also attracted to the organization and its people. As a result, as of now, twenty-one years later, I am still carrying on as a consultant to the company.

Among projects developed during the years was a Management Coordination Program designed to bring to lower management levels more extensive participation in decision-making (1954, 1955a). My activities have included consultation in the development of management training programs and involved, also, a number of studies directed toward the evaluation of these programs. Most exciting among the projects in which I became involved was participation in the organization and administration of a unique program of humanistic education for executives fostered especially by W. D. Gillen, President and J. W. Markle, Vice-President of the company, but involving the entire Bell System.

Within the program, conducted for a period of seven years

(1953-1960), approximately 140 members of the managerial staff of Bell System companies spent a full year at the University of Pennsylvania in an especially designed course (Peckham, 1962) devoted entirely to the humanities. Evaluations, which I conducted at the end of each year, showed that the objectives set for the program were satisfactorily achieved, in that it brought flight from "overconformity," the awareness of social changes in the business environment, the liberalization of opinions, the changes in interest, and the modifications of value systems which were sought in the initiation of the program (1959a). An investigation of the long-range impact of the program, conducted late in 1967, showed further that (1) such changes in attitude persisted and that (2) they had a marked effect on the work of participants as managers in the business (1971).

A FELLOWSHIP FOR STUDY IN USSR (1934-1935)

I have written at length about the earlier years of my career and the forces and incidents which brought development and recognition as an industrial psychologist, but I shall be more sparing in writing about later events. Nevertheless, notes on the highlights of my career and sidelights on my views would be incomplete without consideration of an academic year spent in the USSR during 1934-1935 on a Social Science Research Council Fellowship.

A number of factors combined in 1933 to arouse my interest in spending another year in study abroad. After considering various possibilities, I decided to seek an opportunity to learn what was going on in the USSR—in what was being described as the "great social experiment," particularly its effects upon workers in industry.

In spring 1934 I received a notice from the Social Science Research Council saying that I had been awarded the fellowship for which I had applied. No problems were experienced in obtaining a leave of absence from the university. I anticipated difficulties with the Philadelphia Electric Company, my major industrial employer, but I was not only granted leave, but also allowed half-salary while away, an action reflecting both the quality of leadership and tolerance of the company's two executives, William H. Taylor, President, and Horace P. Liversidge, Vice President.

Portents of Coming Events. I stopped in Prague on route to the USSR in the fall of 1934, to attend a Congress of the International Psychotechnical Association (now the International Association of Applied Psychology) and to take part in the meetings of its Executive Committee, at which Bingham and I were representatives for the United States. The stopover in Prague also provided an opportunity for me to present my wife Rebecca, whom I had married in 1931, to my many European friends.

Already apparent at the meeting was the beginning of the decline of psychology in Germany which took place during the time of the Nazi domination. Representatives from that country included only one psychologist of any note. Members of the delegation created a crisis in the history of the association by devoting their presentations to the exposition of Nazi doctrines. Foreshadowed in the meeting were the later suicide of Otto Lipmann, the flight to South America of the outstanding differential psychologist William Stern, the hounding to death of the French psychologist Lahy during the German occupation of France, and the suffering of many others.

Observations in the USSR. During nine months spent in the USSR, I had an opportunity, through meetings with psychologists such as A. R. Luria, A. N. Leontiev, N. O. Levitov, and others to learn about activities in various fields of psychology. An outstanding privilege was the opportunity to talk at length with Pavlov who, although experiencing some difficulties with the authorities at the time, was nevertheless a "figure" who could lead his life almost as though there had been no change in the political regime.

My attention was naturally focused on industrial psychology. Here I benefited much from help given by I. N. Spielrein who, at the time, was frequently the "leader" of delegations from the USSR to international meetings, and with whom I had established a quite warm friendship. I found that my *Industrial Psychology* had been translated and made available, in mimeographed form, in the university libraries. I was, in fact, asked to participate in the preparation of an official translation for publication by the USSR Press, with royalties, but rejected the offer when informed that this would require rewriting of the two chapters on individual differences to conform to Communist orthodoxy with respect to the origin of individual differences.

I found some research and activity in vocational selection, although this, as well as testing by "pedologists" in the schools, came under attack at the time of my stay in the USSR and was virtually eliminated in 1935. There was interesting work by psychologists in the field of training. Of great interest was research on fatigue, generally involving a team approach which coordinated the efforts of psychologists, physiologists, time-and-motion-study men, and others concerned with the elimination of unnecessary fatigue. Several of the industrial psychologists were concerned with problems of motivation. Paradoxically, however, piece-rate systems and other wage-incentive plans embodying large wage differentials were being used on a scale unknown in "bourgeois capitalistic countries."

In the background of all such activity was the constant danger of offending the "controllers" of thought and action by producing research findings which were not in line with official doctrines. Such restrictions were, however, inconsequential in comparison with the fate of Spielrein who, in 1935, was brought to death, along with many other "old Bolsheviks" and other psychologists, by the Stalin purge.

It was knowledge of such events that led me to conclude an article on industrial psychology in the USSR with the statement, "It is apparent that recent years have brought much progress in industrial psychology in the Soviet Union. This progress is a tribute to the sincerity and integrity of Russian scientists who must struggle not only against the inadequate financial support which hampers scientific workers throughout the world, but also against the intolerance of a political creed and system which denies to them the freedom of thought and opinion that is basic to real accomplishment in every field of science" (1938a).

The stay in the USSR was very valuable, although less in the way of enhancing my background in psychology than as an opportunity to view the great social experiment at first hand. Nothing that I saw or learned there created empathy for the view, as presented by Georges Friedmann (1955), that the "private" profit system and the industrialists' contempt for the working masses represent the prime sources of the evil of mechanization. I agree, as does Friedmann, that "the machines' danger to man is not from the machine itself, but from what man makes of it" (Wiener,

1954). However, unlike Friedmann, I also agree with Wiener's position that "the devil whom the scientist is fighting is the devil of confusion, not of willful malice" (Wiener, 1954). Neither extensive readings nor discussions since my stay in the USSR have convinced me that the way to eliminate the confusion is by substituting for our system that created in USSR, or similar "socialistic" or "Communistic" political systems.

WORLD WAR II ACTIVITIES

The five-year period (1935-1940) following my return from the USSR was a relatively quiet one. Toward the end of the 1930s I started to revise *Industrial Psychology*, for publication in 1942, marking the tenth anniversary of the book. As a result, however, of projects undertaken in connection with the World War II effort, I gave up the revision, although I managed to turn out two chapters on vocational psychology for a book *Fields of Psychology* (1940), edited by J. P. Guilford, and a chapter for a volume entitled *Effective Foremanship* (1941d).

In a sense, I actually became involved in the war effort before the war since, in 1939, I had started research on the development of objective measures of flight performance, supported by a grant from the U.S. Civil Aeronautics Administration, received through the National Research Council. "Standard flights" developed in this project, in collaboration with my student Albert S. Thompson, now at Teachers College, Columbia University, were quickly adapted for military use after entry into the war—as were also photographic techniques for recording flight attitudes and related control movements—as a basis for assessing pilot performance (1945).

Also initiated, and completed, before the Pearl Harbor attack, in collaboration with Kinsley R. Smith, was research on the effects on performance and physiological state of atmospheric conditions and noise, carried on under a U.S. Navy grant and directed toward dealing with the issue of whether to provide air conditioning on warships. This became a secondary issue with the declaration of war. Nevertheless, the study was the first to show that there is a critical area, within the range of 83 and 87.5 degrees effective temperature at which significant decrements in performance occur

(1946), a finding later confirmed in studies by Mackworth (1948, 1950) and by others.

My major activities during World War II were in the field of aviation psychology, most particularly as Chairman of the National Research Council Committee on Aviation Psychology from 1942 to 1951 (1945). In various capacities, including those of Project Director for research carried on through the University of Pennsylvania, member of the Committee on the Selection of Underwater Sound (Sonar) Operators, member of the Applied Psychology Panel of the National Defense Research Committee, and in other connections I became involved in a large variety of programs conducted at naval ground installations along both coasts, and aboard ships. These covered both research and development responsibilities, such as developing tests for the selection of sonar operations, formulating procedures for the assembly and training of small gun crews, preparing doctrine and training manuals covering the operation of the main gun battery on battleships, and many others. An investigation, in 1946, of developments in industrial psychology in Germany during the War and a nationwide survey, in 1951, of opportunities and needs for application of research findings in installations of the newly formed Air Defense Command illustrate further the variety of activities involved in my work with the military services.

Particularly satisfying among efforts in these directions was an opportunity to conduct, in collaboration with Delos Wickens, John H. Gorsuch, A. G. Bayroff, M. H. Rogers, and others (1944a), a rigorous and extensive study of transfer effects. Involved here was a comparison of accuracy in estimating the range of approaching aircraft achieved by Naval gunnery crews through training on a simulator, and that achieved through training on the firing line calling for aircraft in flight, the operation of real guns equipped with ring-sights, etc.

The evidence, in findings from the experiment, that transfer effects from the simulator were without practical significance, in contrast with marked and persisting gains in range-finding skill by training on the firing line led to the substitution of training on the firing line for the use of simulators as a way of preparing gun crews for the combat situation (Rogers et al., 1945). Of even greater consequence was the broader impact of the research project in stimulating action in the way of evaluative research as a preliminary to the use of other simulators in both military and civilian training programs.

The special satisfaction derived from this study came from the fact that I was able to conduct an investigation on a basic problem in learning of a type which is generally not feasible in industry, where change in one specific condition ordinarily elicits others not subject to experimental control. Similarly, the U.S. Navy study on atmospheric conditions and noise provided a satisfying opportunity for research on fatigue—now frequently identified with ergonomics—in which I have a continuing interest.

Except for a foray centering on human factors in the design of electric substations (1939b), my experience in industry did not include work in what is now called engineering psychology, concerned with the psychological aspects of the design and operation of man-machine systems. As Chairman of the National Research Council Committee on Aviation Psychology, I became involved in a project bearing on the design of man-machine systems for the control of air traffic. In fact, I caused much pain to some of the experts in the field by taking sharp issue with their failure to deal with the criterion problem in a report on a study sponsored by the Committee on Aviation Psychology (1951b). However, I have never been attracted to the area, although it represents a field of research and practice that has considerable significance for industrial psychology, and also potential in terms of a rapprochement between "experimental" and "applied" psychology (Melzer, 1972).

There were many intellectual returns and personal satisfactions from involvement in the war effort. In particular, there were gains in the way of an enlargement of experimental sophistication from associations with the many top-notch psychologists, representing diverse areas of psychological research and practice who were engaged in research and consultation with the military services. The fact that experimental and other psychologists worked closely together during the war contributed to mutual understanding and tolerance. Many applied psychologists learned something about the need for sound experimental designs and a theoretical background for research; many experimental psychologists learned that they could do research which had practical objectives without losing their identity as experimentalists.

Participation in the International Scene: Bridging the Gap Between "Scientific" and Applied Psychology. My experiences during the war strengthened the stand which I have consistently taken on the importance of close identification between experimental-theoretical psychology, on the one hand, and applied psychology, on the other. My activities in international associations provided opportunities to do something in the way of bridging the gap between psychologists in the two fields.

Along with Raymond Bonnardel of France, Clifford B. Frisby of Great Britain, and others, I had a hand in bringing to fruition, in 1955, a move to change the name of the International Psychotechnical Association to International Association of Applied Psychology (IAAP). This change in name recorded, in a sense, the growing influence in the association of those concerned with psychology as science as well as profession. It also laid the foundation for what was done, during my ten years of service as President of the association (1958-68)—the first from the United States—to reorganize the objectives and programs of the association, in order to extend the opportunities for meaningful dialogues between applied psychologists and those who are primarily concerned with enlarging the scientific foundations of the discipline (1964, 1968). The establishment of closer relations between the IAAP and the International Union of Scientific Psychology contributed further toward an expansion of a scientific orientation in programs devoted to applied psychology and feed-back to "scientific psychology" of significant research findings in applied psychology.

MOTIVATION AND MORALE IN INDUSTRY

In the late 1940s I turned again to the revision of *Industrial Psychology.* During the decade, my attention had been increasingly attracted, on the one hand, to frequent complaints by management that "few, if any, employees, are working up to their capacity" and, on the other, to an increasing amount of activity in the way of both attitude surveys and experimental studies bearing upon the operation of motives in industrial work (1938b, 1942,

1944b, 1947). As a result, I undertook to deal first with revising the chapter entitled "Motives in Industry." Revision of this chapter, covering fifteen pages in *Industrial Psychology,* became a book of approximately five hundred pages entitled *Motivation and Morale in Industry,* published in 1953.

Early Outlooks on Motivation in Industry. The tremendous growth implied by this enlargement does not mean that the importance of the "will to work" as contrasted with the "capacity to work" was unrecognized in the 1920s and 1930s. There was increasing awareness of the value of financial incentives as recommended in Taylor's proposals for scientific management (Taylor, 1911). Reports by Whiting Williams, a former personnel administrator who had spent many months working in factories and mines in the United States and Europe, strikingly brought into relief the operation and significance of "feelings of worth" and other motives in industrial work (Williams, 1920, 1925). By the end of the 1920s the ground work had been laid for using survey methods to ascertain "what workers want," as illustrated in early studies by Houser (1927) and by investigations conducted in the Hawthorne Works of the Western Electric Company (Putnam, 1930; Mayo, 1930). In addition, psychologists were calling for the use of experimental methodologies characterizing research in science for acquiring information concerning the identity, interrelations, and operation of motives in the work situation (Kornhauser, 1923, 1933; Kornhauser and Sharp, 1932).

Changes in the Paradigms for Research on Motives in Industry. Delay in the development and application of appropriate experimental designs for the study of motives in work was, in large part, the result of wide-spread acceptance of a conceptual framework—commonly called the "instinct hypothesis"—which stated that the "prime movers" in the economic as well as in other activities of man were a variety of instincts, representing innate, unlearned, species-determined psycho-physical dispositions toward behavior (McDougall, 1908). This assumption, promulgated by economists (Veblen, 1914; Tead, 1918; Parker, 1920) as well as psychologists, was not conducive to raising the right questions or to the development of appropriate techniques for the experimental study of human motivation. Present, also, was another handicap in the form of a predominating belief by management that "money alone is the answer" to gaining worker productivity. Under the circumstances, it is not surprising that practically everything of importance in the way of research on motivation could be covered in fifteen pages in the 1932 text.

The vast mass of facts, tentative principles, and theories embodied in *Motivation and Morale in Industry* reflect chiefly a shift in the paradigms of psychology—in the constellation of beliefs, values, techniques, and so on shared by a community of scientists (Kuhn, 1970)—in this case the community of social psychologists. Such shifts, occurring over a number of years produced, in the 1940s, an experimental social psychology. Theories, research techniques, and values underlying research on motivation in industry have come chiefly from this field with, however, substantial additions from personality psychology, psychiatry, sociology, and, to some extent, from applied anthropology.

The Content of Motivation and Morale in Industry. The content of the book reflects such changes, covering topics not even mentioned in *Industrial Psychology* and many terms which were unknown at the time of publication of that book. It includes a detailed treatment of experimental studies and attitude surveys, supplemented by discussion of basic concepts and theories bearing upon motivation in industry. A summary of conclusions is followed by a number of chapters, directed chiefly to management, bearing on the utilization in industry of findings and their implications as covered in earlier chapters.

There was general agreement among reviewers that this volume represented the first comprehensive presentation and evaluation of data bearing on motivation and morale available to psychologists working on industrial problems. Here and there, questions were raised about specific aspects of the book. Thus, in reviews appearing in labor journals, dissatisfaction was expressed with chapters dealing with workers' attitudes toward unions. My view had been shaped by an extensive review of available studies—conducted under union as well as management auspices. These, for example, failed to confirm the bland assertions by Krech and Crutchfield—made without benefit of evidence in 1942—that "the labor union, by and large, can better meet most of the workers needs and demands than can other organizations"; that "most social organizations will generally reflect the major needs of its members and labor unions will therefore be more 'tailored' to the needs of workers than will religious organizations or other less homogeneously composed social organizations" (Krech and Crutchfield, 1942).

The Role of Legends and Miracles in Industrial Psychology. I felt pleased with the reception given to *Motivation and Morale in Industry,* but it did not provide as much pleasure to me as did the writing of earlier books and many of my articles. I was made uncomfortable by the many gray areas in the way of questionable experimental designs; by the extrapolation of meager findings from both surveys and experimental studies into unwarranted generalizations bearing on action; by the frequent substitution of value judgments for facts in the discussion of issues. Again and again, I found it necessary to call attention to the unsubstantial basis for recommendations and programs which were receiving wide acceptance by both professional psychologists and in management circles. My problem was that of avoiding the role of Cassandra, while noting dangers which lay ahead unless steps were taken to correct defects in experimental approaches and to seek verification of findings and conclusions reported in the book.

Within this frame of reference, for example, I noted the significant outcome of the Hawthorne Studies, and of the social philosophy of Elton Mayo (1946) in drawing attention to the great importance of the *small group* as a source of motivation at work. Nevertheless, I found it necessary to deal also with the inadequacies of the experimental design and unsubstantiated conclusions bearing on financial incentives, etc., "derived" from a study which I have come to call the *Legend of the Hawthorne Works* (1959b). In a similar context, there was strong need to deal with errors in the design of experiments on participation in decision making—in what I have named the Miracle of the Harwood Manufacturing Company—which make it impossible to separate the effect of participation in decision making from that of knowledge of results.

Apparent also, at the time, and requiring consideration, was the overextension of theory—an application of the view, as expressed by one social psychologist, that "It doesn't matter how badly conceived an experiment is, so long as it produces a 'sound' theory." Evident was a personal "cultism," expressed both in the tendency to neglect alternative theories and that of subordinating empiricism to theory, which continues to create problems in industrial psychology as both science and profession (1959b, 1969).

It was such aspects of the new field that produced the difficulties in writing the book to which I have referred. I am reminded, in this connection, of the suggestion by one reviewer that I appeared to be uneasy in dealing with the field. I, myself, felt that I had perhaps become a little "soft," because of a desire to present the possibilities rather than to deal too harshly with the very apparent weaknesses of a new and highly important field of research and practice. Evidence that I may have succeeded in presenting strengths without concealing weaknesses appears in a letter, dated March 22, 1954, from a highly knowledgeable, capable, and critical colleague, not an industrial psychologist, which reads, in part: "You have somehow managed to write in this difficult field without introducing any nonsense, which is a triumph in itself. What is perhaps most important, you have upheld high standards of scientific evaluation while simultaneously offering much that seems to be of great practical significance to everyone who has decisions to make in industry, both men and management . . ." (Francis W. Irwin).

A Note on Organizational Psychology. The period covered in *Motivation and Morale in Industry* was one in which the influence of the small group, as formally organized by management or as spontaneously developing on the job, came to the foreground. In contrast, one of the most significant developments of approximately the past two decades has been the systematic study of the influence of the larger business organization. Involved here, in part, is the problem of developing an organizational structure and patterns of interrelations within the organization which will permit full satisfaction of individual needs and complete self-realization, without sacrificing the economic goals of industry (1955b, 1962a).

In a characteristic fashion, the approach to the problems of the total organization takes the form, at one extreme, of an effort on the part of professional industrial psychologists to use what appears to be applicable from research in psychology to "cure the monsters" (Dunnette, 1971). At the other extreme, is the development of a complex theoretical background, yielding a wide series of hypotheses bearing upon steps that might be taken in the reorganization of the company structure, channels of communications, and the behavior of executives, in order to increase the concordance between the satisfaction of individual needs and the achievement of company objectives.

Such developments have been brought together under the rubric of organizational psychology. This has on occasion been treated, along with engineering psychology, ergonomics, and personnel psychology, as though each were a separate field lying outside of industrial psychology. Such fragmentation has been countered, in part, by changing the name of Division 14 of the American Psychological Association from Division of Industrial Psychology to Division of Industrial and Organizational Psychology. In contrast is the separation of engineering psychology from industrial psychology implied in the organization, within APA, of The Society of Engineering Psychologists (Division 21).

Do these developments foreshadow the passing of industrial psychology? This issue has recently been considered by Ross Stagner who notes that "dirges [have] been sounded for the death of industrial psychology. If by this," he adds, "we mean the passing of a specialty devoted to test scores, stanines, and predictive validity coefficients, its departure will be mourned by but a few. The new industrial psychology, however, appears to be lusty and vigorous. It has already enriched social psychology in important ways, and it promises valuable new insights into the human personality functioning in a highly structured environment. Without benefit of a regression equation, I predict for it," Stagner writes, "a valuable and exciting future" (Stagner, 1966).

INDUSTRIAL PSYCHOLOGY: A CREDIBILITY GAP

There are many reasons for agreeing with this prediction. It is supported by gains in knowledge and improvements in methodology which enrich the potential of the field—even that of the specialty which Stagner describes as moribund. I have no doubt, also, that the psychologists entering the field are just as capable, as well motivated and sincere, as were the pioneers in the field and, in addition, immeasurably better informed (1959b). Nevertheless, how "valuable" psychology becomes in their hands depends, in part, on what can be accomplished to overcome a *credibility gap* in the field created by their predecessors. The credibility gap finds expression in increasing doubts as to the extent to which what psychologists do in industry as practitioners has a solid basis in psychology as science. Reflected here is a frequency with which what is recommended as good practice turns out to be without established merit insofar as scientific foundations are concerned. *Vocational Selection and Classification.* The seriousness of this problem appears clearly in the field of vocational selection and placement. The number and variety of tests available to the psychologist in industry provide an impressive spectacle, especially as presented in the often elaborate catalogues distributed by those who publish and sell tests. There have been significant developments in the form of statistical tools for use in test construction, and of conceptualizations bearing upon decision making in the utilization of testing instruments. However, there is reason to question whether such developments have been paralleled by significant improvements in the quality of the testing instruments. For example, there are no indications that the problem of low intercorrelations among tests of general intelligence, which I reported fifty years ago, has been dealt with. In fact, as noted recently (Barrett, 1970), evidence is now available of similar low intercorrelations among tests of job satisfaction (Mukherjee, 1969) and among personality tests. In contrast, intercorrelations among subtests in differential aptitude test batteries remain high, in spite of the requirement for tests measuring "unique" factors (1961). Here, as in the case of personal "cultism" in theory (1959b, 1969), appears the influence of what Barrett has called the "immortality syndrome"—the need of the individual to devise his own instrument and place his name upon it while, concurrently, replication and verification of the work of others in the area are avoided.

The credibility gap in the area of vocational selection and classification is considerably enlarged by the frequent failure of the psychologist to do what he well knows needs to be done in the way of establishing the reliability and validity of psychological tests and other predictions (1959b, 1961, 1964). The problem of the criterion—its objectivity, reliability, and pertinence or *real-*

ism—has been sadly neglected by psychologists concerned with testing in industry. Furthermore, tests which must be viewed as only experimental instruments are thrown into the market and presented to potential consumers as though they were, in fact, thoroughly reliable and validated instruments capable of performing the socially useful tasks for which they were, presumably, designed. The situation is exacerbated by the clinical psychologist who, acting as an "instrument of prediction" (Barrett, 1970), bypasses the need for even the slightest of scientific evaluations of the selection procedure—as very frequently appears to be the practice where the "insights" of the clinical psychologist are used in the selection, evaluation, and promotion of managerial personnel (1958).

Concern with respect to such problems in the construction and use of psychological tests and of other predictives is not limited to their application in industry. Thus, Pius XII found it necessary, in 1958, to remind psychologists of the disregard of ethical principles in the invasion of privacy and of danger to the individual in the uncritical use of inadequately validated personality tests in psychological research and practice. To the further shame of psychologists, it has been found necessary by the Supreme Court of the United States to remind them of the obligation to validate tests against objective and realistic criteria as a condition to their use for selection and classification purposes in industry (U.S. Supreme Court, 1970).

It is clear that management is in some part to blame for what is questionable or improper both in employee selection and in other applications of psychology in industry. There are many indications that management is much less critical in the assessment of proposed employee selection programs and of other proposals dealing with the human problems in industry than it is in appraising the quality of materials, machines, and other physical resources.

Through the years, for example, management has been duped by proponents of physiognomic systems, handwriting analysis, and other non-validated programs for the evaluation of capacity and "character." Personnel managers—even those high in the industrial echelon who frequently make the decisions as to whether psychological tests should or should not be used—have been found to be at least as gullible as students in accepting evaluations based on unsubstantiated character analysis systems (Viteles and Smith, 1932b; Stagner, 1958).

The inclination toward gullibility in the acceptance of psychological programs of questionable value is reinforced by the practice of "one-upmanship"—a drive on the part of executives to "be in" on new developments and even "get ahead" of a colleague in another organization who has boasted on the golf course, or at a luncheon meeting, about what is new in his company. It seems possible that such competitiveness among organizations and their executives is a quite potent factor in the proliferation of psychological programs that turn out to be no more than fads. This, indeed, may be what is behind the current rush of industry to send its executives to learn "brain-wave control" as a way of preparing them to become "better business men" (Smith, 1972), in spite of the meagerness of existing knowledge concerning the full implications and long-range effects of "biofeedback" upon the behavior of man (Luce and Peper, 1971).

The gullibility of executives helps to explain why "innovations" in industrial psychology "can be sold to organizations with little or no demonstration of their effectiveness" (Barrett, 1970). Even more important is the behavior of industrial psychologists who introduce and market their wares within the context of *caveat emptor* (1941a), under a sort of false scientism which lends a halo of respectability to tools, techniques, and programs which have little if any scientific foundation (1950b, 1964).

Human Relations Programs: Fact or Fable? It is within such a context that "titillating therapy" (Gomberg, 1967) in the form of sensitivity training in T-groups or other encounter and confrontation situations has been widely marketed. In fact, practitioners involved in such programs seem, even more than other groups, to believe that the usefulness of their efforts to increase self-awareness and release human potential is self-evident, and needs no verification (Eddy and Lubin, 1971). Significantly, evaluative studies conducted in spite of such beliefs show a recurrent pattern of immediate enthusiasm followed by little beneficial effect (Back, 1972).

Programs brought into industry by psychologists include a large variety directed toward improving the climate of "human relations" in industry. These involve, basically, efforts to use what is known about the determinants of collaboration, knowledge concerning factors which lead people to work together, and so on for increasing the effectiveness of groups in industry in achieving common goals (Schoen, 1957). Fear has been expressed that such management development courses have adverse effects in the way of turning the American business manager into an organizational conformist; that such programs are simply mechanisms to "form an elite of skilled leaders who will guide men back, benevolently, to 'group belongingness'—to cement a closer relationship between the individual and The Organization" (Whyte, 1956; see also Fromm, 1957). It is my opinion that such adverse effects and dangers of human relations training have been grossly exaggerated. Even if the objectives were what they are claimed to be, there is no reason for great concern, since there is little firm evidence that human relations training influences many people to any great extent (1959a). Here, as in many other instances, the immense superstructure of psychological practice in industry rests on a foundation of scattered, splintered, and tinderlike data which could fall apart with essays in the way of further and highly necessary exploration through the use of available scientific techniques (1955c, 1959b).

Many factors have combined to produce this situation, including a paucity of basic research; inappropriate design of the pioneering study or investigations on which practice is based; the dependence on studies conducted in laboratories instead of in industry; the generalization to industrial workers and managers of studies conducted with students and children; and so on. There is, in addition, the persisting practice of subordinating empiricism to theory in the elaboration of programs for dealing with human problems and issues in industry (1969). Only too frequently, as recently noted by Barrett (1970), "a theory may take on the characteristics of a 'received doctrine' and become an unanalyzed article of faith" (Means, 1965).

As I have noted in a number of articles (1959b, 1964, 1969), one way of perpetuating such faith is by designing experiments in such a way that no source of variance appears that throws doubt on the theory. Another is to resist experiments designed within the context of multiple theories. Still another way is to neglect data from experiments by others which are in contradiction with those considered crucial to the support of the theory. Most effective of all steps is that of avoiding virtually any research designed to investigate the tenability of a theory, as appears most strikingly, for example, in the case of Abraham Maslow's hierarchical theory of motivation (Maslow, 1954) and in Douglas McGregor's postulation of theories *X* and *Y* (McGregor, 1960)—both representing influential "received doctrines" underlying the programing of human relations activities by industrial psychologists (Barrett, 1970; Fein, 1970).

Psychologists have been gently chided by Norman R. F. Maier for such practices through the formulation of Maier's Law which states "If facts do not support theory they must be disposed of." It follows that "that theory must supersede the facts. It is the facts that must conform" (Maier, 1960). With contrasting truculence, I have suggested that what applied psychology (along with basic psychology) needs most at the moment is a moratorium on new theory, until those now in the books have gone through a process of digestion which either fortifies the body of psychological knowledge or is discarded as waste (1969).

A CRISIS OF IDENTITY IN PSYCHOLOGY

Resort to theory, in the absence of facts, to support the practice of psychology is neither peculiar to industrial psychology nor of recent origin. It is merely one example of a long-existing tendency on the part of professional psychologists to make assumptions with respect to what might be useful without a firm foundation of knowledge about human behavior, or of specific research findings to support either their assumptions or their practices.

Currently, this tendency is intensified by a growing indecision on the part of experimental, scientifically oriented psychologists as to what is basically most relevant for psychology—service or research; community action or enhancement of knowledge; participation in movements of firming-up the foundations of academe; the advancement of science or the construction of "instant Utopias," and so on. Such uncertainty intensifies what I have called a "crisis of identity"—the uncertainty as to whether psychology is to be primarily science or action; fact or fiction; cult or knowledge; a scholarly discipline or a medium for frequently premature application of views and methods of highly doubtful validity in dealing with highly complex individual social, economic, and political situation (1972).

Within this context, the quarter-century-old crusade by B. F. Skinner "to grasp this sorry Scheme of Things entire . . . and then to remold it nearer to (his) Heart's desire" is only one example, on a grand scale, of what other psychologists have undertaken in the way of piecemeal social engineering. His recent book, *Beyond Freedom and Dignity* (1971)—projecting a supposedly scientific foundation for proposals earlier presented in his novel, *Walden II* (1948)—and the current barrage of discussion in newspapers, in journals, and on radio and television clearly serve to underline the confounding of fact with fiction, science with value judgments, knowledge with good intentions, which occurs as the psychologist turns into social reformer.

In citing Skinner as an example I am not implying that he fails to meet the criteria of a conscientious and even notable scientist in his research, or that he is anything other than a man of good will. Nor are his views on the control of man necessarily more disturbing than those, for example, of Delgado, whose opinions and prophecies with respect to use of remote electrical stimulation of the brain (ESB) as a control mechanism may present an even more distressing prospect for mankind (Delgado, 1969; Scarf, 1970). Nevertheless, both Skinner's publications and public appearances again bring into relief the tendency on the part of the psychologist to confound speculations with scientific content (Chomsky, 1971) and to inject value judgments in a manner that makes it increasingly difficult to know when the psychologist speaks with the authority of science, or when he is playing the role of the social reformer while clothed—or even disguised—in the garb of the scientist (1955c).

In saying this, I am not denying the right of the psychologist to his opinions—to his own value judgments. I am also not denying the need—and even the obligation—of psychology to deal with the problems of society. It may be appropriate that psychologists, along with other scientists, "emerge," in the words of Sinsheimer, "from their laboratories to exercise their prophetic vision—to become responsible prophets to the people, as were in earlier times oracles and priests, warriors and industrialists" (Sinsheimer, 1967).

However, prophecy, often representing expression of great moral principles, is not to be confused with science, which involves predictions, grounded on theory and supported by knowledge derived from research.

The unhappy fact is that the professional psychologist and also the laboratory psychologist transmuted into a man of action disregard this distinction. It is almost as though an insecurity associated with the crisis of identity leads us to enter the affairs of the world not with a sense of humility, but, like Scaphio and Phantis in the delightful comedy *Utopia, Ltd,* by W. S. Gilbert, to the voice of a chorus that sings:

> O make way for the Wise Men.
> They are the prizemen –
> . . . .
> They're the pride of Utopia –
> Cornucopia
> Is each in his mental fertility
> O they never make a blunder,
> and no wonder,
> For they're the triumph of infallibility.

L'ENVOI

Perhaps the time has come for the psychologist to substitute wisdom for the appearance of wisdom–at least, for distinguishing *what we know* from *what we do*–on a broader scale, for separating our thinking and wishes with respect to ordinary affairs from the "critical habits of thinking" (Hill, 1951) that characterize the true scientist and establish the inherent integrity of a science.

The challenge available to young people interested in industrial psychology today is that of widening the road to wisdom. In many ways, the challenge is even more exciting than that which I faced on entering the narrow pathways which led me into the field of industrial psychology.

REFERENCES

Selected Author's Publications

1919 The children of a Jewish orphanage: a preliminary report of a psychological survey. *Psychological Clinic, 12,* 5–9.

1921 Tests in industry. *Journal of Applied Psychology, 5,* 57–63.

1922 (a) A comparison of three tests of general intelligence. *Journal of Applied Psychology, 6,* 392–401.

(b) Job specifications and diagnostic tests of job competency designed for the auditing division of a street railway company. *Psychological Clinic, 14,* 83–105.

(c) Sergeant X., a study in vocational guidance. *Psychological Clinic, 14,* 36–47.

1923 (a) Instruction in psychology in Paris. *Psychological Bulletin, 20,* 545–552.

(b) Psychology in business—in England, France, and Germany. *Annals of the American Academy of Political and Social Sciences, 110,* 209–220.

1924 (a) Vocational guidance and job analysis: the psychological viewpoint. *Psychological Clinic, 15,* 157–182.

(b) Selecting cashiers and predicting length of service. *Journal of Personnel Research, 2,* 467–473.

1925 (a) Research in the selection of motormen, Part I. *Journal of Personnel Research, 3,* 110–115; Part II, *Journal of Personnel Research, 4,* 173–197.

(b) A psychological clinic for vocational guidance. *Vocational Guidance Magazine, 1925, 4,* 78–79.

1926 Psychology in industry. *Psychological Bulletin, 23,* 631–680.

1928 (a) Psychology in industry. *Psychological Bulletin, 25,* 6, 309–340.

(b) The clinical approach in vocational guidance. *Vocational Guidance Magazine, 7,* 1–9.

(c) The mental status of the Negro. *Annals of the American Academy of Political and Social Sciences, 140,* 166–177.

(d) With H. M. Gardner. Women taxicab drivers; sex differences in proneness to motor vehicle accidents. *Personnel Journal, 7,* 349–355.

1929 (a) Validating the clinical method in vocational guidance. *Psychological Clinic, 19,* 69–77.

(b) The human factor in substation operation: specifications and tests for substation operators, *Personnel Journal, 8,* 81–114.

1930 (a) Psychology in industry. *Psychological Bulletin, 27,* 567–635.

(b) Die "gestalt"—betrachtsungsweise in der angewändte psychologie, *Zeitschrift für Angewändte Psychologie, 35,* 525–531.

1931 Clinical problems in the vocational guidance of the mentally deficient. *Psychological Clinic, 20,* 33–41.

1932 (a) *Industrial Psychology.* New York: W. W. Norton, 1932.

(b) With K. R. Smith. The prediction of vocational aptitude and success from photographs. *Journal of Experimental Psychology, 15,* 615–629.

1933 (a) Adjustment in industry through training. *Personnel Journal, 11,* 295–306.

(b) Training and unemployment. *The Human Factor, 7,* 307–311.

1934 (a) *The Science of Work.* New York: W. W. Norton.

(b) Psychology and reemployment. *Scientific Monthly, 39,* 271–273.

(c) With S. W. Fernberger and W. R. Carlson. The effect of changes in illumination upon visual perception. *Journal of Applied Psychology, 18,* b11–b17.

(d) (ed.) Analysis of occupations. *Occupations, 12,* 10, 5–85.

1935 Le point de vue psychologique du chomage aux Etats-Unis. *Le Travail humain, 3,* 129–138.

1936 (a) A dynamic criterion. *Occupations* (Section 1), *14,* 1–5.

(b) How technological changes affect employees. *Mechanical Engineering,* 1936, *58,* 302–303.

1938 (a) Industrial psychology in Russia. *Occupational Psychology,* spring issue, 1–19.

(b) The application of psychology in American business. Washington, D.C. *Proceedings 7th International Management Congress: Personnel-Management Section,* 78–83.

(c) With F. J. Keller. *Vocational Guidance Throughout the World.* New York: W. W. Norton.

1939 (a) Man and the machine. *Power Plant Engineering, 43,* 51–53.

(b) Design of substations for accident prevention. *Edison Electrical Institute Bulletin,* March, 101–106.

1940 Vocational psychology. In J. P. Guilford (ed.), *Fields of Psychology.* New York: D. Van Nostrand. (Revised Edition, 1950), 507–627.

1941 (a) Caveat emptor. *Journal of Consulting Psychology, 5,* 118–122.

(b) The role of industrial psychology in defending the future of America. *Annals of the American Academy of Political and Social Sciences,* July, 156–162.

(c) Psychological practice and research in vocational guidance. *Journal of Consulting Psychology, 5,* 258–264.

(d) The human element in industrial relations. In H. B. Maynard (ed.), *Effective Foremanship.* New York: McGraw-Hill Book Co., 71–87.

1942 The application of psychology in business and industry. *Occupational Psychology, 16,* 55–60.

1944 (a) With J. H. Gorsuch, K. R. Smith, A. G. Bayroff, M. H. Rogers, D. D. Wickens, et al. *An Investigation of the Range Estimation Trainer . . .,* Washington, D.C., OSRD Contract OEM ar-7000, Report No. 4263.

(b) Postlude to the application of psychology in industry. *Journal of Consulting Psychology, 8,* 182–186.

1945 The aircraft pilot: five years of research: a summary of outcomes. *Psychological Bulletin, 42,* 489–526.

1946 With K. R. Smith. An experimental investigation of the effect of changes in atmospheric conditions and noise upon performance. *Transactions of the American Society of Heating and Ventilating Engineers, 52,* 167–180.

1947 The measurement of employee attitudes. In C. W. Churchman, R. L. Ackoff, and M. Wax (eds.), *Measurement of Consumer Interest.* Philadelphia: University of Pennsylvania Press, 177–197.

1949 (a) The use of psychological methods in the selection and the classification of employees in the United States; guiding principles and current trends. In F. Baumgarten, *Progrès de la Psychotechnique.* Bern, Verlag A. Francke, 146–164.

(b) Selection and placement of employees. In Industrial Relations Research Association, *Psychology of Labor Management Relations.* New York: American Book-Stanford Press, 9–21.

1951 (a) Man and machine relationships: the problem of boredom. In *Proceedings 1950 Annual Fall Conference.* New York: Society for Advancement of Management, 129–138.

(b) Editorial foreword. In P. M. Fitts (ed.) *Human Engineering for an Effective Air Navigation and Control System.* Washington, D.C.: Committee on Aviation Psychology, National Research Council.

1953 *Motivation and Morale in Industry.* New York: W. W. Norton.

1954 What raises a man's morale? *Personnel, 30,* 302–313.

1955 (a) Motivation and morale—whose responsibility? *Personnel Practice Bulletin* (Australia), *11,* 27–42.

(b) The human factor in organization. *University of Minnesota Industrial Relations Research and Technical Report, 17,* 19–26.

(c) The new Utopia. *Science, 122,* 1167–1171.

1958 L'Identification du potentiel du personnel d'encadrement. *Bulletin de l'Association internationale de Psychologie appliquée, 7,* 44–79.

1959 (a) "Human relations" and "humanities" in the education of business leaders: evaluation of a program of humanistic studies for executives. *Personnel Psychology, 12,* 1–28.

(b) Fundamentalism in industrial psychology. *Occupational Psychology, 33,* 98–110.

1961 Psychological perspectives in vocational guidance. In M. S. Viteles (A. H. Brayfield and L. E. Tyler), *Vocational Counseling: A Reappraisal in Honor of Donald G. Paterson,* Minnesota Studies in Student Personnel Work No. 11, University of Minnesota Press.

1962 (a) Personality and organization: the individual and the system: an introduction. In G. Nielsen (ed.), *Industrial and Business Psychology.* Munksgaard, 97–100.

(b) Man, mind, and machines. In G. Nielsen (ed.), *Industrial and Business Psychology.* Munksgaard, 9–25.

1964 Experimental foundations of applied psychology. *Bulletin of the International Association of Applied Psychology, 13,* 31–38.

1968 The International Association of Applied Psychology. *International Journal of Psychology, 3,* 307–311.

1969 The two faces of applied psychology. *International Review of Applied Psychology, 18,* 5–10.

1970 The humanistic teaching of psychology: opportunity and dilemma. *Newsletter Division 2, American Psychological Association,* March 5–11.

1971 The long-range impact of a programme of humanistic studies for executives on managerial attitudes and behavior. *International Review of Applied Psychology, 20,* 5–24.

1972 Psychology today: fact and foible. *American Psychologist, 27,* 601–607.

Other Publications Cited

Anon. Advertising strategy and theories of motivation. *Cost and Profit Outlook,* 1956, *9,* 12, 4ff.

Aubrey, E. E. *Humanistic Teaching and the Place of Ethical and Religious Values in Higher Education.* Philadelphia: University of Pennsylvania Press, 1959.

Back, K. W. *Beyond Words: The Story of Sensitivity Training and the Encounter Movement.* New York: Basic Books, 1972.

Baritz, L. *The Servants of Power.* New York: John Wiley, 1965.

Barrett, G. V., Characteristics and requirements of research in industrial and organizational psychology. In G. V. Barrett, B. M. Bass, M. D. Dunnette. *Industrial Psychology in the Seventies and Beyond.* Arlington, Va.: Office of Naval Research, 1970, 1–14.

Bingham, W. V. Army personnel work. *Journal of Applied Psychology,* 1919, *3,* 1–12.

——. On the possibility of an applied psychology. *Psychological Review,* 1923, *30,* 289–305.

Borow, H. *Man in a World at Work.* Boston: Houghton Mifflin, 1964.

Brewer, J. M. *History of Vocational Guidance.* New York: Harper & Bros., 1942.

Brigham, C. *A Study of American Intelligence.* Princeton: Princeton University Press, 1923.

Canaday, J. A Wasp's progress. *New York Times Magazine,* March 19, 1972, 30 ff., 41.

Cohen, J. *Humanistic Psychology.* London: George Allen & Unwin, 1958.

Crichton, M. *The Terminal Man.* New York: Knopf, 1972.

Dawis, R. V., Lofquist, L. H., and Weiss, D. T. *A Theory of Work Adjustment, Minnesota Studies in Vocational Rehabilitation No. XXIII.* Minneapolis, University of Minnesota, 1968.

Delgado, J. M. *Physical Control of the Mind.* New York: Harper & Row, 1969.

Dunnette, M. D. Curing the Monsters (review). *Contemporary Psychology,* 1971, *16,* 113–115.

Eddy, W. B., and Lubin, B. Laboratory training and encounter groups. *Personnel and Guidance Journal,* 1971, *49,* 625–635.

Fein, M. Approaches to Motivation. Hillsdale, N.J. (unpublished manuscript), 1970.

Finch, F. Chimpanzee frustration responses. *Psychosomatic Medicine,* 1942, *4,* 233–251.

Friedmann, G. *Industrial Society.* Glencoe, Ill.: The Free Press, 1955.

Fromm, E. Man is not a thing. *The Saturday Review,* March 16, 1957, 9–11.

Gomberg, W. Titillating therapy: management development's most fashionable fad. (unpublished manuscript; University of Pennsylvania), 1967.

Hill, A. V. The social responsibilities of scientists. *Bulletin of Atomic Scientists,* 1951, *7,* 371.

Hollingworth, H. L. *Vocational Psychology: Its Problems and Methods.* New York: Appleton-Century-Crofts, 1916.

Houser, J. D. *What the Employer Thinks.* Cambridge, Mass.: Harvard University Press, 1927.

Hull, C. L. *Aptitude Testing.* Yonkers-on-the-Hudson: World Book Co., 1928.

Kuhn, T. S. *The Structure of Scientific Revolutions.* (2nd ed.) Chicago: University of Chicago Press, 1970.

Kornhauser, A. The motives-in-industry problem. *Annals of the American Academy of Political and Social Sciences,* 1923, *110,* 105ff.

——. Worker's motivation and production. *Personnel Service Bulletin,* 1933, *2,* 1–3.

——., and Sharp, A. A. Employees' attitudes. *Personnel Journal,* 1932, *10,* 393–404.

——. *Mental Health of the Industrial Worker.* New York: John Wiley, 1965.

Krech, D., and Crutchfield, R. S. *Theories and Patterns of Social Psychology.* New York: McGraw-Hill, 1942.

Link, H. C. *Employment Psychology.* New York: Macmillan, 1919.

Luce, G., and Peper, F. Mind over body: mind over mind. *New York Times Magazine,* September 21, 1971, 34ff.

Mackworth, N. H. Definition of the upper limit of environmental warmth by psychological tests of human performance. *The Royal Society, Empire Scientific Conference Report,* 1948, *1,* 423–441.

——. Researches on the measurement of human performance. *Medical Research Council Special Report Series,* No. 268, H.M. Stationery Office, 1950, 119–133.

Maier, N. R. F. Maier's Law. *American Psychologist,* 1960, *15,* 208–12.

Mann, F. C. Shift work and the shorter work week. In C. E. Dankert, F. C. Mann, and H. R. Northrup. *Hours of Work.* New York: Harper & Row, 1965.

Maslow, A. H. *Motivation and personality.* New York: Harper and Brothers, 1954.

Maugham, W. S. *Cake and Ale.* New York: Doubleday and Co., 1930.

Mayo, E. Changing methods in industry. *Personnel Journal,* 1930, *8,* 326–332.

——. *The Human Problem of an Industrial Civilization.* Cambridge, Mass.: The Harvard Business School, 1946.

McGregor, D. M. *The Human Side of Enterprise.* New York: McGraw-Hill, 1960.

Means, R. S. Weber's thesis of the Protestant ethic: the ambiguities of received doctrine. *The Journal of Religion*, 1965, *45*, 1–11.

Melzer, H. Review of reviews in industrial psychology. 1950–69, *Personnel Psychology*, 1972, *55*, 201–222.

Menotti, G. C. Conversation with Menotti. *New York State Theatre Magazine*, April 1971, 31–33.

Moore, B. V., Viteles, Morris S. Industrial psychology: a review. *Journal of Personnel Research*, 1933, *11*, 258–259.

Mott, P. E., Mann, F. C., McLoughlin, Q., and Warwick, D. P. *Shift Work*. Ann Arbor: University of Michigan Press, 1965.

Mukherjee, B. N. Interrelationships among measures of job satisfaction and job involvement. Washington, D.C., *Experimental Publication System*, 1969, *1*, Ms. No. 036 A, 1–14.

Münsterberg, H. *Psychology and Industrial Efficiency*. Boston: Houghton Mifflin, 1913.

Myers, C. S., *Mind and Work*. London: University of London Press, 1920.

———. *Industrial Psychology in Great Britain*. London Jonathan Cape, 1926.

Myers, C. S. (ed.). *Industrial Psychology*. New York: Henry Holt, 1929.

Parker, C. *The Casual Laborer and Other Essays*. New York: Harcourt, Brace and Howe, 1920.

Peckham, M. *Humanistic Education for Business Executives*. Philadelphia, University of Pennsylvania (Unpublished report), 1962.

Poffenberger, A. T. *Applied Psychology*. New York: Appleton, 1927.

Pope Pius XII. A discourse to the International Association of Applied Psychology. *Occupational Psychology*, 1958, *32*, 218–228.

Putnam, M. L. Improving employee relations. *Personnel Journal*, 1930, *8*, 314–325.

Reisman, J. M. *The Development of Clinical Psychology*. New York: Appleton-Century-Crofts, 1966.

Rogers, M. J., Sprol, S. J., Viteles, M. S., Voss, A. A., and Wicken, D. D. *Evaluation of Methods of Training in Estimating a Fixed Opening Range*. Washington, D.C.: OSRD Contract OEM ar-7000, Report No. 5675, 1945.

Rosen, S. D., Weiss, D. J., Hendel, D. D., Davis, R. V., and Lofquist, L. H. *Occupational Reinforcer Patterns*, Vol. II, *Minnesota Studies in Vocational Rehabilitation XXIX*. Minneapolis: University of Minnesota, 1972.

Scarf, M. Brain researcher Jose Delgado asks "What kind of human being would we like to construct?" *New York Times Magazine*, November 15, 1970, 46ff.

Schoen, D. R. Human relations: Boon or boggle. *Harvard Business Review*, 1957, *35*, 6, 41–47.

Schrag, P. The decline of the WASP. *Harper's Magazine*, April, 1970, 85–91.

Scott, W. C. *Influencing Men and Business*. New York: Ronald Press, 1911.

Shartle, C. L. *Occupational Information: Its Development and Application*. New York: Prentice-Hall, 1946.

Shellow, S. M. Research in the selection of motormen. *Journal of Personnel Research*, 1925, *4*, 222–237.

Sinsheimer, R. L., The end of the beginning. In E. Hutchings and E. Hutchings (eds.), *Scientific Progress and Human Values*. New York: American Elsevier, 1967.

Skinner, B. F. *Walden II*. New York: Macmillan, 1948.

——. *Beyond Freedom and Dignity*. New York: Knopf, 1971.

Smith, W. D. Can man control his mind? *New York Times*, April 6, 1972, Section P, 3.

Spearman, C. *The Abilities of Man*. New York: Macmillan, 1927.

Stagner, R. The gullibility of personnel managers. *Personnel Psychology*, 1958, *11*, 347–352.

——. New design for industrial psychology. *Contemporary Psychology*, 1966, *11*, 145–150.

Taylor, F. W. *Principles of Scientific Management*. New York: Harper & Bros., 1911.

Tead, O. *Instincts in Industry*. New York: McGraw-Hill, 1918.

Thirring, H. The steps from knowledge to wisdom. *American Scientist*, 1956, *44*, 445ff.

Thorndike, E. L. The curve of work and the curve of satisfyingness. *Journal of Applied Psychology*, 1917, *1*, 266.

Twitmyer, E. B. A Study of the Knee Jerk (Ph.D. dissertation, University of Pennsylvania), 1902.

——. Knee jerks without stimulation of the patellar tendon. *Psychological Bulletin*, 1905, *2*, 43ff.

U.S. Supreme Court, *Opinion No. 124*, October Term, 1970.

Veblen, T. *The Instinct of Workmanship*. New York: Augustus M. Kelley, 1914.

Wainwright, *History of the Philadelphia Electric Company, 1881–1961*. Philadelphia: Philadelphia Electric Co., 1961.

Wiener, N. *The Human Use of Human Beings*, 2nd ed. New York: Doubleday and Co., 1954.

Whyte, W. H., Jr. *The Organization Man*. New York: Simon and Schuster, 1956.

Williams, W. *What's on the Worker's Mind*. New York: Charles Scribner's Sons, 1920.

——. *Mainsprings of Men*. New York: Charles Scribner's Sons, 1925.

Witmer, L. Clinical psychology. *Psychological Clinic*, 1907, *1*, 1–9.

——. Psychological diagnosis and the psychonomic orientation in analytic science: An epitome. *Psychological Clinic*, 1925, *16*, 1–18.

Yoakum, C. S., and Yerkes, R. M. (eds.) *Army Mental Tests*. New York: Holt, 1920.

Selected Biographical Index

Adams, Donald K. (1906-), was an active psychologist concentrating his energies in the areas of development, learning, and personality theory. He acted as a Research Psychologist for the Strategic Bombing Survey in Japan in 1945 and is now Professor Emeritus of Duke University. 27,28

Adler, Alexandra (1901-), M.D., daughter of Alfred Adler, is a practicing psychiatrist in New York City and Medical Director of the Alfred Adler Mental Hygiene Clinic. Her writings include *Guiding Human Misfits.* 12

Adler, Alfred (1870-1937), although an important member of Freud's weekly seminars from 1902 to 1911, was destined to develop a drastically different personality theory which emphasized learning (especially of a conceptual sort), interpersonal relations, and motives of a more exclusively emotional sort (drive for superiority, social feeling). 3, 4, 5, 6, 7, 8, 9, 10, 12, 13, 16, 22, 26, 27, 29-36, 40-42, 141, 286, 298, 310, 429

Adrian, Lord (1889-), is one of the founders of the modern study of electrophysiology by means of the electronic amplifier and the oscillograph. With Keith Lucas, he established the characteristics of "all or none" conduction and relative refractory periods of nerve. He next went on to characterize the electrophysiology of the sense organs culminating in his classical little book, *Basis of Sensation.* Then he pioneered the study of evoked potentials from sensory fields from cerebral cortex along with many other important "firsts" in electrophysiology. For many years, he was Professor of Physiology at Cambridge, later Master at Trinity College, and now Chancellor of Cambridge University. He was awarded, with Sherrington, the Nobel Prize in 1932. 408, 410, 411

Alexander, Hartley Burr (1873-1939), was Professor of Philosophy at the University of Nebraska from 1908 to 1927 and later at Scripps College. He was President of the American Philosophical Association (1919), President of the Southwestern Archeological Federation (1928-29), and Honorary Member of the American Institute of Architecture. He planned the symbolism of the architectural sculpture of Nebraska's State Capitol. 136

Allen, Chauncey N. (1900-), is a Professor of Psychology at Dartmouth College. His areas of study include child and abnormal psychology, sex differences, and advertising. 349

Allison, John Moore (1905-), is an Ambassador Emeritus. He was deputy to John Foster Dulles in negotiating the Japanese Peace Treaty and has been Assistant Secretary of State for Far Eastern Affairs, Ambassador to Japan, Indonesia, and Czechosovakia. 135, 137

Allport, Floyd (1890-), is Professor Emeritus at Syracuse University. He contributed extensively to social psychology, scientific methodology, and the theories of personality. 142, 308-9

Allport, Gordon W. (1897-1967), was a vigorous and appealing proponent of an "ideographic" conception of personality, stressing the study of the whole person and the "uniqueness of the individual." 14, 21, 32, 42, 105, 128, 334, 348

Anastasi, Anne (1908-), has been Chairman of the department of psychology at Fordham University since 1968. She received a Ph.D. from Columbia University. Her scholarly efforts are directed to differential psychology. She was president of the APA in 1972. 174

Angyal, Andreas (1902-60), came to America in 1932 as a Rockefeller Fellow with a Ph.D. in psychology and an M.D. He served at Worcester State Hospital (1933-45) as Psychiatrist and later as Director of Research from which he entered private psychiatrical practice in Boston. His investigations of the relation of schizophrenic hallucinations to kinesthesis and hypnogogic states were very interesting. 149, 150

Ansbacher, Rowena Ripin (1906-), is the Associate Editor of the *Journal of Individual Psychology*. Aside from the journal and her work with Heinz Ansbacher, Rowena is interested in intelligence testing, the personality theory, and child development. 3, 6

Arnold, Magda (1903-), is a Professor at Loyola University where she devotes her efforts to the study of the function of the brain and theories of emotions. In 1962-63 she was in Germany as a Fulbright Research Professor. 293-94

Asch, Solomon E. (1907-), is an American-trained psychologist who extended and refined theoretical principles of Gestalt psychology to the psychology of learning, cognitive and social psychology. Currently, Dr. Asch is Professor of Psychology at Rutgers University in Newark. 251-55

Bare, John K. (1917-), is a Professor at Carleton College. His work is concentrated in the area of motivation and the specific hunger behavior in man and animals. 424, 427

Beck, Samuel Jacob (1896-), is Professorial Lecturer Emeritus in the departments of psychology and psychiatry at the University of Chicago and an Associate at Michael Reese Hospital. He pioneered with Rorschach's Test in America and authored *Introduction to the Rorschach Method* (1937), also *Personality Structure in Schizophrenia* (1938), and *Rorschach's Test* (3 vols.). He was President of the Clinical Division of the APA (1952). 149, 153

Beebe-Center, J. G. (1897-1958), was a lifetime Lecturer in psychology at Harvard University. He was best known for his experimental approach to affectivity. 105, 423

Benedict, Ruth (1887-1948), was a Columbia University anthropologist. She wrote *Patterns of Culture* and the *Chrysanthemums and the Sword.* 93, 330-31

Bentham, Jeremy (1748-1832), was the father of English utilitarianism with its doctrine of the greatest good for the greatest number. 88

Bentley, Madison (1870-1955), was among the first to earn a Ph.D. (1898) with E. B. Titchener at Cornell. He taught at Cornell until 1912, when he became Professor and Director of the Psychological Laboratories at the University of Illinois. There he remained until 1928 when, following Titchener's death, he was invited to be Sage Professor of Psychology at Cornell. He was President of the APA (1925), Chairman of the Division of Anthropology and Psychology of the National Research Council (1930-31), Editor of the *American Journal of Psychology,* and Consultant in Psychology to the Library of Congress (1938-40). He authored *The Field of Psychology* and *The New Field of Psychology,* in which he expounded his version of functional psychology, and numerous articles. 143-49, 153, 337

Berg, Irwin A. (1913-), concentrated his studies in the area of adjustment mechanisms, personality tests, and the hormonal induction of behavior. He was a Professor and department Chairman at Louisiana State University in 1955 and is now Dean of Arts and Science at Louisiana State University. 122, 128

Berger, Hans (1873-1941), was a neurologist in Jena. He was the first to record and report on the electrical activity of the brain of the human subject from surface electrodes simply pasted on the external surface of the skull in awake and conscious subjects. He studied the electroencephalogram extensively. For many years brain waves were called "Berger rhythms." 406

Bergmann, Gustav (1906-), is a Viennese philosopher of science who has published influential articles, some coauthored with Kenneth W. Spence, about methodological and historical problems in psychology. Currently Dr. Bergmann is Professor of Philosophy at the University of Iowa. 260

Berlyne, Daniel Ellis (1924-), is Professor of Psychology at the University of Toronto. Earlier he was Assistant and Associate Professor at Boston University (1959-62), Fellow at the Center for Advanced Study and at the Centre International d' Epistemologie Génétique (Geneva), and Visiting Scientist (NIMH) (1956-62), and Lecturer at the University of St. Andrews, Aberdeen (1953-56). He earned his Ph.D. (1953) from Yale. He is the author of many papers on motivation, of *Conflict, Arousal, and Curiosity* (1960), and of *Aesthetics and Psychobiology* (1972). 183

Bingham, Walter Van Dyke (1880-1952), contributed to the development of industrial psychology as Director of the Division of Applied Psychology, Carnegie Institute of Technology; Director of the Personnel Research Federation; Chief Psychologist of the U.S. Adjutant General's Office, Editor of the *Personnel Journal.* He was the author of *Aptitudes and Aptitude Testing. How To Interview* (with B. V. Moore). 21, 233, 452, 461, 468, 476

Bonnardel, Raymond G. (1901-), was Professor at l'Institut de Psychologie à L'Université de Paris; Director of the Laboratoire de Psychologie Appliquée de L'École des Hautes Études, etc. He was the Editor of *Le Travail Humain* and author of publi-

psychological) terms. 288-89

Cronbach, Lee (1916-), one of the leading contemporary educational psychologists, is now Vidadachs Professor of Education at Stanford University. 351

Crook, Mason N. (1904-), was an Instructor of Psychology at Dartmouth College (1930-31), Associate Professor at Skidmore College (1935-45), a Research Psychologist at Columbia University (1944-46), a Resident Associate at the Institute for Psychological Research at Tufts University (1946-), and the Science Director of the American Association for the Advancement of Science (1952). He has concentrated his studies in the area of vision, legibility, and perception. 299

Dallenbach, Karl M. (1887-1971), was Distinguished Professor of Psychology (Emeritus after 1958) and Head of the department at the University of Texas after serving at Cornell (1916-48), where he earned his Ph.D. (1913), in ranks ranging from Instructor to Sage Professor (1945-48). At Cornell he inducted many students into investigation with his studies of the receptors in the skin. He purchased the *American Journal of Psychology* in 1918, brought it to Cornell for E. B. Titchener to edit, and then edited it from 1926 to 1968 when he gave the *Journal* to the department of psychology at the University of Illinois, where he had earned his B.A. (1910). The American Psychological Foundation gave him its Gold Medal Award in 1969. 144-45, 418

Darley, John G. (1910-), Professor and, since 1963, Chairman of the department of psychology at the University of Minnesota, is coauthor of *Vocational Interest Measurement* (1955) and author of *Promise and Performance* (1962). 58

Dashiell, John F. (1888-), is an American psychologist who emphasized objective methods of investigation. His position, which tended to be eclectic, is represented in an influential introductory psychology textbook, *Fundamentals of Objective Psychology,* the first edition of which was published in 1928. 250

Davies, Stanley Powell (1892-), is General Director Emeritus of the Community Service Society of New York (1939-57). Earlier, he had held a similar post in the Charity Organization Society (1933-39) (which merged with the Association for the Improvement of the Condition of the Poor to form the CSS), Associate Secretary of the State Charities Aid Association (1924-33), and Professor of Sociology at Bucknell University (B.A., 1912), after earning his Ph.D. from Columbia (1923). He is the author of *The Mentally Retarded in Society* (1959). 167

Dembo, Tamara (1902-), is Professor and Director of the Rehabilitation Training Program at Clark University. She has served on the faculties of Smith College, Cornell, Mt. Holyoke, Harvard, Stanford, and the New School for Social Research. Born in Russia, she earned her Ph.D. in Berlin (1930), joined Kurt Koffka as a Research Associate at Smith College (1930-32) and later became a Research Associate at Worcester State Hospital (1932-36). 149, 295

Dennis, Wayne (1905-), was Professor and department Head of Psychology at Brooklyn College. His publications are in child psychology, history of psychology, and social psychology. 189, 299, 310

Deutsch, Danica (1890-), is Executive Director and cofounder of the Alfred Adler Mental Hygiene Clinic, New York, and long-time Adlerian student, teacher, practitioner, and writer. 34

Deutsch, Martin (1923-), is Professor of Psychology and Director of New York University's Institute of Developmental Studies, which he founded in 1960. He is one of the pioneers in early childhood education. He is coeditor of *Social Class, Race, and Psychological Development* (1968) and of *The Disadvantaged Child* (1967). 188

Dodge, Joan S. (1925-), received her Ph.D. in psychology at Illinois in 1955. She was a Research Psychologist in the department of child development and family relations from 1958-59. Presently, she is a Principal Investigator at the Sloan Institute Hospital Administration. She has written articles concerning the relation of interpersonal attitudes to interpersonal behavior, and on the nature of these relationships in patient care. 360

Dollard, John (1900-), is Professor Emeritus of Psychology at Yale. Following receipt of his Ph.D. in sociology (1931) at the University of Chicago, he joined the staff of the Institute of Human Relations at Yale (1931). He is the author of *Criteria of a Life History* (1935), *Caste and Class in a Southern Town* (1937, with Allison Davis), *Social Learning and Imitation* (with N. E. Miller, 1941), and *Personality and Psychotherapy* (1950), *Steps in Psychotherapy* (with others, 1953), and *Scoring Human Motives* (1959). He has been elected to the American Academy of Arts and Sciences. 164, 166-69, 176, 180, 182, 430

Dreikurs, Rudolf (1897-1972), M.D., was Professor Emeritus of Psychiatry at Chicago Medical School and founder of the Alfred Adler Institutes in Chicago and Tel-Aviv, child guidance centers, and what is now the *Journal of Individual Psychology*. An indefatigable lecturer and demonstrator, he attracted many followers and also wrote numerous books and articles. 12, 33-34, 36

Duncan, Carl P. (1921-), is Professor of Psychology at Northwestern University, where he has been since he completed his Ph.D. at Brown University in 1947. He has been President of the Midwestern Psychological Association. 163

Dysinger, Donald Warren (1904-), is Professor Emeritus and Chairman of the psychology department at the University of Nebraska, where he went from Iowa (Ph.D., 1932). 152

Eccles, J.C. (1903-), is a Nobel laureate for his work on synaptic transmission in the spinal cord and of other brain areas. He showed that the polarization and depolarization of nerve cells was related to excitability and inhibition of cells and synaptic transmission. He is one of the younger members of the famous Sherrington group of neurophysiologists at Oxford. 408

Ellis, Albert (1913-), founder of the School of Rational Psychotherapy, is Executive Director of the Institute of Rational Living. Of his numerous books and other publications, *Reason and Emotion in Psychotherapy* is outstanding. 33

Endler, Norman Solomon (1931-), is Professor of Psychology at York University in Toronto, where he has been since 1960. He was a Clinical Counselor at the Division of Counseling at Pennsylvania State University (1958-60) and Research Assistant Professor during summers (1963-68) at the University of Illinois, where he earned his Ph.D. (1958). 187-88

Erickson, Raymond L. (1925-), is Professor of Psychology at the University of New Hampshire. Research in verbal learning is a major interest. 414-15, 419

Eysenck, Hans J. (1916-), is Professor of Psychology at the University of London. He is a leading re-

tor of the Center of Sociological Studies, etc. He was the author of *Humanisme du travail et humanité*, *Industrial society*, *Le Travail en miettes*, etc. 467, 477

Frisby, Clifford B. (1902-), a Ph.D. from the University of London, with interests in vocational guidance and job satisfaction, succeeded C. S. Myers as Director of the National Institute of Industrial Psychology. President of the International Association of Applied Psychology from 1953-58, he was the first from Great Britain to hold this office. 481

Furtmüller, Carl (1880-1951), was a Viennese educator, close friend, early coworker, and biographer of Alfred Adler. 33

Galton, Sir Francis (1822-1911), was an English anthropologist who is considered the founder of eugenics. He also has made great contributions to meteorology; founded the modern technique of weather-mapping and invented the term anticyclone. Among other developments, he invented Galton's whistle to determine the upper limit of hearing ability with regard to high frequency tones, and he devised the system of fingerprint identification. 112, 177, 181

Gardner, John William (1912-), is founder and President of Common Cause. He was earlier Secretary of Health, Education, and Welfare (1965-67), Executive Associate to the President of the Carnegie Corporation of New York (1945-65), and President of the Carnegie Foundation for the Advancement of Teaching (1955-65), OSS (1942-45), and Assistant Professor at Mt. Holyoke (1940-42). He is the author of *Excellence* and of *Self-Renewal*, and editor of *To Turn the Tide*. His many honors include the Award for Distinguished Service to Higher Education (1959), and election to the American Academy of Arts and Sciences and to the Royal Society of Arts. 189

Garner, Harry H. (1910-73), M.D., was Professor and Chairman of the departments of psychiatry and behavioral science at Chicago Medical School, and a proponent of the confrontation problem-solving technique of brief psychotherapy. 36

Garrett, Henry Edward (1894-1973), was Professor Emeritus of Psychology at Columbia where he rose from Teaching Assistant (Ph.D., 1923) to Professor and Executive Head of the department (1920-56). He authored a widely used textbook entitled *Statistics in Psychology and Education*, and *Great Experiments in Psychology*, a popular introduction. He has been President of the Eastern Psychological Association (1944) and of the APA (1946). 17, 140, 148

Geldard, Frank A. (1904-), was Professor and Chairman of the department of psychology at the University of Virginia. He held a seat on the Research and Development Board, was Chairman of the Advisory Panel to the Assistant Secretary of Defense, and also has contributed to personnel and training research. Currently he is Stuart Professor at Princeton University, working in the area of sensory psychophysiology. 299

Ghiselli, Edwin E. (1907-), since 1939 Professor and for a period department Chairman at the University of California at Berkeley. He has done research in the areas of psychological measurement, employee selection, etc. He is the author of *Personnel and Industrial Psychology*, and of *Scientific Method in Psychology* (both with C. W. Brown). 470

Gibb, Jack Rex (1914-), was a Research Professor for Fels Group Dynamics Center in Delaware. He is a psychological statistician, clinical psychologist, and consultant and has researched and written on such areas as group behavior, human learning, and problem solving. 111, 127

Glanville, Albert Douglas (1906-), is Professor Emeritus and Head of the department of psychology at the University of Maine, where he has served since 1937. Following receipt of his Ph.D. at Cornell (1932), he investigated motor patterns and electroencephalographic signs in the mentally retarded at Vineland Training School and in psychiatric patients at Delaware State Hospital. 144

Goodenough, Florence L. (1886-), Professor at the University of Minnesota, has to her credit numerous books, including *Developmental Psychology* (2nd ed., 1945), *Mental Testing* (2nd ed., 1949), and *Exceptional Children* (1956). 58

Gorsuch, John H. (1910-), is a Research Associate and Industrial Psychologist at the U.S. Steel Corporation. He is best known for his studies of criminal psychology and executive-personnel administration. 112, 479

Graham, Clarence Henry (1906-71), was perhaps the outstanding investigator and teacher of his generation in the psychology of vision. He earned his Ph.D. (1930) at Clark University but found his field of investigation while working with Halden Keffer Hartline at the Johnson Foundation of Medical Physics at the University of Pennsylvania (1931-32). After teaching at Clark, he became Associate and then Professor at Brown (1936-45), then Professor at Columbia until his all too early death. 19, 150, 158, 299, 310

Grinker, Roy Richard (1900-), is Chairman Emeritus of the Division of Psychiatry at Michael Reese Hospital where he has been since 1936 and also, since 1951 the Director of the Institute of Psychosomatic and Psychiatric Research and Training. He is author of *Neurology*, a textbook, *Psychosomatic Research,* and *Men Under Stress, War Neuroses, and Anxiety and Stress* (with Spiegel). 151

Guilford, Joy Paul (1897-), is Professor Emeritus at the University of Southern California where he has been since 1940 after 12 years as Professor and Head of the department of psychology at the University of Nebraska (B.A. 1922; Ph.D. Cornell, 1927). He is author of *Psychometric Methods* (1936, 1954), a textbook of statistics, and he has used factor analysis to develop descriptive theories of *The Nature of Human Intelligence* (1967), *The Analysis of Intelligence* (1971 with Hoepfner), and *Personality* (1959). He has been President of the Psychometric Society (1938), and the APA (1950) and has been elected to the National Academy of Sciences. 57, 101, 114, 122, 127-28, 137, 139-43, 152-53, 478

Gulliksen, Harold (1903-), is currently a Professor of Psychology at Princeton. He also serves as a Research Advisor for the Educational Testing Service. In the past, he had been Director of the U.S. Navy and National Defense Research Council Projects and a Research Associate for the Mooseheart Laboratory of Child Research. His studies include learning, transfer, and psychological tests. 25, 362

Hall, Stanley G. (1846-1924), was the founder and Editor of the *American Journal of Psychology* in 1887; the founder of The American Psychological Association; and the author of many works such as *The Contents of Children's Minds, Educational Problems, Jesus the Christ, in the Light of Psychology, The Life and Confessions of a Psychologist,* and *Senes-*

cence. Hall is also remembered as a pioneer in child psychology and for the establishment of the psychological laboratory at Johns Hopkins. 91, 174, 177-78, 181

Halstead, Ward Campbell (1908-), is Professor of Medical Psychology in the departments of psychology and medicine at the University of Chicago where he has been on the faculty since 1936. He is noted for his identification and assessments of disturbed function associated with brain injuries. 151

Hanfmann, Eugenia (1905-), is Professor at the Student Counseling Center at Brandeis University. Earlier, she was Lecturer in Clinical Psychology at Harvard (1946-52), at OSS (1944-46), Assistant Professor at Mt. Holyoke (1939-46), Research Psychologist at the Masonic Foundation for Research in Schizophrenia (1936-39), and Research Associate at Worcester State Hospital (1932-36), and Smith College (1930-32), whence she migrated to work with Kurt Koffka from the University of Jena (Ph.D., 1927). Among her investigations is one using Vigotsky's blocks to investigate the thinking of schizophrenic patients. 17, 149

Harlow, Harry Frederick (1905-), is George Cary Comstock Professor of Psychology and Director of the Primate Laboratory at the University of Wisconsin, where he has been since he earned his Ph.D. at Stanford (1930), except for two years as Chief of Human Resources Research in the Department of the Army (1950-52). He uncovered the phenomenon of "learning sets" in monkeys and has demonstrated effects of early experience on the sexual and social behavior of chimpanzees and monkeys. He edited the *Journal of Comparative and Physiological Psychology* (1951-63), was president of the APA (1958), and has been elected to the National Academy of Sciences. 182-83

Harman, Harry H. (1913-), is greatly involved in the fields of statistics and psychometrics. He has contributed to the research of psychological statistics, factor analysis, and electronic computers in man-machine systems. He was the manager of the Systems Simulation Research Laboratory of the System Development Corporation in 1959. 128

Hartley, Eugene L. (1912-), social psychologist at New York City College, 1939-69, wrote and edited several books with his wife Ruth. He is now Dean at the College of Community Science of the University of Wisconsin at Green Bay. 12, 24, 329, 332

Hartline, H. K. (1903-), is a biophysicist and physiologist. He was an early colleague of D. W. Bronk at the Johnson Foundation, at Johns Hopkins, and at Rockefeller University. He is a Nobel laureate for his work on the electrophysiology of single photo receptors in the limulus polyphemus and particularly showed the lateral inhibitory interactions among neighboring photoreceptors. 411

Hebb, Donald Olding (1904-), has been Professor of Psychology at McGill University since 1947, and in 1970 was elected Chancellor. His work with the patients of Wilder Penfield demonstrated that brain tissue is unnecessary for the maintenance of tested intelligence even though it is necessary for its development. He is author of the classic neuropsychological monograph entitled *Organization of Behavior* (1949) and a *Textbook of Psychology* (1958, 2nd ed., 1966). He was President of the APA (1960) and has been honored by the award of the Warren Medal of the Society of Experimental Psychologists (1958) and election to the Royal Societies of

Canada and London (1966). 161, 178, 182-85

Heider, Fritz (1896-), is Professor of psychology at the University of Kansas. He received the Lewin Memorial Award in 1959. His studies include perception and interpersonal relations. Hc wrote *Psychology of Interpersonal Relations.* 357

Helson, Harry (1898-), is Emeritus John C. Peterson Distinguished Professor of Psychology at Kansas State University. Earlier, he was Professor at the University of Texas (1951-61), Professor and Chairman of the department at Brooklyn College (1949-51), and Associate and Professor at Bryn Mawr (1928-49). He earned his Ph.D. (1924) at Harvard. He is the author of *The Psychology of Gestalt* (1926) and *Adaptation-Level Theory* (1964), and editor of *Theoretical Foundations of Psychology* (1951). He received the Warren Medal of the Society of Experimental Psychologists (1959) and the Distinguished Scientific Award of the APA (1962). 183-84

Hertzler, Joyce Oramel (1895-), earned his B.A. at Baldwin Wallace College in 1916, and his Ph.D. in sociology at the University of Wisconsin in 1920. He was Professor of Sociology and Head of the department at the University of Nebraska where he has authored a series of books. Among them are: *A History of Utopian Thought* (1923), *Social Progress* (1928), *Social Institutions* (1929), and the *Social Thought of Ancient Civilizations* (1936). His most recent books are *A Sociology of Language* (1965) and *Laughter: A Socio-scientific Analysis* (1970). 136-37, 139

Heyer, Albert W. (1921-), was an Instructor at Colorado from 1947-48 and a Consultant for Rohrer, Hibler, and Replogle from 1950-56. Presently, he is a partner for Swartzlander and Heyer. Most of his studies were centered on the application of psychological knowledge to industrial management development; motivation and learning of the normal human being; and team dynamics in industrial management. 358, 361

Hoagland, Hudson (1899-), is the founder of the Worcester Foundation for Experimental Biology and was its Executive Director from its inception in 1944 until he became Director Emeritus in 1969. Earlier he was Professor of Physiology at Clark University (1931-44). He earned his Ph.D. (1927) in psychology at Harvard after a B.A. (1921) from Columbia. His investigations (with Gregory Pincus) of stress in relation to the renal cortex have had therapeutic implications. 150

Hobbs, Nicholas (1915-), is Professor of Psychology and Provost of Vanderbilt University. He was Professor and Chairman of Human Development (1951-65) and Director of the Kennedy Center (1965-67) at Peabody College for Teachers, Chairman of the department of psychology at Louisiana State University (1950-51), and Associate Professor and Director of Training in Clinical Psychology at Teachers College, Columbia (1946-50). He has also been Director of the Southern Regional Education Board, a member of the President's Panel on Mental Retardation, and President of the APA (1956). 189

Hollingworth, Harry L. (1880-1957), was a student of Cattell and of Woodworth. He was Head of Psychology at Barnard College and widely known for his theory of reintegration (to the effect that every specific experience functions for the situation of which it was earlier a part). 7, 450, 453

Holtzman, Wayne Harold (1923-), is Professor of Education and Psy-

having served as Assistant Professor at Cornell (1930-37). He was the author of *Psychology in Business and Industry* (1935) and directed the aviation psychology section of the Navy's Bureau of Medicine and Surgery during World War II. At Cornell he was an outstanding lecturer in the introductory course. 144

Jenness, Arthur Freeman (1901-), is Professor Emeritus and Chairman of the psychology department at Williams College. His doctoral dissertation at Syracuse University (Ph.D., 1930) brought the phenomena of the group mind under individual influence and set the pattern for later work on social conformity. Later, at Nebraska University, where he was successively Counselor of Freshmen, Professor and Head of the psychology department (1930-46), he investigated various aspects of hypnotism and group behavior. He now resides in Palo Alto, California. 142, 152, 175

Jones, Mary C. (1896-), was the Research Associate at the Institute for Human Development in California in 1928. In 1946 she was Lecturer of Psychology at the University of California at Berkeley. She centered her efforts on studying the patterns of development in the adolescent, the interrelationship of physical, social, and emotional factors, and in family life and child-rearing practices. 331

Jung, Carl G. (1875-1961), was an early pupil of Freud who later founded his own School of Analytic Psychology studying primordial archetypes and the racial unconsciousness. 141, 299, 429

Karwoski, Theodore F. (1896-1957), was an Instructor in Psychology at the University of North Dakota and an Assistant Professor at Dartmouth College (later to be Professor and Chairman of the department). Most of his studies dealt with color vision, color, music, and thinking. 348

Kaufmann, Walter (1921-), Professor of Philosophy at Princeton University and author of *Nietzsche: Philosopher, Psychologist, Antichrist*, has also edited and retranslated Nietzsche's works. His further numerous books range from existentialism to religion and poetry. 35-36

Keller, Fred S. (1899-), concentrated his efforts on reinforcement theory and is currently working on teaching techniques. He received his Ph.D. in experimental psychology from Harvard in 1928 and in 1949 became Fulbright Lecturer at the University of São Paulo, Brazil. 429

Kelly, George Alexander (1905-68), was Professor of Psychology at Brandeis University when he died. Earlier, he had been Professor and Director (1946-65) and Director of the Psychological Clinic (1946-51) at Ohio State University and rose from Instructor to Associate Professor of Psychology at Fort Hays Kansas State College (1931-45). He received his Ph.D. (1931) from the University of Iowa. He authored *The Psychology of Personal Constructs* (1955). He was an inspiration to many graduate students. 33, 182, 184, 298

Kemp, Edward Harris (1908-), is Professor and Head of the department of psychology at Ohio State University in Dayton. Earlier, he was head of the Human Factors Division of the Electronics Laboratory of the U.S. Navy in San Diego (1956-70), Technical Director of the Observer Laboratory at the Air Force Pilot Training Research Center (1951-56), Associate Professor at Rochester University (1946-51), and Assistant Professor at Duke (1940-42) and Brown (1936-40). 150, 156-58

Kendler, Tracy S. (1918-), was a

albino rats" and "A blind analysis of a case of multiple personality using the semantic differential." 360

Lynd, Robert (1892-1970), and Lynd, Helen (1895-), are the authors of the celebrated *Middletown* (1929) study and of *Middletown in Transition* (1937). They are identified with the multidisciplinary approach to the study of an American community. 331, 333-34, 340

McDougall, William (1871-1938), completed his career as Professor of Psychology at Duke University after a period (1920-27) at Harvard, to which post he had migrated from England where he had already served on the faculties of Cambridge, Oxford, and London Universities and had been elected a Fellow of the Royal Society. He was the author of many books, the first of which was *Physiological Psychology* (1905). His *Social Psychology* (1908) was based on a theory of instincts which set off the controversy over instincts of the 1920's. Later books concerned the relations of psychology to ethics, e.g., *Ethics and Some Modern World Problems* (1924), *World Chaos: The Responsibilities of Science* (1931), and his last was *The Energies of Men* (1933). 102, 124, 141, 143, 482

McGraw, Myrtle, (1899-), is Professor Emeritus of Briarcliff College where she taught from 1953. She was Associate Director of the Study of Normal Child Development at Babies Hospital, Columbia-Presbyterian Medical Center in New York (1930-42), She is the author of *Growth: A Study of Johnny and Jimmy* (1935) and of many papers. 173, 185

Maddi, Salvatore R. (1933-), Professor of Psychology at the University of Chicago, is the author of *Personality Theories: A Comparative Analysis,* a new conception of the field, which has been very successful. 33

Madison, Peter (1918-), was trained in personality and clinical psychology in the Department of Social Relations at Harvard after World War II. His work, which has centered on intensive studies of personality processes and changes in students during their college years, is summarized especially in his *Personality Development in College* published in 1969. 298, 316

Maier, Norman R. F. (1900-), is Professor Emeritus of Psychology at the University of Michigan. He has written extensively in the field of management psychology. 298, 491

Marquis, Donald (1908-73), was Professor in the Sloan School of Management, MIT. One of the youngest men ever elected President of the APA, he is more than any other person responsible for the remarkable development of the Massachusetts Institute of Technology's Department of Psychology after World War II. 349

Marx, Melvin Herman (1919-), was a Professor at the University of Missouri where he taught after completing his Ph.D. (1943) at Washington University in St. Louis. He edited a book on theory in psychology and several topical books for Macmillan. 163, 297-98, 317

Matthews, Sir Bryan (1906-), is Professor of Physiology at Cambridge University. He invented one of the earliest rugged oscillographs adapted for physiological work and did the classic early work on the muscle spindle and other proprioceptive endings in muscle. 409

May, Rollo (1909-), Ph.D., practicing psychotherapist in New York, is widely known as author of numerous books, among them *Love and Will* and *Power and Innocence*; and for the work *Existence: A New Dimension in Psychiatry and Psychol-*

ogy, edited with Ernest Angel and Henri F. Ellenberger. 35-36

Mayo, Elton (1880-1945), was a social philosopher who provided the intellectual setting for the Hawthorne studies and for the doctrine propounded by the "Harvard group" in industrial relations. He was largely responsible for drawing attention to the significance of the small, and especially of the informally organized, group in setting production standards and otherwise influencing the motivation and morale of industrial workers. He was the author of *The Human Problems of an Industrial Civilization, The Social Problems of an Industrial Civilization,* and *The Political Problems of an Industrial Civilization.* 482, 484.

Mead, Margaret (1901-), is the former Columbia anthropologist who did so much to make crosscultural thinking meaningful to social psychologists. 93, 330-31, 333, 341

Meeland, Tor (1922-), served as a staff member for the Lincoln Laboratory at the Massachusetts Institute of Technology in 1958 and as a Research Psychologist for Mitre Corp. in 1959. He is currently a Research Psychologist for the Stanford Research Institute and has written articles such as "Reactions of men under stress to a picture projective test" and "Sociometric effects of race and combat performance." 111

Messick, Samuel J. (1931-), is Vice-President of Research at the Educational Testing Service. He is also an Adjunct Professor at CUNY. 128

Metcalf, John T. (1889-1973), was Professor Emeritus and former Chairman of the department of psychology at the University of Vermont. 28, 30

Metzger, Wolfgang (1899-), Professor Emeritus of Psychology at the University of Münster, Germany, is best known for his work and books on Gestalt psychology. One of the founders of the new German Society of Individual (Adlerian) Psychology, he has in recent years edited the new German paperback editions of Adler's works. 26

Mierke, Karl (1896-1971), was Professor of Psychology and Chairman of the department at the University of Kiel, Germany. Previously he was Director of Personnel Selection in the German Navy. He wrote several books on education and mental health. 26

Miller, Neal Elgar (1909-), since 1966 has been Professor of Psychology at Rockefeller University. He served on the psychology faculty at Yale (1935-66), where he earned his Ph.D. (1935). With John Dollard, he showed in *Social Learning and Imitation* (1941) and in *Personality and Psychotherapy* (1950) how the conditions and laws of learning can explain important aspects of social learning, imitation, neurotic behavior, and psychotherapy. His later work has combined physiological techniques with behavioral to show that direct electrical stimulation of certain parts of the brain will elicit motivation with the functional properties of fear, pain, and pleasure. He was president of the APA in 1961, and his honors include the Newcomb-Cleveland Prize (1951), the Warren Medal (1954), election to the National Academy of Sciences, and the National Medal of Science (1964). 164, 176, 180, 182, 430

Moede, Walther (1890-1950), was responsible for a series of pioneering studies is social psychology, initiated in 1914, covering the influence of the group and of rivalry upon the rate and vigor of muscular activity. As founder of the Psychotechnishe Institut at the Charlottenburg Technische Hochschule, and through associations with business firms, he played a leading role in furthering

founded while Professor of Psychology (1919-36), Chairman of the department (1924-36) at Clark University, and Director of the Clark University Press where he edited and/or published also a series of handbooks for branches of psychology. He was a major innovator in scientific journalism. 164-65

Murphy, Lois Barclay (1902-), grew up in Iowa, Illinois, and Ohio, always retaining her love of the Iowa farm, and the influences of both stimulating parents deeply concerned with religious and social issues. A graduate of Vassar College, she had begun college teaching in the year that Sarah Lawrence College was founded (1928), initiated a nursery school there in 1937, and conducted—with a congenial group of colleagues—a series of studies of individuality at the preschool level as seen through direct observation and projective methods. She served as Director of Developmental Studies in the Menninger Foundation Research Department. Her major publication in Menninger days was *The Widening World of Childhood* (1962). One of her salient contributions to the conceptualization of psychological advances is in the concept of coping; the individual does more than "defend" himself against life's pressures; he develops his own strategy and "copes" both with threats and with challenges. She has nearly finished a book describing her longitudinal studies at the Menninger Foundation, on children's ways of coping with their problems. 189, 323, 330-32, 334, 336-37

Myers, Charles S. (1873-1946), a B.A., M.A. and M.D. from Cambridge, made contact with psychology through research on the sensory and motor responses and the music of primitive tribes. He taught at King's College and at Cambridge, where he was also Director of the Psychological Laboratory. As a founder (1921) and First Director of the National Institute of Industrial Psychology, he was largely responsible for the emphasis upon an experimental approach and upon the interrelations between "pure" and "applied" science characterizing industrial psychology in Great Britain during the earlier decades of the century. He was the author of *Experimental Psychology, Contributions to the Study of Shell Shock, Industrial Psychology in Great Britain, In the Realm of Mind,* etc. 461-62

Odbert, Henry S. (1909-), was Program Director for the Psychology-Biology National Science Foundation. His work includes the studies in psychology of language and communication; personality; personnel; experimental psychology, and animal behavior. 348

O'Kelly, Lawrence I. (1913-), is Professor of Psychology at the University of Illinois. He is known for his work in motivation and learning; brain mechanisms in motivation; and water metabolism, and for having been Chairman at Michigan State University. 358

Papanek, Helene (1901-), M.D., practices psychiatry in New York City, including group therapy. She is director of the Alfred Adler Institute there and author of numerous contributions to the field. 34, 36

Papez, James Wenceslas (1883-1958), served as Assistant and Professor of Neuroanatomy at Cornell (1920-51) after earning his B.A. (1908) and his M.D. (1911) at the University of Minnesota and serving as Professor of anatomy at Emory's Medical College (1911-20). His many contributions

was one of the earliest investigator-teachers of the projective methods, and is an authority in the domain of psychiatric prognosis. A native of Poland, he earned his Ph.D. (1927) at the University of Poznan, was an Associate in Psychiatry at Columbia's College of Physicians and Surgeons (1931-54), Research Psychologist at the New Jersey Department of Agencies (1954-57), and has been Professor at Jefferson Medical College since 1960. 148

Poffenberger, Albert Theodore (1885-), is Professor Emeritus of Psychology at Columbia University where he was on the staff from the time he earned his Ph.D. (1912) until 1950. He is the author of *Applied Psychology* (1917), *Psychology in Advertising* (1925), and *Principles of Applied Psychology* (1942) and edited *J. McKeen Cattell: Man of Science* (1947). He was elected President of the APA (1935) and of the American Association of Applied Psychology (1944). 17, 18, 148, 462

Postman, Leo (1918-), is Professor of Psychology at the University of California at Berkeley. He received his Ph.D. from Harvard and has concentrated his efforts in the area of perception and human learning. 336

Pribram, Karl H. (1919-), is a physiological psychologist who has concentrated on neurophysiology and neuropsychology. In 1948 he was Resident Assistant Professor of Physiology and Psychology at Yale Medical School. At present he is a Professor in the departments of psychology and psychiatry at Stanford University. 293

Prosser, Clifford Ladd (1907-), is Professor of Physiology at the University of Illinois where he has been on the faculty since 1939 and was Head of the department (1960-70). Earlier, he was Assistant Professor at Clark (1934-39) and Parker Fellow in Physiology at Harvard Medical School. He received his Ph.D. (1932) from Johns Hopkins and his B.A. (1929) from Dartmouth. An investigator of neuromuscular relations across species, he is the author of *Comparative Animal Physiology* and has been President of both the Zoological Society of America (1961) and the Society of General Physiology (1958). 150

Raines, George Neely (1908-), after earning his B.S. at the University of Mississippi (1928) and his M.D. from Northwestern (1930), interned at the U.S. Naval Hospital at Mare Island, California (1930-31), and did residencies at the U.S. Naval Medical School (1934-35) and St. Elizabeth's Hospital (1935-36) and received psychoanalytic training at the Washington-Baltimore Institute. After serving in various posts and having various commands, he headed the neuropsychiatric branch of the Bureau of Medicine and Surgery in the Department of the Navy and was Professor of Psychiatry at Georgetown University Medical Center. 155-56

Riggs, Lorin Andres (1912-), is L. Herbert Ballou Professor of Psychology at Brown University where he had made his career since 1941 after earning his Ph.D. (1936) from Clark and teaching at the University of Vermont (1937-41). He has used a plastic contact lens to fix an electrode to the human eye to get electroretinograms which he related to subjective reports obtained with traditional procedures to explicate the neural basis for visual experience, and he has solved the problem of motionless vision to show that the image disappears. He has been elected to the National Academy of Sciences (1961). 19, 28, 158

Rock, Irvin (1919-), was Professor of Experimental and Clinical Psychology in the Graduate School of Education at Yeshiva University. His research work is in the areas of perception, learning, and thinking. At present he is Professor at Rutgers University. 288

Roff, Merrill (1909-), is Professor of Psychology in the Institute of Child Development at the University of Minnesota where he has been utilizing factor analysis in the study of psychological development. Following a B.A. from Witchita University (1929) and a Ph.D. from Cornell (1933), he became Research Assistant to L. L. Thurstone at the University of Chicago and was Assistant and then Associate Professor at Indiana University (1935-47) until he moved to Minnesota. 144

Rogers, Carl Ransom (1902-), is Resident Fellow at the Western Behavioral Science Institute and Professor Emeritus of Psychology and Psychiatry (1957-63) at the University of Wisconsin. Earlier, he was Professor and Director of the Counseling Center at the University of Chicago (1946-57), Professor at Ohio State University (1940-45), and Director of various clinics (1930-40). He introduced the phonographic recording of therapeutic interviews and developed client-centered therapy and is the author of *Counseling and Psychotherapy* (1951), *Psychotherapy and Personality Change* (1954, with others), and *On Becoming a Person* (1961). He was President of both the American Association of Applied Psychology (1945) and the APA (1947), also the American Academy of Psychotherapists (1957), and was among the first to receive a Distinguished Scientific Award of the APA (1956). 182, 184, 298, 310

Rom, Paul (1902-), is an educator, psychologist in private practice in London, and editor, He is the author of a book on Adler, and Editor of the *Individual Psychology Newsletter*. 34

Rosenstein, Alvin Jay (1931-), is Corporate Marketing Research Associate of General Foods. Earlier, he was Assistant Director of the Division of Personnel and Marketing Research of the Psychological Corporation (1961-64), Director of TV research for McCann Erickson, Inc. (1960-61), and Senior Clinical Psychologist at Norwich State Hospital, Connecticut (1958-60). He earned his Ph.D. (1958) at the University of Illinois. 187

Rotter, Julian B. (1916-), Professor and Director of the Clinical Psychology Training Program at the University of Connecticut, is the author of *Social Learning and Clinical Psychology* and initiator of research on internal versus external control of reinforcement. 33

Royce, Joseph R. (1921-), is the Director of the Center for Advanced Study in Theoretical Psychology at the University of Alberta, Canada. One of his major concerns is that of a theory-oriented generalist in a time of empirical specialists. 122, 128

Ruggles, Arthur Hiler (1881-1961), was Superintendent Emeritus of Butler Hospital in Providence, R.I., where he was Assistant Physician (1909-22) and then Superintendent (1922-43) and also Director of the Emma Pendleton Bradley Home in East Providence (1931-41). A leader in the mental-hygiene movement, he was President of the American Psychiatric Association (1943) and of the National Committee of Mental Hygiene (1948-60), and Salmon Lecturer (1955). 157-58, 161

Rychlak, Joseph F. (1928-), Professor of Psychology at Purdue University, is the author of the very profound *A Philosophy of Science for*

Personality Theory and of *Introduction to Personality and Psychotherapy: A Theory-construction Approach.* 33

Saunders, David R. (1923-), received his Ph.D. from the University of Illinois in 1950. He was a Visiting Lecturer at Rutgers University from 1956-60 and a Visiting Professor at the University of Hawaii in 1960. He is presently in private practice. 97

Schlosberg, Harold, (1904-64), was a long-time member of the psychology department at Brown from Assistant Professor through the ranks to Professor and Chairman. He was an experimental physiological psychologist and one of the early workers on conditioning and one of the first to call attention to the differences between classical and instrumental conditioning with regard to the contingencies of reinforcement. He influenced many students. He also investigated the facial expressions of emotion, and (with J. McV.Hunt) the effects of early experience. He edited the second edition of Woodworth's *Experimental Psychology.* The colleagues of his adult career saw him crippled by arthritis; few knew that he had won his P for both marksmanship with the pistol and polo as an undergraduate at Princeton. He was President of the Eastern Psychological Association (1954) and the Experimental Division of the APA (1952) and was elected to the American Academy of Arts and Sciences. 19, 158-60, 162-63, 166, 174, 377, 406, 429

Schwarz, Frederick August Otto (1902-), is a partner in the New York law firm of Davis, Polk, Wardwell, Sunderland, & Kiendl, a director of F. A. O. Schwarz (toy manufacturers and distributors) and of other firms. Formerly, he was a Trustee of the Community Service Society of New York and Chairman of the Board for the Institute of Welfare Research. He continues as a trustee of other religious and welfare organizations. He earned his B.A. (1924) and his LL.B. (1927) at Harvard. He was General Counsel to the U.S. High Commissioner in Germany (1953-54). 167

Sears, Robert Richardson (1908-), has been Professor of Psychology at Stanford University since 1953 where he was also Head of the department (1953-62) and Dean of the School of Humanities and Sciences (1962-70) and where he also earned his B.A. (1929). He was Professor at Harvard (1949-53), Director of the Iowa Child Welfare Research Station (1942-49), and Assistant Professor at Yale (1936-42), where he earned his Ph.D. (1932). He has authored *Frustration and Aggression* (1939, with others), *Objective Studies of Psychoanalytic Concepts* (1943), and *Patterns of Child Rearing* (1958, with others) and served as a consultant to various foundations and federal agencies. He was president of the APA (1951) and the Society for Research in Child Development (1964-66). 164, 176, 180

Sells, Saul B. (1913-) is Research Professor at Texas Christian University and Director of the Institute of Behavioral Research. He had been with the School of Aviation Medicine at Randolph Air Force Base as a Research Psychologist and continues to specialize in aviation psychology and in studies using multivariate design. Along with Charles Berry he edited *Human Factors in Jets and Space Travel.* 12, 14, 17, 101, 128

Shakow, Davis (1901-), is Senior Research Psychologist at the intramural psychological laboratory of the National Institute of Mental Health where he served as Chief

tematic theoretical approach that attempted to extend principles of conditioning to more complex forms of behavior. 255-60, 267-68, 274, 276

Stagner, Ross (1909-), a personality and social psychologist who has taught at Akron, Dartmouth, and Illinois, is currently Professor and Chairman at Wayne State. He is the author of *Psychology of Personality, Psychology of Industrial Conflict,* and other publications bearing on labor relations and organizational psychology. 14, 26, 348-51, 486, 489

Stellar, Eliot (1919-), is Professor of Physiological Psychology in the School of Medicine at the University of Pennsylvania. Before going to Pennsylvania, he advanced from Instructor to Associate Professor at Johns Hopkins (1947-54). He earned his B.A. (1941) from Harvard and his Ph.D. (1947) from Brown. His investigations of the physiology of motivation and of memory have been outstanding. He has been President of the Eastern Psychological Association and of the Experimental Division of the APA and has been elected to the National Academy of Science. 160, 162-63

Stevens, Stanley S. (1906-73), was a psychophysicist. He was noted for his early work on the physiological and psychological aspects of auditory perception. He developed subjective scaling methods and in most recent years developed the so-called magnitude estimate procedure by which a direct measure of sensation magnitude can be obtained. He was a longtime Professor at Harvard University. 105, 297, 317, 418

Stice, Glen F. (1919-), received his Ph.D. in psychology from the University of Illinois in 1951. He has been employed as a Resident Psychologist for the Crew Research Laboratory of the U.S. Air Force Department (1951-53) as well as a Research Associate for the Educational Testing Service (1954-60). Currently he is in private practice. 111

Suci, George J. (1925-), received his Ph.D. in psychology at Illinois in 1951 and is currently Professor in the department of human development and family studies at Cornell. 358-62, 364

Sweney, Arthur B. (1923-), received his Ph.D. in Houston in 1958. Currently he is a Professor and Director of the Center for Human Appraisal at Wichita State University. 98, 101

Symonds, Percival M. (1893-1960), was Professor of Psychology at Teachers College, Columbia University; his early work was largely in educational and psychological measurement (*Diagnosing Personality and Conduct,* 1932); later he turned to psychoanalytic personality theory (*Dynamics of Human Adjustment,* 1946); as author of more than 20 books in these fields, his influence was most evident in the area of overlap between educational and clinical psychology. 205-8, 212

Tannenbaum, Percy H. (1927-), is Professor and Director of the Mass Communications Research Center in Wisconsin. Various articles that were written by him such as "Principle of Congruity in the Prediction of Attitude Change," "Indexing Process in Communication," and "Measurement of Meaning" centered on his studies of attitude change and measurement, psycholinguistics, and mass media effects. 357-58, 360-62

Taylor, Frederick Winslow (1856-1915), was an American engineer known as the Father of Scientific Management. His success in raising individual efficiency by the selection of qualified workers, systematic training, and motivation through financial incentives laid the groundwork for the acceptance of industrial psychology by management and influenced research and practice in the field. He was the author of *Shop Management* and *Principles of Scientific Management.* 451, 482

Thomson, Sir Godfrey H. (1881-1955), was Professor of Educational Psychology at the University of Edinburgh in Scotland. He was a pioneer in the development of factor analysis and espoused the so-called "sampling theory" of mental abilities, whereby abilities are viewed as basically small, independent learned units of behavior which are sampled in different proportions by various mental tests, in contrast to Spearman's theory of *g* as a general mental energy which enters into all forms of intellectual activity. 104, 108-9, 128, 210

Thorndike, Edward L. (1874-1949), was a Columbia University psychologist who gave a new direction to educational psychology. 90-91, 325, 462

Thorne, Frederick C. (1909-), Ph.D., M.D., has been Editor and Publisher of the *Journal of Clinical Psychology* since he founded it in 1945. His concern is the development of an eclectic system of clinical psychology practice. Among his numerous books, *Integrative Psychology* presents his position best. 12, 33, 128

Thurstone, Louis Leon (1887-1955), will be remembered for his psychophysical measurement of attitudes, the development of multiple-factor analysis, and its use on tests of intelligence to isolate the primary mental abilities. He was originally an engineer (M.E., Cornell, 1912) who invented a motion picture projector which led Thomas A. Edison to invite him to serve as an assistant. Then he taught descriptive geometry at the Engineering School of the University of Minnesota before turning to psychology (Ph.D., Chicago, 1917). After eight years at the Carnegie Institute of Technology (1915-23), he was invited to Chicago where he was Associate Professor, Professor, and Charles F. Grey Distinguished Service Professor until his retirement (1953) when he accepted a professorship in education at the University of North Carolina. His honors include the Presidency of the APA (1932) and election to the American Philosophical Society and the National Academy of Sciences. 16, 101, 104, 108, 114, 122, 128, 208, 210, 359

Tolman, Edward C. (1886-1959), was an American Behaviorist who formulated an influential cognitive theory of animal behavior. His basic postulates of learning were influenced by Gestalt perceptual principles while maintaining a strong methodological commitment to objective psychology. 104, 258, 288, 294, 298-99, 310

Triandis, Harry C. (1926-), is currently Professor at Illinois. Some of his articles include "Comparative factor analysis of job semantic structures of managers and workers" and "Some determinants of interpersonal communication." 382

Troland, L. T. (1889-), is a product of M.I.T. and of Harvard. He was a brilliant scientist in the field of psychophysiology and an inventor of colored motion pictures. He was one of the most maturely integrated psychologists. 328, 335

Twitmyer, Edwin B. (1873-1943), Professor of Psychology and Director of the Psychological Laboratory and Clinic at Pennsylvania for many years, was the first in the U.S. to observe and report upon the "conditioned" reflex (1902). He founded, in 1914, the first psychological clinic for the treatment of speech defects and was the author of *Defective Speech* (with Y. S. Nathanson). 446, 448

Undeutsch, Ulo (1917-), is Professor of Psychology at the University of Cologne, Germany. His interests are in educational and forensic psychology. 25

Uzgiris, Ina Cepenas (1937-), is Professor of Psychology at Clark University. Earlier she was Research Assistant Professor at the University of Illinois (1962-66), where she earned her Ph.D. (1962). She is the author of *Toward Ordinal Scales of Psychological Development in Infancy* (with J. McV. Hunt). 186, 189

Virtue, George Olien (1861-1954), earned his B.A. (1892) and his Ph.D. (1897) at Harvard University. He was Professor of Economics at the University of Nebraska from 1909 to 1939. There he published many articles on the history of economic development and taught an outstanding course in the history of economic thought. He continued scholarly activity long after his retirement and published his last article on the history of land economics in the American colonies in 1951 at the age of ninety. 137

Waller, Willard (1901-47), was a Professor of Sociology at Pennsylvania State University. Earlier he was Assistant Professor of Sociology at the University of Nebraska (1929-32). He earned his Ph.D. at the University of Pennsylvania (1929). He authored a dissertation on divorce entitled *The Old Love and the New* and a book on the sociology of the schools. 141

Walton, William Edward (1902-), is Chief Psychologist at the Psychological Guidance Center in Los Angeles and Consulting Psychologist at the Michael Kent School. He was Assistant Professor at the University of Nebraska (1931-42), where he earned his Ph.D. (1931). 152

Watson, John B. (1878-1958), was the founder of American Behaviorism who viewed psychology as "a purely objective experimental branch of natural science" with its goal being "the prediction and control of behavior." 268-69

Watson, Robert I. (1909-), is Professor of Psychology at the University of New Hampshire. He has published books on the history of psychology and on clinical and child psychology. 78

Wellek, Albert (1904-72), was Professor of Psychology and Chairman of the department at the University of Mainz, Germany. A student of Felix Krueger, he considered himself a representative of "the American 'third force' [of Maslow], which in Germany was always the first force." 25

Wertheimer, Max (1880-1943), was the founder, along with Kurt Koffka and Wolfgang Köhler, of Gestalt psychology, a movement that rebelled against analyzing conscious experience without reference to its meaning for the individual. 11, 12, 22, 26, 251-53

White, William Alanson (1870-1937), is the psychiatrist for whom the Psychoanalytic Institute in Washington, D.C., is named. After undergraduate work at Cornell, he earned his M.D. at Long Island Medical College in 1891. After 11 years as Assistant Physician at Binghamton State Hospital, he became in 1903 Superintendent of the U.S. Government Hospital for the Insane (renamed St. Elizabeth's Hospital around 1910), and in 1904 a Professor of Psychiatry at George Washington University. With Smith E. Jelliffe, he founded and edited the *Psychoanalytic Review,* the Nervous and Mental Disease Monograph Series, and authored a number of books. He also authored *Outlines of Psychiatry* and other books. 155-56

Whitney, David Day (1878-1953), was Professor (1916-46) and Chairman (1934-46) of the department of zoology, which he joined in 1911 after earning his Ph.D. at Columbia (1909) and instructing at Wesleyan. He taught a popular course in evolution and genetics. 138

Witmer, Lightner (1867-1956), one of the dissenters among Wundt's students, originated the term "clinical psychology" and gave direction to the field. He founded the first Psychological Clinic in the world in 1896, at the University of Pennsylvania. For many years, he was Professor and Director of the Psychological Laboratory and Clinic at Pennsylvania, and Editor of the journal *The Psychological Clinic,* which he also founded. 445-48

Wolcott, Robert Henry (1868-1934), came to Nebraska from Michigan in 1894 to teach anatomy in the school of medicine, but in 1909 he became Head Professor of Zoology, a post which he held till his death. His lectures in the subject were spellbinding. 136

Wolfe, Harry Kirke (1858-1918), was the third American student to earn his Ph.D. with Wundt at Leipzig (1886). He earned his B.A. from the University of Nebraska in 1880, studied first with Ebbinghaus in Berlin, then with Wundt. He returned to Nebraska as Professor of Philosophy in 1889 and founded what is claimed to be the third laboratory of "new psychology" in the United States. He was also a charter member of the APA. In the course of his career, he devoted a great deal of his attention to education and served as Superintendent of Schools for Omaha and Dean of Nebraska's College of Education. 137

Woodrow, Herbert (1883-), received his Ph.D. from Columbia University in 1909. He also served as a Professor and as Head of the psychology department from 1928 to 1950. He is now a Professor Emeritus at the University of Illinois. 98

Woodruff, Joseph L. (1913-), has done extensive research in extrasensory perception, psychometric methods, and in counseling techniques. He is a Professor of Psychology at City College of New York. 392, 335.

Woodworth, R. S. (1869-1962), trained with Sherrington and shared with Cattell the development of the psychological laboratory at Columbia. He became widely known as a leader of the "middle-of-the-road" psychology of 1900-1962. Woodworth had perhaps the longest productive life among psychologists. Following a B.A. (1891) from Amherst College, he taught mathematics at Washburn College, began graduate work in psychology and physiology at Harvard (1895). There he met W. B. Conant and E. L. Thorndike and earned his M.A. (1897). After a year of teaching physiology at Harvard's Medical School, he transferred to Columbia where he earned his Ph.D. with J. McK. Cattell. While teaching physiology at Columbia's Medical School, he collaborated (1897-1902) with Thorndike on the well-known studies of the transfer of training which yielded the theory of "identical elements." Following a year with Sherrington at the University of Liverpool, he was invited back to Columbia where he remained. He revised Ladd's *Physiological Psychology,* devised the first association tests (1911) and the first psychoneurotic inventory (1913). He introduced the concept of drive to America in his *Dynamic Psychology* (1918), wrote a popular textbook (1921) and his compendious *Experimental Psychology* (1938). After becoming Professor Emeritus in 1945 at the age of